The ETS Test Collection Catalog

The ETS Test Collection Catalog

Volume 3: Tests for Special Populations

Compiled by Test Collection,
Educational Testing Service

Table of Contents

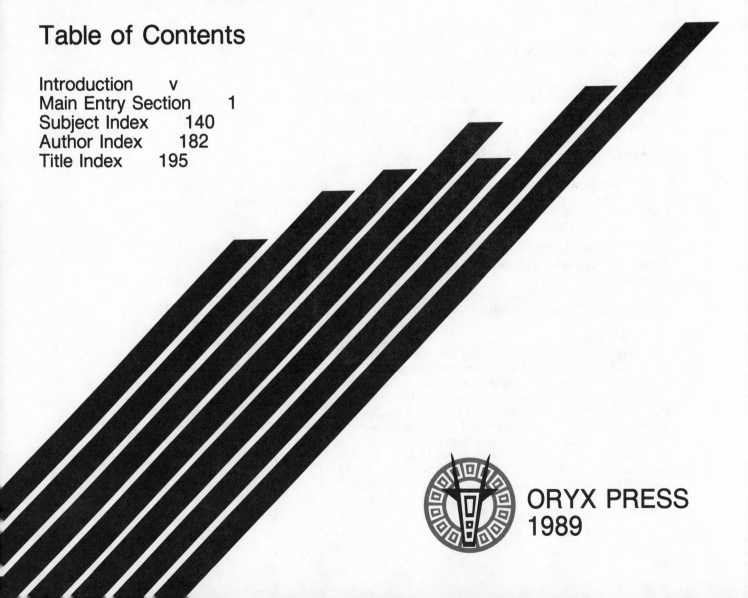

ORYX PRESS
1989

The rare Arabian Oryx is believed to have inspired the myth of the unicorn. This desert antelope became virtually extinct in the early 1960s. At that time several groups of international conservationists arranged to have 9 animals sent to the Phoenix Zoo to be the nucleus of a captive breeding herd. Today the Oryx population is nearly 800, and over 400 have been returned to reserves in the Middle East.

Copyright © 1989 by Educational Testing Service
Published by The Oryx Press
2214 North Central at Encanto
Phoenix, Arizona 85004-1483

Published simultaneously in Canada

Printed and Bound in the United States of America

∞ The paper used in this publication meets the minimum requirements of American National Standard for Information Science—Permanence of Paper for Printed Library Materials, ANSI Z39.48, 1984.

Library of Congress Cataloging-in-Publication Data
(Revised for vol. 3)

The ETS Test Collection catalog.

Includes indexes.
Contents: v. 1. Achievement tests and measurement devices—v. 2. Vocational tests and measurement devices—v. 3. Tests for special populations.
1. Educational tests and measurements—United States—Catalogs. 2. Achievement tests—United States—Catalogs. 3. Educational Testing Service—Catalogs. I. Educational Testing Service. Test Collection.
LB3051.E79   1986   016.3712'6   86-678
ISBN 0-89774-248-6 (pbk. : v. 1)

ISBN 0-89774-477-2 (pbk. : v. 3)

INTRODUCTION

The Test Collection, Educational Testing Service, is an extensive library of approximately 15,500 tests and other measurement devices. It was established to provide information on tests and assessment materials to those in research, advisory services, education, and related activities. As part of its function, the Test Collection acquires and disseminates information on hard-to-locate research instruments as well as on commercially available, standardized tests. Because the Test Collection deals only with tests and evaluation tools, it has been able to provide a reasonable amount of bibliographic control over what has historically been a scattering of information among many diverse sources.

This catalog describes approximately 1,700 tests for special populations. The information is drawn from the Test Collection's computer-retrievable database. The tests described cover all age and grade levels from elementary school through adults.

Special populations encompass a variety of groups, such as older adults; physically handicapped, mentally handicapped, emotionally disturbed, speech-handicapped, and sensory-impaired persons; gifted individuals; limited-English-speaking, non-English-speaking, and bilingual persons; psychiatric patients; those with learning problems or behavior problems; and various ethnic populations. Examples of the kinds of tests described in this volume include developmental assessment instruments of at-risk children; screening tests for potentially learning-disabled, physically or emotionally disturbed persons; tests for older adults to screen for depression or personal adjustment; tests to assess the level of daily living skills of mentally retarded persons; tests for English-as-a-second-language individuals; diagnostic tests for those with brain damage or various speech problems; screening tests for neurological or motor dysfunction; and assessment instruments for use with emotionally and socially disturbed children and adolescents.

For each entry in the main entry section of the directory, the following information is always present: test title, author, descriptors and/or identifiers (subject indexing terms), availability source, age or grade level, and abstract. Other information, which is provided when available, includes publication or copyright date, subtests, number of test items, and the time required for an individual to complete the test. The test descriptions are arranged sequentially by the Test Collection's identification number in the main entry section.

There are three indexes that provide access to the main entry section: subject, author, and test title. The subject index uses ERIC descriptors from the *Thesaurus of ERIC Descriptors*, 11th edition. Each test title and its unique identification number is listed under the major descriptors assigned to it, so that there are several subject access points. In addition, some tests may be indexed under major identifiers, which are additional subject indexing terms not found in the *Thesaurus of ERIC Descriptors* that help in describing the content of the test. In the author index, tests and their corresponding identification numbers are listed under the author's name. The title index is an alphabetical list of all tests included in the directory and their identification numbers.

At the time the test catalog was compiled, all the tests included were still available from the test distributors indicated in the availability source. However, distribution of certain tests may be discontinued by test publishers and new tests developed and published.

The staff of the Test Collection will be happy to answer any questions about this catalog or other products and services. Inquires may be addressed to Test Collection, Educational Testing Service, Princeton, NJ 08541.

Sample Entry

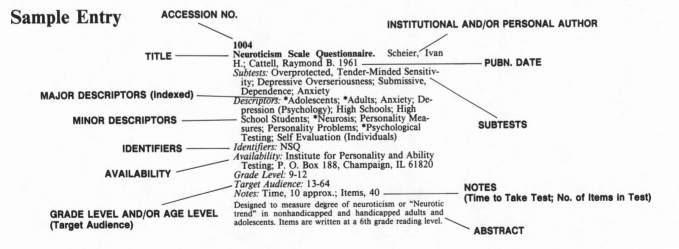

MAIN ENTRY SECTION

27
Geist Picture Interest Inventory. Geist, Harold 1968
Subtests: Persuasive; Clerical; Mechanical; Musical; Scientific; Outdoor; Literary; Computational; Artistic; Social Service; Dramatic; Personal Service
Descriptors: *Adults; Disadvantaged; *Educationally Disadvantaged; Females; *Interest Inventories; Males; Nonverbal Tests; Pictorial Stimuli; Secondary Education; *Secondary School Students; Visual Measures; *Vocational Interests
Identifiers: GPII
Availability: Western Psychological Services; Order Dept., 12031 Wilshire Blvd., Los Angeles, CA 90025
Target Audience: 12-64

Designed to identify vocational and avocational interests using a minimum of language. Examinee selects appropriate pictures. Useful with disadvantaged and educationally deprived population. Separate forms for males and females. Test is untimed. A Motivation Questionnaire can be administered separately to explore motivations behind occupational choice. May be individually or group administered. Manual was revised in 1975.

88
Picture Story Language Test. Myklebust, Helmer 1965
Subtests: Productivity Scale; Syntax Scale; Abstract-Concrete Scale
Descriptors: Adolescents; Children; Diagnostic Tests; *Elementary School Students; Elementary Secondary Education; *Language Acquisition; *Language Tests; Mental Retardation; Neurological Impairments; *Secondary School Students; *Sensory Integration; *Writing Skills; *Written Language
Availability: Grune and Stratton; 111 Fifth Ave., New York, NY 10003
Grade Level: 2-12
Target Audience: 7-17
Notes: Time, 20 approx.

Consists of a picture about which a story is written. Measures one's facility with the written word. The instrument studies language developmentally and diagnostically. Valuable in the appraisal and classification of nonhandicapped and handicapped children. The Picture Story Language Test is contained in Helmer Myklebust's DEVELOPMENT AND DISORDERS OF WRITTEN LANGUAGE. Vol. I. New York: Grune and Stratton, 1965.

157
Standardized Road-Map Test of Direction Sense. Money, John 1976
Descriptors: Adolescents; Adults; Children; Educational Diagnosis; *Elementary School Students; Handicap Identification; Individual Testing; Learning Disabilities; *Neurological Impairments; *Orientation; *Patients; *Secondary School Students; Verbal Tests; Visual Measures; *Visual Stimuli
Identifiers: *Directionality; Oral Tests; *Right Left Discrimination; Road Map Test; Turners Syndrome
Availability: United Educational Services; P.O. Box 357, E. Aurora, NY 14052
Target Audience: 7-64
Notes: Time, 15 approx.; Items, 32

Untimed, individually administered instrument originally designed to assess the right-left directional orientation of patients with Turner's syndrome. Now more widely used as a measure of right-left discriminatory ability and as an aid to evaluating disorders involving defective directional orientation, such as specific type of dyslexia and certain types of brain damage and cytogenetic anomaly. The subject is given a map with a specific route traced on it. Without turning the map, the subject is to tell the test administrator whether he would turn right or left at each corner. Also used in evaluating children who appear to be underachievers and as part of a full neuropsychological battery. Restricted distribution.

158
An Integrated Articulation Test for Use with Children with Cerebral Palsy. Irwin, Orvis C. 1961
Descriptors: *Adolescents; *Articulation (Speech); *Cerebral Palsy; *Children; Consonants; Diagnostic Tests; Individual Testing; Neurological Impairments; *Speech Tests; Speech Therapy; *Verbal Stimuli; Vowels

Availability: Cerebral Palsy Review; v22 n3 p3-24 May-Jun 1961
Target Audience: 3-16
Notes: Items, 87

Five short tests of articulation for use with cerebral palsy children. Tests should be administered in different sittings because of the generally brief attention span of this population. Four tests measure consonant articulation, and one measures vowel articulation. Designed for diagnostic use by speech therapists. Two alternate forms are available.

260
Minnesota Test for Differential Diagnosis of Aphasia (1965 Revision). Schuell, Hildred 1965
Subtests: Auditory Disturbances; Visual and Reading Disturbances; Speech and Language Disturbances; Visuomotor and Writing Disturbances; Disturbances of Numerical Relations and Arithmetic Processes
Descriptors: *Adults; *Aphasia; Clinical Diagnosis; Diagnostic Tests; *Handicap Identification; Language Handicaps; *Neurological Impairments; *Patients; Perceptual Handicaps
Availability: University of Minnesota Press; 2037 University Ave. S.E., Minneapolis, MN 55455
Target Audience: 18-64

Designed as a method to explore language disturbances resulting from brain damage in adults. Specifically useful in forming observations about language behavior of aphasic patients.

415
Escala de Inteligencia Wechsler para Ninos. Wechsler, David 1967
Subtests: Verbal; Performance
Descriptors: *Elementary School Students; Elementary Secondary Education; Individual Testing; *Intelligence; Intelligence Quotient; *Intelligence Tests; *Secondary School Students; *Spanish; *Spanish Speaking
Identifiers: *Puerto Rico; *Wechsler Intelligence Scale for Children
Availability: The Psychological Corporation; 555 Academic Ct., San Antonio, TX 78204-0952
Target Audience: 5-15
Notes: Time, 60 approx.

Spanish-American translation and adaptation of the WISC (1949), developed in Puerto Rico. Uses same set of materials for Performance Scale. Spanish-language manual and verbal items.

610
Tests of General Educational Development: High School Level. American Council on Education, Washington, DC, General Educational Development Testing Service 1975
Subtests: Writing Skills Test; Social Studies Test; Science Test; Reading Skills Test; Mathematics Test
Descriptors: *Academic Achievement; Adults; Braille; *Dropouts; *Educational Certificates; *Equivalency Tests; French; General Education; Grade Equivalent Scores; Older Adults; Reading Skills; *Secondary Education; Secondary School Mathematics; Secondary School Science; Social Studies; Spanish; Timed Tests; Writing Skills
Identifiers: GED; General Certificate of Education; General Educational Development Tests; Lindquist (E F); Test Batteries
Availability: American Council on Education; One Dupont Circle, N.W., Washington, DC 20036, GED Testing Service
Target Audience: 18-80
Notes: Time, 405 approx.; Items, 290

This battery of 5 tests is used to determine a candidate's eligibility to receive a high school equivalency certificate. The context of the test items attempts to measure skills relevant to adult experience. Items require understanding of broad concepts and generalizations and measure the general ability to evaluate, synthesize, and draw conclusions. GED battery is available in French, Spanish, Braille, large print, and on audio cassettes. The Writing Skills test consists of 80 items and requires 75 minutes. The Social Studies test consists of 60 items and requires 90 minutes. The Science test consists of 60 questions and requires 90 minutes. The Reading Skills test consists of 40 questions and requires 90 minutes. These tests were originally developed by the Examination Staff of the United States Armed Forces Institute (a committee of civilian educators under the direction of E. F. Lindquist and Ralph W. Tyler) as a method of evaluating military personnel who

lacked a high school diploma. After the Second World War, the use of the test battery was extended to civilians as well. Tests are updated periodically.

706
School Interest Inventory. Cottle, William C. 1966
Descriptors: *Attitude Measures; *Dropout Characteristics; Dropout Prevention; Females; Males; Predictive Measurement; *School Attitudes; Secondary Education; *Secondary School Students; *Student Attitudes
Availability: The Riverside Publishing Co.; 8420 Bryn Mawr Ave., Chicago, IL 60631
Grade Level: 7-12
Notes: Time, 20 approx.; Items, 150

Designed for use in the early detection, and possible prevention, of potential school dropouts. Scales established for males and females. Separate scoring masks available for each sex.

710
California Life Goals Evaluation Schedules. Hahn, Milton E. 1969
Descriptors: *Adolescents; *Adults; Attitude Measures; *Career Planning; Counseling Techniques; Higher Education; High Schools; *Individual Needs; *Majors (Students); *Motivation; *Older Adults; Rating Scales; Retirement
Identifiers: CLGES; Self Scoring Tests
Availability: Western Psychological Services; 12031 Wilshire Blvd., Los Angeles, CA 90025
Target Audience: 15-75
Notes: Time, 45 approx.; Items, 150

Assesses life goals in 10 areas including Esteem, Profit, Fame, Leadership, Power, Security, Social Service, Interesting Experiences, Self-Expression, and Independence. Useful for career and college planning, adjusting to aging or retirement, and career counseling. May be self- or examiner-scored and administered to individuals or groups.

714
Demos D Scale. Demos, George D. 1965
Subtests: Attitudes toward Teachers; Attitudes toward Education; Influences by Peers or Parents; School Behavior
Descriptors: *Attitude Measures; Dropout Characteristics; *Potential Dropouts; Rating Scales; *School Attitudes; Secondary Education; *Secondary School Students; *Student Attitudes; Student Behavior
Identifiers: DDS; Self Administered Tests
Availability: Western Psychological Services; 12031 Wilshire Blvd., Los Angeles, CA 90025
Grade Level: 7-12
Notes: Items, 29

Designed to assess school attitudes of students in junior and senior high school. Scores may be converted to probabilities of dropping out of school.

715
Oregon Academic Ranking Test. Derthick, Charles H. 1965
Subtests: Making Sentences; Making Comparisons; Numbers; Secret Words; Working Problems; Reasoning; Completing Sentences; Sayings
Descriptors: *Ability Identification; Abstract Reasoning; Academic Ability; *Academically Gifted; Aptitude Tests; Creativity; Elementary Education; *Elementary School Students; Individual Testing; Screening Tests; Special Education
Identifiers: OART
Availability: Western Psychological Services; 12031 Wilshire Blvd., Los Angeles, CA 90025
Grade Level: 3-7
Notes: Time, 30 approx.

Designed to identify exceptionally bright children. Measures creativity and abstract thinking as indices of brightness. May be used as individual or group test. Useful for selection and placement of students into enriched programs and for identification of highly creative youngsters.

718
Buttons; a Projective Test for Pre-Adolescents and Adolescents. Rothman, Esther P.; Berkowitz, Pearl H. 1963

Descriptors: Behavior Problems; Constructed Response; *Diagnostic Tests; Educational Diagnosis; Emotional Problems; Individual Testing; Junior High Schools; *Junior High School Students; Mental Disorders; Personality Problems; Pictorial Stimuli; Problem Children; *Projective Measures; Psychological Evaluation; School Counseling; Student Adjustment; *Student Attitudes; *Student Behavior; Student Characteristics; Student Evaluation; *Student Problems; Visual Measures
Identifiers: Oral Tests
Availability: Western Psychological Services; 12031 Wilshire Blvd., Los Angeles, CA 90025
Grade Level: 7-9
Notes: Time, 45 approx.; Items, 12

A projective test for preadolescent and adolescent boys and girls, which identifies those students with gross deviations in personality, attitudes, and behavior. In a group testing situation, the test identifies those students in need of guidance, counseling, or psychological or psychiatric services; in an individual testing situation, the test enables the administrator to make personality evaluation and differential diagnosis studies. In the group setting, the students write their answers in the booklet; in the individual test situation, it is up to the administrator to decide whether the student writes his or her own answers. Although it requires limited reading ability, the test administrator may read it aloud for the student with reading difficulties. Each item consists of a series of cartoon strip frames, depicting the rabbit Buttons and to others in a specific situation. In the last frame, the student writes (or tells) his or her response to the unfinished sequence of what Buttons says and why and to other questions. Three different scores are obtained: Initial score (number of unacceptable or blank responses), Content score (evaluation of responses in 7 diagnostic areas), and Clinical Observations.

791
Achenbach-Lewis Symptom Checklist. Achenbach, Thomas M.; Lewis, Melvin 1974
Descriptors: Adolescents; *Behavior Patterns; Check Lists; Child Psychology; Children; *Emotional Disturbances; *Personality Traits; Physical Health; *Psychopathology
Identifiers: ALSC; TIM(A)
Availability: Tests in Microfiche; Test Collection, Educational Testing Service, Princeton, NJ 08541
Target Audience: 4-16
Notes: Items, 115

A list of symptoms covers the kinds of behavior that typically are of enough concern to make a child a candidate for treatment. The checklist is intended to be filled out for children aged 4 to 16 by parents, interviewers, therapists, and people who know the child well.

792
Developmental Checklist. Bornstein, Susan; Zimmerman, Ruth 1974
Subtests: Self Help Skills; Receptive Language Skills; Expressive Language Skills; Social Skills; Gross Motor Skills; Fine Motor Skills; Pre-Orientation and Mobility Skills
Descriptors: Check Lists; Developmental Tasks; Diagnostic Tests; Interpersonal Competence; Language Processing; *Multiple Disabilities; Observation; Psychomotor Skills; Self Care Skills; *Visual Impairments; *Young Children
Availability: Boston Center for Blind Children; 147 S. Huntington Ave., Boston, MA 02130
Target Audience: 1-8

Designed to assess a child's present skills and to generate educational goals. Useful for visually impaired multihandicapped children. May be used to evaluate progress by using the checklist to establish a base line and readministering it at established intervals.

841
Arthur Point Scale of Performance, Form I. Arthur, Grace 1943
Subtests: Mare-Foal Formboard; Sequin-Goddard Formboard; Pintner-Paterson 2 Figure Formboard; Casuist Formboard; Pintner Manikin Test; Knox-Kempf Feature Profile Test; Knox Cube Imitation Test; Healy Pictorial Completion Test; Kohs Block and Design Cards; and Porteus Mazes
Descriptors: *Adults; Deafness; Disabilities; *Elementary School Students; Elementary Secondary Education; Emotional Disturbances; Individual Testing; *Intelligence; *Intelligence Tests; Nonverbal Tests; Performance Tests; *Preschool Children; *Secondary School Students
Identifiers: Arthur Point Scale of Performance Tests
Availability: Stoelting Co.; 1350 S. Kostner Ave., Chicago, IL 60623
Target Audience: 4-64

Nonverbal measure of intelligence designed to supplement Binet tests. Useful for subjects with speech defects, language difficulties, or emotional problems.

842
Arthur Point Scale of Performance Tests, Revised Form II. Arthur, Grace 1947
Subtests: Knox Cube Test (Arthur Revision); Sequin Form Board (Arthur Revision); Arthur Stencil Design Test I; Porteus Maze Test (Arthur Revision); Healy Picture Completion Test II
Descriptors: *Adolescents; *Children; Deafness; *Individual Testing; *Intelligence Tests; Non English Speaking; *Nonverbal Tests; Reading Difficulties; Speech Handicaps
Identifiers: Test Batteries
Availability: Stoelting Co.; 1350 S. Kostner Ave., Chicago, IL 60623
Target Audience: 4-17
Notes: Time, 90 approx.

Designed to furnish an Intelligence Quotient comparable to that obtained with the Binet Scales. Tests afford a means of measuring adequately the ability of deaf children, those suffering from reading disabilities, those with delayed or defective speech, and non-English speaking students.

863
Inter-American Series: Test of Reading, Level 1, Primary. Manuel, Herschel T. 1966
Subtests: Vocabulary; Comprehension
Descriptors: *Achievement Tests; *Elementary School Students; Pictorial Stimuli; Primary Education; *Reading Achievement; *Reading Comprehension; *Spanish; *Spanish Speaking; Vocabulary
Availability: Guidance Testing Associates; 1 Camino, Santa Maria, San Antonio, TX 78284
Grade Level: 1-2
Notes: Time, 18 approx.; Items, 80

Designed to measure achievement in reading. Parallel English and Spanish editions have 2 alternative forms each. Designed for students in second semester of grade 1 and beginning grade 2.

864
Inter-American Series: Test of Reading, Level 2, Primary. Manuel, Herschel T. 1962
Subtests: Level of Comprehension; Speed of Comprehension; Vocabulary
Descriptors: *Achievement Tests; *Elementary School Students; *French; Primary Education; *Reading Achievement; *Reading Comprehension; *Spanish; Spanish Speaking; Vocabulary
Availability: Guidance Testing Associates; P.O. Box 28096, San Antonio, TX 78228
Grade Level: 2-3
Notes: Time, 23 approx.; Items, 110

Designed to measure reading achievement in second semester of grade 2 and grade 3. Parallel editions are published in English, Spanish, and French. The French edition was published in 1973. Two alternate forms are available for the English and Spanish editions.

865
Inter-American Series: Test of Reading, Level 3, Elementary. Manuel, Herschel T. 1962
Subtests: Vocabulary; Speed of Comprehension; Level of Comprehension
Descriptors: *Achievement Tests; *Elementary School Students; Intermediate Grades; *Reading Achievement; *Reading Comprehension; *Spanish; Spanish Speaking; *Vocabulary
Availability: Guidance Testing Associates; P.O. Box 28096, San Antonio, TX 78228
Grade Level: 4-6
Notes: Time, 41 approx.; Items, 125

Designed to measure reading achievement in grades 4-6. Parallel editions are published in English and Spanish with 2 alternate forms available. Separate English or Spanish answer sheets are required.

866
Inter-American Series: Test of Reading, Level 4, Intermediate. Manuel, Herschel T. 1962
Subtests: Vocabulary; Speed of Comprehension; Level of Comprehension
Descriptors: *Achievement Tests; Junior High Schools; *Junior High School Students; *Reading Achievement; *Reading Comprehension; *Spanish; Spanish Speaking; *Vocabulary
Availability: Guidance Testing Associates; P.O. Box 28096, San Antonio, TX 78228
Grade Level: 7-9
Notes: Time, 41 approx.; Items, 125

Designed to measure reading achievement in grades 7-9. Parallel editions are published in English and Spanish with 2 alternate forms available. Separate English or Spanish answer sheets are required.

867
Inter-American Series: Test of Reading, Level 5, Advanced. Manuel, Herschel T. 1962
Subtests: Vocabulary; Speed of Comprehension; Level of Comprehension
Descriptors: *Achievement Tests; High Schools; *High School Students; *Reading Achievement; *Reading Comprehension; *Spanish; Spanish Speaking; *Vocabulary
Availability: Guidance Testing Associates; P.O. Box 28096, San Antonio, TX 78228
Grade Level: 10-12
Notes: Time, 41 approx.; Items, 125

Designed to measure reading achievement in grades 10-12. Parallel editions are published in English and Spanish with 2 alternate forms available. Separate English or Spanish answer sheets are required.

888
Test of English as a Foreign Language. Educational Testing Service, Princeton, NJ 1982
Subtests: Listening Comprehension; Structure and Written Expression; Reading Comprehension and Vocabulary
Descriptors: Adults; College Admission; *English (Second Language); *Foreign Students; Graduate Students; Grammar; Higher Education; High School Students; *Language Proficiency; *Language Tests; Listening Comprehension Tests; Multiple Choice Tests; Reading Comprehension; Secondary Education; Sentence Structure; Undergraduate Students; Vocabulary Skills; Writing Skills
Identifiers: Test of Written English; *TOEFL; TWE
Availability: TOEFL; Box 2877, Educational Testing Service, Princeton, NJ 08541
Grade Level: 11-18
Notes: Time, 120; Items, 150

Designed to evaluate the English proficiency of non-native speakers, primarily at the secondary level, who are preparing to study at North American colleges or universities. Administered worldwide at designated test centers. The Listening Comprehension section is administered with spoken material on reel-to-reel or cassette tapes. Multiple-choice questions require test taker to answer questions based on spoken material, choose correct words and phrases, identify improper usage, answer questions based on reading passages, and choose correct word in context. Updated periodically. Beginning in 1986, the Test of Written English (TWE) was administered as part of TOEFL. The TWE provides candidates with opportunity to demonstrate their ability to compose in standard written English. The writing sample is scored on a 1 to 6 holistic scale, and the score is included in the official TOEFL score report.

1004
Neuroticism Scale Questionnaire. Scheier, Ivan H.; Cattell, Raymond B. 1961
Subtests: Overprotected, Tender-Minded Sensitivity; Depressive Overseriousness; Submissive, Dependence; Anxiety
Descriptors: *Adolescents; *Adults; Anxiety; Depression (Psychology); High Schools; High School Students; *Neurosis; Personality Measures; Personality Problems; *Psychological Testing; Self Evaluation (Individuals)
Identifiers: NSQ
Availability: Institute for Personality and Ability Testing; P. O. Box 188, Champaign, IL 61820
Grade Level: 9-12
Target Audience: 13-64
Notes: Time, 10 approx.; Items, 40

Designed to measure degree of neuroticism or "Neurotic trend" in nonhandicapped and handicapped adults and adolescents. Items are written at a 6th grade reading level.

1007
Pictorial Study of Values. Shooster, Charles N. 1957
Descriptors: Adult Literacy; *Adults; Culture Fair Tests; Higher Education; High Schools; *High School Students; *Illiteracy; *Non English Speaking; *Pictorial Stimuli; Political Attitudes; Religion; Social Values; *Undergraduate Students; *Values; *Visual Measures
Availability: Psychometric Affiliates; P.O. Box 807, Murfreesboro, TN 37133
Target Audience: 14-64
Notes: Time, 20 approx.; Items, 60

Designed to measure reactions to aesthetic, social, political, economic, religious, and theoretical basic value areas. Nonlanguage test is composed of photographs. Suitable for illiterate and non-English-speaking persons as well as for literates.

1141
ATDP. Yuker, Harold E.; And Others 1970
Descriptors: Adults; *Attitude Measures; *Disabilities; Rating Scales; *Social Attitudes

Identifiers: Attitude toward Disabled Persons Scale
Availability: Human Resources Center; Albertson, NY 11507
Target Audience: Adults
Notes: Time, 15 approx.; Items, 30
Measures attitudes of disabled and nondisabled persons toward disabled individuals.

1190
Minnesota Multiphasic Personality Inventory: Form R. Hathaway, Starke R.; McKinley, J. C. 1966
Subtests: Lie, Infrequency; Defensiveness; Hypochondriasis; Depression; Hysteria; Psychopathic Deviate; Masculinity-Femininity; Paranoia; Psychasthenia; Schizophrenia; Hypomania; Social Introversion; Anxiety; Repression; Ego Strength; MacAndrew Addiction
Descriptors: *Adolescents; *Adults; Clinical Psychology; Computer Assisted Testing; Emotional Adjustment; Microcomputers; *Older Adults; *Personality Assessment; *Personality Measures; Personality Problems; Personality Traits; *Psychological Evaluation; Psychological Testing; Psychopathology; Screening Tests; Self Evaluation (Individuals)
Identifiers: MMPI
Availability: NCS Interpretive Scoring Systems; P.O. Box 1416, Minneapolis, MN 55440
Target Audience: 16-85
Notes: Time, 90 approx.; Items, 566
Designed for use with adolescents and adults who have psychological or psychiatric difficulties. Provides clinical psychologist with information regarding treatment decisions and treatment evaluation. Identifies psychiatric symptomatology and personality dynamics. Form R consists of 566 true-false items which may be administered in approximately 90 minutes to an adolescent or adult with a minimum 6th grade reading level. Also available for computer-administered testing from Integrated Professional Systems, 5211 Mahoning Ave., Suite 135, Youngstown, OH 44515.

1201
Stanford Multi-Modality Imagery Test. Dauterman, William L. 1972
Descriptors: Adolescents; Adults; *Blindness; Geometric Constructions; *Imagination; Individual Testing; Rehabilitation; *Spatial Ability; *Visual Impairments
Identifiers: SMIT
Availability: American Foundation for the Blind; 15 W. 16th St., New York, NY 10011
Target Audience: 16-64
Designed to measure ability of blind and visually handicapped subjects to imagine geometric patterns. This aptitude is believed to be related to success in rehabilitation.

1318
Bender-Gestalt Test. Bender, Lauretta 1951
Descriptors: Adolescents; Adults; Aptitude Tests; Children; Clinical Diagnosis; Cognitive Development; Individual Development; Individual Testing; Intelligence; *Maturity (Individuals); Maturity Tests; Medical Evaluation; Mental Retardation; Motor Development; *Neurological Impairments; Patients; Perceptual Development; Perceptual Motor Coordination; *Perceptual Motor Learning; *Performance Tests; Personality Measures; *Personality Traits; *Prognostic Tests; Psychological Characteristics; *Psychological Evaluation; *Psychomotor Objectives; Visual Measures; Visual Perception; Visual Stimuli
Identifiers: The Bender
Availability: Pascal, Gerald R.; Suttell, Barbara J. The Bender-Gestalt Test. New York: Grune and Stratton, 1951.
Target Audience: 5-64
Notes: Time, 10 approx.; Items, 9
Untimed, individually administered instrument with many uses. Has been used to estimate maturation, intelligence in children but not adults, psychological disturbances, effects of injury to the cortex; as a repetitive visuomotor test; and to follow the effects of convulsive therapy. The instrument consists of 9 designs which the subject is asked to copy on a sheet of paper; the designs were originally used by Wertheimer (1921) in his studies of visual perception. According to the authors, one may think of the performance as a work sample, which involves certainly the cortical capacity to perceive the designs as presented and the psychomotor capacity to reproduce them; but it also involves (especially with subjects of normal intelligence) a factor that seems to be best described as an attitude toward reality. Requires the use of a set of cards with the designs depicted thereon. Used with patients and nonpatients. The 9 designs adapted from the Wertheimer version were simplified and adapted to accentuate a particular Gestalt feature. The original version required only a verbal description of figures.

1319
Bender Visual Motor Gestalt Test for Children. Bender, Lauretta; Clawson, Aileen 1962
Descriptors: Child Development; *Children; *Emotional Disturbances; Individual Development; *Individual Testing; Maturity (Individuals); Mental Health; *Neurological Impairments; *Perceptual Motor Learning; *Performance Tests; *Psychomotor Skills; Visual Measures; Visual Perception; Visual Stimuli
Identifiers: BVMGT
Availability: Western Psychological Services; 12031 Wilshire Blvd., Los Angeles, CA 90025
Target Audience: 7-11
Notes: Time, 15 approx.; Items, 9
Provides an index of structural and functional aspects of perceptual motor development. Uses the same BVMGT figures. Used as an aid in diagnosing the difficulties of emotionally disturbed children and identifying organic brain damage. Requires copying of 9 designs. These 9 figures were adapted from the original Wertheimer (1921) version which required only a verbal description of the figures. The figures were simplified and adapted to accentuate particular Gestalt figures.

1330
Marianne Frostig Developmental Tests of Visual Perception (3rd Edition). Frostig, Marianne; And Others 1961
Subtests: Eye Motor Coordination; Figure Ground; Constancy of Shape; Position in Space; Spatial Relationships
Descriptors: Children; *Clinical Diagnosis; Deafness; Diagnostic Tests; Educational Diagnosis; Elementary School Students; English (Second Language); *Learning Problems; Mental Retardation; Minimal Brain Dysfunction; Minimum Competencies; *Neurological Impairments; Perception Tests; Perceptual Handicaps; *Perceptual Motor Coordination; *Performance Tests; Preschool Children; *Screening Tests; Slow Learners; Spatial Ability; Visual Discrimination; Visual Measures; *Visual Perception; Visual Stimuli
Identifiers: Developmental Test of Visual Perception; DTVP; Frostig Developmental Test of Visual Perception; Oral Tests
Availability: Consulting Psychologists Press; 577 College Ave., Palo Alto, CA 94306
Target Audience: 3-10
Notes: Time, 30 approx.; Items, 44
To be used as an aid in the evaluation of strengths and handicaps of perceptual skills in young children. May be given to small groups and to individual children. Used as a screening test for preschool through first graders and as an evaluative instrument for children with learning difficulties or neurological handicaps such as cerebral palsy or with mentally retarded children. There is an adaptation of the administrative manual available for use with deaf, hard-of-hearing, and non-English-speaking children. Has also been used as an aid in evaluating the visual perceptual abilities of adult victims of stroke or other brain injury. Requires the use of demonstration cards; and a blackboard is required for group administration.

1384
Cain-Levine Social Competency Scales. Cain, Leo F.; And Others 1963
Subtests: Self Help; Initiative; Social Skills; Communication
Descriptors: Adolescents; *Behavior Rating Scales; *Children; Communication Skills; *Daily Living Skills; Individual Testing; *Interpersonal Competence; Interviews; *Mild Mental Retardation; *Moderate Mental Retardation; Prosocial Behavior; *Skill Analysis; Skill Development
Identifiers: CLSCS
Availability: Consulting Psychologists Press; 577 College Ave., Palo Alto, CA 94306
Target Audience: 5-13
Notes: Time, 40 approx.; Items, 44
Behavior rating scale for measuring the social competence of trainable mentally retarded children. Uses the interview technique for obtaining the data from teacher, parent, or counselor. The authors define social competency as the development of learned skills which ultimately permits the child to achieve self-sufficiency and socially contributory behaviors. Includes motor performance, the degree of self-directed behavior and of interpersonal relationships, and the degree to which the children make themselves and their wants known.

1479
Full Range Picture Vocabulary Test. Ammons, R.B.; Ammons, H.S. 1948
Descriptors: Adolescents; Adults; *Children; *Comprehension; *Disabilities; Individual Testing; Intelligence; *Intelligence Tests; *Nonverbal Tests; Pictorial Stimuli; Screening Tests; *Young Children
Identifiers: FRPV

Availability: Psychological Test Specialists; Box 9229, Missoula, MT 59807
Target Audience: 2-34
Notes: Time, 10 approx.; Items, 16
Designed to measure intelligence based on verbal comprehension. Useful for age levels from 2 through adulthood. No reading or writing is required of examinee. Subject points to picture which corresponds to word given by examiner. Words were organized in approximate order of difficulty. May be used with physically handicapped subjects and those with speech defects. Forms A and B are available.

1486
Organic Integrity Test. Tien, H.C. 1965
Descriptors: Adolescents; Adults; Children; Diagnostic Tests; *Neurological Impairments; Patients; Psychiatric Hospitals; Psychosis; Schizophrenia; *Screening Tests
Identifiers: OIT (Tien)
Availability: Psychodiagnostic Test Co.; Box 859, E. Lansing, MI 48823
Target Audience: 5-64
Notes: Time, 3 approx.; Items, 10
Designed to detect the ability of the central nervous system in a subject to perceive gestalt. Inability to perceive gestalt, or form, would indicate cortical damage as a result of any brain disease.

1546
Cornell Word Form 2. Weider, Arthur 1955
Descriptors: Adjustment (to Environment); *Adults; Emotional Problems; Forced Choice Technique; *Psychological Evaluation; *Screening Tests
Identifiers: CWF2; Psychiatric Patients; *Psychiatric Problems
Availability: Dr. Arthur Weider; 823 United Nations Plaza, Ste. 404, New York, NY 10017
Target Audience: Adults
Notes: Items, 80
A modification of the individually administered word association technique designed for group administration. Designed as a screening test to identify neuropsychiatrically ill subjects.

1547
Valett Developmental Survey of Basic Learning Abilities. Valett, Robert E. 1966
Subtests: Motor Integration and Physical Development; Tactile Discrimination; Auditory Discrimination; Visual-Motor Coordination; Visual Discrimination; Language Development and Verbal Fluency; Conceptual Development
Descriptors: Auditory Discrimination; Child Development; *Cognitive Development; Cognitive Measurement; Cognitive Style; Concept Formation; Developmental Stages; *Developmental Tasks; Individual Testing; Language Acquisition; *Learning; *Learning Disabilities; Perception; Performance Tests; *Physical Development; *School Readiness; Skill Development; Visual Discrimination; *Young Children
Identifiers: Valett Survey
Availability: Consulting Psychologists Press; 577 College Ave., Palo Alto, CA 94306
Target Audience: 2-7
Notes: Items, 233
Individually administered, untimed instrument to evaluate the various developmental abilities of young children. Includes those developmental tasks which are a prerequisite to formal learning. Useful in working with children who have specific learning disabilities and in developing remedial or preventive education. Also used for determining the need for complete diagnostic evaluation and for planning individualized learning programs. Requires the purchase of a specially designed card set; and a collection of toys and objects must be gathered together by the administrator.

1548
The Jesness Inventory. Jesness, Carl F. 1962
Subtests: Social Maladjustment; Value Orientation; Immaturity; Autism; Alienation; Manifest Aggression; Withdrawal; Social Anxiety; Repression; Denial; Asocial Index
Descriptors: *Adolescents; Autism; Behavior Problems; Children; *Delinquency; *Personality Measures; Personality Problems; Personality Traits; *Social Adjustment
Availability: Consulting Psychologists Press; 577 College Ave., Palo Alto, CA 94306
Target Audience: 8-18
Notes: Time, 30 approx.; Items, 155
Designed to distinguish disturbed children from others and provide the basis for a personality typology useful with children and adolescents. Inventory was developed as part of a 5-year study of delinquency, the Fricot Research Project. Yields scores on 11 personality characteristics.

1557
SRA Pictorial Reasoning Test. McMurry, Robert N.; Arnold, Phyllis D. 1966
Descriptors: *Abstract Reasoning; Adults; Aptitude Tests; *Blacks; Concept Formation; *Culture Fair Tests; Entry Workers; High Schools; *High School Students; *Hispanic Americans; Screening Tests; *Vocational Aptitude; *Whites
Identifiers: PRT; Self Administered Tests; Self Scoring Tests
Availability: Science Research Associates, Inc.; 155 N. Wacker Dr., Chicago, IL 60606
Grade Level: 9-12
Target Audience: 14-64
Notes: Time, 15; Items, 80

Designed as a test of general ability to measure learning potential of individuals from diverse backgrounds with reading difficulties. Instrument is culturally fair and predictive of job success. Most useful as a screening test for entry level jobs. Directions have been written at a 6th grade reading level to facilitate understanding.

1563
Maxfield-Buchholz Scale of Social Maturity for Use with Preschool Blind Children. Maxfield, Kathryn E.; Bucholz, Sandra 1957
Subtests: Self-Help General; Self-Help Dressing; Self-Help Eating; Communication; Socialization; Locomotion; Occupation
Descriptors: *Blindness; Interviews; *Maturity (Individuals); *Preschool Children; Preschool Education; *Self Care Skills; *Social Development; *Young Children
Identifiers: MB Scale
Availability: American Foundation for the Blind, Inc.; 15 W. 16th St., New York, NY 10011
Target Audience: 1-6
Notes: Items, 95

Designed to determine a social quotient for young blind children. The social quotient represents the relationship between chronological age and social age. An informant familiar with the child is interviewed to gather information to assess social maturity.

1596
Anton Brenner Development Gestalt of School Readiness. Brenner, Anton 1964
Subtests: Number Producing; Number Recognition; Ten Dot Gestalt; Sentence Gestalt; Draw-a-Man
Descriptors: *Concept Formation; Disadvantaged; Non English Speaking; *Perceptual Development; *Preschool Children; Preschool Education; *School Readiness; *School Readiness Tests
Identifiers: BGT; Gestalt Psychology
Availability: Western Psychological Services; 12031 Wilshire Blvd., Los Angeles, CA 90025
Target Audience: 5-6
Notes: Time, 10 approx.; Items, 40

Predicts success in kindergarten and first grade. Almost culture free; can be used with culturally deprived and non-English speaking children. Provides quantitative and qualitative evaluation of child's perceptual and conceptual development. Uses Gestalt and developmental principles, and can be used to identify early maturing and/or gifted; slowly maturing and/or retarded; and emotionally disturbed children. The child's performance is then interpreted through readiness rating scales.

1659
Culture Fair Intelligence Test, Scale 1. Cattell, Raymond B.; Cattell, A. K. S.
Subtests: Substitution; Classification; Mazes; Selecting Named Objects; Following Directions; Wrong Pictures; Riddles; Similarities
Descriptors: Adolescents; *Adults; Children; Culture Fair Tests; *Elementary School Students; *Individual Testing; *Institutionalized Persons; *Intelligence; *Intelligence Tests; *Mental Retardation; Spatial Ability; Timed Tests
Identifiers: Cattell Culture Fair Intelligence Test; CFIT
Availability: Institute for Personality and Ability Testing; P.O. Box 188, Champaign, IL 61820
Target Audience: 4-64
Notes: Time, 22 approx.; Items, 96

Designed to measure individual intelligence. Only 4 of 8 subtests are culture fair. Scale 1 is to be used with children 4 to 8 years of age and with retarded adults who are institutionalized.

1660
Culture Fair Intelligence Test, Scale 2. Cattell, Raymond B.; Cattell, A.K.S. 1961
Subtests: Series; Classifications; Matrices; Conditions; Topology

Descriptors: *Adults; *Culture Fair Tests; *Elementary School Students; Elementary Secondary Education; Individual Testing; *Intelligence; *Intelligence Tests; *Junior High School Students; *Non English Speaking; *Nonverbal Tests; *Spatial Ability; Timed Tests
Identifiers: Cattell Culture Fair Intelligence Test; CFIT
Availability: Institute for Personality and Ability Testing; P.O. Box 188, Champaign, IL 61820
Target Audience: 8-64
Notes: Time, 13 approx.; Items, 46

Designed to measure individual intelligence in a manner designed to reduce the influence of verbal fluency, cultural climate, and educational level. May be administered to groups or individuals. Scale consists of 4 subtests, involving different perceptual tasks. Forms A and B are available. May be used with children ages 8-14 years and with adults in average intelligence range. Scale 2 is appropriate for majority of subjects.

1661
Culture Fair Intelligence Test, Scale 3. Cattell, Raymond B.; Cattell, A.K.S. 1963
Subtests: Series; Classifications; Matrices; Conditions (Topology)
Descriptors: *Adults; *College Students; *Culture Fair Tests; Higher Education; High Schools; *High School Students; Individual Testing; *Intelligence; *Intelligence Tests; *Non English Speaking; Nonverbal Tests; *Spatial Ability; Timed Tests
Identifiers: Cattell Culture Fair Intelligence Test; CFIT
Availability: Institute for Personality and Ability Testing; P.O. Box 188, Champaign, IL 61820
Target Audience: 15-64
Notes: Time, 13 approx.; Items, 50

Designed to measure individual intelligence in a manner designed to reduce the influence of verbal fluency, cultural climate, and educational level. May be administered to groups or individuals. Scale consists of 4 subtests, involving different perceptual tasks. Forms A and B are available. Scale 3 is more difficult than Scales 1 or 2 and obtains a greater refinement in the higher intelligence ranges. Useful with high school and college students and with adults of superior intelligence.

1668
Memory-for-Designs Test. Graham, Frances K.; Kendall, Barbara S. 1960
Descriptors: Adolescents; Adults; Children; Diagnostic Tests; *Neurological Impairments; *Perceptual Motor Coordination; *Screening Tests; *Short Term Memory
Identifiers: MFD
Availability: Psychological Test Specialists; Box 9229, Missoula, MT 59807
Target Audience: 8-60
Notes: Time, 10 approx.; Items, 15

Drawing test of perceptual motor coordination, which depends on immediate memory. Differentiates between groups of patients with brain disorders including those with focal and diffuse lesions. Useful as a screening device to identify patients with functionally based behavior disorders from those associated with brain injury. Subject is shown a series of 15 designs which he/she reproduces immediately from memory.

1688
Purdue Handicap Problems Inventory. Wright, George N.; Remmers, H.H. 1960
Subtests: Personal; Family; Social Vocational
Descriptors: Adjustment (to Environment); *Adolescents; *Adults; *Counseling Techniques; *Diagnostic Tests; Family Problems; *Physical Disabilities; *Problems; Self Evaluation (Individuals); Vocational Adjustment
Identifiers: HPI
Availability: University Book Store; Dept. 974; 360 State St., W. Lafayette, IN 47096
Target Audience: 13-64
Notes: Time, 35 approx.; Items, 280

Designed for use with physically disabled adolescents and adults who have attained a 5th grade educational level or above. Significance subjects attach to their physical impairment is revealed by problems they believe are a result of their handicap. Useful diagnostic instrument for counselors of physically disabled individuals.

1715
Interpersonal Adjustment Rating Form. Megargee, Edwin I. 1970
Descriptors: Adults; Behavior Rating Scales; Emotional Adjustment; *Interpersonal Relationship; Maturity (Individuals); *Prisoners
Availability: Dr. Edwin I. Megargee; Psychology Dept., Florida State University, Tallahassee, FL 32306
Target Audience: Adults
Notes: Items, 8

Designed to assess interpersonal behavior and adjustment of inmates in correctional settings.

1716
Work Performance Rating Form. Megargee, Edwin I. 1970
Descriptors: Adults; Behavior Rating Scales; Correctional Institutions; Interpersonal Competence; *Job Performance; Motivation; *Observation; *Prisoners
Identifiers: TIM(A)
Availability: Tests in Microfiche; Test Collection, Educational Testing Service, Princeton, NJ 08541
Target Audience: Adults
Notes: Items, 9

Assesses the adjustment and behavior of inmates in their work in a correctional setting. It contains 9, 5-point scales pertaining to quality and quantity of work, job motivation, and interpersonal behavior.

1717
Procedures in Dealing with Children. Cromwell, Rue L. 1966
Subtests: Milieu and Collateral Information (39); Dealing with Specific Behaviors (13); Patterns or Sequences of Response to the Child's Behavior (5)
Descriptors: Arousal Patterns; Behavior Rating Scales; *Child Caregivers; *Children; *Emotional Disturbances; Emotional Response; Institutionalized Persons; *Observation; Problem Children; Psychotherapy; *Responses; *Teachers; *Therapists
Identifiers: PDC; TIM(A)
Availability: Tests in Microfiche; Test Collection, Educational Testing Service, Princeton, NJ 08541
Target Audience: Children
Notes: Items, 57

Assesses the responses which children arouse in adults. The scale is in 3 parts: general aspects of the treatment center, family, and community, as they are experienced by the child; situations which require some response to the child; and sequences and patterns of adult response. It is intended for use by teachers, therapists, and other workers who deal with emotionally disturbed children.

1723
Thurston Sentence Completion Form. Thurston, John R. 1959
Descriptors: Adults; *Attitude Measures; Child Rearing; Children; *Disabilities; Institutionalized Persons; *Parent Attitudes; *Parents; Projective Measures
Identifiers: TIM(C); TSCF
Availability: Tests in Microfiche; Test Collection, Educational Testing Service, Princeton, NJ 08541
Target Audience: Adults
Notes: Items, 45

Designed to elicit the attitudes and emotional reactions of the parents of handicapped children in 7 areas: personal reactions and concerns; attitudes regarding the child's satisfactions—discomfitures; reactions of brothers and sisters; reactions of community, friends, neighbors; attitudes toward the institution-hospital-treatment center and staff; attitudes relating to the hopes and expectations of the parent for the handicapped; and attitudes of a general nature.

1726
Denver Articulation Screening Exam. Frankenburg, William K.; Drumwright, Amelia F. 1973
Descriptors: *Articulation (Speech); *Articulation Impairments; Individual Testing; *Preschool Children; *Screening Tests; *Speech Tests; Young Children
Identifiers: DASE; *Denver Screening Tests for Preschoolers
Availability: Denver Developmental Materials; P.O. Box 6919, Denver, CO 80206-0919
Target Audience: 2-6
Notes: Time, 5; Items, 30

Brief screening test designed to detect articulation disorders in children ages 2-1/2 to 6 years. Measures ability to pronounce 30 sound elements and rates a child's intelligibility in conversation. Developed and standardized with Anglo, Afro, and Mexican-American preschoolers. DASE Manual/Workbook and Training Film or Videotape are designed to train paraprofessionals in test administration.

1727
Denver Audiometric Screening Test: 1972 Edition. Drumwright, Amelia F.; Frankenburg, William K. 1972
Descriptors: *Audiometric Tests; Auditory Tests; *Hearing Impairments; Individual Testing; *Preschool Children; *Screening Tests; Young Children

Identifiers: DAST; *Denver Screening Tests for Preschoolers
Availability: Denver Developmental Materials; P.O. Box 6919, Denver, CO 80206-0919
Target Audience: 3-6
Notes: Time, 10 approx.

Brief screening procedure designed to identify preschool children, ages 3-6 years, who are likely to have a serious hearing loss. DAST Manual/Workbook and Training Film is part of instructional module for paraprofessionals. A puretone audiometer is used to administer test.

1728
Denver Eye Screening Test. Barker, John; And Others 1973
Subtests: Vision Test (Age Appropriate); Cover Test; Pupillary Light Reflex Test
Descriptors: Ametropia; Individual Testing; *Infants; *Preschool Children; *Screening Tests; Strabismus; *Vision Tests; Visual Acuity; *Visual Impairments; Young Children
Identifiers: *Denver Screening Tests for Preschoolers; DEST
Availability: Denver Developmental Materials; P.O. Box 6919, Denver, CO 80206-0919
Target Audience: 0-6
Notes: Time, 10 approx.

Brief screening test used to detect problems in visual acuity and nonstraight eyes (strabismus refractive error and amblyopia). Useful for children 6 months to 6 years of age. Vision test differs for different age groups. "E" test for ages 3-6 years. Picture Card Test for 2-1/2 to 2-11/12 years. Fixation Test for children younger than 2-1/2 years. DEST Manual/Workbook and Training Film or Video Cassettes are available for training in test administration.

1741
Behavior Rating Scale. Kenny, Thomas J.; And Others 1968
Descriptors: *Adjustment (to Environment); *Behavior Problems; Behavior Rating Scales; Children; Elementary Education; *Elementary School Students; *Exceptional Persons
Availability: Thomas J. Kenny; University of Maryland Hospital, University of Maryland, 22 S. Green St., Baltimore, MD 21201
Target Audience: 6-12
Notes: Items, 16

Designed to assess behavior and adjustment of exceptional children.

1763
Correctional Institutions Environment Scale. Moos, Rudolf H. 1974
Subtests: Involvement; Support; Expressiveness; Autonomy; Practical Orientation; Personal Problem Orientation; Order and Organization; Clarity; Staff Control
Descriptors: *Adolescents; *Adults; Attitude Measures; *Correctional Institutions; *Institutional Environment; *Institutionalized Persons; Secondary Education; Secondary School Students; Social Environment
Identifiers: CIES; Social Climate Scales
Availability: Consulting Psychologists Press; 577 College Ave., Palo Alto, CA 94306
Grade Level: 7-12
Target Audience: 13-64
Notes: Time, 20 approx.; Items, 90

Designed to assess the effects of programs, staff training, and other factors on the social environment of juvenile and adult correctional facilities. The 3 dimensions assessed are relationship dimensions, treatment program dimensions, and system maintenance dimensions. This scale has been adapted to measure the ideal social environment (Form I), or the expectations one has of an environment (Form E). Short form (Form S) may be adapted from standard Form R. Alternate scales and their construction are described in the manual.

1769
Carrow Elicited Language Inventory. Carrow-Woolfolk, Elizabeth 1974
Descriptors: Articulation (Speech); *Audiotape Recorders; Audiotape Recordings; *Diagnostic Tests; Individual Testing; *Language Handicaps; Linguistic Performance; *Speech Skills; Young Children
Identifiers: CELI
Availability: DLM Teaching Resources; P.O. Box 4000, One DLM Park, Allen, TX 75002
Target Audience: 3-7
Notes: Time, 5; Items, 52

Designed to measure a child's productive control of grammar. Uses technique of eliciting imitations of a sequence of sentences systematically developed to include basic sentence construction types and specific grammatical morphemes. Used to identify children with language problems. May be administered by a speech pathologist, or by any trained examiner with background in psycholinguistics and language disorders.

1770
Self Observation Scales: Primary Level. Stenner, A. Jackson; Katzenmeyer, William G. 1974
Subtests: Self-Acceptance; Social Maturity; School Affiliation; Self Security; Achievement Motivation
Descriptors: *Elementary School Students; Interpersonal Relationship; Maturity (Individuals); Primary Education; School Attitudes; *Self Concept; *Self Concept Measures; Spanish; *Spanish Speaking; Student Adjustment; Student Attitudes
Identifiers: SOS
Availability: Publishers Test Service; 2500 Garden Rd., Monterey, CA 93940
Grade Level: K-3
Notes: Time, 25 approx.; Items, 50

Designed to measure 5 dimensions of student's self-concept. Assesses relationships with student's teachers and peers. Alternate forms A and B are available in English. Form 5 is Spanish language version.

1773
Preschool Behavior Questionnaire. Behar, Lenore; Stringfield, Samuel 1974
Subtests: Hostile-Aggressive; Anxious-Fearful; Hyperactive-Distractible
Descriptors: Affective Behavior; Aggression; Anxiety; *Behavior Problems; *Behavior Rating Scales; *Emotional Disturbances; Hyperactivity; Observation; Physical Characteristics; Preschool Education; Screening Tests; Social Behavior; *Young Children
Identifiers: Childrens Behavior Questionnaire; PBQ; Rutter (Michael)
Availability: Lenore Behar; Division of Mental Health, Alb Bldg., 325 N. Salisbury St., Raleigh, NC 27610
Target Audience: 3-6
Notes: Items, 30

Screening device designed for use by teachers and child care workers to identify children who show symptoms of emotional disturbance. A modification of Rutter's Children's Behavior Questionnaire. Observer rates frequency of interpersonal, emotional, and physical behaviors.

1777
Environmental Support Questionnaire. Lyon, Keith E.; Zucker, Robert A. 1974
Descriptors: Adults; *Daily Living Skills; Employment Problems; Interpersonal Competence; *Mental Disorders; Questionnaires; *Social Adjustment; *Social Influences
Identifiers: TIM(B)
Availability: Tests in Microfiche; Test Collection, Educational Testing Service, Princeton, NJ 08541
Target Audience: Adults

Designed to measure the amount of support available in the expatient's environment. The semistructured interview covers 13 environmental support variables: residential living involvement, residential living pressure, employment involvement, employment pressure, employment perception, responsibility involvement, responsibility pressure, responsibility perception, visitor involvement, visitor perception, visitor pressure, professional involvement, and medication involvement.

1782
Student Drug Survey. Hays, J. Ray 1971
Descriptors: Dropout Characteristics; *Drug Abuse; *Questionnaires; Secondary Education; *Secondary School Students; *Student Attitudes
Identifiers: TIM(B)
Availability: Tests in Microfiche; Test Collection, Educational Testing Service, Princeton, NJ 08541
Grade Level: 7-12
Notes: Items, 88

Designed to provide information on drug abuse among secondary school students and to identify similar characteristics among drug abusers. Also used to provide information on drug abuse and its correlation with prevalance of dropouts.

1785
Crawford Psychological Adjustment Scale. Crawford, Paul L. 1968
Subtests: Social-Economical-Environmental Competence; Derangement of Thought Process; Physical Behavior; Communications; Social Acceptability of Behavior; Management of Hostility
Descriptors: Adults; *Behavior Patterns; *Emotional Adjustment; Hostility; *Interpersonal Competence; *Mental Disorders; *Personality Measures; *Social Adjustment
Identifiers: TIM(B)
Availability: Tests in Microfiche; Test Collection, Educational Testing Service, Princeton, NJ 08541

Target Audience: Adults
Notes: Items, 25

Measures behavioral indices of personality adjustment in adults. Yields scores for 6 factors: social-economic-environmental competence, derangement of thought processes/peculiar behavior, physical behavior, communication skills, social acceptability, and management of hostility. Ratings should be made by person with knowledge of the patient; however, anamnestic data may be used to supplement first-hand knowledge. The rater should consider the patient's behavior within a specific time period, e.g., the most recent 6 months or so.

1793
DIAL. Mardell-Czudnowski, Carol D.; Goldenberg, Dorothea S. 1975
Subtests: Gross Motor Skills; Fine Motor Skills; Concepts; Communication Skills
Descriptors: *Ability Identification; Concept Formation; Individual Testing; Language Skills; *Learning Disabilities; Observation; Performance Tests; *Preschool Children; Preschool Education; Psychomotor Skills; *Screening Tests; Special Education
Identifiers: Development Indicators for Assessment of Learning
Availability: Childcraft Education Corporation; 20 Kilmer Rd., Edison, NJ 08818
Target Audience: 2-5
Notes: Time, 30 approx.; Items, 28

A team-administered, individual observation for screening preschool children's gross motor, fine motor, concepts, and communication skills. The team should consist of a coordinator and 4 operators. Used to identify children who should be referred for diagnosis of special educational needs.

1822
Adult Basic Learning Examination: Level I Forms A and B. Karlsen, Bjorn; And Others 1967
Subtests: Vocabulary; Reading; Spelling; Arithmetic
Descriptors: Academic Achievement; *Achievement Tests; *Adult Basic Education; Adults; *Arithmetic; *Basic Vocabulary; *Reading Achievement; *Spelling
Identifiers: ABLE; Test Batteries
Availability: The Psychological Corporation; 555 Academic Ct., San Antonio, TX 78204-0952
Target Audience: Adults
Notes: Time, 130 approx.; Items, 178

Battery of tests designed to measure general educational level of adults who have not completed a formal 8th grade education. Level I tests achievement levels equivalent to grades 1-4.

1823
Adult Basic Learning Examination—Level II. Karlsen, Bjorn; And Others 1967
Subtests: Vocabulary; Reading; Spelling; Arithmetic
Descriptors: Academic Achievement; *Achievement Tests; *Adult Basic Education; Adults; *Arithmetic; *Computation; Problem Solving; *Reading Achievement; *Spelling; *Vocabulary
Identifiers: ABLE; Test Batteries
Availability: The Psychological Corporation; 555 Academic Ct., San Antonio, TX 78204-0952
Target Audience: Adults
Notes: Time, 135 approx.; Items, 198

Battery of tests designed to measure general educational level of adults who have not completed a formal 8th grade education. Level II tests achievement levels equivalent to grades 5-8. Forms A and B are available.

2041
Quick Screening Scale of Mental Development. Banham, Katharine M. 1963
Subtests: Bodily Coordination; Manual Performance; Speech and Language; Listening Attention and Number; Play Interests
Descriptors: Behavior Rating Scales; *Children; *Cognitive Ability; Individual Testing; Infant Behavior; *Infants; *Intelligence; *Intelligence Tests; *Special Education
Identifiers: QSS
Availability: Psychometric Affiliates; P.O. Box 807, Murfreesboro, TN 37133
Target Audience: 0-10
Notes: Time, 30 approx.

Designed to provide a preliminary estimate of a child's level of mental development. Used for children ages 6 months to 10 years in clinics, hospitals, and special schools.

2047
Proverbs Test: Forms I, II and III. Gorham, Donald R. 1956

Descriptors: *Abstract Reasoning; Adolescents; *Adults; *Cognitive Tests; Emotional Disturbances; Essay Tests; Higher Education; High Schools; *High School Students; Individual Testing; *Patients; Proverbs; Psychiatric Hospitals; Schizophrenia
Identifiers: Schizophrenic Patients; Verbal Reasoning
Availability: Psychological Test Specialists; Box 9229, Missoula, MT 59807
Target Audience: 16-64
Notes: Time, 30 approx.; Items, 12
Designed to measure verbal comprehension and abstract reasoning by requiring subjects to explain the meaning of several proverbs. May be used with hospitalized mental patients as well as with nonhandicapped populations. Instrument is sensitive to temporary intellectual impairment associated with severe emotional disturbance or schizophrenic disorganization. Forms I, II, and III are equivalent, and each is scaled for difficulty.

2048
Proverbs Test: Best Answer Form. Gorham, Donald R. 1956
Subtests: Abstract; Concrete
Descriptors: *Abstract Reasoning; *Adolescents; *Adults; *Children; *Cognitive Tests; *Elementary School Students; Emotional Disturbances; Higher Education; Intermediate Grades; Multiple Choice Tests; Proverbs; Schizophrenia; Secondary Education; Secondary School Students; Undergraduate Students
Identifiers: Schizophrenic Patients; Verbal Reasoning
Availability: Psychological Test Specialists; Box 9229, Missoula, MT 59807
Grade Level: 5-16
Target Audience: 10-64
Notes: Time, 40 approx.; Items, 40
Designed to measure verbal comprehension and abstract reasoning, or intelligence. Useful in clinical research and evaluation, screening and survey. Subject must select response which indicates meaning of given proverb. May be used with hospitalized mental patients, as well as with nonhandicapped populations.

2068
Benton Revised Visual Retention Test. Benton, Arthur L. 1974
Descriptors: Adolescents; Adults; Children; *Diagnostic Tests; *Memory; *Neurological Impairments; *Visual Perception
Identifiers: BVRT
Availability: The Psychological Corporation; 555 Academic Ct., San Antonio, TX 78204-0952
Target Audience: 8-64
Notes: Time, 5 approx.; Items, 10
Clinical and research instrument designed to assess visual perception and visual memory. Useful in experimental research and as a supplement to mental examinations of persons suspected of abnormality or impairment. Three forms, C, D, and E, are available.

2082
Porteus Mazes: Vineland Revision. Porteus, Stanley D. 1959
Descriptors: *Adolescents; *Adults; Aptitude Tests; *Children; *Cognitive Ability; *Language Handicaps; *Nonverbal Tests; Psychological Evaluation; Spatial Ability
Identifiers: *Mazes; Porteus Maze Test (Original)
Availability: The Psychological Corporation; 555 Academic Ct., San Antonio, TX 78204-0952
Target Audience: 3-12; 14; 18-64
Notes: Time, 15 approx.; Items, 12
A nonlanguage test of mental ability used with verbally handicapped subjects in anthropological studies and in research on the effects of drugs and psychosurgery. Basic tests consisting of 12 mazes used in routine clinical examinations.

2083
Porteus Mazes: Extension. Porteus, Stanley D. 1965
Descriptors: *Adolescents; *Adults; Aptitude Tests; *Children; *Cognitive Ability; *Language Handicaps; *Nonverbal Tests; Psychological Evaluation; Spatial Ability
Identifiers: *Mazes; Porteus Maze Test; *Retesting
Availability: The Psychological Corporation; 555 Academic Ct., San Antonio, TX 78204-0952
Target Audience: 7-12; 14; 18-64
Notes: Time, 25 approx.; Items, 8
A nonlanguage test of mental ability used with verbally handicapped subjects in anthropological studies and in research on the effects of drugs and psychosurgery. Developed to provide for retesting a series of 8 mazes, each slightly more difficult than the one for matching year in the Vineland series. Should not be used as an initial test.

2084
Porteus Mazes: Supplement. Porteus, Stanley D. 1965
Descriptors: *Adolescents; *Adults; Aptitude Tests; *Children; *Cognitive Ability; *Language Handicaps; *Nonverbal Tests; Psychological Evaluation; Spatial Ability
Identifiers: *Mazes; Porteus Maze Test; *Retesting
Availability: The Psychological Corporation; 555 Academic Ct., San Antonio, TX 78204-0952
Target Audience: 7-12; 14; 18-64
Notes: Time, 25 approx.
A nonlanguage test of mental ability used with verbally handicapped subjects in anthropological studies and in research on the effects of drugs and psychosurgery. Developed to meet need for a third testing in certain clinical and research situations. For use with subjects who have previously been tested with both the Vineland Revision and the Extension. Mazes are slightly more difficult than those in extension series.

2100
Ohio Penal Classification Test. Sell, DeWitt E. 1954
Subtests: Block Counting; Digit Symbol; Number Series; Memory Span for Objects
Descriptors: *Adult Literacy; Adults; Correctional Institutions; *Culture Fair Tests; Disadvantaged; *Illiteracy; Intelligence Quotient; *Intelligence Tests; Mental Age; *Nonverbal Ability; Nonverbal Tests; *Prisoners; Semiskilled Workers; Timed Tests; Unskilled Workers; Visual Stimuli
Identifiers: OPCT; Power Tests
Availability: Psychometric Affiliates; P.O. Box 807, Murfreesboro, TN 37133
Target Audience: Adults
Notes: Time, 15; Items, 230
A culture fair, timed instrument designed to measure the mental ability of inmates in penal institutions. Measures the spatial, perceptual, numerical, memory, and reasoning aspects of intellectual functioning. Though timed for 14.5 minutes, it is considered a power rather than speed test. Standardized on penal inmates and 9th grade males; considered applicable in industrial and other nonacademic situations. Available as Form F.

2101
Ohio Classification Test. Sell, DeWitt E.; And Others 1957
Subtests: Block Counting; Digit Symbol; Number Series; Memory Span
Descriptors: *Adult Literacy; Adults; *Culture Fair Tests; Disadvantaged; *Illiteracy; Intelligence Quotient; *Intelligence Tests; *Job Applicants; Mental Age; *Nonverbal Ability; Nonverbal Tests; Personnel; *Semiskilled Workers; Timed Tests; *Unskilled Workers; Visual Stimuli
Identifiers: OCT; Power Tests
Availability: Psychometric Affiliates; P.O. Box 807, Murfreesboro, TN 37133
Target Audience: Adults
Notes: Time, 15; Items, 230
A timed, culture fair, group-administered adult intelligence test for the general adult population which minimizes verbal factors and which emphasizes power rather than speed. Basically the same test as the Ohio Penal Classification Test (TC002100); this slightly changed version includes industrial norms as well as some specific validation evidence from industry. Used for factory workers, sales and managerial applicants, middle management personnel, graduate engineers, scientific students, and technical students, the authors feel this may be administered to near-illiterates or non-English-language applicants.

2128
Pictorial Test of Intelligence. French, Joseph L. 1964
Subtests: Picture Vocabulary; Form Discrimination; Information and Comprehension; Similarities; Size and Number; Immediate Recall
Descriptors: *Disabilities; Individual Testing; *Intelligence; *Intelligence Tests; *Pictorial Stimuli; *Preschool Children; Preschool Education; Primary Education; Recall (Psychology); *Young Children
Identifiers: PTI
Availability: Riverside Publishing Co.; 8420 Bryn Mawr Ave., Chicago, IL 60631
Target Audience: 3-8
Notes: Time, 45 approx.; Items, 137
Designed to assess general intellectual level of nonhandicapped and handicapped children, ages 3 to 8. A shorter form is available for 3- and 4-year-olds which reduces administration time by about 15 minutes.

2203
PTI Oral Directions Test. Langmuir, Charles R. 1954

Descriptors: Adults; Audiotape Recordings; *Educationally Disadvantaged; *English (Second Language); Job Applicants; *Listening Comprehension; Listening Comprehension Tests; *Occupational Tests; Spanish; *Unskilled Workers
Identifiers: CAST; Controlled Administration of Standardized Tests; Personnel Tests for Industry
Availability: The Psychological Corporation; 555 Academic Ct., San Antonio, TX 78204-0952
Target Audience: 18-64
Notes: Time, 15; Items, 16
Designed to measure ability to understand and follow oral directions. Suitable for applicants for maintenance and service work. Measures general mental ability of individuals with limited education or a limited knowledge of English. Test is administered on audiotape, so reading ability is not required. Two English forms, S and T, are available. A Spanish-language edition of Form S is also available. Tapes for administering PTI-ODT in a "CAST" system are also available.

2267
Domino Test, D48 Form. Anstey, E.; And Others 1962
Descriptors: Adolescents; Adult Literacy; Adults; Children; *Culture Fair Tests; *Illiteracy; Intelligence Quotient; *Intelligence Tests; Mental Age; *Nonverbal Ability; Nonverbal Tests; Timed Tests; *Visual Stimuli
Identifiers: British Army Dominoes Test; D48 Test; Dominoes Test; Group Test 100
Availability: Consulting Psychologists Press; 577 College Ave., Palo Alto, CA 94306
Target Audience: 10-64
Notes: Time, 25; Items, 44
Timed, group-administered, nonverbal, cross-cultural instrument that measures the "g" or general factor in intelligence. Based upon the British Army Dominoes Test and Group 100. Each item contains a number of dominoes with a black domino. The subject is to determine the number of dots appropriate for each half of the blank domino. Each item (group of dominoes) depicts a principle of progression. First developed in 1943 by Anstey and Illing for the British War Office; later, various revisions were developed. French and Italian adaptations were prepared in the 1940s, and this American version was first published in the U.S. in 1962. The manual for the U.S. edition prepared by John D. Black. Experimental and research edition.

2328
California Medical Survey. Snow, Harold L.; Manson, Morse P. 1962
Subtests: Chronicity; Emotional; Familial; Medical; Psychiatric; Specific; Organic Medical; Genito-Urinary; Neuro-Muscular Skeletal; Cardio-Vascular-Blood; Sensory; Digestive; Respiratory; Gynecology-Menstruation; Gynecology-Surgery; Gynecology-Menopause; Gynecology-Sterility; Gynecology-Pregnancy; Anxiety-Stress; Psychiatric; Habits-Traits; Sexual-Social; Energy Level
Descriptors: Adolescents; Adults; *Biographical Inventories; Case Records; Children; Females; Males; Mental Health; *Patients; Personality Traits; Physical Health; Stress Variables
Identifiers: CMS; Self Report Measures; Symptoms
Availability: Western Psychological Services; 12031 Wilshire Blvd., Los Angeles, CA 90025
Target Audience: 10-64
Notes: Time, 20 approx.
Designed to provide physicians with medical, psychiatric, and psychological information about a patient. Patient completes the instrument prior to initial interview with clinician or physician. Forms available for children, men, and women. Form C contains 218 items. Form M contains 275 items. Form W contains 295 items. Based upon Cornell Medical Index (TC001545).

2346
Purdue Perceptual Motor Survey. Roach, Eugene G.; Kephart, Newell C. 1966
Subtests: Balance and Posture; Body Image and Differentiation; Perceptual-Motor Match; Ocular Control; Form Perception
Descriptors: Children; Elementary Education; *Elementary School Students; *Handicap Identification; Lateral Dominance; Perceptual Handicaps; *Perceptual Motor Coordination; Performance Tests; *Screening Tests
Identifiers: Directionality; PPMS
Availability: The Psychological Corporation; 555 Academic Ct., San Antonio, TX 78204-0952
Target Audience: 5-10
Notes: Items, 22
Designed to identify children with perceptual motor disabilities that hinder school performance.

2351
Leavell Hand-Eye Coordinator Tests. Leavell, Ullin W. 1961
Subtests: Hand Food Preference Tests; Eye Ear Preference Tests; Hand Dexterity Preference Test; Visual Imagery Pointed Objects; Visual Imagery, Incomplete Objects; Visual Imagery, Moving Objects
Descriptors: Adolescents; Children; Diagnostic Teaching; Diagnostic Tests; *Elementary School Students; Elementary Secondary Education; *Eye Hand Coordination; *Lateral Dominance; *Reading Difficulties; *Secondary School Students
Identifiers: Leavell Language Development Program; *Visual Motor Functioning
Availability: Keystone View; 2212 E. 12th St., Davenport, IA 52803
Target Audience: 8-14

Designed to determine cause of reading difficulties. If problem is a result of confusion arising from lack of eye-hand coordination, exercises are suggested. Program is useful with mirror writers, nonverbal children, and reversal speech cases.

2399
Leiter International Performance Scale. Leiter, Russell Graydon 1966
Descriptors: *Adolescents; *Adults; *Children; Culture Fair Tests; Disabilities; Disadvantaged; Hearing Impairments; Individual Testing; *Intelligence; *Intelligence Tests; Neurological Impairments; *Nonverbal Tests; Preschool Children; Spatial Ability
Identifiers: LIPS
Availability: Stoelting Co.; 1350 S. Kostner Ave., Chicago, IL 60623
Target Audience: 2-64

Nonverbal intelligence test designed for ages 2 through adult. Does not require speech by examiner or subject. Suitable for use with mentally retarded through intellectually gifted subjects. Binet-type year scale has 4 tests at each year-level from Year II through Year XVI, and 6 tests at Year XVIII. Examination is begun with the first test in the year-level which is 2 year-levels below that of the subject's estimated mental age.

2421
Fransworth-Munsell 100-Hue Test. Farnsworth, Dean
Descriptors: *Adolescents; *Adults; *Color; *Performance Tests; Vision Tests; *Visual Discrimination; *Visual Impairments; *Visual Measures; Visual Stimuli
Identifiers: *Color Blindness
Availability: Munsell Color; 2441 N. Calvert St., Baltimore, MD 21218
Target Audience: 12-64
Notes: Time, 10 approx.; Items, 93

Untimed instrument used to determine one's color vision anomalies and color aptitude. The equipment required for this instrument consists of 4 trays, each containing a segment of 85 color reference disks mounted in recessed area of individual black plastic caps. The subject is to place these caps into hue order. The aforementioned trays are contained in a wooden carrying case. Its basic uses are (1) to separate persons with normal color vision into classes according to their color discrimination; and (2) to determine the areas of color confusion of color defective persons. Has also been used as part of an inspector-of-color-goods exam, for exam of colorgraders and dye and paint mixers, to detect poor color vision in salespersons, and as a measurement of effects of medical treatments.

2428
Quick Test. Ammons, R.B.; Ammons, C.H. 1958
Descriptors: Adolescents; Adults; Children; *Disabilities; Individual Testing; *Intelligence; *Intelligence Tests; Mental Retardation; Preschool Children; *Screening Tests
Identifiers: QT
Availability: Psychological Test Specialists; Box 9229, Missoula, MT 59807
Target Audience: 2-64
Notes: Time, 10 approx.; Items, 50

Designed to estimate general level of intellectual ability in a brief time. Words are defined nonverbally as examinee selects appropriate drawings. Assesses intelligence levels from 2 years to superior adult. May be used with any subject able to see the drawings, hear or read word items, and indicate yes-no. Requires no reading, writing, or speaking. Useful with severely handicapped individuals and as screening procedure with mentally retarded subjects.

2435
Human Relations Inventory. Bernberg, Raymond E. 1954
Descriptors: *Adults; Attitude Measures; *Conformity; *Delinquency; Higher Education; High Schools; *High School Students; Personality Measures; *Social Attitudes; *Social Behavior; *Undergraduate Students
Identifiers: HRI
Availability: Psychometric Affiliates; P.O. Box 807, Murfreesboro, TN 37133
Grade Level: 9-16
Target Audience: Adults
Notes: Items, 34

Designed to measure social conformity so that a prediction of antisocial behavior may be made. Discriminates between law violators and ordinary conformists.

2451
Kasanin-Hanfmann Concept Formation Test. Kasanin, Jacob; Hanfmann, Eugenia
Descriptors: *Abstract Reasoning; *Adolescents; *Adults; *Children; Classification; Cognitive Tests; *Concept Formation; *Educationally Disadvantaged; Patients; *Performance Tests; *Psychosis
Identifiers: Blocks; Vigotsky Test
Availability: Stoelting Co.; 1350 S. Kostner Ave., Chicago, IL 60623
Target Audience: 3-64
Notes: Items, 22

Designed to measure ability to think in abstract concepts. Subject must find common factor in a set of 22 blocks of different colors, shapes, and sizes. Useful with children, disadvantaged adults, and special populations.

2466
Sixteen Personality Factor Questionnaire, Form E. Cattell, Raymond B.; Eber, Herbert W. 1970
Subtests: Reserved/Outgoing; Dull/Bright; Affected by Feelings/Emotionally Stable; Humble/Assertive; Sober/Happy-Go-Lucky; Expedient/Conscientious; Shy/Venturesome; Tough-Minded/Tender-Minded; Trusting/Suspicious; Practical/Imaginative; Forthright/Astute; Self-Assured/Apprehensive; Conservative/Experimenting; Group Dependent/Self-Sufficient; Undisciplined Self-Conflict/Controlled; Relaxed/Tense
Descriptors: Adolescents; *Adults; *Educationally Disadvantaged; Forced Choice Technique; *Functional Reading; Grade 3; Personality Assessment; *Personality Measures; *Personality Traits; Readability
Identifiers: Test Batteries; The 16 PF Test
Availability: Institute for Personality and Ability Testing; P.O. Box 188, Champaign, IL 61820
Target Audience: 16-64
Notes: Time, 60 approx.; Items, 128

Designed to measure levels of primary personality traits. Test is designed for individual or group administration. Form E is the lower reading level form written at a 3.3 reading grade level. Designed for use with the most educationally disadvantaged individuals.

2574
Minnesota Multiphasic Personality Inventory: Individual (Card) Form. Hathaway, Starke R.; McKinley, J. C. 1951
Subtests: Lie, Infrequency; Defensiveness; Hypochondriasis; Depression; Hysteria; Psychopathic Deviate; Masculinity-Femininity; Paranoia; Psychasthenia; Schizophrenia; Hypomania; Social Introversion; Anxiety; Repression; Ego Strength; MacAndrew Addiction
Descriptors: *Adolescents; *Adults; Clinical Psychology; *Emotional Adjustment; Individual Testing; Older Adults; Patients; *Personality Assessment; *Personality Measures; Personality Problems; Personality Traits; Psychiatric Hospitals; *Psychological Evaluation; Psychological Testing; Psychopathology; Screening Tests; Self Evaluation (Individuals); Visual Impairments
Identifiers: Card Sort; MMPI
Availability: NCS Interpretive Scoring Systems; P.O. Box 1416, Minneapolis, MN 55440
Target Audience: 16-85
Notes: Items, 550

Designed for use in hospital settings and with visually impaired subjects with psychological or psychiatric difficulties. Provides clinical psychologist with information regarding treatment decisions and treatment evaluation. Identifies psychiatric symptomatology and personality dynamics.

2585
Otis-Lennon Mental Ability Test, Level I, Primary. Otis, Arthur S.; Lennon, Roger T. 1967
Descriptors: Abstract Reasoning; *Academic Aptitude; Aptitude Tests; *Cognitive Ability; Cognitive Measurement; *Intelligence Tests; Kindergarten; *Kindergarten Children; Large Type Materials; Pictorial Stimuli; Primary Education; Visual Impairments
Identifiers: OLMAT; Oral Testing; *Reasoning Ability; Verbal Comprehension; Verbal Reasoning
Availability: American Printing House for the Blind; 1839 Frankfort Ave., Louisville, KY 40206
Grade Level: K
Notes: Time, 30 approx.; Items, 55

Designed to provide assessment of general mental ability or scholastic aptitude. Parallel forms J and K are available at each level. Two parts of test should be administered in separate sittings. No reading is required by examinee. Level I is designed for use with pupils in the last half of kindergarten. Each test item is presented orally by the examiner. Samples mental processes of classification, following directions, quantitative reasoning, and comprehension of verbal concepts. Available in large-type print for visually impaired subjects.

2586
Otis-Lennon Mental Ability Test, Level II, Primary. Otis, Arthur S.; Lennon, Roger T. 1967
Descriptors: Abstract Reasoning; *Academic Aptitude; Aptitude Tests; *Cognitive Ability; Cognitive Measurement; Elementary School Students; *Grade 1; *Intelligence Tests; Large Type Materials; Pictorial Stimuli; Primary Education; Visual Impairments
Identifiers: OLMAT; Oral Testing; *Reasoning Ability; Verbal Comprehension; Verbal Reasoning
Availability: American Printing House for the Blind; 1839 Frankfort Ave., Louisville, KY 40206
Grade Level: 1
Notes: Time, 35 approx.; Items, 55

Designed to provide assessment of general mental ability or scholastic aptitude. Parallel forms J and K are available at each level. Two parts of test should be administered in 2 sittings separated by a brief rest period. Each test item is presented orally by the examiner and requires no reading by the examinee. Primary Level II is designed for students in the first half of grade 1. The content is identical to Primary Level I (TC002585), only the method of hand scoring differs. Instrument samples mental processes of classification, following directions, quantitative reasoning, and comprehension of verbal concepts. Available in large-type print for visually impaired subjects.

2587
Otis-Lennon Mental Ability Test, Level I, Elementary. Otis, Arthur S.; Lennon, Roger T. 1967
Descriptors: Abstract Reasoning; *Academic Aptitude; Aptitude Tests; *Cognitive Ability; Cognitive Measurement; *Elementary School Students; Grade 1; Grade 2; Grade 3; *Intelligence Tests; Large Type Materials; Pictorial Stimuli; Primary Education; Visual Impairments
Identifiers: Analogical Reasoning; OLMAT; Oral Testing; *Reasoning Ability; Verbal Comprehension; Verbal Reasoning
Availability: American Printing House for the Blind; 1839 Frankfort Ave., Louisville, KY 40206
Grade Level: 1-3
Notes: Time, 60 approx.; Items, 80

Designed to provide assessment of general mental ability or scholastic aptitude. Parallel forms J and K are available. This 3-part test should be administered in 2 separate sittings. Elementary Level I is designed for students in the last half of first grade through the end of grade 3. May be used in early grade 4 with pupils who are experiencing reading difficulties. Pictorial items sample the mental processes of classification, following directions, quantitative reasoning, comprehension of verbal concepts, and reasoning by analogy. No reading is required by examinee. Available in large-type print for visually impaired subjects.

2588
Otis-Lennon Mental Ability Test, Level II, Elementary. Otis, Arthur S.; Lennon, Roger T. 1967
Descriptors: *Abstract Reasoning; *Academic Aptitude; Aptitude Tests; *Cognitive Ability; Cognitive Measurement; Cognitive Processes; *Elementary School Students; Grade 4; Grade 5; Grade 6; *Intelligence Tests; Intermediate Grades; Large Type Materials; Visual Impairments
Identifiers: Analogical Reasoning; OLMAT; *Reasoning Ability; Verbal Comprehension; Verbal Reasoning
Availability: American Printing House for the Blind; 1839 Frankfort Ave., Louisville, KY 40206
Grade Level: 4-6
Notes: Time, 50 approx.; Items, 80

Designed to provide assessment of general mental ability or scholastic aptitude. Parallel forms J and K are available at each level. Elementary Level II is designed for use with students in grades 4 through 6. Items are verbal and nonverbal in nature and are arranged in spiral omnibus form. Available in large-type print for visually impaired subjects.

2589

Otis-Lennon Mental Ability Test, Intermediate Level. Otis, Arthur S.; Lennon, Roger T. 1967
Descriptors: *Abstract Reasoning; *Academic Aptitude; Aptitude Tests; *Cognitive Ability; Cognitive Measurement; Cognitive Processes; *Intelligence Tests; Junior High Schools; *Junior High School Students; Large Type Materials; Visual Impairments
Identifiers: Analogical Reasoning; OLMAT; *Reasoning Ability; Verbal Comprehension; Verbal Reasoning
Availability: American Printing House for the Blind; 1839 Frankfort Ave., Louisville, KY 40206
Grade Level: 7-9
Notes: Time, 50 approx.; Items, 80

Designed to provide assessment of general mental ability or scholastic aptitude. Parallel forms J and K are available at each level. Intermediate Level is recommended for use with students in grades 7 through 9. Items are verbal and nonverbal in nature and are arranged in spiral omnibus form. Available in large-type print for visually impaired subjects.

2590

Otis-Lennon Mental Ability Test, Advanced Level. Otis, Arthur S.; Lennon, Roger T. 1967
Descriptors: *Abstract Reasoning; *Academic Aptitude; Aptitude Tests; *Cognitive Ability; Cognitive Measurement; Cognitive Processes; High Schools; *High School Students; *Intelligence Tests; Large Type Materials; Visual Impairments
Identifiers: Analogical Reasoning; OLMAT; *Reasoning Ability; Verbal Comprehension; Verbal Reasoning
Availability: American Printing House for the Blind; 1839 Frankfort Ave., Louisville, KY 40206
Grade Level: 10-12
Notes: Time, 50 approx.; Items, 80

Designed to provide assessment of general mental ability or scholastic aptitude. Parallel forms J and K are available at each level. Advanced Level is recommended for use with students in grades 10 through 12. Items are verbal and nonverbal in nature and are arranged in spiral omnibus form. Available in large-type print for visually impaired subjects.

2591

The Behavior Cards: A Test-Interview for Delinquent Children. Stogdill, Ralph M. 1950
Descriptors: Adolescents; Children; *Delinquency; Individual Testing; *Self Evaluation (Individuals)
Identifiers: Stogdill Behavior Cards
Availability: Stoelting Co.; 1350 S. Kostner Ave., Chicago, IL 60623
Target Audience: 9-19
Notes: Time, 30 approx; Items, 150

Items cover range of delinquencies and background experiences. Use of the cards often uncovers delinquent experiences not previously mentioned by child or revealed in social history. Individually administered.

2616

Test of Aural Perception for Latin-American Students. Lado, Robert; Fries, Charles C. 1949
Descriptors: *Achievement Tests; Audiolingual Skills; *College Students; Diagnostic Tests; *English (Second Language); Higher Education; Interference (Language); Language Tests; *Latin Americans; Listening Comprehension; *Listening Comprehension Tests; *Phonemes; *Pronunciation; Second Language Learning; Threshold Level (Languages)
Identifiers: Oral Tests
Availability: English Language Institute; 2001 N. University Bldg., University of Michigan, Ann Arbor, MI 48109
Grade Level: 13-16
Notes: Time, 50; Items, 100

Designed to measure how well a student has learned to hear the significant sound differences of the English language. Used by teachers of English as a second or foreign language when the teachers are concerned with pronunciation problems. Administered orally by a native American speaker of standard American English or via a mechanical recording of truly high fidelity. The authors feel that the test should be administered to small groups of no more than 20 people unless the room has extremely good acoustics.

2631

A Test of Sound Discrimination for Use with Cerebral Palsied Children. Irwin, Orvis C.; Jensen, Paul J. 1963
Descriptors: Adolescents; *Auditory Discrimination; Auditory Tests; *Cerebral Palsy; Children; Disabilities; *Elementary School Students; Elementary Secondary Education; *Individual Testing; Neurological Impairments; *Secondary School Students
Availability: Cerebral Palsy Review; v24 n2 Mar-Apr 1963
Target Audience: 6-16
Notes: Items, 30

Designed to measure ability of cerebral palsied children to discriminate speech sounds. Parallel forms A and B are available.

2632

An Abstraction Test for Use with Cerebral Palsied Children. Irwin, Orvis C.; Hammill, Donald D. 1964
Descriptors: *Abstract Reasoning; Adolescents; *Cerebral Palsy; Children; Cognitive Tests; *Disabilities; *Elementary School Students; Elementary Secondary Education; Individual Testing; Neurological Impairments; Secondary School Students
Availability: Cerebral Palsy Review; v25 n4 Jul-Aug 1964
Target Audience: 6-17
Notes: Items, 25

Designed to assess ability of cerebral palsied children. Measures levels of abstraction and categorization. Parallel forms X and Y are available.

2686

Cornell Index. Weider, Arthur; And Others 1949
Descriptors: *Adolescents; *Adults; Anxiety; *Patients; *Psychological Evaluation; Psychosomatic Disorders; Questionnaires
Identifiers: CI Form N2; Self Administered Tests; *Symptoms
Availability: Dr. Arthur Weider; 823 United Nations Plaza, Ste. 404, New York, NY 10017
Target Audience: 13-64
Notes: Time, 15 approx.; Items, 101

Developed as an adjunct to the psychiatric interview to differentiate persons with serious personal and psychosomatic disturbances from the rest of the population. Items refer to neuropsychiatric and psychosomatic symptoms.

2698

Examination in Structure (English as a Foreign Language). Lado, Robert; Fries, Charles C. 1947
Descriptors: *Achievement Tests; *College Students; Diagnostic Tests; *English (Second Language); *Grammar; Higher Education; *Language Proficiency; *Language Skills; Language Tests; Language Usage; Multiple Choice Tests; Second Language Learning; Timed Tests
Availability: English Language Institute; 2001 N. University Bldg., University of Michigan, Ann Arbor, MI 48109
Grade Level: 13-16
Notes: Time, 60; Items, 150

Designed to measure the achievement level of English language grammar and other basic structures of English. Over half of the items are multiple choice; the remaining items are completion, for testing question words, negation, sentence order, etc. May be useful for assisting in the diagnosis of problem areas in grammar. Comes in 3 forms: Form A, B, and C. All forms are copyrighted 1947; the answer sheets are copyrighted 1946. Instructions are in English, Spanish, Portuguese, and French.

2699

Test of Aural Perception in English for Japanese Students. Lado, Robert; Andrade, Richard D. 1950
Descriptors: Achievement Tests; Audiolingual Skills; *College Students; Diagnostic Tests; *English (Second Language); Higher Education; Interference (Language); *Japanese; Language Tests; Listening Comprehension; *Listening Comprehension Tests; *Phonemes; *Pronunciation; Second Language Learning; Threshold Level (Languages)
Identifiers: Oral Tests; Test of Aural Perception for Japanese Students
Availability: English Language Institute; 2001 N. University Bldg., University of Michigan, Ann Arbor, MI 48109
Grade Level: 13-16
Notes: Time, 50; Items, 100

Designed to diagnose the sound perception difficulties of Japanese speakers who are learning English. Measures how well the Japanese have learned to hear and distinguish significant sounds in the English language especially those sounds which are not significant in Japanese language. Also measures the ability to hear consonant clusters and combinations. Administered orally by a native American speaker of standard American English or via a mechanical recording of truly high fidelity. The authors feel that the test should be administered to small groups of no more

than 20 people unless the room has extremely good acoustics. For each item the administrator reads 3 sentences; the Japanese-speaking test takers are to encircle the sentences which are exactly the same; if none of the sentences is the same, they encircle the zero. Useful when working on pronunciation problems and as an aid to isolating the special problems of the class or individual students.

2703

Grooved Pegboard Test. Lafayette Instrument Co., Lafayette, IN 1965
Descriptors: Adolescents; Adults; Children; Employees; *Eye Hand Coordination; Individual Testing; *Job Applicants; Job Skills; *Motor Development; *Neurological Impairments; Object Manipulation; Occupational Tests; *Patients; Performance Tests; Psychomotor Skills; Reaction Time; *Screening Tests; Timed Tests; Vocational Aptitude
Identifiers: *Manual Dexterity
Availability: Lafayette Instrument Co.; P.O. Box 5729, Sagamore Pwy., Lafayette, IN 47903
Target Audience: 10-64

A manipulative dexterity test which, according to the publisher, requires more complete visual motor coordination than most pegboards. Used in neuropsychological test batteries as an indicator of brain damage, movement disorders; to distinguish between normal, neurologic, and pseudoneurologic patients; in student labs; and as a screening test in industry. Requires the use of a special board and pegs.

2709

Western Personality Inventory. Manson, Morse P. 1963
Subtests: Manson Evaluation; Alcadd Test
Descriptors: Adjustment (to Environment); *Adults; *Alcoholism; Anxiety; Behavior Patterns; *Drug Addiction; Emotional Adjustment; *Personality Measures; Personality Traits
Availability: Western Psychological Services; 12031 Wilshire Blvd., Los Angeles, CA 90025
Target Audience: Adults
Notes: Items, 137

Combines the Manson Evaluation (TC002710) and the Alcadd Test (TC002711) into one test booklet to measure both the potential alcoholic personality and the extent of alcohol addiction in alcoholics.

2710

Manson Evaluation. Manson, Morse P. 1948
Subtests: Anxiety; Depressive Fluctuations; Emotional Sensitivity; Resentfulness; Incompleteness; Aloneness; Interpersonal Relations
Descriptors: Adjustment (to Environment); *Adults; *Alcoholism; Anxiety; Depression (Psychology); Emotional Adjustment; Interpersonal Relationship; *Personality Measures; Personality Traits
Identifiers: Self Administered Tests
Availability: Western Psychological Services; 12031 Wilshire Blvd., Los Angeles, CA 90025
Target Audience: Adults
Notes: Time, 10 approx.; Items, 72

Designed to identify maladjusted individuals, especially alcoholics and potential alcoholics.

2711

Alcadd Test. Manson, Morse P. 1949
Subtests: Regularity of Drinking; Preference for Drinking over Other Activities; Lack of Controlled Drinking; Rationalization of Drinking; Excessive Emotionality
Descriptors: Adjustment (to Environment); *Adults; *Alcoholism; Behavior Patterns; *Drug Addiction; *Emotional Adjustment; *Personality Measures
Availability: Western Psychological Services; 12031 Wilshire Blvd., Los Angeles, CA 90025
Target Audience: Adults
Notes: Time, 10 approx.; Items, 65

Designed to assess the extent of alcohol addiction and measure areas of maladjustment. Identifies traits unique to alcoholics.

2717

Minnesota Rate of Manipulation Tests, 1969 Edition. Minnesota Univ., St. Paul. Employment Stabilization Research Institute 1969
Subtests: Placing; Turning; Displacing; One-Hand Turning and Placing; Two-Hand Turning and Placing
Descriptors: Adolescents; Adults; Blindness; *Employees; Employment Potential; *Eye Hand Coordination; Individual Testing; Job Applicants; *Motor Development; *Object Manipulation; *Occupational Tests; *Performance Tests; Physical Disabilities; Secondary School Students; Timed Tests
Identifiers: *Manual Dexterity; MRMT

Availability: American Guidance Service; Publishers' Bldg., Circle Pines, MN 55014
Target Audience: 13-64
Notes: Time, 20 approx.; Items, 60

Timed battery of tests which measure arm, hand, and finger dexterity. Designed as an aid in the selection of personnel for job requiring manual dexterity such as assembly line tasks that require the manipulation or sorting of parts. Usually only 2 tests are given with several timed trials recorded for each test; time to administer is about 10 minutes per test. May be administered either to a group or to an individual. The Displacing and the Turning tests have been modified for use with blind persons. Requires the use of a test board and special blocks. Has also been used with students in elementary through university levels and with physically handicapped persons. Available in French under title, Test de Dexterite Manuelle de l'Universite du Minnesota (TC840013).

2743
Harris Tests of Lateral Dominance. Harris, Albert J. 1958
Subtests: Knowledge of Right and Left; Hand Preferences; Simultaneous Writing; Handwriting; Tapping; Dealing Cards; Strength of Grip; Monocular Tests; Binocular Tests; Stereoscopic Tests; Foot Dominance
Descriptors: *Adolescents; *Adults; *Children; Elementary School Students; Elementary Secondary Education; Handwriting; Individual Testing; *Language Handicaps; *Lateral Dominance; *Neurological Impairments; Performance Tests; Secondary School Students; *Speech Handicaps
Identifiers: Handedness
Availability: The Psychological Corporation; 555 Academic Ct., San Antonio, TX 78204-0952
Target Audience: 7-64

Series of tests designed to assess hand dominance, eye dominance, and foot dominance. Designed for use in examining subjects with reading, spelling or writing disabilities, speech defects, or neurological difficulties.

2767
Pennsylvania Bi-Manual Worksample. Roberts, John R. 1969
Descriptors: Adolescents; Adults; *Blindness; *Employees; *Eye Hand Coordination; *Job Applicants; Job Skills; *Motor Development; *Object Manipulation; Occupational Tests; *Performance Tests; Reaction Time; Timed Tests; Vocational Aptitude; Work Sample Tests
Identifiers: *Manual Dexterity
Availability: American Guidance Service; Publishers' Bldg., Circle Pines, MN 55014
Target Audience: 16-64
Notes: Time, 12; Items, 80

Evaluates finger dexterity of both hands, whole movement of both arms, eye-hand coordination, and bi-manual coordination. The subject is seated in front of a board with nuts at one end and bolts at the other. He or she grasps a nut between the thumb and index finger of the left hand and a bolt with the thumb and index finger of the right hand. After screwing the 2 together, applicant places the bolt-nut into a small hole in the board. Requires the use of the test board, nuts, and bolts. The procedures include practice before the timed test. Recommends giving the test to no more than 4 people at a time. A special supplement is available for blind persons.

2768
Emotional Factors Inventory. Bauman, Mary K.
Subtests: Sensitivity; Somatic Symptoms; Social Competency; Attitudes of Distrust; Feelings of Inadequacy; Depression; Attitudes re Blindness
Descriptors: *Adults; Affective Behavior; Audiotape Recordings; Blindness; Interpersonal Competence; *Large Type Materials; Personality Assessment; Personality Measures; *Self Concept; Self Concept Measures; *Visual Impairments
Identifiers: EFI
Availability: Associated Services for the Blind; Rm. 400, 919 Walnut St., Philadelphia, PA 19107 Attn: Testing
Target Audience: Adults
Notes: Time, 170

Designed to assess self-concept and emotionality of visually impaired adults. An equivalent form of 150 items is available for students in grades 7-16.

2879
Devereux Adolescent Behavior Rating Scale. Spivack, George; And Others 1967
Subtests: Unethical; Defiant Resistive; Domineer Sadistic; Heterosexual Interest; Hyperactivity Expansive; Poor Emotional Control; Needs Approval Dependency; Emotional Distance; Physical Inferiority Timidity; Schizoid Withdrawal; Bizarre Speech and Cognition; Bizarre Action

Descriptors: *Adolescents; Behavior; *Behavior Problems; *Behavior Rating Scales; *Child Caregivers; *Emotional Disturbances; Residential Institutions
Identifiers: DAB
Availability: Devereux Foundation Press; 19 S. Waterloo Rd., Devon, PA 19333
Target Audience: 13-17
Notes: Items, 84

Developed as a standard method of describing and communicating overt behavior symptoms which help define the total clinical picture of disturbed adolescents. Designed for use by clinicians, rehabilitation counselors, nurses, hospital aides, and others working with adolescents in a residential setting.

2920
Sloan Achromatopsia Test. Sloan, Louise L.
Descriptors: Adolescents; Adults; Children; *Color; Congenital Impairments; Screening Tests; *Vision Tests; Visual Impairments; *Visual Perception
Identifiers: *Color Blindness
Availability: Munsell Color; 2441 N. Calvert St., Baltimore, MD 21218
Target Audience: 6-64
Notes: Items, 7

Designed for screening of congenital achromat (color-blind individuals). Subject selects shade of gray on scale which matches color reference mounted behind it. Colors differ from one another only in lightness and darkness to the totally color blind. Scales are produced to order only.

3082
Human Figure Drawings Test. Koppitz, Elizabeth Munsterberg 1968
Descriptors: *Child Development; Children; *Elementary School Students; Individual Testing; Interpersonal Competence; Patients; *Personality Development; Psychiatric Hospitals; *Psychological Evaluation; School Readiness
Identifiers: HFD; Psychiatric Patients
Availability: Grune and Stratton; 111 Fifth Ave., New York, NY 10003
Target Audience: 5-12
Notes: Time, 30 approx.

School-age child is asked to draw a whole figure of a person. The drawing is interpreted for individual maturation and emotional development. May be used to screen school beginners, predict academic achievement, and in diagnosing, treating, and assessing the progress of psychiatric patients.

3103
Early Detection Inventory. McGahan, F.E.; McGahan, Carolyn 1967
Subtests: Social-Emotional Behavior Responses; School Readiness Tasks; Motor Performance; Personal History
Descriptors: *Biographical Inventories; Child Development; Cognitive Development; Concept Formation; Developmental Disabilities; Educational Diagnosis; Individual Testing; *Learning Problems; *Maturity Tests; Motor Development; Observation; Perceptual Development; Perceptual Motor Coordination; Performance Tests; *Preschool Children; School Readiness; *School Readiness Tests; *Screening Tests; Young Children
Identifiers: EDI
Availability: N.E.T. Educational Services, Inc.; 3065 Clark Ln., Paris, TX 75460
Target Audience: 4-6
Notes: Items, 101

Screening instrument used to identify potential academic underachievers by evaluating a child's social, emotional, physical, and intellectual development. The social and emotional development are based on observation; the physical development on information supplied by parents; and the intellectual development on the child's performance of motor tasks. Individually administered. While designed for preschool children, it is useful with children in ungraded primary classes and transitional classes.

3130
Straus Rural Attitudes Profile. Straus, Murray A. 1956
Descriptors: Adults; *Attitude Measures; Forced Choice Technique; *Rural Population; *Social Values
Identifiers: TIM(B)
Availability: Tests in Microfiche; Test Collection, Educational Testing Service, Princeton, NJ 08541
Target Audience: Adults
Notes: Time, 12; Items, 48

Inventory measures 4 variables which are hypothesized to be important value dimensions in contemporary American rural life: innovation proneness, rural life preference, primary group preference, and economic motivation. It is

designed for self-administration by individuals with minimal reading skill. There are male and female forms of the test.

3242
Hooper Visual Organization Test. Hooper, H. Elston 1958
Descriptors: *Adolescents; *Adults; *Clinical Diagnosis; *Handicap Identification; *Neurological Impairments; Pictorial Stimuli; Visual Measures
Identifiers: VOT
Availability: Western Psychological Services, Order Dept.; 12031 Wilshire Blvd., Los Angeles CA 90025
Target Audience: 12-64
Notes: Time, 15 approx.; Items, 30

Designed to diagnose organic brain pathology. Differentiates between functional and motivational disorders. Minimizes speed and recent memory items by use of items in which level of difficulty is low. Language functions are not important factors in the test. May be administered to groups or individuals.

3247
Self Interview Inventory. Hovey, H. Birnet 1958
Subtests: Current Complaints; Emotional Insecurity; Guilt Feelings; Prepsychotic or Psychotic; Behavior Problems; Childhood Illness; Lack of Carefulness; Lack of Truthfulness
Descriptors: *Adjustment (to Environment); *Adults; Biographical Inventories; Emotional Disturbances; *Males; Personality Measures; *Self Evaluation (Individuals)
Identifiers: *Psychiatric Patients
Availability: Psychometric Affiliates; P.O. Box 807, Murfreesboro, TN 37133
Target Audience: Adults
Notes: Items, 185

Designed to measure potentially maladjusted men by eliciting information about their past histories and experiences.

3256
Triadal Equated Personality Inventory. Psychometric Affiliates, Murfreesboro, TN 1961
Subtests: Dominance; Self-Confidence; Decisiveness; Independence; Toughness; Suspicion; Conscientious; Introversion; Restlessness; Solemnity; Foresight; Industrious; Warmth; Enthusiasm; Conformity; Inventiveness; Persistance; Sex Drive; Recognition; Cooperativeness; Self-Control; Humility-Tolerance.
Descriptors: Adults; Alcoholism; College Students; Counseling; Forced Choice Technique; Personality Measures; Sales Occupations; Sales Workers; *Personality Traits; *Self Concept; Self Concept Measures
Availability: Psychometric Affiliates; Box 807, Murfreesboro, TN 37133
Target Audience: Adults
Notes: Time, 120 approx.; Items, 633

Yields 21 self-image scores including dominance, self-confidence, decisiveness, independence, toughness, suspicion, introversion, warmth, enthusiasm, conformity, inventiveness, persistence, sex drive, recognition drive, cooperativeness, humility-tolerance, and self-control. Has national norms for sales personnel, alcoholics, counselees, and college students.

3257
Goldstein-Scheerer Tests of Abstract and Concrete Thinking. Goldstein, Kurt; Scheerer, Martin 1951
Subtests: Cube; Color Sort; Object Sort; Color Form Sort; Stick
Descriptors: *Abstract Reasoning; Adults; Clinical Diagnosis; *Cognitive Style; Cognitive Tests; *Diagnostic Tests; *Individual Testing; Logical Thinking; *Neurological Impairments; *Patients; *Performance Tests; Problem Solving
Identifiers: Gelb Goldstein Color Sorting Test; Gelb Goldstein Weigl Scheerer Object Sorting Test; Goldstein Scheerer Cube Test; Goldstein Scheerer Stick Test; *Reasoning Ability; Test Batteries; Weigl Goldstein Scheerer Color Form Sorting Test
Availability: The Psychological Corporation; 555 Academic Ct., San Antonio, TX 78204-0952
Target Audience: Adults

Group of instruments to evaluate abstract and concrete reasoning of brain damaged patients. Requires the use of specialized test materials or common household items. Copyright date of instruments varies from 1941 to 1951. Individually administered performance tests.

3329
Porch Index of Communicative Ability. Porch, Bruce E. 1981

Subtests: Writes Function in Sentences; Writes Names of Objects; Names (Spelling Dictated); Names (Copies); Geometric Forms; Demonstrates Function; Demonstrates Function (Ordered); Describes Function; Names Objects; Sentence Completion; Imitative Naming; Reads Function and Position; Reads Name and Position; Points to Object by Function; Points to Objects by Name; Matching Pictures with Object; Matching Objects with Object
Descriptors: *Adults; *Aphasia; Cognitive Development; *Cognitive Style; Communication (Thought Transfer); *Communication Disorders; Individual Development; *Individual Testing; Perception Tests; *Perceptual Handicaps; Perceptual Motor Learning; Performance Tests; Sensory Integration; Verbal Tests; Visual Stimuli
Identifiers: Oral Tests; PICA
Availability: Consulting Psychologists Press; 577 College Ave., Palo Alto, CA 94306
Target Audience: Adults

Designed to quantify and describe certain verbal, gestural, and graphic abilities in aphasic adults. Individually administered. Requires much training by the test administrator. Approximately 40 hours of work with the manual, etc., is suggested. Requires the use of specialized sets of cards, various items found in any home, etc.

3482
Auditory Tests W-1 and W-2: Spondaic Word Lists. Central Institute for the Deaf, St. Louis, MO
Descriptors: Adolescents; Adults; Auditory Discrimination; Auditory Tests; Children; *Diagnostic Tests; *Hearing Impairments; Individual Testing; *Speech Communication; *Speech Evaluation; *Speech Tests
Identifiers: Auditory Test No 9; Auditory Test Records; CID Auditory Tests W1; CID Auditory Test W2; Oral Tests; *Speech Reception Threshold
Availability: Technisonic Studios, Inc.; 1201 Brentwood Blvd., St. Louis, MO 63117
Target Audience: 7-64
Notes: Items, 36

Recorded word tests used to determine an individual's threshold of intelligibility for speech. Each form, the W-1 and W-2, contains a list of spondaic words; a spondaic word has 2 syllables with each syllable equally stressed. These words were selected from a larger number of words used in the Harvard Psycho-Acoustic Laboratory Auditory Test No 9. In Form W-1 the words have been recorded at the same intensity; in W-2 the words have been recorded in a descending level of intensity. Requires the following equipment: phonograph turntable and pickup with backback characteristic, an amplifier, a meter for monitoring the amplifier's output, an attenuator, and a calibrated earphone or loud speaker. Administered individually.

3511
Wechsler Memory Scale. Wechsler, David; Stone, C. P. 1974
Subtests: Personal and Current Information; Orientation; Mental Control; Logical Memory; Memory Span; Visual Reproduction; Associate Learning
Descriptors: Adults; *Clinical Diagnosis; *Cognitive Processes; Cognitive Tests; *Individual Testing; *Neurological Impairments; *Patients; *Short Term Memory
Identifiers: *Psychiatric Patients; WMS
Availability: The Psychological Corporation; 555 Academic Ct., San Antonio, TX 78204-0952
Target Audience: Adults
Notes: Time, 15 approx.

Individually administered instrument to measure adult memory. Used to detect memory defects in certain specific organic brain damage and with certain psychiatric patients, and senile and other subjects. Available as Form I or II.

3613
Slosson Drawing Coordination Test for Children and Adults. Slosson, Richard L. 1967
Descriptors: *Adults; *Elementary School Students; Elementary Secondary Education; *Eye Hand Coordination; *Handicap Identification; *Neurological Impairments; Performance Tests; Preschool Education; Screening Tests; *Secondary School Students; *Young Children
Identifiers: SDCT
Availability: Slosson Educational Publications; P.O. Box 280, E. Aurora, NY 14052
Target Audience: 2-64
Notes: Time, 15 approx.

Designed to identify individuals with various forms of brain dysfunction or perceptual disorders where eye hand coordination is involved. May be administered to groups or individuals. Used to supplement Slosson Intelligence Test (TC011187).

3617
Screening Test for the Assignment of Remedial Treatments. Ahr, A. Edward 1968
Subtests: Visual Memory; Auditory Memory; Visual Copying; Visual Discrimination
Descriptors: Auditory Perception; *Diagnostic Teaching; *Diagnostic Tests; *Memory; *Preschool Children; Preschool Education; Psychomotor Skills; Remedial Instruction; *Screening Tests; *Visual Discrimination
Identifiers: Oral Testing; START
Availability: Priority Innovations; P.O. Box 792, Skokie, IL 60076
Target Audience: 2-5
Notes: Time, 60 approx.; Items, 50

Designed to assess development of preschool children in areas of visual and auditory memory, visual motor coordination, and visual discrimination. Used to identify children demonstrating extremely slow development for further diagnosis and treatment at earliest phases of formal education.

3628
Denver Developmental Screening Test. Frankenburg, William K.; Dodds, Josiah B. 1967
Subtests: Gross Motor; Fine Motor-Adaptive; Language; Personal-Social
Descriptors: Child Development; Developmental Tasks; Individual Testing; *Infants; *Language Acquisition; *Learning Disabilities; Motor Development; *Preschool Children; *Psychomotor Skills; *Screening Tests; *Social Development; Young Children
Identifiers: DDST; *Denver Screening Tests for Preschoolers
Availability: Denver Developmental Materials; P.O. Box 6919, Denver, CO 80206-0919
Target Audience: 0-6
Notes: Time, 20 approx.; Items, 105

Designed as a screening device to identify infants and preschool children with serious developmental delays. The test is to be used only for screening purposes to alert professional child workers to the possibility of developmental delays so that appropriate diagnostic studies may be pursued. A child at any given age is administered only 20 or so simple items.

3734
Diagnostic Reading Examination for Diagnosis of Special Difficulty in Reading. Monroe, Marion
Subtests: Alphabet Repeating and Reading; Iota Word Test; b,d,p,q,u,n Test; Recognition of Orientation; Mirror Reading; Mirror Writing; Number Reversal; Word Discrimination; Sounding; Handedness
Descriptors: *Diagnostic Tests; *Elementary School Students; Elementary Secondary Education; Individual Testing; *Mental Retardation; *Reading Achievement; *Reading Difficulties; *Secondary School Students
Identifiers: Monroe Diagnostic Reading Test
Availability: Stoelting Co.; 1350 S. Kostner Ave., Chicago, IL 60623
Grade Level: 1-10
Notes: Time, 75 approx.

Designed to measure student's achievement in reading as compared with that in arithmetic and spelling, and with that expected from his or her chronological and mental ages. The educational profile is the result of the arrangement of data on a quantitative scale. The arrangement of data on a quantitative scale yields the profile of errors in reading. Valuable tool in determining effective methods for remedial instruction.

3810
Leiter Adult Intelligence Scale. Leiter, Russell Graydon 1964
Subtests: Similarities-Differences; Digits Forward and Backward; Recall; Pathways; Stencil Design; Painted Cubes
Descriptors: *Adults; *Disabilities; Individual Testing; *Intelligence; *Intelligence Quotient; *Intelligence Tests; Psychological Evaluation; Verbal Ability
Identifiers: LAIS
Availability: Stoelting Co.; 1350 S. Kostner Ave., Chicago, IL 60623
Target Audience: 18-64
Notes: Time, 40 approx.

Designed to measure general adult intelligence. Sensitive to deficits in cognitive, psychophysical, or social areas; therefore, provides a measure of functional efficiency for psychologically disabled or superior subjects. Yield verbal, performance, and full-scale intelligence quotient.

3817
Ward Behavior Inventory. Burdock, Eugene I.; Hardesty, Anne S. 1968

Descriptors: Adults; Allied Health Personnel; Behavior Problems; Behavior Rating Scales; *Mental Disorders; Nurses; Observation; *Patients; *Psychiatric Hospitals
Identifiers: *Psychiatric Patients; WBI
Availability: Springer Publishing Co.; 200 Park Ave. S., New York, NY 10003
Target Audience: Adults
Notes: Items, 138

An observation technique used to measure the severity of psychopathological disturbance shown in ward behaviors of hospitalized adult psychiatric patients. Only observed behavior during a specified observational period is assessed. Instrument is also available in ERIC Document Reproduction Service, ED171763.

3822
Gilmore Oral Reading Test. Gilmore, John V.; Gilmore, Eunice C. 1968
Descriptors: *Achievement Tests; Braille; Elementary Education; *Elementary School Students; Individual Testing; Large Type Materials; *Oral Reading; Reading Achievement; *Reading Rate; *Reading Skills; Reading Tests; Visual Impairments
Availability: The Psychological Corporation; 555 Academic Ct., San Antonio, TX 78204-0952
Grade Level: 1-8
Notes: Time, 20 approx.; Items, 50

Designed to measure 3 aspects of oral reading ability—accuracy, comprehension, and rate. Equivalent forms C and D are available. Available in large-type print or Braille for visually impaired subjects from American Printing House for the Blind, 1839 Frankfort Ave., Louisville, KY 40206.

3839
Test of Non-Verbal Reasoning, Long Form. Richardson, Bellows, Henry and Co., Washington, DC 1963
Descriptors: *Abstract Reasoning; *Adults; *Concept Formation; *Culture Fair Tests; *Educationally Disadvantaged; Intelligence Tests; Job Applicants; *Nonverbal Tests; *Skilled Workers
Identifiers: RBH Nonverbal Reasoning Test Long Form
Availability: Richardson, Bellows, Henry and Co., Inc.; 1140 Connecticut Ave., N.W., Washington, DC 20036
Target Audience: 18-64
Notes: Time, 15; Items, 45

A nonverbal and nonlanguage test of abstract reasoning and intelligence. Useful for low educational level personnel in the United States and foreign countries. Has also been useful with technical and managerial personnel with a high level of education. Examinee need not read English but must read numbers to record answers properly. May be used as part of a test battery for industrial personnel for whom language presents a problem.

3854
Test of Non-Verbal Reasoning, Short Form. Richardson, Bellows, Henry and Co., Washington, DC 1963
Descriptors: *Abstract Reasoning; *Adults; *Concept Formation; *Culture Fair Tests; *Educationally Disadvantaged; Intelligence Tests; *Job Applicants; *Nonverbal Tests; *Unskilled Workers
Identifiers: RBH Non Verbal Reasoning Test Short Form
Availability: Richardson, Bellows, Henry and Co., Inc.; 1140 Connecticut Ave., N.W., Washington, DC 20036
Target Audience: 18-64
Notes: Time, 10; Items, 24

A shortened version of RBH Non-Verbal Reasoning Test (TC003839) designed for inclusion in industrial test batteries. Test measures intelligence and abstract reasoning ability with nonverbal and nonlanguage items. A mirror image of the test is available for cultures where reading is done from right to left.

4029
Devereux Elementary School Behavior Rating Scale. Spivack, George; Swift, Marshall 1967
Subtests: Classroom Disturbance; Impatience; Disrespect-Defiance; External Blame; Achievement Anxiety; External Reliance; Comprehension; Inattentive-Withdrawn; Irrelevant-Responsiveness; Creative Initiative; Need Closeness to Teacher
Descriptors: Academic Achievement; *Behavior Problems; *Behavior Rating Scales; Elementary Education; *Elementary School Students; Elementary School Teachers; Learning Problems
Identifiers: DESB
Availability: The Devereux Foundation Press; 19 S. Waterloo Rd., Devon, PA 19333
Grade Level: K-6

Notes: Items, 47

Designed for use by classroom teacher to assist in focusing on behavioral difficulties affecting academic performance.

4030
Devereux Child Behavior Rating Scale. Spivack, George; Spotts, Jules 1966

Subtests: Distractability; Poor Self Care; Pathological Use of Senses; Emotional Detachment; Social Isolation; Poor Condition and Body Tonus; Incontinence; Messiness, Sloppiness; Inadequate Need for Independence; Unresponsiveness to Stimulation; Proneness to Emotional Upset; Need for Adult Contact; Anxious-Fearful Ideation; "Impulse" Ideation; Inability to Delay; Social Aggression; Unethical Behavior

Descriptors: Behavior; *Behavior Problems; *Behavior Rating Scales; *Child Caregivers; *Children; *Emotional Disturbances; *Mental Retardation; Residential Institutions

Identifiers: DCB; *Latency Age Children

Availability: The Devereux Foundation Press; 19 S. Waterloo Rd., Devon, PA 19333

Target Audience: 8-12

Notes: Items, 97

Designed to assist in description and communication to others the behavioral syndromes of atypical (emotionally disturbed and mentally retarded) latency age children. Intended for use in institutions and clinics by anyone who has knowledge of the child's day-to-day behavior. Profile yields scores on 17 behavior factors.

4031
Specific Language Disability Tests: Grades Six, Seven, and Eight. Malcomesius, Neva 1968

Subtests: Visual to Motor (Distance); Visual to Motor (Near); Visual Discrimination; Visual Memory; Visual Memory to Motor; Auditory Discrimination; Auditory Memory to Motor; Auditory to Visual; Comprehension; Spelling-Auditory to Motor

Descriptors: Auditory Perception; *Dyslexia; Elementary Education; *Elementary School Students; Grade 6; Grade 7; Grade 8; Handwriting; *Language Handicaps; Learning Disabilities; *Middle Schools; *Screening Tests; Visual Perception

Identifiers: SLDT; Slingerland Screening Tests; Test Batteries

Availability: Educators Publishing Service; 75 Moulton St., Cambridge, MA 02238-9101

Grade Level: 6-8

Designed to screen those children with some degree of specific language disability. May be administered individually or to groups. Subtests I-V evaluate perception in visual discrimination, visual memory, and visual-motor coordination. Subtests VI to X evaluate perception in auditory discrimination, auditory visual coordination, auditory motor coordination, and comprehension. All written tests check handwriting, and each test checks ability to follow directions. Upward extension of Slingerland Screening Tests.

4115
SRA Reading Index. Science Research Associates, Chicago, IL 1968

Subtests: Picture-Word Association; Word Decoding; Phrase Comprehension; Sentence Comprehension; Paragraph Comprehension

Descriptors: Achievement Tests; Adolescents; Adults; *Disadvantaged; *Entry Workers; Job Applicants; *Reading Achievement; Reading Tests; *Screening Tests; *Semiskilled Workers; *Unskilled Workers

Identifiers: RAI

Availability: Science Research Associates, Inc.; 155 N. Wacker Dr., Chicago, IL 60606

Target Audience: 14-64

Notes: Time, 25 approx.; Items, 50

Measures general reading achievement of adults and adolescents. Designed for use with applicants for entry-level jobs and special training programs, where the basic skills of applicants are too low to be reliably evaluated by typical selection tests.

4116
SRA Arithmetic Index. Science Research Associates, Chicago, IL 1968

Subtests: Addition and Subtraction of Whole Numbers; Multiplication and Division of Whole Numbers; Fractions; Decimals and Percentages

Descriptors: Achievement Tests; Adolescents; Adults; *Arithmetic; Computation; Decimal Fractions; *Disadvantaged; *Entry Workers; Fractions; Mathematics Tests; *Screening Tests; Semiskilled Workers; *Unskilled Workers

Identifiers: RAI

Availability: Science Research Associates; 155 N. Wacker Dr., Chicago, IL 60606

Target Audience: 14-64

Notes: Time, 25 approx.

Measures computational achievement of adolescents and adults. Designed as a screening device for applicants for entry-level jobs and special training programs where the basic skills of applicants are too low to be reliably evaluated by typical selection tests.

4128
Tests of Reading and Number, Level 3. Manuel, Herschel T. 1969

Subtests: Reading; Number

Descriptors: *Achievement Tests; *Bilingual Students; Elementary Education; *Elementary School Mathematics; Elementary School Students; *Grade 3; *Grade 4; *Reading; *Spanish Speaking

Availability: Guidance Testing Associates; P.O. Box 28096, San Antonio, TX 78228

Grade Level: 3-4

Notes: Time, 34 approx.; Items, 100

Designed to provide an estimate of achievement in reading and simple numerical operations. Should be administered at end of grade 3 or early grade 4 for placement and guidance. Spanish and English editions are available. One of several tests included in the Inter-American Series.

4135
Hiskey Nebraska Test of Learning Aptitude. Hiskey, Marshall S. 1966

Subtests: Bead Patterns; Memory for Colors; Picture Identification; Picture Association; Paper Folding Patterns; Visual Attention Span; Block Patterns; Completion of Drawings; Memory for Digits; Puzzle Blocks; Picture Analogies; Spatial Reasoning

Descriptors: Academic Ability; *Elementary School Students; Elementary Secondary Education; *Hearing Impairments; Individual Testing; Intelligence; *Intelligence Tests; Language Handicaps; Nonverbal Tests; *Preschool Children; Preschool Education; *Secondary School Students; *Speech Handicaps

Identifiers: HNTLA

Availability: The Hiskey Nebraska Test; 5640 Baldwin, Lincoln, NE 68507

Target Audience: 2-18

Notes: Time, 60 approx.

Designed to evaluate learning potentials of hearing-impaired, speech-impaired, or language-impaired children. Separate norms for deaf and hearing subjects, ages 2.5 to 18.5 years. All responses are nonverbal. Is a revision and restandardization of the Nebraska Test of Learning Aptitude for Young Deaf Children.

4136
Haptic Intelligence Scale for Adult Blind. Shurrager, Harriett C.; Shurrager, Phil S. 1964

Subtests: Digit Symbol; Object Assembly; Block Design; Plan-of-Search; Object Completion; Pattern Board; Bead Arithmetic

Descriptors: *Adults; *Blindness; *Intelligence; *Intelligence Tests; *Nonverbal Tests; Performance Tests; *Tactual Perception; Visual Impairments

Identifiers: HISab

Availability: Stoelting Co.; 1350 S. Kostner Ave., Chicago, IL 60623

Target Audience: 18-64

Notes: Time, 90 approx.; Items, 88

A nonverbal intelligence test designed to measure intelligence of blind adults. May be used in conjunction with the Verbal Scale of the Wechsler Adult Intelligence Scale (TC000413).

4192
Western Personnel Test: Spanish. Gunn, Robert L.; Manson, Morse P. 1964

Descriptors: Adults; Aptitude Tests; *Cognitive Ability; Cognitive Tests; Computation; Employment Qualifications; *Intelligence; *Learning; *Mathematical Applications; Mathematical Concepts; Multiple Choice Tests; Spanish; *Spanish Speaking; Timed Tests; *Verbal Ability; Vocational Aptitude

Identifiers: Los Tests Western Para Personal; WPT

Availability: Western Psychological Services; Order Dept., 12031 Wilshire Blvd., Los Angeles, CA 90025

Target Audience: Adults

Notes: Time, 5; Items, 24

A quickly administered instrument used to evaluate general mental ability and learning ability. Includes both verbal and mathematical abilities. Items require a brief answer based upon one's mathematical calculations or are multiple choice. Used with the general population, professional, college, clerical, skilled, and unskilled populations to evaluate general ability and for screening by personnel departments. Scores are given in terms of percentiles. This edition is in Spanish, but the manual is in English. Also available in English (TC000712).

4205
Behavior Status Inventory. Martin, William T. 1971

Subtests: Personal Appearance; Manifest (Obvious) Behavior; Attitude; Verbal Behavior; Social Behavior; Work or School Behavior; Cognitive Behavior

Descriptors: Adults; *Behavior; *Behavior Rating Scales; *Emotional Disturbances; *Mental Retardation; *Neurological Impairments; *Psychiatric Hospitals

Identifiers: BSI; *Psychiatric Patients

Availability: Psychologists and Educators; P.O. Box 513, St. Louis, MO 63017

Target Audience: 18-64

Notes: Items, 91

Designed for use only in psychiatric clinic or hospital setting. Suitable for evaluating behavior of emotionally disturbed, brain damaged, and mentally retarded patients.

4206
Test of Perceptual Organization. Martin, William T. 1969

Descriptors: Abstract Reasoning; *Adolescents; *Adults; Clinical Diagnosis; *Emotional Disturbances; *Handicap Identification; Psychomotor Skills; Spatial Ability; *Timed Tests

Identifiers: TPO

Availability: Psychologists and Educators; P.O. Box 513, St. Louis, MO 63017

Target Audience: 12-64

Notes: Time, 10

Designed to measure abstract reasoning, psychomotor functioning, and ability to follow specific, exacting instructions in an accurate manner. Disturbances in these areas are indicative of emotional and organic pathology. Useful as a clinical research tool and a screening instrument for use in clinical and counseling settings. May be administered to groups or individuals.

4212
Goldman-Fristoe Test of Articulation. Goldman, Ronald; Fristoe, Macalyne 1972

Subtests: Sounds in Words; Sounds in Sentences; Stimulability

Descriptors: Adolescents; *Articulation (Speech); Children; Consonants; Diagnostic Tests; Filmstrips; Individual Testing; *Mental Retardation; Referral; *Speech Evaluation; *Speech Tests; *Young Children

Availability: American Guidance Service; Publishers' Bldg., Circle Pines, MN 55014

Target Audience: 2-16

Notes: Items, 79

Designed to assess subject's articulation of consonant sounds. Evaluation may be made by classroom teacher to determine candidates for referral to speech therapy. Evaluation done by a speech pathologist may be used to determine prognosis and course of therapy. Test materials are contained in an Easel-Kit for ease of administration. Filmstrip version is also available. All 3 subtests may be given or any one or combination depending upon the examiner's purposes.

4233
Polyfactorial Study of Personality. Stark, Ronald H. 1959

Subtests: Hypochondriasis; Sexual Identification; Anxiety; Social Distance; Sociopathy; Depression; Compulsivity; Repression; Paranoia; Schizophrenia; Hyperaffectivity

Descriptors: Adults; Anxiety; Depression (Psychology); *Patients; *Personality Measures; *Prisoners; Psychiatric Hospitals; *Psychological Patterns; Schizophrenia

Identifiers: PFSP; Self Administered Tests

Availability: Martin M. Bruce, Publishers; 50 Larchwood Rd., Box 248, Larchmont, NY 10538

Target Audience: Adults

Notes: Time, 45 approx.; Items, 300

Designed to offer diagnostic profiles approximating those which would be obtained with projective instruments. Scores for 11 categories of diseases are obtained.

4244
Fear Survey Schedule. Wolpe, Joseph; Lang, Peter J. 1969

Descriptors: *Adjustment (to Environment); *Adults; Anxiety; Counseling Techniques; Emotional Response; *Fear; *Patients; Rating Scales; Self Evaluation (Individuals)

Identifiers: FSS; Guilt

Availability: Educational and Industrial Testing Service; P.O. Box 7234, San Diego, CA 92107

Target Audience: Adults

Notes: Items, 108

Designed to identify patients' reactions to a variety of possible sources of maladaptive emotional reactions. Reactions are all fear related.

4270
Psychotic Inpatient Profile. Lorr, Maurice; Vestre, Norris D. 1968
Subtests: Excitement; Hostile Belligerence; Paranoid Projection; Anxious Depression; Retardation; Seclusiveness; Care Needed; Psychotic Disorganization; Grandiosity; Perceptual Distortion; Depressive Mood; Disorientation
Descriptors: Adults; *Behavior Disorders; Behavior Rating Scales; Nurses; Observation; *Patients; Psychiatric Aides; Psychiatric Hospitals; *Psychosis
Identifiers: PIP; *Psychiatric Patients
Availability: Western Psychological Services; 12031 Wilshire Blvd., Los Angeles, CA 90025
Target Audience: Adults
Notes: Time, 30 approx.; Items, 96
Designed for use by experienced nursing hospital personnel familiar with patient's behavior. Rater should observe patient's behavior and interaction with other patients and staff for a 3-day period before assessment. Instrument measures 12 syndromes of currently observable psychotic behavior.

4271
The Houston Test for Language Development. Crabtree, Margaret 1963
Subtests: Infant Scale; Self Identity; Vocabulary; Body Orientation; Gesture; Auditory Judgments; Oral Monitoring with Toys; Sentence Length; Temporal Content; Syntax; Prepositions; Serial Counting; Counting Objects; Imitates Linguistic Structure; Imitates Prosodic Patterns; Imitates Geometric Designs; Drawing; Oral Monitoring while Drawing; Tells about Drawing
Descriptors: *Communicative Competence (Languages); *Diagnostic Tests; *Disabilities; Individual Testing; Language Acquisition; Speech Skills; Young Children
Availability: Stoelting Co.; 1350 S. Kostner Ave., Chicago, IL 60623
Target Audience: 0-6
Notes: Time, 30 approx.
Assesses linguistic and nonverbal communication ability. Infant scale composed of check sheet for observing linguistic and prelinguistic skills of those up to 18 months. The 2-6 year test is administered through subtests. Designed to assist in diagnosis of problems resulting from emotional deprivation, neurological disabilities, retardation, auditory or visual motor deficits, or environmental linguistic influence.

4286
Language-Structured Auditory Retention Span Test. Carlson, Luis 1973
Descriptors: *Adolescents; *Adults; Auditory Stimuli; *Children; *Individual Testing; Learning Disabilities; Memory; *Recall (Psychology); *Retention (Psychology)
Identifiers: LARS; Oral Tests
Availability: Academic Therapy Publications; 20 Commercial Blvd., Novato, CA 94947
Target Audience: 3-64
Notes: Time, 15 approx.; Items, 58
Designed to provide an estimate of the optimum length of a meaningful aural message from which a person can profit during a learning experience. Sentences of increasing length are read orally. Testing is discontinued when subject reaches the upper limit of his or her memory. Useful in diagnosing learning disabilities. Equivalent forms A and B are available.

4295
Vocational Interest and Sophistication Assessment. Parnicky, Joseph J.; And Others 1968
Descriptors: Adolescents; Adults; *Career Awareness; *Career Exploration; Individual Testing; *Interest Inventories; *Mild Mental Retardation; *Pictorial Stimuli; Verbal Tests; Visual Measures; *Vocational Interests
Identifiers: Oral Tests; VISA
Availability: Nisonger Center; Ohio State University, Publications Dept., 434 McCampbell Hall, Columbus, OH 43210
Target Audience: 14-35
Notes: Time, 30 approx.; Items, 85
Measures mildly retarded adolescents and young adults' knowledge of job conditions and requirements and job interest. Identifies those job areas to which a subject is attracted because of high interest. Individually and orally administered. Requires the use of test books (which consists of pictures depicting occupations) and other forms; testbooks are of 2 forms: one form for females has 60 items; and the other for males has 85 items.

4298
Goldman-Fristoe-Woodcock Auditory Memory Test. Goldman, Ronald; And Others 1974
Subtests: Recognition Memory; Memory for Content; Memory for Sequence

Descriptors: Adolescents; Adults; Audiotape Recordings; *Children; *Diagnostic Tests; Individual Testing; Learning Disabilities; *Memory; *Older Adults; Recall (Psychology); Recognition (Psychology)
Identifiers: *Auditory Memory; G F W Auditory Memory Tests; G F W Battery; Test Batteries
Availability: American Guidance Service; Publishers' Bldg., Circle Pines, MN 55014
Target Audience: 3-85
Notes: Items, 140
Goldman-Fristoe-Woodcock Auditory Skills Battery consists of a wide range of diagnostic instruments for identifying and describing deficiencies in auditory functioning. Designed for use by teachers of learning-disabled children, reading specialists, speech and hearing clinicians, and school psychologists. Useful with preschool through geriatric populations. Use of earphones is recommended to reduce distraction. Designed to assess aspects of short-term auditory memory performance including recognition memory, memory for content, and memory for sequence.

4299
Goldman-Fristoe-Woodcock Auditory Selective Attention Test. Goldman, Ronald; And Others 1974
Subtests: Quiet; Fan-like Noise; Cafeteria Noise; Voice
Descriptors: Adolescents; Adults; *Attention; Audiotape Recordings; *Auditory Perception; *Children; *Diagnostic Tests; Individual Testing; *Learning Disabilities; *Listening Comprehension; Listening Skills; *Older Adults
Identifiers: G F W Attention; G F W Battery; Test Batteries
Availability: American Guidance Service; Publishers' Bldg., Circle Pines, MN 55014
Target Audience: 3-85
Notes: Items, 110
Goldman-Fristoe-Woodcock Auditory Skills Battery consists of a wide range of diagnostic instruments for identifying and describing deficiencies in auditory functioning. Designed for use by teachers of learning-disabled students, reading specialists, speech and hearing clinicians, and school psychologists. Useful with preschool through geriatric populations. Use of earphones is recommended to reduce distraction. GFW attention is designed to assess ability to attend under increasingly difficulty listening conditions. Provides an index of individual's ability to listen to and to understand a message in the presence of competing sound that is varied in intensity and type.

4300
Goldman-Fristoe-Woodcock Diagnostic Auditory Discrimination Tests—Parts I, II and III. Goldman, Ronald; And Others 1974
Descriptors: Adolescents; Adults; Audiotape Recordings; *Auditory Discrimination; Auditory Perception; *Children; *Diagnostic Tests; Individual Testing; *Learning Disabilities; *Older Adults
Identifiers: G F W Battery; G F W Diagnostic Discrim; Test Batteries
Availability: American Guidance Service; Publishers' Bldg., Circle Pines, MN 55014
Target Audience: 3-85
Notes: Items, 300
Goldman-Fristoe-Woodcock Auditory Skills Battery consists of a wide range of diagnostic instruments for identifying and describing deficiencies in auditory functioning. Designed for use by teachers of learning-disabled students, reading specialists, speech and hearing clinicians, and school psychologists. Useful with preschool through geriatric populations. Use of earphones is recommended to reduce distraction. Designed for diagnostic assessment of speech-sound discrimination problems. Used to determine individual's ability to discriminate speech-sounds and provide a description of sound confusions. Parts II and III are separately bound from Part I and administered only to subjects who have experienced difficulty with speech-sound discrimination in Part I. A Sound Confusion Inventory (SCI) shows the pattern of a subject's responses and is included for all parts. SCI simplifies identification and analysis of specific speech-sound discrimination errors.

4301
Goldman-Fristoe-Woodcock Sound-Symbol Tests. Goldman, Ronald; And Others 1974
Subtests: Sound Mimicry; Sound Recognition; Sound Analysis; Sound Blending; Sound-Symbol Association; Reading of Symbols; Spelling of Sounds
Descriptors: Adolescents; Adults; Audiotape Recordings; Auditory Perception; *Children; *Diagnostic Tests; Individual Testing; *Language Skills; *Learning Disabilities; *Older Adults
Identifiers: G F W Battery; G F W Sound Symbol; Test Batteries
Availability: American Guidance Service; Publishers' Bldg., Circle Pines, MN 55014
Target Audience: 3-85
Notes: Items, 321

Goldman-Fristoe-Woodcock Auditory Skills Battery consists of a wide range of diagnostic instruments for identifying and describing deficiencies in auditory functioning. Designed for use by teachers of learning-disabled students, reading specialists, speech and hearing clinicians, and school psychologists. Useful with preschool through geriatric populations. Use of earphones is recommended to reduce distraction. Designed to measure several basic abilities which are prerequisite to advanced language skills, including reading and spelling. Identification and analysis of specific difficulties in phonic and structural analysis is simplified by completion of Reading Error Inventory (REI).

4333
Behavioral Expectations Scale. Golding, Stephen L; And Others
Descriptors: Adults; *Expectation; Interaction; *Interpersonal Relationship; *Mental Disorders; *Patients; *Predictive Measurement; Social Behavior
Identifiers: *Attendant Attitudes; BES; TIM(B)
Availability: Tests in Microfiche; Test Collection, Educational Testing Service, Princeton, NJ 08541
Target Audience: Adults
Notes: Items, 28
This behaviorally specific expectation scale was developed to facilitate investigations of behavior-expectation effects in social interactions with mentally ill subjects. The authors feel that, when peers and professionals respond to mentally ill people in sick-role inducing ways, it reinforces deviant behavior.

4342
Harris Articulation Test. Harris, Gail S. 1973
Descriptors: *American Indians; *Articulation Impairments; *Children; *Diagnostic Tests; Individual Testing; *Pictorial Stimuli; *Speech Tests
Identifiers: Articulation Test; TIM(B)
Availability: Tests in Microfiche; Test Collection, Educational Testing Service, Princeton, NJ 08541
Target Audience: Children
Notes: Items, 67
Designed for use with American Indians, the test identifies what sounds the child has difficulty producing and in what position those sounds are in words (beginning, middle, or end of word). The test consists of pictures of objects that are stimuli for testing sounds and requires that the tester go over the pictures with the entire class assembled as a group several days before conducting the individual tests. The Articulation Test Check Sheet is the Revised Edition, 1974.

4732
Word Association Test. Campbell, Joel T.; Belcher, Leon 1968
Descriptors: *Association Measures; *Black Students; *Cognitive Style; Cognitive Tests; Disadvantaged; Higher Education; *Undergraduate Students
Identifiers: Word Associations
Availability: Psychological Reports; v23 p119-34, 1968
Grade Level: 13-16
Notes: Items, 100
Designed to assess word association responses of Black college students. Subjects were asked to write their response to stimulus words.

4744
Religious Behavior Questionnaire. Apfeldorf, Max 1969
Descriptors: Adults; *Behavior; Multiple Choice Tests; Patients; *Religion; *Veterans
Identifiers: TIM(E)
Availability: Tests in Microfiche; Test Collection, Educational Testing Service, Princeton, NJ 08541
Target Audience: Adults
Notes: Items, 36
Designed to assess a person's religious behavior as he or she perceives it. The questionnaire is multidenominational and covers activities related to membership in and interaction with a religious congregation, prayers, Bible reading, other religious reading, and relationship with one's fellow man. One of 3 instruments developed for use in a study of how and to what extent religious beliefs influence behavior. Data were collected from veterans at a Veterans Administration center and VA hospital.

4745
Religious Behavior Check List. Apfeldorf, Max 1969
Descriptors: Adults; Behavior; Behavior Rating Scales; *Observation; Patients; *Religion; *Veterans
Identifiers: TIM(E)
Availability: Tests in Microfiche; Test Collection, Educational Testing Service, Princeton, NJ 08541
Target Audience: Adults

Notes: Items, 15

Designed to assess a person's religious behavior as perceived by an observer. The checklist is multidenominational and covers activities related to membership in and interaction with a religious congregation, prayers, Bible reading, other religious reading, and relationship with one's fellow-man. One of 3 instruments developed for use in a study of how and to what extent religious beliefs influence behavior. Data were collected on 60 veterans in Veterans Administration hospitals.

4795
Religious Belief Questionnaire. Apfeldorf, Max; Smith, Walter J. 1969
Descriptors: Adolescents; Adults; *Attitudes; Behavior; *Beliefs; Patients; Rating Scales; *Religion; *Veterans
Identifiers: TIM(E)
Availability: Tests in Microfiche; Test Collection, Educational Testing Service, Princeton, NJ 08541
Target Audience: 13-65
Notes: Items, 64

Designed to assess an individual's religious beliefs, attitudes, feelings, and practices. The questionnaire is multidenominational and covers God, prayer, Bible, good and evil and their consequences, organized religion, religious practices, and duties of daily living. One of 3 instruments developed for use in a study of how and to what extent religious beliefs influence behavior. Data were collected from 53 veterans in a Veterans Administration hospital and 122 male and female high school students. Two parallel forms are available.

4811
Attitudes Inventory for Youth. French, J. L.; Cardon, B. W. 1969
Subtests: Planning (6); Attitudes toward School and Teachers (45); Personal Traits (36); Goals (17)
Descriptors: *Attitude Measures; *Dropouts; High Schools; *High School Students; Objectives; Personality Traits; Planning; Rating Scales; School Attitudes; Self Concept; *Student Attitudes; Teachers
Identifiers: TIM(A)
Availability: Tests in Microfiche; Test Collection, Educational Testing Service, Princeton, NJ 08541
Grade Level: 9-12
Notes: Items, 104

Designed for use in a study of bright dropouts. A 325-item long form was also used. Students responded to statements on a 5-point agree/disagree scale and checked off traits they felt they possessed.

4891
Wisconsin Card Sorting Test. Grant, David A.; Berg, Esta A.
Descriptors: *Abstract Reasoning; *Adolescents; *Adults; *Children; Computer Assisted Testing; Computer Software; Individual Testing; *Neurological Impairments; Performance Tests; *Preschool Children; *Screening Tests
Identifiers: WCST
Availability: Psychological Assessment Resources, Inc.; P.O. Box 998, Odessa, FL 33556
Target Audience: 4-64
Notes: Items, 64

Designed to assess perseveration and abstract thinking in subjects from preschool children through adults. Provides objective measure of particular difficulty on card sorting task. Instrument is useful in identifying cerebral dysfunction, except where local lesions do not involve frontal areas. Useful screening test for brain damage. A computerized version is available for Apple IIe, II Plus and IIc.

4936
Purpose in Life Test. Crumbaugh, James C.; Maholick, Leonard T. 1969
Descriptors: *Adults; Alcoholism; Attitude Measures; Counseling Techniques; *Disabilities; High Schools; *High School Students; *Life Satisfaction; Neurosis; Older Adults; Quality of Life; Rating Scales
Identifiers: PIL; Sentence Completion Tests
Availability: Psychometric Affiliates; Box 807, Murfreesboro, TN 37133
Grade Level: 9-12
Target Audience: Adults
Notes: Items, 33

Designed to measure the degree to which meaning in life has been found. Constructed from the orientation of logotherapy, a system of existential therapy originated by Viktor E. Frankl of the University of Vienna Medical School. Instrument is designed to detect an existential vacuum. Especially pertinent to alcoholics, retired, and handicapped populations. The Seeking of Noetic Goals Test (TC005869) was developed to complement this instrument.

4944
Group Psychotherapy Evaluation Scale. Kew, Clifton E. 1965
Subtests: Amount of Communication (1); Quality of Communication (1); Quality of Content (1); Capacity for Change (1); Amount of Therapist Verbal Activity (1); Direction of Therapist Verbal Activity (1)
Descriptors: Adolescents; Adults; Behavior Change; Communication (Thought Transfer); *Group Therapy; Patients; *Psychotherapy; *Screening Tests; Therapists
Identifiers: TIM(A)
Availability: Tests in Microfiche; Test Collection, Educational Testing Service, Princeton, NJ 08541
Target Audience: 16-65
Notes: Items, 6

Rater selects from 5 statements describing the behavior of the patient and the focus of the therapist. Designed to evaluate the suitability of patients for group psychotherapy.

4947
The Stockton Geriatric Rating Scale. Meer, Bernard; Baker, James A. 1966
Subtests: Physical Disability; Apathy; Communication Failure; Socially Irritating Behavior
Descriptors: Apathy; *Behavior Patterns; Behavior Rating Scales; Communication Problems; *Geriatrics; Observation; *Older Adults; *Patients; Physical Disabilities
Identifiers: SGRS
Availability: Journal of Gerontology; v21 n3 p392-403 Jul 1966
Target Audience: 65-99
Notes: Items, 33

Designed to assess geriatric patient's behavior after a one-week observation by rater. Instrument is also available from Stockton State Hospital; Research Dept., 510 E. Magnolia St., Stockton, CA 95202.

4948
Zip Test. Scott, Norval C.
Subtests: Language Facility Section; Word Recognition; Reading Comprehension; Word Opposites; Math Section; English Language Facility
Descriptors: Children; *Elementary School Students; English (Second Language); *Individual Testing; Language Fluency; Mathematics Achievement; *Migrant Children; Mathematics Tests; Reading Achievement; Reading Tests; *School Readiness Tests; *Screening Tests; *Spanish Speaking; *Student Placement
Availability: ASIS/NAPS, c/o Microfiche Publications; P.O. Box 3513, Grand Central Station, New York, NY 10163-3513 (NAPS Document 0070)
Target Audience: 5-12
Notes: Time, 30

Determines grade placement of a migrant child in reading and math and assesses the child's English-language facility. The test locates the instructional level at which a child can effectively use a mathematics book and a reader and should not be used for chronological grade placement.

5153
Slingerland Screening Tests for Identifying Children with Specific Language Disability: Form D. Slingerland, Beth H. 1974
Descriptors: *Auditory Perception; *Elementary School Students; Expressive Language; Intermediate Grades; *Kinesthetic Perception; *Language Handicaps; *Learning Disabilities; Receptive Language; *Screening Tests; *Visual Perception
Availability: Educators Publishing Service, Inc.; 75 Moulton St., Cambridge, MA 02238-9101
Grade Level: 5-6
Notes: Time, 120 approx.; Items, 199

Designed to screen those children who show indications of having a specific language disability in reading, handwriting, spelling, or speaking. May be used for individual testing as well as for group testing. Subtests 1-5 evaluate visual motor coordination, visual memory, visual discrimination, and visual memory linked with motor coordination. Subtests 6-8 evaluate auditory-visual discrimination and auditory memory to motor ability. All forms contain individual auditory tests to identify those who are unable to recall or pronounce words correctly or are unable to express organized thoughts in either spoken or written language. Form D contains a ninth subtest for evaluating personal orientation in time and space.

5155
Deaf-Blind Program and Ability Screening Test. Lyall, J.; And Others 1972
Subtests: Vision; Hearing; Gross Motor Skills; Fine Motor Skills; Self-Help Skills; Communication; Socialization

Descriptors: Adolescents; Children; *Deaf Blind; Hearing Impairments; Individual Testing; Multiple Disabilities; Preschool Children; Psychomotor Skills; *Screening Tests; Self Care Skills; Socialization; Visual Impairments; Young Adults
Availability: Mississippi Deaf-Blind Evaluation Center; Ellisville State School, Ellisville, MS 39437
Target Audience: 2-25
Notes: Time, 10 approx.

Designed as a screening instrument for placement of children and adults with multiple handicaps of visual and auditory impairment. Instrument is based on Gessell's Developmental Theory. Subjects are identified and grouped in 3 levels of functioning.

5156
Cutrona Child Study Profile of Psycho-Educational Abilities. Cutrona, Michael P. 1970
Subtests: General Behavior; Gross Motor Development; Fine Motor Development; Body Image and Awareness; Tactile Kinesthetic Development; Visual Motor Perception; Auditory Perception; Time Orientation; Non Verbal Conceptualization; Numerical Conceptualization
Descriptors: Academic Aptitude; Child Development; *Elementary School Students; Handicap Identification; Individual Development; Individual Testing; *Learning Problems; Learning Readiness; *Observation; Performance; *Primary Education; Rating Scales; *School Readiness; School Readiness Tests; Screening Tests; *Student Adjustment; *Student Behavior; Student Evaluation
Availability: Cutronics Educational Institute Publications; 128 W. 56th St., Bayonne, NJ 07002
Grade Level: K-3
Notes: Items, 98

Screening device used to provide a psychoeducational profile of the child. Used as part of complete child study diagnostic evaluation, in planning preschool and primary grade educational programs and for special education programs. According to the author, the instrument indicates general behavioral trends and the child's adequacy of ability or competency in psychoeducational areas.

5167
Self Rating Depression Scale. Zung, William W. K. 1965
Descriptors: Adults; Affective Behavior; *Depression (Psychology); *Patients; Self Concept Measures; *Self Evaluation (Individuals)
Identifiers: SDS
Availability: ERIC Document Reproduction Service; 3900 Wheeler Ave., Alexandria, VA 22304 (ED 171 763, 842 pages)
Target Audience: 20-64
Notes: Items, 20

This volume consists of a series of psychosocial and physiological clinical nursing instruments. The instruments were selected from the published literature in health care, education, psychology, and social sciences. Instruments focus on nursing practice and stress patient variables. Instrument is a self-rating scale which measures patient's feelings of depression. A 22-minute, 16 mm sound and color film on use of the scale is available. Suggested use in conjunction with Depression Status Inventory, (TC010080).

5175
Elizur Test of Psycho-Organicity: Children and Adults. Elizur, Abraham 1969
Subtests: Drawings; Digits; Blocks
Descriptors: Adolescents; *Adults; Auditory Perception; Children; *Diagnostic Tests; *Elementary School Students; Elementary Secondary Education; Intelligence; Memory; *Neurological Impairments; *Secondary School Students; Visual Perception
Identifiers: ETPO
Availability: Western Psychological Services; 12031 Wilshire Blvd., Los Angeles, CA 90025
Target Audience: 6-64
Notes: Time, 10 approx.

Designed to differentiate between subjects with organic and nonorganic brain damage. Separate administration directions for children and adults.

5224
University Alienation Scale. Burbach, Harold J. 1972
Descriptors: *Attitude Measures; *Black Students; College Environment; Higher Education; Social Attitudes; *Student Alienation; *Undergraduate Students
Identifiers: Likert Scales; UAS
Availability: Harold J. Burbach; Foundations of Education, School of Education, University of Virginia, Charlottesville, VA 22093
Grade Level: 13-16

Notes: Items, 24

Designed to assess feelings of alienation among Black students at various institutions of higher education. Alienation in this context was defined as the concept of powerlessness, meaninglessness, and social estrangement.

5235
Walker Problem Behavior Identification Checklist.
Walker, Hill M. 1970
Subtests: Acting Out; Withdrawal; Distractability; Disturbed Peer Relations; Immaturity
Descriptors: *Behavior Problems; Behavior Rating Scales; *Elementary School Students; Elementary School Teachers; Intermediate Grades; Observation; *Student Behavior
Identifiers: Disruptive Behavior; WPBIC
Availability: Western Psychological Services; 12031 Wilshire Blvd., Los Angeles, CA 90025
Grade Level: 4-6
Notes: Items, 50

Designed for completion by classroom teachers after 2 months of observation. Used to identify students with behavior problems who are in need of specialized educational services or further evaluation and treatment. Ratings from other educational specialists who have worked directly with the child can be obtained for comparative analysis.

5271
Primary Visual Motor Test. Haworth, Mary R. 1970
Descriptors: Child Development; Clinical Diagnosis; Cognitive Development; Deafness; *Developmental Disabilities; Diagnostic Tests; Educational Diagnosis; Individual Testing; Mental Retardation; Motor Development; Perceptual Development; *Perceptual Motor Coordination; *Performance Tests; *Primary Education; *Psychomotor Skills; School Readiness; Speech Handicaps; Visual Measures; *Visual Perception; Visual Stimuli; *Young Children
Identifiers: Oral Tests; PVM
Availability: Haworth, Mary R. The Primary Visual Motor Test. New York: Grune and Stratton, 1970
Target Audience: 4-8
Notes: Time, 15 approx.; Items, 16

As the author explains this instrument was designed to serve 2 functions: the assessment of visual motor development in the preschool and early primary grades and the evaluation of deviations in visual motor functioning during the developmental process and at earlier ages than has previously been possible. The subject is presented with 16 designs, one at a time, and asked to copy each. Useful with nonhandicapped children through 7 years of age and with mentally retarded persons whose mental age is 8 or 9 years. Not intended as an intelligence test but to indicate the child's status in the visual motor area. May also be used with deaf and speech-handicapped children. Requires the use of a set of cards and sheets of papers with lines dividing each into 8 parts.

5362
Mutually Responsible Facilitation Inventory.
Gnagey, Thomas D. 1973
Subtests: Importance as a Person; Ability to Conform; Removal of Negative Interaction; Involvement with Others
Descriptors: *Adjustment (to Environment); Adolescents; Adults; *Behavior Problems; Children; *Constructed Response; *Helping Relationship; Individual Development; Measures (Individuals); *Personality Problems; Prognostic Tests; Psychological Testing; *Social Cognition
Identifiers: MRFI
Availability: Psychologists and Educators; P.O. Box 513, St. Louis, MO 63017
Target Audience: 6-64
Notes: Time, 20 approx.; Items, 15

Untimed questionnaire in which an untrained person as a helper can assist an emotionally or socially maladjusted individual. This instrument analyzes this type of helping relationship, how the helper interacted with the individual in the past, and what he or she can do to encourage self-help and to aid the individual's personal and social adjustment in the present and future. Used by teachers, parents, and in marital counseling and in work environments to assist problem employees in the improvement of the basic adjustment to the work situation; also by doctors, psychologists, counselors, special education teachers, etc.

5363
Personal Opinions Inventory. Sistrunk, Frank; McDavid, John W. 1971
Descriptors: *Adolescents; *Adults; Blacks; *Conformity; Females; Males; Personality Measures; Social Behavior; *Social Influences; Whites
Identifiers: POI
Availability: Professor Frank Sistrunk; Dept. of Psychology, University of S. Florida, Tampa, FL 33620

Target Audience: 15-64
Notes: Items, 65

Designed to measure conformity or socially influenced behavior. Subjects were studied on basis of race and sex. They were asked to agree or disagree with responses to items given by an identified majority.

5367
Threshold by Identification of Pictures. Siegenthaler, Bruce M.; Haspiel, George S. 1970
Descriptors: Audiometric Tests; *Auditory Discrimination; Auditory Tests; Elementary Education; *Elementary School Students; Hearing (Physiology); *Hearing Impairments; Mental Retardation; *Preschool Children; Preschool Education
Identifiers: *Speech Reception Threshold; TIP
Availability: Speech and Hearing Clinic; Pennsylvania State University, 110 Psychology Bldg., University Park, PA 16802
Target Audience: 2-8
Notes: Items, 25

Designed to assess speech hearing for hearing-impaired or mentally retarded children. Measures speech reception threshold. Forms A and B are available.

5372
Toy Sorting Task. Hess, Robert D.; Shipman, Virginia 1967
Descriptors: Black Mothers; *Classification; Concept Formation; *Interaction Process Analysis; Parent Child Relationship; Parent Participation; *Performance Tests; *Preschool Children; Preschool Education; Psychological Testing; Task Analysis; *Urban Youth
Identifiers: *Cognitive Environments Project
Availability: ERIC Document Reproduction Service; 3900 Wheeler Ave., Alexandria, VA 22304 (ED 018 264, 6 pages)
Target Audience: 3-4
Notes: Items, 3

Designed to assess the cognitive environment of preschool urban children. Pairs of mothers and preschool children from 3 socioeconomic classes were selected for the study, according to the father's occupation. A 4th group was composed of father-absent families. This toy sorting task consisted of grouping 9 toys into 3 groups based on kind of toy or color. The mother was shown how to sort the toys and then was observed as she taught her child.

5373
Etch-a-Sketch Interaction Test. Hess, Robert D.; Shipman, Virginia 1967
Descriptors: Black Mothers; *Interaction Process Analysis; *Parent Child Relationship; *Performance Tests; *Preschool Children; Preschool Education; Psychological Testing; Teaching Skills; *Urban Youth
Identifiers: *Cognitive Environments Project
Availability: ERIC Document Reproduction Service; 3900 Wheeler Ave., Alexandria, VA 22304 (ED 018 267, 16 pages)
Target Audience: 3-4

Designed to assess the cognitive environment of preschool urban children. Pairs of mothers and preschool children from 3 socioeconomic classes were selected for the study, according to the father's occupation. A 4th group was composed of father-absent families. This task involved instructing the mother in the use of an Etch-a-Sketch toy. She then instructed her child in the use as they were observed. The mother and child cooperated in copying 5 figures of increasing complexity using the toy.

5374
Eight-Block Sorting Task. Hess, Robert D.; Shipman, Virginia C. 1967
Descriptors: Black Mothers; Classification; Concept Formation; *Interaction Process Analysis; Parent Child Relationship; *Parent Participation; Performance Tests; *Preschool Children; Preschool Education; Psychological Testing; Task Analysis; *Teaching Skills; *Urban Youth
Identifiers: *Cognitive Environments Project
Availability: ERIC Document Reproduction Service; 3900 Wheeler Ave., Alexandria, VA 22304 (ED018 265, 9 pages)
Target Audience: 3-4

Designed to assess the cognitive environment of preschool urban children. Pairs of mothers and preschool children from 3 socioeconomic classes were selected for the study, according to the father's occupation. A 4th group included father-absent families. The block sorting task was taught to the mother while the child was out of the room. The mother was observed teaching her child the basis of the groupings so that additional blocks could be included in the groupings. Two rating scales accompanied the task. Observer used a 9-item rating scale to assess the child's cooperation with the mother as teacher. The observer also used a 13-item rating scale for maternal affection during the teaching session.

5378
Gilliland Learning Potential Examination: 1970 Revision. Gilliland, Hap 1970
Subtests: Visual Memory; Symbol Identification; Symbol Interpretation; Relationships; Listening Comprehension; Picture Completion; General Information and Interests; Symbol Representation
Descriptors: *Academic Aptitude; Adults; American Indians; *Aptitude Tests; *Culture Fair Tests; *Disadvantaged; Elementary School Students; Elementary Secondary Education; Intelligence; Nonverbal Tests; *Reading Difficulties; *Reservation American Indians; Secondary School Students
Identifiers: Culturally Specific Tests
Availability: Montana Council for Indian Education; 517 Rimrock Rd., P.O. Box 31215, Billings, MT 59107
Target Audience: 6-16

Designed to determine scholastic aptitude, particularly in reading. Designed for nonreaders and culturally different students from age 6 to 16. May be used with older teenagers and adults with reading difficulties. Areas assessed include visual memory, listening comprehension, ability to use symbols, and to see relationships. Noncultural and nonreading scores can be computed. A slightly adapted version is being used with Indian tribes north of the Arctic Circle and in the Amazon jungles.

5436
Work Adjustment Rating Form. Bitter, James A.; Bolanovich, D.J. 1969
Descriptors: Adults; *Behavior Rating Scales; *Employment Potential; *Mental Retardation; Rehabilitation Programs; Vocational Rehabilitation
Identifiers: TIM(B); WARF
Availability: Tests in Microfiche; Test Collection, Educational Testing Service, Princeton, NJ 08541
Target Audience: Adults
Notes: Time, 7 approx.; Items, 40

Developed to assess the job readiness behaviors of individuals involved in vocational rehabilitation programs. Designed for use with mentally retarded adults. It includes 8 subscales: amount of supervision required, realism of job goals, teamwork, acceptance of rules/authority, work tolerance, perseverance in work, extent trainee seeks assistance, and importance attached to job training.

5438
Anxiety Scale for the Blind. Hardy, Richard E. 1968
Descriptors: *Adolescents; *Adults; *Affective Measures; *Anxiety; *Blindness; Diagnostic Tests
Identifiers: ASB; Oral Tests
Availability: American Foundation for the Blind; 15 W. 16th St., New York, NY 10011
Target Audience: 13-64
Notes: Time, 45 approx.; Items, 78

Orally, group-administered true-false test designed to measure manifest anxiety among blind people. Uses a connected, consecutively numbered roll of tickets. The placement of each ticket indicates the blind person's answer as true or false. Though originally designed for high school students, the author feels that the instrument is useful in rehabilitation organizations and hospitals, and in other counseling situations. Available only to clinical psychologists, rehabilitation and school counselors, and others who can establish their competency to utilize clinical material.

5470
Student Evaluation Scale. 1970
Subtests: Education Response; Social-Emotional Response
Descriptors: *Disabilities; *Disadvantaged; *Elementary School Students; Elementary School Teachers; Elementary Secondary Education; Rating Scales; *Secondary School Students; Secondary School Teachers; Special Education; Student Evaluation; Young Adults
Identifiers: SES
Availability: Psychologists and Educators; P.O. Box 513, St. Louis, MO 63017
Grade Level: 1-12
Target Audience: 6-21
Notes: Time, 5 approx.; Items, 52

Designed to evaluate student behavior and approaches to the learning process in regular and special education classes. May be used in psychiatric and correctional facility training programs also.

5471
Psychiatric Interview Checklist. Psychologists and Educators, Inc., Jacksonville, IL 1970
Descriptors: Adults; *Check Lists; Counseling Techniques; Interviews; *Patients; *Psychiatric Hospitals; Records (Forms)
Identifiers: *Psychiatric Patients

Availability: Psychologists and Educators; P.O. Box 513, St. Louis, MO 63017
Target Audience: Adults

Designed to indicate the major psychiatric symptoms of a patient or client. Checklist format incorporates basic items appropriate in conducting a psychiatric diagnostic interview.

5520
Family Interaction Questionnaire. Greenberg, Irwin M.
Descriptors: Adults; *Family Life; *Institutionalized Persons; *Mental Disorders; *Nuclear Family; Patients; Questionnaires
Identifiers: TIM(B)
Availability: Tests in Microfiche; Test Collection, Educational Testing Service, Princeton, NJ 08541
Target Audience: Adults
Notes: Items, 13

Designed primarily to distinguish between pathological families and relatively well-functioning families, this instrument is intended for use with pathological families by their assigned social workers. The questionnaire measures the amount and kind of interaction within the family covering such variables as medical and psychiatric illness, social isolation, physical or emotional disruption of the home, adequacy of income, work performance of bread winner, degree of aggression in the father and mother, and degree of acceptance by father and mother.

5526
Bristol Social Adjustment Guides. Stott, D. H.; Sykes, E. G. 1970
Descriptors: Adolescents; *Behavior Problems; *Behavior Rating Scales; Children; Elementary Secondary Education; *Emotional Disturbances; *Social Adjustment
Identifiers: BSAG
Availability: Educational and Industrial Testing Service; P.O. Box 7234, San Diego, CA 92107
Target Audience: 5-16
Notes: Time, 20 approx.

Designed to detect behavior disturbance and to diagnose its type and extent. Separate forms for boys and girls. British version available (TC810094).

5569
Grassi Block Substitution Test for Measuring Organic Brain Pathology. Grassi, Joseph R. 1970
Descriptors: Adults; Cognitive Style; *Diagnostic Tests; Individual Testing; Minimal Brain Dysfunction; *Neurological Impairments; *Patients; Performance Tests; Psychiatric Hospitals; Psychological Evaluation
Identifiers: *Psychiatric Patients; Schizophrenic Patients
Availability: Charles C. Thomas, Publisher; 2600 S. First St., Springfield, IL 62717
Target Audience: 18-64

Designed to demonstrate impairment of concrete and abstract performance because of organic brain dysfunction. Especially useful to detect early and minimal organic changes so that defects may be diagnosed in early stages of the disease process.

5613
Walker Readiness Test for Disadvantaged Pre-School Children in the United States. Walker, Wanda 1969
Subtests: Similarities; Differences; Numerical Analogies; Missing Parts
Descriptors: *Concept Formation; Culture Fair Tests; *Disadvantaged Youth; English; French; *Individual Testing; Nonverbal Tests; Number Concepts; *Preschool Children; *Preschool Tests; *School Readiness Tests; Spanish Speaking; Young Children
Identifiers: Project Head Start
Availability: ERIC Document Reproduction Service; 3900 Wheeler Ave., Alexandria, VA 22304 (ED 037 253, 147 pages)
Target Audience: 4-6
Notes: Items, 50

An individually administered culture-fair, nonverbal readiness test, directions for which are available in English, Spanish, or French. (Included in ERIC Document ED037253, 147 pages.) Test population is rural and urban disadvantaged preschool children.

5649
Photos Preference Test. Campbell, Donald Thomas; And Others 1964
Descriptors: *Adolescents; *Adults; *Mental Disorders; Patients; Projective Measures; Psychiatric Hospitals; Psychological Testing; Schizophrenia
Identifiers: PPT
Availability: Stockton State Hospital; Research Dept., 510 E. Magnolia St., Stockton, CA 95202
Target Audience: 13-50

Notes: Items, 100

Designed to determine whether deviant responses to facial photographs were related to psychological disturbances.

5671
Preschool Inventory Revised Edition—1970. Caldwell, Bettye M. 1970
Subtests: Personal-Social Responsiveness; Associative Vocabulary; Concept Activation-Numerical; Concept Activation-Sensory
Descriptors: Achievement Tests; *Disadvantaged Youth; Individual Testing; *Preschool Children; Preschool Education; School Readiness; *Screening Tests
Identifiers: *Cooperative Preschool Inventory
Availability: Publishers Test Service; 2500 Garden Rd., Monterey, CA 93940
Target Audience: 3-6
Notes: Time, 15 approx.; Items, 64

Designed to reveal the degree of disadvantage of the child entering school. Reveals child's knowledge of self, ability to follow directions, verbal expression, basic numerical concepts, and sensory attributes. This test is individually administered. For current psychometric information, see Journal of Applied Developmental Psychology; v3 p217-45, 1982.

5754
Illinois Index of Self-Derogation: Form 3. Meyerowitz, Joseph H. 1962
Descriptors: *Mental Retardation; *Mild Mental Retardation; Preschool Education; Primary Education; *Self Concept Measures; *Self Esteem; *Young Children
Identifiers: IISD; *Self Derogation; TIM(A)
Availability: Tests in Microfiche; Test Collection, Educational Testing Service, Princeton, NJ 08541
Target Audience: 2-8
Notes: Items, 22

Measures the tendency toward and specific nature of self derogation. The test may be group-administered.

5775
Test of Nonverbal Auditory Discrimination. Buktenica, Norman A. 1975
Subtests: Pitch; Loudness; Rhythm; Duration; Timbre
Descriptors: *Auditory Discrimination; Auditory Stimuli; Auditory Tests; Discrimination Learning; *Learning Problems; Nonverbal Tests; *Perception Tests; *Primary Education; *Screening Tests; *Young Children
Identifiers: TENVAD
Availability: Follett Publishing Co.; 1010 W. Washington Blvd., Chicago, IL 60607
Target Audience: 6-8
Notes: Time, 15 approx.; Items, 50

Designed to measure first, second, and third graders' auditory discrimination and to identify those children with auditory discrimination problems which will affect their school success. In each item, the child hears 2 sounds; he or she must decide whether the sounds are the same or different. Requires the use of the phonograph record and playback equipment. May be administered to entire classes for second and third graders; but should be given in small groups to first graders. If played without stopping, the entire record takes about 13 minutes.

5812
Sentence Repetition Task. Anastasiow, Nicholas J.; Hanes, Michael J. 1974
Descriptors: Code Switching (Language); Cognitive Development; *Culture Fair Tests; *Developmental Tasks; *Disadvantaged Youth; *Elementary School Students; Individual Testing; *Language Acquisition; *Language Tests; *Nonstandard Dialects; Primary Education; *Verbal Development; Verbal Tests
Identifiers: Oral Tests; SRT
Availability: Anastasiow, Nicholas J.; Language and Reading Strategies for Poverty Children, Baltimore, MD: University Park Press, 1982.
Target Audience: 4-12
Notes: Time, 25 approx.; Items, 28

Designed as an aid to teachers in distinguishing between children who speak with a different dialect and are normal in language development and children who speak a different dialect and are developmentally delayed. Authors recommend the use of a prerecorded tape and necessary equipment for playback. Individually administered.

5826
I.P.E. Juvenile. Eysenck, Sybil B. G. 1968
Subtests: Extraversion; Neuroticism; Lie
Descriptors: *Adolescents; Affective Measures; *Children; Elementary Secondary Education; Emotional Adjustment; Mental Health; Personality Assessment; *Personality Measures; *Personality Traits; *Self Evaluation (Individuals); *Spanish; *Spanish Speaking

Identifiers: *Extraversion Introversion; *Lie Scale
Availability: Educational and Industrial Testing Service; P.O. Box 7234, San Diego, CA 92107
Target Audience: 7-16
Notes: Time, 10 approx.; Items, 60

Spanish-language version of Junior Eysenck Personality Inventory (TC001009). Questionnaire is in Spanish, manual is in English. Designed to measure personality dimensions of children ages 7 to 16. Twenty-four items measure extraversion, 24 measure neuroticism, and 12 constitute a falsification scale for the detection of response distortion.

5914
State-Trait Anxiety Inventory. Spielberger, Charles D.; And Others 1970
Subtests: Trait Anxiety; State Anxiety
Descriptors: Adolescents; *Adults; Affective Measures; *Anxiety; *College Students; Emotional Disturbances; Emotional Response; Higher Education; High Schools; High School Students; *Personality Traits; Self Evaluation (Individuals)
Identifiers: Self Evaluation Questionnaire; STAI
Availability: Consulting Psychologists Press; 577 College Ave., Palo Alto, CA 94306
Grade Level: 9-16
Target Audience: 14-64
Notes: Time, 20 approx.; Items, 40

Designed to measure anxiety proneness (trait) and current level of tension and apprehension (state). Scales are self-administered. May be used with emotionally disturbed individuals as well as with the general population.

5950
Learner Self-Concept Test. DiLorenzo, Louis T. 1975
Descriptors: *Disadvantaged; Individual Testing; *Preschool Children; Preschool Education; *Self Concept; *Self Concept Measures; *Teacher Student Relationship
Identifiers: LSCT; TIM(A)
Availability: Tests in Microfiche; Test Collection, Educational Testing Service, Princeton, NJ 08541
Target Audience: 3-4
Notes: Items, 12

Designed to measure self-concept of pre-kindergarten, disadvantaged children ages 3.5 to 4.5 years in terms of teachers, peers, and classroom materials. There are 4 separate sets of drawings. There is one each for the following groups of subjects: White Males; Nonwhite Males; White Females; and Nonwhite Females. Instrument is administered orally to individual children.

6001
Adult Basic Learning Examination—Level III. Karlsen, Bjorn; And Others 1971
Subtests: Vocabulary; Spelling; Reading; Arithmetic
Descriptors: Academic Achievement; *Achievement Tests; *Adult Basic Education; Adults; *Arithmetic; *Reading Comprehension; *Spelling; *Vocabulary
Identifiers: ABLE; Test Batteries
Availability: The Psychological Corporation; 555 Academic Ct., San Antonio, TX 78204-0952
Target Audience: Adults
Notes: Time, 207 approx.; Items, 254

Battery of tests designed to measure level of educational achievement of adults who have not completed formal 12th grade education. Form A and Form B are available. Level III tests achievement levels equivalent to grades 9-12.

6020
Purcell Incomplete Sentences: A Projective Test for Children. Purcell, John Wallace 1967
Descriptors: Elementary Education; *Elementary School Students; *Emotional Disturbances; *Low Achievement; *Projective Measures
Identifiers: TIM(A)
Availability: Tests in Microfiche; Test Collection, Educational Testing Service, Princeton, NJ 08541
Grade Level: K-8
Target Audience: 6-14
Notes: Items, 30

Structured clinical interview provides general information about the child who is of fair to high intelligence. Designed for children within the approximate ages of 6-14, who are nonachievers in school. It can be used to establish initial rapport between the child and the psychologist and/or to introduce a battery of tests.

6028
Children's Locus of Control Scale. Bialer, Irv; Cromwell, Rue
Descriptors: Adults; Children; Elementary Education; *Elementary School Students; *Locus of Control; *Mental Retardation; Questionnaires
Identifiers: TIM(A)

Availability: Tests in Microfiche; Test Collection, Educational Testing Service, Princeton, NJ 08541
Grade Level: 1-8
Notes: Items, 23

Scale designed to measure children's conception of locus of control. A reverse form of the scale has been administered to mentally retarded adults.

6055
Ecological Assessment of Child Problem Behavior. Wahler, Robert G.; And Others 1976
Descriptors: *Behavior Problems; *Behavior Rating Scales; Classroom Observation Techniques; Elementary School Students; Elementary Secondary Education; *Emotional Disturbances; Observation; Secondary School Students; Social Behavior; *Social Environment
Availability: Pergamon Press, Inc.; Maxwell House, Fairview Park, Elmsford, NY 10523
Grade Level: K-9
Notes: Time, 30 approx.

Designed to be used in home and school settings to observe emotionally disturbed children displaying problem behavior. Children are studied in relation to their social environment.

6069
Diagnostic Checklist for Behavior Disturbed Children: Form E-2. Rimland, Bernard 1965
Subtests: Behavior; Speech
Descriptors: *Autism; *Behavior Disorders; Biographical Inventories; Check Lists; Child Development; Parents; *Preschool Children; Schizophrenia
Availability: Bernard Rimland, Director; Institute for Child Behavior Research, 4182 Adams Ave., San Diego, CA 92116
Target Audience: 3-5
Notes: Items, 109

Designed for completion by parents of young children who have been, or might be, diagnosed as having severe behavior disorders such as "autism," "childhood schizophrenia," "childhood psychosis," or as "severely emotionally disturbed." Instrument is used to differentiate cases of early infantile autism or Kanner's syndrome. Instrument is also available in French, Spanish, German, Italian, Japanese, Hebrew, Turkish, and Croatian.

6112
Kansas Neurological Institute Developmental Check List. Woellhof, Eldene 1965
Descriptors: *Behavior Rating Scales; *Communicative Competence (Languages); Competence; *Institutionalized Persons; *Mental Retardation; *Motor Development; *Socialization; Young Children
Identifiers: KNI Developmental Scale (Woellhof); TIM(D)
Availability: Tests in Microfiche; Test Collection, Educational Testing Service, Princeton, NJ 08541
Target Audience: 0-5
Notes: Items, 80

Developed to help estimate the mentally retarded child's level of functioning within 4 major areas: socialization, communication, physical development, and self-help. Items are separated into age-level intervals.

6113
Oral English/Spanish Proficiency Placement Test. Moreno, Steve 1974
Descriptors: Adolescents; Adults; Bilingualism; Children; *Diagnostic Tests; Elementary Education; *English (Second Language); *Individual Testing; *Language Proficiency; Pretests Posttests; *Spanish Speaking; *Student Placement
Identifiers: *Oral Tests
Availability: Moreno Educational Co.; 7050 Belle Glade Ln., San Diego, CA 92119
Target Audience: 4-20
Notes: Time, 5 approx.; Items, 151

Test measures oral English proficiency as it relates to H200 Curriculum materials to identify the lesson on which the student should be started for instruction, to provide diagnostic information, and to provide achievement information. The test is based on the student's ability to produce basic linguistic structures in sentence patterns and measures oral English, oral Spanish, and bilingualism. The oral English test is administered in English. Only the initial directions are given in the student's native language. The test is useful for students of various language backgrounds. The test can be administered to children from ages 4 to 20. The test has also shown validity when used with adults.

6119
Prueba de la Terminacion de la Frase de Fehrenbach. Fehrenbach, Alice 1974

Subtests: Self Attitudes (14); Attitudes toward Others (12); Attitudes toward Authority (17); Attitudes toward School (17); Self Adequacy (15); Past and Future (11)
Descriptors: *Attitude Measures; *Emotional Adjustment; Individual Testing; *Leadership; Projective Measures; School Attitudes; Secondary Education; Self Concept; *Social Adjustment; Spanish Speaking
Identifiers: Authority; Frustration; Future; Past; *Sentence Completion Form; TIM(G)
Availability: Tests in Microfiche; Test Collection, Educational Testing Service, Princeton, NJ 08541
Grade Level: 7-12
Notes: Time, 60; Items, 100

Discriminates between students with potential leadership qualities in terms of outstanding or average adjustment or those who have adjustment difficulties. Can be used to gather information prior to counseling or to provide teachers with insight into the hopes, fears of children. Manual and inventory are in Spanish. Can be administered individually or to groups. Group administration in which the students themselves write in the information often exposes more difficulties in communication that the student may have.

6157
Referral Form Checklist. Wood, Mary M. 1972
Subtests: Behavior; Communication; Socialization; Academic or Pre-Academic Skills
Descriptors: *Adolescents; *Behavior Disorders; Behavior Rating Scales; *Children; Diagnostic Tests; Elementary Secondary Education; *Emotional Disturbances; Parents; *Preschool Children; Preschool Education; Special Education; Teachers
Identifiers: RFCL; Rutland Center GA
Availability: ERIC Document Reproduction Service; 3900 Wheeler Ave., Alexandria, VA 22304 (ED 087 703, 305 pages)
Target Audience: 2-14

Designed to assess and identify problem behaviors of children ages 2-14 with severe emotional and behavioral disorders. The checklist is used as part of the diagnostic process. It may be completed by a child's parent or teacher. Part II is completed by professional staff. It consists of Diagnostic Classification and View of the Problem including a rating of severity and prognosis.

6162
Bannatyne System: Early Screening and Diagnostic Tests—Phase I. Bannatyne, Alexander D. 1975
Subtests: Symbol to Sound—Phonemes; Tactile Finger Sensing; Pictorial Mistakes Test; Sound Blending Test; Coding Speed Test; Symbol to Sound Words; Parent Questionnaire; Examiner's Checklist
Descriptors: *Elementary School Students; Gifted; Grade 1; *Handicap Identification; High Risk Students; Individual Testing; *Learning Disabilities; *Preschool Children; Preschool Education; Preschool Tests; Primary Education; Psychomotor Skills; *Screening Tests; Spatial Ability; Student Placement; *Talent Identification
Identifiers: BS ESDT; Test Batteries
Availability: Learning Systems Press; P.O. Box 91108, Lafayette, LA 70509
Target Audience: 3-6
Notes: Time, 25 approx.

Designed for individual screening of all students before, on, or immediately after school entry. Determines which students are "at risk," potentially learning disabled, or gifted. These students identified in Phase I screening assessment are then specifically diagnosed using Bannatyne System: Early Screening and Diagnostic Tests—Phase II (TC008030).

6174
Prison Fantasy Questionnaire. Beit-Hallahmi, Benjamin
Subtests: Daydreaming; Nightdreaming; Adjustment; Sex; Satisfaction; Self Destruction; Aggression; Food; Security; Religion; Unreal; Bizarre; Nurturance; Sadism; Escape; Release; Achievement
Descriptors: Adults; *Fantasy; *Males; *Prisoners; Questionnaires
Identifiers: PFQ; TIM(C)
Availability: Tests in Microfiche; Test Collection, Educational Testing Service, Princeton, NJ 08541
Target Audience: Adults
Notes: Items, 82

Developed to measure self-reported conscious fantasies in male prisoners. The 70 fantasy-content items are divided into 14 content scales: sex, satisfaction, self-destruction, aggression, food, security, religion, unreal, bizarre, nurturance, sadism, escape, release, and achievement. The 12 other items cover frequency of daydreaming, nightdream recall, and adjustment to prison.

6175
Bilingual Syntax Measure. Burt, Marina K.; And Others 1975
Descriptors: Bilingual Students; Culture Fair Tests; Elementary School Students; *English (Second Language); Language Dominance; *Language Proficiency; *Primary Education; Spanish; *Spanish Speaking; Visual Measures
Identifiers: BSM
Availability: The Psychological Corporation; 555 Academic Ct., San Antonio, TX 78204-0952
Grade Level: K-2

Designed to measure childrens' oral proficiency in English and/or Spanish grammatical structure by using natural speech as a basis for making judgments. The test is available in both English and Spanish.

6186
Cornell Learning and Study Skills Inventory: Secondary School. Pauk, Walter; Cassell, Russell N. 1970
Subtests: Goal Orientation; Activity Structure; Scholarly Skills; Lecture Mastery; Textbook Mastery; Examination Mastery; Self Mastery
Descriptors: *Learning Problems; Objective Tests; Secondary Education; *Secondary School Students; *Study Skills
Identifiers: CLASSIC
Availability: Psychologists and Educators; P.O. Box 513, St. Louis, MO 63017
Grade Level: 7-12
Notes: Time, 45 approx.; Items, 120

True-false format designed to assess problems in learning based on factors apart from reading speed and reading comprehension. The 7 partial scores yield a total score which represents one's overall study efficiency. The Reading Validity Index (RVI) is a measure to indicate whether a student has read and deliberated on the items contained in CLASSIC or whether one's scores are an accumulation of random marks. Where RVI falls below 35 or above 65, the CLASSIC profile has little meaning.

6190
Fehrenbach Children's Questionnaire. Fehrenbach, Alice 1957
Descriptors: *Attitude Measures; *Children; Elementary School Students; Parent Child Relationship; Peer Relationship; Questionnaires; School Attitudes; School Counselors; School Psychologists; *Self Evaluation (Individuals); *Spanish; Spanish Speaking; Teacher Student Relationship
Identifiers: TIM(I)
Availability: Tests in Microfiche; Test Collection, Educational Testing Service, Princeton, NJ 08541
Target Audience: 6-12
Notes: Items, 60

A questionnaire which may be administered individually or to groups. Responses to questions will reflect children's attitudes toward themselves, peers, parents, teachers, school, degree of frustration. Questionnaire is also available in Spanish. Is not intended as a diagnostic instrument, but to serve as a point of departure for counseling or therapy.

6211
Ego Strength Scale. Jacobs, Martin A. 1968
Subtests: Impulse Control; Interpersonal Relations; Autonomy; Frustration Tolerance; Self Esteem
Descriptors: Adults; Coping; Emotional Disturbances; *Patients; *Personality Change; Psychiatric Hospitals; Psychotherapy; Rating Scales; *Self Concept; Self Concept Measures; Self Evaluation (Individuals)
Identifiers: ESS; *Psychiatric Patients
Availability: Dr. Martin A. Jacobs; 346 Boston Post Rd., P.O. Box 95, Sudbury, MA 01776
Target Audience: Adults
Notes: Items, 50

A self-rating index of ego strength designed to measure personality change as a result of psychotherapy. Also provides a profile of pathology in coping mechanisms. Measure may be used to discriminate functioning normal subjects from psychiatric patients.

6213
Ego Strength Rating Scale. Jacobs, Martin A. 1968
Descriptors: Adults; Coping; Depression (Psychology); Emotional Disturbances; Patients; *Personality Change; Personality Measures; Psychiatric Hospitals; *Psychiatrists; Psychotherapy; Rating Scales
Identifiers: *Psychiatric Patients
Availability: Dr. Martin A. Jacobs; Community Health Program, Waltham Hospital, Hope Ave., Waltham, MA 02154
Target Audience: Adults

Designed to assess personality change as a result of psychotherapy. Patient is evaluated by a psychiatrist or other hospital personnel upon admission and at several points thereafter.

6244
Zeitlin Early Identification Screening. Zeitlin, Shirley 1974
Descriptors: Body Image; Cognitive Development; *Individual Testing; Language Acquisition; *Learning Problems; Memory; *Preschool Children; Questionnaires; *Screening Tests; Young Children
Identifiers: TIM(B); ZEIS
Availability: Tests in Microfiche; Test Collection, Educational Testing Service, Princeton, NJ 08541
Target Audience: 3-7
Notes: Items, 12

Individually administered instrument is designed to identify children who may have special learning needs. The screening consists of items relating to language, cognitive development, visual motor, auditory and visual memory, gross motor, body image, directionality, and laterality. The questions are divided into 3 parts, including verbal tasks, paper-and-pencil tasks, and nonverbal performance. Checklists for recording relevant observable behaviors and emotional indicators are included. Research instrument.

6270
Specific Stress Index. Michaux, William W. 1967
Descriptors: Adjustment (to Environment); Adults; Interviews; Mental Disorders; *Patients; *Stress Variables
Identifiers: *Psychiatric Patients
Availability: Dr. William Michaux; 501 Colleen Rd., Baltimore, MD 21229
Target Audience: Adults
Notes: Items, 8

Designed to assess stress levels of psychiatric patients through use of a structured interview.

6345
Fehrenbach Language Perception Test, Revised. Fehrenbach, Alice 1983
Descriptors: *Adolescents; Language Processing; *Psychological Patterns; Psychological Testing; Remedial Instruction; School Counselors; School Psychologists; Secondary School Students; *Student Adjustment
Identifiers: Fehrenbach Language Concept Test; *Sentence Completion Method; TIM(I)
Availability: Tests in Microfiche; Test Collection, Educational Testing Service, Princeton, NJ 08541
Target Audience: 13-17
Notes: Items, 20

Valuable as a screening device for teachers of English, communications, and guidance, as well as for school counselors, school psychologists, and clinical psychologists. Results can be used to delineate remedial groups, counseling groups, and those adolescents who need intensive psychological evaluation.

6421
Experiential World Inventory. El-Meligi, A. Moneim; Osmond, Humphry 1970
Subtests: Sensory Perception; Time Perception; Body Perception; Self Perception; Perception of Others; Ideation; Dysphoria; Impulse Regulation
Descriptors: *Adolescents; *Adults; *Mental Disorders; *Neurological Impairments; Personality Measures; Psychopathology; Self Concept Measures; Social Experience
Identifiers: EWI; *Psychiatric Patients
Availability: Mens Sana Publishing Inc.; 4965 Lionel-Groulx, St. Augustin De Quebec, P.Q. Canada G3A 1V2
Target Audience: 11-64
Notes: Time, 50 approx.; Items, 400

Designed to assess abnormality as reflected in the immediate experience of disturbed individuals. Useful in helping a clinician learn how patients perceive the world about them, how they view themselves in relation to it, and how they think and feel about the changes occurring within themselves. Not designed for use with normal populations.

6472
Adaptive Behavior Scale (For Adults 13 Years or Older). Nihira, Kazuo; And Others 1969
Subtests: Independent Functioning; Physical Development; Economic Activity; Language Development; Number and Time Concept; Occupation (Domestic); Occupation (General); Self Direction; Responsibility; Socialization; Violent and Destructive Behavior; AntiSocial Behavior; Rebellious Behavior; Untrustworthy Behavior; Withdrawal; Stereotyped Behavior and Odd Mannerisms; Inappropriate Interpersonal Manners; Unacceptable Vocal Habits; Unacceptable or Eccentric Habits
Descriptors: *Adjustment (to Environment); Adolescents; Adults; Behavior Problems; *Behavior Rating Scales; *Coping; *Emotional Adjustment; *Emotional Disturbances; Institutionalized Persons; *Mental Retardation; *Observation; *Patients; Personality Measures; Personality Traits; Psychological Evaluation; Psychological Testing
Identifiers: ABS; AB Scale; Adaptive Behavior Project
Availability: American Association on Mental Deficiency; 5101 Wisconsin Ave., N.W., Washington, DC 20015
Target Audience: 13-65
Notes: Time, 45 approx.; Items, 113

Originally designed for institutional use, though it may be used by any appropriate adult who has observed closely or personally knows the behavioral pattern of the ratee. Designed to provide, via a behavior rating scale, objective description and assessment of the adaptive behavior of mentally retarded and emotionally maladjusted individuals. The authors define adaptive behavior as the effectiveness with which the individual copes with natural and social demands of his or her environment.

6473
Adaptive Behavior Scale (for Children 12 Years or Younger). Nihira, Kazuo; And Others 1969
Subtests: Independent Functioning; Physical Development; Economic Activity; Language Development; Number and Time Concept; Occupation Domestic; Occupation General; Self Direction; Responsibilities; Socialization; Behavior and Habits
Descriptors: *Adaptive Behavior (of Disabled); *Adjustment (to Environment); Behavior Problems; Behavior Rating Scales; *Children; Coping; Emotional Adjustment; *Emotional Disturbances; Institutionalized Persons; *Mental Retardation; *Observation; *Patients; Personality Measures; Personality Traits; Psychological Evaluation; Psychological Testing
Identifiers: ABS; AB Scale; Adaptive Behavior Project
Availability: American Association on Mental Deficiency; 5101 Wisconsin Ave., N.W., Washington, DC 20015
Target Audience: 3-12
Notes: Items, 111

Originally designed for institutional use, though it may be used by any appropriate adult who has observed closely or personally knows the behavioral pattern of the ratee. Designed to provide, via a behavior rating scale, objective description and assessment of the adaptive behavior of mentally retarded and emotionally maladjusted individuals. The authors define adaptive behavior as the effectiveness with which the individual copes with natural and social demands of his or her environment.

6513
Slingerland Screening Tests for Identifying Children with Specific Language Disability: Form A. Slingerland, Beth H. 1970
Descriptors: *Auditory Perception; *Elementary School Students; Expressive Language; Grade 1; Grade 2; *Kinesthetic Perception; *Language Handicaps; *Learning Disabilities; Primary Education; Receptive Language; *Screening Tests; *Visual Perception
Availability: Educators Publishing Service, Inc.; 75 Moulton St., Cambridge, MA 02238-9101
Grade Level: 1-2
Notes: Time, 60 approx.

Designed to screen those children who show indications of having a specific language disability in reading, handwriting, spelling, or speaking. May be used for individual testing as well as for group testing. Subtests 1-5 evaluate visual-motor coordination, visual memory, visual discrimination, and visual memory linked with motor coordination. Subtests 6-8 evaluate auditory-visual discrimination and auditory memory to motor ability. All forms also contain individual auditory tests to identify those who are unable to recall or pronounce words correctly or are unable to express organized thoughts in either spoken or written language. Designed for use with children of average or superior intelligence.

6514
Slingerland Screening Tests for Identifying Children with Specific Language Disability: Form B. Slingerland, Beth H. 1970
Descriptors: *Auditory Perception; *Elementary School Students; Expressive Language; Grade 2; Grade 3; *Kinesthetic Perception; *Language Handicaps; *Learning Disabilities; Primary Education; Receptive Language; *Screening Tests; *Visual Perception
Availability: Educators Publishing Service, Inc.; 75 Moulton St., Cambridge, MA 02238-9101
Grade Level: 2-3
Notes: Time, 60 approx.

Designed to screen those children who show indications of having a specific language disability in reading, handwriting, spelling, or speaking. May be used for individual testing as well as for group testing. Subtests 1-5 evaluate visual-motor coordination, visual memory, visual discrimination, and visual memory linked with motor coordination. Subtests 6-8 evaluate auditory-visual discrimination and auditory memory to motor ability. All forms also contain individual auditory tests to identify those who are unable to recall or pronounce words correctly or are unable to express organized thoughts in either spoken or written language. Designed for use with children of average or high intelligence.

6515
Slingerland Screening Tests for Identifying Children with Specific Language Disability: Form C. Slingerland, Beth H. 1970
Descriptors: *Auditory Perception; Elementary Education; *Elementary School Students; Expressive Language; Grade 3; Grade 4; *Kinesthetic Perception; *Language Handicaps; *Learning Disabilities; Receptive Language; *Screening Tests; *Visual Perception
Availability: Educators Publishing Service, Inc.; 75 Moulton St., Cambridge, MA 02238-9101
Grade Level: 3-4

Designed to screen those children who show indications of having a specific language disability in reading, handwriting, spelling, or speaking. May be used for individual testing as well as for group testing. Subtests 1-5 evaluate visual-motor coordination, visual memory, visual discrimination, and visual memory linked with motor coordination. Subtests 6-8 evaluate auditory-visual discrimination and auditory memory to motor ability. All forms also contain individual auditory tests to identify those who are unable to recall or pronounce words correctly or are unable to express organized thoughts in either spoken or written language. Designed for use with children of average or superior intelligence.

6559
Manual for Assessing Minor Physical Anomalies. Waldrop, Mary F.
Subtests: Anomalies in the Area of the Head; Anomalies in the Area of the Eyes; Anomalies in the Area of the Ears; Anomalies in the Area of the Mouth; Anomalies in the Area of the Hand; Anomalies in the Area of the Feet
Descriptors: Behavior Problems; Children; *Downs Syndrome; *Hyperactivity; *Measures (Individuals); *Physical Characteristics
Identifiers: TIM(D)
Availability: Tests in Microfiche; Test Collection, Educational Testing Service, Princeton, NJ 08541
Target Audience: 0-12
Notes: Items, 18

A symptom checklist that provides for the rating of a child on 18 minor physical anomalies which have been associated with problem behavior.

6692
S-D Proneness Checklist. Martin, William T. 1970
Subtests: Suicidal Aspects; Depressive Aspects
Descriptors: Adolescents; Adults; Behavior Rating Scales; *Depression (Psychology); *Patients; *Suicide
Availability: Psychologists and Educators; P.O. Box 513, St. Louis, MO 63017
Target Audience: 14-64
Notes: Time, 5 approx.; Items, 30

Designed to assess patient's level of depression and suicidal tendencies. Rating scale is designed for use during, or following, an interview with patient. Useful for suicide prevention centers.

6693
Martin S-D Inventory. Martin, William T. 1970
Descriptors: Adolescents; Adults; *Depression (Psychology); Patients; Self Concept; *Self Concept Measures; *Suicide
Identifiers: Self Report Measures
Availability: Psychologists and Educators; P.O. Box 513, St. Louis, MO 63017
Target Audience: 14-64
Notes: Time, 15 approx.; Items, 50

Designed to assess patient's self-concept and tendency toward depression and suicide. Useful for suicide prevention centers.

6704
Inventario De Habilidades Para Aprender a Leer. Shelquist, Jack; And Others 1975
Subtests: Secuencia De Memoria Auditiva; Discriminacion De Las Palabras; Conocimiento Corporal; Conceptos De Direccion Y Posicion; Discriminacion De Los Colores; Coordinacion Visual Motora; Percepcion Visual De Las Letras; Nombres De Las Letras

Descriptors: Bilingual Students; Concept Formation; Educationally Disadvantaged; *Grade 1; Individual Testing; *Kindergarten Children; Learning Disabilities; Mental Retardation; Perceptual Development; *Preschool Children; Preschool Education; Primary Education; Remedial Programs; *School Readiness; School Readiness Tests; *Spanish Speaking; *Student Placement
Identifiers: Inventory of Readiness Skills
Availability: Educational Programmers; P.O. Box 332, Roseburg, OR 97470
Target Audience: 2-6
Notes: Time, 20 approx.; Items, 102

Diagnostic instrument which assesses a child's readiness for learning with the corresponding strengths and weaknesses. Spanish version of the Inventory of Readiness Skills (TC011360) for use with Spanish speaking children in a bilingual program. Individually administered. Adapted for Spanish customs. A manual is also available for developing those learning skills in which the children are deficient. Requires the use of a set of letters (capital and small).

6740
Institutional Behavior Rating Scale. Leibowitz, Gerald; Chorost, Sherwood 1970
Descriptors: Adolescents; *Affective Behavior; Behavior Rating Scales; Children; *Cognitive Ability; *Institutionalized Persons; *Social Attitudes
Identifiers: TIM(A)
Availability: Tests in Microfiche; Test Collection, Educational Testing Service, Princeton, NJ 08541
Target Audience: 3-19
Notes: Items, 42

Screening device is designed for use in institutional settings where a large number of children may be in need of clinical attention. Ratings are made by the teacher or child care worker. Factors assessed are aggressive-excitability, cognitive efficiency, prosocial avoidance, and passive-aggressive.

6748
T.M.R. Performance Profile for the Severely and Moderately Retarded. DiNola, Alfred J.; And Others 1978
Subtests: Social Behavior; Self-Care; Communication; Basic Knowledge; Practical Skills; Body Usage; Habilitation Level
Descriptors: Adolescents; Adults; Behavior Rating Scales; Children; *Developmental Tasks; Diagnostic Tests; *Individual Development; Individual Testing; Learning Disabilities; *Learning Readiness; Maturity Tests; *Moderate Mental Retardation; Observation; *Severe Mental Retardation; Student Development; Student Evaluation
Availability: Educational Performance Associates; 600 Broad Ave., Ridgefield, NJ 07657
Target Audience: 5-65
Notes: Items, 240

Provides a rating of severely and moderately retarded individual's performance on 240 specific developmental items. Supplies needed information about adaptive behavior for individualized curriculum planning. Evaluation is based on the teacher's observations. Individual development is measured against specific developmental items on a 5-point scale.

6749
Y.E.M.R. Performance Profile for the Young Moderately and Mildly Retarded. DiNola, Alfred J.; And Others 1967
Subtests: Social Behavior; Self-Help; Safety; Communication; Motor Skills; Manipulative Skills; Perceptual and Intellectual Development; Academics; Imagination and Creative Expression; Emotional Behavior; Habilitation Level
Descriptors: Behavior Rating Scales; Children; *Developmental Tasks; Diagnostic Tests; *Elementary School Students; *Individual Development; Individual Testing; Learning Disabilities; *Learning Readiness; Maturity Tests; *Mild Mental Retardation; *Moderate Mental Retardation; Observation; *Primary Education; School Readiness; Student Evaluation
Availability: Educational Performance Associates; 600 Broad Ave., Ridgefield, NJ 07657
Target Audience: 5-11

Based on the author's T.M.R. Performance Profile, the test is designed to identify performance and personal development levels of moderately and mildly retarded children in a variety of (scaled) daily tasks and to identify those areas and levels where the children are deficient and where they show readiness for new learning. Evaluation is based on the teacher's observations. The authors feel that certain developmental abilities are necessary for adjustment and growth of these children to their social and intellectual environment before and after they enter the public school program.

6763
Key Math Diagnostic Arithmetic Test. Connolly, Austin J.; And Others 1976
Subtests: Numeration; Fractions; Geometry and Symbols; Addition; Subtraction; Multiplication; Division; Mental Computation; Numerical Reasoning; Word Problems; Missing Elements; Money; Measurement; Time
Descriptors: Criterion Referenced Tests; *Diagnostic Tests; Elementary Education; *Elementary School Mathematics; *Elementary School Students; *Individual Testing; *Mild Mental Retardation; Mathematics Tests
Availability: American Guidance Service, Inc.; Publishers' Bldg., Circle Pines, MN 55014
Grade Level: K-6
Notes: Time, 30 approx.

Provides a comprehensive assessment through 14 subtests covering 3 basic areas—Content, Operations, and Applications. There are a total of 209 items. However, the test is individually administered so that the examiner uses only those items which are of appropriate difficulty for the student being tested. Especially useful for diagnosing academic deficits in children with learning disabilities. No upper age limit for remedial use. The optional Key Math Metric Supplement (TC008347) assesses progress in metric measurement. Thirty-one test items cover linearity, mass capacity, area, and temperature.

6782
Tests for Colour Blindness. Ishihara, Shinobu 1967
Descriptors: *Adolescents; *Adults; *Children; Congenital Impairments; *Vision Tests; *Visual Impairments; Visual Perception
Identifiers: *Color Blindness; Ishihara Test Chart Books
Availability: Graham-Field Surgical Co., Inc.; New Hyde Park, NY 11040
Target Audience: 6-64

Designed to assess congenital color blindness of 2 types: total color blindness and red-green blindness. Examinee is shown special color plates to determine the kind and degree of defect in color vision. Available in books of 8, 14, 24, and 38 plates.

6818
Columbia Mental Maturity Scale—Levels A-H. Third Edition. Burgemeister, Bessie B. 1972
Descriptors: Children; *Cognitive Ability; *Cognitive Tests; *Disabilities; *Disadvantaged; Individual Testing; *Neurological Impairments; *Non English Speaking; Nonverbal Tests; *Pictorial Stimuli; *Preschool Children; Spanish; Spanish Speaking
Identifiers: CMMS; *Reasoning Ability
Availability: The Psychological Corporation; 555 Academic Ct., San Antonio, TX 78204-0952
Target Audience: 3-10
Notes: Time, 20 approx.; Items, 92

Designed to yield estimate of general reasoning ability of children aged 3-5 through 9-11. Child takes level indicated for his or her chronological age. From 51 to 65 items are actually presented depending on level administered. Requires no verbal response and a minimal motor response. CMMS is suitable for use with brain damaged children, as well as with those with mental retardation, visual handicaps, speech impairment, or hearing loss. Instrument does not depend on reading or language skills, making it suitable for non-English speakers. Spanish directions are included in manual.

6821
Boston Diagnostic Aphasia Test. Goodglass, Harold; Kaplan, Edith 1972
Subtests: Conversational and Expository Speech; Word Discrimination; Body-Part Identification; Commands; Complex Ideational Material; Oral Agility; Automatized Sequences; Recitation, Singing, and Rhythm; Repetition of Words; Repeating Phrases; Word-Reading; Responsive Naming; Visual Confrontation Naming; Body-Part Naming; Animal-Naming (Fluency in Controlled Association); Oral Sentence-Reading; Symbol and Word Discrimination; Phonetic Association; Comprehension of Oral Spelling; Word-Picture Matching; Reading Sentences and Paragraphs; Mechanics of Writing; Recall of Written Symbols; Primer-Level Dictation; Written Word-Finding; Written Formulation
Descriptors: Adults; *Aphasia; *Communication Disorders; *Diagnostic Tests; Individual Testing; Medical Evaluation; *Patients; Pictorial Stimuli; Verbal Communication; Verbal Tests
Identifiers: Aphasia Test; Assessment of Aphasia and Related Disorders; *Oral Tests; Rating Scale Profile of Speech Characteristics
Availability: Lea & Febiger; 600 Washington Square, Philadelphia, PA 19106
Target Audience: Adults
Notes: Items, 280

Designed for 3 purposes: (1) to diagnose the existence and type of aphasic syndrome; (2) to measure the level of performance over a diversified group of items; and (3) to determine the assets and liabilities of the patient as a guide to therapy. The authors recommend tape-recording to assist the administrator in completing the Rating Scale Profile of Speech Characteristics. Requires some materials: the use of printed set of cards and several sheets of blank paper. The authors also describe supplementary language and nonlanguage tests.

6823
Oliphant Auditory Discrimination Memory Test. Oliphant, Genevieve G. 1971
Descriptors: *Auditory Discrimination; Auditory Tests; Elementary Education; *Elementary School Students; Learning Disabilities; *Screening Tests
Availability: Educators Publishing Service; 75 Moulton St., Cambridge, MA 02238-9101
Grade Level: 1-6
Notes: Items, 20

Designed for use in screening the auditory discrimination ability of groups of children. Useful as an aid in identification of those children whose auditory perceptual abilities require more careful analysis.

6824
Oliphant Auditory Synthesizing Test. Oliphant, Genevieve G. 1971
Subtests: Two-Phoneme Words; Three-Phoneme Words; Four-Phoneme Words
Descriptors: *Auditory Perception; Auditory Tests; *Diagnostic Tests; Elementary Education; *Elementary School Students; Individual Testing; *Language Handicaps; Learning Disabilities; Screening Tests
Availability: Educators Publishing Service; 75 Moulton St., Cambridge, MA 02238-9101
Grade Level: 1-6
Notes: Items, 30

Designed to assess child's ability to listen to a word spoken in separate phonemes, retain them in memory in correct sequence, and to blend these phonemes mentally and assign them a linguistic meaning. Especially useful in the establishment of a differential diagnosis of perceptual functioning in evaluation of specific language, or learning, disabilities.

6825
School Entrance Check List. McLeod, John 1968
Descriptors: *Dyslexia; Elementary School Students; *Grade 1; *Kindergarten Children; Primary Education; *Reading Difficulties; School Entrance Age; School Readiness; *Screening Tests
Availability: Educators Publishing Service; 75 Moulton St., Cambridge, MA 02238-9101
Grade Level: K-1
Notes: Items, 18

Recommended for routine survey and screening for use as part of school enrollment procedures. Contains most pertinent questions from the Dyslexia Schedule (TC006826). Designed for completion by parents.

6826
Dyslexia Schedule. McLeod, John 1968
Descriptors: *Biographical Inventories; Case Records; *Dyslexia; Elementary Education; *Elementary School Students; *Learning Disabilities; Questionnaires; *Reading Difficulties
Availability: Educators Publishing Service; 75 Moulton St., Cambridge, MA 02238-9101
Grade Level: K-6
Notes: Items, 89

Designed to be completed for children who have been referred to a special class, school, or reading clinic because of learning disabilities. Parents should complete the questionnaire before child is seen by the psychologist. Responses should be discussed with parents in an interview situation.

6868
Balthazar Scales of Adaptive Behavior: Scales of Functional Independence. Balthazar, Earl E. 1971
Subtests: Dependent Feeding; Finger Foods; Spoon Usage; Fork Usage; Drinking; Total Eating Scale; Total Dressing Scale; Total Toileting Scale
Descriptors: *Adjustment (to Environment); Adults; Behavior Rating Scales; Children; *Institutionalized Persons; *Self Care Skills; *Severe Mental Retardation
Identifiers: BSAB I
Availability: Consulting Psychologists Press; 577 College Ave., Palo Alto, CA 94306
Target Audience: 5-57
Notes: Items, 131

Measures functional independence of severely and profoundly mentally retarded persons in institutional settings.

6870
The Instant Word Recognition Test. Fry, Edward 1977
Descriptors: *Achievement Tests; Criterion Referenced Tests; *Elementary School Students; Individual Testing; Primary Education; *Reading Achievement; *Remedial Reading; *Word Recognition
Availability: Jamestown Publishers; P.O. Box 6743, Providence, RI 02940
Grade Level: 1-3
Notes: Items, 48

Measures a student's sight recognition of 600 most common words. May be used for individual or group administration in primary grades and remedial reading situations. Tests are self-scoring.

6900
The Teaching Research Motor-Development Scale for Moderately and Severely Retarded Children. Fredericks, H.D.; And Others 1972
Descriptors: *Children; Elementary Education; Elementary School Students; Individual Testing; *Mental Retardation; Motor Development; Performance Tests; Physical Education; *Psychomotor Skills
Availability: Charles C. Thomas, Publisher; 2600 S. First St., Springfield, IL 62717
Target Audience: 7-12

Designed to measure motor proficiency of mentally retarded children. May be used with children who are very severely retarded as well as with those with mild retardation. Examiner must ensure the children understand the task they must perform, using verbal directions and demonstration as necessary.

6903
McCarthy Scales of Children's Abilities. McCarthy, Dorothea 1972
Subtests: Verbal; Perceptual-Performance; Quantitative; General Cognitive; Memory, and Motor
Descriptors: Academic Aptitude; Cognitive Tests; Elementary Education; *Elementary School Students; *Handicap Identification; Motor Development; Predictive Measurement; *Preschool Children; Preschool Education; Psychomotor Skills; *Talent Identification
Identifiers: MSCA
Availability: The Psychological Corporation; 555 Academic Ct., San Antonio, TX 78204-0952
Target Audience: 2-9
Notes: Time, 60 approx.

Designed to assess the intellectual and motor development of children 2.5 through 8.5 years of age. Useful in identification of children with learning disabilities, or auditory, visual or speech defects, or gifted children. Eighteen tests have been grouped into 6 scales.

6921
Clinical Analysis Questionnaire. Institute for Personality and Ability Testing, Inc., Champaign, IL 1970
Descriptors: Adolescents; Adults; *Behavior Problems; *Behavior Rating Scales; *Clinical Diagnosis; Computer Assisted Testing; Diagnostic Tests; *Mental Disorders; Microcomputers; *Patients; *Personality Assessment; Personality Measures; Personality Problems; Psychological Evaluation; Psychological Testing
Identifiers: CAQ
Availability: Institute For Personality And Ability Testing; P.O. Box 188, Champaign, IL 61820
Target Audience: 16-64
Notes: Time, 120 approx.; Items, 272

Designed and developed in order to provide clinical psychologists with an objective measurement of primary behavioral dimensions. Measures 28 first-primary factors and the 9 principal second orders that may be derived from them. Thus, 16 normal personality dimensions are included. For the use with neurotic and psychotic patients. Used in general clinical diagnosis for initial diagnosis and for evaluating therapeutic progress; also used for clinical research. Because it is so long, the authors recommend giving it in 2 sessions. Untimed. May also be computer administered on an Apple IIc, IIe, II, and compatibles or on an IBM/PC, IBM-PC/XT, and compatibles. Distributors of software are Integrated Professional Systems, 5211 Mahoning Ave., Ste. 135, Youngstown, OH 44515, and Psychological Assessment Resources, Box 998, Odessa, FL 33556-0998.

6924
Photo Articulation Test. Pendergast, Kathleen; And Others 1969
Descriptors: *Articulation (Speech); Articulation Impairments; Children; Elementary Education; *Elementary School Students; *Pictorial Stimuli; *Preschool Children; Preschool Education; Speech Tests; Speech Therapy
Identifiers: PAT
Availability: Interstate Printers and Publishers, Inc.; Jackson at Van Buren, Danville, IL 61832
Target Audience: 3-12
Notes: Items, 72

Designed for use by speech therapists with children who have articulation problems. The set of color photographs are used to stimulate interest and evoke spontaneous speech response. Available as pages of 9 pictures each or as individual cards.

6925
Motor-Free Visual Perception Test. Colarusso, Ronald P.; Hammill, Donald D. 1972
Subtests: Spatial Relationship; Visual Discrimination; Figure Ground; Visual Closure; Visual Memory
Descriptors: *Cerebral Palsy; Diagnostic Tests; Elementary School Students; Individual Testing; Learning Problems; Learning Readiness; Multiple Choice Tests; Perception Tests; *Primary Education; Reading Readiness; *Screening Tests; Visual Learning; Visual Measures; *Visual Perception; *Visual Stimuli; *Young Children
Identifiers: *Motor Impairment; MVPT; Oral Tests
Availability: Academic Therapy Publications; 20 Commercial Blvd., Novato, CA 94947
Target Audience: 4-8
Notes: Time, 10 approx.; Items, 36

Measures the overall visual perceptual processing ability in children without requiring a motor response. Used for identifying learning disabilities, as a screening, diagnostic, and research instrument. Untimed, individually administered multiple-choice instrument. Used with nonhandicapped children and with children with motor problems such as cerebral palsy, not with mentally retarded or sensorially handicapped children.

6927
Meeting Street School Screening Test. Hainsworth, Peter K.; Siqueland, Marian L. 1969
Subtests: Motor Patterning; Visual Perceptional and Motor; Language
Descriptors: Child Development; Cognitive Development; Elementary School Students; *Grade 1; Individual Development; *Individual Testing; *Kindergarten Children; Learning Disabilities; Learning Readiness; Performance; Performance Tests; *Primary Education; Reading Readiness; School Readiness; School Readiness Tests; *Screening Tests
Identifiers: MSSST; Oral Tests
Availability: Easter Seal Society of Rhode Island, Inc.; Meeting St. School, 667 Waterman Ave., East Providence, RI 02914
Grade Level: K-1
Notes: Time, 20 approx.

Untimed, individually administered screening test designed to identify kindergarten and first grade students with learning disabilities and, thus, avoid a mismatch of the student's skill and the school curriculum. Requires the use of specialized set of cards with pictures, designs, etc.

6968
Pre Kindergarten Scale. Flynn, Tim 1970
Subtests: Cognitive Skills; Self Control; Relationship with Achievement Model; Dependency
Descriptors: *Behavior Rating Scales; *Migrant Children; Multiple Choice Tests; *Preschool Children; Preschool Education; *Preschool Teachers; *Student Behavior; *Teacher Aides
Identifiers: PKS; TIM(C)
Availability: Tests in Microfiche; Test Collection, Educational Testing Service, Princeton, NJ 08541
Target Audience: 4-5
Notes: Items, 25

Designed for use by teachers and teacher aides to rate the behavior of migrant children in preschool programs. Factors assessed include cognitive skills, self-control, relationships with achievement model, dependency. Rater needs only grade school reading level. Suitable for teacher aides with limited educational background.

6975
Behavior Category Observation System. Gottfried, Nathan W.; Seay, Bill
Subtests: Object Directed Behavior Categories; Socially Directed Categories
Descriptors: *Behavior Rating Scales; Black Youth; Day Care; *Lower Class Students; *Peer Relationship; *Preschool Children; *Rural Youth; *Social Behavior
Identifiers: TIM(C)
Availability: Tests in Microfiche; Test Collection, Educational Testing Service, Princeton, NJ 08541
Target Audience: 3-5
Notes: Time, 15

An observational technique devised to study peer-social behavior in young children. The system includes 6 categories of object-directed behavior (transport, sit on, manipulate, oral contact, project, embrace) and 9 categories of social behavior (touch, hit with object, hit, vocalize, verbalize, withdraw, approach, smile, frown). The child is placed in a seminaturalistic setting and is observed for a 15-minute period. The observations are recorded at 15-second intervals.

6998
Test De Comprension Mecanica Bennett. Bennett, George K. 1970
Descriptors: Adolescents; Adults; *Aptitude Tests; College Applicants; College Science; College Students; Engineering Education; *High School Students; Industrial Education; Job Applicants; *Mechanics (Physics); *Mechanics (Process); Occupational Tests; Secondary School Science; *Skilled Workers; *Spanish; *Spanish Speaking; Technical Education; Timed Tests; Trade and Industrial Education; Vocational Aptitude; Vocational High Schools
Identifiers: Bennett Mechanical Comprehension Test; BMCT
Availability: The Psychological Corporation; 555 Academic Ct., San Antonio, TX 78204-0952
Target Audience: 14-64
Notes: Time, 30; Items, 68

In Spanish. Designed to measure the ability to perceive and comprehend the relationship of mechanical elements and physical law and to apply this knowledge to new, practical situations. Administered to high school students, candidates and students in engineering schools, applicants and current employees of mechanical jobs, for other adult males of comparable ability and education and for all women competing for or currently in comparable jobs or educational levels. Includes both Form S and Form T, which are revisions of earlier Forms AA, BB, CC, and W1. Forms S and T have a wider range of difficulty, are for both men and women, and are timed. Scoring is the number correct, with no reduction of score for incorrect answers. Directions and instructions are available as Spanish Language Tape Recording.

7002
Physical and Mental Impairment of Function Evaluation Scale. Gurel, Lee; And Others 1972
Subtests: Self-Care Dependent; Belligerent/Irritable; Mentally Disorganized/Confused; Anxious/Depressed; Bedfast/Moribund; Behaviorally Deteriorated; Paranoid/Suspicious; Sensorimotor Impaired; Withdrawn/Apathetic; Ambulatory
Descriptors: Adults; *Behavior Patterns; Behavior Rating Scales; Disabilities; Diseases; *Geriatrics; *Nursing Homes; Older Adults; Patients
Identifiers: PAMIE
Availability: Dr. Lee Gurel; 3123 S. 14th St., Arlington, VA 22204
Target Audience: 18-85
Notes: Items, 77

Designed to assess behavioral characteristics of disabled aged or chronically ill patients in nursing homes.

7006
Ott Test of Oral Language: English and Spanish. Ott, Elizabeth 1970
Subtests: Phonemic Analysis (33); Fluency (24)
Descriptors: *Language Fluency; Language Tests; *Oral Language; Second Language Learning; *Spanish Speaking; Speech Tests; *Visual Measures; Young Children
Identifiers: OTOLES; TIM(A)
Availability: Tests in Microfiche; Test Collection, Educational Testing Service, Princeton, NJ 08541
Target Audience: 0-8
Notes: Items, 57

Designed to assess the level of proficiency in oral language production of young children from non-English-speaking backgrounds. Part I, Phonemic Analysis, covers common phonemic differentiations recognized as problems for Spanish speakers learning English. Part II, Fluency, assesses fluency including elaboration and intonation. Part II has been translated into Spanish. The test may be administered to small groups of no more than 4 children. Electronic equipment is needed to administer the test.

7012
Academic Readiness Scale. Burks, Harold F. 1968
Subtests: Motor; Perceptual-Motor; Cognitive; Motivational; Social Adjustment
Descriptors: *Grade 1; *Handicap Identification; *Intellectual Development; *Kindergarten Children; Learning Readiness; Primary Education; Rating Scales; *School Readiness; *School Readiness Tests; Slow Learners; Student Evaluation; Young Children
Identifiers: ARS
Availability: Arden Press; Box 2084, Palm Springs, CA 92262
Grade Level: K-1

Developed for identification of students with potential learning handicaps. To be administered at end of kindergarten year or beginning of first grade year.

7014
End of First Grade Progress Scale. Burks, Harold F. 1968
Descriptors: Behavior Rating Scales; Elementary School Students; *Grade 1; *Handicap Identification; Intellectual Development; Learning Disabilities; Primary Education; Psychomotor Skills; *Student Evaluation
Availability: Arden Press; Box 2084, Palm Springs, CA 92262
Grade Level: 1
Notes: Items, 51
Designed to assess student progress at the end of first grade. Assesses academic, perceptual motor, and social/emotional progress. May be used to identify students with learning disabilities or those suspected of mental retardation. Purposes, construction, and format are similar to the Academic Readiness Scale (TC007012). Items in this progress scale are suitable for older children.

7068
Henderson Environmental Learning Process Scale. Henderson, Ronald W.; And Others 1972
Descriptors: Academic Achievement; Adults; Attitude Measures; Cultural Influences; *Family Environment; *Parent Attitudes; Rating Scales; *School Attitudes; Spanish; *Spanish Speaking; Young Children
Identifiers: HELPS; TIM(A)
Availability: Tests in Microfiche; Test Collection, Educational Testing Service, Princeton, NJ 08541
Target Audience: Adults
Notes: Time, 30 approx.; Items, 55
HELPS (Henderson Environmental Learning Process Scale) is designed to measure characteristics of the home environment related to the intellectual and scholastic performance of young children. The interview schedule elicits information on the aspiration level of the home, the range of environmental stimulation available to the child, the parental guidance or direct teaching provided, the range of adult models available, and the nature of reinforcement practices used to influence the child's behavior. Both English and Spanish forms of the scale are available, and the interview is conducted in the language of choice of the respondents.

7075
Appraisal of Language Disturbance. Emerick, Lon L. 1971
Subtests: Aural-Oral; Aural-Visual; Aural-Gesture; Aural-Graphic; Gesture-Visual; Visual-Gesture; Visual-Oral; Visual-Graphic; Central Language Comprehension; Related Factors
Descriptors: Adults; *Aphasia; Auditory Stimuli; *Communication Disorders; Diagnostic Tests; Language Handicaps; *Neurological Impairments; Older Adults; Speech Handicaps; Speech Tests; Visual Stimuli
Identifiers: ALD
Availability: Northern Michigan University Bookstore; University Center, Marquette, MI 49855
Target Audience: 18-80
Designed to evaluate language impairment in adult aphasic patients.

7080
Children's English Proficiency Test. Webster, Sallye L. 1972
Descriptors: *Comprehension; *English (Second Language); Individual Testing; *Performance Tests; *Preschool Children; Preschool Education; Questionnaires; *School Readiness; Spanish; *Spanish Speaking
Identifiers: CEPT; TIM(A)
Availability: Tests in Microfiche; Test Collection, Educational Testing Service, Princeton, NJ 08541
Target Audience: 2-5
Notes: Time, 7 approx.; Items, 37
Experimental instrument designed to assess the degree to which preschool Spanish-speaking children comprehend spoken English. Most of the questions require behavioral rather than verbal responses. The test is individually administered and requires props. Both English and Spanish versions are available. The translations are in the Spanish most frequently used by Mexican-Americans in the Houston, Texas area.

7094
Parents' Behavioral Rating Scale. Strag, Gerald A.
Descriptors: *Behavior Rating Scales; Elementary Education; *Elementary School Students; *Learning Disabilities; Neurological Impairments; Parent Attitudes; Parents; *Severe Mental Retardation
Availability: Dr. Gerald A. Strag; P.O. Box 88, New Bern, NC 28560
Grade Level: K-6
Notes: Items, 30

Designed to be completed by parents of children with potential learning disabilities or severe mental retardation. Parents' perceptions are used to identify children who may require special educational programs.

7101
Oral Placement Test for Adults. Ferrel, Allen 1971
Descriptors: Achievement Tests; Adult Basic Education; Adults; Adult Students; Individual Testing; *Language Proficiency; *Listening Comprehension; *Oral Language
Availability: Southwestern Cooperative Educational Laboratory Publishers; 229 Truman, N.E., Albuquerque, NM 87108
Target Audience: 18-64
Designed to determine ability to use English as a functional tool of communication. Proficiencies are measured in a structured individual interview of potential adult basic education learners. A videotape is available to use in training teachers to administer and score the test. Test may be recorded for later scoring or scored during administration. Proficiency levels are elementary, intermediate, advanced, and exempt.

7121
Purdue Elementary Problem Solving Inventory. Feldhusen, John F.; And Others
Subtests: Sensing and Identifying; Clarification I; Clarification II; Problem Parts; Presolution; Solving Problems I; Solving Problems II; Solving Problems III
Descriptors: Audiotape Recordings; Cognitive Processes; *Cognitive Tests; *Disadvantaged; Elementary Education; *Elementary School Students; Filmstrips; Group Testing; Individual Testing; Multiple Choice Tests; *Problem Solving
Identifiers: TIM(C)
Availability: Tests in Microfiche; Test Collection, Educational Testing Service, Princeton, NJ 08541
Grade Level: 2-6
Notes: Time, 45 approx.; Items, 49
Designed to assess the general problem-solving ability of culturally different disadvantaged children. Real-life problem situations are used to measure the following abilities: sensing that a problem exists, identifying and defining the problem, asking questions, guessing causes, clarifying the goal of the problem situation, judging whether more information is needed, analyzing details of the problem and identifying critical elements, redefining familiar objects for unusual uses, seeing implications, solving single- and multiple-solution problems, and verifying solutions. Cartoons presented on a film strip are used as the stimuli for each problem task, and all the instructions are presented on an audio tape. Individual or group administration.

7170
Differential Aptitude Tests: Forms S and T. Bennett, George K.; And Others 1972
Subtests: Verbal Reasoning; Numerical Ability; Abstract Reasoning; Clerical Speed and Accuracy; Mechanical Reasoning; Space Relations; Spelling; Language Usage
Descriptors: Abstract Reasoning; *Aptitude Tests; Arithmetic; *Career Counseling; *Educational Counseling; Language Usage; Large Type Materials; Mechanical Skills; Problem Solving; Secondary Education; *Secondary School Students; Spatial Ability; Spelling; Verbal Ability; Visual Acuity; Visual Impairments
Identifiers: Analogies; Clerical Aptitude; DAT; Test Batteries
Availability: The Psychological Corporation; 555 Academic Ct., San Antonio, TX 78204-0952
Grade Level: 8-12
Notes: Time, 180 approx.; Items, 630
Integrated battery of aptitude tests designed for educational and vocational guidance in junior and senior high schools. Yields 8 scores dealing with various facets of intelligence. Each of the tests in the battery can be separately administered. Test battery is given over a period of time, preferably within a one- or 2-week period. Form S is available in large print for visually impaired subjects from American Printing House for the Blind, 1839 Frankfort Ave., Louisville, KY 40206.

7171
Escala De Inteligencia Wechsler Para Adultos. Green, R.F.; Martinez, J.N. 1968
Subtests: Informacion; Compresion; Aritmetica; Analogias; Repeticion De Digitos; Vocabulario; Digito Simbolo; Dibujos Para Completar; Disenos Con Cubos; Ordenamiento De Dibujos; Composicion De Objetos
Descriptors: Adults; *Cognitive Ability; Cognitive Tests; Hispanic Americans; *Individual Testing; Intelligence Quotient; *Intelligence Tests; Latin Americans; *Spanish; *Spanish Americans; *Spanish Speaking; Timed Tests

Identifiers: EIWA; WAIS; Wechsler Adult Intelligence Scale
Availability: The Psychological Corporation; 555 Academic Ct., San Antonio, TX 78204-0952
Target Audience: 16-64
Notes: Time, 60 approx.; Items, 305
An authorized Spanish-American version of the Wechsler Adult Intelligence Scale. Type of item varies; some require computation, completion, or performance. The translators call attention to the fact that the Spanish- and English-language materials for WAIS are not interchangeable. Not all subtests are timed.

7174
Activity Level Rating Scale: Infant Form. Banham, Katharine M. 1967
Descriptors: Attention Span; *Behavior Rating Scales; *Cerebral Palsy; *Individual Testing; *Infants; Observation; Physical Activities; *Psychological Testing; Social Behavior
Identifiers: *Activity Analysis; TIM(B)
Availability: Tests in Microfiche; Test Collection, Educational Testing Service, Princeton, NJ 08541
Target Audience: 0-2
Notes: Time, 60 approx.; Items, 10
Designed to assist in the psychological assessment of cerebral palsied children. Categories of activity that are rated are bodily activity, concentration of attention, exploratory and inquisitive, social responsive, vocalizing and speech, avoidance, smiling and laughing, distressful crying and whimpering, persistent striving, and aggressive and assertive. Because it involves recorded observations, the test can be administered to only one child at a time.

7175
Activity Level Rating Scale: Preschool Form. Banham, Katharine M. 1967
Descriptors: Attention Span; *Behavior Rating Scales; *Cerebral Palsy; *Individual Testing; *Observation; Physical Activities; *Preschool Children; *Psychological Testing; Social Behavior
Identifiers: *Activity Analysis; TIM(B)
Availability: Tests in Microfiche; Test Collection, Educational Testing Service, Princeton, NJ 08541
Target Audience: 2-5
Notes: Time, 60 approx.; Items, 10
Designed to assist in the psychological assessment of cerebral palsied preschool children. Categories of activity rated are bodily activity, concentration of attention, exploratory and inquisitive, social responsive, vocalizing and speech, avoidance, smiling and laughter, distressful crying and whimpering, persistent striving, and aggressive and assertive. Because it involves recorded observations, the test can be administered to only one child at a time.

7184
Child Behavior Checklist. Walker, Richard N. 1963
Descriptors: *Behavior Rating Scales; Children; Emotional Disturbances; *Parent Attitudes; *Personality Traits; Preschool Children; *Young Children
Identifiers: TIM(A)
Availability: Tests in Microfiche; Test Collection, Educational Testing Service, Princeton, NJ 08541
Target Audience: Young Children
Notes: Items, 68
Device by which parents may rate their children's behavior. It covers characteristics in 8 areas: energetic, active; curious, thoughtful; aggressive, assertive; fearful, anxious; social, friendly; excitable, tense; cooperative, conforming; and cheerful, expressive. The checklist is appropriate for children ages 2.5-5.0 but is also used with emotionally disturbed children aged 6-14 years.

7193
Analysis of Readiness Skills: Reading and Mathematics. Rodriques, Mary C.; And Others 1972
Subtests: Visual Perception of Letters; Letter Identification; Mathematics-Identification; Mathematics-Counting
Descriptors: *Elementary School Mathematics; Elementary School Students; English; English (Second Language); *Grade 1; *Kindergarten Children; *Learning Readiness; *Letters (Alphabet); Mathematical Concepts; *Numbers; Pictorial Stimuli; Primary Education; Mathematics Tests; *Reading Readiness; Reading Readiness Tests; Second Language Programs; *Spanish; Spanish Speaking; Visual Measures
Identifiers: Oral Tests
Availability: Riverside Publishing Co.; 3 O'Hare Towers, 8420 Bryn Mawr Ave., Chicago, IL 60631
Grade Level: K-1
Notes: Time, 40 approx.; Items, 35

To determine whether a child is ready to enter reading and mathematics programs by testing the child's knowledge of the alphabet and numbers. The test instructions are written in both English and Spanish; the results for Spanish-speaking children would determine their readiness for placement in an English-as-a-Second-Language program. The authors recommend administering to no more than 15 students at a time.

7202
Diagnostic Test of Speechreading. Myklebust, Helmer R.; Neyhus, Arthur I. 1970
Subtests: Words; Phrases; Sentences
Descriptors: Children; *Deafness; *Diagnostic Tests; Films; Individual Testing; *Lipreading; *Receptive Language
Availability: Grune and Stratton; 111 Fifth Ave., New York, NY 10003
Target Audience: 4-9
Notes: Items, 64
Designed to measure the deaf child's ability to comprehend the spoken word. The test is available on 2 technicolor film cassettes. The child must point to the proper corresponding picture. The instrument was developed for objective study of visual receptive language.

7204
Rystrom Dialect Test. Rystrom, Richard C. 1969
Descriptors: *Black Dialects; *Dialect Studies; *Grade 1; Individual Testing; *Language Tests; Nonstandard Dialects; Primary Education
Availability: Reading Research Quarterly; v4 n4 p501-11 Sum 1969
Grade Level: 1
Notes: Items, 24
Test developed to differentiate Black dialect from standard English. See also Dialect Training and Reading: A Further Look, included in Reading Research Quarterly, v5, n4 p581-90, Sum 1970.

7205
Rystrom Dialect Deviation Test. Rystrom, Richard C.
Descriptors: Audiotape Recorders; *Beginning Reading; *Black Dialects; *Black Youth; Dialects; *Grade 1; Individual Testing; Primary Education
Identifiers: TIM(C)
Availability: Tests in Microfiche; Test Collection, Educational Testing Service, Princeton, NJ 08541
Grade Level: 1
Notes: Items, 25
Devised to measure differences in dialect between speakers of standard English dialect and speakers of Black dialects. The individual administration requires 2 tape recorders. The simple sentences which the child is to imitate are recorded on one. The other is used to record both the cues and the child's responses.

7228
Prereading Expectancy Screening Scale. Hartlage, Lawrence C.; Lucas, David G. 1973
Subtests: Sequencing Test; Spatial-Aural-Visual; Memory; Letter Identification
Descriptors: *Beginning Reading; *Diagnostic Tests; *Elementary School Students; *Grade 1; Primary Education; *Reading Difficulties; Reading Readiness
Identifiers: PRESS
Availability: Psychologists and Educators; P.O. Box 513, St. Louis, MO 63017
Target Audience: 6-9
Notes: Time, 35 approx.
Group diagnostic battery used to predict reading problems in beginning readers. Developed to identify learning disabilities in early school years.

7229
Black Intelligence Test of Cultural Homogeneity. Williams, Robert L. 1972
Descriptors: Adolescents; Adults; *Black Culture; *Black Dialects; *Blacks; Cultural Awareness; *Intelligence Tests; Multiple Choice Tests; Vocabulary
Identifiers: BITCH; *Culturally Specific Tests
Availability: Williams and Associates, Inc.; Educational and Psychological Services, 6374 Del Mar Blvd., St. Louis, MO 63130
Target Audience: 13-64
Notes: Time, 30 approx.; Items, 100
Culturally specific, multiple-choice, vocabulary and intelligence test which uses items drawn from the Black Experience. The test may be used as a measure of learning potential or as a measure of sensitivity and responsiveness of Whites to the Black Experience.

7241
Student Instructional Report. Educational Testing Service, Princeton, NJ 1973

Descriptors: *College Students; *Course Evaluation; *Higher Education; Questionnaires; Spanish; *Spanish Speaking; Student Attitudes; *Student Evaluation of Teacher Performance; Teacher Student Relationship; *Two Year Colleges; *Vocational Schools
Availability: ETS College and Univ. Programs; Educational Testing Service, Princeton, NJ 08541
Grade Level: 13-16
Notes: Items, 49
Questionnaire designed to measure student perceptions of the organization and structure of courses, teaching techniques and student-teacher rapport for 2- and 4-year colleges, universities, and technical institutions. Thirty academic fields are represented. Also available in Spanish.

7242
Themes Concerning Blacks. Williams, Robert L. 1972
Descriptors: *Adolescents; *Adults; Attitude Measures; *Black Attitudes; *Blacks; Pictorial Stimuli; *Projective Measures
Identifiers: TCB
Availability: Williams and Associates; Black Community Psychology, 6373 Del Mar Blvd., St. Louis, MO 63130
Target Audience: 13-64
Notes: Items, 15
Designed to elicit from Black subjects themes of achievement, pride, awareness, as well as negative themes of hate, aggression, and depression. Subject is shown a picture and asked to construct a story about what took place prior to the picture, what is occurring in the picture, and what will be the outcome.

7243
Williams Awareness Sentence Completion. Williams, Robert L. 1972
Descriptors: Adolescents; Adults; *Attitude Measures; *Black Attitudes; *Blacks; Projective Measures; Racial Bias; Whites
Identifiers: Sentence Completion Tests; WASC
Availability: Williams and Associates; Black Community Psychology, 6373 Del Mar Blvd., St. Louis, MO 63130
Target Audience: 13-64
Notes: Items, 40
Designed to elicit feelings of conflict of Black people regarding their race and prejudicial and/or positive White attitudes toward Blacks.

7263
Developmental Screening Questionnaire for Preschool Children. Sharp, Elizabeth Y. 1973
Subtests: Physical Development; Care of Self; Social Responses; Language; Speech; Visual Impairment; Hearing Impairment; General Health
Descriptors: Behavior Rating Scales; *Learning Problems; Observation; *Physical Development; *Preschool Children; *Reservation American Indians; *Screening Tests; *Self Care Skills; *Social Development
Identifiers: Kirk (Samuel A); Project Head Start; TIM(B)
Availability: Tests in Microfiche; Test Collection, Educational Testing Service, Princeton, NJ 08541
Target Audience: 3-5
Notes: Items, 39
Developed for use by Head Start Programs on Indian reservations in Arizona to identify children who may have mental, speech, sensory, emotional, physical, or developmental learning problems. The questionnaire was developed from the work described in Samuel A. Kirk's book entitled You and Your Retarded Child (Palo Alto, CA, Pacific Books, 1955). Included are forms for 3-year olds, 4-year olds, and 5-year olds.

7275
Patient Reputation Scale. Fontana, Alan F. 1971
Descriptors: Adults; *Behavior Patterns; Behavior Rating Scales; Nurses; *Patients; Physicians; Psychiatric Hospitals; Reputation
Identifiers: Manipulative Behavior; *Psychiatric Patients
Availability: Archives of General Psychiatry; v25 p88-93 Jul 1971
Target Audience: Adults
Notes: Items, 18
Designed to assess behavior of psychiatric patients through observation by nurses and physicians. Patients were determined to have reputations of critical manipulator, involved helper, or model patient. Instrument may also be obtained from the author: Dr. Alan F. Fontana; Psychology Service, Veterans Administration Hospital, West Haven, CT 06516.

7284
Auditory Sequential Memory Test. Wepman, Joseph M.; Morency, Anne 1973

Descriptors: Academic Aptitude; Cognitive Ability; Cognitive Tests; *Elementary School Students; Individual Testing; Learning Disabilities; *Learning Processes; *Learning Readiness; *Primary Education; *Retention (Psychology); *School Readiness; Young Children; Short Term Memory
Identifiers: Memory for Digits; Perceptual Test Battery (PTB)
Availability: Western Psychological Services; 12031 Wilshire Blvd., Los Angeles, CA 90025
Target Audience: 5-8
Notes: Time, 5 approx.; Items, 14
Individualized test to measure a perceptual auditory ability, more specifically, ability to recall the exact order of group of digits that are given orally. Sometimes called Memory-for-Digits. Used to determine a student's readiness for learning to read, speak, and to do arithmetic processes. Also useful in determining specific auditory learning disabilities. According to the author, the longer span of immediate memory in exact order a child can use the more accurate, more intelligible, and more adaptive his or her learning is likely to be. Comes in Form I and II. The 6 perceptual test may be used in combination as a Perceptual Test Battery consisting of Spatial Orientation Memory Test (TC007127), The Auditory Discrimination Test (TC007283), Auditory Memory Span Test (TC007285), Auditory Sequential Memory Test (TC007284), Visual Discrimination Test (TC008090), Visual Memory Test (TC008091).

7298
Reading/Everyday Activities in Life. Lichtman, Marilyn 1972
Descriptors: Adult Literacy; *Adults; Audiotape Cassettes; Audiotape Recorders; *Diagnostic Tests; Elementary Secondary Education; *Functional Literacy; Group Testing; Individual Testing; *Minority Groups; Students
Identifiers: REAL
Availability: Westwood Press, Inc.; 76 Madison Ave., New York, NY 10016
Target Audience: 10-64
Notes: Items, 45
Used to assess functional literacy suitable for minority populations and those who have been singled out by the bias of standardized reading achievement tests. May be used with adults at basic education levels. May be used for diagnostic and evaluative purposes.

7314
Test of Creative Potential. Hoepfner, Ralph; Hemenway, Judith 1973
Subtests: Writing Words; Picture Decoration; License Plate Words
Descriptors: *Adolescents; Adults; Aptitude Tests; Children; *Creativity; *Creativity Tests; *Elementary School Students; Elementary Secondary Education; *Secondary School Students; Timed Tests; *Verbal Ability
Identifiers: TCP
Availability: Monitor; P.O. Box 2337, Hollywood, CA 90028
Target Audience: 7-64
Notes: Time, 30 approx.
Designed to assess general creative potential of subjects from 7 years of age through adolescence and adulthood. Assesses factors of fluency, flexibility, and elaboration of verbal, symbolic, and figural materials. Available in 2 parallel forms.

7321
Thinking Creatively with Sounds and Words: Level I. Torrance, E. Paul; And Others 1973
Subtests: Sounds and Images; Onomatopoeia and Images
Descriptors: *Auditory Stimuli; *Creativity; *Creativity Tests; *Elementary School Students; Elementary Secondary Education; *Secondary School Students; Verbal Ability; *Verbal Stimuli
Identifiers: TCSW; Test Batteries
Availability: Scholastic Testing Service, Inc.; 480 Meyer Rd., Bensenville, IL 60106
Grade Level: 3-12
Notes: Time, 30 approx.
A battery of 2 tests are designed to assess creativity by measuring the originality of ideas stimulated by abstract sounds and spoken onomatopoeic words. Tests must be administered using 2 long playing records on which are presented instructions to the subjects and the auditory and verbal stimuli. The recordings also maintain the timing of the tests. Parallel forms are available for Level I.

7322
Thinking Creatively with Sounds and Words: Level II. Torrance, E. Paul; And Others 1973
Subtests: Sounds and Images; Onomatopoeia and Images
Descriptors: *Adults; *Auditory Stimuli; *Creativity; *Creativity Tests; Verbal Ability; *Verbal Stimuli
Identifiers: TCSW; Test Batteries

Availability: Scholastic Testing Service, Inc.; 480 Meyer Rd., Bensenville, IL 60106
Target Audience: 18-64
Notes: Time, 30 approx.

A battery of 2 tests are designed to assess creativity by measuring the originality of ideas stimulated by abstract sounds and spoken onomatopoeic words. Tests must be administered using 2 long playing records on which are presented instructions to the subjects and the auditory and verbal stimuli. The recordings also maintain the timing of the tests. Parallel forms are available for Level II.

7329

Structured and Scaled Interview to Assess Maladjustment. Gurland, Barry J.; And Others 1974
Subtests: Work; Social and Leisure; Family of Origin; Marriage; Sex; Overall
Descriptors: Adults; Interpersonal Competence; Interviews; Mental Health; *Patients; Psychotherapy; *Social Adjustment; Stress Variables
Identifiers: Psychiatric Patients; SSIAM
Availability: Springer Publishing Co.; 200 Park Ave. S., New York, NY 10003
Target Audience: Adults
Notes: Time, 30 approx.; Items, 60

A structured interview designed to assess deviant behavior, friction with others, and subjective distress within 5 fields of maladjustment. Also assessed are the degree of emotional stress, prognostic issues, and aspects of positive mental health. Enables interviewer to quantitatively rate problems in social adjustment.

7332

Home Bilingual Usage Estimate. Skoczylas, Rudolph V. 1971
Descriptors: *Bilingual Students; *Elementary School Students; Elementary Secondary Education; English (Second Language); Family Life; Interviews; *Language Dominance; Listening Comprehension; *Secondary School Students; *Spanish; Spanish Speaking
Availability: R.V. Skoczylas; 7649 Santa Inez Ct., Gilroy, CA 95020
Grade Level: K-12
Notes: Time, 6 approx.

Designed to measure language usage in the home-family domain of students. Yields a single score which classifies subject as English dominant, English monolingual, apparent bilingual, Spanish dominant or Spanish monolingual. Adult is interviewed concerning child's home language environment.

7338

Test for Auditory Comprehension of Language. Carrow-Woolfolk, Elizabeth 1973
Descriptors: Bilingual Students; Diagnostic Tests; Individual Testing; *Language Handicaps; Listening Comprehension; *Listening Comprehension Tests; Pictorial Stimuli; *Preschool Children; Preschool Education; *Receptive Language; *Spanish Speaking
Identifiers: TACL
Availability: DLM Teaching Resources; P.O. Box 4000, One DLM Park, Allen, TX 75002
Target Audience: 3-6
Notes: Time, 20 approx.; Items, 101

Measures receptive language in English or Spanish. Encompasses areas of vocabulary, morphology, and syntax. Child is asked to respond to pictorial stimuli by pointing to correct response. Permits assessment of oral language comprehension without requiring language expression from the child. Examiner should hold at least a bachelor's degree in education, psychology, or sociology and have significant testing experience. Individually administered.

7341

Spanish-English Dominance Assessment Test. Spolsky, Bernard 1970
Subtests: Entrevista Part A; Word Availability Part B; Interview Part C; Word Availability Part D; Taped Speech Sample Part E
Descriptors: *Bilingual Students; *Elementary School Students; English (Second Language); *Language Dominance; *Language Tests; Primary Education; *Spanish Speaking
Identifiers: TIM(A)
Availability: Tests in Microfiche; Test Collection, Educational Testing Service, Princeton, NJ 08541
Grade Level: 1-2
Notes: Time, 10; Items, 29

Designed to classify children who are bilingual in Spanish and English or monolingual in one of the above. Administrator of test and recorder should both be bilingual.

7342

Navajo-English Language Dominance Interview. Spolsky, Bernard; Holm, Wayne 1973
Descriptors: Elementary School Teachers; English (Second Language); *Grade 1; Individual Testing; Interviews; *Language Dominance; Language Tests; *Navajo; Young Children

Identifiers: Oral Tests; TIM(B)
Availability: Tests in Microfiche; Test Collection, Educational Testing Service, Princeton, NJ 08541
Grade Level: 1
Target Audience: 6
Notes: Items, 24

An experimental instrument was developed to provide validity data on teacher rating in a study of the language use of Navajo children. The instrument should be administered by 2 bilingual interviewers, one of whom speaks only English while the other uses only Navajo during the interview. The test is administered to one child at a time.

7360

Short Term Auditory Retrieval and Storage Test. Flowers, Arthur 1972
Descriptors: Audiotape Recordings; Auditory Stimuli; *Auditory Tests; Clinical Diagnosis; Cognitive Tests; Diagnostic Tests; Elementary Education; *Elementary School Students; *Learning Disabilities; *Mild Mental Retardation; *Short Term Memory
Identifiers: Auditory Memory; STARTS; Tests of Central Auditory Abilities
Availability: Perceptual Learning Systems; P.O. Box 864, Dearborn, MI 48121
Grade Level: 1-6
Notes: Time, 25 approx.; Items, 55

Designed to assess short-term auditory storage and retrieval function within the central mechanism of hearing. Testing procedure utilizes the concept of simultaneously spoken verbal material presented binaurally (all test stimuli going into both ears simultaneously). Limited norms are provided for various classifications of handicapped children. STARS Teaching Programs are available for remediation of problems identified with the STARS Test.

7368

Flowers Auditory Test of Selective Attention. Flowers, Arthur 1972
Descriptors: *Attention; Attention Span; Audiotape Recordings; Auditory Perception; Auditory Stimuli; *Auditory Tests; Diagnostic Tests; Elementary Education; *Elementary School Students; *Learning Disabilities; *Listening Skills; *Mild Mental Retardation
Identifiers: FATSA; Tests of Central Auditory Abilities
Availability: Perceptual Learning Systems; P.O. Box 864, Dearborn, MI 48121
Grade Level: 1-6
Notes: Time, 30 approx.; Items, 33

Designed to assess auditory attention span with emphasis on auditory "vigilance." Used to assess listening-language skills of young children. Auditory attention deficit identified with this instrument may be remediated with the Auditory Vigilance Teaching Program. Norms are provided for various classifications of handicapped children as well as for children in regular classes.

7371

Advanced Tests of Central Auditory Abilities. Flowers, Arthur; And Others 1972
Subtests: Competing Messages; Low Pass Filtered Speech
Descriptors: Audiotape Recordings; *Auditory Evaluation; Auditory Perception; *Auditory Tests; *Elementary School Students; Elementary Secondary Education; Individual Testing; *Learning Disabilities; *Screening Tests; *Secondary School Students
Identifiers: Tests of Central Auditory Abilities
Availability: Perceptual Learning Systems; P.O. Box 864, Dearborn, MI 48121
Grade Level: 2-12
Notes: Time, 10 approx.; Items, 62

Designed as a screening measure to identify subjects with general auditory perceptual dysfunction. May be used as a criterion-referenced test to identify specific auditory phonemic identification deficiencies.

7379

Visual Efficiency Scale. Barraga, Natalie C. 1970
Descriptors: *Diagnostic Teaching; Diagnostic Tests; Elementary Education; *Elementary School Students; Partial Vision; *Preschool Children; Preschool Education; *Vision Tests; Visual Discrimination; *Visual Impairments; *Visual Perception
Identifiers: VES; Visual Aptitude
Availability: American Printing House for the Blind; 1839 Frankfort Ave., Louisville, KY 40206-0085
Target Audience: 3-12
Notes: Items, 48

Designed to assess whether a child is fully utilizing his or her residual vision. Teacher's guide provides background for the teacher's understanding and motivation as well as suggested activities and materials for prescriptive programs.

7382

Screening Test for Auditory Comprehension of Language. Carrow-Woolfolk, Elizabeth 1973
Descriptors: Bilingual Students; *Language Handicaps; Listening Comprehension; Listening Comprehension Tests; *Preschool Children; Preschool Education; *Receptive Language; *Screening Tests; *Spanish Speaking
Identifiers: STACL
Availability: DLM Teaching Resources; P.O. Box 4000, One DLM Park, Allen, TX 75002
Target Audience: 3-6
Notes: Items, 25

Identifies children who have receptive language problems in English or Spanish. A group-administered test which samples vocabulary, morphology, and syntax. Used to identify children who require in-depth testing with TACL, assess basic competence in language, and establish dominant language of the child.

7385

Whitaker Index of Schizophrenic Thinking. Whitaker, Leighton C. 1973
Subtests: New Inventions; Word Pairs; Similarities
Descriptors: Adults; *Cognitive Processes; Individual Testing; *Patients; Psychiatric Hospitals; Psychological Testing; *Schizophrenia; Screening Tests
Identifiers: *Psychiatric Patients; WIST
Availability: Western Psychological Services; 12031 Wilshire Blvd., Los Angeles, CA 90025
Target Audience: Adults
Notes: Time, 15 approx.; Items, 25

Designed to provide a brief, objective index of schizophrenic thinking. May be used for intake screening as part of mental status examination or as part of battery of psychological tests. May be completed by anyone with at least an 8th grade education. Discriminates between schizophrenics and nonschizophrenics. Two forms are available.

7387

Forty-Eight Item Counseling Evaluation Test: Revised. McMahon, Frank B. 1971
Subtests: Anxiety-Tension-Stress; Compulsive-Obsessive-Rigid Behavior; Depressive-Defeatist Thoughts and Feelings; Friendship-Socialization; Goals; Religious-Philosophical; Inadequacy; Feelings and Behavior
Descriptors: Adolescents; *Adults; Anxiety; *College Students; Counseling Techniques; Depression (Psychology); *Emotional Problems; Higher Education; High Schools; *High School Students; *Personality Measures; Stress Variables
Identifiers: 48 ICET; Self Administered Tests
Availability: Western Psychological Services; 12031 Wilshire Blvd., Los Angeles, CA 90025
Grade Level: 9-16
Target Audience: Adults
Notes: Time, 20 approx.; Items, 48

Designed to aid counselors in the identification of personal and emotional problems of adolescents and adults. Each item is composed of a double question. The Introductory Question probes a specific aspect of behavior or personality. The Contingency Question qualifies and amplifies the Introductory Question. May be administered to individuals or groups.

7388

Symbol Gestalt Test: Form A Revised. Stein, Kenneth B. 1970
Descriptors: Adults; *Cognitive Style; Cognitive Tests; Group Testing; *Individual Testing; *Neurological Impairments; *Perception Tests; *Perceptual Motor Coordination; Timed Tests
Identifiers: SG; TIM(B)
Availability: Tests in Microfiche; Test Collection, Educational Testing Service, Princeton, NJ 08541
Target Audience: Adults
Notes: Time, 3; Items, 120

Perceptual motor test for brain damage involves the duplication of a series of geometrical designs and figures. Completion of the task emphasizes both speed and accuracy and reveals individual differences in perception, cognitive ordering, and processing stimuli.

7390

Delinquency Check List. Stein, Kenneth B.; And Others
Subtests: Delinquent Role; Drug Usage; Parental Defiance; Assaultiveness
Descriptors: Antisocial Behavior; *Delinquency; Drug Abuse; High Schools; *High School Students; Institutionalized Persons; *Males; Questionnaires; Recidivism
Identifiers: DCL
Availability: Kenneth B. Stein; 517 Moraga Ave., Piedmont, CA 94611
Grade Level: 9-12

Notes: Items, 54

Designed to assess frequency of antisocial or delinquent behaviors in adolescent males. Study was conducted on incarcerated juveniles.

7410
Symbol Digit Modalities Test. Smith, Aaron 1973
Descriptors: Adolescents; Adults; Children; *Culture Fair Tests; *Developmental Disabilities; *Handicap Identification; *Learning Disabilities; *Neurological Impairments; *Perceptual Handicaps; *Screening Tests; Timed Tests
Identifiers: SDMT
Availability: Western Psychological Services; 12031 Wilshire Blvd., Los Angeles, CA 90025
Target Audience: 8-64
Notes: Time, 2; Items, 120

A screening instrument used to identify cerebral dysfunction or other learning disorders. May be individually, orally administered, or written, group administered. The subjects are shown a key in which different geometric shapes are used to represent specific numbers. In the test, the subject is to substitute (by writing or saying) the appropriate number for the presented shape. Timed for 90 seconds. May be used with subject having manual motor handicaps; to predict and identify children with potential reading difficulties; and to identify covert manual motor, visual, learning or other cerebral defects in apparently normal people. Considered a culture-free instrument because it uses only geometric shapes and Arabic numbers.

7411
Southern California Sensory Integration Tests. Ayres, A. Jean 1972
Subtests: Space Visualization; Figure-Ground Perception; Position in Space; Design Copying; Motor Accuracy; Kinesthesia; Manual Form Perception; Finger Identification; Graphesthesia; Localization of Tactile Stimuli; Double Tactile Stimuli Perception; Imitation of Postures; Crossing Mid-Line of Body; Bilateral Motor Coordination; Right-Left Discrimination; Standing Balance, Eyes Open; Standing Balance, Eyes Closed
Descriptors: Cerebral Palsy; Children; *Disabilities; Emotional Disturbances; *Handicap Identification; Individual Testing; Learning Problems; *Minimal Brain Dysfunction; Motor Development; Neurological Impairments; *Perception; Perception Tests; *Psychomotor Skills; *Screening Tests; *Sensory Integration; Visual Measures
Identifiers: Apraxia (Speech); Ayres Space Test; Oral Tests; SCSIT; Southern California Motor Accuracy Test; Southern California Perceptual Motor Tests
Availability: Western Psychological Services; Order Dept., 12031 Wilshire Blvd., Los Angeles, CA 90025
Target Audience: 4-10
Notes: Time, 90 approx.; Items, 209

To evaluate the amount and type of disorder (sensory integrative dysfunction) which is often associated with learning and emotional problems and with minimal brain dysfunction. The tests measure visual, tactile, and kinesthetic perception, and various types of motor performances. This battery of tests may be administered in more than one session and can be used with cerebral palsied children. Combines a battery of 17 different tests and includes the former Ayres Space Test, Southern California Motor Accuracy Test, Southern California Figure-Ground Visual Perception Test, Southern California Kinesthesia and Tactile Perception Tests, and the Southern California Perceptual-Motor Tests. Various equipment (e.g., formboards, stimulus cards, shield of cardboard, etc.) are required; specialized materials are included. The author feels that the administration of the tests requires skill and experience by the administrator; until proficient, the examiner should be checked by a second person who has gained considerable skill in the use of these tests. The Kinesthesia Chart and the Perception Forms are dated 1973. The author prefers to have the tests given in 2 45-minute sessions rather than in one session of about 1 1/2 hours.

7425
Koontz Child Development Program. Koontz, Charles W. 1974
Subtests: Gross Motor; Fine Motor; Social; Language (Receptive); Language (Expression)
Descriptors: *Child Development; Cognitive Development; Cognitive Measurement; Communication Skills; *Developmental Stages; Hearing Impairments; Individual Development; Individual Testing; *Mental Retardation; Mild Disabilities; *Motor Development; *Observation; *Perceptual Development; Perceptual Motor Learning; Profiles; Socialization; *Verbal Development; Visual Impairments; Young Children
Identifiers: Child Development Program; KCDP
Availability: Western Psychological Services; 12031 Wilshire Blvd., Los Angeles, CA 90025
Target Audience: 0-4
Notes: Items, 25

Individualized instrument which evaluates (with recommendations for improvement) the developmental abilities of nonhandicapped children less than 48 months of age and of retarded children who function between the developmental ages of one month and 48 months. The child is observed at routine activities by a parent, teacher, or therapist and rated 22 times, i.e., at specified ages between the ages of one month and 48 months. Thus, a profile of the child's development is obtained. Also includes modification of activities for use with hearing- and vision-impaired children.

7435
CPH Patient Attitude Scale. Kahn, Marvin W.; Jones, Nelson F. 1974
Descriptors: Adults; *Attitude Measures; Group Testing; Individual Testing; *Mental Disorders; *Patients; *Psychiatric Hospitals; Rating Scales
Identifiers: Patient Attitudes; TIM(A)
Availability: Tests in Microfiche; Test Collection, Educational Testing Service, Princeton, NJ 08541
Target Audience: Adults
Notes: Items, 45

Designed to measure the attitudes of mental patients toward mental hospital activities and personnel. Also measures their attitudes about the nature, cause, and treatment of mental illness. Scale can be administered individually or in groups.

7454
Louisville Behavior Checklist. Form E2. Miller, Lovick C. 1977
Subtests: Infantile Aggression; Hyperactivity; Antisocial Behavior; Aggression; Social Withdrawal; Sensitivity; Fear; Inhibition; Academic Disability; Immaturity; Learning Disability; Normal Irritability; Prosocial Deficit; Rare Deviance; Neurotic Behavior; Psychotic Behavior; Somatic Behavior; Sexual Behavior; Severity Level
Descriptors: Antisocial Behavior; *Behavior Disorders; Check Lists; *Children; Parents; Personality Measures; Prosocial Behavior; *Psychopathology; Social Behavior
Identifiers: LBC
Availability: Western Psychological Services; 12031 Wilshire Blvd., Los Angeles, CA 90025
Target Audience: 7-12
Notes: Items, 164

Designed to facilitate parents' perceptions of their children's behaviors. Inventory covers wide range of social and emotional behaviors indicative of psychopathological disorders in children.

7461
Wechsler Intelligence Scale for Children—Revised. Wechsler, David 1974
Subtests: Information; Similarities; Arithmetic; Vocabulary; Comprehension; Picture Completion; Picture Arrangement; Block Design; Object Assembly; Coding (or Mazes); Digit Span
Descriptors: Adolescents; Children; *Elementary School Students; Elementary Secondary Education; *Gifted; Hearing Impairments; Individual Testing; *Intelligence; Intelligence Quotient; *Intelligence Tests; Performance Tests; *Secondary School Students; Talent Identification; Verbal Ability
Identifiers: Test Batteries; WISCR
Availability: The Psychological Corporation; 555 Academic Ct., San Antonio, TX 78204-0952
Target Audience: 6-16
Notes: Time, 60 approx.; Items, 328

Designed for use by school psychologists and other trained clinical examiners to measure intelligence of children ages 6.0 to 16.11. WISC-R is a revision of the earlier WISC (TC000414) and requires new materials. It cannot be administered with WISC materials. The verbal and performance subtests are administered alternately. WISC-R may be used as part of System of Multicultural Pluralistic Assessment (SOMPA) (TC009044). Available in special edition for hearing-impaired subjects from Office of Demographic Studies, Gallaudet College, Washington, DC 20002.

7464
Bryant-Schwan Design Test. Bryant, Antusa S.; Schwan, LeRoy B. 1971
Subtests: Line; Shape; Color; Value; Texture
Descriptors: *Achievement Tests; *Art; *Design; Diagnostic Tests; Elementary School Students; Elementary Secondary Education; Knowledge Level; Mental Retardation; Secondary School Students; Visual Literacy
Identifiers: BSDT
Availability: Antusa Santos Bryant; Dept. of Special Education, Mankato State University, Mankato, MN 56001
Grade Level: 1-12
Notes: Time, 10 approx.; Items, 50

Geared to measuring achievement in design knowledge of mentally retarded children. Can be used with normal children for the same purpose. Can be used as a diagnostic tool to identify what elements of art are known or not known by children. Test results may also be used to develop measurable goals for an art curriculum. Matching and identification items for each of 5 design elements are included.

7469
Lyons Relationship Scales. Goucher, Elizabeth L.; Efron, Herman Y.
Subtests: The Relationship from the Viewpoint of the Patient; The Relationship from the Viewpoint of the Relative
Descriptors: Adults; Family Attitudes; *Family Relationship; Interaction; *Interviews; *Patients; *Psychiatric Hospitals; Rating Scales
Identifiers: Patient Attitudes; *Psychiatric Patients; TIM(C)
Availability: Tests in Microfiche; Test Collection, Educational Testing Service, Princeton, NJ 08541
Target Audience: Adults
Notes: Time, 45 approx.; Items, 29

Designed to assess changes in the psychiatric patient-family relationship. The instrument consists of 2 parts: Schedule I, the relationship from the viewpoint of the patient; and Schedule II, the relationship from the viewpoint of the relative. The scales are intended for use after an interview with both the patient and the relative.

7471
Suicide Detection Test. Efron, Herman Y. 1960
Descriptors: Adults; *Patients; Predictive Measurement; Predictor Variables; Projective Measures; *Psychiatric Hospitals; Screening Tests; *Suicide
Identifiers: *Psychiatric Patients; Sentence Completion Tests
Availability: Herman Y. Efron; 909 Brentwood Ln., Silver Spring, MD 20902
Target Audience: Adults
Notes: Time, 60 approx.; Items, 54

Designed to detect patients who are morbidly preoccupied with depressive thoughts and may be suicidal.

7476
Group Dynamics Sentence Completion Test. Michaux, William W. 1961
Descriptors: Adults; Group Behavior; *Group Dynamics; *Patients; Projective Measures
Identifiers: Sentence Completion Tests
Availability: Group Psychotherapy; v14 p48-49 1961
Target Audience: Adults

A projective technique designed to elicit information for diagnostic study of groups. Each member completes a sentence stem and composes a new stem for the next member. The first stem may be provided by the examiner or a designated group member.

7487
Personal Skills Scale. Vogel, William; And Others
Descriptors: Adolescents; Adults; *Behavior Change; *Behavior Rating Scales; Children; *Developmental Disabilities; Individual Development; Individual Testing; Maturity (Individuals); *Mental Retardation; Observation; Patients; Personality Measures; Prognostic Tests; Psychological Testing; *Responsibility; *Self Care Skills; Verbal Development
Identifiers: Personal Skills; PS Scale
Availability: Professor William Vogel; Dept. of Psychology, Worcester State Hospital, Worcester, MA 01713
Target Audience: 9-64
Notes: Time, 5 approx.; Items, 15

Specifically designed for rating retarded individuals' behavior from the records of the Wrentham State School. The authors feel that the PS Scale may be too imprecise when working with the retarded persons themselves rather than with the records. Rates the degree to which retarded subjects have acquired those perceptual, motoric, and verbal skills which enable them to assume personal responsibility for themselves and their possessions. Used to reevaluate after treatment to determine the degree of adaptive behavior and change.

7488
Social and Emotional Behavior Scale. Vogel, William; And Others

Descriptors: Adolescents; Adults; Affective Behavior; *Behavior Change; *Behavior Rating Scales; Children; *Developmental Disabilities; *Emotional Disturbances; Individual Development; Individual Testing; *Interpersonal Competence; *Mental Retardation; Observation; Patients; Personality Measures; Prognostic Tests; Prosocial Behavior; Psychological Testing; *Self Control
Identifiers: SEB Scales
Availability: Professor William Vogel; Dept. of Psychiatry, University of Mass. Medical Center, 55 Lake Ave. N., Worcester, MA 01605
Target Audience: 9-64
Notes: Time, 5 approx.; Items, 15

Specifically designed for rating retarded individuals' behavior from the records of the Wrentham State School. The authors feel that the SEB Scale may be too imprecise when working with the retarded persons themselves rather than with the records. Measures the acquisition of self-control over uncontrolled emotional responses and the ability to interact and relate socially to others. Used to reevaluate after treatment to determine the degree of adaptive behavior and change.

7517
Screening Test of Spanish Grammar. Toronto, Allen S. 1973
Subtests: Receptive; Expressive
Descriptors: Individual Testing; *Language Proficiency; *Screening Tests; *Spanish; *Spanish Speaking; *Young Children
Identifiers: STSG
Availability: Northwestern University Press; 1735 Benson Ave., Evanston, IL 60201
Target Audience: 3-7
Notes: Items, 46

Designed to identify Spanish-speaking children who do not demonstrate native syntactic proficiency commensurate with their age. Not to be used as an in-depth or complete language assessment.

7518
Mertens Visual Perception Test. Mertens, Marjorie K. 1974
Subtests: Design Copying; Design Reproduction; Framed Pictures; Design Completion; Spatial Recognition; Visual Memory
Descriptors: *Diagnostic Tests; Elementary School Students; *Grade 1; Individual Testing; *Kindergarten Children; *Learning Problems; Learning Readiness; Perception Tests; Perceptual Motor Learning; Performance; *Primary Education; *Reading Readiness; Reading Readiness Tests; Visual Learning; Visual Measures; *Visual Perception; *Visual Stimuli
Identifiers: MVPT; Oral Tests; Visual Perception Test
Availability: Western Psychological Services; 12031 Wilshire Blvd., Los Angeles, CA 90025
Grade Level: K-1
Notes: Time, 30 approx.; Items, 36

Measures 6 areas of visual perception which are prerequisites for reading; used to identify those kindergarten and first grade children who appear likely to develop reading or learning disabilities as a result of problems with visual perception. The Framed Pictures and Visual Memory are timed subtests; the others are not. May be group- or individually administered. Requires the use of charts and the booklets.

7526
A Study of Young People. Blacker, Edward; And Others
Descriptors: Adolescents; *Alcoholism; *Attitude Measures; *Delinquency; *Drinking; *Males; Social Attitudes
Identifiers: TIM (A)
Availability: Tests in Microfiche; Test Collection, Educational Testing Service, Princeton, NJ 08541
Target Audience: Adolescents
Notes: Items, 174

Designed to collect information regarding the drinking attitudes and practices of male adolescents, particularly among delinquent male adolescents, among whom alcoholism is a problem.

7529
Mental Status Examination Record. Spitzer, Robert L.; Endicott, Jean 1970
Descriptors: Adolescents; Adults; *Behavior Rating Scales; *Case Records; Institutionalized Persons; Mental Disorders; *Observation; *Patients; *Psychiatric Hospitals; *Psychological Evaluation; Psychological Patterns; Records (Forms)
Identifiers: MSER; Multi State Information System for Psych Pat Proj; *Psychiatric Patients
Availability: Eugene Laska; Rockland Research Institute, Orangeburg, NY 10962
Target Audience: 14-64

Computerized form used to record the current mental status of a mentally ill patient. Information is drawn from the rater's observations and interaction with the patient over the period of a week. May be compared with previous week's evaluation. Does not include prognosis.

7530
Periodic Evaluation Record—Community Version. Spitzer, Robert L.; Endicott, Jean 1969
Descriptors: Adolescents; Adults; *Behavior Rating Scales; *Case Records; *Deinstitutionalization (of Disabled); Mental Disorders; *Patients; *Psychological Evaluation; *Psychological Patterns; Records (Forms)
Identifiers: Multi State Information System for Psych Pat Proj; PER C; *Psychiatric Patients
Availability: Eugene Laska; Rockland Research Institute, Orangeburg, NY 10962
Target Audience: 14-64

Computerized medical recording form to be used with mentally ill patients who live in the community. Records the current mental status based on information from various sources. Based on a one-week study period; does not include prognosis.

7531
Periodic Evaluation Record. Spitzer, Robert L.; Endicott, Jean 1969
Descriptors: Adolescents; Adults; *Behavior Rating Scales; *Case Records; Institutionalized Persons; Mental Disorders; *Observation; *Patients; *Psychiatric Hospitals; *Psychological Evaluation; *Psychological Patterns; Records (Forms)
Identifiers: Multi State Information System for Psych Pat Proj; PER; *Psychiatric Patients
Availability: Eugene Laska; Rockland Research Institute, Orangeburg, NY 10962
Target Audience: 14-64

Computerized medical form to evaluate a patient's condition and functioning during the past week. Information obtained by observations, previous records, and other inhouse medical files, etc. To be conducted over a period of one week. Does not include prognosis. To be used periodically, not weekly.

7533
Psychiatric Anamnestic Record. Spitzer, Robert L.; Endicott, Jean
Descriptors: Adolescents; Adults; *Institutionalized Persons; *Medical Case Histories; Medical Evaluation; *Patients; *Psychiatric Hospitals; *Psychological Characteristics; *Psychological Evaluation
Identifiers: Multi State Information System for Psych Pat Proj; PAR; *Psychiatric Patients; Psychiatric Problems
Availability: Eugene Laska; Rockland Research Institute, Orangeburg, NY 10962
Target Audience: 13-64

Computerized form for recording the medical case history of psychiatric patients. Information may be obtained from hospital or clinical records, reports from the family or close friends, or from the patients themselves. Used to obtain a narrative account of the patient's psychiatric history and for systematic evaluation of individual patients.

7535
Psychiatric Evaluation Form. Spitzer, Robert L.; And Others 1968
Subtests: Comprehensive Psychopathology Scales; Role Impairment Scales
Descriptors: Adults; Audiotape Recordings; Behavior Rating Scales; *Institutionalized Persons; Interviews; *Medical Evaluation; *Patients; *Psychiatric Hospitals; Psychopathology
Identifiers: PEF; *Psychiatric Patients
Availability: Research Assessment and Training Unit, New York State Psychiatric Institute; 722 W. 168th St., New York, NY 10032
Target Audience: 18-64

Designed to record scaled judgments of a subject's functioning during a one-week period. Part I consists of judgments made on 19 dimensions of psychopathology called Comprehensive Psychopathology Scales. Degree of Role Impairment is assessed if subject meets criteria for roles of Employed Wage Earner, Housekeeper, Student Trainee, Mate, or Parent. Part II is completed when a subject is newly admitted to a psychiatric facility. Demonstration training audiotape is included.

7536
Psychiatric Status Schedule: Second Edition. Spitzer, Robert L.; And Others 1968
Descriptors: Adults; Audiotape Recordings; Behavior; Institutionalized Persons; Interviews; *Patients; *Psychiatric Hospitals; *Self Concept
Identifiers: PSS; *Psychiatric Patients
Availability: Research Assessment and Training Unit, New York State Psychiatric Institute; 722 W. 168th St., New York, NY 10032
Target Audience: 18-64

Notes: Items, 321

Designed to gather information from psychiatric patients. Information is gleaned from patient responses, as well as by interviewer's observations of patient behavior. Patients are judged on all items except optional sections, wage earner role or housekeeper role, if they are not applicable. Demonstration audiotape is used for interviewer training.

7545
Dos Amigos Verbal Language Scales. Critchlow, Donald E. 1974
Descriptors: *Bilingual Students; Elementary Education; *Elementary School Students; *English (Second Language); Individual Testing; *Language Acquisition; *Language Dominance; Language Proficiency; *Language Tests; Second Language Learning; *Spanish
Identifiers: Oral Tests
Availability: United Educational Services; P.O. Box 357, E. Aurora, NY 14052
Grade Level: K-6
Target Audience: 5-13
Notes: Time, 20 approx.; Items, 170

Designed to determine cognitive level of language functioning, in both English and Spanish, among individual students. Useful where mixed language proficiency exists to determine child's dominant language. Reveals comparative scores in Spanish and English development and identifies functional language levels. Examiner must be fluent in both English and Spanish.

7570
The Kindergarten Questionnaire. Perlman, Evelyn; Berger, Susan 1976
Descriptors: Cognitive Development; Emotional Development; *Kindergarten; Language Acquisition; Learning Problems; *Maturity (Individuals); Physical Health; *Preschool Children; Preschool Education; Psychomotor Skills; *School Readiness; *Screening Tests
Availability: Evelyn Perlman; 10 Tyler Rd., Lexington, MA 02173
Target Audience: 4-5
Notes: Time, 30; Items, 65

Designed for use in identifying children who might have learning, emotional, behavioral, or language deficiencies. Used in the spring of the year prior to kindergarten entrance so that they may be deferred. Consists of a parent report of health and physical information and a series of drawing, copying, and gross motor tasks to be performed by the child.

7599
Lower Level Job Interest Test. Robinson, Ernest L.; Grigg, Austin E. 1964
Subtests: Service; Business Contact; Organizational; Technological; Outdoor; Scientific; Arts and Entertainment
Descriptors: Adults; *Educationally Disadvantaged; *Interest Inventories; Prisoners; *Semiskilled Workers; *Unskilled Workers; *Vocational Interests
Identifiers: Roe Occupational Classification
Availability: Dr. Robert J. Filer; Psychological Consultants Inc., 6724 Patterson Ave., Richmond, VA 23229
Target Audience: Adults
Notes: Time, 10 approx.; Items, 98

An occupational interest inventory designed for population with limited educational backgrounds. Job areas are those defined by Anne Roe as Levels 3, 4, and 5. Level 3 jobs involve a low level of responsibility for others, and a high school plus technical education. Level 4 consists of skilled occupations requiring apprenticeship or experience. Level 5 jobs are represented by semiskilled occupations. Classifications were made on basis of focus of activity and level of responsibility, skill, and training required.

7609
Ward Atmosphere Scale. Moos, Rudolf H. 1974
Subtests: Involvement; Support; Spontaneity; Autonomy; Practical Orientation; Personal Problem Orientation; Anger and Aggression; Order and Organization; Program Clarity; Staff Control
Descriptors: Adults; Attitude Measures; Hospital Personnel; *Hospitals; *Patients; Psychiatric Hospitals; *Psychiatric Services; *Social Environment
Identifiers: *Psychiatric Patients; Social Climate Scales; WAS
Availability: Consulting Psychologists Press; 577 College Ave., Palo Alto, CA 94306
Target Audience: Adults
Notes: Time, 20 approx.; Items, 100

Designed to assess the social environment of hospital-based psychiatric treatment programs. The subscales are arranged in dimensions of relationship, treatment program, and system maintenance. May be completed by patients or staff members. This scale has been adapted to measure the ideal social environment (Form I), or the expectations one has of an environment (Form E). Short form (Form S) may be adapted from standard Form R. Alternate scales and their construction are described in the manual.

7610
Community Oriented Programs Environment Scale. Moos, Rudolf H. 1974
Subtests: Involvement; Support; Spontaneity; Autonomy; Practical Orientation; Personal Problem Orientation; Anger and Aggression; Order and Organization; Program Clarity; Staff Control
Descriptors: *Adults; Attitude Measures; *Community Health Services; Group Homes; *Psychiatric Services; Rehabilitation Centers; Sheltered Workshops; *Social Environment
Identifiers: COPES; Patient Attitudes; *Psychiatric Patients; Social Climate Scales
Availability: Consulting Psychologists Press; 577 College Ave., Palo Alto, CA 94306
Target Audience: Adults
Notes: Time, 20 approx.; Items, 100

Designed to assess the social environment of community-based psychiatric treatment programs, such as halfway houses and sheltered workshops. This scale has been adapted to measure the ideal social environment (Form I) or the expectations one has of an environment (Form E). Short form (Form S) may be adapted from standard Form R. Alternate scales and their construction are described in the manual.

7620
Geriatric Rating Scale. Plutchik, Robert; And Others 1970
Descriptors: *Behavior Rating Scales; *Daily Living Skills; *Geriatrics; Health Personnel; *Interpersonal Competence; *Older Adults; Patients
Identifiers: GRS
Availability: ERIC Document Reproduction Service; 3900 Wheeler Ave., Alexandria, VA 22304 (ED 171 763, 842 pages)
Target Audience: 65-99
Notes: Items, 31

This volume consists of a series of psychosocial and physiological clinical nursing instruments. The instruments were selected from the published literature in health care, education, psychology, and the social sciences. Instruments focus upon nursing practice and stress patient variables. Instrument was designed to assess level of physical and mental functioning of geriatric patients. Observable behavior was rated by health care personnel.

7621
Geriatric Interpersonal Evaluation Scale. Plutchik, Robert; And Others
Descriptors: Adults; Cognitive Processes; *Cognitive Style; *Geriatrics; Individual Testing; Interviews; *Older Adults; *Patients; Psychiatric Hospitals
Identifiers: GIES; *Psychiatric Patients
Availability: Dr. Robert Plutchik; 1131 N. Ave., New Rochelle, NY 10804
Target Audience: 18-99
Notes: Items, 16

Designed to assess the degree of cognitive functioning of highly regressed patients through the use of a semistructured interview. Also measures perceptual motor ability. Used primarily with geriatric ward patients.

7622
Columbia M-D Scale. Plutchik, Robert; And Others
Descriptors: Adults; Affective Behavior; *Depression (Psychology); *Patients; Personality Measures; *Psychiatric Hospitals; Self Evaluation (Individuals)
Identifiers: *Psychiatric Patients
Availability: Dr. Robert Plutchik; 1131 N. Ave., New Rochelle, NY 10804
Target Audience: Adults

Designed to assess manic-depressive patients. Two scores may be obtained—one score for discriminating depression from normalcy and another score for discriminating mania from normalcy.

7625
Body Discomforts Questionnaire. Plutchik, Robert; And Others 1971
Descriptors: Adults; *Body Image; *Geriatrics; *Older Adults; *Patients; Questionnaires; Rating Scales
Identifiers: *Discomfort; Psychiatric Patients
Availability: Dr. Robert Plutchik; 1131 N. Ave., New Rochelle, NY 10804
Target Audience: 18-85
Notes: Items, 23

Designed to assess frequency with which individuals reported various body discomforts. May be used for all adult populations. However, instrument was developed to assess the nature of body image in aged persons with different types of psychiatric or medical experiences. Re-

sults of the instrument's use in a research study demonstrate that impaired body image is a major correlate of mental illness, rather than a function of the aging process.

7626
Body Worries Questionnaire. Plutchik, Robert; And Others 1971
Descriptors: Adults; *Body Image; *Geriatrics; *Older Adults; *Patients; Questionnaires
Identifiers: Psychiatric Patients
Availability: Dr. Robert Plutchik; 1131 N. Ave., New Rochelle, NY 10804
Target Audience: 18-85
Notes: Items, 15

Designed to assess frequency with which individuals reported various body worries or concerns with bodily dysfunctions. May be used with all adult populations. However, instrument was developed to assess the nature of body image in aged persons with different types of psychiatric or medical experiences. Results of the instrument's use in a research study demonstrate that impaired body image is a major correlate of mental illness, rather than a function of the aging process.

7627
Body Feelings Questionnaire. Plutchik, Robert; And Others 1973
Subtests: Evaluative; Potency; Activity
Descriptors: Adults; *Body Image; *Geriatrics; *Older Adults; *Patients; Psychiatric Hospitals; Self Concept; Self Concept Measures; Semantic Differential
Identifiers: Psychiatric Patients
Availability: Dr. Robert Plutchik; 1131 N. Ave., New Rochelle, NY 10804
Target Audience: 18-85
Notes: Items, 23

Designed to assess significance individual body parts have to one's body image. A semantic differential technique representing the evaluative, potency, and activity dimensions was used to assess body feelings. May be used for all adult populations. However, instrument was developed to assess the nature of body image in aged persons with different types of psychiatric or medical experiences. Results of a research study using this instrument, demonstrate that impaired body image is a major correlate of mental illness, rather than a function of the aging process.

7630
The Long Term Family Interview Schedule. Blum, Richard H.
Subtests: Section 1 Family Description; Section 2 Mother Interview; Father Interview; Section 3 Child Description; Section 4 Family Organization; Section 5 Whole Family Observation; Section 6 Family Study; Student Interview; Dealer Section; Interview for Children Under 13; Drug and Medicine Survey
Descriptors: Adolescents; Adults; Children; *Drug Abuse; *Family Attitudes; *Family Counseling; *Family Environment; *Family Relationship; Lysergic Acid Diethylamide; Marijuana; *Parent Attitudes; Questionnaires; Sedatives; Stimulants
Identifiers: TIM(A)
Availability: Tests in Microfiche; Test Collection, Educational Testing Service, Princeton, NJ 08541
Target Audience: 5-64
Notes: Items, 277

Designed to investigate and identify those familial variables related to the development of drug problems and illicit drug use in children. Ten-part questionnaire.

7675
Auditory Pointing Test. Fudala, Janet Baker; And Others 1974
Subtests: Memory Span; Sequential Memory
Descriptors: Auditory Perception; Auditory Tests; Cognitive Processes; *Diagnostic Tests; Educational Diagnosis; Elementary Education; *Elementary School Students; *Individual Testing; *Learning Disabilities; *Learning Problems; Pictorial Stimuli; *Sensory Integration; Sequential Learning; *Short Term Memory; Visual Perception
Identifiers: APT; Oral Tests
Availability: United Educational Services; P.O. Box 357, E. Aurora, NY 14052
Grade Level: K-5
Notes: Items, 151

Individually administered instrument which measures and distinguishes between span and sequential short-term memory. The subject is shown a picture containing many objects and, first, asked to point out a specific object, then asked to point out 2 objects in the same order as the test administrator said them. The test is stopped when the number of errors is too high. The longest list of named objects is 10. Comes in form A and B; requires the use of set of cards depicting the objects. Used as an aid in identifying specific learning disabilities such as deficiencies in auditory and visual sequential memory.

7679
Vocational Opinion Index. Wolf, Abraham 1973
Descriptors: Adults; *Attitude Measures; Biographical Inventories; *Spanish; Spanish Speaking; Vocational Maturity; *Work Attitudes
Identifiers: *Job Readiness; Likert Scales; VOI
Availability: Associates for Research in Behavior: The Science Center, 34 and Market St.s, Philadelphia, PA 19104
Target Audience: Adults
Notes: Time, 45 approx.; Items, 42

The Vocational Opinion Index (VOI) is designed to measure an individual's job readiness posture. A diagnostic and remediation system based on the use of the VOI would provide individuals who do not have workers' job readiness posture with appropriate training modules. The English or Spanish version of the test may be administered to an individual who can read at or above the 5th grade reading level.

7686
Revised Scale of Employability. Bolton, Brian 1970
Subtests: Workshop Scale; Counseling Scale
Descriptors: Adults; Disabilities; Emotional Disturbances; Employment Potential; Interpersonal Competence; Mental Retardation; Physical Disabilities; Rating Scales; Rehabilitation; Vocational Evaluation; Work Attitudes
Identifiers: TIM(A)
Availability: Tests in Microfiche; Test Collection, Educational Testing Service, Princeton, NJ 08541
Target Audience: Adults
Notes: Items, 11

Assesses the potential employability of mentally, physically, and emotionally handicapped adults who are clients of rehabilitation workshops. It is in 2 parts. The Counseling Scale assesses 5 dimensions of vocational competence: adequacy of work history, appropriateness of job demands, interpersonal competence-vocational, interpersonal competence-social, and prominence of handicap. The Workshop Scale assesses 5 dimensions of job competence: attitudinal conformity to work role, maintenance of quality, acceptance of work demands, interpersonal security, and speed of production.

7687
Schematic Concept Formation Task. Evans, Selby H. 1973
Descriptors: Adolescents; Adults; *Aptitude Tests; Children; *Cognitive Ability; Concept Formation; Culture Fair Tests; *Disadvantaged; Elementary Secondary Education; Higher Education; Nonverbal Tests; *Predictive Measurement
Identifiers: SCF; TIM(B)
Availability: Tests in Microfiche; Test Collection, Educational Testing Service, Princeton, NJ 08541
Target Audience: 6-65
Notes: Items, 210

Designed to measure aptitude for spontaneous classification of stimuli on the basis of similarity, this nonverbal cognitive aptitude measure may be useful in predicting a person's learning ability or academic potential independently of his or her cultural background or educational level. The items consist of computer generated graph-like and language-like patterns.

7695
Behavioral Developmental Profile. Donohue, Mike; And Others 1972
Descriptors: Cognitive Development; *Developmental Stages; *Disabilities; *Disadvantaged; Emotional Development; Language Acquisition; Physical Development; Social Development; *Young Children
Availability: ERIC Document Reproduction Service; 3900 Wheeler Ave., Alexandria, VA 22304 (ED079917, 35 pages)
Target Audience: 0-6

Developed for use with handicapped and disadvantaged children ages 0-6. Covers receptive and expressive language, cognitive, fine, and gross motor skills, personal-social skills, self-help skills, and emotions. Profile format used with a guide listing behaviors occurring at set ages. Establishes a baseline and ceiling while indicating areas for intervention. Not timed. From 2 to 10 items of behavior are listed for each age range.

7717
Location Activity Inventory. Schooler, Carmi; and Others
Subtests: Location Dimension; Position Dimension; Activity Dimension; Posture Disposition
Descriptors: Adults; *Behavior Patterns; *Behavior Rating Scales; *Institutionalized Persons; Observation; *Patients; *Schizophrenia
Identifiers: LAI; *Psychiatric Patients; TIM(C)
Availability: Tests in Microfiche; Test Collection, Educational Testing Service, Princeton, NJ 08541

Target Audience: Adults
Notes: Time, 15 approx.

Developed to measure objectively the overt ward adjustment of neuropsychiatric patients. Systematic observations provide behavioral profiles of patients in the areas of patterns of patient location on the ward, characteristic orientation to major architectural features, posture, and patterns of activities or response to the social and nonsocial stimuli on the ward.

7722
Base Expectancy Inventory. Gottfredson, Don M.; Bonds, Jack A. 1961
Descriptors: Adjustment (to Environment); Adults; *Correctional Rehabilitation; *Criminals; Predictive Measurement; Probationary Period
Availability: Don M. Gottfredson, Dean; School of Criminal Justice, Rutgers University, 53 Washington St., Newark, NJ 07102
Target Audience: Adults

Designed to assess probability of favorable parole adjustment of convicted criminals. May be used to determine treatment of incarcerated individuals to prepare them for better parole adjustment.

7740
Sensory Deprivation Rating Indices. Adams, Henry B.; And Others 1972
Subtests: Behavioral Anxiety; Gross Symptomatology; Sympton Reduction; Symptom Increase
Descriptors: Adults; *Behavior Rating Scales; *Institutionalized Persons; *Interviews; Measures (Individuals); *Mental Disorders; Observation; *Patients; Psychological Evaluation; *Sensory Deprivation
Identifiers: *Symptoms
Availability: Perceptual and Motor Skills; v34 p199-217 1972
Target Audience: Adults

Four behavioral rating indices developed to evaluate the effects of sensory deprivation on mentally ill patients. As the author explains, these indices were derived from ratings of interview behavior before and after sensory deprivation and from ratings of observable behavior during the sensory deprivation experience. The authors have not given this group of indices a specific name.

7742
Ferriera-Winter Questionnaire for Unrevealed Differences. Winter, William D.; Ferriera, Antonio T.
Subtests: Spontaneous Agreement; Decision Time; Choice Fulfillment
Descriptors: Adolescents; Adults; Children; Criminals; *Decision Making; Emotional Problems; *Family Problems; *Family Relationship; *Fathers; *Mothers; Rating Scales
Identifiers: TIM(E)
Availability: Tests in Microfiche; Test Collection, Educational Testing Service, Princeton, NJ 08541
Target Audience: 9-50
Notes: Items, 17

Designed for use in studies of decision making in normal and abnormal families. Abnormal families are defined as those in which a family member has emotional or criminal problems and who might have had psychotherapy within 5 years. It contains 17 situations with 10 alternatives. The family must pick 3 alternatives they like the least and the 3 they like the most. First, all family members complete questionnaire separately, then as a family unit.

7755
Preschool Disability Identification and Prevention. Metzger, H. Bruce 1973
Subtests: Language; Pre-Reading and Reading Skills; Math; Perceptual-Motor
Descriptors: *Behavioral Objectives; Behavior Rating Scales; Developmental Tasks; *Identification; *Learning Disabilities; *Preschool Children; Preschool Education; Preschool Teachers; *Preschool Tests; Reading Readiness
Identifiers: TIM(C)
Availability: Tests in Microfiche; Test Collection, Educational Testing Service, Princeton, NJ 08541
Target Audience: 2-5

Preschool curriculum, based on behavioral objectives, provides the teacher with a day-to-day evaluation tool that can facilitate decision making related to program planning for the child. Tasks are provided in 4 basic areas. As the child acquires a skill, the date is recorded so that the child's development is plotted on a continual basis.

7756
In-Community Evaluation Interview. Lorei, Theodore W. 1965
Subtests: Descriptive Data; Interview with Veteran; Interview with Significant Other

Descriptors: *Adjustment (to Environment); Adults; Interviews; Job Applicants; *Patients; *Psychiatric Hospitals; Schizophrenia; Veterans; *Vocational Adjustment
Identifiers: *Discharged Patients; ICE; Psychiatric Patients; TIM(C)
Availability: Tests in Microfiche; Test Collection, Educational Testing Service, Princeton, NJ 08541
Target Audience: Adults
Notes: Items, 235

Intended for use with Veterans Administration schizophrenic patients to assess their adjustment 3 months after their release from the hospital. It is designed specifically to collect information on the individual's job-seeking progress and societal adjustment. The interview consists of 3 parts: general information about the household in which the patient lives, a self-report of the patient's job-seeking activities, and a report from a significant other on the patient's adjustment.

7757
Work/Adjustment Criterion Information. Lorei, Theodore W. 1971
Descriptors: *Adjustment (to Environment); Adults; Interviews; Job Applicants; *Patients; *Psychiatric Hospitals; Schizophrenia; Veterans; *Vocational Adjustment
Identifiers: *Discharged Patients; Psychiatric Patients; TIM(C); WACI
Availability: Tests in Microfiche; Test Collection, Educational Testing Service, Princeton, NJ 08541
Target Audience: Adults
Notes: Items, 307

Intended for use with schizophrenic patients in the Veterans Administration's Psychiatric Evaluation Project. It was designed to assess patients' adjustment 9 months after their release from the hospital and has been used to investigate factors in mental hospital effectiveness.

7770
Means-End Problem Solving Procedure. Platt, Jerome J.; Spivack, George 1975
Descriptors: Adolescents; Adults; Interpersonal Relationship; Logical Thinking; *Patients; *Problem Solving; Projective Measures; *Psychiatric Hospitals
Identifiers: *Psychiatric Patients; Self Administered Tests; The MEPS Procedure
Availability: George Spivack, Hahnemann University (MS 626) Broad & Vine St., Philadelphia, PA 19102
Target Audience: 15-64
Notes: Items, 10

Designed to assess appropriate problem-solving methods. Subject is presented with a situation involving an interpersonal conflict. The beginning and end of the situation are given. The patient must supply the means of achieving the goal. Stories may be scored for relevant means, obstacles, enumeration of means, time, irrelevant means, no-means responses, as well as for story content.

7775
Behavior Check List. Rubin, Eli Z; And Others 1966
Subtests: Disorientation and Maladaptation to the Environment; Antisocial Behavior; Unassertive, Overconforming Behavior; Neglect; Infantile Behavior; Immature Social Behavior; Irresponsible Behavior
Descriptors: *Behavior Rating Scales; Elementary Education; *Elementary School Students; *Emotional Disturbances; *Social Behavior; *Student Behavior; *Teacher Attitudes
Identifiers: TIM(C)
Availability: Tests in Microfiche; Test Collection, Educational Testing Service, Princeton, NJ 08541
Grade Level: 1-6
Notes: Items, 39

Provides a method by which teachers' ratings can be used to identify maladjusted children and facilitate their placement in remedial education. The checklist is comprised of 39 items describing behavior indicative of maladjustment in the classroom situation. The teacher indicates whether each behavior is typical of the child and, if so, how frequently it occurs. The checklist encompasses 7 factors.

7778
Stroop Color and Word Test. Golden, Charles J. 1978
Subtests: Word Page; Color Page; Word-Color Page
Descriptors: *Adults; Culture Fair Tests; *Elementary School Students; Elementary Secondary Education; Individual Testing; *Neurological Impairments; Older Adults; *Personality Assessment; *Screening Tests; *Secondary School Students; Stress Variables

Availability: The Stoelting Co.; 1350 S. Kostner Ave., Chicago, IL 60623
Target Audience: 8-80
Notes: Time, 5 approx.; Items, 300

Designed to differentiate normal subjects, non-brain damaged psychiatric subjects, and brain damaged subjects. May be used alone or in conjunction with a larger screening battery. Useful in locating precise area of brain dysfunction. May be administered individually or to groups. Also used to investigate personality, cognition, stress response, and other psychological phenomena.

7802
Essential Math and Language Skills. Sternberg, Les; And Others 1978
Subtests: Language Skills; Sets and Operations; Numbers and Operations; Part and Whole Relations; Spatial Relations; Measurement; Patterns
Descriptors: Academic Aptitude; Children; *Cognitive Ability; Cognitive Development; Cognitive Tests; *Concept Formation; *Diagnostic Tests; Disabilities; *Individual Testing; Language Skills; Learning Readiness; Mathematical Concepts; *Preschool Children; *Primary Education; *School Readiness; School Readiness Tests; Visual Measures; Visual Stimuli
Identifiers: EMLS Program; Numbers and Operations; Part Whole Relations; Pattern Recognition Skills Inventory; Sets and Operations; Spatial Relations
Availability: Hubbard; 1946 Raymond Dr., Northbrook, IL 60062
Target Audience: 4-10

Individually administered instrument used to (1) assess a student's ability to recognize various pattern sequences and (2) measure the cognitive readiness of handicapped (or nonhandicapped) students relating to mathematical and language concepts. Pattern Recognition Skills Inventory was incorporated into the Program.

7809
Motor Fitness Test for the Moderately Mentally Retarded. Johnson, Leon; Londeree, Ben 1976
Descriptors: *Adolescents; *Children; *Moderate Mental Retardation; *Performance Tests; *Physical Fitness; Psychomotor Skills; *Young Adults
Availability: American Alliance for Health, Physical Education, Recreation, and Dance, 1900 Association Dr., Reston, VA 22091
Target Audience: 6-20

Designed to provide a physical fitness profile of moderately retarded children and adolescents. A battery of 6 items is suggested including flexed arm hang; situps, standing long jump, softball throw for distance, 50-yard dash, and 300-yard run-walk. Additional items are described in manual for use at examiner's discretion.

7812
New Physician's Rating List (for Outpatients). Free, Spencer M.
Subtests: Anxiety Manifestations; Associated Symptomatology
Descriptors: Adults; Anxiety; *Drug Therapy; Medical Services; *Patients; *Personality Problems; *Physicians; Rating Scales
Identifiers: TIM(C)
Availability: Tests in Microfiche; Test Collection, Educational Testing Service, Princeton, NJ 08541
Target Audience: Adults
Notes: Items, 19

Designed to rate the symptoms manifested by out-patients. The items represent 3 symptom complexes: anxiety, depression, and somatic complaints.

7820
Assessment of Children's Language Comprehension, 1973 Revision. Foster, Rochana; And Others 1973
Subtests: Vocabulary; Two Critical Elements; Three Critical Elements; Four Critical Elements
Descriptors: Communication Skills; *Diagnostic Tests; Language Acquisition; *Language Handicaps; Language Processing; Listening Comprehension; Pictorial Stimuli; *Picture Books; *Receptive Language; *Visual Measures; *Young Children
Identifiers: ACLC; *Oral Tests
Availability: Consulting Psychologists Press; 577 College Ave., Palo Alto, CA 94306
Target Audience: 3-7
Notes: Time, 10 approx.; Items, 40

To determine the receptive language difficulties of children ages 3 to 7 and to indicate the guidelines for correction of language disorders. The subject points to the correct picture as his/her response. Used for both nonhandicapped and handicapped children. Includes material for administering both to individuals and to groups. Group form is abstracted from individual form and has only 12 items.

7821
Porch Index of Communicative Ability in Children.
Porch, Bruce E. 1974
Descriptors: Auditory Perception; Children; Cognitive Style; Communication Disorders; Elementary Education; *Elementary School Students; Individual Testing; Perception Tests; Perceptual Handicaps; *Performance Tests; *Preschool Children; Preschool Education; Verbal Communication
Identifiers: PICAC; Test Batteries
Availability: Consulting Psychologists Press; 577 College Ave., Palo Alto, CA 94306
Target Audience: 3-12
Notes: Time, 60 approx.
Clinical tool designed to assess and quantify verbal, gestural, and graphic abilities. Basic battery is for use with children ages 3 to 6 and has 15 subtests. The advanced battery is for students aged 6 to 12 and consists of 20 subtests. Advanced battery has more auditory and reading tasks.

7824
Balthazar Scales of Adaptive Behavior: II. Scales of Social Adaptation. Balthazar, Earl E. 1973
Subtests: Unadaptive Self-Directed Behaviors; Unadaptive Interpersonal Behaviors; Adaptive Self-Directed Behaviors; Adaptive Interpersonal Behaviors; Verbal Communication; Play Activities; Response to Instructions; Checklist Items
Descriptors: Adjustment (to Environment); Adults; Behavior Rating Scales; Children; *Coping; *Severe Mental Retardation; *Social Adjustment
Identifiers: BSAB II
Availability: Consulting Psychologists Press; 577 College Ave., Palo Alto, CA 94306
Target Audience: 5-57
Notes: Items, 19
Designed to yield objective measures of coping behaviors.

7826
Basic Occupational Literacy Test. United States Employment Service, Washington, DC 1973
Subtests: Reading Vocabulary; Reading Comprehension; Arithmetic Computation; Arithmetic Reasoning
Descriptors: Achievement Tests; Adults; *Arithmetic; *Basic Skills; Computation; *Educationally Disadvantaged; *Reading Achievement; Reading Comprehension; *Reading Skills
Identifiers: USES Basic Occupational Literacy Test (BOLT)
Availability: State Employment Office
Target Audience: 18-64
Notes: Time, 150 approx.
Designed for use with educationally disadvantaged adults to test basic reading and arithmetic skills. Four levels of difficulty for reading vocabulary, reading comprehension, and arithmetic computation. Levels are advanced, high intermediate, basic intermediate, and fundamental. Arithmetic reasoning forms are available at advanced, intermediate, and fundamental levels. Reading vocabulary tests contain 14 items. Reading Comprehension tests contain 12 items. The advanced and high intermediate levels of arithmetic computation have 14 items each; basic intermediate level has 15 items; and fundamental level has 20 items. Advanced and intermediate arithmetic reasoning forms have 12 items; fundamental level has 14 items. The Wide Range Scale is a screening test which can be administered in approximately 15 minutes. It determines the level of BOLT to use with the individual being tested. The BOLT is intended for use primarily by State Employment Security Agencies. This test is available for release to certain individuals and organization at the discretion of the appropriate State Employment Security representative.

7827
Vocabulary Comprehension Scale. Bangs, Tina E. 1975
Subtests: Pronouns; Quality; Position; Size; Quantity
Descriptors: Achievement Tests; *Diagnostic Tests; Individual Testing; *Learning Disabilities; Performance Tests; Preschool Tests; *School Readiness; School Readiness Tests; *Verbal Development; Verbal Tests; *Vocabulary Development; *Young Children
Identifiers: Oral Tests
Availability: DLM Teaching Resources; P.O. Box 4000, One DLM Park, Allen, TX 75002
Target Audience: 2-6
Orally and individually administered test to determine a child's comprehension of various words regarding size, position, number, etc. Used to give teachers of language- or learning-handicapped children baseline information needed to plan activities for helping these children develop vocabulary acquired for kindergarten or first grade.

Requires the child to manipulate various materials upon spoken directions by the test administrator. Test packet includes the materials (tea set, trees, people, fence, ladder, cubes, buttons, etc.) to be manipulated.

7839
Bilingual Center Parent Questionnaire. Chicago Area Bilingual Centers, IL 1974
Subtests: Background and Language; About the Bilingual Center; Parents Feelings
Descriptors: Adults; Arabic; *Attitude Measures; *Bilingualism; *Bilingual Students; Chinese; Greek; Italian; Japanese; Korean; *Parent Attitudes; Parents; *Program Evaluation; Spanish; Spanish Speaking; Tagalog
Identifiers: TIM(E)
Availability: Tests in Microfiche; Test Collection, Educational Testing Service, Princeton, NJ 08541
Target Audience: Adults
Notes: Items, 38
Designed to assess the attitudes of parents, whose children attend the Chicago Area Bilingual Centers, toward the centers themselves. Questions are included which gather information on dominant language, language used in various situations, and communication ease in English. Forms are available in English, Greek, Chinese, Arabic, Italian, Korean, Japanese, and Tagalog.

7847
French Achievement Test: Language Arts, Kindergarten. Comeaux, Jane B. 1973
Subtests: Vocabulary-Oral Comprehension; Paragraph Meaning; Prereading Skills
Descriptors: *Achievement Tests; *Bilingual Education; *Criterion Referenced Tests; *French; *Kindergarten Children; *Language Skills; Preschool Education; Reading Readiness; *Visual Measures
Identifiers: TIM(C)
Availability: Tests in Microfiche; Test Collection, Educational Testing Service, Princeton, NJ 08541
Grade Level: K
Notes: Items, 21
One of a series of criterion-referenced tests based on Bilingual Education instructional objectives. Designed to assess language skills in French. Tests are available for kindergarten through grade 5. Directions for administration are in French.

7848
French Achievement Test: Language Arts, Grade 1.
Comeaux, Jane B.; And Others 1973
Subtests: Vocabulary-Oral Comprehension; Comprehension-Categories; Comprehension-Stories; Word Reading; Paragraph Meaning; Grammar-Syntax
Descriptors: *Achievement Tests; *Beginning Reading; *Bilingual Education; *Criterion Referenced Tests; Elementary School Students; *French; *Grade 1; Grammar; *Language Skills; Primary Education; Reading Comprehension; Vocabulary Skills; Young Children
Identifiers: TIM(C)
Availability: Tests in Microfiche; Test Collection, Educational Testing Service, Princeton, NJ 08541
Grade Level: K
Notes: Items, 53
One of a series of criterion-referenced tests based on Bilingual Education instructional objectives. Designed to assess language skills in French. Tests are available for kindergarten through grade 5. Directions for administration are in French.

7849
French Achievement Test: Language Arts, Grade 2.
Comeaux, Jane B.; And Others 1973
Subtests: Vocabulary-Oral Comprehension; Comprehension-Categories, Word Reading; Paragraph Meaning; Spelling; Language Analysis; Reading Comprehension
Descriptors: *Achievement Tests; *Bilingual Education; *Criterion Referenced Tests; Elementary School Students; *French; *Grade 2; *Language Skills; Primary Education; Reading Comprehension; Vocabulary Skills; Young Children
Identifiers: TIM(C)
Availability: Tests in Microfiche; Test Collection, Educational Testing Service, Princeton, NJ 08541
Grade Level: 2
Notes: Items, 85
One of a series of criterion-referenced tests based on Bilingual Education instructional objectives. Designed to assess language skills in French. Tests are available for kindergarten through grade 5. Directions for administration are in French.

7850
French Achievement Test: Language Arts, Grade 3.
Comeaux, Jane B.; And Others 1973
Subtests: Vocabulary; Spelling; Language Analysis; Reading Comprehension
Descriptors: *Achievement Tests; *Bilingual Education; *Criterion Referenced Tests; Elementary School Students; *French; *Grade 3; *Language Skills; Primary Education; Reading Comprehension; Vocabulary Skills; Young Children
Identifiers: TIM(C)
Availability: Tests in Microfiche; Test Collection, Educational Testing Service, Princeton, NJ 08541
Grade Level: 3
Notes: Items, 68
One of a series of criterion-referenced tests based on Bilingual Education instructional objectives. Designed to assess language skills in French. Tests are available for kindergarten through grade 5. Directions for administration are in French.

7851
French Achievement Test: Language Arts, Grade 4.
Comeaux, Jane B.; And Others 1974
Subtests: Vocabulary; Spelling; Language Analysis; Reading Comprehension
Descriptors: *Achievement Tests; *Bilingual Education; Children; *Criterion Referenced Tests; Elementary School Students; *French; *Grade 4; Intermediate Grades; *Language Skills; Reading Comprehension; Vocabulary Skills
Identifiers: TIM(C)
Availability: Tests in Microfiche; Test Collection, Educational Testing Service, Princeton, NJ 08541
Grade Level: 4
Notes: Items, 75
One of a series of criterion-referenced tests based on Bilingual Education instructional objectives. Designed to assess language skills in French. Tests are available for kindergarten through grade 5. Directions for administration are in French.

7852
French Achievement Test: Language Arts, Grade 5.
Guidry, Richard; Cluet, Jean Marc 1974
Subtests: Vocabulary; Spelling; Language Analysis; Reading Comprehension
Descriptors: *Achievement Tests; *Bilingual Education; Children; *Criterion Referenced Tests; Elementary School Students; *French; *Grade 5; Intermediate Grades; *Language Skills; Reading Comprehension; Vocabulary Skills
Identifiers: TIM(C)
Availability: Tests in Microfiche; Test Collection, Educational Testing Service, Princeton, NJ 08541
Grade Level: 5
Notes: Items, 80
One of a series of criterion-referenced tests based on Bilingual Education instructional objectives. Designed to assess language skills in French. Tests are available for kindergarten through grade 5. Directions for administration are in French.

7853
French Achievement Test: Mathematics, Kindergarten. Comeaux, Jane B.; And Others 1974
Descriptors: *Achievement Tests; *Bilingual Education; *Criterion Referenced Tests; *Elementary School Mathematics; *French; *Kindergarten Children; Number Concepts; Preschool Education; *Mathematics Tests
Identifiers: TIM(C)
Availability: Tests in Microfiche; Test Collection, Educational Testing Service, Princeton, NJ 08541
Grade Level: K
Notes: Items, 22
One of a series of criterion-referenced tests based on Bilingual Education instructional objectives. Designed to assess mathematical skills in French and emphasizes numerical concepts at the kindergarten level. Tests are available for grades K-5. Directions for administration are in French.

7854
French Achievement Test: Mathematics, Grade 1.
Comeaux, Jane B.; And Others 1974
Subtests: Numerical Concepts; Numerical Concepts and Fractions; Recognition of Numbers; Problem Solving
Descriptors: *Achievement Tests; *Bilingual Education; *Criterion Referenced Tests; *Elementary School Mathematics; Elementary School Students; *French; *Grade 1; Primary Education; *Mathematics Tests
Identifiers: TIM(C)

Availability: Tests in Microfiche; Test Collection, Educational Testing Service, Princeton, NJ 08541
Grade Level: 1
Notes: Items, 47

One of a series of criterion-referenced tests based on Bilingual Education instructional objectives. Designed to assess mathematical skills in French. Tests are available for kindergarten through grade 5. Directions for administration are in French.

7855
French Achievement Test: Mathematics, Grade 2.
Comeaux, Jane B.; And Others 1974
Subtests: Numerical Concepts; Problem Solving
Descriptors: *Achievement Tests; *Bilingual Education; *Criterion Referenced Tests; *Elementary School Mathematics; *French; *Grade 2; Primary Education; *Mathematics Tests
Identifiers: TIM(C)
Availability: Tests in Microfiche; Test Collection, Educational Testing Service, Princeton, NJ 08541
Grade Level: 2
Notes: Items, 52

One of a series of criterion-referenced tests based on Bilingual Education instructional objectives. Designed to assess mathematical skills in French. Tests are available for kindergarten through grade 5. Directions for administration are in French.

7856
French Achievement Test: Mathematics, Grade 3.
Comeaux, Jane B.; And Others 1974
Subtests: Numerical Concepts; Problem Solving
Descriptors: *Achievement Tests; *Bilingual Education; *Criterion Referenced Tests; *Elementary School Mathematics; *French; *Grade 3; Primary Education; *Mathematics Tests
Identifiers: TIM(C)
Availability: Tests in Microfiche; Test Collection, Educational Testing Service, Princeton, NJ 08541
Grade Level: 3
Notes: Items, 66

One of a series of criterion-referenced tests based on Bilingual Education instructional objectives. Designed to assess mathematical skills in French. Tests are available for kindergarten through grade 5. Directions for administration are in French.

7857
French Achievement Test: Mathematics, Grade 4.
Comeaux, Jane B.; And Others 1974
Subtests: Numerical Concepts; Problem Solving
Descriptors: *Achievement Tests; *Bilingual Education; *Criterion Referenced Tests; *Elementary School Mathematics; Elementary School Students; *French; *Grade 4; Intermediate Grades; *Mathematics Tests
Identifiers: TIM(C)
Availability: Tests in Microfiche; Test Collection, Educational Testing Service, Princeton, NJ 08541
Grade Level: 4
Notes: Items, 66

One of a series of criterion-referenced tests based on Bilingual Education instructional objectives. Designed to assess mathematical skills in French. Tests are available for kindergarten through grade 5. Directions for administration are in French.

7858
French Achievement Test: Mathematics, Grade 5.
Comeaux, Jane B.; And Others 1974
Subtests: Numerical Concepts; Problem Solving
Descriptors: *Achievement Tests; *Bilingual Education; *Criterion Referenced Tests; *Elementary School Mathematics; Elementary School Students; *French; *Grade 5; Intermediate Grades; *Mathematics Tests
Identifiers: TIM(C)
Availability: Tests in Microfiche; Test Collection, Educational Testing Service, Princeton, NJ 08541
Grade Level: 5
Notes: Items, 70

One of a series of criterion-referenced tests based on Bilingual Education instructional objectives. Designed to assess mathematical skills in French. Tests are available for kindergarten through grade 5. Directions for administration are in French.

7859
Ivie Attitudinal Test. Ivie, Richard P. 1975
Subtests: Self Concept; Attitude toward School; Peer Relations

Descriptors: *Elementary School Students; Elementary Secondary Education; *Peer Relationship; Personality Measures; Personality Traits; Psychological Testing; *Rating Scales; *Secondary School Students; Self Concept; *Self Concept Measures; *Spanish; Spanish Speaking; Student Adjustment; *Student Attitudes; Student Characteristics
Identifiers: IAT; Ivie Prueba De Comportamiento
Availability: Bilingual Leadership through Speech and Drama; Pomona Unified School District, 800 S. Garey Ave., P.O. Box 2900, Pomona, CA 91769
Grade Level: 6-12
Notes: Time, 15 approx.; Items, 59

Questionnaire and rating scale designed to measure student activities and feelings toward school, home, parents, and community. Available in both Spanish and English.

7890
Preschool Profile. Lynch, Linda L.; O'Conor, Mary Ruth 1975
Descriptors: *Developmental Disabilities; *Expressive Language; Infants; *Preschool Children; Preschool Education; Profiles; *Psychomotor Skills; *Receptive Language; Young Children
Availability: Experimental Education Unit; University of Washington, Seattle, WA 98195
Target Audience: 0-6

Designed for use with children who are developmentally delayed or have developmental disabilities. Profile may be used for assessment, programming, reporting, and curriculum planning. Child's level of functioning in psychomotor skills, pre-academic skills, self-help skills, language skills, creative skills, and social and play skills is assessed.

7896
Short Tests of Linguistic Skills: Pilot Version Spanish-English. Frederickson, Charles 1975
Subtests: Listening; Reading; Writing; Speaking
Descriptors: *Bilingual Students; Culture Fair Tests; Elementary Education; *Elementary School Students; *English (Second Language); *Language Dominance; Language Proficiency; *Spanish; Spanish Speaking
Identifiers: STLS; TIM(C)
Availability: Tests in Microfiche; Test Collection, Educational Testing Service, Princeton, NJ 08541
Grade Level: 3-8
Notes: Time, 90 approx.; Items, 80

Measure has been developed in English and 10 other languages by teachers and language specialists. Tests in other languages are not translations from the English version. Parallel format is used throughout all the tests using the same linguistic areas, subtests, and parallel selection of items. Items are culturally specific and language specific. Tests are available in Arabic, Chinese, Greek, Italian, Japanese, Korean, Filipino, Polish, and Vietnamese as well as Spanish. Uses a contrastive linguistic approach to determine language dominance and proficiency of children bilingual in English and Spanish. Listening, reading, and writing subtests are administered in groups. Speaking subtest is individually administered and requires about 8 minutes.

7904
Comprehensive Identification Process. Zehrbach, R. Reid 1975
Descriptors: Cognitive Ability; *Disabilities; Expressive Language; *Handicap Identification; Hearing (Physiology); Individual Testing; Interviews; *Parent Participation; *Preschool Children; Preschool Education; Psychomotor Skills; Screening Tests; *Special Education; Vision
Identifiers: CIP
Availability: Scholastic Testing Service; 480 Meyer Rd., Bensenville, IL 60106
Target Audience: 2-5
Notes: Time, 30 approx.

Developed to identify all children in a community who are eligible for special preschool programs or need medical attention or therapy to function at full potential in kindergarten or grade one. Parent and child are individually interviewed. Areas of child's ability which are assessed include cognitive-verbal, fine motor, gross motor, speech and expressive language, hearing, vision, social/effective behavior, and medical history.

7919
Social Learning Environment. Rating Scale. Warshow, Joyce P.; And Others 1976
Descriptors: Adults; Audiotape Recordings; *Children; Classroom Environment; *Classroom Observation Techniques; *Mild Mental Retardation; *Self Evaluation (Individuals); Socialization; Teacher Student Relationship; *Teacher Evaluation; Teachers
Identifiers: SLOR; Social Learning Curriculum; TIM(C)

Availability: Tests in Microfiche; Test Collection, Educational Testing Service, Princeton, NJ 08541
Target Audience: Adults
Notes: Items, 103

Classroom observation instrument is designed to examine teacher-student behavior within the framework of the Social Learning Curriculum, a large-scale curriculum for educable mentally handicapped children. Scale items are organized around the major objectives of the SLC: critical thinking, independent action, and teacher use of curriculum. The scale comprises 5 factors: problem emergence, problem clarification, problem resolution, application of learning, and the social learning environment.

7926
Structure Tests—English Language: Advanced, Forms 1 and 2. Best, Jeanette; Ilyin, Donna 1976
Descriptors: *Achievement Tests; Adult Education; *Adults; College Students; *English (Second Language); *Equivalency Tests; Higher Education; *Language Skills; Secondary Education; Secondary School Students; *Student Placement
Identifiers: STEL
Availability: Newbury House Publishers; 54 Church St., Cambridge, MA 02138
Target Audience: 12-64
Notes: Time, 30; Items, 50

STEL can be used as an achievement and as a placement test. Improvement in skills is not to be expected until after 350 to 500 hours of instruction for most adult high school programs. High school and college students achieve gain at a faster rate, however.

7927
Structure Tests—English Language: Intermediate, Forms 1 and 2. Best, Jeanette; Ilyin, Donna 1976
Descriptors: *Achievement Tests; Adult Education; *Adults; College Students; *English (Second Language); *Equivalency Tests; Higher Education; *Language Skills; Secondary Education; Secondary School Students; *Student Placement
Identifiers: STEL
Availability: Newbury House Publishers; 54 Church St., Cambridge, MA 02138
Target Audience: 12-64
Notes: Time, 30; Items, 50

STEL can be used as an achievement and as a placement test. Improvement in skills is not to be expected until after 350 to 500 hours of instruction for most adult high school programs. High school and college students achieve gain at a faster rate, however.

7928
Structure Tests—English Language: Beginning, Forms 1 and 2. Best, Jeanette; Ilyin, Donna 1976
Descriptors: *Achievement Tests; Adult Education; *Adults; College Students; *English (Second Language); *Equivalency Tests; Higher Education; *Language Skills; Secondary Education; Secondary School Students; *Student Placement
Identifiers: STEL
Availability: Newbury House Publishers; 54 Church St., Cambridge, MA 02138
Target Audience: 12-64
Notes: Time, 30; Items, 50

STEL can be used as an achievement and as a placement test. Improvement in skills is not to be expected until after 350 to 500 hours of instruction for most adult high school programs. High school and college students achieve gain at a faster rate, however.

7929
Wisconsin Test of Adult Basic Education. Wisconsin Univ., Madison, Univ. Extension 1971
Subtests: Word Meaning; Reading; Arithmetic; Life Coping Skills; The World around Me
Descriptors: Achievement Tests; Adult Basic Education; Adults; Cognitive Style; *Computation; *Daily Living Skills; *Functional Literacy; *Rural Population; *Verbal Ability
Identifiers: Rural Family Development Project; TIM(C); WITABE
Availability: Tests in Microfiche; Test Collection, Educational Testing Service, Princeton, NJ 08541
Target Audience: Adults
Notes: Time, 90 approx.; Items, 68

Developed for use in monitoring the achievement of basic educational and coping skills by persons enrolled in the Rural Family Development Program. It consists of 3 subtests. Subtests one and 2 focus on basic reading and computational skills. Subtest 3 deals with the coping skills an adult normally needs in his or her daily life. It includes such tasks as using a road map, ordering by mail, filling out a tax return, using a phone book, and writing a letter of application.

7933
Scales for Rating the Behavioral Characteristics of Superior Students. Renzulli, Joseph S. 1976

Subtests: Learning Characteristics; Motivational Characteristics; Creativity Characteristics; Leadership Characteristics; Artistic Characteristics; Musical Characteristics; Dramatics Characteristics; Communication Characteristics-Precision; Communication Characteristics-Expressiveness; Planning
Descriptors: *Ability Identification; Academically Gifted; Behavior Rating Scales; *Diagnostic Teaching; *Elementary School Students; *Gifted; Intermediate Grades; Screening Tests; Special Education; *Student Characteristics
Identifiers: SRBCSS
Availability: Creative Learning Press; P.O. Box 320, Mansfield Center, CT 06250
Grade Level: 4-6
Designed to provide an objective and systematic instrument to be used as an aid to guiding teacher judgment in identification of superior students. Learning experiences should be developed to capitalize on student's strengths. The scores obtained for each dimension yield a profile. They should not be added to yield a total score.

7938
Marysville Test of Language Dominance. Thonis, Eleanor 1973
Subtests: Test of Listening Comprehension; Speaking; Reading; Writing; Cultural Variables
Descriptors: *Bilingual Students; *Cultural Traits; Elementary Education; Elementary School Students; Individual Testing; *Language Dominance; *Language Proficiency; *Language Tests; Preschool Children; Preschool Education; *Spanish; Spanish Speaking
Identifiers: Oral Testing
Availability: Marysville Joint Unified School District; 1919 B St., Marysville, CA 95901
Target Audience: 3-10
Designed to determine extent of English-language and native-language proficiency. Children in preschool and kindergarten should be tested on oral sections (listening and speaking) and the cultural variables only.

7939
Oral Language Assessment for Diagnosis and Planning. Marysville Joint Unified School District, CA
Subtests: Receptive Language-Listening Comprehension; Expressive Language-Speaking Fluency
Descriptors: *Bilingual Students; *Diagnostic Tests; Elementary Education; Elementary School Students; *Expressive Language; Individual Testing; Preschool Children; Preschool Education; *Receptive Language; *Spanish; Spanish Speaking
Identifiers: Oral Testing
Availability: Marysville Joint Unified School District; 1919 B St., Marysville, CA 95901
Target Audience: 3-10
Designed to measure receptive and expressive language competencies of bilingual students. Forms available in English and Spanish.

7941
Checklist for Anxiety-Behavior Observation. Zeisset, Ray M. 1966
Descriptors: Adults; *Anxiety; Behavior Rating Scales; *Interviews; *Patients; *Psychiatric Hospitals
Identifiers: CABO; *Psychiatric Patients; TIM(C)
Availability: Tests in Microfiche; Test Collection, Educational Testing Service, Princeton, NJ 08541
Target Audience: Adults
Notes: Time, 5 approx.; Items, 13
Designed to measure the anxiety of subjects during an interview. The checklist consists of 13 observable indicators of anxiety. The presence or absence of each indicator is recorded by 2 observers at 30-second intervals during the interview.

7942
Vocational Adjustment Rating Scale. Daniels, Lloyd K.; Stewart, James A. 1971
Descriptors: Adults; Behavior Rating Scales; *Mental Retardation; Sheltered Workshops; *Vocational Adjustment; Vocational Education
Availability: American Institute for Mental Studies; The Training School Bulletin; v69 n2, Aug 1972
Target Audience: 18-64
Designed to assess vocational adjustment of potentially employable mentally retarded adults engaged in vocational adjustment training. Traits of vocational adjustment are defined as direct or indirect. The worker traits also indicate the direction of scoring as positive or negative. A 62-item scale composed of 39 "directly" related items and 23 "indirectly" related items may be drawn from the 127 items originally developed.

7955
Personal Inventory. Hill, Harris E.; Monroe, Jack J. 1975
Descriptors: Adults; *Attitudes; Biographical Inventories; *Drug Abuse; *Drug Addiction; *Males; Personality Traits; Predictive Measurement; Psychotherapy; *Self Concept
Identifiers: *Drug Addicts; PI; TIM(D)
Availability: Tests in Microfiche; Test Collection, Educational Testing Service, Princeton, NJ 08541
Target Audience: Adults
Notes: Items, 220
Designed to measure personality and drug-related experiences of opiate addicts, with the intent of predicting their suitability for psychotherapy. The items cover personality characteristics, drug preference, effect of drugs on personal experiences, and history of use.

7956
Inventory of Habits and Attitudes. Monroe, Jack J.; Hill, Harris E. 1970
Descriptors: Adults; *Alcoholism; *Attitude Measures; *Attitudes; Biographical Inventories; *Males; Personality Traits
Identifiers: *Alcoholism Questionnaire; IHA; TIM(D)
Availability: Tests in Microfiche; Test Collection, Educational Testing Service, Princeton, NJ 08541
Target Audience: Adults
Notes: Items, 200
Developed for the evaluation and description of presumably stable characteristics of alcoholics. Covers experiences, sentiments, and attitudes concerning alcohol and alcoholics as well as a variety of demographic variables, personality, adjustment, familial relationships, and attitudes about treatment.

7957
Drug Association Test. Haertzen, Charles A. 1973
Descriptors: *Adults; *Drug Abuse; Drug Addiction; Multiple Choice Tests
Identifiers: *Drug Addicts
Availability: Dr. Charles A. Haertzen; NIDA Addiction Research Center, c/o Baltimore City Hospital, Bldg. D-5W, 4940 Eastern Ave., Baltimore, MD 21224
Target Audience: Adults
Notes: Items, 278
A word-association technique used in assessing drug habit strength. Opiate and heroin addicts were asked to indicate to which of 5 drugs they associated 278 words or sentences.

7962
Costello-Comrey Anxiety Scale. Costello, Charles G.; Comrey, Andrew L. 1967
Descriptors: Adults; *Anxiety; *Patients; Psychiatric Hospitals; Rating Scales
Identifiers: Psychiatric Patients; Self Report Measures
Availability: Journal of Psychology; v66 p303-13 1967
Target Audience: 18-55
Notes: Items, 14
Designed to measure a predisposition to develop anxious-affective states.

7963
Costello-Comrey Depression Scale. Costello, Charles G.; Comrey, Andrew L. 1967
Descriptors: Adults; *Depression (Psychology); *Patients; Psychiatric Hospitals; Rating Scales
Identifiers: Psychiatric Patients; Self Report Measures
Availability: Journal of Psychology; v66 p303-13 1967
Target Audience: 18-55
Notes: Items, 14
Designed to measure intensity of depression within clinical and normal populations. Developed to measure depression which would be independent of anxiety.

7970
Bender-Purdue Reflex Test. Bendix, Miriam L. 1976
Descriptors: Children; Educational Diagnosis; *Elementary School Students; Individual Testing; *Learning Disabilities; Learning Problems; *Motor Development; *Neurological Impairments; Observation; *Screening Tests
Identifiers: *Locomotor Patterns; Reflexes; *Symmetric Tonic Neck Reflex Immaturity; TNR
Availability: United Educational Services; P.O. Box 357, E. Aurora, NY 14052
Target Audience: 6-12
Motor test which assesses the presence and amount (level) of symmetric tonic neck reflex activity. Used for children, who are suspected of having learning disabilities, to deter-

mine the extent to which the unsuppressed tonic reflex interferes with the children's scholastic learning. The child is to watch a visual target while rocking or crawling backward and forward and while pushing or pulling against manual resistance. Requires a strip along which the child moves, knee pads, and the targets. An optional walking test may be added. Useful for screening those who need a motor training program, a program which will stimulate reflex maturation, develop correct motor patterns, and increase eye-fixation ability.

7971
Metropolitan Readiness Tests: 1976 Edition, Level I. Nurss, Joanne R.; McGauvran, Mary E. 1976
Subtests: Auditory Memory; Rhyming; Letter Recognition; Visual Matching; School Language and Listening; Quantitative Language
Descriptors: *Academic Ability; *Grade 1; *Kindergarten Children; Language Acquisition; Large Type Materials; Preschool Education; Reading Readiness; Reading Readiness Tests; *School Readiness; *School Readiness Tests; Visual Impairments
Identifiers: MRT
Availability: The Psychological Corporation; 555 Academic Ct., San Antonio, TX 78204-0952
Grade Level: K-1
Notes: Time, 95 approx.; Items, 76
Designed to provide a skill-based assessment of those underlying or enabling skills that are important for early school learning, particularly reading, mathematics, and language development. Level I is for use during kindergarten year and early grade 1 with groups judged to be at a relatively low level of skill development. Forms P and Q are available. An optional subtest, coping, is also available at this level. Test is administered in 7 sittings. Available in large-type print for visually impaired children from American Printing House for the Blind, 1839 Frankfort Ave., Louisville, KY 40206.

7972
Metropolitan Readiness Tests: 1976 Edition, Level II. Nurss, Joanne R.; McGauvran, Mary E. 1976
Subtests: Beginning Consonants; Sound-Letter Correspondence; Visual Matching; Finding Patterns; School Language; Listening; Quantitative Concepts; Quantitative Operations
Descriptors: *Academic Ability; Elementary School Students; *Grade 1; *Kindergarten Children; Language Acquisition; Large Type Materials; Primary Education; Reading Readiness; Reading Readiness Tests; *School Readiness; *School Readiness Tests; Visual Impairments
Identifiers: MRT
Availability: The Psychological Corporation; 555 Academic Ct., San Antonio, TX 78204-0952
Grade Level: K-1
Notes: Time, 105 approx.; Items, 97
Designed to provide a skill-based assessment of those underlying or enabling skills that are important for early school learning, particularly reading, mathematics, and language development. Level II is for use at the end of kindergarten and early in grade 1. The test can be administered in 5 sittings if optional quantitative tests are used. Administration can be completed in 4 sittings if quantitative tests are omitted. An optional coping test is also available. Forms P and Q are available at this level. Available in large-type print for visually impaired children from American Printing House for the Blind, 1839 Frankfort Ave., Louisville, KY 40206.

7975
Eysenck Inventario De Personalidad. Eysenck, H. J.; Eysenck, Sybil B. G. 1972
Subtests: Extraversion; Neuroticism; Lie
Descriptors: Adolescents; Adults; *Affective Measures; Emotional Adjustment; Forced Choice Technique; *Mental Health; Personality Measures; *Personality Traits; Psychological Testing; Questionnaires; *Spanish; *Spanish Speaking; Students
Identifiers: EPI; *Extraversion Introversion; Eysenck Personality Inventory; *Lie Scale
Availability: Educational and Industrial Testing Service; P.O. Box 7234; San Diego, CA 92107
Target Audience: 14-64
Notes: Time, 10 approx.; Items, 57
Measures 2 independent dimensions of personality: (1) extraversion-introversion; and (2) neuroticism-stability. Each of these traits is measured by 24 questions to which the respondent must answer either yes or no. A response distortion (Lie Scale) is also included to detect attempts to falsify responses. Forms A and B available. Also available in English (TC003239). Although test is in Spanish, the manual and other related material are in English.

7976
Employee Aptitude Survey: Prueba 2—Habilidad Numerica. Grimsley, G.; And Others 1969
Subtests: Integers; Decimals; Fractions

Descriptors: Adults; *Aptitude Tests; Career Choice; Career Counseling; College Students; Computation; Employees; Employment Potential; *High School Seniors; *Job Applicants; Job Placement; Job Skills; Mathematics; Multiple Choice Tests; *Occupational Tests; *Mathematics Tests; *Spanish; Spanish Speaking; Timed Tests; Vocational Aptitude; Vocational Education
Identifiers: EAS; *Mathematical Aptitude; Number Operation
Availability: Psychological Services, Inc.; 3450 Wilshire Blvd., Ste. 1200, Los Angeles, CA 90010
Target Audience: 17-64
Notes: Time, 10; Items, 75

A battery of 3 tests, integers, decimal fractions, and common fractions, each is timed separately. Designed to measure skill in the 4 basic operations of addition, subtraction, multiplication, and division. Also measures the ability to work easily with numbers and to do arithmetic fast and accurately. Executives, supervisory engineering, accounting, sales, and many types of clerical jobs require good ability in this area. Also available in English. Scoring is the number right minus 1/4 the wrong answers.

7977
Employee Aptitude Survey: Prueba 3—Continuidad Visual. Grimsley, G.; And Others 1969
Descriptors: Adults; *Aptitude Tests; Career Choice; Career Counseling; College Students; Employees; Employment Potential; *High School Seniors; *Job Applicants; Job Placement; Job Skills; Occupational Tests; *Perceptual Motor Learning; *Spanish; Spanish Speaking; Timed Tests; *Visual Discrimination; Visual Measures; Vocational Aptitude; Vocational Education
Identifiers: EAS; *Visual Pursuit
Availability: Psychological Services, Inc.; 3450 Wilshire Blvd., Ste. 1200, Los Angeles, CA 90010
Target Audience: 17-64
Notes: Time, 5; Items, 30

Designed to measure the ability to make rapid scanning movements of the eyes without being distracted by other, irrelevant visual stimulation. Involves the visual tracing of lines through an entangled network. Must be done with speed and accuracy. According to the authors, this is a special type of perceptual ability which is valuable for draftsmen, design engineers, engineering drawing checkers, electronic technicians, and other personnel who work with complex schematic diagrams. The prototype of this test was the Pursuit subtest of the MacQuarries Tests for Mechanical Ability (1925). Comes in both English and Spanish.

7978
Employee Aptitude Survey: Prueba 4—Rapidez Y Precision Visual. Grimsley, G.; And Others 1969
Descriptors: Adults; *Aptitude Tests; Career Choice; Career Counseling; Clerical Workers; College Students; Employees; Employment Potential; *High School Seniors; *Job Applicants; Job Placement; Job Skills; *Occupational Tests; *Spanish; Spanish Speaking; Timed Tests; *Visual Discrimination; Vocational Aptitude; Vocational Education
Identifiers: Clerical Aptitude; Clerical Skills; EAS; *Perceptual Speed
Availability: Psychological Services, Inc.; 3450 Wilshire Blvd., Ste. 1200, Los Angeles, CA 90010
Target Audience: 17-64
Notes: Time, 5; Items, 30

Designed to measure the ability to see minute details quickly and accurately, as in performing visual inspection tasks and in handling routine clerical work. The authors feel that ability in this area is important for bookkeepers, accountants, general office clerks, typists, stenographers, operators of most types of office machines, and most sales, supervisory, and executive positions. The test consists of 2 columns of numbers; the respondent decides whether the number in the first column is exactly the same as the number in the second column. Comes in 2 English-language forms and in Spanish.

7979
Employee Aptitude Survey: Prueba 5—Visualizacion De Espacio (Forma a Rev.). Grimsley, G.; And Others
Descriptors: Adults; *Aptitude Tests; Career Choice; Career Counseling; Cognitive Ability; Cognitive Tests; College Students; Employees; Employment Potential; *High School Seniors; *Job Applicants; Job Placement; Job Skills; *Occupational Tests; *Spanish; Spanish Speaking; *Spatial Ability; Timed Tests; Visual Measures; *Visual Perception; Vocational Aptitude; Vocational Education
Identifiers: EAS
Availability: Psychological Services, Inc.; 3450 Wilshire Blvd., Ste. 1200, Los Angeles, CA 90010
Target Audience: 17-64
Notes: Time, 5; Items, 50

Designed to measure the ability to visualize forms in space and to manipulate these forms or objects mentally. The test taker is shown a group of numbered, piled blocks and must determine, for a specifically numbered block, how many other blocks touch it. The authors feel that this test is a requirement for draftsmen, engineers, and personnel in technical positions. They refer to space visualization as a strong component of mechanical aptitude. Comes in both English and Spanish.

7980
Employee Aptitude Survey: Prueba 6—Razonamiento Numerico (Forma A, Revisada). Grimsley, G.; And Others 1969
Descriptors: Adults; *Aptitude Tests; Career Choice; Career Counseling; Cognitive Ability; Cognitive Tests; College Students; Employees; Employment Potential; *High School Seniors; *Induction; Intelligence; *Job Applicants; Job Placement; Job Skills; *Occupational Tests; Mathematics Tests; *Serial Ordering; *Spanish; Spanish Speaking; Timed Tests; Vocational Aptitude; Vocational Education
Identifiers: EAS; *Reasoning Ability
Availability: Psychological Services, Inc.; 3450 Wilshire Blvd., Ste. 1200, Los Angeles, CA 90010
Target Audience: 17-64
Notes: Time, 5; Items, 20

Designed to measure the ability to analyze logical relationships and to see the underlying principles of such relationships. This is also known as the process of inductive reasoning—making generalizations from specific instances. The authors feel that this ability is an important part of general intelligence and is a valuable ability in technical, supervisory, and executive positions. The test taker is given a series of numbers and determines what the next number will be. Scoring is the number right minus 1/4 the number wrong. Comes in 2 English Forms (A and B) and in Spanish.

7981
Employee Aptitude Survey: Prueba 7—Razonamiento Verbal (Forma a Rev.). Grimsley, G.; And Others 1969
Descriptors: Adults; *Aptitude Tests; Career Choice; Career Counseling; Cognitive Ability; Cognitive Tests; College Students; *Decision Making Skills; Employees; Employment Potential; *High School Seniors; *Job Applicants; Job Placement; Job Skills; *Logical Thinking; *Occupational Tests; *Spanish; Spanish Speaking; Timed Tests; Verbal Tests; Vocational Aptitude; Vocational Education
Identifiers: EAS; Reasoning; *Reasoning Ability
Availability: Psychological Services, Inc.; 3450 Wilshire Blvd., Ste. 1200, Los Angeles, CA 90010
Target Audience: 17-64
Notes: Time, 5; Items, 30

Designed to measure the ability to analyze verbally stated facts and to make valid judgments on the basis of the logical implications of such facts; and thus, the ability to analyze available information to make practical decisions. An important feature of the test is the measurement of the ability to determine whether the available facts provide sufficient information to draw a definite conclusion. The authors recommend this ability for executive, administrative, supervisory, scientific, accounting, and technical maintenance personnel. Scoring is the number of right answers minus 1/2 the wrong answers. Comes in both English and Spanish.

7982
Employee Aptitude Survey: Prueba 9—De Movimientos Manuales. Psychological Services, Inc., Los Angeles, CA 1969
Descriptors: Adults; *Aptitude Tests; Career Choice; Career Counseling; College Students; Employees; Employment Potential; *Eye Hand Coordination; *High School Seniors; *Job Applicants; Job Placement; Job Skills; Occupational Tests; Performance Tests; Psychomotor Skills; *Spanish; Spanish Speaking; Timed Tests; Vocational Aptitude; Vocational Education
Identifiers: Clerical Aptitude; Clerical Skills; EAS; *Manual Dexterity
Availability: Psychological Services, Inc.; 3450 Wilshire Blvd., Ste. 1200, Los Angeles, CA 90010
Target Audience: 17-64
Notes: Time, 5; Items, 750

Designed to measure the ability to make rapid and precise movements with the hands and fingers. Also measures, according to the authors, the temperamental willingness to perform highly repetitive, routine, and monotonous work. Recommended for office workers involved with filing and the operation of many kinds of office machines, and for such personnel as dental technicians, watch repairmen, and similar precision jobs that require fine finger movements. The test taker is to put a pencil dot in as many circles as possible in 5 minutes, without letting the dots touch the sides of the small circles. Comes with English or Spanish instructions.

7983
Employee Aptitude Survey: Prueba 10—Razonamiento Simbolico (Forma A). Ruch, F. L.; Ford, J. S. 1969
Descriptors: *Abstract Reasoning; Adults; *Aptitude Tests; Career Choice; Career Counseling; Cognitive Ability; Cognitive Tests; College Students; Employees; Employment Potential; *High School Seniors; *Job Applicants; Job Placement; Job Skills; *Logical Thinking; Occupational Tests; *Spanish; Spanish Speaking; Timed Tests; Vocational Aptitude; Vocational Education
Identifiers: EAS; Reasoning Ability
Availability: Psychological Services, Inc.; 3450 Wilshire Blvd., Ste. 1200, Los Angeles, CA 90010
Target Audience: 17-64
Notes: Time, 5; Items, 30

Designed to measure the ability to think and reason abstractly, using symbols rather than words or numbers; to manipulate abstract symbols mentally; and to make judgments and decisions which are logical and valid. Each problem contains a statement and a conclusion and uses certain symbols such as the equal sign and mathematical symbols for greater than and smaller than, etc. The test taker determines whether the conclusion is definitely true, definitely false, or impossible to determine on the basis of the statement. Scoring is the number of right answers minus 1/2 the wrong answers. Comes in 2 English-language forms and in Spanish.

7986
Tests of Adult Basic Education, 1976 Edition, Level E (Easy). CTB/McGraw-Hill, Monterey, CA 1978
Subtests: Vocabulary; Comprehension; Computation; Concepts; Problems
Descriptors: Achievement Tests; *Adult Basic Education; Adults; Computation; *Equivalency Tests; Mathematical Concepts; *Mathematics; *Reading Comprehension; Vocabulary
Identifiers: TABE 76E
Availability: CTB/McGraw-Hill; Del Monte Research Park, Monterey, CA 93940
Target Audience: 18-64
Notes: Time, 88; Items, 202

Measures adult proficiency in the basic skills of reading, mathematics, and language. Evaluates needs of adults who wish to undertake vocational-technical training or general literacy and self-improvement study. Adapted from Level 2 of California Achievement Tests (CAT-70), grades 2.5-4.9. Forms 3 and 4 are available.

7987
Tests of Adult Basic Education, 1976 Edition, Level M (Medium). CTB/McGraw-Hill, Monterey, CA 1978
Subtests: Vocabulary; Comprehension; Computation; Fractions; Concepts; Problems; Capitalization; Punctuation I and II; Expression; Spelling
Descriptors: Achievement Tests; *Adult Basic Education; Adults; Computation; *Equivalency Tests; *Language Skills; Mathematical Concepts; *Reading Comprehension; Spelling; Vocabulary
Identifiers: TABE 76M
Availability: CTB/McGraw-Hill; Del Monte Research Park, Monterey, CA 93940
Target Audience: 18-64
Notes: Time, 149; Items, 331

Measures adult proficiency in the basic skills of reading, mathematics, and language. Evaluates needs of adults who wish to undertake vocational-technical training or general literacy and self-improvement study. Results help to establish level at which instruction should begin, as well as to identify individual's instructional needs in the basic skills. Adapted from Level 3 of California Achievement Tests (CAT-70), grades 4.0-6.9. Equivalent forms 3 and 4 are available.

7988
Tests of Adult Basic Education, 1976 Edition, Level D (Difficult). CTB/McGraw-Hill, Monterey, CA 1978
Subtests: Vocabulary; Comprehension; Computation; Concepts; Problems; Capitalization; Punctuation; Expression; Spelling
Descriptors: Achievement Tests; *Adult Basic Education; Adults; Computation; *Equivalency Tests; Language Skills; Mathematical Concepts; *Reading Comprehension; Spelling; Vocabulary
Identifiers: TABE 76D
Availability: CTB/McGraw-Hill; Del Monte Research Park, Monterey, CA 93940

Target Audience: 18-64

Notes: Time, 137; Items, 315

Measures adult proficiency in the basic skills of reading, mathematics, and language. Evaluates needs of adults who wish to undertake vocational-technical training or general literacy and self-improvement study. Results help to establish level at which instruction should begin, as well as to identify individual's instructional needs in the basic skills. Adapted from Level 4 of California Achievement Tests (CAT-70), grades 6.0-9.9. Parallel forms 3 and 4 are available at this level.

7989

Tests of Adult Basic Education, 1976 Edition, Practice Exercise and Locator Test. CTB/ McGraw-Hill, Monterey, CA 1978

Subtests: Practice Exercise; Locator Test

Descriptors: *Adult Basic Education; Adults; Mathematics; Multiple Choice Tests; *Screening Tests; *Test Wiseness; Vocabulary

Identifiers: TABE 76

Availability: CTB/McGraw-Hill; Del Monte Research Park, Monterey, CA 93940

Target Audience: 18-64

Notes: Time, 35 approx.; Items, 52

Designed to accomplish preliminary practice and screening. Practice Exercise usually requires about 20 minutes. If students have had some experience in taking tests, examiner may omit Practice Exercise. Locator Test requires approximately 15 minutes and is used to determine appropriate test level. Testing should be discussed in advance with students to stimulate their interest without arousing undue stress.

7990

Social and Prevocational Information Battery. Halpern, Andrew; And Others 1975

Subtests: Purchasing Habits; Budgeting; Banking; Job Related Behavior; Job Search Skills; Home Management; Health Care; Hygiene and Grooming; Functional Signs

Descriptors: *Daily Living Skills; Home Management; *Job Skills; *Mild Mental Retardation; *Money Management; Objective Tests; Secondary Education; *Secondary School Students; Self Care Skills

Identifiers: Oral Testing; SPIB

Availability: CTB/McGraw-Hill; Del Monte Research Park, Monterey, CA 93940

Grade Level: 7-12

Notes: Items, 277

Series of 9 tests measuring areas included in secondary educable mentally retarded (EMR) education. Tests vary in length from 26 to 36 items and require 15-25 minutes each to administer. Response format is true-false or picture selection so students are not penalized for reading deficiencies. Long-range goals assessed are employability, economic, self-sufficiency, family living, personal habits, and communication. Orally administered tests administered to groups not exceeding 20. A student adult ratio of 7 to 1 is recommended.

8002

Ilyin Oral Interview. Ilyin, Donna 1976

Descriptors: Adult Education; Adults; *Adult Students; *English (Second Language); Individual Testing; Interviews; *Oral Language; Secondary Education; *Secondary School Students

Availability: Newbury House Publishers; 54 Church St., Cambridge, MA 02138

Target Audience: 14-64

Notes: Items, 50

Designed for use with standard English-as-a-Second-Language (ESL) programs. Designed to measure ability to use English orally in response to hearing it, in a controlled situation. Student is not required to do any reading or writing.

8004

Test of Grammatically Correct Spanish/English. Las Cruces School District No. 2, NM 1976

Descriptors: *Achievement Tests; Bilingual Education; *Bilingual Students; Elementary Education; *Elementary School Students; *Grammar; *Spanish Speaking; Verbal Tests; *Writing Skills

Identifiers: *Oral Tests; TIM(C)

Availability: Tests in Microfiche; Test Collection, Educational Testing Service, Princeton, NJ 08541

Grade Level: K-6

Notes: Time, 22 approx.

Consists of both oral and written tests assessing grammar skills in English and Spanish. The tests cover vocabulary, sentence patterns, grammar, and usage.

8023

Test of Auditory Discrimination. Risko, Victoria 1975

Subtests: Initial Consonants; Initial Consonant Blends and Digraphs; Final Consonant Sounds; Final Consonant Blend and Digraph Sounds; Vowels; Auditory Blending

Descriptors: *Auditory Discrimination; *Auditory Perception; Auditory Stimuli; Auditory Tests; *Diagnostic Tests; Elementary Education; *Elementary School Students; *Individual Testing; Learning Problems; *Learning Readiness; Perception Tests; Reading Diagnosis; *Reading Difficulties; Reading Skills; Verbal Tests

Identifiers: Oral Tests; TAD

Availability: United Educational Services; P. O. Box 357, E. Aurora, NY 14052

Grade Level: K-6

Notes: Time, 45 approx.; Items, 180

Untimed, individually administered measure of auditory discrimination and blending skills. Includes the ability to distinguish between sounds within words and their position within words; to relate a sound or part of one word to another word; to identify spoken sounds at the beginning, middle, or end of words as being the same or different; and to identify and blend sound units with words. Used for diagnosis; includes activities for improving deficient skills. Used with nonhandicapped students and with those having reading problems.

8030

Bannatyne System: Early Screening and Diagnostic Tests—Phase II. Bannatyne, Alexander D. 1975

Subtests: Recall Vocabulary; Design Matching; Balance Test; Auditory Closure; Form/Motor Memory; Auditory Vocal Sequencing Memory; Dexterity Parallels; Spatial Form Recognition; Echo Words

Descriptors: *Diagnostic Teaching; Diagnostic Tests; Elementary School Students; Grade 1; *High Risk Students; Individual Testing; Intelligence Quotient; Language Skills; *Learning Disabilities; *Memory; *Preschool Children; Preschool Education; Preschool Tests; Primary Education; Spatial Ability

Identifiers: BS ESDT; Test Batteries

Availability: Learning Systems Press; P.O. Box 91108, Lafayette, LA 70509

Target Audience: 3-6

Notes: Time, 25 approx.

Designed to obtain an accurate diagnostic profile of the strengths and deficits of "at-risk," learning-disabled, and gifted students. Profile may be used in prescriptive planning of student's academic program. Assesses skills in reading, spelling, language, and spatial ability. Composite quotients may be derived for intelligence, language, or spatial ability.

8031

Jansky Screening Index. Jansky, Jeannette

Descriptors: Handicap Identification; *High Risk Students; Individual Testing; Kindergarten; *Kindergarten Children; Primary Education; *Reading Readiness; Screening Tests

Identifiers: Test Batteries

Availability: Matt-Jansky; 120 E. 89th St., New York, NY 10028

Grade Level: K

A test battery designed to identify children of kindergarten age who are at risk of failing in reading. Five tests in the battery are Picture Naming; Gates Word Matching; Bender Motor Gestalt Cards; Letter Naming; and Binet Sentence Memory.

8038

Parental Attitude Research Instrument (Glasser-Radin Revision). Glasser, Paul; Radin, Norma 1965

Descriptors: Adults; *Attitude Measures; *Child Rearing; Disadvantaged; Low Income; *Mothers; *Parent Attitudes; *Parent Education; Preschool Children; Rating Scales

Identifiers: Likert Scales; PARI; TIM(E)

Availability: Tests in Microfiche; Test Collection, Educational Testing Service, Princeton, NJ 08541

Target Audience: Adults

Notes: Items, 36

Revision of the original instrument for measuring child rearing attitudes by Schaefer and Bell was developed for use in a study of disadvantaged parents. Statements are evaluated on a 4-point, Likert-type forced-choice scale from strongly agree to strongly disagree.

8045

Speech Sound Discrimination Test. Peisach, Estelle; Victor, Jack 1969

Descriptors: *Auditory Discrimination; *Auditory Tests; *Disadvantaged Youth; Elementary School Students; *Grade 1; *Kindergarten Children; Primary Education; Speech

Identifiers: Institute for Developmental Studies; SSDT

Availability: Institute for Developmental Studies; Press Bldg., New York University, Washington Square, New York, NY 10003

Grade Level: K-1

A group administered speech sound test to assess speech sound discrimination ability of disadvantaged children. Instrument is also available from Estelle Peisach, Dept. of Art Therapy, Pratt Institute, 215 Ryerson St., Brooklyn, NY 11205.

8077

Stanford Diagnostic Mathematics Test: Blue Level. Beatty, Leslie S.; And Others 1976

Subtests: Number System and Numeration; Computation; Applications

Descriptors: Achievement Tests; Community Colleges; Computation; *Diagnostic Tests; High Schools; Junior High Schools; *Low Achievement; Mathematical Applications; *Mathematics Achievement; Number Systems; Mathematics Tests; *Secondary School Students; Two Year Colleges; *Two Year College Students

Identifiers: SDMT

Availability: The Psychological Corporation; 555 Academic Ct., San Antonio, TX 78204-0952

Grade Level: 8-14

Notes: Time, 90 approx.; Items, 117

Designed to identify instructional needs of students in grades 8-12 and community college with respect to basic mathematics. Most useful for students who are weak in mathematics. Two parallel forms, A and B, are available.

8078

Stanford Diagnostic Reading Test: Red Level. Karlsen, Bjorn; And Others 1976

Subtests: Auditory Vocabulary; Auditory Discrimination; Phonetic Analysis; Word Reading; Reading Comprehension

Descriptors: Achievement Tests; Auditory Discrimination; *Diagnostic Tests; *Elementary School Students; *Low Achievement; Phonetic Analysis; Primary Education; *Reading Achievement; *Reading Comprehension; Vocabulary

Identifiers: SDRT

Availability: The Psychological Corporation; 555 Academic Ct., San Antonio, TX 78204-0952

Grade Level: 1-3

Notes: Time, 110 approx.; Items, 206

Measures major components of reading process. Designed to diagnose weaknesses of low achieving pupils in grades 1.5 through 3.5. Areas assessed include auditory discrimination, phonics skills, auditory vocabulary, word recognition, and comprehension of short sentences and paragraphs. Parallel forms A and B are available. An optional practice test requires 20 minutes additional time.

8079

Stanford Diagnostic Reading Test: Green Level. Karlsen, Bjorn; And Others 1976

Subtests: Auditory Vocabulary; Auditory Discrimination; Phonetic Analysis; Structural Analysis; Reading Comprehension

Descriptors: Achievement Tests; Auditory Discrimination; *Diagnostic Tests; Elementary Education; *Elementary School Students; *Low Achievement; Phonetic Analysis; *Reading Achievement; *Reading Comprehension; Vocabulary

Identifiers: SDRT

Availability: The Psychological Corporation; 555 Academic Ct., San Antonio, TX 78204-0952

Grade Level: 2-5

Notes: Time, 125 approx.; Items, 232

Designed to measure auditory discrimination, phonetic and structural analysis, auditory vocabulary, and literal and inferential comprehension. Intended for use in grades 3 and 4 and with low-achieving pupils in grade 5 and beyond. Most useful in accurately assessing low-achieving pupils. Parallel forms A and B are available. Optional practice test requires an additional 20 minutes.

8080

Stanford Diagnostic Reading Test: Brown Level. Karlsen, Bjorn; And Others 1976

Subtests: Auditory Vocabulary; Reading Comprehension; Phonetic Analysis

Descriptors: Achievement Tests; *Diagnostic Tests; *Elementary School Students; Intermediate Grades; Junior High Schools; *Junior High School Students; *Low Achievement; Phonetic Analysis; *Reading Achievement; Reading Comprehension

Identifiers: SDRT

Availability: The Psychological Corporation; 555 Academic Ct., San Antonio, TX 78204-0952

Grade Level: 4-9

Notes: Time, 103 approx.; Items, 248

Measures phonetic and structural analysis, auditory vocabulary, literal and inferential comprehension, and reading rate. Designed for use in grades 5-8 and with low achieving high school students. Parallel forms A and B are available.

8081

Educational Goal Attainment Tests. Tuckman, Bruce W.; Montare, Alberto P.S. 1975

Descriptors: *Achievement Tests; Attitude Measures; *Bilingual Students; *Educational Objectives; Knowledge Level; *Needs Assessment; Secondary Education; *Secondary School Students
Identifiers: EGAT
Availability: Phi Delta Kappa, Center for the Dissemination of Innovative Programs; 8th and Union, Box 789, Bloomington, IN 47401
Grade Level: 7-12
Notes: Time, 100

Designed to assess educational goals common to many communities. The purpose of broad needs assessment is primarily program improvement; therefore tests were not designed for diagnosis of individual student performance. Test booklets are randomly distributed to students and are administered anonymously. Each student completes only one of 10 booklets. Spanish editions are available for all test booklets except English Language.

8083
Educational Goal Attainment Tests: Spanish Version. Tuckman, Bruce W.; Montare, Alberto P.S. 1975
Subtests: Arts and Leisure; Careers; Civics; General Knowledge; Human Relations; Life Skills; Reasoning, Self Test; Latin America
Descriptors: *Achievement Tests; Attitude Measures; *Bilingual Students; *Educational Objectives; Knowledge Level; Needs Assessment; Secondary Education; *Secondary School Students; *Spanish
Identifiers: EGAT
Availability: Phi Delta Kappa, Center for the Dissemination of Innovative Programs; 8th and Union, Box 789, Bloomington, IN 47401
Grade Level: 7-12
Notes: Time, 100 approx.

Designed to assess the broad range of educational goals common to many communities. Tests were designed for program improvement rather than for diagnosis of individual student performance. Test booklets are randomly distributed to students, and they do not identify themselves on test booklets. Spanish-speaking students should have both Spanish and English versions unless they are clearly dominant in the use of one language.

8084
Kaufman Developmental Scale. Kaufman, H. 1974
Subtests: Gross Motor; Fine Motor; Receptive; Expressive; Personal Behavior; Interpersonal Behavior
Descriptors: *Child Development; *Children; Developmental Stages; *Diagnostic Teaching; Expressive Language; Individual Testing; *Mental Retardation; Psychomotor Skills; Receptive Language; School Readiness
Identifiers: KDS
Availability: Stoelting Co.; 1350 S. Kostner Ave., Chicago, IL 60623
Target Audience: 0-10
Notes: Items, 270

Designed to assess developmental behavior of normal children through age 9 and for mentally retarded individuals of all ages. Six developmental level modalities yield a Developmental Age (DA) and Developmental Quotient (DQ). Developmental stages include infancy, early childhood, play age, middle childhood, early adolescence, and later adolescence and beyond. A prescription for teaching objectives may be formulated from the evaluation.

8090
Visual Discrimination Test. Wepman, J. M.; And Others 1975
Descriptors: Compensatory Education; *Diagnostic Tests; Individual Testing; Learning Disabilities; *Reading Readiness; Remedial Instruction; *Screening Tests; *Visual Perception; Young Children
Identifiers: Perceptual Test Battery (PTB)
Availability: Western Psychological Services; 12031 Wilshire Blvd., Los Angeles, CA 90025
Target Audience: 5-8
Notes: Items, 20

Test explores a child's ability to compare nonalphabetic forms demonstrating how well a child with auditory imperception can use his or her other major modality—visual perception—in compensatory or remedial education. The 6 perceptual tests may be used in combination as a Perceptual Test Battery consisting of Spatial Orientation Memory Test (TC007127), The Auditory Discrimination Test (TC007283), Auditory Memory Span Test (TC007285), Auditory Sequential Memory Test (TC007284), Visual Discrimination Test (TC008090), Visual Memory Test (TC008091).

8091
Visual Memory Test. Wepman, Joseph M.; And Others 1975
Descriptors: *Elementary School Students; Individual Testing; Nonverbal Tests; Pictorial Stimuli; Primary Education; Reading Difficulties; *Reading Readiness; *Short Term Memory; *Visual Measures; *Young Children
Availability: Western Psychological Services; 12031 Wilshire Blvd., Los Angeles, CA 90025
Target Audience: 5-8
Notes: Items, 16

Designed to measure ability to retain visually presented nonalphabetic forms in immediate memory. Verbal responses are not required. Students experiencing difficulty in this perceptual task may have problems in learning to read. Low score may indicate necessity of further evaluation.

8094
AAMD Adaptive Behavior Scale: Public School Version, 1974 Revision. Lambert, Nadine; And Others 1975
Subtests: Independent Functioning; Physical Development; Economic Activity; Language Development; Numbers and Time; Domestic Activity; Vocational Activity; Self-Direction; Responsibility; Socialization; Violent and Destructive Behavior; Antisocial Behavior; Rebellious Behavior; Untrustworthy Behavior; Withdrawal; Stereotyped Behavior and Odd Mannerisms; Inappropriate Interpersonal Manners; Unacceptable Vocal Habits; Unacceptable or Eccentric Habits; Self-Abusive Behavior; Hyperactive Tendencies; Sexually Aberrant Behavior; Psychological Disturbances; Use of Medications
Descriptors: *Adjustment (to Environment); Behavior Rating Scales; *Children; *Daily Living Skills; Developmental Disabilities; Elementary Education; Elementary School Students; Emotional Problems; Individual Testing; *Mild Mental Retardation; *Moderate Mental Retardation; *Social Adjustment
Availability: Publishers Test Service; 2500 Garden Rd., Monterey, CA 93940
Target Audience: 7-13

A 2-part scale designed to assess adaptive behavior of students aged 7-13 years. Part I is designed to evaluate an individual's skills and habits in 10 behavior domains considered important to the development of personal independence in daily living. Part II is designed to measure maladaptive behavior related to personality and behavior disorders. Designed to obtain information from teachers, parents, and other professional or paraprofessional school personnel who have had an opportunity to closely observe the child's behavior.

8095
AAMD Adaptive Behavior Scale for Adults and Children, 1975 Revision. Nihira, Kazuo; And Others 1975
Subtests: Violent and Destructive Behavior; Antisocial Behavior; Rebellious Behavior; Untrustworthy Behavior; Withdrawal; Stereotyped Behavior and Odd Mannerisms; Inappropriate Interpersonal Manners; Unacceptable Vocal Habits; Unacceptable or Eccentric Habits; Self Abusive Behavior; Hyperactive Tendencies; Sexually Aberrant Behaviors; Psychological Disturbances; Use of Medication; Independent Functioning; Physical Development; Economic Activity; Language Development; Numbers and Time; Domestic Activity; Vocational Activity; Self Direction; Responsibility; Socialization
Descriptors: Adolescents; Adults; Affective Behavior; *Behavior Rating Scales; Children; *Daily Living Skills; Developmental Disabilities; *Emotional Disturbances; *Mental Retardation; Observation; Older Adults; Personality Problems; *Social Adjustment
Availability: American Association on Mental Deficiency; Central Office, 2501 Connecticut Ave., N.W., Washington, DC 20015
Target Audience: 0-70
Notes: Items, 44

Behavior rating scale for mentally retarded, emotionally and developmentally disabled individuals, but can be used with other handicapped persons as well. Designed to provide objective descriptions and evaluations of an individual's adaptive behavior, to the social expectation of his or her environment. There are 2 parts to the scale. Part one is concerned with the evaluation of the individual's skills and habits important to the development of personal independence in daily living. Part 2 deals with the social expectations placed upon retarded persons, both in residential institutions and in the community, and is designed to provide measures of maladaptive behavior related to personalities and behavior disorders.

8105
Physical Fitness Test Battery for Mentally Retarded Children. Fait, Hollis 1967
Subtests: Speed; Static Muscular Endurance of Arm and Shoulder Girdle; Muscular Endurance of Leg and Abdominal Muscles; Static Balance; Agility; Cardiorespiratory Endurance
Descriptors: Adolescents; Children; *Measures (Individuals); *Mild Mental Retardation; *Moderate Mental Retardation; *Physical Fitness; Young Adults
Identifiers: Test Batteries; TIM(D)
Availability: Tests in Microfiche; Test Collection, Educational Testing Service, Princeton, NJ 08541
Target Audience: 9-20
Notes: Items, 6

Designed to measure physical fitness levels of retarded persons, aged 9 through 20, independent of intelligence factors. The test assesses speed, static muscular endurance of leg and abdominal muscles, static balance, agility, and cardiorespiratory endurance.

8106
School Behavior Profile: Revised. Balow, Bruce; Rubin, Rosalyn A. 1974
Subtests: Poor Control; Developmental Immaturity; Anxious-Neurotic Behavior
Descriptors: Anxiety; Behavior Rating Scales; Elementary Education; *Elementary School Students; Emotional Problems; Individual Testing; Maturity (Individuals); *Observation; *Screening Tests; Self Control; Social Behavior; Student Adjustment; *Student Behavior
Identifiers: SBP; TIM(C)
Availability: Tests in Microfiche; Test Collection, Educational Testing Service, Princeton, NJ 08541
Grade Level: K-5
Notes: Items, 58

Developed to aid the teacher and other school personnel in the effective identification of children with social and emotional problems. In this testing situation the teacher rates the student; the lower the score, the worse the child's behavior. Useful for identifying those students who are likely to require special attention such as placement in special programs, retention in grade, referral to school psychologist or social worker, remedial reading instruction, or individual tutoring. May also be used to assess the behavior of the child who has had problems and who is being returned to the regular classroom. Individually administered.

8175
Hall Occupational Orientation Inventory: Adult Basic Form. Hall, L.G.; Tarrier, Randolph B. 1976
Descriptors: *Adults; *Career Choice; Decision Making; Rating Scales; Readability; *Reading Difficulties
Identifiers: HALL; Maslows Hierarchy of Needs; Self Administered Tests; Self Scoring Tests
Availability: Scholastic Testing Service; 480 Meyer Rd., Bensenville, IL 60106
Target Audience: 18-64
Notes: Time, 40 approx.; Items, 110

Adaptation of Hall Occupational Orientation Inventory (TC009783) for reading-handicapped adults. A shorter inventory, world-of-work oriented, with controlled readability levels. Focuses on several job and personality characteristics. Scales assess values and needs, job characteristics, and worker-traits.

8266
Khatena—Torrance Creative Perception Inventory. Khatena, Joe; Torrance, E. Paul 1976
Subtests: What Kind of Person Are You?; Something about Myself
Descriptors: *Adults; Biographical Inventories; *Creative Thinking; Creativity Tests; *Gifted; Personality Traits; Secondary Education; *Secondary School Students; *Self Concept Measures; Student Placement
Identifiers: KTCPI; SAM; Test Batteries; WKOPAY
Availability: Stoelting Co.; 1350 S. Kostner Ave., Chicago, IL 60623
Grade Level: 7-12
Target Audience: 12-64
Notes: Time, 45 approx.; Items, 100

Designed to identify creative individuals. May be used to select individuals for participation in special educational programs or job assignments. Two biographical components may be administered independently or together as a test battery. "What Kind of Person Are You?" assesses acceptance of authority, self-confidence, inquisitiveness, awareness of others, and discipline imagination. "Something about Myself" assesses environmental sensitivity, initiative, self-strength, intellectuality, individuality, and artistry.

8276
Melvin-Smith Receptive Expressive Observation. Smith, Joan M. 1976

Subtests: Visual Vocal Tasks; Visual Motor Tasks; Auditory Vocal Tasks; Auditory Motor Tasks
Descriptors: Auditory Discrimination; *Diagnostic Teaching; *Diagnostic Tests; Elementary Education; *Elementary School Students; Individual Testing; *Learning Modalities; Perception; *Perceptual Handicaps; Short Term Memory; Visual Discrimination
Identifiers: Receptive Expressive Observation; REO
Availability: Academic Therapy Publications; 20 Commercial Blvd., Novato, CA 94947
Target Audience: 6-12
Notes: Time, 15 approx.; Items, 68

Designed to assess simple memory and memory coding across sensory channels among individual students. May also be used with adults. Yields an accurate estimate of student deficiencies in perceptual areas addressed.

8297
Motor Academic Perceptual Skill Development Checklist. Smith, Donna K. 1973
Subtests: Motor Skills; Academic Skills; Perceptual Skills
Descriptors: *Academic Aptitude; Behavior Rating Scales; Children; *Multiple Disabilities; Observation; *Perceptual Development; *Psychomotor Skills; Reading Readiness; *School Readiness; Visual Discrimination; *Young Children
Identifiers: MAP; TIM(D)
Availability: Tests in Microfiche; Test Collection, Educational Testing Service, Princeton, NJ 08541
Target Audience: 2-8

Designed to provide the teacher of multiply handicapped children with a behavior-oriented evaluation of the child's existing skills in the following areas: motor (gross motor, manipulative, self-care, exhibiting body awareness), academic (general readiness, communication, early skill development), and perceptual (visual discrimination, nonvisual discrimination). The checklist is completed through teacher observation of children as they are involved in classroom activities.

8298
Scientific New Uses Test. Gough, Harrison G. 1975
Descriptors: Adults; Creative Thinking; *Creativity; Creativity Tests; *Engineers; *Scientists
Availability: Journal of Creative Behavior; v9 n4 p245-52 Fourth Quarter 1975
Target Audience: 18-64
Notes: Time, 30; Items, 20

Designed to measure creativity of scientists and engineers. Examinees are asked to think of as many new scientific uses as possible for each of 20 items.

8299
Scientific Word Association Test. Gough, Harrison G. 1976
Descriptors: Adults; *Association (Psychology); *Creativity; Divergent Thinking; *Engineers; Projective Measures; *Scientists
Identifiers: TIM(E)
Availability: Tests in Microfiche; Test Collection, Educational Testing Service, Princeton, NJ 08541
Target Audience: Adults
Notes: Time, 10 approx.; Items, 200

Employs the word association technique to provide a measure of associational fluency and creative thinking in scientists.

8300
Generalized Contentment Scale. Hudson, Walter W. 1974
Descriptors: Adolescents; Adults; Attitudes; *Depression (Psychology); *Mental Health Clinics; *Patients; *Psychological Patterns; Psychological Testing; *Rating Scales
Identifiers: GCS; Patient Response Form; TIM(D)
Availability: Tests in Microfiche; Test Collection, Educational Testing Service, Princeton, NJ 08541
Target Audience: 12-65
Notes: Time, 5 approx.; Items, 25

Designed to monitor and evaluate client responses to treatment over time, the scale measures the degree or magnitude of nonpsychotic depression in individuals. Items elicit the respondent's feelings about a number of behaviors, attitudes, events, affect states, and conditions that are associated with depression. Part of a battery of tests intended to be administered periodically to enable therapists to monitor and evaluate their clients' response to treatment.

8301
Index of Self Esteem. Hudson, Walter W. 1974
Descriptors: Adolescents; Adults; Affective Behavior; *Mental Health Clinics; *Patients; Psychological Testing; Rating Scales; Self Concept; *Self Concept Measures; *Self Esteem
Identifiers: ISE; TIM(D)
Availability: Tests in Microfiche; Test Collection, Educational Testing Service, Princeton, NJ 08541
Target Audience: 12-65
Notes: Time, 5 approx.; Items, 25

Designed to reflect the extent to which persons (ages 12 and older) feel positive about themselves and their social interactions. It is intended to be administered at regular intervals to enable therapists to monitor and evaluate their clients' responses to treatment. Self-administered. One of a battery of 4 scales.

8309
Pennsylvania Assessment of Creative Tendency. Rookey, Thomas J. 1973
Descriptors: *Attitude Measures; *Creativity; *Curiosity; *Divergent Thinking; *Elementary School Students; Evaluative Thinking; Intermediate Grades; Rating Scales
Identifiers: PACT; TIM(D)
Availability: Tests in Microfiche; Test Collection, Educational Testing Service, Princeton, NJ 08541
Grade Level: 4-6
Notes: Items, 45

An attitude inventory developed to measure students' creative tendencies. Creativity is defined as the conception by an individual of an event or relationship which, in the experience of that individual, did not exist previously. The items were constructed in terms of 9 traits derived from a profile of the creative child: self-direction, evaluative ability, flexible thinking, original thinking, elaborative thinking, willingness to take risks, ease with complexity, curiosity, and fluent thinking ability. Five alternate forms of this test are included: Form 39, Form 19A, Form 19B, Form 13A, Form 13B.

8313
Performance Test of Activities of Daily Living. Kuriansky, Judith B.; Gurland, Barry J.
Descriptors: Cross Cultural Studies; *Geriatrics; Older Adults; *Patients; *Performance Tests; *Psychiatric Hospitals; *Self Care Skills
Identifiers: PADL; *Psychiatric Patients; TIM(D)
Availability: Tests in Microfiche; Test Collection, Educational Testing Service, Princeton, NJ 08541
Target Audience: Older Adults
Notes: Time, 20 approx.; Items, 16

An objective performance test measuring geriatric patients' functional independence in activities of daily living. It requires patients to demonstrate ability to perform tasks considered essential for functional independence. On the basis of scores, patients can be placed in one of 3 categories of self-care: independent, moderately dependent, and dependent.

8314
Interpretation Test. Watt, Norman F.; Benjamin, Thomas B.
Descriptors: Adolescents; Adults; Aphasia; Cognitive Processes; *Language Processing; *Linguistic Performance; Multiple Choice Tests; *Neurological Impairments; *Patients; *Psychiatric Hospitals; *Semantics
Identifiers: *Psychiatric Patients; TIM(D)
Availability: Tests in Microfiche; Test Collection, Educational Testing Service, Princeton, NJ 08541
Target Audience: 13-65
Notes: Items, 48

Measures certain forms of semantic confusion in interpreting the meaning of ambiguous words. The test consists of 48 items that require the respondents to choose which of 3 answers seems to be the best interpretation of the sentence they have just read. Each sentence contains a homograph for which more than one meaning is possible. Used to measure linguistic regression in aphasic, alcoholic, and schizophrenic patients.

8315
Repertory Test. Watt, Norman F.; Benjamin, Thomas B.
Descriptors: Adolescents; Adults; Cognitive Processes; *Language Processing; *Linguistic Performance; Multiple Choice Tests; *Neurological Impairments; *Patients; *Psychiatric Hospitals; *Semantics
Identifiers: *Psychiatric Patients; TIM(D)
Availability: Tests in Microfiche; Test Collection, Educational Testing Service, Princeton, NJ 08541
Target Audience: 13-65
Notes: Items, 24

Assesses knowledge of various meaning of homographs, which are words that have 2 or more semantically distinguishable meanings. For each item, the respondent is re-

quired to select from among 5 options the one closest in meaning to the stem word. The correct response is often an unusual meaning of the word and not the first meaning that comes to mind. Used to measure linguistic regression in aphasic, alcoholic, and schizophrenic patients.

8331
Creative Response Matrices Test. Vernon, Philip E. 1969
Descriptors: *Cognitive Processes; Cognitive Style; *Culture Fair Tests; Elementary Education; *Elementary School Students; *English (Second Language); *Logical Thinking; Nonverbal Tests
Identifiers: Oral Testing; TIM(D)
Availability: Tests in Microfiche; Test Collection, Educational Testing Service, Princeton, NJ 08541
Target Audience: 6-12
Notes: Time, 15 approx.; Items, 24

A general reasoning test developed for use with culturally different children who would understand instructions presented in oral (but not written) English and who are probably unfamiliar with the multiple-choice format. Each item involves the completion of a figural series. The test is intended to be self-instructing because the respondent learns the instructions by having earlier test items explained.

8336
Vocational Interest Inventory. Lokan, Janice J. 1969
Descriptors: *Disadvantaged; Foreign Countries; *High Risk Students; High Schools; *Interest Inventories; *Job Training; Low Achievement; *Noncollege Bound Students; Rating Scales; Semiskilled Occupations; Slow Learners; Trade and Industrial Education; *Vocational High Schools; *Vocational Interests
Identifiers: Canada; Likert Scales; Ottawa Board of Education (Ontario)
Availability: ERIC Document Reproduction Service; 3900 Wheeler Ave., Alexandria, VA 22304 (ED078012, 53 pages)
Grade Level: 9-12
Notes: Time, 15 approx.; Items, 30

Untimed instrument developed to identify suitable careers for vocational high school students with limited reading ability, from disadvantaged backgrounds, and who are low academic achievers. Measures vocational interest by having the subject indicate his or her preference of job tasks on a 4-point scale. Each task is represented pictorially and verbally with a 5th to 6th grade reading level. Used to place these students in the appropriate job training programs. Comes in 2 forms: a 30-item form for boys and a 28-item form for girls. Adapted from Freeberg's Test booklet on assessment of disadvantaged adolescents.

8346
Pictorial Test of Bilingualism and Language Dominance. Nelson, Darwin; And Others 1975
Subtests: Oral Vocabulary; Oral Language Production
Descriptors: *Bilingualism; *Bilingual Students; *Elementary School Students; English (Second Language); Grade 1; Grade 2; Individual Testing; *Kindergarten Children; *Language Dominance; *Language Tests; Preschool Children; Preschool Education; Primary Education; *Spanish; Spanish Speaking
Availability: Stoelting Co.; 1350 S. Kostner Ave., Chicago, IL 60623
Grade Level: K-2
Target Audience: 4-8
Notes: Time, 30 approx.; Items, 40

Designed to measure child's language development in English and Spanish (bilingualism) and to determine language dominance. Utilizes a series of pictures in which each picture depicts a single concept. Results are plotted on a Diagnostic Grid which categorizes a child as English Dominant, Spanish Dominant, Bilingual, Pseudobilingual, Language Deficient, and Suspected Mental Retardation or Language/Learning Disability.

8347
Key Math Diagnostic Arithmetic Test: Metric Supplement. Connolly, Austin J. 1976
Descriptors: Criterion Referenced Tests; *Diagnostic Tests; Elementary Education; *Elementary School Mathematics; *Elementary School Students; Individual Testing; *Metric System; *Mild Mental Retardation; Mathematics Tests
Availability: American Guidance Service; Publishers' Bldg., Circle Pines, MN 55014
Grade Level: K-6
Notes: Time, 40 approx.; Items, 31

Designed to assess student progress in metric measurement. May be used with Keymath Diagnostic Arithmetic Test. Items cover 5 instructional clusters: linearity, mass, capacity, area, and temperature. Especially useful for diagnosing academic deficits in children with learning disabilities. No upper age limit for remedial use.

8349
Pittsburgh Auditory Tests. Craig, Helen B.; And Others 1975
Subtests: Duration of Gross Sounds; Duration of Words and Phrases; Vowel Discrimination; Simple Vocabulary Discrimination; Sentence Discrimination; Transition Test; Intonation in Conversation; Simple Commands; 5 Syllable Sentence Test; 10 Syllable Sentence Test
Descriptors: *Adolescents; *Auditory Discrimination; *Auditory Tests; *Children; Elementary Secondary Education; *Hearing Impairments; *Individual Testing; Preschool Education
Identifiers: PAT; TIM(D)
Availability: Tests in Microfiche; Test Collection, Educational Testing Service, Princeton, NJ 08541
Target Audience: 2-18
A battery of tests designed to measure the specific auditory discrimination skills of hearing-impaired children from preschool through grade 12. Subtests should be selected appropriate to the age of child being evaluated and to concepts under investigation.

8350
Craig Lipreading Inventory. Craig, William N.
Subtests: Word Recognition; Sentence Recognition
Descriptors: *Adolescents; Adults; *Children; Communication Skills; Elementary Secondary Education; *Hearing Impairments; Lipreading; Preschool Education; Residential Schools; Verbal Tests; *Word Recognition
Identifiers: TIM(D)
Availability: Tests in Microfiche; Test Collection, Educational Testing Service, Princeton, NJ 08541
Target Audience: 2-15
Notes: Items, 57
Intended to aid in the assessment of the communication level of deaf children and adults. A word test is used to inventory selected phonemes and a sentence test to assess lipreading for more complete language patterns. Two forms of the test are available.

8359
Basic Inventory of Natural Language. Herbert, Charles H. 1979
Descriptors: *Bilingual Students; *Criterion Referenced Tests; *Elementary School Students; Elementary Secondary Education; English (Second Language); *Language Dominance; *Language Fluency; *Language Proficiency; Pictorial Stimuli; *Secondary School Students
Identifiers: BINL
Availability: CHECpoint Systems, Inc.; 1520 N. Waterman Ave., San Bernardino, CA 92404
Grade Level: K-12
A criterion-referenced language assessment system designed to measure language dominance, fluency, complexity of language, and language development or growth. Forms A and B are kits designed for grades K-6. Forms C and D are kits designed for grades 7-12. Computer scoring and analysis are available. Tests may be scored in 32 different languages. May be administered to groups or individuals. Found to be particularly useful in bilingual, English-as-a-Second-Language, and language development programs. Also used in speech and language remediation programs by therapists and language specialists.

8360
Situation Avoidance Behavior Checklist. Cooper, Eugene B. 1976
Descriptors: *Adolescents; *Adults; Behavior Patterns; Check Lists; *Children; Self Evaluation (Individuals); Speech Handicaps; Speech Therapy; *Stuttering
Identifiers: *Avoidance Behavior
Availability: Eugene B. Cooper; Chairman, Dept. of Communicative Disorders, P.O. Box 1965, The University of Alabama, University, AL 35486
Target Audience: 3-64
Notes: Items, 50
A checklist of 50 situations which a stutterer might wish to avoid. Client indicates which situations are of most concern.

8361
Concomitant Stuttering Behavior Checklist. Cooper, Eugene B. 1976
Subtests: Posturing Behaviors; Respiratory Behaviors; Facial Behaviors; Syntactic and Semantic Behaviors; Vocal Behaviors
Descriptors: Adolescents; Adults; *Behavior; Behavior Modification; *Check Lists; Children; *Diagnostic Tests; *Observation; *Prognostic Tests; Speech Evaluation; Speech Habits; Speech Therapy; *Stuttering
Identifiers: Personalized Fluency Control Therapy; PFC Therapy
Availability: DLM Teaching Resources; P.O. Box 4000, One DLM Park, Allen, TX 75002
Target Audience: 4-64
Notes: Items, 32
Part of the Personalized Fluency Control Therapy, a program of behavioral and attitudinal therapy, designed for stuttering modification in both children and adults. This instrument requires an observor to check each behavior that accompanies moments of stuttering. Used as an aid in identifying stuttering behaviors and in assessing behavior changes resulting from therapy.

8362
Stuttering Chronicity Prediction Checklist. Cooper, Eugene B. 1976
Subtests: Historical Indicators; Attitudinal Indicators; Behavioral Indicators
Descriptors: *Check Lists; *Children; *Observation; *Predictive Measurement; Speech Evaluation; *Speech Habits; Speech Therapy; *Stuttering
Identifiers: Personalized Fluency Control Therapy; PFC Therapy
Availability: DLM Teaching Resources; P.O. Box 4000, One DLM Park, Allen, TX 75002
Target Audience: 3-12
Notes: Items, 27
Part of the Personalized Fluency Control Therapy, a program of behavioral and attitudinal therapy, designed to modify stuttering in adults and children. This instrument aids in the differentiation between the spontaneous and the episodic child stutterer. To be completed by an appropriate adult.

8364
Client and Clinician Perceptions of Stuttering Severity Ratings. Cooper, Eugene B. 1976
Subtests: Client Perceptions; Clinical Perceptions
Descriptors: Adolescents; Adults; *Behavior Rating Scales; Children; *Interviews; *Observation; Self Concept; *Self Evaluation (Individuals); *Speech Evaluation; Speech Habits; Speech Therapy; *Stuttering
Identifiers: Likert Scales; Personalized Fluency Control Therapy; PFC Therapy
Availability: DLM Teaching Resources; P.O. Box 4000, One DLM Park, Allen, TX 75002
Target Audience: 9-64
Notes: Items, 7
Part of the Personalized Fluency Control Therapy, a program of behavioral and attitudinal therapy, designed to modify stuttering in adults and in children. This instrument, through an interview, is designed to elicit information on the severity of a person's stuttering based on the clinician's observations and the client's own perceptions. Uses a Likert-type scale.

8366
Stuttering Frequency and Duration Estimate Record. Cooper, Eugene B. 1976
Subtests: Answering Questions; Reciting Letters of Alphabet; Reading Paragraph
Descriptors: *Adolescents; *Children; *Diagnostic Tests; *Observation; Speech Evaluation; Speech Habits; *Speech Tests; Speech Therapy; *Stuttering
Identifiers: Oral Tests; Personalized Fluency Control Therapy; PFC Therapy
Availability: DLM Teaching Resources; P.O. Box 4000, One DLM Park, Allen, TX 75002
Target Audience: 9-16
Notes: Time, 40 approx.; Items, 40
Part of the Personalized Fluency Control Therapy, a program of behavioral and attitudinal therapy, designed for stuttering modification in both children and adolescents. This instrument requires the verbal responses of a stuttering subject, which is then recorded by the observor. Basically used to elicit information on the nature of the subject's stuttering.

8367
Psycho-Educational Battery. Pope, Lillie 1976
Subtests: Gross Motor Performance; Fine Motor Coordination; Awareness of Place and Time; Probe of Interests; Sight Words; Decoding and Reading Comprehension; Basic Reading Skills; Spelling; Concept Development; Ability to Classify and Language Usage; Auditory Memory; Auditory Word Discrimination; Speech; Handicapping Behavior; Helpful Characteristics; Physical Status and Appearance
Descriptors: Adolescents; Adults; Children; Cognitive Tests; *Diagnostic Tests; Educational Diagnosis; High Risk Students; Individual Testing; *Learning Problems; *Psychoeducational Methods; Psychological Characteristics; Psychological Evaluation; *Screening Tests; *Student Evaluation; Student Problems; *Students
Identifiers: Oral Tests; PEB
Availability: Stoelting Co.; 1350 S. Kostner, Chicago, IL 60623
Target Audience: 5-64
Designed to help improve educational planning for individual learners by providing performance data that enable the teacher to pinpoint the needs of the individual. Used for (1) early screening and identification of children who are likely to have learning problems, sometimes called high-risk children; (2) psychoeducational assessment of skills and deficits of children who cannot seem to handle the demands of kindergarten or the early grades; and (3) psychoeducational assessment of skills and deficits of learners of any age who seem to have difficulty with reading skills, etc. with a view to educational planning for remediation and avoidance of further problems. Available in 2 forms: Level Y for kindergarten through 6 grade; and Level O for grade 7 through adult years; subtests vary slightly for each form. In Form Y, the first section is a group, orally administered test. Those whose responses are inadequate, unusual, or questionable are further tested individually. Reading sections are the same as those in Deborah Edel's Informal Evaluation of Oral Reading.

8368
Inventory of Language Abilities. Minskoff, Esther H.; And Others 1972
Subtests: Auditory Reception; Visual Reception; Auditory Association; Visual Association; Verbal Expression; Manual Expression; Auditory Memory; Visual Memory; Grammatic Closure; Visual Closure; Auditory Closure and Sound Blending
Descriptors: Auditory Stimuli; *Elementary School Students; *Expressive Language; *Kindergarten Children; Language Proficiency; *Learning Disabilities; Primary Education; *Receptive Language; *Screening Tests; Verbal Ability; Visual Stimuli
Availability: Educational Performance Associates; 600 Broad Ave., Ridgefield, NJ 07657
Grade Level: K-2
Notes: Items, 132
Screening device for use by classroom teacher in identifying children with possible language-learning disabilities. Has a separate checklist for each of the language areas in the MWM Program for Developing Language Abilities, except for auditory closure and sound blending which are combined. Each of the checklists contains examples of everyday social and academic behaviors common in the lives of most children in the primary grades. Designed for use by teachers in primary grades and by teachers of special classes for handicapped children.

8369
Arithmetic Concept Individual Test. Melnick, Gerald I.; And Others 1972
Subtests: Seriation; Classification and Inclusion of Class; Rotation of Landscape; Conservation of Number; Perception of Differences in Length; One to One Correspondence
Descriptors: *Elementary School Students; *Individual Testing; *Mathematical Concepts; *Mild Mental Retardation; Primary Education; *Mathematics Tests; Young Children
Identifiers: ACIT; Piagetian Tasks; TIM(D)
Availability: Tests in Microfiche; Test Collection, Educational Testing Service, Princeton, NJ 08541
Grade Level: K-3
Notes: Time, 50 approx.; Items, 72
Based on Piagetian concepts, the test is designed to assess the process by which primary level educable retarded children handle quantitative relations and to diagnose why particular children do not progress in their arithmetic skills. It consists of tasks related to seriation, classification, class inclusion, differentiation of length and number concepts, one-to-one correspondence, conservation of number, and spatial relations. Individually administered. The test is intended as a followup to the group-administered Arithmetic Concept Screening Test (008370).

8370
Arithmetic Concept Screening Test. Melnick, Gerald I.; And Others 1974
Descriptors: *Arithmetic; Children; *Disadvantaged Youth; Elementary Education; *Elementary School Students; *Mathematical Concepts; *Mild Mental Retardation; Nonverbal Tests; Pictorial Stimuli; School Readiness; *Screening Tests; Student Placement
Identifiers: ACST; Oral Testing; TIM(D)
Availability: Tests in Microfiche; Test Collection, Educational Testing Service, Princeton, NJ 08541
Grade Level: K-6
Designed for placement and evaluation of educable mentally retarded children with respect to their arithmetic skills. The test items are arranged into 6 separate tests to reflect levels of difficulty. Major factors covered by the test include basic concepts, one-to-one correspondence, form and size discrimination, rational counting, more and less, visual clustering, before and after, identification of symbols, reversibility of addends, number sequence, rule of likeness, ordinal numbers, addition and subtraction facts, multiplication and division readiness, and money

concepts. Although developed for use with an EMR population, the test may also be appropriate for culturally different young children. Each of 6 tests requires approximately 30 minutes to administer.

8373
Matric Test of Referential Communication.
Greenspan, Stephen; Barenboim, Carl 1974
Descriptors: *Cognitive Development;
*Egocentrism; Elementary Education;
*Elementary School Students; Emotional Adjustment; *Emotional Disturbances; *Individual Testing; Nonverbal Tests; Residential Schools;
*Verbal Communication
Identifiers: *Piagetian Stages; TIM(D)
Availability: Tests in Microfiche; Test Collection, Educational Testing Service, Princeton, NJ 08541
Grade Level: 1-6

Assesses communicative egocentrism using a 3 X 3 matrix board and colored, geometric shapes. The child is asked to dictate instructions that would enable a hypothetical other child who is unable to see the subject's board to replicate a design that the subject has made on his or her matrix board. Scoring of these instructions provides a measure of the child's cognitive-developmental level in an area of functioning significant to Piagetian theory.

8375
Test of Language Development. Newcomer, Phyllis L.; Hammill, Donald D. 1977
Subtests: Picture Vocabulary; Oral Vocabulary; Grammatic Understanding; Sentence Imitation; Grammatic Completion; Word Discrimination; Word Articulation
Descriptors: *Elementary School Students; Expressive Language; Individual Testing; *Language Acquisition; *Language Handicaps; *Language Tests; Phonology; *Preschool Children; Preschool Education; Primary Education; Receptive Language; Semantics; Syntax
Identifiers: TOLD
Availability: Western Psychological Services; 12031 Wilshire Blvd., Los Angeles, CA 90025
Target Audience: 4-9
Notes: Time, 40 approx.; Items, 190

Developed upon a linguistic model of language to provide a standardized measure of children's language competencies as well as specific strengths and weaknesses. Used to identify children who have significant problems in understanding or using spoken language; to isolate specific types of language difficulty; and to serve as a basis for planning programs.

8378
Child Behavior Characteristics: Form 3. Borgatta, Edgar F.; Fanshel, David 1970
Descriptors: *Adolescents; *Behavior Development; *Behavior Rating Scales; *Children; Elementary Secondary Education; *Patients;
*Psychiatric Hospitals
Identifiers: CBC; *Psychiatric Patients; TIM(D)
Availability: Tests in Microfiche; Test Collection, Educational Testing Service, Princeton, NJ 08541
Target Audience: 7-17
Notes: Items, 115

Provides for the rating of the behavior of children ages 7 through 17. The 115 items can be divided into 27 component scores. These can be further consolidated into 16 component scores: alertness-intelligence, learning difficulty, responsibility, unmotivated-laziness, agreeableness, appetite, sex precociousness, overcleanliness, sex inhibition, activity, assertiveness, defiance-hostility, emotionality-tension, infantilism, withdrawal, and likeability.

8383
Quick Language Assessment Inventory. Moreno, Steve 1974
Descriptors: *Bilingual Education Programs;
*Biographical Inventories; Children; Elementary Education; *Elementary School Students; English (Second Language); *Non English Speaking;
*Preschool Children; Preschool Education;
*Screening Tests; *Spanish Speaking
Availability: Moreno Educational Co.; 6837 Elaine Way, San Diego, CA 92120
Target Audience: 2-11
Notes: Time, 1 approx.; Items, 11

Designed for use with children suspected of needing ESL instruction or those being screened for bilingual education. Provides information about a student's English- and Spanish-language background. Inventory may also be used with students whose native language is other than Spanish. Interviewer should substitute student's native language for Spanish in all questions.

8404
Burks' Behavior Rating Scales: Parent Form.
Burks, Harold F. 1975

Descriptors: Anxiety; Behavior Problems;
*Behavior Rating Scales; Disabilities; Elementary Education; *Elementary School Students; Junior High Schools; *Junior High School Students; Mild Mental Retardation; Parents; Prognostic Tests; Special Education
Availability: Western Psychological Services; 12031 Wilshire Blvd., Los Angeles, CA 90025
Grade Level: 1-8
Notes: Items, 110

Designed for completion by parents or teachers to record observed behavior. Used to identify behavior problems and facilitate differential diagnosis with special groups such as educable mentally retarded or educationally, orthopedically, speech-, hearing-handicapped persons.

8410
Flexibility in Finding Meanings Test. MacGinitie, Walter H.
Descriptors: Adolescents; Children; *Deafness; Elementary Secondary Education; Language Acquisition; *Verbal Tests; *Vocabulary; *Vocabulary Development
Identifiers: FFM; TIM(D)
Availability: Tests in Microfiche; Test Collection, Educational Testing Service, Princeton, NJ 08541
Target Audience: 9-20
Notes: Items, 100

Designed to measure the ability to shift conceptual sets to find an appropriate meaning for a multiple-meaning word. It is in the form of a vocabulary test in which the correct answer is embedded among other words that are associated with a different meaning. The respondent must be able to recognize word meanings in these misleading contexts. Developed for use in an investigation of the vocabulary development of deaf children. There are 3 forms of this instrument.

8429
Oral Vibrotactile Stimulation for Threshold Sensitivity Instrument. Fucci, Donald J.; Kelly, Dan H. 1972
Descriptors: Adolescents; Adults; *Articulation Impairments; Children; Discrimination Learning;
*Electromechanical Aids; *Hearing Impairments; *Sensory Experience; *Tactual Perception
Identifiers: *Tactile Tests; *Vibrotactile Stimulation
Availability: Dr. Donald Fucci; School of Hearing and Speech Sciences, College of Health and Human Services, Lindley Hall, Ohio University, Athens, OH 45701
Target Audience: 3-64

Designed to measure the vibrotactile stimulation of the tongue and the tongue's sensitivity to vibration. Based upon the theory that the tongue is the major articulatory organ. Thus the process of articulation involves an interaction between sensory and motor systems; this interaction is critical for the development of correct speech sound production. Used for evaluation of the lingual-tactile sensory feedback system in children, adolescents, and adults with speech and hearing handicaps. Requires the use of specialized equipment. Earlier versions of the equipment required the use of a tongue clamp, which was eliminated from the current model. The exact name for the equipment is never stated.

8432
Watts Articulation Test for Screening. Watts, Shirley Ann; Paynter, Earlene Tash 1971
Descriptors: *Articulation (Speech); *Articulation Impairments; *Individual Testing; *Pictorial Stimuli; *Speech Tests; *Visual Measures;
*Young Children
Identifiers: Oral Tests; WATS
Availability: Dr. Earlene Tash Paynter; Dept. of Speech And Theatre Arts, Texas Tech. University, Box 4266, Lubbock, TX 79409-4266
Target Audience: 3-8
Notes: Time, 3 approx.; Items, 28

An orally, individually administered instrument used to identify those children with articulation defects. Requires the use of a picture containing objects and colors that the child names.

8440
T.M.R. School Competency Scales: Forms I and II. Levine, Samuel; And Others 1976
Subtests: Perceptual-Motor; Initiative-Responsibility; Cognition; Personal-Social; Language
Descriptors: *Adolescents; *Behavior Rating Scales; *Children; *Cognitive Measurement; Competence; Elementary Secondary Education; Interpersonal Competence; Language Skills;
*Moderate Mental Retardation; *Perceptual Motor Coordination; *Student Evaluation;
*Student Responsibility
Identifiers: TMRSCS
Availability: Consulting Psychologists Press; 577 College Ave., Palo Alto, CA 94306

Target Audience: 5-17

Designed to provide evaluation of trainable mentally retarded students on school-related activities. Separate forms are available. Form I rates students from 5-10 years of age, divided into scales for ages 5-7 and 8-10. Form I has 91 items. Form II covers ages 11-17, divided into scales for ages 11-13, 14-16, and 17 and above. It contains 103 items. Sixty-six items are common to both scales. Competency ratings are to be based on cumulative experience with the student.

8443
Sapir Developmental Scale and Profile. Sapir, Selma G. 1968
Descriptors: Auditory Discrimination; Body Image; *Child Development; *Handicap Identification; Lateral Dominance; *Learning Disabilities;
*Screening Tests; Visual Discrimination;
*Young Children
Availability: Selma Sapir; Special Education-Learning Disabled, Graduate Programs, Bank St. College of Education, 610 W. 112th St., New York, NY 10025
Target Audience: 4-7

Designed to assess child's development in areas of perceptual motor skills, bodily schema, and language. Used to identify children who may have potential learning disabilities.

8452
Basic Motor Fitness Test. Hilsendager, Donald R.
Descriptors: Adolescents; Children; *Emotional Disturbances; *Mental Retardation; *Motor Development; *Neurological Impairments;
*Performance Tests; Physical Education; Psychomotor Skills
Identifiers: TIM(D)
Availability: Tests in Microfiche; Test Collection, Educational Testing Service, Princeton, NJ 08541
Target Audience: 4-18
Notes: Time, 40 approx.; Items, 32

Developed to evaluate the motor performance of emotionally disturbed, brain impaired, and mentally retarded children. The test was designed to be meaningful both with normal and handicapped children to provide a ready comparison of the latter with the former without bias induced by mental ability. Level I measures specific skills important to the successful performance of the everyday activities of normal children through age 5. Level II includes items that are based on the assumption of generality of physical performance.

8453
Language Assessment Battery: Level 1. New York City Board of Education, Brooklyn, NY; Office of Educational Evaluation 1976
Subtests: Listening and Speaking; Reading; Writing
Descriptors: *Bilingual Students; *Diagnostic Tests; *Elementary School Students; English (Second Language); Individual Testing;
*Kindergarten Children; *Language Proficiency; Language Tests; Primary Education; Spanish;
*Spanish Speaking
Identifiers: LAB
Availability: Riverside Publishing Co.; 3 O'Hare Towers, 8420 Bryn Mawr Ave., Chicago, IL 60631
Grade Level: K-2
Notes: Time, 10 approx.; Items, 40

Designed for use in New York City Public Schools to determine student's effectiveness in English and Spanish. Student is assessed for English competencies and compared against a monolingual English-speaking norm group. A Spanish version is used to determine whether child is more effective in Spanish than in English. Main purpose of battery is student classification. Spanish-language skills may be measured by using Spanish-language battery.

8454
Language Assessment Battery: Level II. New York City Board of Education, Brooklyn, NY; Office of Educational Evaluation 1976
Subtests: Listening; Reading; Writing; Speaking
Descriptors: *Bilingual Students; *Diagnostic Tests; Elementary Education; *Elementary School Students; English (Second Language);
*Language Proficiency; Language Tests; Spanish;
*Spanish Speaking
Identifiers: LAB
Availability: Riverside Publishing Co.; 3 O'Hare Towers, 8420 Bryn Mawr Ave., Chicago, IL 60631
Grade Level: 3-6
Notes: Time, 41 approx.; Items, 92

Designed to assess reading, writing, listening comprehension, and speaking in English and Spanish. Used for classification of students to determine whether their learning is more effective in English or Spanish. Spanish-language skills may be measured by use of the Spanish-language battery. All subtests are group administered with the exception of Speaking which is individually administered.

8455

Language Assessment Battery: Level III. New York City Board of Education, Brooklyn, NY; Office of Educational Evaluation 1976
Subtests: Listening; Reading; Writing; Speaking
Descriptors: *Bilingual Students; *Diagnostic Tests; English (Second Language); *Language Proficiency; Language Tests; Secondary Education; *Secondary School Students; *Spanish; *Spanish Speaking
Identifiers: LAB
Availability: Riverside Publishing Co.; 3 O'Hare Towers, 8420 Bryn Mawr Ave., Chicago, IL 60631
Grade Level: 7-12
Notes: Time, 41 approx.; Items, 92

Designed to assess reading, writing, listening comprehension, and speaking in English and Spanish. Used for classification of students to determine whether their learning is more effective in English or Spanish. Spanish language skills may be measured by use of the Spanish language battery. All subtests are group administered with the exception of the speaking test, which is individually administered.

8460

Incomplete Sentences Task. Lanyon, Barbara J. 1970
Subtests: Hostility; Anxiety; Dependency
Descriptors: *Anxiety; *Emotional Disturbances; *Hostility; Junior High Schools; *Junior High School Students; Personality Traits; Projective Measures; *Screening Tests
Identifiers: *Dependency (Personality); IST
Availability: Stoelting Co.; 1350 S. Kostner Ave., Chicago, IL 60623
Grade Level: 7-9
Notes: Items, 39

Designed to identify junior high school age children with emotional problems that might interfere with classroom learning. Three basic personality variables are assessed: hostility, anxiety, and dependency.

8468

Behavioral Characteristics Progression. Santa Cruz County Office of Education, CA 1973
Descriptors: *Adults; Basic Skills; Behavior Rating Scales; Communication Skills; Criterion Referenced Tests; Daily Living Skills; *Diagnostic Teaching; *Disabilities; *Elementary School Students; Elementary Secondary Education; Exceptional Persons; *Individualized Education Programs; Individual Testing; Interpersonal Competence; Learning Modules; Mental Retardation; Physical Disabilities; *Preschool Children; Preschool Education; Psychomotor Skills; Secondary School Students; Spanish; *Special Education; Student Educational Objectives
Identifiers: BCP
Availability: VORT Corporation; P.O. Box 60132, Palo Alto, CA 94306
Target Audience: 2-18

Developed as part of the Santa Cruz County Special Education Management Project. Nonstandardized continuum of behaviors in chart form. Twenty-four hundred observable behavioral characteristics are grouped into categories referred to as behavioral strands. Fifty-nine strands begin with most primary characteristics and progress through the complex characteristics which society considers appropriate or acceptable adult behaviors. Guide for special educators to be used as an assessment, instructional, and communication device. DBP Binder is used for individual assessment. BCP Observation Booklet may be used to assess up to 6 individuals. BCP Binder is also available in Spanish.

8469

Delco-Elfman Developmental Achievement Test: Clinical and Research Edition. Elfman, Rose Marks 1974
Subtests: Physical; Social; Intellectual; Visual-Motor Coordination
Descriptors: Behavior Rating Scales; *Child Development; *Child Development Specialists; *Disabilities; Individual Testing; Infants; Interpersonal Competence; Psychomotor Skills; Young Children
Identifiers: DEDAT
Availability: Delaware County Intermediate Unit; State Bldg., 6th and Olive St.s, Media, PA 19063
Target Audience: 1-6

Designed to evaluate child's present functioning levels. May be used to develop a descriptive educational prescription. Items are designed for ages 6 months to 6 years. May also be used for older children who function in this

age range. May require more than one testing session with children who are distractible or have a short attention span.

8477

Child Task/Social Relations Competence Scale. Thomas, George 1972
Subtests: Task; School Mate; Cottage Mate; Teacher; Cottage Parent
Descriptors: *Adolescents; *Children; *Elementary School Students; Elementary Secondary Education; *Institutionalized Persons; *Interpersonal Competence; Peer Relationship; *Secondary School Students; *Self Concept; Self Concept Measures
Identifiers: Effectiveness of Child Caring Institutions; TSRCS
Availability: Regional Institute of Social Welfare Research, Inc.; 455 N. Milledge Ave., P.O. Box 152, Athens, GA 30603
Grade Level: 3-12
Notes: Items, 46

One of a series of instruments developed for use in a research study on community-oriented care in children's institutions. Designed to measure children's self-concept and social relationship competence. A modified form of the instrument suitable for students in regular school settings in grades 3-8 consists of 37 items.

8483

PPP Copying Test. Levine, Eleanor; Fineman, Carol 1972
Subtests: Partial Letters (Straight Lines); Partial Letters (Curved Lines); Partial Numerals
Descriptors: *Children; Elementary Education; *Elementary School Students; *Eye Hand Coordination; *Handicap Identification; Individual Testing; *Learning Disabilities; Perceptual Handicaps; *Perceptual Motor Coordination; Performance Tests; Psychomotor Skills
Identifiers: Prescriptive Profile Procedure; TIM(D)
Availability: Tests in Microfiche; Test Collection, Educational Testing Service, Princeton, NJ 08541
Target Audience: 5-12
Notes: Items, 27

Developed in connection with the Prescriptive Profile Procedure for Children with Learning Disabilities, the test is intended to assess pure fine motor copying skills in an untimed task involving no memory function. The task may reveal reversals, orientations, and other indicators of perceptual motor dysfunction. It can be individually or group administered to children ages 5-12. Special allowances must be given for inadequate eye-hand coordination in children 8-years old and younger when scoring.

8488

Fargo Preschool Screening Test. Fargo Public Schools, ND 1975
Descriptors: Associative Learning; Compensatory Education; Individual Testing; Interpersonal Competence; Learning Problems; Mathematical Concepts; Memory; *Preschool Children; *Preschool Tests; *School Readiness Tests; *Screening Tests
Identifiers: Elementary Secondary Education Act Title IV
Availability: Fargo Public Schools; 1104 2nd Ave. S., Fargo, ND 58102
Target Audience: 4
Notes: Time, 15 approx.; Items, 42

Developed as part of the Pre-Kindergarten Prescriptive Teaching Program for Learning Disabled Children. Intended to identify preschool children with learning problems, covering 6 areas: associate skills, math concepts, memory skills, motor skills, sensory skills, and social responsiveness. During the 1974-75 and 1975-76 school years, the test was administered to all identified 4-year-olds in the City of Fargo (approximately 800).

8497

Group Visual-Motor Screening Figures. Kelly, George R. 1974
Descriptors: *Concept Formation; *Elementary School Students; *Eye Hand Coordination; *Language Handicaps; Primary Education; Psychomotor Skills; *Screening Tests; *Visual Perception
Identifiers: Kelly Test; TIM(D)
Availability: Tests in Microfiche; Test Collection, Educational Testing Service, Princeton, NJ 08541
Grade Level: K-3
Notes: Time, 25 approx.; Items, 5

Designed to identify those children who need individual diagnosis of visual perception and visual-motor expressive difficulties. The children are asked to label and copy each of 5 figures. Because the figures are developmental in nature, if a child can copy them adequately after one demonstration, he or she does not require intensive developmental diagnosis or training. Follow-up evaluation with the Frostig test is recommended.

8501

Primary Grade Retarded-Trainable Children's Referral and Behavior Rating Form. Peterson, Rolf A.; And Others 1973
Subtests: Walking; Stairs-up; Stairs-down; Toilet Training-Soiling; Toilet Training-Wetting; General Toilet Behaviors; Eating Behavior-Motor; Drinking; General Language Use; Language-Response Behavior; Commands; Dressing; Socialization-Free Play; Eating Behaviors; Communication Behaviors; Response to Commands; Group Activity Behaviors; Individual Task Behaviors; Personal-Social Behaviors
Descriptors: *Behavior Problems; Behavior Rating Scales; Check Lists; *Developmental Disabilities; *Elementary School Students; Individual Development; *Moderate Mental Retardation; Primary Education; *Referral; *Special Education
Identifiers: Barker (Roberta A); PGRC Profile Form; PGRC Referral and Behavior Rating Form; TIM(E)
Availability: Tests in Microfiche; Test Collection, Educational Testing Service, Princeton, NJ 08541
Grade Level: 1-3
Notes: Items, 129

Developed as a way of quickly and accurately obtaining both developmental and behavior problem data from parents and teachers for referral agencies' use. Consists of 2 parts: (1) 82 statements, divided into 13 subparts, rating developmental level; and (2) 47 statements, divided into 6 groups, describing behavior ratings. The respondents check those statements that fit the child. The authors feel that this test can serve as a diagnostic guide by identifying the child's special needs, can be evaluated for the appropriateness of the referral, and does distinguish between the referral and the nonreferral cases. Also included is the P-G-R-C Profile Form developed by Roberta A. Barker and Rolf A. Peterson to plot developmental scores and record behavior problem scores.

8504

Global Baseline Checklist. Watson, Luke S. 1978
Subtests: Self Help; Motor Coordination; Undesirable Behavior; Language; Social-Recreation; Academic; Vocational
Descriptors: *Adolescents; *Adults; Antisocial Behavior; Check Lists; *Children; *Daily Living Skills; *Emotional Disturbances; Interviews; *Mental Retardation; *Older Adults; Psychomotor Skills; *Psychosis; Social Behavior
Identifiers: Global Evaluation Scale; *Psychiatric Patients
Availability: BMT; 1379 Sautern Dr. S.W., Fort Myers, FL 33907
Target Audience: 1-85
Notes: Items, 353

Interview procedure designed to provide an overview of an individual's behavior in several areas. Someone who knows the subject very well, such as a parent or psychiatric aide, is asked whether subject exhibits specific behaviors. Proficiency and progress in 7 behavioral skill areas are assessed.

8518

The Coleman Test of Visual-Perceptual-Motor Skills. Coleman, Howard M. 1975
Subtests: Writing Abilities; Body-Image Concepts; Number Sequences and Number Concepts; Visual Memory and Recall; Laterality and Directionality; Spatial Orientation; Brain-Eye-Hand Coordination; Graphesthesia; Stereopsis Testing
Descriptors: Body Image; *Disabilities; *Educational Diagnosis; Elementary Education; *Elementary School Students; Eye Hand Coordination; Individual Testing; Motor Development; *Perception Tests; Psychomotor Skills; Recall (Psychology); *Spatial Ability
Availability: Children's Perceptual Achievement Center, Inc.; 428 Pawtucket Ave., Rumford, RI 02916
Grade Level: K-6
Notes: Time, 20 approx.

Designed to reveal child with potential learning disabilities. Measures visual, perceptual, and motor development.

8523

Creativity Self Report Scale. Feldhusen, John F.; and Others 1965
Descriptors: *Creativity; *Creativity Tests; Higher Education; Secondary Education; *Secondary School Students; Self Evaluation (Individuals); *Undergraduate Students
Identifiers: CR; Survey
Availability: John F. Feldhusen; Purdue University-SCC-G, Educational Psychology Section, W. Lafayette, IN 47906
Grade Level: 7-16
Notes: Time, 15 approx.; Items, 67

Designed to assess creative behavior and attributes of students. Eight factor scores are applicable to junior and senior high school populations: self-descriptive items; socially conforming self-image; socially nonconforming self-image; dynamic, energetic aspects of self-image; fluency; diffidence in self-image; flexibility; global items. Six factor scores are applicable to college level populations: self-descriptive items; cognitive complexity, innovation, and curiosity; risk-taking, impulsive behavior; creative imagination; fluency; flexibility, global items. Instrument is titled "Survey" to avoid revelation of its purpose to examinee.

8527
Situation Exercises. Thurston, John R. 1964
Descriptors: *Behavior Problems; Elementary Secondary Education; *Emotional Adjustment; Individual Testing; *Psychological Evaluation; *Responses; *Situational Tests; Social Behavior; Stimulation; *Student Adjustment
Identifiers: Eau Claire County Youth Study WI; Feldhusen (John F); TIM(E)
Availability: Tests in Microfiche; Test Collection, Educational Testing Service, Princeton, NJ 08541
Grade Level: 3-9
Notes: Time, 16 approx.; Items, 4
Designed to help understand the behavioral and psychological nature of misbehaving children in the classroom. Calls for written responses—to write all the things that you can think the character in each situation might do or say to anyone—to the frustrations depicted in 4 situations. Each response of each item is scored individually and twice: (1) rated as maladaptive, adaptive, or indeterminate; (2) evaluated for his or her inner state of mind, the pressure imposed, and the nature of the child's need. The authors give a warning: use this test for diagnosing classroom aggression only with utmost caution. Part of a larger project, the Eau Claire County Youth Study.

8528
Kahn Intelligence Test: A Culture-Minimized Experience. Kahn, Theodore C. 1975
Subtests: Brief Placement Scale; Main Scale; Concept Formation; Recall; Motor Coordination; Sign Language; Scale for Use with Blind Subjects
Descriptors: Adolescents; Adults; *Blindness; Children; Concept Formation; *Culture Fair Tests; Deafness; Disadvantaged; Individual Testing; Infants; *Intelligence Tests; *Mental Retardation; Performance Tests; Retention (Psychology); *Sign Language
Identifiers: KIT EXP
Availability: Psychological Test Specialists; Box 9229, Missoula, MT 59807
Target Audience: 0-64
Designed to assess intelligence requiring a minimum of verbalization and no reading, writing, or verbal knowledge. Consists of a brief placement scale to determine entry into the main scale and special shorter scales to estimate ability in areas of concept formation, recall, and motor coordination. Special scales are suggested for administration by sign language and for testing sight-handicapped and blind persons. Distribution is restricted to psychologists, psychiatrists, counselors, and others with comparable training, as well as qualified researchers.

8535
Portage Guide to Early Education: Revised Edition. Bluma, Susan M.; And Others 1976
Subtests: Infant Stimulation; Socialization; Language; Self-Help; Cognitive; Motor
Descriptors: Behavior Rating Scales; *Child Development; Cognitive Ability; Daily Living Skills; *Diagnostic Teaching; Diagnostic Tests; *Disabilities; Infant Behavior; *Infants; Language Acquisition; *Preschool Children; Preschool Education; Psychomotor Skills; Social Development; *Spanish
Identifiers: PGEE
Availability: The Portage Project; P.O. Box 564, Portage, WI 53901-0564
Target Audience: 0-6
Designed to assess child's behavior in 6 developmental areas. May be used to plan realistic curriculum goals. Developed for use with preschool children with mental ages of birth to 6 years. Older children and adults with behaviors common to preschool children might also be assessed with the checklists. Behaviors are developmentally sequenced. Card file of suggested teaching activities for each behavior on the checklist. Available in English and Spanish.

8536
Dallas Pre-School Screening Test. Percival, Robert R. 1972
Subtests: Language Scale; Articulation Scale; Psychological; Auditory; Visual; Motor

Descriptors: Auditory Perception; *Handicap Identification; Individual Testing; Language Acquisition; *Learning Disabilities; Number Concepts; *Preschool Children; Preschool Education; Psychomotor Skills; *Screening Tests; Speech; Visual Perception; Vocabulary
Availability: Dallas Educational Services; P.O. Box 1254, Richardson, TX 75080
Target Audience: 3-6
Designed to discover learning disabilities in children 3 to 6 years of age. Measures developmental levels in 6 areas. Instrument is almost culture free.

8538
The Magic Kingdom: A Preschool Screening Program. Kallstrom, Christine 1975
Descriptors: Concept Formation; Diagnostic Tests; *Handicap Identification; Interpersonal Competence; Kindergarten; *Kindergarten Children; Language Acquisition; *Learning Disabilities; *Preschool Children; Preschool Education; Psychomotor Skills; *Screening Tests
Identifiers: Screening Programs
Availability: Red River Human Services Foundation; 15 Broadway, Ste. 510, Fargo, ND 58126
Target Audience: 3-6
Notes: Time, 90 approx.
Screening program for preschool children in several developmental areas. These include motor, visual, auditory, language, conceptual, and social-emotional. Designed primarily to identify children with special needs. Parents are involved in the screening process.

8541
Sequenced Inventory of Communication Development. Hedrick, Dona Lea 1975
Subtests: Receptive Scale; Expressive Scale
Descriptors: *Communication Skills; *Diagnostic Tests; *Disabilities; Expressive Language; Individual Testing; Infants; *Language Handicaps; Mental Retardation; Preschool Children; Receptive Language; Remedial Programs; *Young Children
Identifiers: SICD
Availability: University of Washington Press; P.O. Box 5569, Seattle, WA 98105
Target Audience: 0-4
Notes: Items, 210
Designed to evaluate communication abilities of normal and retarded children who are functioning between 4 months and 4 years of age. Useful in remedial programing of young child with sensory impairments, language disorders, and varying degrees of mental retardation.

8562
Dallas Pre-School Screening Test: Spanish Version. Percival, Robert R. 1972
Subtests: Auditory; Language; Motor; Visual; Psychological; Articulation
Descriptors: Auditory Perception; *Bilingual Teachers; *Handicap Identification; Individual Testing; Language Acquisition; *Learning Disabilities; Number Concepts; *Preschool Children; Preschool Education; Psychomotor Skills; *Screening Tests; *Spanish; Speech; Visual Perception; Vocabulary
Availability: Dallas Educational Services; P.O. Box 1254, Richardson, TX 75080
Target Audience: 3-6
Designed to identify learning disabilities in children 3 to 6 years of age. Spanish edition is identical to English except that pupil record form is in Spanish. Assumption is made that test administrators are bilingual.

8635
Hartford Scale of Clinical Indicators of Cerebral Dysfunction in Child Psychiatric Patients. Graffagnino, Paul N.; And Others 1968
Subtests: Related to Impulsivity or Direct Aggression; Related to Compensatory Adjustments against Impulsivity or Aggression; Obtained from Child's Early History
Descriptors: *Adolescents; Check Lists; *Children; Conceptual Tempo; *Neurological Impairments; Patients; Psychiatric Hospitals
Identifiers: Psychiatric Patients
Availability: Dr. Paul N. Graffagnino, Director; Child Psychiatric Services, Institute of Living, 400 Washington St., Hartford, CT 06106
Target Audience: 2-17
Notes: Items, 30
A rating scale of 30 symptoms which may indicate cerebral dysfunction or organic brain damage.

8639
El Inventario de Ayuda Para Aprendizaje: Forma Primario. Markoff, Annabelle 1976
Subtests: Destreza Social y Emocional; Comportamiento de Aprendizaje; Destrezas Fisicas; Destrezas de Languaje; Escuchar; Hablar; Leer; Deletrear; Escribir; Destrezas Aritmeticos

Descriptors: Arithmetic; Behavior Rating Scales; *Diagnostic Teaching; *Diagnostic Tests; Elementary School Students; Elementary School Teachers; Individualized Instruction; *Language Skills; Primary Education; Psychomotor Skills; *Spanish; Spanish Speaking
Availability: Learning Resources, Inc.; The Markoff School, 1810 Charing Cross Rd., San Mateo, CA 94402
Grade Level: K-3
Developed to aid teachers in observing children to facilitate individualized instruction. Designed to be used to set teaching goals directly from behaviors with which teachers are familiar. Items and teacher's manual are written in Spanish.

8640
Wist-Arnold Auditory Discrimination Test. Arnold, Richard D.; Wist, Anne Hope 1968
Subtests: Mexican-American Scale; Anglo-American Scale; Control
Descriptors: Audiotape Recordings; *Auditory Discrimination; Auditory Tests; *Disadvantaged; *Elementary School Students; Primary Education; *Spanish Speaking
Availability: Richard D. Arnold; Professor of Education, Purdue University, Lafayette, IN 47907
Grade Level: 1-3
Target Audience: 6-9
Notes: Time, 8 approx.; Items, 40
Designed to determine differences between disadvantaged Mexican-American and disadvantaged Anglo-American children in their respective abilities to auditorily discriminate between certain speech sounds. Instrument consists of 30 phonemes plus 10 like word pairs which serve as a control for validity.

8646
Behavior Rating Instrument for Autistic and Other Atypical Children. Ruttenberg, Bertram A. 1977
Subtests: Relationship to an Adult; Communication; Drive for Mastery; Vocalization and Expressive Speech; Sound and Speech Reception; Social Responsiveness; Body Movement; Psychological Development
Descriptors: *Autism; *Behavior Rating Scales; Children; Clinical Diagnosis; *Emotional Disturbances; Speech Evaluation
Identifiers: BRIAAC
Availability: Stoelting Co.; 1350 S. Kostner Ave., Chicago, IL 60623
Target Audience: 3-12
Designed to evaluate status of low-functioning, atypical, and autistic children by standardized behavior observation procedure. May be used with autistic children of all ages. Eight scales, each of which begins with the most severe autistic behavior and progresses to behavior comparable to that of a normal child ages 3.5 to 4.5.

8671
Triple Mode Test of Categorization. Silverman-Dresner, Toby R. 1966
Subtests: Functional; Associative; Superordinate
Descriptors: Adolescents; Children; *Classification; *Cognitive Measurement; Cognitive Processes; *Deafness; *Pictorial Stimuli; Visual Measures
Identifiers: Silverman (Toby R); TIM(D); Vygotsky (Lev S)
Availability: Tests in Microfiche; Test Collection, Educational Testing Service, Princeton, NJ 08541
Target Audience: 7-15
Notes: Time, 45 approx.; Items, 126
Based upon Lev S. Vygotsky's 3 major roles of categorization. Designed to reveal the ways in which deaf children categorize stimuli and to determine whether there are different developmental patterns in deaf vs. hearing children. Each item consists of 3 pictures; the child is to place the center picture (an object) into either the right or left picture, i.e., where he/she thinks the center picture belongs.

8674
Shutt Primary Language Indicator Test (Spanish-English). Shutt, D. L. 1976
Subtests: Listening Comprehension—Spanish; Listening Comprehension—English; Verbal Fluency—Spanish; Verbal Fluency—English; Reading Comprehension and Grammar—Spanish; Reading Comprehension and Grammar—English
Descriptors: *Bilingual Students; Cubans; Elementary Education; *Elementary School Students; English; Hispanic American Culture; Hispanic Americans; Individual Testing; *Language Dominance; *Language Fluency; Language Proficiency; *Language Tests; Listening Comprehension; Mexican Americans; Puerto Rican Culture; Puerto Ricans; Reading Comprehension; *Spanish; Spanish Speaking
Identifiers: SPLIT

Availability: McGraw Hill Book Co.; Webster Division, 1221 Ave. of the Americas, New York, NY 10020
Grade Level: K-6

Designed to assess the child's primary language proficiency. Items are appropriate for Cuban, Puerto Rican, and Mexican-American children. Listening Comprehension in Spanish and English and Reading Comprehension in Spanish and English must be administered as individual tests by bilingual examiners. The reading comprehension tests are suitable only for students in grades 3 to 6.

8676

Gallistel-Ellis Test of Coding Skills. Gallistel, Elizabeth; Ellis, Karalee 1974
Subtests: Giving Sounds for Letters; Reading; Spelling
Descriptors: Criterion Referenced Tests; Diagnostic Tests; Elementary Education; *Elementary School Students; *Handicap Identification; Individual Testing; *Learning Disabilities; Phonics; *Reading Skills; *Spelling
Availability: Montage Press, Inc.; P.O. Box 4322, Hamden, CT 06514
Grade Level: 1-6
Notes: Time, 35 approx.

Designed to measure coding skills in reading and spelling. Assesses child's ability to give sounds for various letters and units. Student's ability to recognize and spell words made up of these sounds is also measured. Useful in identification of children with learning disabilities.

8677

SORTS Test for Sampling Children's Organization and Recall Strategies. Riegel, R. Hunt 1976
Descriptors: *Classification; *Cluster Grouping; Concept Formation; *Elementary School Students; *Individual Testing; Learning Disabilities; *Learning Strategies; Mild Mental Retardation; Perceptual Handicaps; Primary Education; *Recall (Psychology); Visual Measures
Identifiers: SORTS Test (Riegel)
Availability: Montage Press; P.O. Box 4322, Hamden, CT 06514
Grade Level: K-3

Series of picture cards presented to a child with instructions to identify and sort animals/objects, to give reasons for groupings, to test recall and organizational skills. Not to be group administered or used with children with severe visual or physical handicaps; test requires good vision and physical coordination to handle cards.

8678

Micro Tower System of Vocational Evaluation. ICD Rehabilitation & Research Center, New York, NY 1977
Subtests: Electronic Connector Assembly; Bottle Capping and Packing; Lamp Assembly; Blueprint Reading; Graphics Illustration; Mail Sorting; Filing; Zip Coding; Record Checking; Message Taking; Want Ads Comprehension; Payroll Computation; Making Change
Descriptors: *Adolescents; *Adults; Aptitude Tests; Clerical Occupations; *Disabilities; Mathematical Concepts; Mental Retardation; Physical Disabilities; Psychomotor Skills; *Semiskilled Occupations; Spatial Ability; *Unskilled Occupations; Verbal Ability; *Vocational Aptitude; *Vocational Evaluation; Work Sample Tests
Availability: International Center for the Disabled; Micro Tower Research, 340 E. 24th St., New York, NY 10010
Target Audience: 15-64

A series of work sample tests designed to measure aptitudes required in unskilled and semiskilled jobs. Assesses motor skills, clerical perception, spatial perception, as well as job-related verbal and numerical skills. Designed for vocational guidance for clients in vocational rehabilitation programs, as well as for students.

8694

Ann Arbor Learning Inventory, Skill Level A. Bullock, Waneta B.; Meister, Barbara 1978
Subtests: Body Image; Visual Discrimination Skills; Visual Motor Coordination Skills; Visual Sequential Memory Skills; Aural Discrimination Skills; Aural Sequential Memory Skills; Aural Conceptual Skills
Descriptors: Auditory Discrimination; *Diagnostic Teaching; *Diagnostic Tests; Elementary School Students; *Grade 1; *Kindergarten Children; *Learning Disabilities; Perceptual Motor Coordination; Primary Education; Remedial Instruction; Screening Tests; Visual Discrimination
Availability: Ann Arbor Publishers; P.O. Box 7249, Naples, FL 33940
Grade Level: K-1

Designed to identify students with learning disabilities. Remediation programs are available for those students requiring them.

8696

Woodcock-Johnson Psycho-Educational Battery. Woodcock, Richard W.; Johnson, Mary B. 1977
Subtests: Picture Vocabulary; Spatial Relations; Memory for Sentences; Visual-Auditory Learning; Blending; Quantitative Concepts; Visual Matching; Antonyms and Synonyms; Analysis-Synthesis; Numbers Reversed; Concept Formation; Analogies; Letter Word-Identification; Word Attack; Passage Comprehension; Calculations; Applied Problems; Dictation; Proofing; Science; Social Studies; Humanities; Reading Interest; Mathematics Interest; Written Language Test; Physical Interest; Social Interest
Descriptors: *Achievement Tests; Adolescents; Adults; *Aptitude Tests; Children; *Cognitive Tests; Individual Testing; *Interest Inventories; Older Adults; Standardized Tests; Testing Programs
Identifiers: Antonyms; Quantitative Thinking; Synonyms; Test Batteries
Availability: DLM Teaching Resources; P.O. Box 4000, One DLM Park, Allen, TX 75002
Notes: Time, 120 approx.

Individually administered battery is composed of 27 subtests (over 877 items), divided according to 3 major areas of assessment: cognitive ability/scholastic aptitude, scholastic achievement, and interest level. Norms are provided from preschool to the geriatric level. Cassette recorder and stop-watch are required for portions of the test. Primary application is student evaluation. May also be used for vocational rehabilitation counseling and as a research instrument. Special feature: Part I subtests Quantitative Concepts and Antonyms-Synonyms, requiring about 15 minutes to administer and score, correlate highly with measures of intelligence as well as with school achievement.

8717

Spanish Oral Proficiency Test. Apodaca, Edwards; and Others 1971
Subtests: Oral Comprehension of Commands; Visual Oral Comprehension; Oral Comprehension of Common Verbs; Oral Questions
Descriptors: *Achievement Tests; Comprehension; Elementary Education; *Elementary School Students; *Language Fluency; Oral Language; *Spanish; *Spanish Speaking
Availability: National Hispanic Center/BABEL; 255 E. 14th St., Oakland, CA 94606
Grade Level: K-6
Notes: Items, 40

Comprehensive Spanish exam to measure oral comprehension and level of proficiency.

8787

Test of Oral Language Proficiency. Southwestern Cooperative Educational Laboratory, Albuquerque, NM 1976
Subtests: Vocabulary; Pronunciation; Structure
Descriptors: *Achievement Tests; American Indians; Elementary Education; *Elementary School Students; *English (Second Language); Individual Testing; *Language Proficiency; Language Tests; *Linguistic Performance; Pretests Posttests; Pronunciation; Spanish Speaking; *Syntax; Vocabulary Skills
Identifiers: SWCEL Test of Oral Language Proficiency
Availability: Southwestern Cooperative Educational Laboratory; 229 Truman, N.E., Albuquerque, NM 87108
Grade Level: K-8
Notes: Time, 25 approx.

Designed to assess performance of elementary school age children as speakers of English by eliciting verbal responses. Measures aspects of vocabulary, pronunciation, and syntactic structures. Useful with non-native speakers of English.

8788

Checklist of Characteristics of Gifted and Talented Children. San Francisco Unified School District, CA 1973
Descriptors: Check Lists; Elementary Education; *Elementary School Students; *Gifted; *Measures (Individuals); Observation; *Screening Tests; *Talent
Identifiers: Cummings (William B); TIM(E)
Availability: Tests in Microfiche; Test Collection, Educational Testing Service, Princeton, NJ 08541
Grade Level: K-6
Notes: Items, 31

A screening device intended to aid teachers in the identification and selection of students for inclusion in gifted programs.

8798

Visual Aural Digit Span Test. Koppitz, Elizabeth M. 1978
Subtests: Aural-Oral; Visual-Oral; Aural-Written; Visual-Written
Descriptors: Auditory Stimuli; *Diagnostic Tests; Elementary Education; *Elementary School Students; *Individual Testing; Learning Disabilities; *Memory; Mental Retardation; School Readiness; Screening Tests; *Short Term Memory; Visual Stimuli
Identifiers: VADS
Availability: Grune and Stratton; 111 Fifth Ave., New York, NY 10003
Grade Level: K-6

Designed to assess intersensory integration, sequencing, and recall and to serve as a diagnostic instrument for identifying learning disabilities in school-age children. Useful for students from end of kindergarten to grade 6. Useful as part of screening battery for school readiness.

8799

Hutt Adaptation of the Bender-Gestalt Test: Third Edition. Hutt, Max L. 1977
Descriptors: Adolescents; Adults; Children; Disadvantaged; Language Handicaps; *Mental Disorders; Mental Retardation; Neurological Impairments; *Nonverbal Tests; Patients; Pictorial Stimuli; *Projective Measures; Psychiatric Hospitals; Visual Perception
Identifiers: Bender Gestalt Test; HABGT
Availability: Grune and Stratton; 111 Fifth Ave., New York, NY 10003
Target Audience: 7-64

Designed for clinical use from the original Wertheimer experimental designs. Provides projective and objective data for a wide range of subjects. Hutt figures are more similar to the original Wertheimer (1921) figures than those of Bender (TC001313) and said by the author not to contain drafting irregularities that might influence the response. Used to estimate maturation and intelligence (children only) and psychological disturbance; to detect mental retardation, brain damage, and psychosis; to predict school achievement, intercultural differences, and the relationship between perceptual-motor behaviors and personality.

8804

Bruininks-Oseretsky Test of Motor Proficiency. Bruininks, Robert H. 1978
Subtests: Running Speed and Agility; Balance; Bilateral Coordination; Strength; Upper Limb Coordination; Response Speed; Visual Motor Control; Upper Limb Speed and Dexterity
Descriptors: *Adolescents; *Children; Individual Testing; Motor Development; Neurological Impairments; *Performance Tests; *Psychomotor Skills
Identifiers: Fine Motor Skills; Gross Motor Skills
Availability: American Guidance Service; Publishers' Bldg., Circle Pines, MN 55014
Target Audience: 4-14
Notes: Time, 60 approx.; Items, 46

Designed to assess a child's level of general motor development. Provides differentiated measures of gross and fine motor skills. May be used to assess neurological development and motor dysfunction. Short form consists of 14 items and yields a single general motor proficiency score. Requires approximately 20 minutes to administer and may be used to screen for motor performance.

8805

Quick Neurological Screening Test. Revised Edition. Mutti, Margaret; And Others 1978
Descriptors: Adults; *Elementary School Students; Elementary Secondary Education; Handicap Identification; Individual Testing; *Learning Disabilities; Motor Development; *Neurological Impairments; Psychomotor Skills; *Screening Tests; *Secondary School Students
Identifiers: QNST
Availability: Academic Therapy Publications; 20 Commercial Blvd., Novato, CA 94947
Grade Level: K-12
Target Audience: 18-64
Notes: Time, 20 approx.; Items, 15

Designed to assess 15 areas of neurological integration as they relate to learning. Measures maturity of motor development, psychomotor skills, motor planning and sequencing, sense of rate and rhythm, spatial organization, visual and auditory perceptual skills, balance and cerebellar-vestibular function, and disorders of attention. Recommended for administration by professional personnel. May be used with adults who have learning problems.

8820

Spanish Reading-Criterion Referenced Test: Kindergarten. National Hispanic Center/BABEL, Oakland, CA 1971

Descriptors: Criterion Referenced Tests; Group Testing; Individual Testing; Kindergarten; *Kindergarten Children; Primary Education; *Reading Readiness; *Spanish; *Spanish Speaking
Availability: National Hispanic Center/BABEL; 255 E. 14th St., Oakland, CA 94606
Grade Level: K

Designed to measure student's readiness skills for reading in Spanish.

8821
Spanish Reading-Criterion Referenced Test: First Grade. National Hispanic Center/BABEL, Oakland, CA 1971
Descriptors: *Beginning Reading; Criterion Referenced Tests; *Elementary School Students; *Grade 1; Primary Education; *Reading Skills; *Spanish Speaking
Availability: National Hispanic Center/BABEL; 255 E. 14th St., Oakland, CA 94606
Grade Level: 1

Designed to measure skills in beginning reading in Spanish. Areas assessed include initial, medial, and ending sounds; comprehension and word association; and objectives.

8822
Spanish Reading-Criterion Referenced Test: Second Grade. National Hispanic Center/BABEL, Oakland, CA 1971
Descriptors: Criterion Referenced Tests; *Elementary School Students; *Grade 2; Primary Education; Reading Achievement; Reading Comprehension; *Reading Skills; *Spanish; *Spanish Speaking
Availability: National Hispanic Center/BABEL; 255 E. 14th St., Oakland, CA 94606
Grade Level: 2

Designed to measure basic reading skills in Spanish. Skills assessed include phonics, vowels, word association, writing, word meaning, plurals, and comprehension. Objectives are outlined.

8823
Spanish Reading-Criterion Referenced Test: Third Grade. National Hispanic Center/BABEL, Oakland, CA 1971
Descriptors: Criterion Referenced Tests; *Elementary School Students; *Grade 3; Primary Education; Reading Achievement; Reading Comprehension; *Reading Skills; Spanish; *Spanish Speaking
Availability: National Hispanic Center/BABEL; 255 E. 14th St., Oakland, CA 94606
Grade Level: 3

Designed to measure basic reading skills in Spanish. Skills assessed include comprehension, vocabulary, syntax, inference, and alphabetical order. Objectives are outlined.

8833
The Selected Creativity Tasks. Abraham, Eugene C.
Subtests: Instances; Alternate Uses
Descriptors: *Creativity; *Creativity Tests; Divergent Thinking; Elementary School Students; *Grade 6; Individual Testing; Measures (Individuals); *Verbal Tests
Identifiers: SCT; TIM(E)
Availability: Tests in Microfiche; Test Collection, Educational Testing Service, Princeton, NJ 08541
Grade Level: 6
Notes: Items, 8

Designed to identify creative ability. Verbal responses are assessed according to the following criteria: fluency, flexibility, originality, and elaboration. The administrator asks the questions orally, and the child answers orally. The administrator records the answer exactly as stated.

8836
Seaman's Attitude Inventory. Seaman, Janet A.
Subtests: Social Aspects; Psychological Aspects; Administrative Aspects; Physical Aspects
Descriptors: *Attitude Measures; *Disabilities; *Elementary School Students; Grade 6; Intermediate Grades; *Physical Education; School Attitudes; Secondary Education; *Secondary School Students; *Student Attitudes
Availability: Educational Studies Center for Adapted Physical Education; Dept. of Physical Education, California State University, 5151 State University Dr., Los Angeles, CA 90032
Grade Level: 6-12
Notes: Items, 40

Designed to assess attitudes of handicapped students toward physical education instruction. Useful with students possessing a minimum reading level of 6th grade.

8839
A-M-L Behavior Rating Scale. Van Vleet, Phyllis P. 1978
Subtests: Aggressive-Outgoing; Moody-Internalized; Learning
Descriptors: *Behavior; Behavior Problems; *Elementary School Students; Elementary Secondary Education; Rating Scales; *Secondary School Students; *Student Adjustment; Student Behavior
Availability: Phyllis P. Van Vleet; 8545 Carmel Valley Rd., Carmel, CA 93923
Grade Level: K-12
Notes: Time, 30 approx.; Items, 11

Designed for completion by classroom teacher to identify students experiencing difficulties in school adjustment.

8847
CSL Profile Level 1. Chew, Laureen; Chung, May 1976
Subtests: Comprehension and Vocabulary; Sentence Structures
Descriptors: Bilingual Students; *Chinese; Elementary Education; *Elementary School Students; Individual Testing; *Language Proficiency; Language Tests
Availability: Chinese Bilingual Pilot Program; ESEA Title VII, San Francisco Unified School District, 950 Clay St., Rm. 204, San Francisco, CA 94108
Grade Level: 1-6

Designed to assess language proficiency in Chinese.

8868
Checklist for Kindergarten. Dade County Public Schools, Hialeah, Florida Dept. of Exceptional Child Education
Descriptors: *Check Lists; Creativity; *Gifted; Interpersonal Competence; *Kindergarten Children; Language Skills; Mathematics; Primary Education; Psychomotor Skills; Talent Identification
Availability: Dade County Public Schools; Coordination for Gifted Programs, 733 E. 57th St., Hialeah, FL 33013
Grade Level: K
Notes: Items, 27

Instrument designed to assist in the identification of gifted kindergarten students. The device in the form of a checklist permits teacher evaluation in the areas of language, psychomotor abilities, mathematics, creativity, and general characteristics.

8875
Revised Beta Examination, Second Edition. Kellogg, C. E.; Morton, N. W. 1978
Subtests: Mazes; Coding; Paper Form Boards; Picture Completion; Clerical Checking; Picture Absurdities
Descriptors: Adolescents; Adults; Aptitude Tests; *Cognitive Ability; Cognitive Tests; *Educationally Disadvantaged; Employees; Employment Potential; *Illiteracy; Job Applicants; Job Skills; *Nonverbal Ability; Nonverbal Tests; Spanish; Spanish Speaking; Timed Tests; Visual Measures; *Visual Stimuli; *Vocational Aptitude
Identifiers: Army Group Examination Beta; BETA II
Availability: The Psychological Corporation; 555 Academic Ct., San Antonio, TX 78204-0952
Target Audience: 13-64
Notes: Items, 210

Nonverbal measure of mental abilities; thus, useful with illiterate, non-English-speaking, or handicapped persons employed in unskilled jobs in industrial organizations. Revision of Army Group Examination Beta (1920). Also available in Spanish BETA (TC885031). Scores yield percentile rank and deviation IQ. Instructions in this version are also given in Spanish.

8885
Multi-Dimensional Aggression Scales. Abramson, Paul R.; And Others 1972
Subtests: Intensity; Agent; Directionality
Descriptors: *Aggression; Antisocial Behavior; Assertiveness; *Black Youth; Individual Testing; Interpersonal Relationship; *Parent Child Relationship; *Preschool Children; Preschool Education; Situational Tests; Violence
Availability: Paul R. Abramson; Dept. of Psychology, University of California, 405 Hilgard Ave., Los Angeles, CA 90024
Target Audience: 3-5
Notes: Items, 10

Designed to assess intensities, agents, and directions of aggressive behavior in response to a structured doll play interview.

8890
Canter Background Interference Procedures for the Bender Gestalt Test. Canter, Arthur 1976

Subtests: Bender Gestalt; Background Interference
Descriptors: Adolescents; Adults; Clinical Diagnosis; *Individual Testing; *Neurological Impairments; *Perceptual Handicaps; Perceptual Motor Coordination; *Performance Tests; *Screening Tests; Visual Measures; *Visual Stimuli
Identifiers: Bender Gestalt Test; Bender Visual Motor Gestalt Test; BIP
Availability: Western Psychological Services; 12031 Wilshire Blvd., Los Angeles, CA 90025
Target Audience: 12-64
Notes: Items, 16

Determines the presence of organic brain damage. After the Bender Test is administered under standard conditions, it is readministered with the subject drawing on paper filled with intersecting lines which provide visual interference. The purpose is to define a level of impairment on the Background Interference Procedure relative to performance on the Bender Test (first administration). Restricted distribution. Individually administered. Requires the use of specific set of cards.

8895
Prescriptive Reading Performance Test. Fudala, Janet B. 1978
Descriptors: Adults; *Diagnostic Tests; *Elementary School Students; Elementary Secondary Education; Individual Testing; *Reading Achievement; *Reading Diagnosis; *Reading Difficulties; *Secondary School Students; Spelling
Identifiers: PRPT
Availability: Western Psychological Services; 12031 Wilshire Blvd., Los Angeles, CA 90025
Grade Level: K-12

Designed to obtain quick assessment of reading level, determine grade level at which to begin testing for paragraph reading comprehension, and facilitate diagnosis of strengths and weaknesses in reading and word attack skills. Provides individual assessment of student reading and spelling performance and classifies patterns into normal and 3 atypical patterns suggestive of subtypes of developmental dyslexia. Graded word lists cover age and grade range from prereading readiness level through adult level.

8896
Southern California Postrotary Nystagmus Test. Ayres, A. Jean 1975
Descriptors: *Children; Diagnostic Tests; Elementary Education; *Elementary School Students; *Eye Movements; Individual Testing; *Learning Disabilities; *Neurological Impairments
Identifiers: SCPNT; Vestibular Stimulation
Availability: Western Psychological Services; 12031 Wilshire Blvd., Los Angeles, CA 90025
Grade Level: K-4
Target Audience: 5-9
Notes: Time, 5 approx.

Designed to evaluate the normalcy of the duration of nystagmus (involuntary, rapid, back and forth movement of the eyeballs) following rotation. This may indicate disorders in the vestibular system. Child is placed on the Nystagmus Rotation Board and passively rotated in each direction. Observer notes and records duration of nystagmus at the end of each rotation.

8900
Crisis Evaluation Form. Sinay, Ruth
Subtests: Crisis; Family; School; Peers; Drugs; Medical; Authorities; Sex
Descriptors: Behavior Problems; Counseling Techniques; *Crisis Intervention; Drug Abuse; Parent Child Relationship; Peer Relationship; Secondary Education; *Secondary School Students; Social Attitudes; Therapists; *Young Adults
Availability: Ruth Sinay; 1025 Carolyn Way, Beverly Hills, CA 90210
Grade Level: 9-12
Target Audience: 13-30

Designed for completion by therapist treating patient after referral for crisis behavior.

8906
Law Encounter Severity Scale. Witherspoon, A.D.; And Others 1973
Descriptors: Adults; *Behavior; Classification; *Criminals; Delinquency; *Records (Forms)
Identifiers: LESS; TIM(E)
Availability: Tests in Microfiche; Test Collection, Educational Testing Service, Princeton, NJ 08541
Target Audience: Adults
Notes: Items, 38

Developed for use in studies of postrelease behavior of exoffenders in the community; to validate the predictive abilities of behavioral assessment instruments used to measure postrelease adjustment; and to rank law encounters which have been verified by checking official court and arrest records.

8908
Weekly Activity Record. Jenkins, W. O.; And Others 1974
Descriptors: Adults; *Behavior; *Criminals; Delinquency; Predictive Measurement; *Recidivism; Rehabilitation
Identifiers: TIM(E); WAR
Availability: Tests in Microfiche; Test Collection, Educational Testing Service, Princeton, NJ 08541
Target Audience: Adults
Notes: Items, 18

Designed to predict criminal behavior and recidivism. It was developed for use in a longitudinal follow-up study of the released offender which emphasized effective intervention and treatment.

8913
Social Interaction and Creativity in Communication System. Johnson, David L. 1975
Descriptors: Audiotape Recordings; *Classroom Observation Techniques; *Communication Skills; *Creativity; *Elementary School Students; Elementary Secondary Education; Gifted; *Secondary School Students; Student Behavior; Teacher Student Relationship; *Talent Identification; Videotape Recordings
Identifiers: SICCS
Availability: Stoelting Co.; 1350 S. Kostner Ave., Chicago, IL 60623
Grade Level: K-12

Designed to identify and evaluate creativity, leadership, and communication skills through structured observation of teacher-student verbal interactions.

8915
Fait Motor Skill Test for Severely and Profoundly Retarded: Texas Revision. Denton, Richard 1978
Descriptors: *Behavior Rating Scales; *Elementary School Students; Elementary Secondary Education; Individual Development; Individual Testing; Measures (Individuals); *Performance Tests; *Physical Activity Level; *Physical Development; Physical Fitness; *Secondary School Students; *Severe Mental Retardation
Identifiers: Basic Movement Performance Profile; Fait (Hollis)
Availability: Fait, Hollis; Special Physical Education, New York: Holt, Rinehart and Winston, 1978
Grade Level: K-12

Measures physical fitness levels and basic movement performance ability of severely retarded students, independent of intelligence factors. Based on observation of the subject, the test administrator records the data on a rating scale. Adapted from Hollis Fait's Physical Fitness Test Battery for Mentally Retarded Children (TC008105).

8933
Creativity Checklist. Johnson, David L.
Descriptors: Classroom Observation Techniques; *College Students; *Creativity; *Creativity Tests; *Elementary School Students; Elementary Secondary Education; Higher Education; Rating Scales; *Secondary School Students; *Talent Identification
Identifiers: CCh
Availability: Stoelting Co.; 1350 S. Kostner Ave., Chicago, IL 60623
Grade Level: K-20
Notes: Time, 15 approx.; Items, 8

Designed to assess individual's creativity on the basis of observation by a teacher or someone else familiar with the subject's behavior. May be used in conjunction with Gifted and Talented Screening Form (TC008980).

8945
Literacy Assessment Battery. Sticht, Thomas G.; Beck, Lawrence J. 1976
Subtests: Paragraphs: Auding; Paragraphs: Reading; Vocabulary: Auding and Reading; Vocabulary: Reading; Decoding
Descriptors: Achievement Tests; *Adult Literacy; Adults; Aptitude Tests; Decoding (Reading); *Listening Comprehension; Listening Comprehension Tests; *Reading Ability; Reading Achievement; *Reading Comprehension; *Reading Diagnosis; *Reading Difficulties; Timed Tests; Vocabulary
Identifiers: LAB; Synonyms
Availability: ERIC Document Reproduction Service; 3900 Wheeler Ave., Alexandria, VA 22304 (ED129900, 166 pages)
Target Audience: Adults
Notes: Time, 50 approx.; Items, 101

Designed for adults who have a reading problem. Experimental battery of tests to determine the relative efficiency with which adults can comprehend language by reading or listening and gives estimates of discrepancies between the ability to aud (listen to speech) and the ability to read. The authors feel that information concerning auding/read-

ing discrepancies are useful in identifying the nature and extent of a reading problem, estimating reading potential and revealing the type of needed remedial training. Requires the use of a stopwatch and cassette recorder. Types of answer are short answer (filling in information), multiple choice, and encircling the spoken error.

8955
Visco Child Development Screening Test. Visco, Susan J.; Visco, Carmela R. 1978
Subtests: Fine Motor Skills; Gross Motor Skills; Visual Sequencing-Body Directions; Auditory Sequencing-Body Directions; Copy Figures; Perceptuomotor-Spatial Directions; Auditory Sequencing; Numerical Counting; Numerical Gestalt; Draw-a-Picture; Language; Articulation
Descriptors: *Elementary School Students; Individual Testing; Language Skills; *Learning Disabilities; Number Concepts; Perceptual Motor Coordination; *Preschool Children; Preschool Education; Primary Education; Psychomotor Skills; *Screening Tests
Identifiers: Piaget (Jean); The Childs Test
Availability: Educational Activities, Inc.; P.O. Box 392, Freeport, NY 11520
Target Audience: 3-7
Notes: Time, 30 approx.

Designed to identify children who are likely to experience significant difficulty with traditional school curriculum. Based on Piaget's stage theory of development and Osgood's communications model showing the child's efficiency in processing information.

8957
Bilingual Oral Language Test. Cohen, Sam; And Others 1976
Descriptors: *Bilingual Students; Elementary School Students; *English (Second Language); Individual Testing; Intermediate Grades; *Language Dominance; Language Proficiency; Language Tests; Oral Language; Secondary Education; Secondary School Students; *Spanish
Identifiers: Bahia Oral Language Test; BOLT
Availability: Bilingual Media Productions Inc.; P.O. Box 9337, N. Berkeley Station, Berkeley, CA 94709
Grade Level: 4-12
Notes: Time, 12 approx.; Items, 20

Designed to assess oral language skills in English or Spanish. BOLT-English and BOLT-Spanish are independent components of the same instrument. Each component requires 6 minutes to administer. When both components are used, the student's level of bilingualism may be assessed.

8967
Self-Appraisal Inventory, Primary Level, Spanish Version. Tilley, Sally D. 1976
Descriptors: Biculturalism; *Bilingual Students; *Elementary School Students; Primary Education; *Self Concept; *Self Concept Measures; *Spanish; Spanish Speaking
Availability: ERIC Document Reproduction Service; 3900 Wheeler Ave., Alexandria, VA 22304 (ED127362, 11 pages)
Grade Level: 1-3
Notes: Items, 36

A Spanish translation of the Self-Appraisal Inventory, Primary Level (TC006151). Designed to assess self-concept of multiethnic Spanish-speaking children.

8977
Verbal Peer Adult Emotional Scale. Streedbeck, Darlene; Hughes, Robert B. 1975
Subtests: Verbal Behavior; Peer Interaction; Adult Interaction; Emotional Behavior
Descriptors: Adjustment (to Environment); Behavior Rating Scales; *Children; Emotional Adjustment; Emotional Disturbances; *Institutionalized Persons; Interpersonal Relationship; Peer Relationship; *Severe Mental Retardation
Identifiers: VPAE
Availability: ERIC Document Reproduction Service; 3900 Wheeler Ave., Alexandria, VA 22304 (ED150162, microfiche only)
Target Audience: 2-9
Notes: Time, 30 approx.; Items, 16

A measure designed to assess progress of institutionalized severely maladaptive children. The behavioral categories assessed are verbal behavior, peer interaction, adult interaction, and emotional behavior.

8980
Gifted and Talented Screening Form. Johnson, David L.

Descriptors: *Academically Gifted; Creativity; Elementary Education; *Elementary School Students; Gifted; Intelligence; Junior High Schools; *Junior High School Students; Leadership; Psychomotor Skills; Rating Scales; *Screening Tests; *Talent Identification
Identifiers: GTSF
Availability: Stoelting Co.; 1350 S. Kostner Ave., Chicago, IL 60623
Grade Level: K-9
Notes: Time, 10 approx.; Items, 24

Designed to screen individuals and groups for gifted and talented school programs. Students are observed and assessed in talent areas of academics, intelligence, creativity, leadership, visual-performing arts, and psychomotor ability.

8983
Bilingual Syntax Measure II. The Psychological Corporation, San Antonio, TX 1978
Descriptors: Bilingual Students; Culture Fair Tests; Elementary Secondary Education; *English (Second Language); *Language Dominance; Language Proficiency; Spanish Speaking; Visual Measures
Identifiers: BSM II
Availability: The Psychological Corporation; 555 Academic Ct., San Antonio, TX 78204-0952
Grade Level: 3-12
Notes: Time, 15 approx.; Items, 26

An extension of the Bilingual Syntax Measure. Measures language dominance (Spanish or English), structural proficiency in English-as-a-Second-Language, and the degree of maintenance or loss of basic Spanish structures.

9016
Adjustment Scale. Carey, Raymond G. 1977
Descriptors: Adults; Counseling Techniques; Depression (Psychology); Emotional Adjustment; *Emotional Problems; Personality Measures; *Psychological Needs; Psychosomatic Disorders; *Widowed
Availability: Dr. Raymond G. Carey; Health Care Evaluation, Parkside Medical Services Corp., 1580 N.W. Hwy., Park Ridge, IL 60068
Target Audience: Adults
Notes: Items, 8

Designed for assessment of adjustment problems experienced by widows or widowers. May be used to determine whether physical complaints are possibly psychosomatic in origin. May also be used in counseling situations.

9039
Visco Tests of Auditory Perception. Visco, Susan J. 1975
Subtests: Attention to Auditory Stimuli; Sound versus No Sound; Sound Localization; Discriminating between Two Sounds; Discriminating Sound Patterns; Auditory Figure Ground; Associating Sound Sources
Descriptors: Audiotape Cassettes; Auditory Evaluation; Auditory Perception; Auditory Tests; *Diagnostic Tests; Elementary Education; *Elementary School Students; High Risk Students; Individual Testing; Nonverbal Tests; Primary Education; *Screening Tests
Identifiers: VI TAP
Availability: Educational Activities, Inc.; P.O. Box 392, Freeport, NY 11520
Grade Level: K-3
Target Audience: 5-14

Designed for use as an individual diagnostic instrument and as a group screening. May be used for screening purposes for kindergarten through grade 3 to identify children who are at high risk for academic failure because of auditory perceptual disorders. VI-TAP Individual Diagnostic Test may be used with children ages 5-14 to evaluate and diagnose disorders for prescriptive programming.

9044
System of Multicultural Pluralistic Assessment. Mercer, Jane R.; Lewis, June F. 1978
Descriptors: *Adjustment (to Environment); Auditory Perception; Biographical Inventories; Black Youth; Children; *Cognitive Ability; *Culture Fair Tests; Disabilities; Elementary Education; *Elementary School Students; Exceptional Persons; Hispanic Americans; Intelligence; Interpersonal Competence; Nondiscriminatory Education; Parents; *Perceptual Motor Learning; Physical Development; Physical Health; Psychomotor Skills; Sociocultural Patterns; *Spanish; Special Education; Student Evaluation; Talent Identification; Visual Acuity; White Students
Identifiers: Adaptive Behavior Inventory for Children; Bender Visual Motor Gestalt Test; SOMPA; Wechsler Intelligence Scale for Children (Revised); Wechsler Preschool Primary Scale of Intelligence

Availability: The Psychological Corporation; 555 Academic Ct., San Antonio, TX 78204-0952
Target Audience: 5-11
Notes: Time, 80 approx.

Comprehensive system for assessment of cognitive and sensorimotor abilities, and adaptive behavior of children ages 5 to 11 years. Parent Interview Materials and Student Assessment Materials are 2 major components. Each component is available as a separate package. Parent Interview is conducted in the home with the principal caretaker of the child, usually the mother. May be conducted in English or Spanish and requires one hour to complete. The measures used in the interview include the Adaptive Behavior Inventory for Children (TC011756); Sociocultural Scales; and Health History Inventories. Student Assessment Materials include Physical Dexterity Tasks; Bender Visual Motor Gestalt Test (TC001319); Weight by Height; Visual Acuity; Auditory Acuity; and WISC-R (TC007461). The system is racially and culturally nondiscriminatory and, thus, fulfills the requirements of the Education for All Handicapped Children Act. Normative data are available for Black, Hispanic, and White children.

9045
Smith-Johnson Nonverbal Performance Scale. Smith, Alathena J.; Johnson, Ruth E. 1977
Subtests: Formboard; Block Building; Pencil Drawing; Bead Stringing; Knot Tying; Color Items; Scissors; Paper Folding; Cube Tapping; Form Discrimination; Completion Items; Manikin; Block Patterns; Sorting
Descriptors: *Developmental Tasks; Diagnostic Tests; *Hearing Impairments; Individual Testing; *Language Handicaps; Nonverbal Tests; Performance Tests; *Preschool Children; Preschool Education
Availability: Western Psychological Services; 12031 Wilshire Blvd., Los Angeles, CA 90025
Target Audience: 2-4
Notes: Time, 45 approx.; Items, 65

Designed to evaluate developmental level of hearing-impaired preschool children. Nonverbal, performance instrument may also be used with delayed language and culturally different children.

9050
Wachs Analysis of Cognitive Structures. Wachs, Harry; Vaughan, Lawrence J. 1977
Subtests: Identification of Objects; Object Design; Graphic Design; General Movement
Descriptors: *Cognitive Development; Culture Fair Tests; *Disadvantaged; Hearing Impairments; Individual Testing; Language Handicaps; *Learning Disabilities; Performance Tests; *Preschool Children; Preschool Education; Psychomotor Skills; School Readiness; Piagetian Theory
Identifiers: WACS
Availability: Western Psychological Services; 12031 Wilshire Blvd., Los Angeles, CA 90025
Target Audience: 3-6
Notes: Time, 45 approx.

Designed to detect quality of a child's actual performance of high level thinking for various body and sense thinking tasks. Fifteen clusters of tasks are grouped into 4 subjects. Inventory activities are presented as challenging games.

9054
School Behavior Checklist. Miller, Lovick C. 1977
Descriptors: Affective Behavior; Antisocial Behavior; Anxiety; Behavior Patterns; Behavior Rating Scales; Cognitive Development; Elementary Education; *Elementary School Students; Elementary School Teachers; *Emotional Disturbances; Social Behavior; *Student Behavior
Identifiers: SBC
Availability: Western Psychological Services; 12031 Wilshire Blvd., Los Angeles, CA 90025
Target Audience: 4-13
Notes: Time, 10 approx.

Teacher assesses student's classroom behavior to provide an objective and standardized evaluation. Assesses need achievement, aggression, anxiety, cognitive or academic deficit, hostile isolation, and extraversion. Form A-1 is for children aged 4-6 years and includes 104 items. It has additional clinical scales for normal irritability, school disturbance, and total disability. Form A-2 is for children aged 7-13 years and includes 96 items. It has one additional clinical scale—total disability. Measures wide range of social and emotional school behaviors from social competence to moderate social deviance indicative of psychopathological disorders.

9058
Test of Grammatically Correct Spanish/English: Written and Oral. Bilingual Education Project, Las Cruces, NM 1976

Descriptors: *Bilingual Students; Elementary Education; *Elementary School Students; *English (Second Language); Grammar; Language Tests; Oral Language; *Spanish; *Spanish Speaking; Writing Skills
Availability: K-12 Bilingual (Spanish/English) Multicultural Demonstration Programs; Las Cruces Public Schools, 301 W. Amador Ave., Las Cruces, NM 88001
Grade Level: K-6
Notes: Time, 10 approx.

Designed to assess oral language ability in students from kindergarten to grade 6. Written language ability is assessed for students in grades 2-6. Written responses are scored for vocabulary, sentence patterns, grammar, and usage. Oral responses are scored for vocabulary, sentence patterns, grammar, and usage. Directions for written test may be given in Spanish or English. Directions for oral test are to be given only in English.

9059
Perceptual-Motor Rating Scale. Garvey, Reba; Kimball, Thomas R. 1978
Subtests: Organization of Work, Perception, Following Directions; Self Sufficiency, Self Confidence; Perceptual Motor Coordination; Body Movement, Gross Motor Control
Descriptors: Adapted Physical Education; Behavior Rating Scales; *Elementary School Students; *Mainstreaming; *Perceptual Handicaps; Perceptual Motor Learning; Primary Education; Psychomotor Skills; Special Programs
Availability: ERIC Document Reproduction Service; 3900 Wheeler Ave., Alexandria, VA 22304 (ED152856, 35 pages)
Grade Level: 1-3
Notes: Items, 28

Designed to assess effects of special perceptual motor training on primary grade pupils with perceptual handicaps.

9069
O'Brien Vocabulary Placement Test. O'Brien, Janet 1977
Descriptors: Achievement Tests; *Disadvantaged; Elementary Education; *Elementary School Students; *Grouping (Instructional Purposes); *Independent Reading; *Reading Achievement; Vocabulary Skills
Availability: Educational Activities, Inc.; P.O. Box 392, Freeport, NY 11520
Grade Level: K-6
Notes: Time, 15 approx.; Items, 60

Designed to assess independent reading level of students by means of a group reading inventory. Culturally unbiased test which discounts guessing. Test is composed of a series of ditto materials with 10 items on each ditto. Students should begin with page one and continue until they reach a page on which they score less than 5 correct answers. Test is also available on floppy disc (Apple II) (TC011468).

9072
Auditory Integrative Abilities Test. Grote, Carole 1976
Subtests: Auditory-Motor; Auditory-Graphic; Auditory-Verbal
Descriptors: Audiotape Cassettes; *Auditory Perception; *Auditory Tests; Diagnostic Teaching; *Diagnostic Tests; Elementary Education; *Elementary School Students; Handwriting; *Learning Disabilities; *Perceptual Handicaps; Perceptual Motor Coordination; Speech Skills; Writing Skills
Identifiers: AIAT
Availability: Educational Activities, Inc.; P.O. Box 392, Freeport, NY 11520
Target Audience: 6-9
Notes: Items, 30

Concise, diagnostic instrument designed to assess auditory perception disorders as they relate to language and learning disabilities. Nonverbal stimuli are used for testing in 3 skill areas: auditory-motor (clapping sound patterns), auditory-graphic (visually reproduce sound patterns), and auditory-verbal (orally reproduce sound patterns).

9075
Test Procedures for Preschool Children. Graham, Frances K.; Ernhart, Claire B. 1962
Subtests: Vocabulary Scale; Block-Sort; Copy-Forms; Motor Coordination; Figure-Ground; Tactual-Localization; Mark-Car Accuracy; Mark-Car Mark; Distraction-Variable Error; Distraction-Constant Error; Parent Questionnaire (Personality)
Descriptors: *Concept Formation; Diagnostic Tests; Individual Testing; *Neurological Impairments; *Perceptual Motor Coordination; Performance Tests; Personality Assessment; *Preschool Children; Preschool Education; *Vocabulary Skills

Identifiers: Test Batteries
Availability: Dr. Frances K. Graham; Dept. of Psychology, University of Delaware, Newark, DE 19716
Target Audience: 2-5
Notes: Time, 60 approx.

Developed to measure vocabulary skills, conceptual ability, perceptual-motor ability, and personality characteristics of preschool children. Designed for use in differentiating brain injured from normal population. Personality characteristics were assessed by parent-completed questionnaires and rating scales completed by examiner.

9104
Steenburgen Quick Math Screening. Steenburgen, Gelb, F. 1978
Descriptors: Criterion Referenced Tests; Elementary Education; *Elementary School Mathematics; *Elementary School Students; Mathematical Concepts; Pretests Posttests; *Mathematics Tests; Remedial Mathematics; *Screening Tests
Availability: Academic Therapy Productions; 20 Commercial Blvd., Novato, CA 94947
Grade Level: 1-6

This criterion-referenced, untimed screening test in basic math functions offers a remedial follow-up program to help children in grades 1 through 6 and older remedial students with math skills at elementary levels. Developed with the needs of distractible students in mind, the spacious presentation of problems does not overstimulate hyperactive or distractible children.

9105
Tree-Bee Test of Auditory Discrimination. Fudala, Janet B. 1978
Subtests: Words; Phrases; Pairs; Comprehension
Descriptors: Adults; *Auditory Discrimination; *Auditory Tests; Elementary Education; Elementary School Students; Individual Testing; Learning Disabilities; Listening Comprehension; Pictorial Stimuli; Preschool Children; Preschool Education; Secondary School Students
Availability: United Educational Services; P.O. Box 357, E. Aurora, NY 14052
Target Audience: 3-64
Notes: Time, 10 approx.; Items, 24

Designed to measure auditory discrimination of persons aged 3 to adult. Norms are available for children ages 3 to 9. The skills tested are normally attained by grade 4. Two forms are available for individual administration and 2 for group administration. Used to identify subjects with auditory discrimination problems. No reading or writing is required of examinee.

9117
McCarthy Screening Test. McCarthy, Dorothea 1978
Subtests: Right-Left Orientation; Verbal Memory; Draw-a-Design; Numerical Memory; Conceptual Grouping; Leg Coordination
Descriptors: Classification; *Handicap Identification; *Learning Disabilities; Memory; Perceptual Handicaps; *Preschool Children; Preschool Education; Primary Education; Psychomotor Skills; *School Readiness; *Screening Tests; Special Education; Young Children
Identifiers: McCarthy Scales of Childrens Abilities; MST
Availability: The Psychological Corporation; 555 Academic Ct., San Antonio, TX 78204-0952
Target Audience: 4-6
Notes: Time, 20 approx.

An adaptation of the McCarthy Scales of Children's Abilities (MSCA) (TC006903). Designed to help schools identify children 4 to 6.5 years of age who may require special educational assistance. MST consists of 6 of the 18 tests which comprise the MSCA. The 6 tests were chosen to be representative of the original instrument.

9121
Author Adaptation of the Leiter International Performance Scale. Arthur, Grace 1952
Subtests: Two Year Tests; Three Year Tests; Four Year Tests; Five Year Tests; Six Year Tests; Seven Year Tests; Eight Year Tests; Nine Year Tests; Ten Year Tests; Eleven Year Tests; Twelve Year Tests
Descriptors: Culture Fair Tests; *Elementary School Students; Individual Testing; *Intelligence; *Intelligence Tests; *Nonverbal Tests; Performance Tests; *Preschool Children; Preschool Education; Primary Education; Speech Handicaps; Young Children
Identifiers: Arthur Adaptation of Leiter Intl Performance Scale; Leiter International Performance Scale
Availability: Western Psychological Services; 12031 Wilshire Blvd., Los Angeles, CA 90025
Target Audience: 3-7

Designed as a nonverbal Binet scale for young children. Tests are untimed, and those at lower end of scale measure ability to learn rather than measure acquired skills or learned material. Ratings obtained from combining scores on this instrument with the Revised Form II of Point of Scale Performance Tests (TC000842) yield a reliable measurement of general intelligence in areas of oral and written response. Results are especially useful with children with a foreign language handicap or delayed speech.

9123
Comparative Language Dominance Test. Southwestern Cooperative Educational Laboratory, Albuquerque, NM 1975
Descriptors: *Adolescents; *Adults; Bilingualism; *Bilingual Students; *Children; *English (Second Language); Individual Testing; *Language Dominance; Language Tests; *Pictorial Stimuli; *Spanish
Identifiers: SWCEL CLD
Availability: Southern Cooperative Educational Laboratory Publishers; 229 Truman, N.E., Albuquerque, NM 87108
Target Audience: 2-64
Notes: Time, 20 approx.; Items, 150

Designed as a comparative measure of language dominance in bilingual individuals aged 2 years to adults. Instrument is structured to sample concept identification in English and Spanish. Items are arranged in order of increasing difficulty. The manual suggests appropriate starting points for several age groups.

9124
Neurological Dysfunctions of Children. Kuhns, James W. 1979
Descriptors: Biographical Inventories; Children; Early Childhood Education; *Elementary School Students; *Handicap Identification; Individual Testing; *Neurological Impairments; *Preschool Children; Psychomotor Skills; *Screening Tests
Identifiers: NDOC
Availability: Publishers Test Service; 2500 Garden Rd., Monterey, CA 93940
Target Audience: 3-10
Notes: Items, 18

Designed to aid professional examiner in the evaluation of neurological signs of central nervous system dysfunction. Useful in determining whether or not a child should be referred for a neurological evaluation. Items 1-16 are a series of tasks children are asked to perform to indicate their neurological functioning. Item 17 is the measurement of the child's head circumference. Item 18 is a parental interview to gather information about the child's developmental history.

9126
Ambiguous Word Language Dominance Test: Spanish/English. Keller, Gary D. 1978
Descriptors: *Adolescents; Bilingual Education; *Bilingual Students; *Children; Elementary School Students; Elementary Secondary Education; *English (Second Language); *Hispanic Americans; Individual Testing; *Language Dominance; *Language Tests; *Pronunciation; Secondary School Students; *Spanish; Word Lists
Identifiers: AWLDT
Availability: Publishers Test Service; 2500 Garden Rd., Monterey, CA 93940
Target Audience: 10-17
Notes: Items, 100

Designed to measure degree of language dominance of Spanish/English bilingual students, 10 years of age and above. Student reads aloud a list of 100 words. The list consists of ambiguous words, which can be pronounced as either Spanish or English words; Spanish words that are not similar to English words; and English words that are not similar to Spanish words. The ambiguous words are the most critical for scoring purposes.

9127
Flexibility Language Dominance Test: Spanish/English. Keller, Gary D. 1978
Descriptors: *Adolescents; Bilingual Education; *Bilingual Students; *Children; Elementary School Students; Elementary Secondary Education; English (Second Language); *Hispanic Americans; *Language Dominance; *Language Tests; Secondary School Students; Spanish; Vocabulary
Identifiers: FLDT
Availability: Publishers Test Service; 2500 Garden Rd., Monterey, CA 93940
Target Audience: 10-17
Notes: Time, 10 approx.

Designed to assess degree of language dominance of Spanish/English bilingual students, 10 years of age and older. Students are allowed equal periods of time (60 seconds) to construct meaningful Spanish and English words from nonsense units. English and Spanish words are

common or have a similar frequency of usage. An identical number of Spanish and English words can be formed from each nonsense unit.

9135
Kindergarten Screening Instrument. Houston Independent School District, TX 1975
Subtests: Vision; Hearing; Eye Hand Coordination; Language Learning; Gross Motor
Descriptors: Child Development; *Cognitive Development; *Individual Development; Individual Testing; *Kindergarten Children; Learning Readiness; *Performance Tests; Primary Education; *Psychomotor Skills; School Readiness; *Screening Tests; Spanish; *Spanish Speaking; Visual Measures; Visual Stimuli; Volunteers
Identifiers: HISD Kindergarten Screening Instrument; in Public Schools (Houston); Oral Tests
Availability: ERIC Document Reproduction Service; 3900 Wheeler Ave., Alexandria, VA 22304 (ED153999, 84 pages)
Grade Level: K

Screening device developed by the Board of Education of the Houston Independent School District through the Volunteers in Public Schools. Used to detect possible difficulties in such areas as perception, discrimination, physical development, and cognitive development. Individually administered by the trained volunteers. Requires the use of numerous items, such as eye chart, cassette tape playback, various drawings and pictures, scissors, a 24-inch hoop, etc. Instructions that are to be given to the child are written in both Spanish and English.

9156
Sensorimotor Integration for Developmentally Disabled Children. Montgomery, Patricia; Richter, Eileen 1977
Descriptors: *Children; *Developmental Disabilities; Elementary Education; Learning Disabilities; Moderate Mental Retardation; Perceptual Development; Perceptual Motor Coordination; Performance Tests; Preschool Education; Psychomotor Skills; *Sensory Integration
Availability: Western Psychological Services; 12031 Wilshire Blvd., Los Angeles, CA 90025
Target Audience: 2-12

A series of activities designed to improve sensory integrative functions of developmentally disabled or delayed children. Designed for use by occupational or physical therapists.

9172
Washington Alcohol Poll Questionnaire. Maxwell, M. 1951
Descriptors: *Adults; *Alcoholic Beverages; Alcoholism; *Attitude Measures; *Behavior Patterns; *Drinking; Interviews; Questionnaires
Identifiers: Alcoholics
Availability: CARRF; Center of Alcohol Studies, Rutgers University, Allison Rd., Piscataway, NJ 08854
Target Audience: Adults
Notes: Items, 77

Designed to assess attitudes toward drinking as well as drinking practices. Developed for use in a quantity-frequency survey of drinking behavior. Instrument is available as entry 2.1/3.

9176
Life History Questionnaire for Alcoholics. Jackson, J. K. 1951
Subtests: Childhood Neighborhood; Family History; School and Adolescence; Adulthood and Work History; Military Service; Hospitalization and Illness
Descriptors: Adults; *Alcoholism; *Biographical Inventories; Discipline; Educational Experience; *Family Characteristics; Family Influence; Family Relationship; Physical Health; Social Background; Work Experience
Identifiers: *Alcoholics; Questionnaire on Drinking Behavior
Availability: CARRF; Center of Alcohol Studies, Rutgers University, Allison Rd., Piscataway, NJ 08854
Target Audience: Adults
Notes: Items, 136

Designed to elicit information from alcoholics concerning personal history and social background. Instrument is available as entry 2.7/215. It is a modified version of a questionnaire by E. M. Jellinek available as entry 2.7/102.

9180
Connor Social Background and Drinking History Questionnaire. Connor, R. G. 1960
Descriptors: Adults; *Alcoholism; Behavior Patterns; *Biographical Inventories; Drinking; Questionnaires; Self Concept; Social Background
Identifiers: *Alcoholics

Availability: CARRF; Center of Alcohol Studies, Rutgers University, Allison Rd., Piscataway, NJ 08854
Target Audience: Adults
Notes: Items, 102

Designed for use with Gough's Adjective Check List (TC002498). Elicits social background data and drinking history of alcoholics. Available as entry 2.7/202.

9188
Alcohol Assessment Interview; Psychosocial Interview Guide. Stone, A. R.; and Others 1963
Descriptors: Adults; *Alcoholism; Behavior Patterns; Drinking; Interviews; *Screening Tests
Identifiers: *Alcoholics
Availability: CARRF; Center of Alcohol Studies, Rutgers University, Allison Rd., Piscataway, NJ 08854
Target Audience: Adults
Notes: Time, 60 approx.; Items, 42

Structured interview used to distinguish between alcoholics and nonalcoholics. Used to determine level of severity of alcoholism. Available as entry 3.1.

9192
Values Inventory for Children. Gilford, Joan S.; And Others 1971
Subtests: Asocial; Social Conformity; Me First; Academic/Health; Masculinity; Adult Closeness; Aesthetics; Sociability
Descriptors: *Childhood Attitudes; Cultural Differences; *Elementary School Students; Ethnic Groups; Forced Choice Technique; Individual Needs; Nonverbal Tests; *Picture Books; Primary Education; *Self Concept Measures; Spanish; Spanish Speaking; *Student Attitudes; *Values; Visual Measures
Identifiers: Faking (Testing)
Availability: ERIC Document Reproduction Service; 3900 Wheeler Ave., Alexandria, VA 22304 (ED050178, 278 pages)
Grade Level: 1-3
Notes: Time, 30 approx.; Items, 30

A nonverbal, self-administering inventory of values, which is used to measure 7 dimensions of value based upon 7 categories of needs: physiological, safety, love, esteem, aesthetic, self-actualization, and aggression. In this instrument, values are interpreted to be reflected by attitudes as determined by the affective responses to the activities and situation presented in the picture books. Moral attitudes (or values) have also been included even though they are not synonymous with the term values as defined herein. There are 2 alternate forms: (1) Form X (the child responds to a single picture by choosing the extent of his or her like or dislike on a graded, 4-point scale; the child circles the face that describes his feelings); and (2) Form Y (the child selects which of the 2 pictures in each item he or she likes better). Instructions for administering the instrument are available in both Spanish and English.

9217
Weiss Comprehensive Articulation Test. Weiss, Curtis E. 1978
Descriptors: *Adolescents; *Adults; *Articulation (Speech); *Children; *Communication Disorders; *Diagnostic Tests; Elementary School Students; Elementary Secondary Education; Individual Testing; Pictorial Stimuli; Preschool Children; Preschool Education; Secondary School Students; *Speech Evaluation; Verbal Stimuli
Identifiers: WCAT
Availability: DLM Teaching Resources; P.O. Box 4000, One DLM Park, Allen, TX 75002
Target Audience: 3-64
Notes: Items, 85

Designed for use by speech professionals in field of communication disorders. Picture form may be used with nonreaders; sentence form for subjects who can read consists of 38 items. Instrument may be administered in its entirety or in part depending on subjects' age and diagnostician's needs.

9238
Behavior and Learning Rate. Keller, Charles 1978
Descriptors: *Antisocial Behavior; Attention Span; Behavior Problems; Behavior Rating Scales; *Elementary School Students; Elementary School Teachers; *Hyperactivity; Neurosis; Parents; Primary Education; Psychosis
Identifiers: BLR
Availability: Dr. Charles Keller; Hilton Family Medicine, P.C., 42 Lake Ave., Hilton, NY 14468
Grade Level: 1-3

Designed for completion by parents and classroom teachers. Subject is assessed on frequency of behaviors symptomatic of hyperactivity, short attention span, aggressive behavior, psychoticism, neuroticism, and seizure equivalents.

9250
Leamos: Orientation and Placement Tests, Fundamental Stage: Primary, Steps 4-15. Los Angeles Unified School District, CA 1976
Descriptors: *Diagnostic Teaching; *Diagnostic Tests; *Elementary School Students; Functional Literacy; Orientation; Primary Education; Reading Tests; *Spanish; *Spanish Speaking; *Student Placement
Identifiers: Spanish Developmental Reading; Test Batteries
Availability: Paul S. Amidon and Associates; 1966 Benson Ave., St. Paul, MN 55116-9990
Grade Level: K-3

Designed to acquaint students with test format and determine appropriate learner entry level on skills continuum. Used as part of Leamos; Spanish Developmental Reading Program (DRP).

9251
Leamos: Diagnostic/Prescriptive Tests, Fundamental Stage: Primary, Steps 1-3. Los Angeles Unified School District, CA 1976
Descriptors: *Diagnostic Teaching; *Diagnostic Tests; *Elementary School Students; Functional Literacy; Pretests Posttests; Primary Education; *Reading Skills; Reading Tests; *Spanish; *Spanish Speaking
Identifiers: Spanish Developmental Reading; Test Batteries
Availability: Paul S. Amidon and Associates; 1966 Benson Ave., St. Paul, MN 55116-9990
Grade Level: K-3

Designed by Spanish Developmental Reading Task Force for use with primary grade children, who are Spanish speakers. The program is based on the idea that, after literacy is achieved in Spanish, the transfer to the reading of English is accomplished with greater ease and assurance of learner success. Step I consists of 21 items. Step II also has 21 items and Step III consists of 24 items. Contents are similar to English Developmental Reading.

9252
Leamos: Diagnostic/Prescriptive Tests, Fundamental Stage: Primary, Steps 4-6. Los Angeles Unified School District, CA 1976
Descriptors: *Diagnostic Teaching; *Diagnostic Tests; *Elementary School Students; Functional Literacy; Pretests Posttests; Primary Education; *Reading Skills; Reading Tests; *Spanish; *Spanish Speaking
Identifiers: Spanish Developmental Reading; Test Batteries
Availability: Paul S. Amidon and Associates; 1966 Benson Ave., St. Paul, MN 55116-9990
Grade Level: K-3

Designed for Spanish-speaking primary grade children by the Spanish-speaking reading consultants of the Developmental Reading Task Force. The program is based on the premise that, after literacy is achieved in Spanish, the transfer to the reading of English is accomplished with greater ease and assurance of learner success. It is the Spanish version of the Developmental Reading Program. Step 4 has 20 items, step 5 has 29 items, and step 6 has 36 items.

9253
Leamos: Diagnostic/Prescriptive Tests, Fundamental Stage: Primary, Steps 7-9. Los Angeles Unified School District, CA 1976
Descriptors: *Diagnostic Teaching; *Diagnostic Tests; *Elementary School Students; Functional Literacy; Pretests Posttests; Primary Education; *Reading Skills; Reading Tests; *Spanish; *Spanish Speaking
Identifiers: Spanish Developmental Reading; Test Batteries
Availability: Paul S. Amidon and Associates; 1966 Benson Ave., St. Paul, MN 55116-9990
Grade Level: K-3

Designed for Spanish-speaking primary grade children by the Spanish-speaking reading consultants of the Developmental Reading Task Force. The program is based on the premise that, after literacy is achieved in Spanish, the transfer to the reading of English is accomplished with greater ease and assurance of learner success. It is the Spanish edition of the Developmental Reading Program. Step 7 has 28 items, step 8 has 27 items, and step 9 has 36 items.

9254
Leamos: Diagnostic/Prescriptive Tests, Fundamental Stage: Primary, Steps 10-12. Los Angeles Unified School District, CA 1976
Descriptors: *Diagnostic Teaching; *Diagnostic Tests; *Elementary School Students; Functional Literacy; Pretests Posttests; Primary Education; *Reading Skills; Reading Tests; *Spanish; *Spanish Speaking
Identifiers: Spanish Developmental Reading; Test Batteries
Availability: Paul S. Amidon and Associates; 1966 Benson Ave., St. Paul, MN 55116-9990
Grade Level: K-3

Designed for Spanish-speaking students by the Spanish-speaking reading consultants of the Developmental Reading Task Force. The program is based on the premise that, after literacy is achieved in Spanish, the transfer to the reading of English is accomplished with greater ease and assurance of learner success. It is the Spanish edition of the Developmental Reading Program (DRP). Step 10 has 19 items, step 11 has 29 items, and step 12 has 20 items.

9255
Leamos: Diagnostic/Prescriptive Tests, Fundamental Stage: Primary, Steps 13-15. Los Angeles Unified School District, CA 1976
Descriptors: *Diagnostic Teaching; *Diagnostic Tests; *Elementary School Students; Functional Literacy; Pretests Posttests; Primary Education; *Reading Skills; Reading Tests; *Spanish; *Spanish Speaking
Identifiers: Spanish Developmental Reading; Test Batteries
Availability: Paul S. Amidon and Associates; 1966 Benson Ave., St. Paul, MN 55116-9990
Grade Level: K-3

Designed for Spanish-speaking students by the Spanish speaking reading consultants of the Developmental Reading Task Force. The program is based on the premise that, after literacy is achieved in Spanish, the transfer to the reading of English is accomplished with greater ease and assurance of learner success. It is the Spanish edition of the Developmental Reading Program (DRP). Step 13 has 25 items, step 14 has 26 items, and step 15 has 20 items.

9265
SOI Learning Abilities Test: Special Edition, K-1. Meeker, Mary; And Others 1975
Subtests: Memory; Divergent Production; Evaluation; Cognition; Convergent Production
Descriptors: *Cognitive Ability; *Diagnostic Teaching; *Diagnostic Tests; *Educational Diagnosis; Elementary School Students; Gifted; *Grade 1; *Kindergarten Children; Learning Disabilities; Mathematical Concepts; Primary Education; Reading Skills; *Special Education
Identifiers: Guilford (JP); *Structure of Intellect
Availability: SOI Institute; 214 Main St.; El Segundo, CA 90245
Grade Level: K-1

Basal level of achievement drawn from regular version of SOI Learning Abilities Test. Designed for young children and those with special needs such as mentally gifted and learning handicapped children. Students who pass all items on any subtest or do extremely well on test, in general, should be tested on regular revision of SOI-LA where there are 2 higher levels of difficulty.

9267
SOI Screening Form for Gifted. Meeker, Mary; Meeker, Robert 1975
Descriptors: *Ability Identification; *Cognitive Ability; Convergent Thinking; Divergent Thinking; Elementary Education; *Elementary School Students; *Gifted; *Screening Tests
Identifiers: Guilford (JP); *Structure of Intellect
Availability: SOI Institute; 214 Main St., El Segundo, CA 90245
Grade Level: 1-6
Notes: Time, 30 approx.

Designed to identify those students who should be tested further for gifted qualification.

9291
Kinsey Interview Schedule for Female Alcoholics. Kinsey, Barry A. 1966
Descriptors: Adults; *Alcoholism; Behavior Patterns; Drinking; *Females; Interviews; Social Attitudes
Identifiers: *Alcoholics
Availability: In: Kinsey, Barry A.; The Female Alcoholic, Springfield, IL: Charles C. Thomas, Publisher, 1966
Target Audience: Adults
Notes: Items, 18

Designed to assess drinking practices, attitudes, and history of female alcoholics. May be adapted for use with males.

9292
Kinsey Questionnaire for Female Alcoholics. Kinsey, Barry A. 1966
Descriptors: Adults; *Alcoholism; *Behavior Patterns; Biographical Inventories; *Drinking; *Females; Parent Attitudes; Questionnaires; Self Concept; Social Attitudes
Identifiers: *Alcoholics
Availability: In Kinsey, Barry A.; The Female Alcoholic, Springfield, IL: Charles C. Thomas, Publisher, 1966
Target Audience: Adults

Designed to assess family background, self-concept, drinking practices, and attitudes of female alcoholics. May be adapted for use with males.

9330
Developmental Reading: Diagnostic/Prescriptive Test, Fundamental Stage: Primary, Steps 16-18. Reading Task Force, Los Angeles Unified School District, CA 1975
Descriptors: *Diagnostic Teaching; *Diagnostic Tests; *Elementary School Students; *Functional Literacy; *Kindergarten Children; Letters (Alphabet); Phonics; Pretests Posttests; Primary Education; *Reading Readiness; Reading Tests; Spelling
Identifiers: Test Batteries
Availability: Paul S. Amidon and Associates, Inc.; 1966 Benson Ave., St. Paul, MN 55116
Target Audience: 5-8

Designed to determine specific skill strengths and weaknesses of each learner as a basis for differentiated instruction. A sequential reading program applicable for learners from prekindergarten through adult level. Designed to measure achievement of functional literacy. The major goals of the program include multisensory readiness skills, alphabetic mastery skills, regular spelling patterns, variant spelling patterns, and phonic generalizations. Step 16 measures skills in hard and soft sounds of c and g; final y sounds; "or" vowel controller; long or short sound of diphthong "oo"; syllabication; sight words; decodable word meanings; context; cause and effect; and inference. Step 17 measures skills in "or" or "ar" vowel controller; compound words; syllabication; concrete and abstract words; sight words; compound word meanings; main idea; sequence; simile; emotional reactions. Step 18 measures skills in vowel controllers (er), (ir), (ur); diphthongs; plural possessive; sight words; decodable word meanings; synonyms and antonyms; details; relationships; conclusions; compare and contrast; and dictionary skills.

9336
Developmental Reading: Diagnostic/Prescriptive Tests, Fundamental Stage: Advanced, Steps 13-18. Reading Task Force, Los Angeles Unified School District, CA 1975
Descriptors: *Adults; *Diagnostic Teaching; *Diagnostic Tests; *Elementary School Students; *Functional Literacy; Intermediate Grades; Letters (Alphabet); Phonics; Pretests Posttests; Reading Tests; Secondary Education; *Secondary School Students; Spelling
Identifiers: Test Batteries
Availability: Paul S. Amidon and Associates, Inc.; 1966 Benson Ave., St. Paul, MN 55116
Target Audience: 9-64

Designed to determine specific skill strengths and weaknesses of each learner as a basis for differentiated instruction. A sequential reading program applicable for learners from prekindergarten through adult level. Designed to measure achievement of functional literacy. The major goals of the program include multisensory skills, alphabetic mastery skills, regular spelling patterns, variant spelling patterns, and phonic generalizations. Step 13 measures skills in long vowel sounds; initial consonant clusters; VCe phonograms; decodable label names; sight words; context; main idea; classification; and relationships. Step 14 measures skills in final consonant clusters; vowel digraphs; VCC phonograms; S-form verbs; sight words; decodable word meanings; antonyms; details; relationships; and inference. Step 15 measures skills in consonant digraphs; VCC phonogram; possessive; decodable word meanings; sight words; main idea; punctuation marks; sequence; and drawing conclusions. Step 16 measures skills in hard and soft sounds of c and g; final y sounds; "ar" vowel controller; long or short sound of diphthong "oo"; syllabication; sight words; decodable word meaning; context; cause and effect; and inference. Step 17 measures skills in "or" or "ar" vowel controller; compound words; syllabication; concrete and abstract words; sight words; main idea; sequence; similes; and emotional reactions. Step 18 measures skills in vowel controllers "er," "ir," "ur"; diphthongs; plural possessive; sight words; meanings of decodable words; synonyms and antonyms; details, relationships; conclusions; compare and contrast; and dictionary skills.

9352
School Referral Report Form. Amble, Bruce R. 1974
Subtests: Type of Referral; Academic Adjustment; Testing Program; Family Contact; Student Information
Descriptors: *Educational Diagnosis; *Elementary School Students; Elementary Secondary Education; Learning Disabilities; *Learning Problems; Questionnaires; *Referral; *Secondary School Students; Teacher Attitudes; Teachers
Identifiers: Student Referral Report Form
Availability: Psychologists and Educators; P.O. Box 513, St. Louis, MO 63017
Grade Level: K-12

Designed for completion by classroom teacher. Useful in referring students to specialists.

9353
Biographical and Personality Inventory. Force, Ronald C. 1972
Descriptors: Adolescents; *Attitudes; *Biographical Inventories; *Delinquency; *Delinquent Rehabilitation; *Drug Abuse; *Personality Assessment; *Recidivism; Young Adults
Availability: Test Systems, Inc.; P.O. Box 18432, Wichita, KS 67218
Target Audience: 13-19
Notes: Time, 60; Items, 200

Invididual or group administered objective test designed to predict the recovery potential of delinquent youth. Low scores indicate need only for housing and care by own or foster family. Highest scores indicate need for controlled environment. Separate forms for boys and girls are available. Items are multiple choice and true/false. Requires 5th grade reading ability. Scoring procedure available indicating drug or alcohol problems. May be administered prior to sentencing or treatment and only by a certified psychologist.

9357
Revised Token Test. McNeil, Malcolm Ray; Prescott, Thomas E. 1978
Descriptors: *Adults; Aphasia; *Auditory Perception; Clinical Diagnosis; Diagnostic Tests; Language Handicaps; *Language Processing; Learning Disabilities; *Neurological Impairments; *Perceptual Handicaps; Performance Tests
Identifiers: RTT; Token Test (Language)
Availability: University Park Press; 300 N. Charles St., Baltimore, MD 21201
Target Audience: 18-64

Designed as a clinical and research tool for assessing central auditory system. Measures auditory deficits resulting from brain dysfunction. Provides an index of the type and severity of processing disorders. Useful with aphasic subjects. Developed as a revision and standardization of DeRenzi and Vignolo's Token Test.

9365
Differential Attitudes of Black and White Patients toward Psychiatric Treatment in Child Guidance. Jackson, Anna M.; And Others 1978
Subtests: Therapist's Attitude toward the Patient; Attitude of Other People in the Clinic; Helpfulness of Therapy; Expectations of Therapy and Reasons for Seeking Help; Resistances; Content of Therapy and Techniques; Psychological Mindedness; Fantasy Expression; Prejudicial Attitudes
Descriptors: Adults; *Attitude Measures; *Blacks; Children; Interviews; *Mental Health Clinics; *Parent Attitudes; Psychiatric Services; *Racial Attitudes; *Whites
Identifiers: TIM(E)
Availability: Tests in Microfiche; Test Collection, Educational Testing Service, Princeton, NJ 08541
Target Audience: Adults
Notes: Items, 141

A parental questionnaire including items on the therapist's attitude toward the patient, the attitudes of other people in the clinic, the effectiveness of therapy, expectations of therapy and reasons for seeking help, problems with having a White therapist, content of therapy and techniques, fantasy expression, and prejudicial attitudes. The questionnaire was prepared for a study designed to test the assumption that, after terminating therapy, Black parents would have different attitudes toward psychiatric clinics and psychotherapy than would White parents.

9376
Juvenile Probationer's Behavior and Attitude Rating Scale. Horejsi, Charles R.
Descriptors: Adults; Attitude Change; *Behavior Change; *Delinquent Rehabilitation; Interviews; *Parents; *Program Evaluation; *Rating Scales; *Volunteers
Identifiers: TIM(E)
Availability: Tests in Microfiche; Test Collection, Educational Testing Service, Princeton, NJ 08541
Target Audience: Adults
Notes: Items, 51

Designed for use with the parents or parental surrogates of adolescents on probation. Thirty-seven items relating to the youngster's behavior and attitudes measure the parents' assessment of positive or negative change resulting from a one-to-one, court-volunteer/probationer relationship. Only those changes attributed to the volunteer's influence are considered in the scoring procedure.

9412
Peer Interaction Recording System. Hops, Hyman 1973
Descriptors: Classroom Observation Techniques; *Disabilities; *Elementary School Students; Elementary Secondary Education; *Interpersonal Competence; Nonverbal Communication; *Peer Relationship; *Secondary School Students; Verbal Communication
Identifiers: Coding Manual; CORBEH; Peer Interaction Recording System; PIRS
Availability: Center at Oregon for Research in the Behavioral Education of the Handicapped; Dept. of Special Education, Clinical Services Bldg., University of Oregon, Eugene, OR 97403
Grade Level: K-12

Designed to observe disabled children in a classroom setting. Social interactions which occur between peers in a classroom setting are systematically tracked. Social interaction is defined as an exchange of verbal or nonverbal signals between 2 or more students.

9427
Symbol Substitution Test. Ben-Zeev, Sandra 1963
Descriptors: *Bilingual Students; Hebrew; Monolingualism; Preschool Education; Primary Education; *Syntax; *Verbal Learning; Verbal Tests; *Young Children
Identifiers: TIM(E); Verbal Symbol Substitution Test
Availability: Tests in Microfiche; Test Collection, Educational Testing Service, Princeton, NJ 08541
Target Audience: 3-8
Notes: Items, 7

Designed to measure the ability of bilingual and monolingual children to use words as flexible units which could be substituted for one another within a general code system and as a measure of word magic, a subject's inability to separate a word from its connection with its referent.

9429
Dental Hygiene Behavior Checklist. Abramson, Edward E.; Wunderlich, Richard A. 1972
Descriptors: Adolescents; Behavior Rating Scales; Children; *Dental Health; *Self Care Skills; *Severe Mental Retardation
Availability: Mental Retardation; v10 n3 p6-8 Jun 1972
Target Audience: 9-14

Designed to assess training of severely mentally retarded persons to brush their teeth. Behavioral techniques used in this study could be used to train this population to perform other personal hygiene tasks.

9432
Phonological Process Analysis. Weiner, Frederick F. 1979
Descriptors: *Articulation (Speech); *Articulation Impairments; *Diagnostic Tests; Individual Testing; Phonology; *Preschool Children; Preschool Education; Speech Evaluation; Speech Tests; *Speech Therapy; Syllables; *Therapists
Identifiers: Harmony; PPA
Availability: University Park Press; 300 N. Charles St., Baltimore, MD 21201
Target Audience: 2-5
Notes: Time, 45 approx.

Designed to aid in diagnosis and assessment of speech of unintelligible child. Child is usually hesitant to speak or engage in conversation. Instrument is based on articulatory responses elicited from action pictures rather than pictures of objects.

9436
Behavior Inventory. Hess, Robert D. 1966
Descriptors: Aggression; Behavior Rating Scales; *Disadvantaged Youth; Interpersonal Relationship; *Personality Assessment; *Preschool Children; Preschool Education; Student Adjustment; Student Behavior
Identifiers: Project Head Start
Availability: ERIC Document Reproduction Service; 3900 Wheeler Ave., Alexandria, VA 22304 (ED015772, 139 pages)
Target Audience: 2-5
Notes: Items, 23

Designed to measure behavioral and emotional tendencies ranging from verbal participation, social interaction, and aggression to general dispositional states. Developed for use with disadvantaged preschool children enrolled in Head Start Programs.

9468
JAW Board. Norton, Jeanette; And Others 1970
Descriptors: Adults; Attitude Measures; Behavior Patterns; Group Therapy; *Males; *Peer Evaluation; *Prisoners; *Problem Solving; Rehabilitation Centers; Sociometric Techniques
Availability: Bernard C. Kirby; Professor of Sociology, Dept. of Sociology, California State University at San Diego, 5402 College Ave., San Diego, CA
Target Audience: Adults

Designed to enable residents of a rehabilitation center to evaluate their peers' problem-solving ability. Enabled residents to learn how their peers perceived their behavior.

9471
Desert Willow Trait Profile. Meketon, Jerry 1973
Descriptors: Adults; American Indians; Individual Characteristics; *Mental Health; *Paraprofessional Personnel; Peer Evaluation; Personality Measures; Personality Traits; Rating Scales; *Reservation American Indians; *Self Concept; Self Evaluation (Individuals)
Identifiers: TIM(E)
Availability: Tests in Microfiche; Test Collection, Educational Testing Service, Princeton, NJ 08541
Target Audience: Adults
Notes: Items, 30

Developed to provide mental health technicians with a clearer understanding of personality traits. Subjects rate themselves as they presently are and the ideal persons they might become in terms of 30 traits to be assessed. Subjects describe their ideal mental health technician, and 5 associates judge subject. Inventory has been used with community health representatives, non-Indian mental health technicians, Indian mental health technicians, Indian community health medics, and non-Indian mental health professionals.

9502
Children's Somatic Apperception Test. Caldwell, Willard E.; Adams, Nancy M. 1963
Descriptors: *Body Image; Children; *Elementary School Students; *Mental Retardation; *Neurological Impairments; Personality Assessment; *Projective Measures; Self Concept
Identifiers: Figure Drawing
Availability: Journal of General Psychology; v68 p43-57 1963
Target Audience: 7-12
Notes: Items, 10

Measures body image in terms of gross anatomy: length of legs, arms, and head. For use in a study of differences in body image in normal, disturbed, and mentally retarded children.

9503
Farm Knowledge Test. Grigg, Austin E. 1948
Descriptors: Achievement Tests; Adults; *Agricultural Laborers; *Farm Occupations; Males; Multiple Choice Tests; *Prisoners
Availability: Journal of Applied Psychology; v32 n5 p452-55 Oct 1948
Target Audience: Adults
Notes: Items, 30

Used as part of a vocational appraisal of male adult prisoners. Designed to identify those with a rural background. Covers crops, fruit trees, livestock, market facts, etc.

9504
Screening Interview. Simon, Alexander; And Others 1966
Descriptors: *Interviews; *Mental Disorders; *Older Adults; Psychiatric Services; Psychiatry; *Screening Tests; *Social Agencies
Availability: Marjorie Fisk Lowenthal; Human Development Program, University of California at San Francisco, 1415-29 Fourth Ave., San Francisco, CA 94143
Target Audience: Older Adults
Notes: Items, 112

Designed for use by nonphysician personnel as a screening instrument to identify cases of psychiatric impairment in adults, aged 65 and over.

9506
Post Interview Questionnaire. Hain, Jack D.; And Others 1966
Descriptors: Adults; Drug Use; *Emotional Response; Interviews; Medical Research; *Patients; Psychiatry; Psychotherapy; Questionnaires
Identifiers: *Psychiatric Research; Symptoms
Availability: Journal of Psychiatric Research; v4 p95-106 1966
Target Audience: Adults
Notes: Items, 20

Used in a study during which drugs were utilized to facilitate psychiatric diagnostic and therapeutic interviews. Filled out by patients 24 and 48 hours after interview. Covers feelings, symptoms, remembrance of interview, sleep.

9510
Teacher Rating Scale. Conners, C. Keith 1969
Subtests: Conduct Problem; Inattentive-Passive; Tension-Anxiety; Hyperactivity and Sociability

Descriptors: Adjustment (to Environment); Antisocial Behavior; Anxiety; Attendance Patterns; *Behavior Patterns; Behavior Problems; *Behavior Rating Scales; Children; *Drug Therapy; *Elementary School Students; Hyperactivity; Teachers
Identifiers: Helpfulness; Shyness; Symptoms; TIM(E)
Availability: Tests in Microfiche; Test Collection, Educational Testing Service, Princeton, NJ 08541
Target Audience: 6-12
Notes: Items, 39

Teacher rating of student behavior designed for use in a study of behavior and learning disorders and hyperactive children medicated with dextroamphetamines.

9511
Parent's Questionnaire. Conners, C. Keith 1970
Subtests: Aggressive-Conduct Disorder; Anxious-Inhibited; Antisocial Reaction; Enuresis; Psychosomatic Problems; Anxious-Immature
Descriptors: Aggression; Antisocial Behavior; Anxiety; *Behavior Patterns; *Behavior Rating Scales; Children; *Elementary School Students; *Hyperactivity; *Neurosis; Parents; Psychosomatic Disorders
Identifiers: Enuresis; Symptoms; TIM(E)
Availability: Tests in Microfiche; Test Collection, Educational Testing Service, Princeton, NJ 08541
Target Audience: Children
Notes: Items, 93

Symptom rating scale completed by parents. Designed for use in identifying hyperkinetic children and in evaluating treatment effects. Appears sensitive to drug treatment effects.

9513
Life Satisfaction Index Z. Havighurst, Robert J. 1971
Descriptors: Attitude Measures; *Attitudes; *Life Style; *Older Adults; *Questionnaires; *Self Evaluation (Individuals); *Life Satisfaction
Availability: Robert J. Havighurst; Graduate School of Education, University of Chicago, 5835 Kimbark Ave., Chicago, IL 60637
Target Audience: Older Adults

Designed to measure older adults' satisfaction with their past and present lives. Three forms of the test are available.

9514
Interview Schedule. Havighurst, Robert J. 1969
Descriptors: Church Programs; Clubs; Industrial Personnel; *Interviews; Leisure Time; Marriage; Older Adults; Parent Role; *Retirement; *Role Perception; Social Life
Availability: Havighurst, Robert J.; And Others. Adjustment to Retirement: A Cross-National Study. New York: Humanities Press, 1969
Target Audience: Older Adults
Notes: Items, 20

An interview to be used with retired steel workers to determine their present activity in a variety of different roles and their feelings toward those roles.

9515
Social Role Rating Scales. Havighurst, Robert J. 1957
Subtests: Present Activity Level in Role (14); Satisfaction with Role (14); Ego-Involvement with Role (14); Reported Change in Activity Level (14); Affect Regarding Reported Change in the Role (14)
Descriptors: Child Role; Church Programs; Citizen Participation; Clubs; Extended Family; Grandparents; Homemakers; Industrial Personnel; Marriage; *Older Adults; Parent Role; *Rating Scales; *Retirement; *Role Perception; Social Life; Spouses
Availability: Robert J. Havighurst; Graduate School of Education, University of Chicago, 5835 Kimbark Ave., Chicago, IL 60637
Target Audience: Older Adults
Notes: Items, 70

Rating scales used to evaluate the role performance of retired workers, based on the information collected with the Interview Schedule.

9517
Rating Scale for Personal Adjustment. Havighurst, Robert J. 1957
Subtests: Personal Intimate Contact (1); Formal Contact (1); Feeling of Importance (1); Emotional Stability (1); Personal Adjustment (1)
Descriptors: *Adjustment (to Environment); Clubs; *Emotional Adjustment; Friendship; *Human Relations; Older Adults; Rating Scales; *Retirement; *Self Esteem; Social Life

Availability: Genetic Psychology Monographs; v56 p297-375 1957
Target Audience: 65
Notes: Items, 5

Nine-point scale used to evaluate 5 areas of personal adjustment for older adults.

9520
Affective Differential. Plutchik, Robert 1967
Subtests: Protection (3); Destruction (3); Deprivation (3); Reproduction (3); Rejection (3); Incorporation (2); Orientation (2); Exploration (3)
Descriptors: *Adults; *Emotional Experience; *Mental Disorders; Neurosis; *Personality Assessment; Psychiatrists; Psychological Characteristics; Psychologists; Psychosis; Rating Scales
Availability: Psychological Reports; v20 n1 p19-25 1967
Target Audience: Adults
Notes: Items, 352

Clinicians were asked to rate the extent to which persons with one of 16 diagnostic labels (manic, neurotic, etc.) would be likely to show each of 22 listed emotions.

9528
Current Status Evaluation: Psychiatric Rating. Plutchik, Robert; And Others 1972
Descriptors: *Adults; *Check Lists; *Clinical Diagnosis; Mental Disorders; *Psychological Evaluation; Social Workers
Availability: Robert Plutchik; Albert Einstein College of Medicine, Yeshiva University, 1300 Morris Park Ave., Bronx, NY 10461
Target Audience: Adults
Notes: Items, 33

A checklist for evaluation of patient symptoms by psychiatrists or social workers.

9531
Automated Tri-Informant Goal Oriented Progress Note (ATGON). Wilson, Nancy C.; And Others 1973
Descriptors: *Adults; Behavior Change; Community Services; *Computer Oriented Programs; *Counseling Effectiveness; *Counseling Objectives; Daily Living Skills; Emotional Disturbances; Evaluation Methods; *Goal Orientation; Human Relations; Medical Services; *Mental Health Programs; Milieu Therapy; Physical Health; *Program Evaluation; Self Concept
Identifiers: ATGON
Availability: Fort Logan Mental Health Center; 3520 W. Oxford Ave., Denver, CO 80236
Target Audience: Adults

Patient treatment goals and methods for achieving them are preselected, followed by a periodic evaluation of goal attainment. The system can be used for systematic evaluation of treatment effectiveness at all administration levels.

9534
Meeker-Cromwell Language and Behavior Development Assessment. Meeker, Mary N.; Cromwell, Rue 1972
Descriptors: Adolescents; *Behavior Development; *Behavior Rating Scales; Children; Cultural Awareness; Elementary Secondary Education; Interpersonal Competence; *Language Acquisition; *Mild Mental Retardation; *Moderate Mental Retardation; Motivation; Self Concept
Identifiers: Hedonism
Availability: SOI Institute; 214 Main St., El Segundo, CA 90245
Target Audience: 1-18

Rating scale covers establishment of basic boundary of self-development, intact hedonism, conceptual motivation system, interpersonal functioning, and development of cultural functioning for educable mentally retarded, trainable mentally retarded, and learning-disabled students.

9540
R-E-P Language Scale. D'Asaro, Michael J.; John, Vera 1961
Descriptors: Behavior Rating Scales; *Cerebral Palsy; *Expressive Language; *Infants; *Language Acquisition; Neurological Impairments; *Phonetics; *Preschool Children; *Receptive Language
Availability: Cerebral Palsy Review; Sep-Oct 1961
Target Audience: 0-6
Notes: Items, 100

Designed for rating language development of the cerebral-palsied child.

9541
Brentwood Socialization Scale. Spiegel, Donald E.
Descriptors: Adults; Interpersonal Competence; *Patients; *Psychiatric Hospitals; *Rating Scales; *Social Adjustment; Socialization
Availability: Donald E. Spiegel; 5143 Tyrone Ave., Sherman Oaks, CA 90073

Target Audience: Adults
Notes: Items, 43

A psychiatric patient is rated on a scale composed of statements made by the patient during an interview. These statements are concerned with the patient's social competence behavior during the interview.

9542
Illinois Children's Language Assessment Test. Arlt, Phyllis B. 1977
Descriptors: Aphasia; Auditory Perception; *Handicap Identification; *Language Handicaps; *Preschool Children; Preschool Evaluation; *Speech Handicaps; Tests; Visual Perception
Availability: Interstate Printers and Publishers, Inc.; 19-27 N. Jackson St., Danville, IL 61834
Target Audience: 3-6
Notes: Time, 40 approx.; Items, 18

A children's version of the Schuell Short Examination for Aphasia.

9543
Operation Communication.
Descriptors: *Behavior Rating Scales; Elementary School Students; Elementary School Teachers; *Handicap Identification; Learning Disabilities; Teacher Attitudes
Availability: CANHC Literature Center; 645 Odin Dr., Pleasant Hill, CA 94523
Grade Level: K-6
Notes: Items, 48

Student rating scale designed to identify children with learning disabilities.

9546
Black Power Sentiments Scale (Modified Form). Tucker, Richard Dennis 1969
Descriptors: *Attitude Measures; *Black Attitudes; *Black Power; College Students; Forced Choice Technique; Higher Education; Political Attitudes; *Racial Attitudes
Identifiers: Black Separatism
Availability: Richard D. Tucker; Dept. of Psychology, University of Central Florida, Orlando, FL 32816
Grade Level: 13-16
Notes: Items, 24

Revision of the Black Power Sentiment Scale (Stenfors and Woodmansee, 1968). Designed to identify Black separatist extremism of the Black Panther variety.

9549
Patient Adjustment Q Sort Technique. Nickerson, Eileen Tressler 1961
Descriptors: Adults; *Physical Disabilities; Physicians; *Q Methodology; Rating Scales; *Social Adjustment
Identifiers: *Paraplegics
Availability: University Microfilms International; Dissertation Copies, P.O. Box 1764, Ann Arbor, MI 48106 (Order No. 61-2664)
Target Audience: Adults

Physicians and rehabilitation staff rate the adjustment of a group of paraplegics on a 9-point continuum from very poor to very good. Paraplegics rate their own adjustment on a 3-point scale. Adjustment in this case is normality of functioning within the limitations of the handicap, preparation, and readiness for reintegration into community life.

9554
Self-Concept Test. Cratty, Bryant J.; And Others 1970
Descriptors: *Ability; *Children; Forced Choice Technique; Minimal Brain Dysfunction; *Neurological Impairments; Physical Characteristics; *Self Concept; Self Concept Measures
Availability: Cratty, Bryant J. and Others. Movement Activities, Motor Ability and the Education of Children. Springfield, IL.: Charles C. Thomas, 1970.
Target Audience: 5-12
Notes: Items, 20

A modification of the Piers-Harris Scale, this questionnaire focuses on self-concept of physical ability and appearance. Designed for use with minimally neurologically handicapped children.

9560
Behavior Checklist. Rienherz, Helen; And Others 1977
Descriptors: *Behavior Rating Scales; *Emotional Disturbances; *Parent Attitudes; *Preschool Children; Preschool Evaluation; Screening Tests; *Social Development
Availability: ERIC Document Reproduction Section; 3900 Wheeler Ave., Alexandria, VA 22304 (ED158451, 23 pages)
Target Audience: 4-5
Notes: Items, 38

Parent questionnaire designed to assess social and emotional dysfunction in children entering kindergarten.

9568
SEARCH: A Scanning Instrument for the Identification of Potential Learning Disability. Silver, Archie A.; Hagin, Rosa A. 1976
Subtests: Lamb Chop Test: Matching (8); Lamb Chop Test: Recall (8); Role Sequencing (10); Auditory Discrimination: Objects (20); Auditory Discrimination (20); Articulation (17); Initials (10); Directionality (10); Finger Schema (8); Designs (6)
Descriptors: Elementary School Students; *Handicap Identification; *Kindergarten Children; *Learning Disabilities; *Preschool Children; Preschool Evaluation; Primary Education; *Screening Tests; Tests
Availability: Walker Educational Book Corporation; 720 Fifth Ave., New York, NY 10019
Grade Level: Kindergarten
Notes: Items, 117

Test battery designed to screen kindergarten children to detect those with potential learning problems, and those with potential for emotional decompensation.

9569
School Problem Screening Inventory (Fifth Edition). Gnagey, Thomas D. 1978
Descriptors: Adjustment (to Environment); *Behavior Problems; *Disadvantaged; *Elementary School Students; Elementary Secondary Education; Learning Problems; *Mental Retardation; Rating Scales; *Screening Tests; *Secondary School Students
Availability: Slosson Educational Publications; P.O. Box 280, E. Aurora, NY 14052
Grade Level: K-12
Notes: Items, 37

Rating scales designed for use by teachers to identify students who are learning disabled, mildly retarded, behavior disordered, socioculturally handicapped, or generally skill deficient or maladjusted.

9575
Work Preference Schedule. Cleland, Charles C.; Swartz, Jon D. 1968
Subtests: Work Preference (12); Pleasure Schedule (10)
Descriptors: Adults; Eating Habits; *Institutionalized Persons; *Mental Retardation; Questionnaires; Recreational Activities; *Vocational Interests; *Work Attitudes
Availability: Charles C. Cleland; University of Texas, 204 Sutton, Austin, TX 78712
Target Audience: Adults
Notes: Items, 22

Series of questionnaires designed to determine preferences in work and nonwork activities and diet in institutionalized adult retarded males. Pictures of actual work scenes in the environment were rated as liked or disliked.

9587
Adolescent Research Project. Smith, Aaron
Subtests: Psychiatric Status (5); Social Interaction (5); Antisocial Behavior (5); Background (53); Drug and Other Treatments (26)
Descriptors: *Adolescents; Adults; Antisocial Behavior; *Background; Children; Drug Therapy; Interpersonal Relationship; *Medical Services; *Mental Disorders; *Patients; *Psychiatric Hospitals; Questionnaires; Rating Scales
Availability: Aaron Smith; Haverford State Hospital, 3500 Darby Rd., Haverford, PA 19041
Target Audience: 11-20
Notes: Items, 94

Questionnaire and rating scale designed to collect descriptive information on adolescent patients in psychiatric hospitals to assist in planning future services and to investigate factors related to increases in adolescent admissions. Covers patient condition, drug and other treatments, psychiatric status, social interaction, antisocial behavior, and background information.

9606
Subject Community Follow-Up Interview. Steadman, Henry J.
Descriptors: *Adjustment (to Environment); Adults; *Community; Institutionalized Persons; *Interviews; Mental Disorders; *Patients
Availability: Henry J. Steadman; Mental Health Research Unit, New York State Dept. of Mental Hygiene, 44 Holland Ave., Albany, NY 12208
Target Audience: Adults
Notes: Items, 55

Interview to be administered one month after subject's release from a maximum security mental hospital. Covers adjustment problems to community, treatment since release, living conditions, contacts with others, incidents reported to police, estimations of stigma.

9607
Pre-Transfer Interview Schedule. Steadman, Henry J.
Descriptors: Adults; *Attitudes; Criminals; Institutionalized Persons; *Interviews; Mental Disorders; *Patients; *Prisoners
Availability: Henry J. Steadman; Mental Health Research Unit, New York State Dept. of Mental Hygiene, 44 Holland Ave., Albany, NY 12208
Target Audience: Adults
Notes: Time, 25; Items, 53

Interview measure to be administered prior to patients' leaving for a state mental hospital. Covers patient perceptions of institution, estimations of their own dangerousness, expectations of future situations, self-concept, interactions with patients, perceptions of stigma.

9608
Competency Hearing Schedule. Steadman, Henry J.
Descriptors: Adults; Court Litigation; *Criminals; Mental Health; *Observation; Psychological Evaluation
Identifiers: Mental Competency
Availability: Henry J. Steadman; Mental Health Research Unit, New York State Dept. of Mental Hygiene, 44 Holland Ave., Albany, NY 12208
Target Audience: Adults
Notes: Items, 29

An observation schedule used to collect information about nontestimony influences and sequences and content.

9609
Philosophy of Treatment Form. Barrell, Robert P.; De Wolfe, Alan S.; Cummings, Jonathan W. 1965
Subtests: Hospital Rules (8); Informing Patients (6); Behavior of Staff Interacting with Patients (3); Patient Needs (7); Staff Relationships (8); Patient Characteristics (8); Adequacy of Staff Performance on the Job (1)
Descriptors: Adults; Attitude Measures; *Attitudes; *Hospital Personnel; Job Satisfaction; *Medical Care Evaluation; Medical Services; Nurses; Nurses Aides; *Patients; Physicians; Practical Nursing; Psychologists; *Questionnaires; Social Workers
Availability: Robert P. Barrell; Psychological Research Laboratory, Veterans Administration Hospital, Dawney, IL 60064
Target Audience: Adults
Notes: Time, 15; Items, 144

Questionnaire in 2 separate forms designed to measure attitudes of staff and patients in general medical and surgical hospitals toward aspects of patient care. Uses 4-point agree/disagree response.

9610
Recreation Participation Rating Scales. Barrell, Robert P.
Subtests: Social Hour Activity (5); Card Games and Other Small Group Activities (5)
Descriptors: Adults; Hospitals; Participation; *Patients; *Rating Scales; *Recreational Activities
Availability: Robert P. Barrell; Psychological Research Laboratory, Veterans Administration Hospital, Downy, IL 60064
Target Audience: Adults
Notes: Items, 10

Staff member rates patient participation in social activities. Concerned with patient's spontaneity, response, conversation, and animation.

9611
Patient's Opinion Form. Barrell, Robert P.
Descriptors: Adjustment (to Environment); Adults; *Hospitals; *Medical Care Evaluation; *Patients; Program Evaluation; *Questionnaires
Availability: Robert P. Barrell; Psychological Research Laboratory, Veterans Administration Hospital, Downy, IL 60064
Target Audience: Adults
Notes: Time, 10; Items, 56

Questionnaires concerned with patients' opinions about care, hospital conditions, treatment, staff, family concerns. Used in conjunction with the Hospital Adjustment Inventory (TC009613) and the Hospital Situation Study (TC009612) to provide an overall "Pleasure-Displeasure Quotient."

9612
Hospital Situation Study. Barrell, Robert P.
Descriptors: Adjustment (to Environment); Adults; *Hospitals; *Patients; Questionnaires; *Situational Tests
Availability: Robert P. Barrell; Psychological Research Laboratory, Veterans Administration Hospital, Downy, IL 60064
Target Audience: Adults
Notes: Items, 8

Patient supplies words missing from a stimulus picture concerned with attitudes toward hospitalization and home problems, from 3 statement choices. Used in conjunction with the Patient's Opinion Form (TC009611) and the Hospital Adjustment Inventory (TC009613) to provide an overall "Pleasure-Displeasure Quotient."

9613
Hospital Adjustment Inventory. Barrell, Robert P.
Descriptors: *Adjustment (to Environment); Adults; *Hospitals; *Patients; *Questionnaires
Availability: Robert P. Barrell; Psychological Research Laboratory, Veterans Administration Hospital, Downy, IL 60064
Target Audience: Adults
Notes: Items, 23

Patient responds yes or no to statements concerned with worries the patient may be having about social problems associated with a hospital stay. Used in conjunction with Patient's Opinion Form (TC009611) and Hospital Situation Study (TC009612) to provide an overall "Pleasure-Displeasure Quotient."

9614
Physician's Rating Form. Barrell, Robert P. 1966
Descriptors: Adults; *Patients; *Physical Health; *Physicians; *Rating Scales
Availability: Psychosomatic Medicine; v28 n3 p197-206 1966
Target Audience: Adults
Notes: Items, 11

To facilitate comparison of patients with different diseases, the form assesses recovery to date, current disability and discomfort, anticipated future recovery, and expected long-term disability.

9615
Change Seeker Index. Garlington, Warren K.; Shimota, Helen E. 1964
Descriptors: Adults; College Students; Military Personnel; Patients; *Personality Assessment; Psychiatric Hospitals; *Questionnaires; *Stimuli
Identifiers: *Change Seeking
Availability: Psychological Reports; v14 p919-24 Jun 1964
Target Audience: Adults
Notes: Items, 95

Designed to investigate the premise that change seeking, the intensity of one's need to vary stimulus input, is a measurable dimension of behavior reflected in certain personality characteristics.

9619
Methods for Coding Family Interaction Process. Wild, Cynthia M.; Shapiro, Linda N. 1973
Descriptors: Adults; Children; *Communication Problems; *Family Relationship; *Interaction Process Analysis; Observation
Availability: Cynthia Wild; Massachusetts Mental Health Center, 74 Fernwood Rd., Boston, MA 02115
Target Audience: Adults; Children
Notes: Time, 60; Items, 6

Developed for use in scoring the interactions of families (mother, father, son) of schizophrenics,, psychiatrically hospitalized nonschizophrenics and normal controls. Covers transactional attention disturbances, closure, problem-solving efficiency, and dominance.

9620
Parent Interview. Seattle Atlantic Street Center, WA Berleman, William C.; Steinburn, Thomas 1964
Subtests: Interpersonal Relations; Parent Employment; Parent Aspirations; Discipline; Relations with Children; Economic Situation; Conditions of Interview
Descriptors: Adults; Background; Blacks; *Delinquency Prevention; Interviews; Junior High Schools; *Junior High School Students; *Occupational Aspiration; *Parent Child Relationship; *Parents; Work Experience
Identifiers: Seattle Atlantic Street Center WA; TIM(E)
Availability: Tests in Microfiche; Test Collection, Educational Testing Service, Princeton, NJ 08541
Grade Level: 7-9
Notes: Items, 283

Designed to elicit data from parents prior to a study of delinquency prevention in youth. Based on theories of anomie, differential association, community disorganization, family disorganization, and parental discipline.

9622
Behavioral Classification Project. Dreger, Ralph Mason 1970
Descriptors: *Adolescents; Check Lists; *Children; *Clinical Diagnosis; *Emotional Disturbances; *Emotional Problems; Parents; *Preschool Children
Identifiers: TIM(F)

Availability: Tests in Microfiche; Test Collection, Educational Testing Service, Princeton, NJ 08541
Target Audience: 0-17

Parent checklist aimed at classifying children's emotional disorders, including psychotic, neurotic, asocial, antisocial, organic, academic, sleeping, eating, developmental, and physical problems. Preschool, children, and adolescent versions are available. Number of items vary with various test levels.

9627
Tests of Basic Language Competence in English and Spanish. Lansing School District, MI 1973
Subtests: Oral Vocabulary (10); Comprehension of Commands and Directions (10); Recognition of Interrogative Patterns and Production of Grammatic Structures (10)
Descriptors: *Bilingual Education; *Communicative Competence (Languages); Elementary School Students; *English (Second Language); *Language Fluency; *Language Tests; Listening Comprehension; *Primary Education; Second Language Learning; Sentence Structure; *Spanish; Vocabulary
Identifiers: Commands
Availability: Lansing School District; Bilingual Education, E.S.E.A. Title VII, 620 Lesher Pl., Lansing, MI 48912
Target Audience: Children
Notes: Items, 30

Designed to measure growth in Spanish as a Second Language. Individually administered. English and Spanish versions of subtests.

9628
Mathematics Criterion Referenced Test. Lansing School District, MI 1973
Subtests: Kindergarten, Forms A and B (10); Grade 1, Forms A and B (10); Grade 2, Forms A and B (10); Grade 3, Forms A and B (10); Grade 4, Forms A and B (10)
Descriptors: Bilingual Education; Criterion Referenced Tests; Elementary Education; Elementary School Mathematics; Elementary School Students; *English (Second Language); *Multiple Choice Tests; *Numbers; *Primary Education; *Spanish
Availability: Lansing School District; Bilingual Education, E.S.E.A. Title VII, 620 Lesher Pl., Lansing, MI 48912
Grade Level: K-4
Notes: Items, 10

Designed to test a child's knowledge of numbers. Spanish and English versions are available.

9629
Cultural Heritage Criterion Referenced Test. Lansing School District, MI 1973
Descriptors: *Bilingual Education; Criterion Referenced Tests; *Cultural Background; Elementary Education; *Elementary School Students; Grade 3; Grade 4; Latin American Culture; *Multiple Choice Tests; *Spanish Culture
Availability: Lansing School District; Bilingual Education, E.S.E.A. Title VII, 620 Lesher Pl., Lansing, MI 48912
Grade Level: 3-4
Notes: Items, 10

Multiple-choice tests designed to measure the child's knowledge of Hispanic cultural heritage.

9633
Behavioral Assertiveness Test. Eisler, Richard M.; And Others 1973
Descriptors: Adults; *Assertiveness; Interpersonal Competence; *Patients; Psychiatric Hospitals; *Role Playing
Availability: Journal of Clinical Psychology; v29 n3 p295-99, Jul 1973
Target Audience: Adults
Notes: Items, 14

Role playing of 14 situations is used to measure a psychiatric patient's assertiveness. Subjects are rated on 9 behavioral components of assertiveness such as duration of reply, loudness of speech, requests for new behavior, etc.

9635
Item Response Test. Southeastern New Mexico Bilingual Program, Artesia 1972
Descriptors: *Bilingual Education; Elementary School Students; English (Second Language); Primary Education; *Response Style (Tests); *Spanish Speaking; *Student Participation
Identifiers: *Sentence Completion Method
Availability: Southeastern New Mexico Bilingual Program; Artesia Public Schools, 1106 W. Quay Ave., Artesia, NM 88210
Grade Level: K-3
Notes: Items, 12

Questionnaire designed to determine whether the student's responsiveness in Spanish and English has increased or decreased during the year's instruction. Based on the observation that, because of cultural factors in the home, Spanish children are less willing to respond in class.

9636
Self Image Test. Southeastern New Mexico Bilingual Program, Artesia 1972
Descriptors: Bilingual Education; Intermediate Grades; Primary Education; Rating Scales; *Self Concept; Self Evaluation (Individuals); *Spanish Speaking
Availability: Southeastern New Mexico Bilingual Program; Artesia Public Schools, 1106 W. Quay Ave., Artesia, NM 88210
Grade Level: K-5
Notes: Items, 11

Measures self-concept relevant to school success. Group administered in English or Spanish. Does not require reading. Factors are aggressiveness/cooperation, peer ostracism/acceptance, intellectual self-image, helpfulness, emotional self, success/nonsuccess.

9637
Sociometric Design Test. Southeastern New Mexico Bilingual Program, Artesia 1972
Descriptors: Bilingual Education; English (Second Language); Peer Relationship; Primary Education; *Sociometric Techniques; *Spanish Speaking
Availability: Southeastern New Mexico Bilingual Program; Artesia Public Schools, 1106 W. Quay Ave., Artesia, NM 88210
Grade Level: 1-3
Notes: Items, 4

Elicits 3 names of class members that each child would select to attend a party, play a game, help complete a drawing, and one whom the child would visit for play.

9640
Mood Scales. Raskin, Allen; And Others 1967
Descriptors: Adults; *Depression (Psychology); Drug Therapy; Emotional Response; *Mental Disorders; *Patients; Psychiatric Hospitals; *Psychological Patterns; *Rating Scales
Identifiers: *Moods
Availability: Allen Raskin, Research Psychologist; National Institute of Mental Health, 5600 Fishers Ln., Rockville, MD 20852
Target Audience: Adults
Notes: Items, 52

An adjective checklist giving particular emphasis to items which have reflected shifts in psychiatric patient mood as a function of drug treatment.

9655
Inventario Personal "Bown." Forma R-3. Bown, Oliver H. 1960
Descriptors: Adults; *Employment Qualifications; *Health Personnel; *Mental Health; *Personality Assessment; Personnel Evaluation; *Screening Tests; Spanish; *Spanish Speaking
Availability: Oliver H. Bown; Research and Development Center for Teacher Education, University of Texas, Austin, TX 78712
Target Audience: Adults
Notes: Time, 15; Items, 48

Measures individuals' reactions and feelings toward situations, other people, and themselves.

9662
Skills Inventory. Frank, Alan R.; And Others 1971
Descriptors: *Adjustment (to Environment); Adolescents; *Informal Assessment; Job Skills; Mental Retardation; *Mild Mental Retardation; Secondary School Students
Availability: Teaching Exceptional Children; p82-86 Win 1971
Target Audience: 14-17
Notes: Items, 7

Informal inventory designed to help the teacher of secondary-level mentally retarded students determine strengths and weaknesses in dealing with daily living activities such as using want ads, a telephone book, buying insurance.

9666
Barrio Test of Primary Abilities (Form A). Oliveria, Arnulfo L. 1972
Descriptors: Adults; Cultural Awareness; *Elementary School Teachers; *Intelligence Tests; *Spanish Speaking; *Testing Problems
Availability: Educational Leadership, p169-70 Nov 1972
Target Audience: Adults
Notes: Items, 16

An intelligence test for teachers working with Spanish-speaking students. Designed to raise the consciousness of teachers about the problems of students from the barrio.

9686
Laurelton Self Attitude Scale. Butler, Alfred J. 1961
Subtests: Buffer Items (6); Physical Appearance (15); Physical Health (15); Interpersonal-Peers (10); Interpersonal-Nonpeers or General (32); Personal Worth (39); Mental Health (28); Lie Scale (10)
Descriptors: Adolescents; Adults; *Females; *Mental Retardation; Personality Assessment; *Questionnaires; *Self Concept
Availability: Laurelton State School and Hospital; Laurelton, PA 17835
Target Audience: 14-22
Notes: Items, 156

Recommended for use only for research purposes to identify patterns of self-attitudes which characterize subgroups of retarded subjects. Self-attitudes are viewed as a major determinant of the behavior and perceptions of retarded persons. A 50-item short form is also available.

9690
Tower System. Institute for the Crippled and Disabled, New York, NY 1967
Descriptors: Adults; *Mental Retardation; *Physical Disabilities; *Vocational Rehabilitation; *Work Sample Tests
Availability: ICD Rehabilitation and Research; 340 E. 24th St.; New York, NY 10010
Target Audience: Adults

A system of work sample tests for use with crippled and disabled clients. Includes 14 broad areas of vocational evaluation: clerical, drafting, drawing, electronics assembly, jewelry manufacturing, leather goods, lettering, machine shop, mail clerk, optical mechanics, pantograph engraving, sewing machine operating, welding, and workshop assembly.

9697
Spanish Criterion Referenced Test. Austin Independent School District, TX Bilingual Program 1974
Descriptors: *Bilingual Students; *Criterion Referenced Tests; Elementary Education; Elementary School Students; *Mastery Tests; Phonetic Analysis; Reading Comprehension; *Reading Tests; *Spanish; *Spanish Speaking; Structural Analysis (Linguistics)
Identifiers: TIM(F)
Availability: Tests in Microfiche; Test Collection, Educational Testing Service, Princeton, NJ 08541
Grade Level: K-5

Designed to assess mastery level in a Spanish-language reading program for bilingual students in grades K-5. Covers phonetic and structural analysis and comprehension.

9708
Information Test of Intelligence. Guthrie, George M. 1970
Descriptors: *Adults; Cultural Influences; *Culture Fair Tests; Foreign Countries; *Intelligence Tests; *Rural Population; Test Bias; Testing Problems
Identifiers: *Philippines
Availability: ERIC Document Reproduction Service; 3900 Wheeler Ave., Alexandria, VA 22304 (ED054212, 11 pages)
Target Audience: Adults
Notes: Items, 25

Constructed for use with rural Filipinos. Questions are based on experiences common to this population. Cannot be used to compare groups from markedly different cultural backgrounds.

9723
Social and Prevocational Information Battery, Form T. University of Oregon, Eugene 1979
Subtests: Pretest (30); Hygiene and Grooming (30); Functional Signs (29); Job Related Behavior (29); Home Management (33); Health Care (32); Job Search Skills (32); Budgeting (35); Banking (32); Purchasing Habits (39)
Descriptors: Communication Skills; *Daily Living Skills; Home Economics Skills; Hygiene; Job Skills; Knowledge Level; *Mild Mental Retardation; *Moderate Mental Retardation; Secondary Education; Secondary School Students
Identifiers: SPIB
Availability: Publishers Test Service; Order Services Center, 2500 Garden Rd., Monterey, CA 93940
Grade Level: 7-12
Notes: Time, 135; Items, 320

This revision is designed for use with trainable and low-functioning mentally retarded students. Nine tests are administered orally to individuals or small groups. Cover skills and competencies necessary for community adjustment. Pretest identifies students who cannot respond.

9725
Spanish-English Reading and Vocabulary Screening. CTB/McGraw-Hill, Monterey, CA 1978
Subtests: Spanish Practice Test (10); English Practice Test (10); Test Terms (14); Sentence Reading (10)
Descriptors: *Bilingual Students; Elementary Education; Elementary School Students; Language Dominance; Primary Education; *Spanish Speaking; *Test Wiseness
Identifiers: *Practice Tests
Availability: CTB/McGraw-Hill; Del Monte Research Park, Monterey, CA 93940
Grade Level: K-8
Notes: Items, 44

Multiple-choice test designed to determine whether a student should be tested with Spanish or English form of achievement test, to give practice in marking responses, to measure oral comprehension of test directions and terms.

9735
Social-Sexual Knowledge and Attitudes Questionnaire. Edmonson, Barbara; And Others 1977
Descriptors: Adults; Mild Mental Retardation; *Moderate Mental Retardation; *Opinions; Parent Attitudes; Questionnaires; Sex Education; *Sexuality; Teacher Attitudes; *Test Construction
Availability: ERIC Document Reproduction Service; 3900 Wheeler Ave., Alexandria, VA 22304 (ED160643, microfiche only).
Target Audience: Adults
Notes: Items, 22

Designed to elicit recommendations of parents, educators, and others as to which sociosexual areas should be sampled prior to the construction of a sex knowledge and attitude test for mildly and moderately mentally retarded subjects.

9744
Dyadic Oral Tests. Findley, Charles A. 1977
Descriptors: *Communication Skills; *Daily Living Skills; Elementary Education; Elementary School Students; *English (Second Language); *Teaching Methods
Identifiers: *Oral Tests
Availability: ERIC Document Reproduction Service; 3900 Wheeler Ave., Alexandria, VA 22304 (ED145692, 41 pages)
Grade Level: 1-6

Groups of tasks to provide experience in purposeful communication for students of English as a Second Language in the form of requests, manipulative instructions, and descriptions. May be used as a test of proficiency.

9757
Preschool Inventory, Spanish Edition. Caldwell, Bettye M. 1974
Descriptors: Academic Achievement; *Learning Readiness; Preschool Education; *School Readiness Tests; *Spanish Speaking
Availability: Publishers Test Service; 2500 Garden Rd., Monterey, CA 93940
Target Audience: 3-5
Notes: Time, 30; Items, 64

Screening test for achievement in areas necessary for success in school. Reveals degree of disadvantage of a child entering school. Covers self-knowledge, ability to follow directions, verbal expression, basic numerical concepts, and sensory attributes. Fall norms are based on a Head Start population.

9760
Learning Staircase. Coughran, Lila; Goff, Marilyn 1976
Subtests: Adjectives (11); Auditory Memory (79); Auditory Perception (34); Body Image (24); Classification (21); Colors (13); Fine Motor (81); Gross Motor (54); Number Concepts (41): Reading Readiness (28); Same and Different (38); Sequence (6); Spatial Relations (23); Time (9); Verbal Comprehension (16); Expression (18); Vocabulary (7); Visual Memory (22)
Descriptors: *Diagnostic Tests; Early Childhood Education; Educational Diagnosis; *Individualized Instruction; *Special Education; Student Evaluation; Young Children
Availability: Learning Concepts, 2501 N. Lamar, Austin, TX 78705
Target Audience: 2-7
Notes: Items, 525

Program developed for early childhood special education classes to provide diagnosis of individual children and evaluation of the results of the individualized curriculum. Tasks are presented on individual cards at each developmental level.

9781
School Readiness Test, Spanish Language Edition. Anderhalter, O. F. 1977

Subtests: Word Recognition (15); Identifying Letters (20): Visual Discrimination (15); Handwriting Readiness (10); Auditory Discrimination (13); Comprehension and Interpretation (12); Number Readiness (30)
Descriptors: Auditory Discrimination; Comprehension; Early Childhood Education; Writing Readiness; *Kindergarten; Letters (Alphabet); Numbers; *School Readiness Tests; *Spanish Speaking; Visual Discrimination; Word Recognition; Handwriting
Availability: Scholastic Testing Service; 480 Meyer Rd. Bensenville, IL 60106
Grade Level: K-1
Notes: Time, 60; Items, 115

Group administered at end of grade K or before third full week of grade 1. Test results place child at one of 6 readiness levels: Long Delay, Short Delay, Marginal, Average Ready, Superior Ready, Gifted Ready.

9786
CTBS Espanol, Level B. Norwalk-La Mirada Unified School District, CA 1978
Subtests: Word Recognition I (19); Word Recognition II (19); Reading Comprehension (24); Mathematics Computation (24): Mathematics Concepts and Applications (16)
Descriptors: *Achievement Tests; *Grade 1; *Mathematical Applications; *Mathematical Concepts; Primary Education; Reading Comprehension; *Reading Tests; Spanish Speaking; Vocabulary; Word Recognition
Availability: CTB/McGraw-Hill; Del Monte Research Park, Monterey, CA 93940
Grade Level: K-1
Notes: Time, 133; Items, 102

Spanish-language adaptation of CTBS/S Reading and Mathematics tests.

9787
CTBS Espanol, Level C. Norwalk-La Mirada Unified School District, CA 1978
Subtests: Reading Vocabulary (33); Reading Comprehension (41); Mathematics Computation (28); Mathematics Concepts and Applications (25)
Descriptors: *Achievement Tests; *Grade 2; *Mathematical Applications; *Mathematical Concepts; Primary Education; Reading Comprehension; *Reading Tests; Spanish Speaking; Vocabulary; Word Recognition
Availability: CTB/McGraw-Hill; Del Monte Research Park, Monterey, CA 93940
Grade Level: 1-2
Notes: Time, 150; Items, 127

Spanish-language adaptation of CTBS/S Reading and Mathematics tests.

9788
CTBS Espanol, Level 1. Norwalk-La Mirada Unified School District, CA 1978
Subtests: Reading Vocabulary (40); Reading Comprehension (45); Mathematics Computation (48); Mathematics Concepts and Applications (50)
Descriptors: *Achievement Tests; Intermediate Grades; *Mathematical Applications; *Mathematical Concepts; Primary Education; Reading Comprehension; *Reading Tests; Spanish Speaking; Vocabulary
Availability: CTB/McGraw-Hill; Del Monte Research Park, Monterey, CA 93940
Grade Level: 2-4
Notes: Items, 183

Spanish adaptation of the Comprehensive Tests of Basic Skills, Form S, Reading and Mathematics.

9789
CTBS Espanol, Level 2. Norwalk-La Mirada Unified School District, CA 1978
Subtests: Reading Vocabulary (40); Reading Comprehension (45); Mathematics Computation (48); Mathematics Concepts and Applications (50)
Descriptors: *Achievement Tests; Intermediate Grades; *Mathematical Applications; *Mathematical Concepts; Reading Comprehension; *Reading Tests; Spanish Speaking; Vocabulary
Availability: CTB/McGraw-Hill; Del Monte Research Park, Monterey, CA 93940
Grade Level: 4-6
Notes: Items, 183

Spanish adaptation of the Comprehensive Tests of Basic Skills, Form S, Reading and Mathematics.

9790
CTBS Espanol, Level 3. Norwalk-La Mirada Unified School District, CA 1978

Subtests: Reading Vocabulary (40); Reading Comprehension (45); Mathematics Computation (48); Mathematics Concepts and Applications (50)
Descriptors: *Achievement Tests; Intermediate Grades; Junior High Schools; *Mathematical Applications; *Mathematical Concepts; Reading Comprehension; *Reading Tests; Spanish Speaking; Vocabulary
Availability: CTB/McGraw Hill; Del Monte Research Park, Monterey, CA 93940
Grade Level: 6-8
Notes: Items, 183

Spanish-language edition of the Comprehensive Tests of Basic Skills, Form S, Reading and Mathematics.

9796
Program for Assessing Youth Employment Skills. Educational Testing Service, Princeton, NJ 1979
Subtests: Job Holding Skills; Attitude toward Supervision; Self Confidence; Job Knowledge; Job Seeking Skills; Practical Reasoning; Vocational Interest Inventory
Descriptors: Adolescents; Adults; Attitude Measures; Business; Clerical Occupations; Creative Activities; Diagnostic Tests; Disadvantaged Youth; Dropouts; *Job Skills; Knowledge Level; Multiple Choice Tests; *Occupational Information; Outdoor Activities; Sciences; Secondary Schools; *Self Esteem; Service Occupations; Sex Fairness; Supervision; Technical Occupations; *Vocational Education; *Vocational Interests; *Work Attitudes; Young Adults
Identifiers: Oral Testing; PAYES; Reasoning
Availability: Cambridge Book Co.; 888 Seventh Ave., New York, NY 10019
Target Audience: 16-21
Notes: Time, 75; Items, 134

Designed to assist program directors, counselors, and teachers in the guidance and counseling of persons with low verbal skills as they prepare for entry-level employment. Used with school dropouts, potential dropouts, and disadvantaged youth.

9797
Hospital Experience Inventory. Meketon, Jerry 1968
Subtests: Experiencing; Desirability
Descriptors: Adults; *Expectation; *Experience; Hospitals; *Institutional Environment; Patients; Questionnaires; Therapeutic Environment
Identifiers: Drug Addicts; TIM(E)
Availability: Tests in Microfiche; Test Collection, Educational Testing Service, Princeton, NJ 08541
Target Audience: Adults
Notes: Items, 44

Administered to patients on arrival and at dismissal from hospital setting to determine the correlation between patients' initial expectations and actual experiences.

9815
Test of Language Dominance. ELNAS Version. Revised Edition. Bass, Willard P. 1977
Subtests: Receptive Skills (English); Receptive Skills (Spanish); Expressive Skills (English); Expressive Skills (Spanish)
Descriptors: Bilingual Students; English (Second Language); *Expressive Language; *Language Dominance; *Language Proficiency; *Language Tests; *Navajo; Primary Education; *Receptive Language; *Spanish Speaking; *Young Children
Identifiers: *ERA Language Needs Assessment
Availability: Southwest Research Associates; P.O. Box 4092, Albuquerque, NM 87106
Target Audience: 5-8

Measures a child's proficiency in each of 2 languages and compares proficiency to determine language dominance. Both receptive and expressive skills are measured in Spanish-English and Navajo-English.

9816
Stanford Early School Achievement Test; Level 1. Navajo Edition. Morgan, William; Harvey, Anthony 1970
Subtests: Environment: Social Studies and Science; Mathematics; Letters and Sounds: English; Letters and Sounds: Navajo; Aural Comprehension
Descriptors: *Achievement Tests; *American Indians; Arithmetic; *Grade 1; *Kindergarten Children; Listening Skills; *Navajo; Oral Reading; Primary Education; Sciences; Social Studies
Availability: Southwest Research Associates; P.O. Box 4092, Albuquerque, NM 87106
Grade Level: K-1
Notes: Time, 90; Items, 126

Test items were adapted, with permission, for Navajo children from the Stanford Early School Achievement Test. Test may be completed in up to 5 sittings.

9837
Liquid Quantity Conservation Task. Hess, Robert D.; Shipman, Virginia C. 1967
Descriptors: Academic Achievement; Black Mothers; *Black Students; Cognitive Development; Conceptual Tempo; Economic Factors; Family Environment; Individual Testing; Longitudinal Studies; *Parent Child Relationship; Parent Influence; *Preschool Children; Preschool Education; Questionnaires; Reading Readiness
Identifiers: Project Head Start
Availability: ERIC Document Reproduction Service; 3900 Wheeler Ave., Alexandria, VA 22304 (ED022550, 68 pages)
Target Audience: 2-5

One of a series of instruments designed to measure child's cognitive abilities, impulsivity, and reading readiness and the mother's attitudes about school, her intelligence level, and her flexibility of thought. The instruments were developed for use in a study of mothers and their preschool children to determine the differential effects of middle and lower socioeconomic group cognitive environments on Black urban preschool children.

9838
Length Conservation Task. Hess, Robert D.; Shipman, Virginia C. 1967
Descriptors: *Black Mothers; *Black Students; Cognitive Development; Conservation (Concept); Economic Factors; Family Environment; Longitudinal Studies; *Parent Child Relationship; Parent Influence; *Preschool Children; Preschool Education
Identifiers: Length; Project Head Start
Availability: ERIC Document Reproduction Service; 3900 Wheeler Ave., Alexandria, VA 22304 (ED022550, 68 pages)
Target Audience: 4-5
Notes: Items, 6

One of a series of instruments designed to measure child's cognitive abilities, impulsivity, and reading readiness and the mother's attitudes about school, her intelligence level, and her flexibility of thought. The instruments were developed for use in a study of mothers and their preschool children to determine the differential effects of middle and lower socioeconomic group cognitive environments on Black urban preschool children.

9839
Number Constancy Test. Hess, Robert D.; Shipman, Virginia C. 1967
Descriptors: *Black Mothers; *Black Students; Cognitive Development; Economic Factors; Family Environment; Longitudinal Studies; Numbers; *Parent Child Relationship; Parent Influence; *Preschool Children; Preschool Education
Identifiers: Project Head Start
Availability: ERIC Document Reproduction Service; 3900 Wheeler Ave., Alexandria, VA 22304 (ED022550, 68 pages)
Target Audience: 4-5
Notes: Items, 3

One of a series of instruments designed to measure child's cognitive abilities, impulsivity, and reading readiness and the mother's attitudes about school, her intelligence level, and her flexibility of thought. The instruments were developed for use in a study of mothers and their preschool children to determine the differential effects of middle and lower socioeconomic group cognitive environments on Black urban preschool children.

9840
Ring Segment Task. Hess, Robert D.; Shipman, Virginia C. 1967
Descriptors: *Black Mothers; *Black Students; Cognitive Development; Economic Factors; Family Environment; Longitudinal Studies; *Parent Child Relationship; Parent Influence; *Preschool Children; Preschool Education
Identifiers: Measurement (Mathematics); Project Head Start
Availability: ERIC Document Reproduction Service; 3900 Wheeler Ave., Alexandria, VA 22304 (ED022550, 68 pages)
Target Audience: 4-5
Notes: Items, 5

One of a series of instruments designed to measure child's cognitive abilities, impulsivity, and reading readiness and the mother's attitudes about school, her intelligence level, and her flexibility of thought. The instruments were developed for use in a study of mothers and their preschool children to determine the differential effects of middle and lower socioeconomic group cognitive environments on Black urban preschool children.

9841
Generic Identity Task. Hess, Robert D.; Shipman, Virginia C. 1967
Descriptors: *Black Mothers; *Black Students; Cognitive Development; Concept Formation; Economic Factors; Family Environment; Longitudinal Studies; *Parent Child Relationship; Parent Influence; *Preschool Children; Preschool Education
Identifiers: Generic Identity; Project Head Start
Availability: ERIC Document Reproduction Service; 3900 Wheeler Ave., Alexandria, VA 22304 (ED022550, 68 pages)
Target Audience: 4-5
Notes: Items, 6

One of a series of instruments designed to measure child's cognitive abilities, impulsivity, and reading readiness and the mother's attitudes about school, her intelligence level, and her flexibility of thought. The instruments were developed for use in a study of mothers and their preschool children to determine the differential effects of middle and lower socioeconomic group cognitive environments on Black urban preschool children.

9842
Class Inclusion Task. Hess, Robert D.; Shipman, Virginia C. 1967
Descriptors: *Black Mothers; *Black Students; Classification; Cognitive Development; Economic Factors; Family Environment; Longitudinal Studies; *Parent Child Relationship; Parent Influence; *Preschool Children; Preschool Education
Identifiers: Project Head Start
Availability: ERIC Document Reproduction Service; 3900 Wheeler Ave., Alexandria, VA 22304 (ED022550, 68 pages)
Target Audience: 4-5
Notes: Items, 7

One of a series of instruments designed to measure child's cognitive abilities, impulsivity, and reading readiness and the mother's attitudes about school, her intelligence level, and her flexibility of thought. The instruments were developed for use in a study of mothers and their preschool children to determine the differential effects of middle and lower socioeconomic group cognitive environments on Black urban preschool children.

9843
Dream Interview. Hess, Robert D.; Shipman, Virginia C. 1967
Descriptors: *Black Mothers; *Black Students; Cognitive Development; Economic Factors; Family Environment; Interviews; Longitudinal Studies; *Parent Child Relationship; Parent Influence; *Preschool Children; Preschool Education
Identifiers: *Dreams; Project Head Start; Reality
Availability: ERIC Document Reproduction Service; 3900 Wheeler Ave., Alexandria, VA 22304 (ED022550, 68 pages)
Target Audience: 4-5

One of a series of instruments designed to measure child's cognitive abilities, impulsivity, and reading readiness and the mother's attitudes about school, her intelligence level, and her flexibility of thought. The instruments were developed for use in a study of mothers and their preschool children to determine the differential effects of middle and lower socioeconomic group cognitive environments on Black urban preschool children. Interview technique designed to assess preschool child's comprehension of dreams versus reality.

9844
Draw a Circle Slowly. Hess, Robert D.; Shipman, Virginia C. 1967
Descriptors: *Black Mothers; *Black Students; Cognitive Development; Economic Factors; Family Environment; Longitudinal Studies; *Parent Child Relationship; Parent Influence; *Preschool Children; Preschool Education
Identifiers: Project Head Start
Availability: ERIC Document Reproduction Service; 3900 Wheeler Ave., Alexandria, VA 22304 (ED022550, 68 pages)
Target Audience: 4-5

One of a series of instruments designed to measure child's cognitive abilities, impulsivity, and reading readiness and the mother's attitudes about school, her intelligence level, and her flexibility of thought. The instruments were developed for use in a study of mothers and their preschool children to determine the differential effects of middle and lower socioeconomic group cognitive environments on Black urban preschool children.

9845
Cusiosity Task. Hess, Robert D.; Shipman, Virginia C. 1967
Descriptors: *Black Mothers; *Black Students; Cognitive Development; *Curiosity; Economic Factors; Family Environment; Individual Testing; Longitudinal Studies; *Parent Child Relationship; Parent Influence; *Preschool Children; Preschool Education
Identifiers: Project Head Start

Availability: ERIC Document Reproduction Service; 3900 Wheeler Ave., Alexandria, VA 22304 (ED022550, 68 pages)
Target Audience: 4-5
Notes: Items, 16

One of a series of instruments designed to measure child's cognitive abilities, impulsivity, and reading readiness and the mother's attitudes about school, her intelligence level, and her flexibility of thought. The instruments were developed for use in a study of mothers and their preschool children to determine the differential effects of middle and lower socioeconomic group cognitive environments on Black urban preschool children. Designed to assess preschool child's curiosity through use of 8 pairs of simple and complex drawings which child examined with a viewing apparatus.

9848
Somato-Chroma Apperception Test. Caldwell, Willard E.; Matoon, Creighton U. 1966
Descriptors: *Adolescents; *Adults; Black Youth; *Body Image; Individual Testing; Projective Measures; *Self Concept; *Self Concept Measures
Availability: Journal of General Psychology; v74 p253-72 1966
Target Audience: 12-40
Notes: Time, 12 approx.; Items, 8

Designed to assess individual's body image with specific interest in the aspect of skin color.

9851
Prueba de Lectura. Wisconsin State Dept. of Public Instruction, Madison Ozete, Oscar 1978
Descriptors: *Bilingual Students; *Cloze Procedure; Elementary Education; Grade 3; Grade 6; *Native Speakers; Reading Comprehension; *Reading Tests; *Spanish; *Spanish Speaking
Identifiers: TIM(F)
Availability: Tests in Microfiche; Test Collection, Educational Testing Service, Princeton, NJ 08541
Grade Level: 3; 6
Notes: Items, 40

Designed to assess reading comprehension in the child's native Spanish for bilingual children as part of a program for developing reading competence in the child's first language before attempting to instruct the child in reading in a second language. Uses cloze procedure and multiple choice to measure literal comprehension and skill in making inferences and obtaining instruction. Has 2 parallel forms.

9854
Language Dominance Survey. San Bernardino City Unified School District, CA 1975
Subtests: Listening; Speaking; Reading; Writing; Home Language Usage
Descriptors: *Bilingual Education; Bilingualism; Bilingual Students; Elementary Secondary Education; *Language Dominance; *Language Tests; *Spanish Speaking
Identifiers: TIM(F)
Availability: Tests in Microfiche; Test Collection, Educational Testing Service, Princeton, NJ 08541
Grade Level: K-12
Notes: Items, 37

This 5-part survey was designed to identify students with problems in the development of English and/or Spanish-language skills and to identify the dominant home language. Covers aural-oral skills in grades K-1 and listening, speaking, reading, writing, and home language usage in the upper grades.

9878
Self-Esteem Inventory. Grobe, Robert P. 1974
Descriptors: Attitude Measures; Black Students; Ethnic Groups; *Minority Groups; *Reading Difficulties; Secondary Education; *Secondary School Students; *Self Concept Measures; *Self Esteem; Teacher Attitudes
Identifiers: TIM(F)
Availability: Tests in Microfiche; Test Collection, Educational Testing Service, Princeton, NJ 08541
Grade Level: 7-12
Notes: Time, 10 approx.; Items, 15

Used in conjunction with a school and reading attitude survey (not included here) in a Secondary Reading Project for students in grades 7-12, who fall far below national norms in reading. Contains questions designed to measure general self-esteem for groups of students with low reading ability. A form is included on which teacher estimates which 5 students have highest and lowest self-esteem. Author recommends cautious use for diagnosis of individuals.

9882
Age Independence Scale. Keith, Robert Allen 1969

Descriptors: Adolescents; Attitude Measures; Cerebral Palsy; Children; Interpersonal Competence; Mental Retardation; *Parent Aspiration; *Parent Attitudes; Physical Disabilities; *Prediction; *Self Care Skills
Identifiers: *Independent Behavior; TIM(F)
Availability: Tests in Microfiche; Test Collection, Educational Testing Service, Princeton, NJ 08541
Target Audience: 2-18

Parent and professional indicate those behaviors a handicapped child now performs, the age at which it is felt the child will be able to perform other behaviors, and those behaviors the child will never be able to perform. Covers motor, cognitive, social, and self-care behaviors. Used in a study of parent's unrealistic expectations for their handicapped child. Preschool Form contains 75 items; the Elementary Form, 105 items; the Adolescent Form contains 60 items. Reliability data were available for the Preschool Form only. Some items of this form were taken from the Vineland Social Maturity Scale as well as other sources.

9887
Escala Internacional de Conducta Adaptiva. Richmond, Bert O.; de la Serna, Marcelo 1978
Subtests: Desarrollo del Lenguaje; Funcionamiento Independiente; Desempeno del Papel Familiar; Actividad Economica-Vocacional; Socializacion
Descriptors: *Adjustment (to Environment); Children; Daily Living Skills; Elementary Education; *Elementary School Students; Language Proficiency; Maturity (Individuals); *Maturity Tests; Mild Mental Retardation; Slow Learners; Social Adjustment; *Spanish; Spanish Speaking
Identifiers: EICA
Availability: Dr. Bert O. Richmond, Counselor; 408 Aderhold, University of Georgia, College of Education, School of Psychology Program, Athens, GA 30602
Grade Level: K-6
Target Audience: 5-10
Notes: Time, 25 approx.; Items, 115

Used to obtain an indication of the children's social competency and adjustment in 5 areas: language proficiency; daily living skills; basic everyday functions; basic economic skills; and social skills. Appropriate for use with children between the ages of 5 and 10. Preliminary studies indicate it can be used with slow learners and educable mentally retarded subjects. Test administrators elicit answers to questions from the children.

9890
Anders Childrearing Scale. Anders, Sarah Frances 1967
Descriptors: Adults; *Attendants; Attitude Measures; *Child Rearing; *Ethnic Origins; *Institutionalized Persons; *Mental Retardation; *Residential Care; Socioeconomic Status
Identifiers: Attendant Attitudes; *Permissiveness; TIM(F)
Availability: Tests in Microfiche; Test Collection, Educational Testing Service, Princeton, NJ 08541
Target Audience: Adults
Notes: Items, 47

Consists of statements concerned with childrearing practices and several alternative courses of action or age levels. Respondent selects choice of action or age level which corresponds to their own practices or beliefs. The scale was used in a study of the relationship between certain ethnic variables and permissive childrearing beliefs of attendants with direct patient care in an institution for mentally retarded patients. Covers practices related to infancy, early childhood, pre-puberty, and adolescence.

9894
Pupil Communication Skills Inventory. Brentwood Union School District, CA
Descriptors: Bilingualism; *Bilingual Students; Children; *Communication Skills; Comprehension; Concept Formation; Grammar; Rating Scales; *Spanish Speaking; Speech Communication
Identifiers: TIM(F)
Availability: Tests in Microfiche; Test Collection, Educational Testing Service, Princeton, NJ 08541
Target Audience: Children

Teacher rating of the frequency with which a child performs a list of behaviors in Spanish or in English. Behaviors are concerned with oral communication, conceptual knowledge, knowledge of grammar, and comprehension skill. Orientation form has 46 items. Transitional form has 47 items.

9896
Criterion Reference Tests for Golden Mountain Reading Series. Sung, Robert 1977
Descriptors: *Bilingual Education; Bilingual Students; *Chinese; *Chinese Americans; *Criterion Referenced Tests; Elementary Education; *Elementary School Students; Language Tests; Pretests Posttests; Reading Achievement; *Reading Tests; Word Recognition
Availability: Bilingual Education Dept.; 300 Seneca Ave., San Francisco, CA 94112
Grade Level: 1-7

A series of pretests and posttests developed to evaluate student progress. The instruments are coordinated with the Golden Mountain Reading Series. All items are written in Chinese.

9903
Criterion Referenced Test: MGS/CRTest Eastern Navajo Agency, Level B. Dougherty, Dan; And Others 1978
Subtests: Language Arts; Mathematics
Descriptors: *Academic Achievement; *American Indians; *Criterion Referenced Tests; Kindergarten; *Kindergarten Children; Language Arts; Mathematics; *Minimum Competencies; Primary Education
Identifiers: *Navajo (Nation); TIM(F)
Availability: Tests in Microfiche; Test Collection, Educational Testing Service, Princeton, NJ 08541
Grade Level: Kindergarten
Notes: Items, 34

Developed for use in instructional planning, diagnosis, and remediation, this series covers grades K-8 and is designed to measure Navajo student progress in the achievement of minimum grade standards (MGS) in basic skills. Level B, for Grade K, covers language arts, listening (Navajo and English), visual skills, classification, and identification of objects; mathematics, counting, writing numbers, shapes, addition. Pictures and items reflect local living environment and culture. This test is untimed.

9904
Criterion-Referenced Test: MGS/CRTest Eastern Navajo Agency, Level C. Dougherty, Don; And Others 1978
Subtests: Language Arts; Mathematics
Descriptors: *Academic Achievement; *American Indians; *Criterion Referenced Tests; *Grade 1; Language Arts; Mathematics; *Minimum Competencies; Primary Education
Identifiers: *Navajo (Nation); TIM(F)
Availability: Tests in Microfiche; Test Collection, Educational Testing Service, Princeton, NJ 08541
Grade Level: 1
Notes: Items, 22

Developed for use in instructional planning, diagnosis, and remediation, this series covers grades K-8 and is designed to measure Navajo student progress in the achievement of minimum grade standards (MGS) in basic skills. Level C covers language arts, sounds, word and sentence recognition, reading comprehension, word skills; mathematics, shapes, time, more and less, numerals, addition, subtraction. Pictures, items reflect local environment and culture. This test is untimed.

9905
Criterion-Referenced Test: MGS/CRTest Eastern Navajo Agency, Level D. Dougherty, Don; And Others 1978
Subtests: Language Arts; Mathematics; Science
Descriptors: *Academic Achievement; *American Indians; *Criterion Referenced Tests; *Grade 2; Language Arts; Mathematics; *Minimum Competencies; Primary Education; Sciences
Identifiers: *Navajo (Nation); TIM(F)
Availability: Tests in Microfiche; Test Collection, Educational Testing Service, Princeton, NJ 08541
Grade Level: 2
Notes: Items, 26

Developed for use in instructional planning, diagnosis, and remediation, this series covers grades K-8 and is designed to measure Navajo student progress in the achievement of minimum grade standards (MGS) in basic skills. Level D covers language arts, punctuation, capitalization, comprehension, consonants, word usage; mathematics, place, equations, addition, time, problems, fractions, money; science, plants, animals, seasons, and energy. Pictures, items reflect local environment and culture. This test is untimed.

9906
Criterion-Referenced Test: MGS/CRTest Eastern Navajo Agency, Level E. Dougherty, Don; And Others 1978
Subtests: Language Arts; Mathematics; Science; Social Studies
Descriptors: *Academic Achievement; *American Indians; *Criterion Referenced Tests; *Grade 3; Language Arts; Mathematics; *Minimum Competencies; Primary Education; Sciences; Social Studies
Identifiers: *Navajo (Nation); TIM(F)
Availability: Tests in Microfiche; Test Collection, Educational Testing Service, Princeton, NJ 08541
Grade Level: 3
Notes: Items, 30

Developed for use in instructional planning, diagnosis, and remediation, this series covers grades K-8 and is designed to measure Navajo student progress in the achievement of minimum grade standards (MGS) in basic skills. Level E covers language arts, parts of speech, punctuation, word usage, comprehension; mathematics, place value, operations, time, shape, money, fractions; science, plants, animals, machines; social studies, office holders, maps. This test is untimed.

9907
Criterion-Referenced Test: MGS/CRTest Eastern Navajo Agency, Level F. Dougherty, Don; And Others 1978
Subtests: Language Arts; Mathematics; Science; Social Studies; Health
Descriptors: *Academic Achievement; *American Indians; *Criterion Referenced Tests; *Grade 4; Health; Intermediate Grades; Language Arts; Mathematics; *Minimum Competencies; Sciences; Social Studies
Identifiers: *Navajo (Nation); TIM(F)
Availability: Tests in Microfiche; Test Collection, Educational Testing Service, Princeton, NJ 08541
Grade Level: 4
Notes: Items, 36

Developed for use in instructional planning, diagnosis, and remediation, this series covers grades K-8 and is designed to measure Navajo student progress in the achievement of minimum grade standards (MGS) in basic skills. Level F covers language arts, synonyms etc., reading comprehension, parts of speech, word skills, reference skills, sentences, punctuation, possessives, capitalization; mathematics, measuring, operations, time, fractions, perimeter, problems; science, habitats, weather, water cycle, man and environment; social studies, office holders, researching, map skills; health, safety, body systems, hygiene. This test is untimed.

9908
Criterion-Referenced Test: MGS/CRTest Eastern Navajo Agency, Level G. Dougherty, Don; And Others 1978
Subtests: Language Arts; Mathematics; Science; Social Studies; Health
Descriptors: *Academic Achievement; *American Indians; *Criterion Referenced Tests; *Grade 5; Health; Intermediate Grades; Language Arts; Mathematics; *Minimum Competencies; Sciences; Social Studies
Identifiers: *Navajo (Nation); TIM(F)
Availability: Tests in Microfiche; Test Collection, Educational Testing Service, Princeton, NJ 08541
Grade Level: 5
Notes: Items, 48

Developed for use in instructional planning, diagnosis, and remediation, this series covers grades K-8 and is designed to measure Navajo student progress in the achievement of minimum grade standards (MGS) in basic skills. Level G covers language arts, synonyms, etc., affixes, reference skills, reading comprehension, sentences, mechanics, usage; mathematics, operations, time, shapes, measures, fractions, money, problems; science, animals, seasons, oxygen/carbon dioxide, oceans, minerals, friction, stars/planets; social studies, peoples, Navajo history, geography, topography; health, body systems, senses, exercises. This test is untimed.

9909
Criterion-Referenced Test: MGS/CRTest Eastern Navajo Agency, Level H. Dougherty, Don; And Others 1978
Subtests: Language Arts; Mathematics; Science; Social Studies; Health
Descriptors: *Academic Achievement; *American Indians; *Criterion Referenced Tests; *Grade 6; Health; Intermediate Grades; Language Arts; Mathematics; *Minimum Competencies; Sciences; Social Studies
Identifiers: *Navajo (Nation); TIM(F)
Availability: Tests in Microfiche; Test Collection, Educational Testing Service, Princeton, NJ 08541
Grade Level: 6
Notes: Items, 45

Developed for use in instructional planning, diagnosis, and remediation, this series covers grades K-8 and is designed to measure Navajo student progress in the achievement of minimum grade standards (MGS) in basic skills. Level H covers language arts, affixes, synonyms, comprehension, parts of speech, mechanics, usage, outlining; mathematics, operations, geometry, fractions, measurement, money, problems; science, earth and man, graph reading; social studies, people, countries, climate, consumer role; health, body systems, drugs, exercise, eating habits, first aid. This test is untimed.

9910
Criterion-Referenced Test: MGS/CRTest Eastern Navajo Agency, Level I. Dougherty, Don; And Others 1978
Subtests: Language Arts; Mathematics; Science; Social Studies
Descriptors: *Academic Achievement; *American Indians; *Criterion Referenced Tests; *Grade 7; Junior High Schools; Language Arts; Mathematics; *Minimum Competencies; Sciences; Social Studies
Identifiers: *Navajo (Nation); TIM(F)
Availability: Tests in Microfiche; Test Collection, Educational Testing Service, Princeton, NJ 08541
Grade Level: 7
Notes: Items, 45

Developed for use in instructional planning, diagnosis, and remediation, this series covers grades K-8 and is designed to measure Navajo student progress in the achievement of minimum grade standards (MGS) in basic skills. Level I covers language arts, vocabulary skills, parts of speech, comprehension, punctuation, directions, reference skills, business forms; mathematics, operations, geometry, operations with fractions, problems; science, animals, insects, plants, body systems, chemistry, space, physical forces; social studies, people, Navajo history, local geography, and economics. This test is untimed.

9911
Criterion-Referenced Test: MGS/CRTest Eastern Navajo Agency, Level J. Dougherty, Don; And Others 1978
Subtests: Language Arts; Mathematics; Science; Social Studies
Descriptors: *Academic Achievement; *American Indians; *Criterion Referenced Tests; *Grade 8; Junior High Schools; Language Arts; Mathematics; *Minimum Competencies; Sciences; Social Studies
Identifiers: *Navajo (Nation); TIM(F)
Availability: Tests in Microfiche; Test Collection, Educational Testing Service, Princeton, NJ 08541
Grade Level: 8
Notes: Items, 49

Developed for use in instructional planning, diagnosis, and remediation, this series covers grades K-8 and is designed to measure Navajo student progress in the achievement of minimum grade standards (MGS) in basic skills. Level J covers language arts, skimming, vocabulary, literary forms, comprehension, analysis, writing letters, job applications; mathematics, operations, geometry, operations with fractions, decimals, percent, metrics, problems; science, chemistry, machines, electricity, weather, pollution, first aid; social studies, tribal history and services, government, consumer education. This test is untimed.

9915
Screening Guide for Exceptionalities. Evans, De Ette Britte 1978
Descriptors: Arithmetic; Daily Living Skills; *Elementary School Students; Elementary Secondary Education; *Handicap Identification; Individualized Education Programs; Job Placement; Language Skills; *Learning Disabilities; Perceptual Motor Coordination; Prevocational Education; Reading Skills; *Screening Tests; *Secondary School Students; *Student Evaluation
Identifiers: IEP
Availability: Chronical Guidance Publications; Moravia, NY 13118
Grade Level: K-12

Series of 9 forms completed by teacher, parent, student, and other school personnel; designed for use as a guide for screening and placement of exceptional children. Forms include Parent Letter, Parent Sociological Review, Student Referral Form, Student Survey, Evaluation Summary, Screening Committee Report, Permission for Placement, Admissions Committee Summary Report, and Admissions Committee Report.

9926
Test of Oral English Production. Luft, Max; And Others 1969
Descriptors: Audiotape Recorders; *Diagnostic Tests; *Elementary School Students; *English (Second Language); *Grammatical Acceptability; Individual Testing; *Language Proficiency; *Oral Language; Pretests Posttests; Primary Education; Program Evaluation
Availability: Southwestern Cooperative Educational Laboratory; 229 Truman, N.E., Albuquerque, NM 87108
Grade Level: K-3
Notes: Time, 15 approx.; Items, 83

Designed to elicit spontaneous responses to assess child's oral language proficiency. Responses are tape recorded for later scoring. Partial scores may be obtained for Vocabulary and Pronunciation and for Use of English Grammatical Structures. Also available in microfiche only from ERIC Document Reproduction Service; P.O. Box 190, Arlington, VA 22210 (ED042793).

9927
Myers-Briggs Type Indicator: Form G. Myers, Isabel Briggs; Briggs, Katherine C. 1977
Subtests: Introversion-Extraversion; Sensing-Intuition; Thinking-Feeling; Judging-Perceptive
Descriptors: *Adults; *Career Counseling; Computer Assisted Testing; *Elementary School Students; Elementary Secondary Education; Family Counseling; Microcomputers; *Personality Assessment; Personality Measures; *Personality Traits; Psychological Evaluation; *Secondary School Students; Spanish Speaking
Identifiers: Jung (Carl); MBTI; Self Administered Tests
Availability: Consulting Psychologists Press; 577 College Ave., Palo Alto, CA 94306
Target Audience: 10-64
Notes: Time, 30 approx.; Items, 126

Measure of personality dispositions and interests based on Jung's theory of types. Scales assessed are Introversion-Extraversion, Sensing-Intuition, and Judging-Perceptive which are identical to Myers Briggs Type Indicator: Form F (TC007901). Thinking-Feeling preference scale is slightly different than Form G. Form G is a shorter version designed for use where time and/or reading level make the longer form inadvisable. Designed to ascertain an individual's basic preferences. Form G is also available in a Spanish-language version. Also available for computer-administered testing from Integrated Professional Systems, 5211 Mahoning Ave., Ste. 135, Youngstown, OH 44515.

9929
Assessment of Skills in Computation. Los Angeles Unified School District, CA 1978
Descriptors: *Computation; Diagnostic Teaching; *Diagnostic Tests; Junior High Schools; *Junior High School Students; *Minimum Competencies; Minimum Competency Testing; *Remedial Mathematics; Secondary School Mathematics
Identifiers: ASC
Availability: CTB/McGraw-Hill; Del Monte Research Park, Monterey, CA 93940
Grade Level: 7-9
Notes: Time, 100 approx.; Items, 72

Designed to assess ability to handle computational problems typically encountered in daily life. Provides basic information needed for a diagnostic prescriptive assessment and instructional program. School systems must set their own passing or cut-off scores. Test should be administered in 2 50-minute sessions. ASC may be used in remedial programs for senior high and adult students.

9933
Speaking Test in Spanish/English. Offenberg, Robert M. 1970
Subtests: Repetition; Questions; Spanish
Descriptors: *Achievement Tests; *Bilingual Education; *Communicative Competence (Languages); *Elementary School Students; *English (Second Language); Grade 1; Kindergarten; Language Tests; *Preschool Children; Preschool Education; Primary Education; Program Evaluation; Spanish Speaking
Availability: ERIC Document Reproduction Service; 3900 Wheeler Ave., Alexandria, VA 22304 (ED046295, microfiche only)
Target Audience: 2-6

Measures speaking skills in English and Spanish for bilingual students in nursery school through grade 1. Developed as part of "Let's Be Amigos" program in Philadelphia schools.

9947
Oral Language Ability Scale. Giuliano, Helen Solana; And Others
Descriptors: Bilingual Students; *Diagnostic Tests; Elementary Education; *Elementary School Students; *English (Second Language); Grammar; *Language Proficiency; *Oral English; Oral Language; Spanish Speaking
Identifiers: OLAS; Oral Tests
Availability: Northeast Regional Curriculum Development Center; I. South 184, Complex 419, 778 Forest Ave., Bronx, NY 10456
Grade Level: 1-8
Notes: Items, 33

Designed to measure English-language proficiency of non-English-speaking children and to provide diagnostic information. Used for instructional placement and grouping, as well as for measuring rate of growth in oral English. Part I determines level of language proficiency by the complexity of structural patterns used and proper use of tense and vocabulary. Part II is administered only to

students who are rated 3 or higher on Part I. Part II assesses ability to produce standard grammatical and phonological features.

9996
Examen en Francais. Caribou Bilingual Project, ME
Subtests: Reading Comprehension; Vocabulary; Sentence Meaning; Scrambled Sentences; Vowel Sounds; Beginning Sounds; Rhymes
Descriptors: *Achievement Tests; Bilingual Students; *French; *Grade 3; *Language Proficiency; *Primary Education; Reading Comprehension; Sentences; Sentence Structure; Vocabulary; Word Recognition
Identifiers: Rhyming Words; TIM(G)
Availability: Tests in Microfiche; Test Collection, Educational Testing Service, Princeton, NJ 08541
Grade Level: 3
Notes: Items, 89

Group-administered test of facility in the French language for bilingual students.

9997
Eau Claire Functional Abilities Test. Heal, Laird W. 1972
Descriptors: *Cerebral Palsy; *Children; Exceptional Child Research; *Neurological Impairments; Performance Tests; Physical Disabilities; Psychomotor Skills
Identifiers: ECFAT
Availability: ERIC Document Reproduction Service; 3900 Wheeler Ave., Alexandria, VA 22304 (ED070237, 63 pages)
Target Audience: 6-13
Notes: Items, 10

Designed to evaluate the motor task-solving ability of neuromotorically severely handicapped children. Especially useful with cerebral palsied individuals.

9998
Wolfe-Bluel Socialization Inventory. Heal, Laird W. 1972
Subtests: Self Care; Environmental Orientation; Independence; Communication; Emotional Maturity; Group Interaction; Intellectual Growth
Descriptors: Behavior Rating Scales; *Cerebral Palsy; Children; *Daily Living Skills; Emotional Development; Exceptional Child Research; Intellectual Development; *Neurological Impairments; Social Development; Speech Communication
Identifiers: WBSI
Availability: ERIC Document Reproduction Service; 3900 Wheeler Ave., Alexandria, VA 22304 (ED070237, 63 pages)
Target Audience: 6-13
Notes: Items, 62

Designed to assess the social development of neuromuscularly handicapped children, especially those with cerebral palsy. Inventory is administered and scored through the utilization of informant sources.

10002
Specific Aptitude Test Battery for Ward Clerk (Medical Services). Manpower Administration (DOL), Washington, DC, U.S. Employment Service 1974
Subtests: General Learning Ability; Numerical Aptitude; Clerical Perception; Motor Coordination
Descriptors: Adults; *Aptitude Tests; Career Guidance; Computation; *Culture Fair Tests; Employment Potential; Employment Qualifications; Ethnic Groups; *Hospital Personnel; Job Applicants; Job Skills; *Job Training; Minority Groups; Multiple Choice Tests; Occupational Tests; Personnel Evaluation; Personnel Selection; Predictive Measurement; Mathematics Tests; Timed Tests; *Vocational Aptitude
Identifiers: GATB; General Aptitude Test Battery; SATB; Specific Aptitude Test Battery; USES; *Ward Clerks (Medical Services)
Availability: Local U.S. Employment Service Office
Target Audience: Adults
Notes: Time, 39; Items, 480

Battery of tests selected from the General Aptitude Test Battery (TC001422). Used in the selection of inexperienced or untrained individuals for training as a ward clerk in a hospital. Through research it has been determined that these combined subtests, used together, are a significant aptitude measure and do predict job performance. Research also indicates that this instrument does not discriminate among minorities or ethnic groups. Number of items excludes the subtest on manual dexterity, which is scored according to the number of successfully completed moves; this subtest requires the use of equipment. Available as Form A or B. A report describing the development of this test can be found in the ERIC system, document ED100969.

10003

Specific Aptitude Test Battery for Drafter, Civil (Profes. and Kin.). Manpower Administration (DOL), Washington, DC, U.S. Employment Service 1974
Subtests: General Learning Ability; Numerical Aptitude; Spatial Aptitude; Clerical Perception
Descriptors: Adults; *Aptitude Tests; Career Guidance; *Culture Fair Tests; *Drafting; Employment Potential; Employment Qualifications; Ethnic Groups; Job Applicants; Job Skills; *Job Training; Minority Groups; Multiple Choice Tests; Occupational Tests; Personnel Evaluation; Personnel Selection; Predictive Measurement; Timed Tests; *Vocational Aptitude
Identifiers: *Civil Draftsmen; GATB; General Aptitude Test Battery; SATB; USES Specific Aptitude Test Battery
Availability: Local U.S. Employment Service Office
Target Audience: Adults
Notes: Time, 44; Items, 390
Battery of tests selected from the General Aptitude Test Battery (TC001422). Used in the selection of inexperienced or untrained individuals for training civil drafters. Through research, it has been determined that these combined subtests, used together, are a significant aptitude measure and do predict job performance. Research also indicates that this instrument does not discriminate among minorities or ethnic groups. Comes as Form A or Form B. A report describing the development of this test can be found in the ERIC system, document ED103489.

10004

Specific Aptitude Test Battery for Teacher Aid, Elementary School. Manpower Administration (DOL), Washington, DC, U.S. Training and Employment Service 1974
Subtests: Verbal Aptitude; Numerical Aptitude; Clerical Perception; Motor Coordination
Descriptors: Adults; *Aptitude Tests; Career Guidance; Computation; *Culture Fair Tests; *Elementary Schools; Employment Potential; Employment Qualifications; Ethnic Groups; Job Applicants; Job Skills; *Job Training; Minority Groups; Multiple Choice Tests; Occupational Tests; Personnel Evaluation; Personnel Selection; Predictive Measurement; Mathematics Tests; *Teacher Aides; Timed Tests; *Vocational Aptitude
Identifiers: GATB; General Aptitude Test Battery; SATB; USES Specific Aptitude Test Battery
Availability: Local U.S. Employment Service Office
Target Audience: Adults
Notes: Time, 33; Items, 415
Battery of tests selected from the General Aptitude Test Battery (TC001422). Used in the selection of inexperienced or untrained individuals for training as an elementary school teacher aid. Through research, it has been determined that these combined subtests, used together, are a significant aptitude measure and do predict job performance. Research also indicates that this instrument does not discriminate among minorities or ethnic groups. Comes in Forms A and B. A report describing the development of this test can be found in the ERIC system, document ED103456.

10005

Specific Aptitude Test Battery for Electronics Assembler (Electronics). Manpower Administration (DOL), Washington, DC, U.S. Employment Service 1974
Subtests: Spatial Aptitude; Form Perception; Clerical Perception; Manual Dexterity
Descriptors: Adults; *Aptitude Tests; *Assembly (Manufacturing); Career Guidance; *Culture Fair Tests; *Electronics Industry; Employment Potential; Employment Qualifications; Ethnic Groups; Job Applicants; Job Skills; *Job Training; Minority Groups; Multiple Choice Tests; Occupational Tests; Performance Tests; Personnel Evaluation; Personnel Selection; Predictive Measurement; Timed Tests; *Vocational Aptitude
Identifiers: *Electronics Assemblers; GATB; General Aptitude Test Battery; SATB; USES Specific Aptitude Test Battery
Availability: Local U.S. Employment Service Office
Target Audience: Adults
Notes: Time, 26; Items, 299
Battery of tests selected from the General Aptitude Test Battery (TC001422). Used in the selection of inexperienced or untrained individuals for training as electronics assemblers. Through research, it has been determined that these combined subtests, used together, are a significant aptitude measure and do predict job performance. Re-

search also indicates that this instrument does not discriminate among minorities or ethnic groups. Number of items does not include the subtest on manual dexterity, which is scored according to the number of completed moves and which requires the use of equipment. Comes as Form A or Form B. A report describing the development of this test can be found in the ERIC system, document ED103492.

10006

Specific Aptitude Test Battery for Teller (Banking). Manpower Administration (DOL), Washington, DC, U.S. Employment Service 1975
Subtests: Numerical Aptitude; Form Perception; Clerical Perception
Descriptors: Adults; *Aptitude Tests; *Banking; Career Guidance; Computation; *Culture Fair Tests; Employment Potential; Employment Qualifications; Ethnic Groups; Job Applicants; Job Skills; *Job Training; Minority Groups; Multiple Choice Tests; Occupational Tests; Personnel Evaluation; Personnel Selection; Predictive Measurement; Mathematics Tests; Timed Tests; *Vocational Aptitude
Identifiers: Aptitude Test Battery for Teller (Banking); *Bank Tellers; GATB; General Aptitude Test Battery; SATB; USES Specific Aptitude Test Battery
Availability: Local U.S. Employment Service Office
Target Audience: Adults
Notes: Time, 31; Items, 334
Battery of tests selected from the General Aptitude Test Battery (TC001422). Used in the selection of inexperienced or untrained individuals for training as bank tellers. Through research, it has been determined that these combined subtests, used together, are a significant aptitude measure and do predict job performance. Research also indicates that this instrument does not discriminate among minorities or ethnic groups. Comes in Forms A and B. A report describing the development of this test can be found in the ERIC system, document ED103495.

10007

Specific Aptitude Test Battery for Utility Hand (Paper Goods). Manpower Administration (DOL), Washington, DC, U.S. Employment Service 1975
Subtests: Form Perception; Clerical Perception; Manual Dexterity
Descriptors: Adults; *Aptitude Tests; Career Guidance; *Culture Fair Tests; Employment Potential; Employment Qualifications; Ethnic Groups; Job Applicants; Job Skills; *Job Training; Minority Groups; Multiple Choice Tests; Occupational Tests; *Paper (Material); Performance Tests; Personnel Evaluation; Personnel Selection; Predictive Measurement; Timed Tests; *Vocational Aptitude
Identifiers: GATB; General Aptitude Test Battery; SATB; USES Specific Aptitude Test Battery; *Utility Hands (Paper Goods)
Availability: Local U.S. Employment Service Office
Target Audience: Adults
Notes: Time, 20; Items, 259
Battery of tests selected from the General Aptitude Test Battery (TC001422). Used in the selection of inexperienced or untrained individuals for training as a utility hand, working with paper goods. Through research, it has been determined that these combined subtests, used together, are a significant aptitude measure and do predict job performance. Research also indicates that this instrument does not discriminate among minorities or ethnic groups. Number of items does not include the manual dexterity subtest, which is scored according to the number of moved objects; this subtest requires the use of equipment. Comes in Forms A and B. A report describing the development of this test can be found in the ERIC system, document ED117132.

10008

Specific Aptitude Test Battery for Nurse, Licensed, Practical (Medical Service). Manpower Administration (DOL), Washington, DC, U.S. Employment Service 1975
Subtests: Verbal Aptitude; Clerical Perception; Motor Coordination; Manual Dexterity
Descriptors: Adults; *Aptitude Tests; Career Guidance; *Culture Fair Tests; Employment Potential; Employment Qualifications; Ethnic Groups; Job Applicants; Job Skills; *Job Training; Minority Groups; Multiple Choice Tests; *Nursing; Occupational Tests; Performance Tests; Personnel Evaluation; Personnel Selection; *Practical Nursing; Predictive Measurement; Timed Tests; *Vocational Aptitude
Identifiers: Aptitude Test for Nurse (Licensed Practical); GATB; General Aptitude Test Battery; SATB; USES Specific Aptitude Test Battery

Availability: Local U.S. Employment Service Office
Target Audience: Adults
Notes: Time, 15; Items, 340
Battery of tests selected from the General Aptitude Test Battery (TC001422). Used in the selection of inexperienced or untrained individuals for training as a licensed practical nurse in medical services. Through research, it has been determined that these combined subtests, used together, are a significant aptitude measure and do predict job performance. Research also indicates that this instrument does not discriminate among minorities or ethnic groups. Number of items does not include subtest for manual dexterity, which requires the use of equipment and is scored according to the number of items manipulated. Comes in Forms A and B. A report describing the development of this test can be found in the ERIC system, document ED117159.

10009

Specific Aptitude Test Battery for Maintenance Repairer, Factory or Mill (Any Industry). Manpower Administration (DOL), Washington, DC, U.S. Employment Service 1975
Subtests: Spatial Aptitude; Clerical Perception; Manual Dexterity
Descriptors: Adults; *Aptitude Tests; Career Guidance; *Culture Fair Tests; Employment Potential; Employment Qualifications; Ethnic Groups; Job Applicants; Job Skills; *Job Training; *Machine Repairers; Minority Groups; Multiple Choice Tests; Occupational Tests; Performance Tests; Personnel Evaluation; Personnel Selection; Predictive Measurement; Timed Tests; *Vocational Aptitude
Identifiers: Aptitude Test Battery for Maintenance Repairer; GATB; General Aptitude Test Battery; SATB; USES Specific Aptitude Test Battery
Availability: Local U.S. Employment Service Office
Target Audience: Adults
Notes: Time, 14; Items, 190
Battery of tests selected from the General Aptitude Test Battery (TC001422). Used in the selection of inexperienced or untrained individuals for training as a factory or mill (any industry) maintenance repairer. Through research, it has been determined that these combined subtests, used together, are a significant aptitude measure and do predict job performance. Research also indicates that this instrument does not discriminate among minorities or ethnic groups. Number of items does not include the subtest on manual dexterity, which is scored according to the number of successfully completed moves; this subtest requires the use of equipment. Comes in Form A and B. A report describing the development of this test can be found in the ERIC system, document ED117160.

10010

Specific Aptitude Test Battery for Nurse Aid (Medical Service). Manpower Administration (DOL), Washington, DC, U.S. Employment Service 1975
Subtests: General Learning Ability; Form Perception; Clerical Perception
Descriptors: Adults; *Aptitude Tests; Career Guidance; *Culture Fair Tests; Employment Potential; Employment Qualifications; Ethnic Groups; Job Applicants; Job Skills; *Job Training; Minority Groups; Multiple Choice Tests; *Nurses Aides; Occupational Tests; Personnel Evaluation; Personnel Selection; Predictive Measurement; Timed Tests; *Vocational Aptitude
Identifiers: GATB; General Aptitude Test Battery; SATB; USES Specific Aptitude Test Battery
Availability: Local U.S. Employment Service Office
Target Audience: Adults
Notes: Time, 37; Items, 384
Battery of tests selected from the General Aptitude Test Battery (TC001422). Used in the selection of inexperienced or untrained individuals for training as a nurse aid in the medical service. Through research, it has been determined that these combined subtests, used together, are a significant aptitude measure and do predict job performance. Research also indicates that this instrument does not discriminate among minorities or ethnic groups. Available as Form A or B. A report describing the development of this test can be found in the ERIC system, document ED118597.

10011

Specific Aptitude Test Battery for Proof-Machine Operator (Banking). Manpower Administration (DOL), Washington, DC, U.S. Employment Service 1975
Subtests: Numerical Aptitude; Clerical Perception; Motor Coordination

Descriptors: Adults; *Aptitude Tests; *Banking; Career Guidance; Computation; *Culture Fair Tests; Employment Potential; Employment Qualifications; Ethnic Groups; Job Applicants; Job Skills; *Job Training; Minority Groups; Multiple Choice Tests; Occupational Tests; Personnel Evaluation; Personnel Selection; Predictive Measurement; Mathematics Tests; Timed Tests; *Vocational Aptitude
Identifiers: GATB; General Aptitude Test Battery; *Proof Machine Operator; SATB; USES Specific Aptitude Test Battery
Availability: Local U.S. Employment Service Office
Target Audience: Adults
Notes: Time, 20; Items, 355

Battery of tests selected from the General Aptitude Test Battery (TC001422). Used in the selection of inexperienced or untrained individuals for training as a proofmachine operator in banking. Through research, it has been determined that these combined subtests, used together, are a significant aptitude measure and do predict job performance. Research also indicates that this instrument does not discriminate among minorities or ethnic groups. Comes in Forms A and B. A report describing the development of this test can be found in the ERIC system, document ED118598.

10012
Specific Aptitude Test Battery for Plumber (const.)/Pipe Fitter (const.). Manpower Administration (DOL), Washington, DC, U.S. Employment Service 1978
Subtests: Verbal Aptitude; Form Perception; Manual Dexterity
Descriptors: Adults; *Aptitude Tests; Career Guidance; *Construction Industry; *Culture Fair Tests; Employment Potential; Employment Qualifications; Ethnic Groups; Job Applicants; Job Skills; *Job Training; Minority Groups; Multiple Choice Tests; Occupational Tests; Performance Tests; Personnel Evaluation; Personnel Selection; *Plumbing; Predictive Measurement; Timed Tests; *Vocational Aptitude
Identifiers: GATB; General Aptitude Test Battery; SATB; USES Specific Aptitude Test Battery
Availability: Local U.S. Employment Service Office
Target Audience: Adults
Notes: Time, 20; Items, 169

Battery of tests selected from the General Aptitude Test Battery (TC001422). Used in the selection of inexperienced or untrained individuals for training as plumbers or pipefitters in the construction industry. Through research, it has been determined that these combined subtests, used together, are a significant aptitude measure and do predict job performance. Research also indicates that this instrument does not discriminate among minorities or ethnic groups. Number of items does not include the subtest for manual dexterity; manual dexterity subtest requires the use of equipment. Available in Forms A and B. A report describing the development of this test can be found in the ERIC system, document ED158039.

10020
Home Interview Instrument. Zirkel, Perry Alan 1973
Descriptors: Adults; Biculturalism; Bilingualism; Educational Background; *Elementary School Students; *Family Characteristics; Family Influence; *Parent Aspiration; *Parent Attitudes; *Parent Role; Parent School Relationship; *Puerto Ricans; *Sociolinguistics; *Spanish Speaking; *State Surveys
Identifiers: Connecticut
Availability: ERIC Document Reproduction Service; 3900 Wheeler Ave., Alexandria, VA 22304 (ED074191, 32 pages)
Target Audience: 18-64
Notes: Items, 47

Deals with parental perceptions and family background factors relating to the education of Spanish-speaking students. This is available in parallel English and Spanish forms. The study was done in 2 large Connecticut cities, and the subjects were Puerto Rican families with children in the schools.

10024
Checklist for Early Recognition of Problems in Classrooms. Schleichkorn, Jacob 1972
Subtests: Coordination and Motor Activities; Behavior Responses (Aural); Communication (Verbal); Conceptual Ability; Perception
Descriptors: Behavior Rating Scales; Check Lists; *Communication Skills; *Elementary School Students; Elementary School Teachers; *Handicap Identification; Perceptual Development; Primary Education; *Psychomotor Skills; *Screening Tests; *Student Behavior
Availability: Journal of Learning Disabilities; v5 n8 p501-03 Oct 1972
Grade Level: K-3

Notes: Items, 121

Designed to assist primary grade teachers to recognize developing problems of students. The checklist is to be used only as a screening device to identify children who are in need of further evaluation.

10034
Behavioral Check List. Daughton, David; Fix, A. James 1978
Descriptors: *Behavior Disorders; *Behavior Patterns; Behavior Rating Scales; Depression (Psychology); Elementary Education; *Elementary School Students; Handicap Identification; Hyperactivity; Learning Disabilities; Mental Disorders
Availability: Journal of Special Education; v12 n1 p37-44 1978
Grade Level: K-6

Designed for use by classroom teachers to assist in identifying children who require medical or psychiatric evaluation. A behavioral cluster system, rather than single behaviors, is used.

10054
Diabetes Mellitus Patient Interview. Bowen, Rhoda G.; And Others 1961
Subtests: Knowledge of Disease; Knowledge of Insulin; Performance in Self-Administration of Insulin; Performance in Urine Testing; Knowledge of Diet and Food Exchange; Attitudes and Knowledge of Personal Hygiene; Attitudes toward the Disease
Descriptors: Adults; Attitude Measures; *Diabetes; Dietetics; Hygiene; Interviews; *Knowledge Level; Medicine; Nutrition; *Patients; Performance Tests
Identifiers: Insulin; *Patient Attitudes
Availability: ERIC Document Reproduction Service; 3900 Wheeler Ave., Alexandria, VA 22304 (ED171763, 842 pages)
Target Audience: Adults
Notes: Items, 100

This volume consists of a series of psychosocial and physiological clinical nursing instruments. The instruments were selected from the published literature in health care, education, psychology, and the social sciences. Instruments focus on nursing practice and stress patient variables. This structured interview assesses a diabetes patient's knowledge and attitudes concerning diabetes and its treatment. The subject is also asked to demonstrate self-administration of insulin and urine testing.

10056
Labor and Delivery Tool. Aguiar, Martha B. 1974
Descriptors: Adults; Attitude Measures; *Birth; Knowledge Level; Mother Attitudes; *Mothers; *Patients; Pregnancy
Identifiers: *Labor (Birth); Postpartum Patients
Availability: ERIC Document Reproduction Service; 3900 Wheeler Ave., Alexandria, VA 22304 (ED171763, 842 pages)
Target Audience: Adults
Notes: Time, 15 approx.; Items, 41

This volume consists of a series of psychosocial and physiological clinical nursing instruments. The instruments were selected from the published literature in health care, education, psychology, and the social sciences. Instruments focus on nursing practice and stress patient variables. Instrument was developed to assess the postpartum patient's perceptions of her labor, and delivery experience. Her general knowledge of pregnancy, labor, and delivery are also measured.

10057
Anxiety Due to Territory and Space Intrusion Questionnaire. Allekian, Constance I. 1973
Subtests: Territorial Space Instrusions; Personal Space Intrusions
Descriptors: Adults; *Anxiety; Attitude Measures; *Hospital Personnel; Hospitals; Interpersonal Relationship; Nurses; Nursing; *Patients; *Personal Space; Proximity; Rating Scales
Identifiers: *Patient Attitudes
Availability: ERIC Document Reproduction Service; 3900 Wheeler Ave., Alexandria, VA 22304 (ED171763, 842 pages)
Target Audience: Adults
Notes: Time, 20 approx.; Items, 27

This volume consists of a series of psychosocial and physiological clinical nursing instruments. The instruments were selected from the published literature in health care, education, psychology, and the social sciences. Instruments focus on nursing practice and stress patient variables. Instrument assesses patient's feelings of anxiety which result from territorial and personal space instrusions by health care personnel.

10062
Loneliness Rating Scale. Francis, Gloria M. 1976
Subtests: Cathectic Investment; Loneliness

Descriptors: Adults; Affective Measures; Attachment Behavior; *Hospitals; Individual Testing; Interviews; *Loneliness; *Patients
Availability: ERIC Document Reproduction Service; 3900 Wheeler Ave., Alexandria, VA 22304 (ED171763, 842 pages)
Target Audience: Adults
Notes: Time, 20 approx.; Items, 25

This volume consists of a series of psychosocial and physiological clinical nursing instruments. The instruments were selected from the published literature in health care, education, psychology, and the social sciences. Instruments focus on nursing practice and stress patient variables. Instrument was designed to measure human secondary loneliness and cathectic investment of hospitalized adults. Cathectic investment was defined as the endowment of social and physical objects with meaning, import, and energy.

10063
Social Psychological Determinants of Patients' Performance in Stroke Rehabilitation. Hyman, Martin D. 1972
Subtests: Feelings of Stigma; Self Esteem; Satisfaction with Occupational Role; Satisfaction with Family Role; Feelings of Social Isolation; Dependency; Belief in Supernatural Causes of Illness; Secondary Gain in Illness
Descriptors: Adults; Attitude Measures; Individual Testing; Interviews; Loneliness; Nurses; *Nursing; *Patients; Rehabilitation; *Self Concept; Self Concept Measures; *Social Isolation
Identifiers: Dependency (Personality); Guttman Scales; Illness; *Patient Attitudes
Availability: ERIC Document Reproduction Service; 3900 Wheeler Ave., Alexandria, VA 22304 (ED171763, 842 pages)
Target Audience: Adults
Notes: Items, 29

This volume consists of a series of psychosocial and physiological clinical nursing instruments. The instruments were selected from the published literature in health care, education, psychology, and the social sciences. Instruments focus on nursing practice and stress patient variables. This instrument assesses patient's self-concept, attitudes toward social isolation, and attitudes toward illness. These social and psychological factors have been proven important to the success of patient rehabilitation.

10064
Psychosocial Problems Inventory. Jacox, Ada; Stewart, Mary 1973
Descriptors: Adults; Affective Measures; Depression (Psychology); Family Relationship; *Loneliness; *Patients
Identifiers: Dependency (Personality); Illness; *Pain; *Psychosocial Problems; Self Administered Tests
Availability: ERIC Document Reproduction Service; 3900 Wheeler Ave., Alexandria, VA 22304 (ED171763, 842 pages)
Target Audience: Adults
Notes: Items, 24

This volume consists of a series of psychosocial and physiological clinical nursing instruments. The instruments were selected from the published literature in health care, education, psychology, and the social sciences. Instruments focus upon nursing practice and stress patient variables. Instrument assesses psychosocial problems associated with pain and illness. Types of problems assessed include feelings of loneliness, fear of pain, depression, dependency, family, and vocation.

10066
Patient's Perception Scale. Palmer, Irene S. 1963
Subtests: Confidence in Family; Faith in God; Skill and Competence of Staff; Body Integrity; Acceptance of Need for Surgery; Financial Security; Understanding, Acceptance, and Support of Others; Dependency-Independency; Postoperative Living Patterns; Expectations about Surgery; Self-Awareness; Anesthesia; Painful Procedures
Descriptors: Adults; Attitude Measures; Nurses; *Nursing; *Patients; *Surgery
Identifiers: *Patient Attitudes
Availability: ERIC Document Reproduction Service; 3900 Wheeler Ave., Alexandria, VA 22304 (ED171763, 842 pages)
Target Audience: Adults
Notes: Time, 15 approx.; Items, 46

This volume consists of a series of psychosocial and physiological clinical nursing instruments. The instruments were selected from the published literature in health care, education, psychology, and the social sciences. Instruments focus on nursing practice and stress patient variables. Instrument is designed to measure adult patient's perceptions of impending general surgery.

10067
Health-Illness (Powerlessness) Questionnaire. Roy, Callista 1976

Descriptors: Adults; Attitude Measures; Hospitals; *Locus of Control; Nurses; Nursing; *Opinions; *Patients; Physicians; Rating Scales
Identifiers: Illness; Patient Attitudes; *Powerlessness
Availability: ERIC Document Reproduction Service; 3900 Wheeler Ave., Alexandria, VA 22304 (ED171763, 842 pages)
Target Audience: Adults
Notes: Items, 8

This volume consists of a series of psychosocial and physiological clinical nursing instruments. The instruments were selected from the published literature in health care, education, psychology, and the social sciences. Instruments focus on nursing practice and stress patient variables. Instrument was designed to elicit patient's perception of his/her control over illness, physicians, nurses, and hospitals.

10068
Hospitalized Patient Decision-Making. Roy, Callista 1976
Descriptors: Adults; *Decision Making; Forced Choice Technique; Hospital Personnel; Hospitals; *Patients
Identifiers: Patient Attitudes
Availability: ERIC Document Reproduction Service; 3900 Wheeler Ave., Alexandria, VA 22304 (ED171763, 842 pages)
Target Audience: Adults
Notes: Items, 15

This volume consists of a series of psychosocial and physiological clinical nursing instruments. The instruments were selected from the published literature in health care, education, psychology, and the social sciences. Instruments focus on nursing practice and stress patient variables. Instrument assesses the patient's perceptions of decisions he or she makes while in a hospital. The patient also indicates the decisions he or she would prefer to make.

10071
Evaluation of Emotional Tension on Admission in Labor. Crawford, Mary I. 1968
Descriptors: Adults; *Anxiety; Birth; Fear; *Mothers; Nurses; Observation; *Patients; Rating Scales
Identifiers: Emotional Tension; *Labor (Birth)
Availability: ERIC Document Reproduction Service; 3900 Wheeler Ave., Alexandria, VA 22304 (ED171763, 842 pages)
Target Audience: Adults
Notes: Items, 4

This volume consists of a series of psychosocial and physiological clinical nursing instruments. The instruments were selected from the published literature in health care, education, psychology, and the social sciences. Instruments focus on nursing practice and stress patient variables. This instrument evaluates emotional tension of a woman in labor at the time of hospital admission.

10072
Evaluation of Muscle Tension Questionnaire. Crawford, Mary I. 1968
Descriptors: Adults; Anxiety; Birth; *Mothers; *Motor Reactions; Nurses; Patients; *Pregnancy; Questionnaires; Self Evaluation (Individuals)
Identifiers: Labor (Birth); *Pain
Availability: ERIC Document Reproduction Service; 3900 Wheeler Ave., Alexandria, VA 22304 (ED171763, 842 pages)
Target Audience: Adults
Notes: Time, 5 approx.; Items, 14

This volume consists of a series of psychosocial and physiological clinical nursing instruments. The instruments were selected from the published literature in health care, education, psychology, and the social sciences. Instruments focus on nursing practice and stress patient variables. Instrument assesses the severity of muscle tension and other subjective symptoms experienced during a 2-week period of the third trimester of pregnancy. Many studies have suggested that anxiety is associated with increased muscle tension.

10073
Behavioral Rating Checklist for Nursing Personnel. Garrity, Thomas F.; Klein, Robert F. 1975
Descriptors: *Adjustment (to Environment); Adults; *Anxiety; Behavior Rating Scales; Depression (Psychology); Hospitals; Hostility; Nurses; *Nursing; Observation; *Patients
Identifiers: Coronary Care; *Heart Attack; Intensive Care Units
Availability: ERIC Document Reproduction Service; 3900 Wheeler Ave., Alexandria, VA 22304 (ED171763, 842 pages)
Target Audience: Adults
Notes: Items, 21

This volume consists of a series of psychosocial and physiological clinical nursing instruments. The instruments were selected from the published literature in health care, education, psychology, and the social sciences. Instruments focus on nursing practice and stress patient variables.

Instrument assesses presence and degree of unresolved emotional distress of coronary care unit patients during acute phase of heart attack. Patient behaviors are observed during the first 5 days after hospitalization.

10074
Symptom Rating Test. Kellner, Robert; Sheffield, Brian F. 1973
Subtests: Anxiety; Depression; Somatic; Inadequacy
Descriptors: Adults; *Anxiety; Check Lists; *Depression (Psychology); Emotional Adjustment; Nurses; *Nursing; *Patients; Self Concept Measures; Self Evaluation (Individuals)
Identifiers: SRT; *Symptoms
Availability: ERIC Document Reproduction Service; 3900 Wheeler Ave., Alexandria, VA 22304 (ED171763, 842 pages)
Target Audience: Adults
Notes: Time, 20 approx.; Items, 60

This volume consists of a series of psychosocial and physiological clinical nursing instruments. The instruments were selected from the published literature in health care, education, psychology, and the social sciences. Instruments focus on nursing practice and stress patient variables. Instrument is designed to assess patients' perceptions of distress. Self-ratings on 4 subcategories of distress are obtained.

10076
Hospital Stress Rating Scale. Volicer, Beverly J.; Bohannon, Mary W. 1975
Descriptors: Adults; Attitude Measures; *Hospitals; Nurses; *Nursing; *Patients; *Stress Variables
Identifiers: Card Sort; *Patient Attitudes
Availability: ERIC Document Reproduction Service; 3900 Wheeler Ave., Alexandria, VA 22304 (ED171763, 842 pages)
Target Audience: Adults
Notes: Items, 49

This volume consists of a series of psychosocial and physiological clinical nursing instruments. The instruments were selected from the published literature in health care, education, psychology, and the social sciences. Instruments focus on nursing practice and stress patient variables. Card sort-technique is used to measure psychosocial stress experienced by short-term hospital patients.

10077
Patient Recovery Inventory. Wolfer, John A.; And Others 1972
Descriptors: Adults; Hospitals; Nurses; Nursing; *Patients; *Physical Health; Rating Scales; *Self Evaluation (Individuals); Surgery
Identifiers: Nursing Care; Pain; *Postoperative Patients; *Recovery (Illness)
Availability: ERIC Document Reproduction Service; 3900 Wheeler Ave., Alexandria, VA 22304 (ED171763, 842 pages)
Target Audience: Adults
Notes: Time, 7 approx.; Items, 15

This volume consists of a series of psychosocial and physiological clinical nursing instruments. The instruments were selected from the published literature in health care, education, psychology, and the social sciences. Instruments focus on nursing practice and stress patient variables. Designed to elicit a patient's evaluation of his/her physical condition while recovering from elective surgery.

10079
Anxiety Status Inventory. Zung, William W. K. 1971
Descriptors: Adults; *Anxiety; Hospitals; *Interviews; *Patients
Identifiers: ASI
Availability: ERIC Document Reproduction Service; 3900 Wheeler Ave., Alexandria, VA 22304 (ED171763, 842 pages)
Target Audience: Adults
Notes: Time, 10 approx.; Items, 20

This volume consists of a series of psychosocial and physiological clinical nursing instruments. The instruments were selected from the published literature in health care, education, psychology, and the social sciences. Instruments focus on nursing practice and stress patient variables. This instrument is designed for a clinician interview. Assesses patient's affective and somatic symptoms of anxiety disorder.

10080
Depression Status Inventory. Zung, William W. K. 1972
Subtests: Affective Disturbances; Physiological Disturbances; Psychomotor Disturbances; Psychological Disturbances
Descriptors: Adults; Affective Measures; *Depression (Psychology); Interviews; *Patients; Psychological Evaluation
Identifiers: DSI

Availability: ERIC Document Reproduction Service; 3900 Wheeler Ave., Alexandria, VA 22304 (ED171763, 842 pages)
Target Audience: 20-64
Notes: Items, 20

This volume consists of a series of psychosocial and physiological clinical nursing instruments. The instruments were selected from the published literature in health care, education, psychology, and the social sciences. Instruments focus on nursing practice and stress patient variables. Instrument is a semistructured interviewer rated assessment of patient's depression characteristics. Questions are based on clinical signs and symptoms of depression. Developed for use with Self-Rating Depression Scale (TC005167).

10081
Adaptation of Clark and Clark Doll Test and Bogardus Social Distance Scale. Anderson, Frances J.; Hamm, N. 1973
Descriptors: American Indians; *Children; *Elementary School Students; Interviews; Peer Relationship; Preschool Children; Primary Education; *Racial Attitudes; *Self Concept; Self Concept Measures; *Sociometric Techniques; Whites
Availability: ERIC Document Reproduction Service; 3900 Wheeler Ave., Alexandria, VA 22304 (ED171763, 842 pages)
Grade Level: 1-3
Target Audience: 3-8
Notes: Items, 20

This volume consists of a series of psychosocial and physiological clinical nursing instruments. The instruments were selected from the published literature in health care, education, psychology, and the social sciences. Instruments focus on nursing practice and stress patient variables. Instrument consists of 16 questions presented in form of doll choosing game, and 4 sociogram questions. Measures racial self-concept determined by peer preference.

10082
Postmyocardial Infarction Patient Semantic Differential Scales. Avillo, Linda J. 1971
Descriptors: Adults; Emotional Adjustment; *Hospitals; Interviews; *Patients; Rating Scales; *Self Concept; *Self Concept Measures; Semantic Differential
Identifiers: *Heart Attack
Availability: ERIC Document Reproduction Service; 3900 Wheeler Ave., Alexandria, VA 22304 (ED171763, 842 pages)
Target Audience: Adults
Notes: Time, 10 approx.; Items, 12

This volume consists of a series of psychosocial and physiological clinical nursing instruments. The instruments were selected from the published literature in health care, education, psychology, and the social sciences. Instruments focus on nursing practice and stress patient variables. Instrument was designed to assess the self-concept of a postmyocardial infarction patient after being transferred from a coronary care unit to a general medical unit. Should be orally administered by an investigator in the hospital setting.

10083
Sick Role Acceptance (Measure 1). Brown, Julia S.; Rawlinson, May E. 1975
Descriptors: Adults; Patients; *Physical Health; *Self Concept; Self Concept Measures; Semantic Differential
Identifiers: Postoperative Patients; Self Administered Tests
Availability: ERIC Document Reproduction Service; 3900 Wheeler Ave., Alexandria, VA 22304 (ED171763, 842 pages)
Target Audience: Adults
Notes: Items, 10

This volume consists of a series of psychosocial and physiological clinical nursing instruments. The instruments were selected from the published literature in health care, education, psychology, and the social sciences. Instruments focus on nursing practice and stress patient variables. Instrument assesses patient's perception of self as resembling sick persons with regard to worthiness, power, activity, and independence.

10084
Health Self-Concept. Jacox, Ada; Stewart, Mary 1973
Descriptors: Adults; Hospitals; *Patients; *Physical Health; Self Concept; Self Concept Measures; *Self Evaluation (Individuals)
Identifiers: Illness; *Pain; Psychosocial Problems
Availability: ERIC Document Reproduction Service; 3900 Wheeler Ave., Alexandria, VA 22304 (ED171763, 842 pages)
Target Audience: Adults
Notes: Time, 10 approx.; Items, 7

This volume consists of a series of psychosocial and physiological clinical nursing instruments. The instruments were selected from the published literature in health care, education, psychology, and the social sciences. Instruments focus on nursing practice and stress patient variables. Instrument was developed for use with hospitalized patients experiencing varying degrees of pain. Assesses one's self-concept as a relatively ill or healthy person.

10085
PARS V Community Adjustment Scales. Ellsworth, Robert B. 1975
Subtests: Interpersonal Involvement; Anxiety-Depression; Confusion; Alcohol/Drug Abuse; Household Management; Relationship to Children; Outside Social Involvement; Employment
Descriptors: Adults; Alcoholism; Anxiety; Behavior Rating Scales; Depression (Psychology); Drug Abuse; Family (Sociological Unit); Family Relationship; Interpersonal Competence; Mental Health Programs; *Patients; Program Evaluation; *Social Adjustment
Identifiers: *Psychiatric Patients
Availability: ERIC Document Reproduction Service; 3900 Wheeler Ave., Alexandria, VA 22304 (ED171763, 842 pages)
Target Audience: Adults
Notes: Items, 57

This volume consists of a series of psychosocial and physiological clinical nursing instruments. The instruments were selected from the published literature in health care, education, psychology, and the social sciences. Instruments focus on nursing practice and stress patient variables. Instrument should be completed by a "significant other" of the patient. Measures community adjustment of discharged psychiatric patients. Pretreatment and Posttreatment forms for males and females are available. Measures effectiveness of mental health services through patient's community adjustment.

10086
Nursing Rating Scale. Hargreaves, William A. 1968
Descriptors: Adults; Behavior Patterns; Behavior Rating Scales; Longitudinal Studies; *Nurses; Nursing; *Patients; *Psychiatric Aides; Psychiatric Hospitals; Psychopathology
Identifiers: NRS; *Psychiatric Patients
Availability: ERIC Document Reproduction Service; 3900 Wheeler Ave., Alexandria, VA 22304 (ED171763, 842 pages)
Target Audience: Adults
Notes: Items, 24

This volume consists of a series of psychosocial and physiological clinical nursing instruments. The instruments were selected from the published literature in health care, education, psychology, and the social sciences. Instruments focus on nursing practice and stress patient variables. Instrument was designed for use by psychiatric nurses or technicians to describe symptoms and ward behavior of psychiatric patients. Scale is intended for longitudinal studies of individual patients.

10087
Pediatric Behavioral Questionnaire. Tasem, Walter M.; And Others 1974
Descriptors: *Adolescents; Adults; Behavior Patterns; *Behavior Problems; *Children; Parent Attitudes; *Parents; Personality Problems; *Preschool Children; *Screening Tests; *Spanish
Identifiers: *Psychiatric Problems
Availability: ERIC Document Reproduction Service; 3900 Wheeler Ave., Alexandria, VA 22304 (ED171763, 842 pages)
Target Audience: 4-14
Notes: Time, 5 approx.; Items, 28

This volume consists of a series of psychosocial and physiological clinical nursing instruments. The instruments were selected from the published literature in health care, education, psychology, and the social sciences. Instruments focus on nursing practice and stress patient variables. Instrument is designed for psychiatric screening. Parents are asked to check areas they believe are serious problems for their children. Assesses problems in areas of eating habits, sleeping, bowel problems, bed-wetting, speech, discipline, sex behavior and education, extreme dependency or independency, size, alcohol, drugs, or recurrent physical complaints. Forms available in Spanish as well as English. Completion of form should be followed by parental interview.

10088
Washington Symptom Checklist. Wimberger, Herbert C.; Gregory, Robert J. 1968
Descriptors: *Adolescents; Adults; Behavior Problems; Behavior Rating Scales; *Children; Emotional Problems; Mental Health Clinics; *Parent Attitudes; *Parents
Identifiers: Psychiatric Patients; WSCL
Availability: ERIC Document Reproduction Service; 3900 Wheeler Ave., Alexandria, VA 22304 (ED171763, 842 pages)
Target Audience: 6-17
Notes: Time, 20 approx.; Items, 76

This volume consists of a series of psychosocial and physiological clinical nursing instruments. The instruments were selected from the published literature in health care, education, psychology, and the social sciences. Instruments focus on nursing practice and stress patient variables. Instrument was developed to assess parents' perceptions of the behaviors of their children for whom they are seeking professional psychiatric help. Also assesses parents' motivation in seeking help. It is preferable for each parent to complete the instrument so that the professional has 2 sources of information about the child.

10091
Recovery Room Activity Schedule. Elms, Roslyn R. 1972
Subtests: Spontaneous Behavior Activity; Spontaneous Behavior Comfort; Response to Stimuli Comfort; Response to Stimuli Positive Responses; Response to Stimuli-Negative Responses
Descriptors: Adults; *Behavior Patterns; Behavior Rating Scales; Hospitals; Motor Reactions; *Observation; *Older Adults; *Patients; Responses; Surgery
Identifiers: *Postoperative Patients
Availability: ERIC Document Reproduction Service; 3900 Wheeler Ave., Alexandria, VA 22304 (ED171763, 842 pages)
Target Audience: 18-85

This volume consists of a series of psychosocial and physiological clinical nursing instruments. The instruments were selected from the published literature in health care, education, psychology, and the social sciences. Instruments focus on nursing practice and stress patient variables. Instrument was developed to assess relationship between patients recovery room behaviors and patterns of convalescence. Observer rates patient on overt behaviors and respective comfort ratings in the recovery room.

10092
Data Collection Sheet for Assessment of Patient's Potential for Pressure Sores. Gosnell, Davina J. 1973
Descriptors: Adults; Nurses; *Nursing; Nutrition; *Older Adults; *Patients; *Physical Health; Physical Mobility; Predictive Measurement; Rating Scales
Identifiers: *Bedsores
Availability: ERIC Document Reproduction Service; 3900 Wheeler Ave., Alexandria, VA 22304 (ED171763, 842 pages)
Target Audience: 18-90
Notes: Time, 5 approx.; Items, 8

This volume consists of a series of psychosocial and physiological clinical nursing instruments. The instruments were selected from the published literature in health care, education, psychology, and the social sciences. Instruments focus on nursing practice and stress patient variables. Developed to gather data which would provide insights into factors causing patients to develop pressure sores. Instrument was designed for use by a nurse as part of patient assessment procedure.

10093
Oral Hygiene Index and Simplified Oral Hygiene Index. Greene, John C.; Vermillion, Jack D. 1963
Subtests: Debris Index; Calculus Index
Descriptors: Adolescents; Adults; Children; *Dental Evaluation; *Dental Health; *Patients
Identifiers: OHI; OHIs; *Oral Hygiene
Availability: ERIC Document Reproduction Service; 3900 Wheeler Ave., Alexandria, VA 22304 (ED171763, 842 pages)
Target Audience: 5-64

This volume consists of a series of psychosocial and physiological clinical nursing instruments. The instruments were selected from the published literature in health care, education, psychology, and the social sciences. Instruments focus on nursing practice and stress variables. Instrument was designed to assess oral hygiene status of patients. It may be used to assess tooth brushing efficiency and study the epidemiology of periodontal disease and oral calculus. The OHIs may be used when the examiner has limited time to conduct the evaluation.

10094
Index of Independence in Activities of Daily Living. Katz, Sidney 1963
Descriptors: Adults; Behavior Rating Scales; *Diseases; *Geriatrics; Observation; *Older Adults; *Patients; *Self Care Skills; Special Health Problems
Identifiers: *Independence; Index of ADL
Availability: ERIC Document Reproduction Service; 3900 Wheeler Ave., Alexandria, VA 22304 (ED171763, 842 pages)
Target Audience: 55-80
Notes: Items, 12

This volume consists of a series of psychosocial and physiological clinical nursing instruments. The instruments were selected from the published literature in health care,

education, psychology, and the social sciences. Instruments focus on nursing practice and stress patient variables. Instrument was designed to measure the independence of chronically ill and aging persons in performance of specific self-care tasks. These include bathing, dressing, toileting, transfer, continence, and feeding.

10097
Sleep Status Observation Form. McFadden, Eileen H. 1968
Descriptors: Adults; Behavior Rating Scales; Nurses; *Nursing; Observation; *Patients; *Sleep; *Surgery
Identifiers: Intensive Care Unit; *Postoperative Patients
Availability: ERIC Document Reproduction Service; 3900 Wheeler Ave., Alexandria, VA 22304 (ED171763, 842 pages)
Target Audience: Adults

This volume consists of a series of psychosocial and physiological clinical nursing instruments. The instruments were selected from the published literature in health care, education, psychology, and the social sciences. Instruments focus on nursing practice and stress patient variables. Instrument was designed to elicit data concerning the possible relationship between sleep deprivation and postoperative cardiac psychoses. Nurses' perceptions of a patient's sleep or wakefulness status are measured.

10098
Rasmussen Pain Description Index. Rasmussen, Susan L. 1974
Descriptors: Adults; Biographical Inventories; *Patients; Rating Scales
Identifiers: *Pain; RPDI; Self Administered Tests
Availability: ERIC Document Reproduction Service; 3900 Wheeler Ave., Alexandria, VA 22304 (ED171763, 842 pages)
Target Audience: Adults
Notes: Items, 16

This volume consists of a series of psychosocial and physiological clinical nursing instruments. The instruments were selected from the published literature in health care, education, psychology, and the social sciences. Instruments focus on nursing practice and stress patient variables. Instrument was designed to assess patient's intensity of pain as it can be verbally described.

10099
Colorado Maternal Health Index. Waller, Mildred; And Others 1968
Descriptors: Adults; Check Lists; Congenital Impairments; Hypertension; Mothers; Neonates; Nurses; *Patients; *Physical Health; *Pregnancy; Prenatal Influences
Availability: ERIC Document Reproduction Service; 3900 Wheeler Ave., Alexandria, VA 22304 (ED171763, 842 pages)
Target Audience: Adults
Notes: Items, 43

This volume consists of a series of psychosocial and physiological clinical nursing instruments. The instruments were selected from the published literature in health care, education, psychology, and the social sciences. Instruments focus on nursing practice and stress patient variables. Instrument consists of 5 parts. First 4 parts are completed during pregnancy. They include demographic data, factors related to unfavorable pregnancy outcomes, patient conditions which indicate a high risk of unfavorable outcomes, and checklist of less important predictors of unfavorable outcomes. Part 5 is completed after delivery. Developed to assess the risk status of a pregnant woman.

10100
Patient Welfare Inventory. Wolfer, John A.; And Others 1970
Descriptors: Adults; Affective Measures; *Emotional Adjustment; Hospitals; Nursing; *Patients; Surgery
Identifiers: Nursing Care; *Patient Attitudes; Postoperative Patients
Availability: ERIC Document Reproduction Service; 3900 Wheeler Ave., Alexandria, VA 22304 (ED171763, 842 pages)
Target Audience: Adults
Notes: Time, 7 approx.; Items, 20

This volume consists of a series of psychosocial and physiological clinical nursing instruments. The instruments were selected from the published literature in health care, education, psychology, and the social sciences. Instruments focus on nursing practice and stress patient variables. Instrument was designed to assess patient's emotional status as he/she recovers from surgery. Self-report instrument used to examine the effects of nursing care on the emotional state of the patient.

10101
Behavior Rating Scale. Brink, Pamela J. 1972
Subtests: Sleep Habits; Activities; Elimination; Socialization; Eating Habits; Grooming; Behaviors
Descriptors: Adults; Behavior Patterns; *Behavior Rating Scales; Drug Addiction; Nurses; *Nursing; Observation; *Patients

Identifiers: *Drug Addicts; Nursing Care
Availability: ERIC Document Reproduction Service; 3900 Wheeler Ave., Alexandria, VA 22304 (ED171763, 842 pages)
Target Audience: Adults
Notes: Items, 50

This volume consists of a series of psychosocial and physiological clinical nursing instruments. The instruments were selected from the published literature in health care, education, psychology, and the social sciences. Instruments focus on nursing practice and stress patient variables. Instrument was designed for completion by nurse observer. Behavioral characteristics of heroin addict inpatients were recorded by nurse. Designed to elicit characteristic behavioral patterns of addict population to facilitate development of a nursing care plan.

10102
Postoperative Convalescence Questionnaire. Elms, Roslyn R. 1972
Subtests: Physical Complaints and Discomforts; Physical Independence; Social Interaction and Diversional Activity; Emotional Responses
Descriptors: Adults; Affective Measures; *Emotional Adjustment; *Hospitals; Interpersonal Competence; Interviews; Nurses; *Nursing; *Patients; Physical Health; Surgery
Identifiers: *Postoperative Patients; *Recovery (Illness)
Availability: ERIC Document Reproduction Service; 3900 Wheeler Ave., Alexandria, VA 22304 (ED171763, 842 pages)
Target Audience: Adults
Notes: Time, 30 approx.; Items, 46

This volume consists of a series of psychosocial and physiological clinical nursing instruments. The instruments were selected from the published literature in health care, education, psychology, and the social sciences. Instruments focus on nursing practice and stress patient variables. Instrument is administered by a trained interviewer. Provides information about postsurgical patient's physical and emotional status. Developed to provide information useful in exploring the relationship between recovery room behaviors and postsurgical patterns of recovery.

10103
Social and Psychological Status of Myocardial Infarction Patients during Recovery Evaluation Questionnaire. Garrity, Thomas F. 1972
Subtests: Physical Health; Social Functioning; Morale
Descriptors: Adults; *Interpersonal Competence; *Morale; *Patients; Physical Health; Questionnaires; *Self Evaluation (Individuals); Well Being
Identifiers: *Heart Attack; Recovery (Illness)
Availability: ERIC Document Reproduction Service; 3900 Wheeler Ave., Alexandria, VA 22304 (ED171763, 842 pages)
Target Audience: Adults
Notes: Items, 81

This volume consists of a series of psychosocial and physiological clinical nursing instruments. The instruments were selected from the published literature in health care, education, psychology, and the social sciences. Instruments focus on nursing practice and stress patient variables. Instrument is designed for completion by heart attack victims 6 months after leaving the hospital. It assesses 3 areas of a respondent's social and psychological status during recovery.

10104
Geriatric Functional Rating Scale to Determine the Need for Institutional Care. Grauer, H.; Birnbom, F. 1975
Subtests: Physical Condition; Mental Condition; Functional Abilities; Support from the Community; Living Quarters; Relatives and Friends; Financial Situation
Descriptors: *Daily Living Skills; Evaluation Criteria; Family Involvement; *Gerontology; Mental Health; *Observation; *Older Adults; Personal Care Homes; Physical Health; Rating Scales
Identifiers: *Independence
Availability: ERIC Document Reproduction Service; 3900 Wheeler Ave., Alexandria, VA 22304 (ED171763, 842 pages)
Target Audience: 65-99
Notes: Items, 30

This volume consists of a series of psychosocial and physiological clinical nursing instruments. The instruments were selected from the published literature in health care, education, psychology, and the social sciences. Instruments focus on nursing practice and stress patient variables. Instrument was designed to assess aged person's ability to care for self and support from family and community. Developed to determine the need for institutional placement for older adults.

10105
Patient Past Pain Experience Interview. Jacox, Ada; Stewart, Mary 1973
Subtests: Pain History and Alleviation: Current Illness; Childhood Experiences Related to Pain
Descriptors: Adults; Affective Behavior; *Early Experience; Hospitals; Interviews; Medical Case Histories; Nurses; *Patients
Identifiers: Illness; *Pain
Availability: ERIC Document Reproduction Service; 3900 Wheeler Ave., Alexandria, VA 22304 (ED171763, 842 pages)
Target Audience: Adults
Notes: Time, 60 approx.; Items, 14

This volume consists of a series of psychosocial and physiological clinical nursing instruments. The instruments were selected from the published literature in health care, education, psychology, and the social sciences. Instruments focus on nursing practice and stress patient variables. Instrument was developed to assess pain of a current illness and how it might be related to a patient's past experiences with pain, particularly in childhood. Authors believe person's interpretation and response to pain are influenced by past experience with pain.

10106
Prenatal Questionnaire. Lowe, Marie L. 1970
Descriptors: Adults; Attitude Measures; Behavior Patterns; Followup Studies; *Medical Services; *Nurses; Nursing; Nutrition; *Patients; *Pregnancy; Public Health
Identifiers: *Patient Attitudes
Availability: ERIC Document Reproduction Service; 3900 Wheeler Ave., Alexandria, VA 22304 (ED171763, 842 pages)
Target Audience: Adults
Notes: Time, 30 approx.; Items, 83

This volume consists of a series of psychosocial and physiological clinical nursing instruments. The instruments were selected from the published literature in health care, education, psychology, and the social sciences. Instruments focus on nursing practice and stress patient variables. Instrument was designed to measure patients' attitudes toward, and behavioral compliance with, a regimen prescribed during prenatal care. Administered at the outset of prenatal care and near the end of pregnancy. There are also 13 items concerning the outcome of delivery and public health nursing followup.

10107
Screening Questionnaire for Health Needs of Older Adults, Stage II. Managan, Dorothy; And Others 1974
Subtests: Physical Functioning; Health Condition; Accessibility of Health Care; Social Isolation; Service Needs; Contentment; Subjective Health Index
Descriptors: Daily Living Skills; Emotional Adjustment; *Health Needs; Health Services; *Interviews; *Older Adults; Physical Health; Social Isolation
Identifiers: Self Report Measures
Availability: DuPage County Health Dept.; 111 N. County Farm Rd., Wheaton, IL 60187 Attn: Olive Vanderbruggen
Target Audience: 65-99
Notes: Time, 45 approx.; Items, 77

Designed to provide information regarding the extent to which older adults who report health problems require help from a secondary support system. If patient is unable to respond to interview because of mental or physical illness, a person familiar with the patient may complete the interview.

10108
Psychosocial Problems of Adolescents with Epilepsy. Richardson, Donald W.; Friedman, Stanford B. 1974
Subtests: Adolescent Questionnaire; Adolescent Interview; Parent Questionnaire; Parent Interview
Descriptors: *Adolescents; Adults; *Epilepsy; Interpersonal Relationship; Interviews; *Parents; Questionnaires; Secondary Education; *Secondary School Students; *Seizures; Social Adjustment; Student Adjustment
Identifiers: *Psychosocial Problems
Availability: ERIC Document Reproduction Service; 3900 Wheeler Ave., Alexandria, VA 22304 (ED171763, 842 pages)
Target Audience: 13-17

This volume consists of a series of psychosocial and physiological clinical nursing instruments. The instruments were selected from the published literature in health care, education, psychology, and the social sciences. Instruments focus on nursing practice and stress patient variables. A series of 4 instruments for adolescents with epilepsy and their parents. The Adolescent Questionnaire consists of 20 items. It is designed to follow the 19 item Adolescent Interview. The Parent Questionnaire consists of 18 items and is designed to follow the 12 item Parent Interview.

Designed to assess problems related to school, career plans, social interaction, and family life. Interviews require approximately 45 minutes.

10109
Screening Tool to Detect Psychosocial Adjustment of Children with Cystic Fibrosis. Rodgers, Beckett M.; And Others 1974
Descriptors: Adults; Attitude Measures; Childhood Attitudes; *Children; Diseases; Emotional Adjustment; Family Attitudes; Interpersonal Relationship; Interviews; *Parent Attitudes; *Parents; Patients; *Special Health Problems; Student Adjustment
Identifiers: *Cystic Fibrosis; *Psychosocial Problems
Availability: ERIC Document Reproduction Service; 3900 Wheeler Ave., Alexandria, VA 22304 (ED171763, 842 pages)
Target Audience: 5-12
Notes: Items, 35

This volume consists of a series of psychosocial and physiological clinical nursing instruments. The instruments were selected from the published literature in health care, education, psychology, and the social sciences. Instruments focus on nursing practice and stress patient variables. Instrument is a semistructured parent interview. Designed to detect psychosocial adjustment problems of school-age children with cystic fibrosis.

10110
Health Status of Rheumatic Patients. Schaefer, Joanne L. 1973
Descriptors: *Adults; *Diseases; Drug Therapy; Medical Services; Mental Health; *Patients; Quality of Life; Questionnaires; *Self Evaluation (Individuals); Social Isolation
Identifiers: Pain; *Rheumatic Patients
Availability: ERIC Document Reproduction Service; 3900 Wheeler Ave., Alexandria, VA 22304 (ED171763, 842 pages)
Target Audience: Adults
Notes: Time, 45 approx.; Items, 64

This volume consists of a series of psychosocial and physiological clinical nursing instruments. The instruments were selected from the published literature in health care, education, psychology, and the social sciences. Instruments focus on nursing practice and stress patient variables. Instrument is designed to assess rheumatic patient's health status as perceived in terms of pain, suffering, physical limitation, and social isolation.

10111
Health Status Questionnaire. Schmid, A. Allan; And Others 1973
Descriptors: *Adolescents; *Adults; Biographical Inventories; *Children; *Clinics; Elementary Secondary Education; Interviews; *Medical Services; Nutrition; *Older Adults; Patients; *Physical Health; *Rural Areas
Availability: ERIC Document Reproduction Service; 3900 Wheeler Ave., Alexandria, VA 22304 (ED171763, 842 pages)
Target Audience: 6-99

This volume consists of a series of psychosocial and physiological clinical nursing instruments. The instruments were selected from the published literature in health care, education, psychology, and the social sciences. Instruments focus on nursing practice and stress patient variables. Designed to assess health status as indicated by data concerning health history and work or school activities. Administered by interviewer. Developed for use in a community survey to assess impact of services of rural health care clinic.

10112
Personal and Social Competence Inventory. Anderson, Catherine J. 1973
Subtests: Personal Competence; Personal Responsibility; Social Competence; Social Responsibility; Community Orientation
Descriptors: Adults; *Daily Living Skills; Institutionalized Persons; Interpersonal Competence; Nurses; *Patients; *Psychosis; Rating Scales; Self Care Skills; *Social Adjustment
Identifiers: Psychiatric Patients
Availability: ERIC Document Reproduction Service; 3900 Wheeler Ave., Alexandria, VA 22304 (ED171763, 842 pages)
Target Audience: Adults
Notes: Time, 30 approx.; Items, 25

This volume consists of a series of psychosocial and physiological clinical nursing instruments. The instruments were selected from the published literature in health care, education, psychology, and the social sciences. Instruments focus on nursing practice and stress patient variables. Instrument was designed to assess personal and social competence among long stay, socially regressed, psychotic patients. Nurses or aides who have observed the patient complete the instrument.

10113
Observed Patient Behavior Rating Scale. Barajas, Judy Doan Kerr 1971
Subtests: Social Competence; Social Interest; Personal Neatness; Depression; Irritability
Descriptors: *Behavior Rating Scales; Depression (Psychology); *Geriatrics; Interpersonal Competence; Nurses; Nursing Homes; Observation; *Older Adults; Patients; Personality Traits; Self Care Skills; *Sensory Deprivation
Availability: ERIC Document Reproduction Service; 3900 Wheeler Ave., Alexandria, VA 22304 (ED171763, 842 pages)
Target Audience: 65-99
Notes: Time, 5 approx.; Items, 25
This volume consists of a series of psychosocial and physiological clinical nursing instruments. The instruments were selected from the published literature in health care, education, psychology, and the social sciences. Instruments focus on nursing practice and stress patient variables. Instrument was developed to assess effects of sensory deprivation in geriatric patients living in a nursing home. Designed for completion by health care personnel who have observed the patient's behavior for at least 2 days prior to the rating.

10114
Functioning Status Assessment Form. Densen, Paul M.; And Others 1973
Descriptors: Adults; Nurses; Nursing Homes; Observation; *Patients; Physical Mobility; Rating Scales; *Self Care Skills
Availability: ERIC Document Reproduction Service; 3900 Wheeler Ave., Alexandria, VA 22304 (ED171763, 842 pages)
Target Audience: Adults
Notes: Items, 14
This volume consists of a series of psychosocial and physiological clinical nursing instruments. The instruments were selected from the published literature in health care, education, psychology, and the social sciences. Instruments focus on nursing practice and stress patient variables. Instrument designed to assess the patient's degree of independence in functioning. Applicable to long-term patients in nursing homes as well as patients in other residential settings.

10115
Health Needs of the Elderly. Hain, Mary Jeanne; Chen, Shu Pi 1974
Descriptors: *Daily Living Skills; *Gerontology; *Health Needs; Interviews; *Older Adults; Physical Health; Physical Mobility
Availability: ERIC Document Reproduction Service; 3900 Wheeler Ave., Alexandria, VA 22304 (ED171763, 842 pages)
Target Audience: 65-99
Notes: Items, 10
This volume consists of a series of psychosocial and physiological clinical nursing instruments. The instruments were selected from the published literature in health care, education, psychology, and the social sciences. Instruments focus on nursing practice and stress patient variables. Instrument is an interview to assess the health needs of elderly living in high rise apartments. Health needs include any factor which, if lacking, impinges on the psychosocial or physiological well-being of an individual.

10116
PULSES Profile. Moskowitz, Eugene 1960
Descriptors: *Adults; Disabilities; *Diseases; *Geriatrics; Mental Health; Observation; *Older Adults; *Patients; Physical Health; Physical Mobility
Identifiers: Nursing Care
Availability: ERIC Document Reproduction Service; 3900 Wheeler Ave., Alexandria, VA 22304 (ED171763, 842 pages)
Target Audience: 18-99
Notes: Items, 6
This volume consists of a series of psychosocial and physiological clinical nursing instruments. The instruments were selected from the published literature in health care, education, psychology, and the social sciences. Instruments focus on nursing practice and stress patient variables. Instrument was designed to assess functional capacity of aged and chronically ill patients. Functions assessed include general physical condition, upper extremity functioning, lower extremity functioning, sensory and excretory functions, and mental and emotional status.

10117
Psychosocial Function Scale. Putnam, Phyllis A. 1973
Descriptors: Adults; *Gerontology; *Interpersonal Competence; Interpersonal Relationship; Nurses; *Nursing; *Older Adults; *Patients; *Personal Care Homes; Rating Scales
Identifiers: Psychosocial Functioning
Availability: ERIC Document Reproduction Service; 3900 Wheeler Ave., Alexandria, VA 22304 (ED171763, 842 pages)

Target Audience: 18-99
Notes: Items, 8
This volume consists of a series of psychosocial and physiological clinical nursing instruments. The instruments were selected from the published literature in health care, education, psychology, and the social sciences. Instruments focus on nursing practice and stress patient variables. Instrument was designed to enable health care personnel to assess psychosocial functions of aged patients. May also be used in ordinary patient care settings. Functions assessed are interaction with nurse and other patients; use of spare time; knowledge of current events; knowledge of daily schedule, hospital resources, and own resources; and expression of needs.

10118
Functional Life Scale. Sarno, John E.; And Others 1973
Subtests: Cognition; Activities of Daily Life; Home Activities; Outside Activities; Social Interaction
Descriptors: *Adults; *Behavior Rating Scales; Cognitive Processes; *Daily Living Skills; *Disabilities; Interpersonal Competence; Nurses; Nursing; *Patients; Rehabilitation
Identifiers: FLS
Availability: ERIC Document Reproduction Service; 3900 Wheeler Ave., Alexandria, VA 22304 (ED171763, 842 pages)
Target Audience: Adults
Notes: Items, 44
This volume consists of a series of psychosocial and physiological clinical nursing instruments. The instruments were selected from the published literature in health care, education, psychology, and the social sciences. Instruments focus on nursing practice and stress patient variables. Instrument was designed to assess patient's ability to participate in basic daily activities. An attempt is made to describe the patient in terms of what he or she actually does, rather than his or her ability. Useful in the investigation of factors related to the recovery (rehabilitation), or lack of it, in a disabled patient.

10119
Mental Health Patient Assessment Record. Vincent, Pauline A.; And Others 1976
Subtests: Physical Behaviors; Psychological Behaviors; Social Behaviors; Medical Behaviors; Household Members; Behaviors with Patient
Descriptors: *Adjustment (to Environment); Adults; *Behavioral Objectives; *Daily Living Skills; Interpersonal Competence; Interpersonal Relationship; *Mental Health; Nurses; Nursing; *Patients; Rating Scales
Identifiers: *Psychiatric Patients; Visiting Nurse Association
Availability: ERIC Document Reproduction Service; 3900 Wheeler Ave., Alexandria, VA 22304 (ED171763, 842 pages)
Target Audience: Adults
This volume consists of a series of psychosocial and physiological clinical nursing instruments. The instruments were selected from the published literature in health care, education, psychology, and the social sciences. Instruments focus on nursing practice and stress patient variables. Instrument was designed to assess the physical, psychological, social, and medical behaviors of psychiatric patients following discharge from the hospital. Two sections of the instrument include a checklist of patient behaviors and a Goals and General Performance Record.

10127
Behavior Observation Scale. Freeman, Betty Jo; And Others 1978
Descriptors: *Autism; Behavior Rating Scales; Developmental Disabilities; *Mental Retardation; Observation; *Preschool Children
Identifiers: BOS
Availability: Journal of the American Academy of Child Psychiatry; p576-88 1978.
Target Audience: 2-5
Notes: Time, 27 approx.; Items, 67
An observation technique used to assist in diagnosis of autism in young children. Subject is observed through one way mirror and coded on 67 objectively defined behaviors.

10128
Clinical Analysis Questionnaire, Part II. Spanish Edition. Delhees, Karl H.; Cattell, Raymond B. 1970
Descriptors: Adults; Clinical Diagnosis; *Mental Disorders; Personality Assessment; *Personality Measures; *Psychological Evaluation; Psychopathology; *Spanish
Identifiers: CAQ
Availability: Institute For Personality and Ability Testing; P.O. Box 188, Champaign, IL 61820
Target Audience: Adults
Notes: Time, 60 approx.; Items, 144

Intended for use in general clinical diagnosis for evaluating therapeutic progress and for basic clinical research, both with neurotics and psychotics. Part II consists of 12 pathological dimensions: low-high hypochondriasis, zestfullness-suicidal disgust; low-high brooding discontent; low-high anxious depression; high energy euphoria-low energy depression; low-high guilt and resentment; low-high bored depression; low-high depression; low-high paranoia, low-high psychopathic deviation; low-high schizophrenia, low-high psychathenia; low-high general psychosis. Untimed test, but estimated that Part II will take approximately 60 minutes.

10140
Socio-Sexual Knowledge and Attitudes Test. Wish, Joel; And Others 1977
Subtests: Anatomy Terminology; Dating; Marriage; Intimacy; Intercourse; Pregnancy, Childbirth and Childbearing; Menstruation; Masturbation; Homosexuality; Alcohol and Drugs; Community Risks and Hazards; Birth Control; Venereal Disease; Terminology Check
Descriptors: *Achievement Tests; Adjustment (to Environment); Adults; *Attitude Measures; Attitudes; Family Life Education; Individual Testing; Institutionalized Persons; *Mild Mental Retardation; *Moderate Mental Retardation; Normalization (Handicapped); *Screening Tests; Self Concept Measures; Self Evaluation (Individuals); Sex Differences; *Sexuality; Social Attitudes; Social Cognition; Social Development
Identifiers: Oral Tests; Sex Knowledge and Attitude Test; SSKAT
Availability: ERIC Document Reproduction Service; 3900 Wheeler Ave., Alexandria, VA 22304 (ED160643, microfiche only)
Target Audience: Adults
Notes: Time, 100 approx.; Items, 250
Developed to measure a mildly or moderately retarded person's sociosexual knowledge and attitudes as well as how much he or she thinks that he or she knows about each subject. Also includes evaluation on the Adaptive Behavior Scale (Nihira et al., rev. 74). Used to determine the sociosexual instruction needed and used as an achievement and attitude test after instruction is given. Based on the trend that returns mentally retarded persons to the community and the corresponding sociosexual adjustment which this return involves. Answers require very short statements, pointing to a picture, and/or selection among multiple choices. Requires the use of pictures and photographs for some subtests. No more than 5 subtests should be given in one session of approximately 30 minutes. Individually administered.

10162
Oral Language Proficiency Scale. Dade County Public Schools, Miami, Florida Division of Elementary and Secondary Education 1978
Subtests: Understanding of Spoken Language; Using Grammatical Structure; Pronunciation; Vocabulary
Descriptors: Bilingual Education; *Elementary School Students; Elementary Secondary Education; *English (Second Language); *Individual Testing; *Language Proficiency; Language Tests; *Secondary School Students; *Student Placement
Identifiers: Dade County Public Schools FL; *Oral Tests; TIM(E)
Availability: Tests in Microfiche; Test Collection, Educational Testing Service, Princeton, NJ 08541
Grade Level: K-12
Notes: Items, 20
Used in an oral interview for student placement in a program of English for Speakers of Other Languages (ESOL). Placement is based on proficiency in 4 areas. Two forms are available—elementary and secondary.

10163
Examen de Lectura en Espanol. Dade County Public Schools, Miami, Florida Division of Elementary and Secondary Education 1975
Descriptors: Bilingual Education; Language Proficiency; Language Tests; Secondary Education; *Secondary School Students; *Spanish; *Student Placement
Identifiers: Dade County Public Schools FL; TIM(E)
Availability: Tests in Microfiche; Test Collection, Educational Testing Service, Princeton, NJ 08541
Grade Level: 7-12
Notes: Items, 30
A Spanish reading placement test for grades 7-12. The test consists of 30 multiple-choice questions, 2 of which are samples.

10164
Examen de Lenguaje en Espanol. Dade County Public Schools, Miami, Florida Division of Elementary and Secondary Education 1975

Subtests: Language Usage; Verbs; Vocabulary
Descriptors: Bilingual Education; *Elementary School Students; Grade 7; Intermediate Grades; Junior High School Students; Language Proficiency; Language Tests; *Spanish; *Student Placement
Identifiers: Dade County Public Schools FL; TIM(E)
Availability: Tests in Microfiche; Test Collection, Educational Testing Service, Princeton, NJ 08541
Grade Level: 5-7
Notes: Items, 48

A Spanish-language placement test for grades 5-7. The multiple-choice test consists of 48 questions divided into 3 sections.

10177
Modes of Learning a Second Language. Bowen, J. Donald 1978
Subtests: Derivational Morphology; Reading List-Monosyllables; Reading List-Polysyllables; Reading List-Letters and Numbers; Imitation-Short Sentences; Response-One Word
Descriptors: Adolescents; *Auditory Stimuli; Cognitive Style; Individual Testing; *Language Acquisition; *Language Tests; Literacy; *Second Language Learning; *Visual Stimuli
Availability: Alatis, James E., ed.. International Dimensions of Bilingual Education. Washington, DC: Georgetown University Press, 1978
Target Audience: Adolescents
Notes: Time, 15 approx.; Items, 96

Used to determine method of acquisition of a second language, taking into account the influence of literacy. Designed to evaluate the English of 3 groups whose language learning experience differs in ways that can perhaps be assigned literacy correlates. Measures certain skills using aural and visual techniques, after which correlations between test performance and cognitive style can be attempted, specifically as related to preliteracy and post-literacy.

10178
Criminal Attitude Scale. Taylor, A.J.W. 1968
Descriptors: Adults; Attitude Change; *Attitude Measures; Crime; Criminal Law; *Criminals
Identifiers: CATS
Availability: Journal of Criminal Law, Criminology, and Political Science; v51 n1 p37-40 1968
Target Audience: Adults
Notes: Items, 15

Measures attitudes and opinions of criminals regarding criminal justice, law enforcement, and feelings of despair. Object is to assess degree of criminality and change of attitude as a result of treatment or contamination.

10179
Children's Personality Questionnaire, Spanish Edition. Porter, Rutherford B.; And Others 1976
Subtests: Reserved-Warmhearted; Less Intelligent-More Intelligent; Affected by Feelings-Emotionally Stable; Phlegmatic-Excitable; Obedient-Assertive; Sober-Happy-Go-Lucky; Expedient-Conscientious; Shy-Venturesome; Tough Minded-Tender Minded; Zestful-Circumspect; Forthright-Shrewd; Self-Assured-Apprehensive; Casual-Controlled; Relaxed-Tense
Descriptors: Academic Achievement; Assertiveness; Children; Delinquency; Diagnostic Tests; Emotional Problems; Individual Testing; Leadership; *Personality Measures; Screening Tests; *Spanish Speaking; Underachievement
Availability: Institute for Personality and Ability Testing; P.O. Box 188, Champaign, IL 61820
Target Audience: 8-12
Notes: Time, 60; Items, 140

A general measure of personality assessing 14 dimensions of personality. Designed to predict academic achievement/ underachievement, delinquency, leadership, and emotional disturbance. Four forms are available. Group or individually administered. Used for diagnosis and screening.

10180
The John Test. Kesper, Ray; And Others 1976
Subtests: Oral Comprehension; Ability to Produce Connected Discourse in Past Tense Narrative; Ability to Ask Questions
Descriptors: Adults; Comprehension; *English (Second Language); Individual Testing; *Language Tests; Pictorial Stimuli; Speech Skills; *Student Placement
Identifiers: Oral Tests
Availability: Language Innovations, Inc.; 2112 Broadway, Rm. 515, New York, NY 10023
Target Audience: 18-65
Notes: Time, 10; Items, 34

Oral placement test for non-native speakers of English. Individually administered. Seven pictures depict occurrences in the typical day of a young man named John.

Simple questions elicit information about him. Parts I and II of the test are sufficient for placement. A shortened form is available.

10196
Bilingual Test Battery. Bilingual Education Service Center, Arlington Heights, IL 1974
Subtests: Mathematics; Social Studies; General Science; Attitude
Descriptors: *Achievement Tests; *Bilingual Students; *Elementary School Students; Elementary Secondary Education; Mathematics; Science Tests; *Secondary School Students; Social Studies; *Spanish; Student Attitudes
Identifiers: TIM(E)
Availability: Tests in Microfiche; Test Collection, Educational Testing Service, Princeton, NJ 08541
Grade Level: 3-10
Notes: Items, 40

Battery consists of English-Spanish bilingual tests in mathematics, social studies, science, and attitudes. Eighty multiple-choice questions are given in both languages. Students are instructed to choose the language they prefer. Three levels are available: Level I (grades 3-4), Level II (grades 5-6), and Level III (grades 7-10).

10197
Self-Care Skill Level Evaluation Checklist. Waukegan Developmental Center, IL 1975
Subtests: Toileting; Showering; Washing Face and Hands; Grooming; Dressing and Undressing Skills; Mealtime Skills
Descriptors: Adults; *Behavior Rating Scales; Developmental Disabilities; *Evaluation Criteria; Residential Care; *Self Care Skills; *Severe Mental Retardation
Identifiers: TIM(E); WDC
Availability: Tests in Microfiche; Test Collection, Educational Testing Service, Princeton, NJ 08541
Target Audience: Adults
Notes: Items, 193

Developed for use as a description of a developmentally disabled student's observed behavior during periodic evaluations. When used with the Initial Skill-Level Evaluation, the results can be used to evaluate the effectiveness of self-care programs. The skills observed are divided into 6 sections.

10203
School Performance Checklist. Macy, Daniel J.
Descriptors: Adults; *Behavior Rating Scales; Children; *Exceptional Persons; *Special Education; Student Behavior; *Student Evaluation; *Teacher Attitudes
Identifiers: TIM(E)
Availability: Tests in Microfiche; Test Collection, Educational Testing Service, Princeton, NJ 08541
Target Audience: Adults
Notes: Items, 27

Developed for use with children in special education classes. Designed to measure teacher perceptions of how special students function within the classroom and school setting.

10211
Early School Personality Questionnaire, Spanish Edition. Coan, Richard W.; And Others 1976
Subtests: Reserved-Warmhearted; Dull-Bright; Affected by Feelings-Emotionally Stable; Undemonstrative-Excitable; Obedient-Dominant; Sober-Enthusiastic; Disregards Rules-Conscientious; Timid-Venturesome; Tough-Tender-Minded; Vigorous-Doubting; Forthright-Shrewd; Self-Assured-Guiltprone; Relaxed-Tense
Descriptors: Counseling; Group Testing; *Personality Measures; Personality Traits; *Spanish Speaking; Young Children
Identifiers: Oral Tests
Availability: Institute for Personality and Ability Testing; P.O. Box 188, Champaign, IL 61820
Target Audience: 6-8
Notes: Time, 60; Items, 160

A general measure of personality for use with school children for counseling and guidance. Measures 13 primary personality traits. Questions are read aloud to child who responds on a nonreading answer sheet. Group administered.

10212
Spanish High School Personality Questionnaire. Cattell, Raymond B.; Cattell, Mary 1968
Descriptors: Adolescents; Assertiveness; Emotional Adjustment; High School Students; Intelligence; Junior High School Students; Personal Autonomy; *Personality Measures; Preadolescents; *Spanish Speaking; Young Adults

Availability: Institute for Personality and Ability Testing, Inc.; P.O. Box 188, Champaign, IL 61820
Target Audience: 12-18; Items, 142

Measures 13 personality dimensions: reserved-warmhearted; less-more intelligent; affected by feelings-emotionally stable; undemonstrative-excitable; obedient-assertive; sober-enthusiastic; disregards rules-conscientious; shy-adventurous; tough-minded-tender-minded; zestful-circumspect; self-assured-apprehensive; sociably group dependent-self-sufficient; uncontrolled-controlled; relaxed-tense. Test itself is in Spanish. All other materials are in English. U.S. norms for males and females.

10224
SEVTC Assessment Scales for Community Integration of the Severely/Profoundly Handicapped, Part IIB, Post Entry Monitoring Instrument. Southeastern Virginia Training Center for the Mentally Retarded, Chesapeake, VA 1977
Subtests: Motor Development; Self-Help Independent Living; Academic/Cognitive; Language; Socialization
Descriptors: Adolescents; Adults; *Behavioral Objectives; Behavior Change; *Cognitive Development; Criterion Referenced Tests; *Daily Living Skills; Institutionalized Persons; *Language Acquisition; *Mental Retardation; Motor Development; *Normalization (Handicapped); Self Care Skills; *Severe Disabilities; *Social Development
Availability: ERIC Document Reproduction Service; 3900 Wheeler Ave., Alexandria, VA 22304 (ED167565, 46 pages)
Target Audience: 8-64
Notes: Items, 110

Criterion-referenced instrument to assess a mentally retarded person's competence in skill areas related to readiness for community integration. Subject's behaviors are observed directly. Some items are scored through indirect reports of behavior.

10230
Dibner System. Dibner, Andrew S.
Descriptors: Adults; *Anxiety; Audiotape Recordings; *Interviews; *Patients; *Psychotherapy; *Speech
Identifiers: TIM(G)
Availability: Tests in Microfiche; Test Collection, Educational Testing Service, Princeton, NJ 08541
Target Audience: Adults

Developed to investigate the relationship between anxiety as a transient, situational phenomenon and speech patterns in the psychotherapeutic process. Eleven speech characteristics were identified as related to situational anxiety: unfinished sentence, breaking in with a new thought, interrupted sentence, repeated words or phrases, stuttering, I don't know, sighing or deep breath, laughing, voice change, questioning the interviewer, and blocking.

10253
The Experiencing Scale. Klein, M. H.; And Others 1970
Descriptors: Adults; Audiotape Recordings; *Participation; *Patients; *Psychotherapy; Rating Scales
Identifiers: EXP Scale
Availability: Bureau of Audio-Visual Instruction; University Extension, The University of Wisconsin, Box 2093, Madison, WI 53701
Target Audience: Adults

Designed to evaluate directly from tape recordings or typescripts the quality of a patient's self-involvement in psychotherapy.

10263
The Projective Assessment of Aging Method. Starr, Bernard D.; And Others 1979
Descriptors: Adult Development; *Aging (Individuals); Attitude Measures; *Gerontology; *Older Adults; Pictorial Stimuli; *Projective Measures
Identifiers: PAAM
Availability: Springer Publishing Co.; 200 Park Ave., S., New York, NY 10003
Target Audience: 65-99
Notes: Time, 45 approx.; Items, 14

A projective technique to assess feelings, attitudes, and perceptions of older adults. Respondent examines a series of pictures depicting scenes related to the aging process and themes of aging.

10290
Disruptive Behavior Scale. Mendelsohn, Mark; Erdwins, Carol 1978
Descriptors: Adolescents; *Antisocial Behavior; Check Lists; Public Schools; Secondary Education; *Secondary School Students; Student Behavior
Identifiers: DBS

Availability: Journal of Clinical Psychology; v34 n2 p426-28 Apr 1978
Grade Level: 7-12
Target Audience: 12-18
Notes: Time, 25 approx.; Items, 26

Designed as an objective index of socially unacceptable public secondary school behavior.

10301
Tentative Drug Use Scale. Horan, John J.; Williams, John M. 1975
Descriptors: *Adults; *College Students; *Drug Abuse; Drug Education; Higher Education; Program Evaluation; Questionnaires
Identifiers: TDUS
Availability: Journal of Drug Education; v5 n4 p381-84 1975
Grade Level: 13-16
Target Audience: Adults
Notes: Items, 9

Designed for use in evaluation of drug abuse prevention programs. May be used as a posttest of a drug abuse prevention project or as a survey research instrument to determine the extent of a drug problem in a given locale.

10304
Mini-Mult. Kincannon, James C. 1968
Descriptors: Adults; Clinical Psychology; Interviews; Mental Health Clinics; *Patients; Personality Measures; *Psychiatric Hospitals; *Psychological Testing; Self Evaluation (Individuals)
Availability: ADI Auxiliary Publications Project; Photoduplication Service, Library of Congress, Washington, DC 20540 (Document No. 9949)
Target Audience: Adults
Notes: Items, 71

Designed for use in situations where a rapid evaluation of personality is needed. Items were chosen as representative of the clinical Minnesota Multiphasic Personality Inventory (TC002462). May also be used with patients who are unable, or unwilling, to complete the longer instrument. Items are administered orally.

10311
Test of English for International Communication. Educational Testing Service, Princeton, NJ 1982
Descriptors: Adults; *Business Communication; *Business English; *Communicative Competence (Languages); *English (Second Language); *Japanese; *Language Tests; Listening Comprehension; Multiple Choice Tests; Reading Comprehension
Identifiers: TOEIC; Woodford (Protase)
Availability: Educational Testing Service, International Office; Princeton, NJ 08541
Target Audience: Adults
Notes: Items, 200

A secure testing program developed for non-English-speaking countries to measure English-language skills outside of the traditional academic context. Used by foreign businesspersons to assess their knowledge and communicative abilities in English. Although currently in use in Japan, the program could be adapted for any other non-English-speaking country. Test is administered at designated centers only, not sold directly.

10314
Coping Ability Scale. Taylor, James Bentley 1970
Descriptors: Adults; Case Studies; *Coping; Rating Scales; *Retirement
Identifiers: Example Anchored Scales
Availability: Educational and Psychological Measurement; v30 p311-18 1970
Target Audience: Adults
Notes: Items, 4

Brief case history vignettes related to the variable being assessed are used as anchor points on a rating scale. Vignettes concern retirees and their ability to cope with various related conditions.

10315
Patient Activity Checklist. Aumack, Lewis 1968
Descriptors: Adults; Behavior Patterns; Daily Living Skills; Hygiene; Interpersonal Relationship; *Patients; Psychiatric Hospitals; Rating Scales
Identifiers: *Psychiatric Patients
Availability: Journal of Clinical Psychology, v25 n2 p134-37 Apr 1969
Target Audience: 18-64
Notes: Items, 24

Rating scale designed to measure the improvement of hospitalized psychiatric patients. A series of observations is made over a period of days or weeks. Covers hygiene, relationships with other patients, eating, and recreational habits.

10322
Expressive One-Word Picture Vocabulary Test. Gardner, Morrison F. 1979

Descriptors: Age Grade Placement; Basic Vocabulary; Bilingual Students; Children; *Cognitive Development; *Elementary School Students; *Expressive Language; Individual Testing; *Intelligence Tests; *Mental Age; Pictorial Stimuli; Preschool Children; School Readiness; *Screening Tests; Student Placement; *Verbal Ability; Verbal Tests; *Visual Measures
Identifiers: EOWPVT; Oral Tests
Availability: Academic Therapy Publications; 20 Commercial Blvd., Novato, CA 94947
Target Audience: 2-12
Notes: Time, 20 approx.; Items, 110

Untimed measure of verbal intelligence for children ages 2 to 12; may also be used with older persons. May also be used for screening of possible speech defects or potential learning disorders, estimation of bilingual students' fluency in English, screening for kindergarten and for kindergarten readiness or placement, and as an appraisal of a student's definitional and interpretational skills. The respondent is presented with 110 pictures, one at a time, and is asked to name each picture. The objects depicted fall into 4 categories of language: general concepts, groupings (plurals), abstract concepts, and descriptive concepts. Distribution is restricted.

10323
Tests for Everyday Living. Halpern, Andrew; And Others 1979
Subtests: Purchasing Habits; Banking; Budgeting; Health Care; Home Management; Job Search Skills; Job Related Behavior
Descriptors: *Achievement Tests; Adolescents; *Adults; Consumer Education; *Daily Living Skills; Health; Home Management; Job Search Methods; Job Skills; *Learning Problems; *Minimum Competencies; Money Management; Multiple Choice Tests; *Secondary School Students; Verbal Tests
Identifiers: *Oral Tests; TEL
Availability: CTB/McGraw-Hill; Del Monte Research Park, Monterey, CA 93940
Target Audience: 12-64
Notes: Time, 140 approx.; Items, 245

Battery of 7 untimed tests that measure knowledge of life skills necessary to successfully perform everyday life tasks. Orally administered so that poor readers are not disadvantaged. Estimated time for each test is 20 minutes. Frequently used in grades 7 through 12 with average or low-achieving students, or remedial and learning-disabled students. Does include some performance items, such as filling out an application form or writing a check where some reading is required.

10325
Bloom Sentence Completion Survey (Student). Bloom, Wallace 1974
Subtests: Age Mates; Physical Self; Family; Psychological Self; Self Directedness; Education; Accomplishment; Irritants
Descriptors: *Attitude Measures; *Elementary School Students; Elementary Secondary Education; Family Attitudes; Individual Testing; *Mild Mental Retardation; *Projective Measures; School Attitudes; *Secondary School Students; Self Concept; *Student Attitudes
Availability: Stoelting Co.; 1350 S. Kostner Ave., Chicago, IL 60623
Grade Level: 1-12
Notes: Time, 25 approx.; Items, 40

Designed to reveal subject's attitudes toward important factors in everyday living. Examiner should offer to record responses so that survey will be completed more quickly; answers will be unedited; and subjects will be allowed to enjoy opportunity to dictate to someone who will do writing for them.

10334
Basic Educational Skills Test. Segel, Ruth; Golding, Sandra 1979
Subtests: Reading; Writing; Mathematics
Descriptors: *Aural Learning; Basic Skills; Diagnostic Tests; Elementary Education; *Elementary School Mathematics; Elementary School Students; *Learning Disabilities; Learning Modalities; *Reading Tests; *Screening Tests; *Speech Skills; *Tactual Perception; *Visual Learning; *Writing Skills
Identifiers: BEST
Availability: United Educational Services; P.O. Box 357, E. Aurora, NY 14052
Grade Level: 1-5
Notes: Time, 60; Items, 75

Individually administered assessment of perceptual abilities and academic skills. May be administered by teacher, aide, or parent. Recording form correlates performance on each item with relevant perceptual modalities.

10390
Pre-School Screening Instrument. Cohen, Stephen Paul 1979

Subtests: Human Figure Drawing; Visual Fine Motor Perception; Visual Gross Motor Perception; Language Development; Speech; Behavior
Descriptors: *Behavior Development; Individual Testing; Language Acquisition; *Learning Problems; Observation; Performance Tests; *Preschool Children; *Psychomotor Skills; Questionnaires; *School Readiness; School Readiness Tests; *Screening Tests; Verbal Communication; *Verbal Development; Verbal Tests; Visual Perception; Young Children
Identifiers: Oral Tests; PSSI
Availability: Stoelting Co.; 1350 S. Kostner Ave., Chicago, IL 60623
Target Audience: 4-5
Notes: Time, 10 approx.; Items, 32

Individually administered screening test for prekindergarten children to identify those with potential learning problems. Includes observation by administrator, performance and some verbal responses by the testee, and a Parental Questionnaire on which the parent gives developmental, medical, behavioral, and general information about the child. Comes with the equipment needed to carry out the performance parts of the test.

10391
Rockford Infant Developmental Evaluation Scales. Project RHISE, Rockford, IL 1979
Subtests: Personal-Social/Self-Help; Fine Motor/Adaptive; Receptive Language; Expressive Language; Gross Motor
Descriptors: Behavior Rating Scales; *Developmental Tasks; *Disabilities; Individual Development; Infant Behavior; *Infants; Intervention; Language Acquisition; Observation; *Preschool Children; Psychomotor Skills; Social Development; Special Education
Identifiers: RIDES
Availability: Scholastic Testing Service, Inc.; 480 Meyer Rd., P.O. Box 1056, Bensenville, IL 60106
Target Audience: 0-4

A checklist of 308 developmental behaviors arranged by age range into 5 skill areas. Designed for use in early intervention and preschool programs to assess developmental functioning of disabled children.

10395
Birth to Three Developmental Scale. Bangs, Tina E.; Dodson, Susan 1979
Subtests: Language Comprehension; Language Expression; Problem Solving; Social/Personal; Motor
Descriptors: Behavior Rating Scales; *Developmental Stages; Expressive Language; *Handicap Identification; Individual Testing; Infant Behavior; *Infants; *Language Acquisition; Preschool Children; Problem Solving; Psychomotor Skills; Receptive Language; *Social Development
Availability: DLM Teaching Resources; P.O. Box 4000, One DLM Park, Allen, TX 75002
Target Audience: 0-3

Designed for the early identification and assessment of developmental delay in 4 behavioral categories. Useful in preparing appropriate educational objectives.

10407
System FORE: Spanish Adaptation. Los Angeles Unified School District, California Division of Special Education 1975
Descriptors: *Children; Evaluation Methods; *Language Acquisition; Measures (Individuals); Morphology (Languages); Phonology; Preschool Children; Semantics; *Spanish; *Spanish Speaking; Syntax
Identifiers: TIM(F)
Availability: Tests in Microfiche; Test Collection, Educational Testing Service, Princeton, NJ 08541
Target Audience: Children

Series of inventories designed to assess a child's linguistic development in the Spanish language for native speakers of developmental age 3-7 years. The inventories accompany instructional objectives arranged by developmental levels as an aid for individualizing and planning instruction. There are 10 developmental levels of this program. Each level is divided into strands to include the 4 aspects of language: phonology, morphology, syntax, and semantics. Level 3 has 34 items; level 4 has 34 items; level 5 has 24 items; level 6 has 22 items; level 7 has 27 items; level 8 has 25 items; level 9 has 14 items; and level 10 has 16 items.

10431
The Socio-Sexual Knowledge and Attitude Test. Wish, Joel; And Others 1976

Subtests: Anatomy Terminology; Menstruation; Dating; Marriage; Intimacy; Intercourse; Pregnancy; Childbirth; Childrearing; Birth Control; Masturbation; Homosexuality; Venereal Disease; Alcohol and Drugs; Community Risks and Hazards; Terminology Check
Descriptors: Adults; *Attitude Measures; Developmental Disabilities; Individual Testing; *Knowledge Level; *Language Handicaps; *Mental Retardation; *Sexuality
Identifiers: SSKAT
Availability: Stoelting Co.; 1350 S. Kostner Ave., Chicago, IL 60623
Target Audience: Adults
Notes: Items, 240

Developed for developmentally disabled persons, including mentally retarded individuals who are not verbally proficient or for those whose speech is unintelligible. Used to determine what this population knows or believes about areas of sociosexual functioning and what their attitudes are toward sociosexual practices. There are 14 subscores for the knowledge section. For the attitude section, there are 10 subscores. Individually administered.

10433
Perceptions of Developmental Skills. Bagnato, Stephen J.; And Others 1977
Descriptors: Communication Skills; Developmental Stages; *Disabilities; *Preschool Children; Preschool Education; *Preschool Teachers; Problem Solving; Psychomotor Skills; Rating Scales; *Screening Tests; Self Care Skills
Identifiers: PODS
Availability: ERIC Document Reproduction Service; 3900 Wheeler Ave., Alexandria, VA 22304 (ED170344, 38 pages)
Target Audience: 2-5

Developed as a screening instrument for standardizing and profiling diverse perceptions of significant adults who interact with handicapped preschoolers. A rating scale of functional skills within developmental areas of communication, social/emotional adjustment, physical, and cognitive development. Instrument was designed for use in HICOMP, a comprehensive outreach model program for handicapped preschoolers.

10438
McCarron-Dial Evaluation System. Dial, Jack G.; And Others 1975
Subtests: Wechsler Adult Intelligence Scale (180); Peabody Picture Vocabulary Test (175); Bender Visual Motor Gestalt Test (9); Haptic Visual Discrimination Test; McCarron Assessment of Neuromuscular Development; Observational Emotional Inventory; Dial Behavior Rating Scale
Descriptors: Adolescents; Adults; *Clinical Diagnosis; *Cognitive Ability; Coping; Diagnostic Tests; *Disabilities; *Educational Diagnosis; Emotional Adjustment; Learning Disabilities; Perceptual Development; Psychomotor Skills; Vocational Aptitude; *Vocational Rehabilitation; Work Sample Tests
Identifiers: Psychiatric Patients; Sensory Motor Skills
Availability: Common Market Press; P.O. Box 45628, Dallas, TX 75245
Target Audience: Adolescents, Adults

Component tests evaluate disabled person's cognitive, emotional-coping and sensorimotor functioning in a neuropsychological approach to vocational, clinical or educational evaluation.

10450
Stress Events Inventory (Revised). Chandler, Louis A. 1980
Descriptors: Check Lists; Children; *Emotional Problems; *Stress Variables
Identifiers: Childrens Life Events Inventory
Availability: Louis A. Chandler; The Psychoeducational Clinic, University of Pittsburgh, Pittsburgh, PA 15260
Target Audience: Children
Notes: Time, 5 approx.; Items, 37

An adaptation of Coddington's Life Events of Children. To be used in schools and clinics as part of intake-referral procedures for children with emotional adjustment problems. Provides a means of identifying sources of psychological stress during the assessment problem. This inventory is currently called the Children's Life Events Inventory.

10453
Test of Syntactic Abilities. Quigley, Stephen P.; And Others 1978
Subtests: Negation; Conjunction; Determiners; Question Formation; Verb Processes; Pronominalization; Relativization; Complementation; Nominalization

Descriptors: Adolescents; Children; *Deafness; *Diagnostic Tests; *Elementary School Students; Hearing Impairments; *High School Students; Language Acquisition; Language Skills; Language Tests; Multiple Choice Tests; *Screening Tests; *Syntax
Identifiers: TSA
Availability: Dormac, Inc.; P.O. Box 752, Beaverton, OR 97075
Target Audience: 8-18
Notes: Time, 60 approx.; Items, 120

To assess the syntactic knowledge of English by deaf students. May also be used with persons who have language problems, mild mental retardation, various types of learning disabilities, and/or minor hearing impairment. It is recommended that the screening test of 120 multiple-choice items be administered first; it takes about one hour. Based upon the results, one or more of the 20 diagnostic tests should be administered; each test takes about 30 minutes.

10466
Creative Behavior Inventory. Hocevar, Dennis 1979
Subtests: Fine Arts; Crafts; Literature; Music; Performing Arts; Mathematics-Science
Descriptors: Adults; *Creativity Tests; Dance; Drama; Graphic Arts; Handicrafts; Higher Education; Literature; Mathematics; Music; Sciences; *Talent Identification; Undergraduate Students
Availability: ERIC Document Reproduction Service; 3900 Wheeler Ave., Alexandria, VA 22304 (ED170350, 15 pages)
Grade Level: 13-16
Notes: Items, 90

Designed to identify creative people by gathering information on their activities and achievements. Covers creativity in literary production, publications, music production and performance, crafts, graphic media, dance, and drama.

10471
Tactile Test of Basic Concepts. Caton, Hilda R. 1971
Descriptors: *Blindness; *Classroom Communication; *Cognitive Development; Cognitive Tests; Concept Formation; Criterion Referenced Tests; *Elementary School Students; Individual Testing; Primary Education; Raised Line Drawings; *School Readiness Tests; *Tactile Adaptation
Identifiers: *Boehm Test of Basic Concepts; BTBC; Oral Tests; TTBC
Availability: American Printing House for the Blind, Inc.; 1839 Frankfort Ave., Louisville, KY 40206-0085
Grade Level: K-2
Notes: Time, 50 approx.; Items, 50

Tactile test designed to evaluate a student's mastery of concepts needed to understand oral classroom communication. Such tests are usually found in commonly used instructional materials. Concepts are classed as Space (location, direction, orientation, dimensions), quantity and number, time, and miscellaneous. Adapted from the Boehm Test of Basic Concepts (TC009434), Form A.

10472
Interethnic Attitude Scale. Stephan, Walter G. 1973
Subtests: Attitude Scale-Mexican American; Black; White; Contact Scale; Background
Descriptors: *Attitude Measures; Blacks; *Elementary School Students; *Ethnic Groups; *Ethnicity; *Ethnic Relations; Intermediate Grades; Mexican Americans; *Racial Attitudes; *Racial Integration; Semantic Differential; Social Integration; Whites
Identifiers: TIM(G)
Availability: Tests in Microfiche; Test Collection, Educational Testing Service, Princeton, NJ 08541
Grade Level: 4-5
Notes: Time, 45; Items, 30

Black, Mexican-American, and White students rate one another via 3 forms of a semantic differential describing students' temperament, social relations, work habits, and other characteristics. Also includes a scale designed to measure frequency of social contacts with other ethnic groups.

10481
Katz Adjustment Scales. Katz, Martin M. 1963
Subtests: Patient-Symptoms and Social Behavior; Socially Expected Activities; Level of Expectations; Free Time Activities; Satisfaction with Free Time Activities; Patient Self Rating Symptom Discomfort; Patient Self Rating Socially Expected Activities; Patient Self Rating Level of Expectations; Patient Self Rating Free Time Activities; Patient Self Rating Satisfaction with Free Time Activities

Descriptors: *Adjustment (to Environment); Adults; Family (Sociological Unit); *Mental Disorders; *Patients; *Psychiatric Hospitals; *Rating Scales; Self Evaluation (Individuals); *Social Behavior
Identifiers: KAS
Availability: Psychological Reports; v13 n2 p503-35 Oct 1963
Target Audience: Adults
Notes: Items, 338

Set of inventories for objectively assessing the adjustment and social behavior of prepsychotic and ex-hospital patients in the community. One set of scales is completed by the ex-patient's relative, and one set of scales is completed by the ex-patient. Designed for application to the problems of describing and classifying patients in accordance with their behavior prior to entrance to the hospital and in the community follow-up evaluation and comparison of psychiatric treatments.

10482
SEVTC Assessment Scales for Community Integration of the Severely/Profoundly Handicapped, Part I, Pre-Entry Screening Instrument. Southeastern Virginia Training Center for the Mentally Retarded, Chesapeake, VA 1977
Descriptors: Adolescents; Adults; Children; Daily Living Skills; *Deinstitutionalization (of Disabled); Interviews; Language Skills; Parents; *Screening Tests; *Severe Disabilities; Social Development
Availability: ERIC Document Reproduction Service; 3900 Wheeler Ave., Alexandria, VA 22304 (ED167564, 31 pages)
Target Audience: 0-64

A screening and selection tool for use with institutionalized mentally retarded individuals to select those suitable for a program that would return them to a less restrictive living environment. Consists of an interview for use with parent or institutional staff member who has worked with the individual. Covers language, personal hygiene, toilet training, dressing, table behavior, gross motor skills.

10483
SEVTC Assessment Scales for Community Integration of the Severely/Profoundly Handicapped, Part II, Post-Entry Monitoring Instrument, Preschool Form. Southeastern Virginia Training Center for the Mentally Retarded, Chesapeake, VA 1977
Subtests: Motor Development; Self-Help Academic/Cognitive; Language; Socialization
Descriptors: Behavioral Objectives; Check Lists; Cognitive Development; Daily Living Skills; *Deinstitutionalization (of Disabled); Language Acquisition; Motor Development; Observation; Preschool Children; *Severe Disabilities; Social Development
Availability: ERIC Document Reproduction Service; 3900 Wheeler Ave., Alexandria, VA 22304 (ED167565, 51 pages)
Target Audience: 0-8

For use in a program to deinstitutionalize mentally retarded individuals and return them to a less restrictive environment. This instrument measures observed behavioral change and progress through a short rehabilitation period. Each subscale has 5 levels from minimal to independent functioning. Each item appears as a behavioral objective. Scoring depends on whether the behavior was self-initiated, cued, or not performed.

10485
MDC Behavior Identification Form. Materials Development Center, Menomonie, WI 1974
Descriptors: Adults; Antisocial Behavior; Behavior Modification; *Behavior Patterns; *Behavior Rating Scales; *Employees; *Sheltered Workshops; *Vocational Adjustment; *Vocational Rehabilitation; Work Attitudes
Availability: Materials Development Center, Stout Vocational Rehabilitation Institute; University of Wisconsin-Stout, Menomonie, WI 54751
Target Audience: 18-64
Notes: Items, 22

Rating system consists of series of judgments made regarding vocational rehabilitation client's behaviors as they relate to employment. Designed to determine whether client's existing work behaviors interfere with his/her ability to hold a job in competitive or sheltered employment.

10489
Peabody Mathematics Readiness Test. Bassler, Otto C.; And Others 1979
Subtests: Discrimination Test; Drawing Test
Descriptors: *Diagnostic Tests; *Elementary School Mathematics; *Grade 1; *Kindergarten Children; Primary Education; Mathematics Tests; *Remedial Mathematics; School Readiness Tests
Identifiers: PMRT

Availability: Scholastic Testing Service; 480 Meyer Rd., Bensenville, IL 60106
Grade Level: K-1
Notes: Time, 20

Provides diagnostic information about the ability of average (4 to 6 years) and special education (4 to 6 mental age) children to complete first-grade mathematics. An activity manual provides activities to assist in prescriptive remediation.

10491
Mohawk Language Checklist—Level I. Steele, Catherine 1979
Descriptors: *American Indian Languages; *Bilingual Students; Check Lists; *Elementary School Students; Individual Testing; Intermediate Grades; Oral Language; Pronunciation; Vocabulary; Word Lists
Identifiers: MLC; *Mohawk
Availability: ERIC Document Reproduction Service; 3900 Wheeler Ave., Alexandria, VA 22304 (ED178573, microfiche only)
Grade Level: 4-6

Designed to evaluate student's progress in picture association and pronunciation of Mohawk language vocabulary.

10492
Texas Environmental Adaptation Measure, Experimental Edition. Corpus Christi Independent School District, TX
Subtests: Family Environment Assessment; Personality Assessment; Adaptive Behavior Assessment
Descriptors: *Adjustment (to Environment); Adolescents; Children; Cultural Influences; *Disadvantaged Environment; *Family Characteristics; Interviews; Parent Attitudes; Parents; Parent Student Relationship; *Personality Assessment; Socioeconomic Background; Special Education; Student Placement
Identifiers: TEAM
Availability: Corpus Christi Independent School District; Consultant for Diagnostic Services, 601 Leopard St., P.O. Drawer 110, Corpus Christi, TX 78043
Target Audience: 5-16
Notes: Time, 60 approx.; Items, 244

The Texas Environmental Adaptation Measure has been used to determine the eligibility of students for special education classes. Team has 4 parts: 2 measure the child's social-emotional environment; one measures personality, and the 4th is a measure of the child's adaptive behavior. It is designed to be administered in its entirety, but the adaptive behavior section can be given separately. This is the only part that provides a numerical score. It was developed as a home interview using the person familiar with the child as respondent. The family environment assessment part covers 7 areas: (1) family background, (2) educational background, (3) medical background, (4) economic information, (5) housing, (6) description of neighborhood, (7) child care. The personality assessment questions concern developmental aspects, response to discipline and frustration, usual mode of interaction with others, recent trauma (if any), and school adjustment. The adaptive behavior assessment investigates activities in 6 areas: autonomous activities, mechanical skills, play and recreation, communication and social skills, responsibility, and economic activity. The interviews are with parents whose children are ages 5-16. The information obtained by TEAM from the parents can be used in setting up individual education programs or compensatory education programs for the child. This instrument was developed by the Corpus Christi Independent School District from a grant from the Texas Education Agency and has been used in that school district.

10529
Revised Pre-Reading Screening Procedures to Identify First Grade Academic Needs. Slingerland, Beth H. 1977
Descriptors: *Academically Gifted; *Auditory Perception; *Grade 1; *Kindergarten Children; *Kinesthetic Perception; Language Handicaps; Learning Disabilities; Learning Modalities; Primary Education; *Screening Tests; *Visual Perception
Identifiers: PSP
Availability: Educators Publishing Service, Inc.; 75 Moulton St., Cambridge MA 02238-9101
Grade Level: K-1

Designed to screen groups of children to identify those for whom specific instruction can prevent failure in learning to read, write, spell, verbalize, and express language in writing. Designed for use at the end of kindergarten or the beginning of first grade when children who have not begun reading instruction. Useful for children of average or superior intelligence. Not meant to be used for diagnosis. There are 6 visual tasks and 6 auditory tasks.

10530
Uniform Performance Assessment System. Child Development and Mental Retardation Center; University of Washington, Seattle 1978
Subtests: Pre-Academic/Fine Motor; Communication; Social/Self Help; Gross Motor; Behavior Management
Descriptors: Behavior Patterns; *Child Development; Cognitive Development; *Disabilities; *Individualized Education Programs; Individual Testing; *Infants; *Language Processing; Mental Retardation; *Preschool Children; Preschool Education; Psychomotor Skills; Young Children
Identifiers: UPAS
Availability: Child Development and Mental Retardation Center, WJ-10; Experimental Education Unit, University of Washington, Seattle, WA 98105
Target Audience: 0-6

A curriculum-referenced instrument designed for use with handicapped children. Assesses skills normally acquired between birth and 6 years of age.

10531
Brief Psychiatric Rating Scale. Overall, John E.; Gorham, Donald R. 1961
Descriptors: Adults; Anxiety; *Behavior Change; Behavior Rating Scales; Interviews; *Patients
Identifiers: *Psychiatric Patients; Symptoms
Availability: Psychological Reports; v10 p799-812 1962
Target Audience: Adults
Notes: Items, 16

Designed to provide a rapid assessment technique especially useful in the evaluation of patient change. The 16-item scale is completed following a 20-minute interview with the psychiatric patient.

10534
A Normalization and Development Instrument. Flynn, Ann G.; Weiss, Sandra K. 1978
Subtests: Program; Rights; Social Integration; Facility; Administration
Descriptors: *Adolescents; *Adults; *Children; *Developmental Disabilities; Normalization (Handicapped); Program Administration; Program Effectiveness; *Program Evaluation; Program Improvement; Residential Programs; *Special Education
Identifiers: ANDI
Availability: ANDI; P.O. Box 60964, Sacramento, CA 95860
Target Audience: 6-64
Notes: Items, 105

A program evaluation instrument designed to assess quality of programs for developmentally disabled children and adults.

10540
Symptom Distress Check List. Mattsson, Nils B.; And Others 1968
Subtests: Neurotic Feelings; Somatization; Performance Difficulty; Fear-Anxiety; Depression
Descriptors: Adults; Anxiety; Check Lists; Depression (Psychology); *Neurosis; *Patients; *Self Evaluation (Individuals)
Identifiers: Psychiatric Patients; SCL; Self Report Measures; *Symptoms
Availability: Multivariate Behavioral Research; v3 n2 p199-212 Apr 1968
Target Audience: Adults
Notes: Items, 58

Designed to assess symptoms of anxious neurotic outpatients. Patient completes the checklist before receiving treatment.

10598
Anonymous Elementary School Referral Questionnaire. Gregory, Mary K.
Subtests: Version a (5); Version B (5)
Descriptors: *Behavior Problems; Elementary Education; *Learning Disabilities; *Rating Scales; Referral
Availability: Mary K. Gregory; Center for Behavioral Studies, University of Milwaukee, P.O. Box 413, Milwaukee, WI 53201
Grade Level: K-6
Notes: Items, 10

Determines kinds of behavioral and/or learning problems for which teachers are most likely to make referrals.

10599
Examen Del Desarrolla Del Nino en Denver. Frankenburg, William and Others 1970
Descriptors: *Child Development; *Developmental Disabilities; *Language Acquisition; *Motor Development; Screening Tests; *Social Development; *Spanish Speaking; Young Children
Identifiers: Denver Developmental Screening Test

Availability: Denver Developmental Materials; P.O. Box 6919, Denver, CO 80206-0919
Target Audience: 0-6
Notes: Items, 105

A Spanish translation of the manual for the Denver Developmental Screening Test, 1970 edition, which was designed to provide a method of screening for evidence of slow development. Covers gross motor, language, fine-motor adaptive, and personal-social functions.

10601
Manual for Administering the Analysis of Developmental Learning Skills. Revised 1977. South Bend Community School Corp., IN 1977
Subtests: Motor Coordination; Visual Performance; Visual Perception; Visual Memory; Auditory Perception; Auditory Memory; Language Development; Conceptual Development; Social Development
Descriptors: Developmental Tasks; *Diagnostic Teaching; Diagnostic Tests; *Individual Development; Individual Testing; Kindergarten; *Kindergarten Children; Learning Disabilities; Perceptual Development; Primary Education; Psychomotor Skills; *School Readiness Tests
Identifiers: ADLS; *Analysis of Developmental Learning Skills
Availability: ERIC Document Reproduction Service; 3900 Wheeler Ave., Alexandria, VA 22304 (ED177175 microfiche only)
Target Audience: 4-5

Designed to identify children with lags in developmental skills. Useful in identification of children with learning disabilities, retardation, social, or emotional problems. Instrument combined Learning Style Screening Instrument (LSSI) and The Inventory of Developmental Tasks (IDT). Available from EDRS only in microfiche.

10604
Racial Attitudes and Perceptions Survey. O'Mara, Francis E.; Tierney, William 1978
Subtests: Incidence of Discriminatory Behaviors; Abridged Racial Perceptions Inventory
Descriptors: Adults; *Attitude Measures; Black Attitudes; Blacks; *Military Personnel; *Racial Attitudes; Racial Bias; Racial Integration; Reverse Discrimination; Whites
Identifiers: RAPS 2
Availability: ERIC Document Reproduction Service; 3900 Wheeler Ave., Alexandria, VA 22304 (ED169098, 80 pages)
Target Audience: Adults
Notes: Items, 68

Designed for use with military personnel to assess racial climate. Racial Attitudes and Perception Survey (RAPS) consisted of 2 scales. RAPS-2 has an abridged version of the RPI.

10605
Oral Language Evaluation. Silvaroli, Nicholas J.; And Others 1977
Subtests: Identification; Assessment; Diagnosis; Prescription
Descriptors: *Diagnostic Teaching; Diagnostic Tests; Elementary Education; *Elementary School Students; English (Second Language); Language Proficiency; Language Skills; *Oral Language; Spanish
Availability: EMC Corporation; 300 York Ave., St. Paul, MN 55101
Grade Level: 1-6

Designed to identify, assess, diagnose, and prescribe the oral language capability of English and Spanish speakers. Instrument enables teachers with limited language evaluation experience and/or structural linguistic training to evaluate children. Forms available in English and Spanish.

10632
Oral Placement Test. Poczik, Robert
Descriptors: *Achievement Tests; *Adult Basic Education; Adults; Communicative Competence (Languages); Diagnostic Tests; *English (Second Language); Individual Testing; Oral English; Speech Communication; *Student Placement
Identifiers: English as a Second Language Tests; Oral Placement Test (Poczik)
Availability: ERIC Document Reproduction Service; 3900 Wheeler Ave., Alexandria, VA 22304 (ED181036, 17 pages)
Target Audience: 18-64
Notes: Time, 5 approx.

Designed to place adult students at various ESL levels solely on the basis of oral language abilities. May be used for diagnostic purposes if student's errors are noted on the test as it is scored. Developed to follow content and sequence of the "Orientation in American English" series.

10633
Oral Production Tests: Levels One-Three. Poczik, Robert

Descriptors: *Achievement Tests; *Adult Basic Education; Adults; Communicative Competence (Languages); Diagnostic Tests; *English (Second Language); Individual Testing; *Listening Comprehension; Oral English; *Speech Skills
Identifiers: English as a Second Language Tests; Oral Production Tests (Poczik)
Availability: ERIC Document Reproduction Service; 3900 Wheeler Ave., Alexandria, VA 22304 (ED181036, 17 pages)
Target Audience: 18-64
Notes: Time, 10 approx.

Developed to assess oral English ability of adults. Three forms at each of 3 levels of difficulty are available. Assesses auditory comprehension and oral production. Tests are based on the "Orientation in American English" series.

10637
Children's Adaptive Behavior Scale. Richmond, Bert O.; Kicklighter, Richard H. 1980
Subtests: Language Development; Independent Functioning; Family Role Performance; Economic-Vocational Activity; Socialization
Descriptors: *Adaptive Behavior (of Disabled); *Children; Family Relationship; Individual Testing; Interpersonal Competence; Language Acquisition; *Mental Retardation; Special Education
Identifiers: CABS; *Independent Behavior
Availability: Humanics Limited; P.O. Box 7447, Atlanta, GA 30309
Target Audience: 5-10
Notes: Time, 30 approx.; Items, 115

Designed to measure skill development and adaptive behavior of mentally retarded children ages 5 to 10.

10639
Grammatical Analysis of Elicited Language: Simple Sentence Level. Moog, Jean S.; Geers, Ann E. 1979
Descriptors: *Children; Expressive Language; *Hearing Impairments; *Language Acquisition; *Language Tests; Oral Language; Sign Language; Total Communication
Identifiers: GAEL(S)
Availability: Central Institute for the Deaf; 818 S. Euclid, St. Louis, MO 63110
Target Audience: 5-9
Notes: Items, 94

Designed to evaluate child's acquisition of specific grammatical structures. Consists of 21 activities used to elicit 94 target sentences exemplifying simple sentence structures. The 21 activities fall into 5 types: opening boxes, manipulating toys, guessing games, picture and/or object descriptions, picture stories. Concentrates on expressive language skills. Has been standardized on hearing-impaired children aged 5 to 9 years and on hearing children aged 2.5 to 5 years. Also useful with children diagnosed as learning disabled, aphasic, mentally retarded, autistic, or language impaired.

10643
Self-Perception Inventory—Student Forms. Soares, Anthony T.; Soares, Louise M. 1980
Subtests: Self-Concept; Reflected Self-Classmates; Reflected Self-Teachers; Reflected Self-Parents; Ideal Concept; Perceptions of Others; Student Self; Perceptions of Others/Student Self
Descriptors: *Disadvantaged Youth; *Elementary School Students; Elementary Secondary Education; Parent Attitudes; Peer Evaluation; Rating Scales; *Secondary School Students; *Self Concept; *Self Concept Measures; Semantic Differential
Identifiers: Classmates; Ideal Self Concept; Reflected Self Concept; Self Concept of Ability
Availability: Soares Associates; 111 Teeter Rock Rd., Trumbull, CT 06611
Grade Level: 1-12
Notes: Time, 60; Items, 288

A self-concept measure using the semantic differential format in which the student rates each concept on a 4-point scale using 2 opposite adjectives or phrases. Six components of self-perception are covered. Included is a term called "Perceptions of Others," which is administered to those mentioned in the reflected-self forms, teachers, classmates, and parents. Administration time varies from 5 to 20 minutes per part depending on age and reading level. Norms are available for advantaged and disadvantaged students.

10648
Bateria de Examenes de Aptitud General. United States Dept. of Labor, Employment and Training Administration, Washington, DC 1974
Subtests: Name Comparison; Computation; Three-Dimensional Space; Vocabulary; Tool Matching; Arithmetic Reasoning; Form Matching; Mark Making; Pegboard; Finger Dexterity Board

Descriptors: *Adults; *Aptitude Tests; Career Guidance; High School Students; Perceptual Motor Coordination; Personnel Evaluation; *Personnel Selection; Professional Occupations; Semiskilled Occupations; Skilled Occupations; Spanish; *Spanish Speaking; Spatial Ability; Unskilled Occupations; Verbal Ability; *Vocational Aptitude; *Vocational Interests
Identifiers: Clerical Aptitude; Finger Dexterity; Manual Dexterity; Mathematical Aptitude
Availability: State Employment Service Offices
Target Audience: 18-64

A Spanish-language version of the General Aptitude Test Battery (GATB) (TC001422) designed for use by State Employment Service Offices for evaluation of applicants for jobs and training programs. Aptitudes measured are general learning ability, verbal aptitude, numerical aptitude, spatial aptitude, form perception, clerical perception, motor coordination, finger dexterity, manual dexterity. Scores on part 1, name comparison, and part 4, vocabulary, are not translations. They use Spanish surnames and vocabulary words and are not comparable to the English version.

10649
Secondary Level English Proficiency Test. Educational Testing Service, Princeton, NJ 1981
Subtests: Listening Comprehension; Reading Comprehension
Descriptors: *Achievement Tests; *Audiotape Recordings; *English (Second Language); *Language Proficiency; Language Tests; *Listening Comprehension; *Reading Comprehension; Secondary Education; *Secondary School Students; Second Language Learning
Identifiers: SLEP
Availability: Secondary Level English Proficiency Test, School Service Program; Publications Order Service Section, Box 2870, Princeton, NJ 08541
Grade Level: 7-11
Notes: Time, 85 approx.; Items, 150

Designed to measure ability of students whose native language is not English to understand spoken and written English. School Service Program enables school to purchase test, administer it, and score locally. May be used in making some placement decisions. ETS sponsors SLEP test and administers it within the Test of English-as-a-Foreign-Language (TOEFL) program. May be administered in its entirety or in 2 sessions to individuals or groups.

10651
Child Abuse Potential Inventory. Milner, Joel S.; Wimberly, Ronald C. 1979
Subtests: Loneliness; Rigidity; Problems; Control
Descriptors: Adults; Attitude Measures; *Child Abuse; Family Problems; *Mental Rigidity; Parent Attitudes; *Parent Child Relationship; *Parents; Personality Traits; Predictive Measurement; Predictor Variables; *Self Control; Loneliness
Identifiers: CAP Inventory
Availability: Journal of Clinical Psychology; v35 n1 p95-100 Jan 1979
Target Audience: Adults
Notes: Items, 37

Designed to discriminate between parents who may or may not abuse their children. Factors of personality known to be possessed by child abusing parents were identified.

10672
Test of Ability to Subordinate. Davidson, David M. 1978
Descriptors: *Adults; Bilingual Students; Diagnostic Tests; *English (Second Language); Higher Education; *Sentence Combining; *Undergraduate Students; *Writing Skills
Identifiers: TAS
Availability: Language Innovations, Inc.; 2112 Broadway, Rm. 515, New York, NY 10023
Grade Level: 13-16
Target Audience: 18-64
Notes: Items, 45

Designed to measure ability of non-native speakers of English to control certain structures of subordination in writing. Developed to assess students' ability to manipulate grammatical structures generally indicative of mature writing.

10673
Luria-Nebraska Neuropsychological Test Battery. Luria, A.R.; And Others 1980
Subtests: Motor Functions; Rhythm; Tactile Functions; Visual Functions; Receptive Speech; Expressive Speech; Writing; Reading; Arithmetic; Memory; Intellectual Processes; Pathognomonic Scale; Left Hemisphere; Right Hemisphere

Descriptors: Adolescents; Adults; Arithmetic; *Clinical Diagnosis; Cognitive Processes; *Diagnostic Tests; Expressive Language; Individual Testing; Memory; *Neurological Impairments; Psychomotor Skills; Reading Skills; Receptive Language; Standardized Tests; Tactual Visual Tests; Writing Skills
Identifiers: *Normal Persons; *Schizophrenic Patients
Availability: Western Psychological Services; 12031 Wilshire Blvd., Los Angeles, CA 90025
Target Audience: 13-64
Notes: Time, 150; Items, 269

Standardized version for use with normal, schizophrenic and brain damaged patients to identify and localize specific areas of brain dysfunction. Picture cards, cassette tape recorder, and simple objects are required. Individually administered.

10676
Task Assessment for Prescriptive Teaching. Hofeditz, Daniel; Wilke, Duane 1979
Descriptors: Criterion Referenced Tests; Diagnostic Teaching; *Diagnostic Tests; Elementary Education; *Elementary School Mathematics; *Elementary School Students; Individual Testing; Learning Disabilities; Mental Disorders; *Reading Achievement; Reading Skills; *Special Education
Identifiers: TAPT
Availability: Scholastic Testing Service; 480 Meyer Rd., Bensenville, IL 60106
Grade Level: 1-6

Designed to identify critical academic and functional skills for classroom diagnosis in reading and mathematics. Twelve separate booklets covering mathematics skills include preskills, addition, subtraction, monetary concepts, time concepts, multiplication, division, fractions, decimals, percentages, weights and measures, and practical skills (with calculator). Eleven separate booklets covering reading skills include preskills, letters, consonant/symbol sound, vowel/symbol sound, blending skills, academic/instructional words, community/functional words, word structure analysis, question orientation and context, thought expression, and informational resources. May be used in regular or special education.

10694
The Callier-Azusa Scale, G. Edition. Stillman, Robert 1978
Subtests: Postural Control; Locomotion; Fine Motor; Visual Motor; Visual Development; Auditory Development; Tactile Development; Undressing and Dressing; Personal Hygiene; Development of Feeding Skills; Toileting; Cognitive Development; Receptive Communication; Expressive Communication; Development of Speech; Interactions with Adults; Interactions with Peers; Interactions with the Environment
Descriptors: Children; *Cognitive Development; *Daily Living Skills; *Deaf Blind; Expressive Language; *Motor Development; *Perceptual Development; *Physical Disabilities; Rating Scales; Receptive Language; *Severe Disabilities; *Social Development; *Speech Communication
Identifiers: *Developmental Scales
Availability: Callier Center for Communication Disorders; 1966 Inwood Rd., Dallas, TX 75235
Target Audience: 0-12
Notes: Items, 800

This edition of the scale now covers cognitive development through the preoperational period. New items were added to the Receptive and Expressive Communication subscales. Designed to aid in the assessment of deaf-blind and severely and profoundly handicapped children so that developmentally appropriate activities can be provided.

10698
REFER: Rapid Exam for Early Referral. Kunzelmann, Harold P.; Koenig, Carl H. 1980
Descriptors: Children; Criterion Referenced Tests; Culture Fair Tests; Developmental Tasks; Kindergarten Children; *Learning Disabilities; Norm Referenced Tests; Preschool Children; *Referral; *Screening Tests
Availability: The Psychological Corporation; 555 Academic Ct., San Antonio, TX 78204-0952
Target Audience: 3-7
Notes: Time, 5; Items, 4

Norm- and criterion-referenced screening instrument for use by teachers to determine need for further diagnosis. Utilizes developmental activities consisting of writing loops, touching body parts, and counting to 10. Reported to be culturally nondiscriminatory.

10700
Denver Prescreening Developmental Questionnaire. Frankenburg, William K.; And Others 1975

Descriptors: *Developmental Tasks; Individual
Testing; *Infants; Language Acquisition; Learn-
ing Disabilities; Motor Development; Parents;
*Preschool Children; *Screening Tests; Social
Development; Young Children
Identifiers: Denver Developmental Screening Test;
Denver Screening Tests for Preschoolers; PDQ
Availability: Denver Developmental Materials;
P.O. Box 6919, Denver, CO 80206-0919
Target Audience: 0-6
Notes: Time, 5 approx.; Items, 97

Designed to be a "prescreening" tool used to identify
those children 3 months to 6 years of age-who will require
further screening with the Denver Developmental Screening Test (TC003628). Used to detect developmental lags
and suggest that more detailed screening is required. Parent selects the10 age-appropriate questions for his or her
child and answers these. Five color-coded forms arrange
items by the chronological age at which most children can
perform certain skills.

10701
**Denver Prescreening Developmental Questionnaire
(French Version).** Frankenburg, William K.; And
Others 1975
Descriptors: *Developmental Tasks; *French; In-
dividual Testing; *Infants; Language Acquisi-
tion; Learning Disabilities; Motor Development;
Parents; *Preschool Children; *Screening Tests;
Social Development; Young Children
Identifiers: Denver Developmental Screening Test;
Denver Screening Test for Preschoolers; PDQ
Availability: Denver Developmental Materials;
P.O. Box 6919, Denver, CO 80206-0919
Target Audience: 0-6
Notes: Time, 5 approx.; Items, 97

Designed to be a "prescreening" tool used to identify
those children 3 months to 6 years of age who will require
further screening with the Denver Developmental Screening Test (TC003628). Used to detect developmental lags
and suggest that more detailed screening is required. Parent selects the 10 age-appropriate questions for his or her
child and answers these. Five color-coded forms arrange
items by the chronological age at which most children can
perform certain skills.

10747
Prueba de Lenguaje Santillana, Level G. Baran-
diaran, Estela 1980
Subtests: Reading Comprehension (25); Grammar
(52); Study Skills (12)
Descriptors: *Bilingual Students; Criterion Re-
ferenced Tests; Grade 5; *Grammar; Intermedi-
ate Grades; *Reading Comprehension;
*Screening Tests; Spanish; *Spanish Speaking;
*Study Skills
Availability: Santillana Publishing Co., Inc.; 257
Union St.; Northvale, NJ 07647
Grade Level: 5
Notes: Items, 89

Designed for bilingual students who have an intermediate
or advanced reading level in Spanish, this group or individual diagnostic placement test covers reading comprehension, grammar, and study skills. Levels G-J available.

10748
Prueba de Lenguaje Santillana, Level H. Baran-
diaran, Estela 1980
Subtests: Reading Comprehension (25); Grammar
(52); Study Skills (10)
Descriptors: *Bilingual Students; Criterion Re-
ferenced Tests; Grade 6; *Grammar; Intermedi-
ate Grades; *Reading Comprehension;
*Screening Tests; Spanish; *Spanish Speaking;
*Study Skills
Availability: Santillana Publishing Co., Inc.; 257
Union St., Northvale, NJ 07647
Grade Level: 6
Notes: Items, 87

Designed for bilingual students who have an intermediate
or advanced reading level in Spanish, this group or individual diagnostic placement test covers reading comprehension, grammar, and study skills.

10749
Prueba de Lenguaje Santillana, Level I. Baran-
diaran, Estela 1980
Subtests: Reading Comprehension (25); Grammar
(52); Study Skills (11)
Descriptors: *Bilingual Students; Criterion Re-
ferenced Tests; Grade 6; Grade 7; *Grammar;
Intermediate Grades; Junior High Schools;
*Reading Comprehension; *Screening Tests;
Spanish; *Spanish Speaking; *Study Skills
Availability: Santillana Publishing Co., Inc.; 257
Union St.; Northvale, NJ 07647
Grade Level: 6-7
Notes: Items, 88

Designed for bilingual students who have an intermediate
or advanced reading level in Spanish, this group or individual diagnostic placement test covers reading comprehension, grammar, and study skills. Levels G-J available.

10750
Prueba de Lenguaje Santillana, Level J. Baran-
diaran, Estela 1980
Subtests: Reading Comprehension (25); Grammar
(52); Study Skills (11)
Descriptors: *Bilingual Students; Criterion Re-
ferenced Tests; Grade 8; *Grammar; Junior
High Schools; *Reading Comprehension;
*Screening Tests; Spanish; *Spanish Speaking;
*Study Skills
Availability: Santillana Publishing Co., Inc; 257
Union St.; Northvale, NJ 07647
Grade Level: 8
Notes: Items, 88

Designed for bilingual students who have an intermediate
or advanced reading level in Spanish, this group or individual diagnostic placement test covers reading comprehension, grammar, and study skills. Levels G-J available.

10752
The Survey Inventory. Tidwell, Romena 1978
Descriptors: Academically Gifted; Biographical In-
ventories; *Gifted; Grade 10; High Schools;
*Interest Inventories
Availability: Romena Tidwell; UCLA Graduate
School of Education, 345 Moore Hall, Los
Angeles, CA 90024
Grade Level: 10
Notes: Items, 20

Developed for use in a study of gifted students, the inventory provides information about how a typical week is
spent.

10753
Test of Lateral Awareness and Directionality.
Lockavitch, Joseph; Mauser, August 1980
Subtests: Lateral Awareness (15); Directionality
(20)
Descriptors: Adults; *Criterion Referenced Tests;
Disabilities; Elementary Secondary Education;
*Individual Testing; Nonverbal Tests; Spatial
Ability
Identifiers: Directionality; Right Left Labeling
Availability: United Educational Services; P.O.
Box 357, E. Aurora, NY 14052
Grade Level: 1-12
Notes: Time, 20; Items, 35

This group or individually administered criterion-referenced test is designed to identify children with right-left
labeling difficulties as high, medium, and low risk. Data
were gathered on normal and special populations. Also
covers spatial concepts. Items require unilateral, con-
tralateral, or crossdiagonal response.

10754
Career Adaptive Behavior Inventory. Lombardi,
Thomas P. 1980
Subtests: Academics (12); Communication (12);
Interest (12); Leisure Time (12); Motor (12);
Responsibility (12); Self-Concept (12); Self-Help
(12); Socialization (12); Task Performance (12)
Descriptors: Academic Achievement; *Adjustment
(to Environment); Adolescents; Children; Child
Responsibility; Communication Skills; *Daily
Living Skills; *Developmental Disabilities; In-
terpersonal Competence; *Job Skills; Leisure
Time; Performance; Psychomotor Skills; Rating
Scales; Self Concept; Vocational Interests
Availability: Special Child Publications; 4535
Union Bay Pl. N.E.; Seattle, WA 98105
Target Audience: 3-15
Notes: Time, 30; Items, 120

A 5-point scale is used to rate developmentally disabled
students on their ability to perform daily living behaviors
necessary prior to vocational courses. Completed by anyone who observes child from memory, observation, or
both; and source of rating is indicated.

10755
Patient Expectations and Perceptions. Chinsky,
Jack M.; Rappaport, Julian 1970
Descriptors: Adults; *Attitude Measures; *Patients;
*Psychiatric Hospitals; Student Volunteers;
Therapists
Availability: Journal of Consulting and Clinical
Psychology; v35 n3 p388-94 1970
Target Audience: Adults
Notes: Items, 25

Designed to measure psychiatric patients perceptions of
the characteristics of college student volunteers in a hospital companionship program as opposed to perceptions of
their therapists.

10756
**Bay Area Functional Performance Evaluation, Re-
search Edition.** Bloomer, Judith S.; Williams,
Susan K. 1979
Subtests: Task Oriented Assessment (11); Social
Interaction Scale (35)
Descriptors: Adults; *Behavior Rating Scales; Cog-
nitive Measurement; *Daily Living Skills;
*Institutionalized Persons; Interpersonal Com-
petence; Mental Disorders; *Perception; Psycho-
motor Skills; *Social Behavior; Verbal Commu-
nication
Identifiers: Dependency (Personality); Independ-
ence (Personality)
Availability: Consulting Psychologists Press, Inc.,
577 College Ave.; Palo Alto, CA 94306
Target Audience: Adults
Notes: Items, 46

Developed to assess, in a consistent and measurable way,
some of the functions that people must be able to perform
in general activities of daily living. The combined results
of the 2 subtests are used as indicators of overall functional performance and provide information about cognitive, affective, and perceptual motor characteristics.
Standardized on an adult psychiatric inpatient population.

10758
**The Fullerton Language Test for Adolescents, Ex-
perimental Edition.** Thorum, Arden R. 1980
Subtests: Auditory Synthesis (20); Morphology
Competency (20); Oral Commands (20); Con-
vergent Production (75); Divergent Production
(5); Syllabication (20); Grammatic Competency
(20); Idioms (20)
Descriptors: Adolescents; Children; Diagnostic
Tests; *Language Handicaps; *Language Pro-
cessing; *Language Proficiency; Language Tests
Availability: Consulting Psychologists Press, Inc.;
577 College Ave.; Palo Alto, CA 94306
Target Audience: 11-18
Notes: Time, 45 approx.; Items, 200

Developed to provide a valid language assessment instrument that could distinguish normal from language-impaired adolescents. Individually administered.

10767
The Developmental Checklist. Hicks, Mack R.
1979
Subtests: Teacher Form (104); Parent Form (110)
Descriptors: *Behavior; *Check Lists; Child Devel-
opment; Children; Diagnostic Tests; Learning
Disabilities; *Observation; Parents; *Screening
Tests; Teachers
Availability: NCS Interpretive Scoring Systems;
P.O. Box 1416, Minneapolis, MN 55440
Target Audience: 6-12
Notes: Time, 15 approx.; Items, 214

Designed for the identification and assessment of developmental problems, this behavioral checklist has forms for
classroom teacher and parent use.

10777
Learning Potential Assessment Device. Feuer-
stein, Reuven; And Others 1979
Subtests: Organization of Data (2); Plateaux Test
(4); LPAD Variations I (5); Representational
Stencil Design Test (20)
Descriptors: Adolescents; Children; *Cognitive
Ability; Diagnostic Tests; *Disabilities; Disad-
vantaged; Disadvantaged Youth; Group Testing;
*Individual Testing; *Intelligence Tests;
*Learning Processes; *Mild Mental Retardation;
*Nonverbal Tests; Training Methods
Identifiers: LPAD
Availability: Feuerstein, Reuven; And Others. The
Dynamic Assessment of Retarded Performers.
Baltimore, MD: University Park Press, 1979
Target Audience: 12-17
Notes: Items, 49

Battery of nonverbal tests designed to measure intellectual
potential of handicapped and disadvantaged adolescents.
Examinee is given training to master series of tasks concerning elementary cognitive principles. Tests the individual in the process of learning.

10778
Psychoeducational Profile. Schopler, Eric 1979
Subtests: Imitation (10); Perception (11); Fine
Motor (10); Gross Motor (11); Eye-Hand In-
tegration (14); Cognitive Performance (14); Cog-
nitive Verbal Skills (39); Pathology Scale (44)
Descriptors: *Autism; Children; *Cognitive Devel-
opment; *Developmental Disabilities; Diagnos-
tic Tests; Individualized Education Programs;
Individual Testing; *Motor Development;
*Perceptual Motor Coordination; *Psychosis
Availability: Schopler, Eric. Individualized Assess-
ment and Treatment for Autistic and Devel-
opmentally Disabled Children. Baltimore, MD:
University Park Press, 1979
Target Audience: 1-12

Notes: Time, 60; Items, 139

This inventory of behavior skills utilizes a set of developmentally ordered toy and play activities to provide information on developmental functioning and degree of psychosis in autistic, psychotic and developmentally disabled children functioning at a preschool level. Aids in planning individual programs.

10783

Butch and Slim. Ward, J. 1972
Descriptors: Adolescents; Children; Deduction; *Gifted; Individual Testing; *Intelligence Tests; Logic
Identifiers: Combinatorial Analysis; Great Britain; Piaget
Availability: British Jorunal of Educational Psychology; v42 p267-89 1972
Target Audience: 10-18
Notes: Time, 24; Items, 32

Individually administered game of propositional logic based on Piaget's combinatorial analysis of children's thinking in adolescence. Discriminates children of high intelligence. Uses theme of 2 bankrobbers.

10821

Patients' Bill of Rights Questionnaire. Pankrantz, Deanna
Descriptors: Adults; Attitude Measures; Nurses; *Nursing; *Patients
Identifiers: *Nurse Attitudes; Self Administered Tests
Availability: ERIC Document Reproduction Service; 3900 Wheeler Ave., Alexandria, VA 22304 (ED171763, 842 pages)
Target Audience: Adults
Notes: Items, 25

This volume consists of a series of psychosocial and physiological clinical nursing instruments. The instruments were selected from the published literature in health care, education, psychology, and the social sciences. Instruments focus upon nursing practice and stress patient variables. Designed to provide information on attitudes toward patients' rights and whether or not these rights are provided in a particular health care setting. No scoring information was provided.

10827

Importance of Nursing Actions Opinionnaire. Walker, Laura C. 1960
Descriptors: Adults; Attitude Measures; *Attitudes; Medical Services; *Nurses; *Nursing; *Patients
Availability: ERIC Document Reproduction Service; 3900 Wheeler Ave., Alexandria, VA 22304 (ED171763, 842 pages)
Target Audience: Adults
Notes: Time, 20 approx.; Items, 16

This volume consists of a series of psychosocial and physiological clinical nursing instruments. The instruments were selected from the published literature in health care, education, psychology, and the social sciences. Instruments focus on nursing practice and stress patient variables. Instrument assesses respondents' perceptions of the relative importance of specific nursing actions relative to patients. A modified q-sort technique is used.

10828

Checklist for Patients. Abdellah, Faye G.; Levine, Eugene 1957
Subtests: Events Indicating Satisfaction with Care; Rest and Relaxation; Dietary Needs; Elimination; Personal Hygiene and Supportive Care; Reaction to Therapy; Contact with Nurses
Descriptors: Adults; *Attitude Measures; Attitudes; Check Lists; Hospitals; Interaction; *Medical Care Evaluation; *Nurses; *Nursing; *Patients
Identifiers: *Nursing Care
Availability: ERIC Document Reproduction Services; 3900 Wheeler Ave., Alexandria, VA 22304 (ED171763, 842 pages)
Target Audience: Adults
Notes: Items, 50

This volume consists of a series of psychosocial and physiological clinical nursing instruments. The instruments were selected from the published literature in health care, education, psychology, and the social sciences. Instruments focus on nursing practice and stress patient variables. Instrument was developed to assess how patients feel about nursing care provided them during a hospital stay. Only events relating to nurse-patient relationship are assessed. Designed for use in conjunction with Checklist for Personnel (TC010829).

10830

Patient Satisfaction Interview Form. Collins, Verla 1975
Descriptors: Adults; Hospitals; Interviews; *Nurses; *Nursing; *Patients
Identifiers: *Nursing Care
Availability: ERIC Document Reproduction Service; 3900 Wheeler Ave., Alexandria, VA 22304 (ED171763, 842 pages)
Target Audience: Adults

Notes: Time, 30 approx.; Items, 20

This volume consists of a series of psychosocial and physiological nursing instruments. The instruments were selected from the published literature in health care, education, psychology, and the social sciences. Instruments focus on nursing practice and stress patient variables. Instrument was designed to elicit patients' opinions about nursing care during hospitalization and their understanding of the illness which resulted in the hospitalization.

10831

Inpatient Psychiatric Treatment Program Evaluation. Freeman, Cynthia K. 1976
Descriptors: Adults; Interaction; Nurses; *Patients; *Program Evaluation; *Psychiatric Hospitals; Rating Scales
Identifiers: *Psychiatric Patients
Availability: ERIC Document Reproduction Service; 3900 Wheeler Ave., Alexandria, VA 22304 (ED171763, 842 pages)
Target Audience: Adults
Notes: Items, 16

This volume consists of a series of psychosocial and physiological clinical nursing instruments. The instruments were selected from the published literature in health care, education, psychology, and the social sciences. Instruments focus on nursing practice and stress patient variables. Instrument was developed to evaluate treatment programs through patients' opinions.

10835

Postoperative Interview Guide. Hegyvary, Sue T. 1974
Subtests: Patient's Level of Understanding of Required Role; Preoperative Stress; Organizational Constraints
Descriptors: Adults; *Attitude Measures; Hospitals; Interviews; *Medical Care Evaluation; Nurses; *Nursing; *Patients; Stress Variables
Identifiers: *Patient Attitudes; *Postoperative Patients
Availability: ERIC Document Reproduction Service; 3900 Wheeler Ave., Alexandria, VA 22304 (ED171763, 842 pages)
Target Audience: Adults
Notes: Items, 21

This volume consists of a series of psychosocial and physiological clinical nursing instruments. The instruments were selected from the published literature in health care, education, psychology, and the social sciences. Instruments focus on nursing practice and stress patient variables. Designed to elicit information from postoperative patients. Should be administered by an interviewer. Developed to examine the relationship between postoperative outcomes and the type of organizational setting characteristic of a hospital.

10836

Patient Satisfaction with Health Care Survey. Linn, Lawrence 1975
Descriptors: Adults; *Attitude Measures; Clinics; *Medical Care Evaluation; Nurses; *Nursing; *Patients; Physicians
Identifiers: Patient Attitudes; *Patient Care; Patient Survey; Satisfaction
Availability: ERIC Document Reproduction Service; 3900 Wheeler Ave., Alexandria, VA 22304 (ED171763, 842 pages)
Target Audience: Adults
Notes: Time, 15 approx.; Items, 21

This volume consists of a series of psychosocial and physiological clinical nursing instruments. The instruments were selected from the published literature in health care, education, psychology, and the social sciences. Instruments focus on nursing practice and stress patient variables. Designed for completion by patient immediately after having received medical care in an outpatient clinic or in a primary care setting. Respondent evaluates treatment received and records sources of satisfaction, or dissatisfaction, with the experience.

10837

Patient Satisfaction Scale. McGivern, Diane O. 1972
Descriptors: Adults; *Attitude Measures; *Hospital Personnel; *Hospitals; Medical Care Evaluation; Nurses; *Nursing; *Patients
Identifiers: *Patient Attitudes; *Patient Care; Satisfaction
Availability: ERIC Document Reproduction Service; 3900 Wheeler Ave., Alexandria, VA 22304 (ED171763, 842 pages)
Target Audience: Adults
Notes: Time, 30 approx.; Items, 21

This volume consists of a series of psychosocial and physiological clinical nursing instruments. The instruments were selected from the published literature in health care, education, psychology, and the social sciences. Instruments focus on nursing practice and stress patient variables. Designed to assess a patient's perceptions of hosptial ex-

periences and health care personnel. Assesses nurses' and physicians' services, hosptial routines and regulations, and general hospital care.

10839

Patient's Perception of Aspects of Health Care. Pankrantz, Deanna
Descriptors: Adults; *Attitude Measures; Hospital Personnel; *Hospitals; *Medical Care Evaluation; Nurses; *Nursing; *Patients; Rating Scales
Identifiers: *Patient Attitudes; Patient Care; Satisfaction
Availability: ERIC Document Reproduction Service; 3900 Wheeler Ave., Alexandria, VA 22304 (ED171763, 842 pages)
Target Audience: Adults
Notes: Items, 14

This volume consists of a series of psychosocial and physiological clinical nursing instruments. The instruments were selected from the published literature in health care, education, psychology, and the social sciences. Instruments focus on nursing practice and stress patient variables. Instrument measures a patient's perceptions of the importance of aspects of health care in hospitals and his or her personal satisfaction with those aspects.

10840

Patient Interview Questionnaire. Pienschke, Darlene 1973
Descriptors: Adults; *Attitude Measures; *Cancer; Hospitals; Interviews; *Medical Care Evaluation; Nurses; *Nursing; *Patients
Identifiers: Nursing Care; Patient Attitudes; Patient Care
Availability: ERIC Document Reproduction Service; 3900 Wheeler Ave., Alexandria, VA 22304 (ED171763, 842 pages)
Target Audience: Adults
Notes: Items, 28

This volume consists of a series of psychosocial and physiological clinical nursing instruments. The instruments were selected from the published literature in health care, education, psychology, and the social sciences. Instruments focus on nursing practice and stress patient variables. Designed to obtain data for indicating the consequences of differing approaches to giving cancer patients information about their diagnosis and prognosis. Patient confidence and satisfaction with health care are assessed. First part of instrument is administered by an interviewer, and second part is self-administered by patient.

10841

Risser Patient Satisfaction Scale. Risser, Nancy 1972
Subtests: Technical-Professional; Interpersonal-Educational; Interpersonal-Trusting
Descriptors: Adults; *Attitude Measures; Clinics; *Medical Care Evaluation; *Nurses; *Nursing; *Patients
Identifiers: Nursing Care; *Patient Attitudes; Satisfaction
Availability: ERIC Document Reproduction Service; 3900 Wheeler Ave., Alexandria, VA 22304 (ED171763, 842 pages)
Target Audience: Adults
Notes: Time, 15 approx.; Items, 28

This volume consists of a series of psychosocial and physiological clinical nursing instruments. The instruments were selected from the published literature in health care, education, psychology, and the social sciences. Instruments focus on nursing practice and stress patient variables. Instrument was developed to evaluate patient care from the patient's perspective. Patients' attitudes toward nurses and nursing care in a primary health care setting are measured.

10842

Quality of Nursing Care Questionnaire-Patient. Safford, Beverly J.; And Others 1960
Subtests: Physical Care; Emotional Care; Nurse-Physician Relationship; Teaching and Preparation for Home Care; Administration; Quality of Nursing Care
Descriptors: Adults; *Attitude Measures; *Hospitals; *Medical Care Evaluation; Nurses; *Nursing; *Patients
Identifiers: *Nursing Care; *Patient Attitudes; Satisfaction
Availability: ERIC Document Reproduction Service; 3900 Wheeler Ave., Alexandria, VA 22304 (ED171763, 842 pages)
Target Audience: Adults
Notes: Items, 45

This volume consists of a series of psychosocial and physiological clinical nursing instruments. The instruments were selected from the published literature in health care, education, psychology, and the social sciences. Instruments focus on nursing practice and stress patient variables. This instrument was developed to provide information regarding relationship between hospital staffing patterns and patients' perceptions of the quality of nursing care received.

10843
Patient Perceptions of Health Services. Triplett, June L.
Subtests: Nurse Disparity; Medical Disparity; Perceived Threat-Past Experience; Social Isolation; Threat; Self Esteem; Perceptions of Others; Demographic Data; Observation
Descriptors: Adults; *Attitude Measures; *Community Health Services; Medical Care Evaluation; *Nurses; *Nursing; *Patients; Physicians; Public Health; Self Esteem
Identifiers: *Patient Attitudes
Availability: ERIC Document Reproduction Service; 3900 Wheeler Ave., Alexandria, VA 22304 (ED171763, 842 pages)
Target Audience: Adults
Notes: Time, 60 approx.; Items, 94
This volume consists of a series of psychosocial and physiological clinical nursing instruments. The instruments were selected from the published literature in health care, education, psychology, and the social sciences. Instruments focus on nursing practice and stress patient variables. Instrument measures patient's perceptions of health services. Designed to be read to subject during home visit by public health nurse-interviewer.

10852
Seizure Survey. Clark, Bernardine A. 1976
Descriptors: Adults; Child Caregivers; Children; *Epilepsy; Interviews; *Parents; Questionnaires; *Seizures
Availability: ERIC Document Reproduction Service; 3900 Wheeler Ave., Alexandria, VA 22304 (ED171763, 842 pages)
Target Audience: Adults
Notes: Items, 54
This volume consists of a series of psychosocial and physiological clinical nursing instruments. The instruments were selected from the published literature in health care, education, psychology, and the social sciences. Instruments focus on nursing practice and stress patient variables. Instrument was designed to assess parents' and caregivers' general knowledge of epilepsy and epileptic seizures in children. The first section of 52 true-false items is concerned with nature of the illness, its physical management, medical management, and psychosocial management. The second section consists of an interview relating to problems experienced by the epileptic child at home and school.

10855
Wife's Perception of Loss after Her Husband's Myocardial Infarction Questionnaire. Smith, Linda S. 1975
Descriptors: Adults; *Affective Measures; Attitudes; *Emotional Adjustment; Emotional Response; *Patients; *Spouses
Identifiers: *Heart Attack
Availability: ERIC Document Reproduction Service; 3900 Wheeler Ave., Alexandria, VA 22304 (ED171763, 842 pages)
Target Audience: Adults
Notes: Time, 35 approx.; Items, 33
This volume consists of a series of psychosocial and physiological clinical nursing instruments. The instruments were selected from the published literature in health care, education, psychology, and the social sciences. Instruments focus on nursing practice and stress patient variables. This instrument assessed the wife's subjective perception of loss in the areas of financial security, emotional closeness to her husband, her husband's physical strength, open communication with her husband, and sexual relations with her husband following his myocardial infarction heart attack.

10856
Aphasia Language Performance Scales. Keenan, Joseph S.; Brassell, Esther G. 1975
Subtests: Listening (10); Talking (10); Reading (10); Writing (10)
Descriptors: Adolescents; Adults; *Aphasia; Children; *Diagnostic Tests; Language Acquisition; Prognostic Tests; Speech Handicaps
Availability: Pinnacle Press; P.O. Box 1122, Murfreesboro, TN 37130
Target Audience: 7-64
Notes: Time, 35; Items, 40
A series of scales for use by speech clinicians in measuring the impairment level of aphasic patients. Results can be useful in prognosis and planning therapy.

10858
Apraxia Battery for Adults. Dabul, Barbara 1979
Subtests: Diadochokinetic Rate (9); Increasing Word Length (30); Limb Apraxia and Oral Apraxia (20); Latency and Utterance Time for Polysyllabic Words (10); Repeated Trials Test (30); Inventory of Articulation Characteristics of Apraxia (15)
Descriptors: *Adults; Articulation Impairments; Psychomotor Skills; Reaction Time; *Speech Handicaps; *Speech Tests; Syllables

Identifiers: *Apraxia (Speech); Repetition (Language)
Availability: C. C. Publications; P.O. Box 23699; Tigard, OR 97223
Target Audience: Adults
Notes: Time, 20 approx.; Items, 114
A revision of an earlier battery which had been administered to 40 adult male patients in various Veterans Administration hospitals in southern California. Purpose of this individually administered test is to verify presence of apraxia in adult patients and to gain an estimate of the severity of the disorder.

10865
Client Attitude Questionnaire, Revised. Morrison, James K. 1977
Descriptors: Adults; *Attitude Measures; Institutionalized Persons; *Mental Disorders; Patients; Professional Personnel; Questionnaires; Student Attitudes
Identifiers: CAQ B; *Medical Viewpoint; *Psychosocial Viewpoint
Availability: Morrison, James K., Ed.; A CONSUMER APPROACH TO COMMUNITY PSYCHOLOGY. Chicago: Nelson-Hall, 1979
Target Audience: Adults
Notes: Items, 20
Designed to measure the respondent's attitudes toward mental illness. Three-point response mode allows use with institutionalized mental patients as well as mental health professionals and students. Distinguishes orientation toward the psychosocial or medical views of mental illness.

10869
Individualized Problem Resolution Checklist. Morrison, James K. 1978
Descriptors: Adults; Check Lists; *Emotional Problems; Formative Evaluation; *Group Therapy; Patients; *Personality Problems; Psychotherapy; Rating Scales; *Social Problems
Identifiers: IPRC
Availability: Morrison, James K., Ed.; A CONSUMER APPROACH TO COMMUNITY PSYCHOLOGY. Chicago; Nelson-Hall, 1979
Target Audience: Adults
Group therapy clients formulate a list of problems they expect to resolve through therapy and rate each problem on its current state of resolution on a 6-point scale.

10870
Interpersonal Improvement Scale. Morrison, James K. 1978
Descriptors: Adults; Check Lists; *Emotional Problems; *Group Therapy; Patients; *Personality Problems; Psychotherapy; Rating Scales; *Social Problems; Summative Evaluation
Identifiers: IIS
Availability: Morrison, James K., Ed.; A CONSUMER APPROACH TO COMMUNITY PSYCHOLOGY. Chicago: Nelson-Hall, 1979
Target Audience: Adults
Notes: Items, 17
A standardized list of common interpersonal problems which group therapy clients rate as to the degree of resolution on a 6-point scale.

10871
Psychotherapy Problem Checklist. Morris, James K. 1979
Descriptors: Adults; Check Lists; *Emotional Problems; Patients; *Personality Problems; Psychotherapy; *Social Problems; Summative Evaluation
Identifiers: *Emotive Reconstructive Therapy; PPC
Availability: Morrison, James K., Ed.; A CONSUMER APPROACH TO COMMUNITY PSYCHOLOGY. Chicago; Nelson-Hall, 1979
Target Audience: Adults
Notes: Items, 21
Self-report measure of client problem resolution. Client responds yes or no to 21 statements concerned with problems such as frequent headaches, excessive anxiety, insomnia, etc.

10872
Client Service Questionnaire. Becker, Roy E.; And Others 1975
Descriptors: Adults; *Attitude Measures; Emotional Problems; *Mental Health Clinics; *Patients; Physical Health; Professional Personnel; *Psychotherapy; Social Problems
Identifiers: CSQ
Availability: Morrison, James K., Ed.; A CONSUMER APPROACH TO COMMUNITY PSYCHOLOGY. Chicago: Nelson-Hall, 1979
Notes: Items, 36
Client responds true/false to items concerned with client attitudes toward staff. [Concerns patients felt needs for contact with staff, physical and emotional symptoms, and social activities.]

10873
Clinic Recognition Test. Morrison, James K.; Yablonowitz, Harold 1979
Descriptors: Adults; Knowledge Level; *Mental Health Clinics; Patients; Professional Personnel; Program Content; *Psychotherapy
Availability: Morrison, James K.; A CONSUMER APPROACH TO COMMUNITY PSYCHOLOGY. Chicago: Nelson-Hall, 1979
Target Audience: Adults
Measures degree to which client of psychiatric clinic is acquainted with staff and programs. Clients supply last names, professions of staff members, indicate those they recognize on sight, and list all clinic programs.

10876
Howell Township Schools Kindergarten Early Identification Test. Howell Township Schools, NJ 1979
Subtests: Shapes; Listening Comprehension; Auditory Memory; Colors; Color Words; Vocabulary; Classification; Letter Identification; Rhyming; Letter Writing; Directionality and Spacial Relationships; Consonant Sounds; Visual Motor; Visual Discrimination; Name; Number Identification; Number Writing; Counting Sets; Math Concepts; Addition and Subtraction; Copying
Descriptors: *Kindergarten Children; Language Arts; Mathematical Concepts; Perception; Remedial Instruction; *Screening Tests; *Student Evaluation
Identifiers: Elementary Secondary Education Act Title I
Availability: Board of Education, Howell Township Schools, Howell, NJ 07731
Grade Level: K
Notes: Time, 120 approx.; Items, 73
Provides for early identification of students needing supportive instructional programs. Test results can be used to help develop a diagnostic supplementary educational plan. It is recommended that the test be administered in 4 sittings over a 2-day period.

10877
Peabody Picture Vocabulary Test—Revised, Form L. Dunn, Lloyd M.; Dunn, Leota M. 1981
Descriptors: *Academic Ability; Academic Aptitude; *Achievement Tests; Adolescents; Adults; Children; *Gifted; Job Placement; *Mental Retardation; *Non English Speaking; Preschool Children; *Screening Tests; *Verbal Ability; Vocabulary Skills
Identifiers: *Aural Vocabulary; PPVT
Availability: American Guidance Service; Publisher's Bldg., Circle Pines, MN 55014
Target Audience: 2-40
Notes: Time, 15; Items, 175
Nationally standardized, individually administered measure of hearing vocabulary. Designed to measure verbal ability or scholastic aptitude. Used for screening special students, job candidates, and to assess vocabulary of non-English-speaking students, ranging in age from 2.5 years to 40.

10878
Peabody Picture Vocabulary Test—Revised, Form M. Dunn, Lloyd M.; Dunn, Leota M. 1981
Descriptors: *Academic Ability; *Achievement Tests; Adolescents; Adults; Children; *Gifted; Job Placement; *Mental Retardation; *Non English Speaking; Preschool Children; *Screening Tests; *Verbal Ability; Vocabulary Skills
Identifiers: *Aural Vocabulary; PPVT
Availability: American Guidance Service; Publisher's Bldg., Circle Pines, MN 55014
Target Audience: 2-40
Notes: Time, 15; Items, 175
Nationally standardized, individually administered measure of hearing vocabulary. Designed to measure verbal ability or scholastic aptitude. Used for screening special students, job candidates, and to assess vocabulary of non-English-speaking students, ranging in age from 2.5 years to 40.

10884
Merrill Language Screening Test. Mumm, Myrna; And Others 1980
Subtests: Expressive Language; Receptive Language; Elicited Language
Descriptors: Early Childhood Education; Expressive Language; *Grade 1; *Kindergarten Children; *Language Handicaps; Primary Education; Receptive Language; *Screening Tests
Identifiers: MLST
Availability: The Psychological Corporation; 555 Academic Ct., San Antonio, TX 78204-0952
Grade Level: K-1
Notes: Time, 5; Items, 15

Designed to identify potential language problems. Examiner tells a story illustrated with pictures. Child retells story and answers questions. Covers production of complete sentences, utterance length, verb-tense agreements, elaboration, communication competence.

10896
The D.A.L.E. System Developmental Assessment of Life Experiences: An Inventory to Assess Competencies in Community Living. Barber, Gertrude A.; And Others 1978
Subtests: Sensory Motor; Language; Self-Help; Cognition; Socialization; Personal Hygiene; Personal Management; Communication Skills; Residence/Home Maintenance; Community Access
Descriptors: Adolescents; Adults; Behavior Rating Scales; Check Lists; Children; Cognitive Ability; Communication Skills; Daily Living Skills; Home Management; Hygiene; Interpersonal Competence; Language Skills; *Mental Retardation; Moderate Mental Retardation; Perceptual Motor Coordination; Residential Care; Severe Mental Retardation
Identifiers: DALE
Availability: Gertrude A. Barber Center, Inc.; 136 E. Ave., Erie, PA 16507
Target Audience: 6-65
Notes: Items, 642

Checklist for recording the quantity and quality of behaviors necessary in institutional transitional or group home settings for exceptional individuals. Level I lists tasks for severely and profoundly mentally retarded subjects. Level II lists higher functioning behaviors.

10899
Stanford Achievement Test: Braille Edition, Primary, Level II. American Printing House for the Blind, Louisville, KY 1972
Subtests: Vocabulary; Reading Comprehension; Mathematics Concepts; Mathematics Computation; Spelling; Word Study Skills; Listening Comprehension; Mathematics Applications; Social Science; Science
Descriptors: *Achievement Tests; *Blindness; *Braille; Elementary School Mathematics; Elementary School Science; Elementary School Students; *Grade 2; *Grade 3; *Listening Comprehension; Primary Education; *Reading Comprehension; Skills; Spelling; Vocabulary; *Word Study Skills
Identifiers: Test Batteries
Availability: American Printing House for the Blind; 1839 Frankfort Ave., Louisville, KY 40206
Grade Level: 2-3
Notes: Time, 260; Items, 442

Achievement test battery for blind children. Battery is to be administered in 12 sessions. All subtests are in braille except science and social studies concepts, spelling, beginning and ending sounds, and numbers and measures which are teacher dictated. Designed for students in grades 2.5 through 3.4. Each subtest is individually timed. Forms A and B are available.

10900
Stanford Achievement Test: Braille Edition, Primary, Level III. American Printing House for the Blind, Louisville, KY 1972
Subtests: Vocabulary; Reading Comprehension; Mathematics Concepts; Mathematics Computation; Spelling; Word Study Skills; Listening Comprehension; Mathematics Applications; Social Science; Science; Language
Descriptors: *Achievement Tests; *Blindness; *Braille; Elementary Education; Elementary School Mathematics; Elementary School Science; Elementary School Students; *Grade 3; *Grade 4; Language Skills; *Listening Comprehension; *Reading Comprehension; Spelling; Vocabulary; Word Study Skills
Identifiers: Test Batteries
Availability: American Printing House for the Blind; 1839 Frankfort Ave., Louisville, KY 40206
Grade Level: 3-4
Notes: Time, 295; Items, 504

Designed to measure important understandings, skills, and abilities for use in improvement of instruction, pupil guidance and evaluation of progress. Each subtest is individually timed. Forms A and B are available for use in grades 3.5 through 4.4. Battery is to be administered in several sittings to blind children.

10901
Stanford Achievement Test: Braille Edition, Intermediate, Level I. American Printing House for the Blind, Louisville, KY 1972

Subtests: Vocabulary; Reading Comprehension; Mathematics Concepts; Mathematics Computation; Spelling; Word Study Skills; Listening Comprehension; Mathematics Applications; Social Science; Science; Language
Descriptors: *Achievement Tests; *Blindness; *Braille; Elementary School Mathematics; *Elementary School Science; *Elementary School Students; *Grade 4; *Grade 5; Intermediate Grades; *Language Skills; Large Type Materials; Listening Comprehension; *Reading Comprehension; Spelling; Visual Impairments; Vocabulary; Word Study Skills
Identifiers: Test Batteries
Availability: American Printing House for the Blind; 1839 Frankfort Ave., Louisville, KY 40206
Grade Level: 4-5
Notes: Time, 320; Items, 588

Designed to measure important understandings, skills, and abilities for use in improvement of instruction, pupil guidance, and evaluation of progress. Test battery is not administered in one sitting. Each subtest is individually timed. Intermediate Level I is for use in grades 4.5 through 5.4. Forms A and B are available. Battery is to be administered to blind students in 18 sessions. Available in large-type print or Braille for visually impaired subjects.

10902
Stanford Achievement Test: Braille Edition, Intermediate, Level II. American Printing House for the Blind, Louisville, KY 1972
Subtests: Vocabulary; Reading Comprehension; Mathematics Concepts; Mathematics Computation; Spelling; Word Study Skills; Listening Comprehension; Mathematics Applications; Social Science; Science; Language
Descriptors: *Achievement Tests; *Blindness; *Braille; *Elementary School Mathematics; Elementary School Science; Elementary School Students; *Grade 5; *Grade 6; Intermediate Grades; Language Skills; Large Type Materials; Listening Comprehension; *Reading Comprehension; Spelling; Visual Impairments; Vocabulary; Word Study Skills
Identifiers: Test Batteries
Availability: American Printing House for the Blind; 1839 Frankfort Ave., Louisville, KY 40206
Grade Level: 5-6
Notes: Time, 320; Items, 595

Achievement test battery for blind children in grades 5.5 through 6.9. Battery is to be administered in 18 sessions. Forms A and B are available. Each subtest is individually timed. Available in large-type print or Braille for visually impaired subjects.

10903
Stanford Achievement Test; Braille Edition, Advanced Level. American Printing House for the Blind, Louisville, KY 1972
Subtests: Vocabulary; Reading Comprehension; Mathematics Concepts; Mathematics Computation; Spelling; Mathematics Applications; Social Science; Science; Language
Descriptors: *Achievement Tests; *Blindness; *Braille; Junior High Schools; *Junior High School Students; *Language Skills; Large Type Materials; *Mathematical Applications; Mathematical Concepts; *Reading Comprehension; Sciences; Social Sciences; Spelling; Visual Impairments; Vocabulary
Identifiers: Test Batteries
Availability: American Printing House for the Blind; 1839 Frankfort Ave., Louisville, KY 40206
Grade Level: 7-9
Notes: Time, 260; Items, 503

Achievement test battery for blind students in grades 7 through 9. Battery is to be administered in 18 sessions. Forms A and B are available. Each subtest is individually timed. Available in large-type print or Braille for visually impaired subjects.

10904
Stanford Test of Academic Skills, Braille Edition, Level I. American Printing House for the Blind, Louisville, KY 1972
Subtests: Reading; English; Mathematics
Descriptors: *Achievement Tests; *Basic Skills; *Blindness; *Braille; Language Skills; Mathematics; Multiple Choice Tests; *Reading Comprehension; Secondary Education; *Secondary School Students; Spelling; Vocabulary
Identifiers: TASK; Test Batteries
Availability: American Printing House for the Blind; 1839 Frankfort Ave., Louisville, KY 46206
Grade Level: 8-10
Notes: Time, 120; Items, 195

Measures basic cognitive enabling skills: reading, English, and mathematics. Content assessed is usually taught before the end of grade 8. TASK may be used to assess minimal competence in the basic skills. Each subtest requires 40 minutes of working time. Two equivalent forms A and B are available for blind students in grades 8 through 10.

10905
Diagnostic Analysis of Reading Tasks. Steinberg, Ethel 1976
Descriptors: *Decoding (Reading); Diagnostic Teaching; *Diagnostic Tests; Elementary Education; *Elementary School Students; Elementary School Teachers; *Phonics; *Reading Diagnosis; *Reading Difficulties; *Structural Analysis (Linguistics)
Identifiers: DART; *Encoding
Availability: Slosson Educational Publications; P.O. Box 280, E. Aurora, NY 14052
Grade Level: 1-6

Designed to help diagnose problems in encoding and decoding, the basic tasks in reading. Part I is designed for use in grades 2-5 or below. Part II is designed for grades 2-5 or above. Useful in prescriptive teaching when administered early in the school year. May be used to identify students with reading disabilities and those requiring remedial instruction.

10909
Individual Assessment. Alpha Plus Corp., Piedmont, CA 1977
Subtests: Language; Cognitive; Gross Motor; Fine Motor; Socio-Emotional; Self-Help
Descriptors: Child Development; *Cognitive Style; *Developmental Disabilities; Early Childhood Education; *Elementary School Students; Exceptional Persons; *Language Skills; Observation; *Preschool Children; Preschool Education; *Psychomotor Skills
Availability: Circle Preschool; 9 Lake Ave., Piedmont, CA 94611
Target Audience: 2-8

Designed to assess 6 skill areas of child development. Observer rates child on skills based upon observation. Assessment is appropriate for children with exceptionalities or developmental delays. Useful in setting objectives for educational development of this population.

10912
Color Pattern Board. Special Education Materials, Inc., Yonkers, NY 1969
Descriptors: Elementary School Students; Elementary Secondary Education; Mental Retardation; *Perception Tests; Perceptual Handicaps; *Perceptual Motor Coordination; Secondary School Students; Spatial Ability; *Special Education; Visual Perception
Identifiers: Visual Memory
Availability: Special Education Materials, Inc.; 484 S. Broadway, Yonkers, NY 10705
Grade Level: 1-12

Designed to evaluate perceptual abilities of educable and trainable mentally retarded children and perceptually handicapped individuals. Assesses color perception, spatial relationship, visual discrimination and memory, and eye-hand coordination.

10913
Burks' Behavior Rating Scales. Burks, Harold F. 1977
Subtests: Excessive Self-Blame; Anxiety; Withdrawal; Dependency; Suffering, Sense of Persecution; Aggressiveness, Resistance; Poor Ego Strength; Physical Strength; Coordination; Intellectuality; Academics; Attention; Impulse Control; Reality Contact; Sense of Identity; Anger Control; Social Conformity
Descriptors: Academic Ability; *Aggression; *Anxiety; Attention Span; *Behavior Problems; *Behavior Rating Scales; Conformity; Diagnostic Tests; Educationally Disadvantaged; *Elementary School Students; Elementary Secondary Education; Emotional Disturbances; Hearing Impairments; Individual Testing; Intellectual Development; *Junior High School Students; Mild Mental Retardation; Muscular Strength; Parent Attitudes; Physical Disabilities; *Psychomotor Skills; *Self Concept; Self Control; Speech Handicaps; *Student Behavior; Teacher Attitudes; Withdrawal (Psychology); Anger
Identifiers: Dependency (Personality); Persecution; Reality; Suffering
Availability: Western Psychological Services; 12031 Wilshire Blvd., Los Angeles, CA 90025
Grade Level: 1-9
Notes: Items, 110

Designed to identify patterns of behavior problems. Parent or teacher rates observed behavior. For diagnosis of individual children. May be used with mentally handicapped, speech and hearing disabled, emotionally disturbed, physically handicapped, educationally disadvantaged, and nonhandicapped children.

10917
Relevant Aspects of Potential. Grant, Thomas E.; Renzulli, Joseph S. 1974
Descriptors: *Academic Aptitude; *College Bound Students; Gifted; High Schools; High School Students; *Minority Groups; *Self Concept; Self Concept Measures; *Talent Identification
Identifiers: RAP
Availability: RAP Researchers, c/o Grant; Gaylord Ln., Burlington, CT 06013
Grade Level: 11-12
Notes: Items, 30
Designed for use in identifying students from low socioeconomic and minority group backgrounds who are potentially gifted or of high scholastic aptitude.

10920
Clinical Evaluation of Language Functions, Elementary Level. Semel, Eleanor Messing; Wiig, Elisabeth H. 1980
Subtests: Elementary Processing (31); Elementary Production (17)
Descriptors: Elementary School Students; Expressive Language; Intermediate Grades; *Language Handicaps; Oral Language; Primary Education; Receptive Language; *Screening Tests
Identifiers: CELF
Availability: The Psychological Corporation; 555 Academic Ct., San Antonio, TX 78204-0952
Grade Level: K-5
Notes: Items, 48
Individually administered test designed to screen for delays and disabilities in language processing and production. Items are presented as oral directions requiring a pointing response and spoken stimuli requiring a spoken response.

10921
Clinical Evaluation of Language Functions, Advanced Level. Semel, Eleanor Messing; Wiig, Elisabeth H. 1980
Subtests: Advanced Processing (34); Advanced Production (18)
Descriptors: Expressive Language; High School Students; Intermediate Grades; Junior High School Students; *Language Handicaps; Oral Language; Receptive Language; *Screening Tests; Secondary Education
Identifiers: CELF
Availability: The Psychological Corporation; 555 Academic Ct., San Antonio, TX 78204-0952
Grade Level: 5-12
Notes: Items, 52
Individually administered test designed to screen for delays and disabilities in language processing and production. Items are presented as oral directions requiring a pointing response and spoken stimuli requiring a spoken response.

10922
Developmental Assessment for the Severely Handicapped. Dykes, Mary K. 1980
Subtests: Social-Emotional (226); Language (342); Sensory-Motor (263); Activities of Daily Living (264); Preacademic (399)
Descriptors: Adolescents; Adults; Children; Criterion Referenced Tests; Daily Living Skills; *Developmental Disabilities; *Diagnostic Tests; Disabilities; Emotional Development; Language Skills; Learning Readiness; Perceptual Motor Coordination; *Screening Tests; Social Development
Identifiers: DASH
Availability: Pro. Ed, Inc.; 5341 Industrial Oaks Blvd., Austin, TX 78735
Target Audience: 0-64
Notes: Time, 150; Items, 1494
Criterion-referenced instrument for measuring programing and tracking skills of nonhandicapped or severely multiply handicapped and developmentally young individuals in 5 developmental areas. For use with those functioning at the developmental age levels of 0-6.

10928
Skills Inventory for Teachers. Garland, Corinne W. 1978
Subtests: Referral, Intake, & Screening; Determining Child Placement; Interdisciplinary Assessment; Interdisciplinary Staffing; Planning the Individualized Developmental Plan; Developing Teaching Skills in Parents (Caretakers); Individualization of Instruction; Managing Child Progress Data; Consultations; Staff Development; Generic Skills

Descriptors: Adults; Behavior Rating Scales; *Disabilities; Homebound; *Special Education Teachers; *Staff Development; Teaching Skills; *Young Children
Identifiers: SIFT
Availability: Child Development Resources; P.O. Box 299, Lightfoot, VA 23090
Target Audience: Adults
Designed to assess needs for staff development activities and evaluate effectiveness of those activities used with very young handicapped children and their families. Useful for personnel decision makers to identify skills needed by persons providing direct services to young handicapped children.

10929
Skills Inventory for Parents. Waltrip, Jean B. 1978
Subtests: Parental Involvement with the Program as a Whole; Home Visits and Prescriptions; Teaching Skills; Encouragement of Language Development; Physical Care; Environment; Broker-Advocacy Skills
Descriptors: Adults; Behavioral Objectives; Behavior Rating Scales; *Disabilities; Homebound; Infants; *Parent Participation; *Parents; Teaching Skills; Young Children
Identifiers: SIP
Availability: Child Development Resources; P.O. Box 299, Lightfoot, VA 23090
Target Audience: Adults
Notes: Items, 115
Designed to measure changes in parental skills as a result of programing in a home based prescriptive program. Developed to encourage development of each parent's skills in child care, teaching, or advocacy on behalf of his/her handicapped or developmentally delayed child from birth to 2 years of age.

10944
Lunchtime Program Evaluation. Gendreau, Joan C. 1980
Descriptors: *Eating Habits; *Evaluation Methods; *Multiple Disabilities; Self Care Skills; *Severe Mental Retardation
Availability: ERIC Document Reproduction Service; 3900 Wheeler Ave., Alexandria, VA 22304 (ED192476, 19 pages)
Grade Level: K-12
Provides for assessment of behavior during school meals of severely mentally retarded and/or multiply handicapped students.

10956
Group Inventory for Finding Creative Talent. Second Edition. Rimm, Sylvia B. 1980
Subtests: Primary Level (32); Elementary Level (34); Upper Elementary Level (33)
Descriptors: Children; *Creativity; Elementary Education; *Elementary School Students; *Gifted; Personality Traits; *Screening Tests
Identifiers: GIFT
Availability: Educational Assessment Service, Inc.; Rt. 1, Box 139-A, Watertown, WI 53094
Grade Level: K-6
Target Audience: 5-12
Notes: Time, 45 approx.; Items, 99
Used to screen elementary school students for programs for the creatively gifted by identifying attitudes and values associated with creativity. Validity studies have been conducted with various socioeconomic, ethnic, and special learning groups as well as with several foreign populations.

10968
The Self Directed Search, Form E. Holland, John L. 1979
Subtests: Realistic; Investigative; Artistic; Social; Enterprising; Conventional
Descriptors: Adolescents; Adults; Educationally Disadvantaged; *Interest Inventories; Reading Difficulties; *Self Evaluation (Individuals); Slow Learners; *Vocational Interests
Availability: Consulting Psychologists Press; 577 College Ave., Palo Alto, CA 94306
Target Audience: 13-65
Notes: Items, 203
Vocational interest measure with directions containing only 4th grade level words for those with limited reading skills. This version uses an easier scoring procedure than earlier versions. Form E is also shorter than other forms and uses two-letter occupational codes.

10970
Florida International Diagnostic-Prescriptive Vocational Competency Profile. Rosenberg, Howard; Tesolowski, Dennis G. 1979

Subtests: Vocational Self Help Skills (14); Social Emotional Adjustment (14); Work Attitudes-Responsibility (7); Cognitive-Learning Ability (14); Perceptual-Motor Skills (12); General Work Habits (9)
Descriptors: Adolescents; Adults; Daily Living Skills; *Diagnostic Tests; *Disabilities; Emotional Adjustment; Interpersonal Competence; Job Performance; Perceptual Motor Coordination; *Vocational Aptitude; Work Attitudes
Availability: Stoelting Co.; 1350 S. Kostner Ave., Chicago, IL 60623
Target Audience: 13-65
Notes: Items, 70
Evaluates individuals' general functional level and 6 specific domains of vocational competency. Was developed to meet individualized needs of handicapped students and clients. Instrument focuses on actual performance or observed behavior demonstrated within the school or rehabilitation center.

10971
Group Inventory for Finding Interests. Level I. Rimm, Sylvia B.; Davis, Gary A. 1979
Descriptors: *Creativity; *Gifted; *Interest Inventories; Junior High Schools; *Screening Tests; Student Interests; *Talent Identification
Availability: Educational Assessment Service, Rt. 1, Box 139-A, Watertown, WI 53094
Grade Level: 6-9
Notes: Time, 35 approx.; Items, 60
Screening test to help select junior high school students for programs for the creatively gifted. Identifies students with attitudes and interests usually associated with creativity, such as independence, curiosity, perseverance, flexibility, breadth of interest, risk taking, and sense of humor.

10972
Here I Am—Where Do I Want to Go? A Career Interest Survey for Native Americans. Graves, Mary A. 1980
Descriptors: Adults; *American Indians; *Interest Inventories; *Vocational Interests
Availability: United Indians of All Tribes Foundation; Daybreak Star Indian Cultural-Educational Center, P.O. Box 99253, Discovery Park, Seattle, WA 98199
Target Audience: Adults
Self-rating inventory for determining individual's inclination in one of the following career areas: artistic, business, inquiring, social, vocational, enterprising. For each area, a list of possible jobs is given.

10974
Weller-Strawser Scales of Adaptive Behavior. Elementary Scale. Weller, Carol; Strawser, Sherri 1981
Subtests: Social Coping; Relationships; Pragmatic Language; Production
Descriptors: *Adjustment (to Environment); *Behavior Patterns; Behavior Rating Scales; Children; *Communicative Competence (Languages); *Coping; Elementary Education; *Interpersonal Competence; *Learning Disabilities
Availability: Academic Therapy Publications; 20 Commercial Blvd., Novato, CA 94947
Grade Level: 1-6
Target Audience: 6-12
Notes: Items, 35
Assesses adaptive behavior of learning-disabled students. Scales serve several purposes: discriminates severity of problem; measures adaptive functioning in 4 areas; provides profile of adaptive behaviors; provides awareness of adaptive capabilities; identifies most commonly found adaptive behaviors; enhances placement options of students; and identifies specific behaviors which may be addressed with specialized programing and environmental changes.

10975
Screening Test for Auditory Perception. Revised Edition. Kimmell, Geraldine M.; Wahl, Jack 1981
Subtests: Vowel Sounds (12); Initial Single Consonant Sounds (12); Rhyming and Nonrhyming Words (12); Rhythmic Sound Patterns (6); Paired Words (12)
Descriptors: Adolescents; *Auditory Perception; Elementary Education; Norm Referenced Tests; Remedial Instruction; *Screening Tests
Availability: Academic Therapy Publications; 20 Commercial Blvd., Novato, CA 94947
Grade Level: 1-6
Notes: Time, 45 approx.; Items, 54
Norm-referenced test for detection of weaknesses in auditory perception of elementary grade students and for older students in remedial classes. Total test scores may be converted to percentiles, grade equivalents, and age equivalents.

10976
Learning Disability Rating Procedure. Spadafore, Gerald J.; Spadafore, Sharon J. 1981
Descriptors: Attention Span; Decoding (Reading); Elementary Secondary Education; Intelligence Quotient; Interpersonal Competence; *Learning Disabilities; Learning Motivation; Listening Comprehension; Rating Scales; Severe Disabilities; *Student Evaluation; *Student Placement; Verbal Development; Writing Skills
Availability: Academic Therapy Publications; 20 Commercial Blvd., Novato, CA 94947
Grade Level: K-12

Evaluation method by which a student is systematically rated on each of 10 indicators associated with learning disabilities. Yields a placement score which indicates student's suitability for inclusion in a program for learning disabled students.

10977
Adult Basic Education/Learning Disabilities Screening Test. Vaillancourt, Beverly 1979
Subtests: Word Recognition; Arithmetic; Spelling; Writing Sample; Reading Comprehension
Descriptors: *Adult Basic Education; Adults; Arithmetic; Communication Skills; *Diagnostic Tests; *Learning Disabilities; Reading Tests; *Screening Tests; Spelling; Writing Skills
Availability: ERIC Document Reproduction Service; 3900 Wheeler Ave., Alexandria, VA 22304 (ED193433, 233 pages)
Target Audience: Adults
Notes: Items, 66

Designed to determine competencies in reading, written communication, and mathematics. For use with adults who cannot complete a reading placement test. Group or individually administered.

10978
Weller-Strawser Scales of Adaptive Behavior. Secondary Scale. Weller, Carol; Strawser, Sherri 1981
Subtests: Social Coping (9); Relationships (7); Pragmatic Language (9); Production (10)
Descriptors: *Adjustment (to Environment); Adolescents; *Behavior Patterns; Behavior Rating Scales; *Communicative Competence (Languages); *Coping; *Interpersonal Competence; *Learning Disabilities; Secondary Education
Availability: Academic Therapy Publications; 20 Commercial Blvd., Novato, CA 94947
Grade Level: 7-12
Target Audience: 13-18
Notes: Items, 35

Assesses adaptive behavior of learning-disabled students. Scales serve several purposes: discriminate severity of problem; measure adaptive functioning in 4 areas; provide profile of adaptive behaviors; provide awareness of adaptive capabilities; identify most commonly found adaptive behaviors; enhances placement options of students; and identify specific behaviors which may be addressed with specialized programing and environmental changes.

10979
Group Inventory for Finding Interests. Level 2. Rimm, Sylvia B.; Davis, Gary A. 1979
Descriptors: *Creativity; *Gifted; High Schools; *Interest Inventories; *Screening Tests; Student Interests; *Talent Identification
Availability: Educational Assessment Service, Rt. 1, Box 139-A, Watertown, WI 53094
Grade Level: 9-12
Notes: Time, 35 approx.; Items, 60

Screening test to help select senior high school students for creatively gifted programs. Identifies students with attitudes and interests usually associated with creativity, such as independence, curiosity, perserverance, flexibility, breadth of interest, risk taking, and sense of humor.

10984
Acculturation Rating Scale for Mexican Americans. Cuellar, Israel; Jasso, Ricardo 1979
Descriptors: *Acculturation; Adults; Mental Disorders; *Mexican Americans; Patients; Rating Scales
Identifiers: Likert Scales
Availability: Israel Cuellar; 1715 Dulcinea, Edinburg, TX 78539
Target Audience: Adults
Notes: Items, 20

Acculturation scale for Mexican Americans that can be administered in English, Spanish, or both languages to either psychiatric inpatients or normals.

10985
EPB: Environmental Prelanguage Battery. 1978
Descriptors: *Child Language; Children; Diagnostic Tests; *Disabilities; Individual Testing; *Language Acquisition; *Language Handicaps; Nonverbal Communication; Training Methods; Verbal Communication
Identifiers: *Environmental Language Intervention Program; EPB; *Prelinguistics
Availability: The Psychological Corporation; 555 Academic Ct., San Antonio, TX 78204-0952
Target Audience: Children

Series of diagnostic tests to assess and train prelinguistic skills judged necessary for a child to develop spoken language. Intended for program evaluation and individual diagnostic use with language-delayed children functioning below or at the single-word level. Covers prelanguage and early language skills usually learned by a child from 12-30 months.

10986
ELI: Environmental Language Inventory. MacDonald, James D. 1978
Descriptors: *Child Language; Children; *Clinical Diagnosis; Diagnostic Tests; *Disabilities; *Expressive Language; Individual Testing; Language Acquisition; *Language Handicaps; Training Methods
Identifiers: ELI; *Environmental Language Intervention Program
Availability: The Psychological Corporation; 555 Academic Ct., San Antonio, TX 78204-0952
Target Audience: Children

Part of the Environmental Language Intervention Program. A professionally administered inventory for handicapped learners of all ages who function at or beyond the use of 2-word phrases. Three essential design components include semantic-grammatical rule content, parallel linguistic and nonlinguistic eliciting cues, and assessment in the 3 production modes of imitation, conversation, and free play. Basic purpose of test is to sample client's optimal natural language and to serve as guidelines for training.

10990
Independent Living Behavior Checklist. Walls, Richard T.; And Others 1979
Subtests: Mobility Skills (42); Self-Care Skills (63); Home Maintenance and Safety Skills (46); Food Skills (75); Social and Communication Skills (69); Functional Academic Skills (48)
Descriptors: Accident Prevention; Adults; *Behavioral Objectives; Check Lists; *Daily Living Skills; Homemaking Skills; Interpersonal Competence; *Mental Retardation; Minimum Competencies; Physical Mobility; Self Care Skills
Availability: West Virginia Research and Training Center; One Dunbar Plaza, Ste. E, Dunbar, WV 25064
Target Audience: Adults
Notes: Items, 343

Assesses skills deemed necessary for emotionally and mentally handicapped persons to function in society. Checklist can be used to define independent living skills; specify range of skills applicable to variety of necessary activities; determine standards for skill mastery; document client progress and training procedure effectiveness; provide objective means to determine program accountability and cost effectiveness; determine means of goal setting and documentation; and outline an objectively specified curriculum.

11000
Community Home Assessment for Low-Functioning Persons. Appalachia Intermediate Unit 08, Edensburg, PA 1979
Subtests: Communication; Behavioral Compliance and Manageability; Self Help (Toileting); Feeding; Dressing and Undressing; Bodily Hygiene
Descriptors: Adaptive Behavior (of Disabled); *Adolescents; Behavior Change; *Behavior Rating Scales; *Daily Living Skills; *Deinstitutionalization (of Disabled); *Diagnostic Tests; *Individual Testing; Observation; Pretests Posttests; *Severe Mental Retardation; Social Behavior
Identifiers: Kelly (Mary P)
Availability: Appalachia Intermediate Unit 08, 313 W. High St., Ebensburg, PA 15931
Target Audience: Adolescents
Notes: Items, 83

Designed for use with the severely and profoundly mentally retarded institutionalized adolescents at Cresson Center. An individually administered, untimed rating scale and assessment device to determine an adolescent's strengths and weaknesses in home and community living skills in preparation to returning this mentally retarded adolescent to the community (to deinstitutionalize). The instrument consists of pretesting and posttesting; preferrably both testings should be done by the same person. The instrument includes both observation and interaction with the subject. Used as a basis for program planning and implementation and was developed as a workable model that could be used in other similar situations.

11014
Expressive One-Word Picture Vocabulary Test. Spanish Edition. Gardner, Morrison F. 1980
Descriptors: Children; Expressive Language; *Spanish Speaking; *Verbal Ability; *Verbal Development; *Verbal Tests; *Vocabulary
Availability: Academic Therapy Publications; 20 Commercial Blvd., Novata, CA 94947
Target Audience: 2-12
Notes: Time, 20; Items, 110

Estimates child's verbal intelligence through child's ability to form and to express an idea or concept of a picture or object. May also be used to screen for possible speech defects, estimate bilingual student's fluency in English; screen for prekindergarten or kindergarten readiness or placement. Is individually administered. May be used with subjects older than standardization population.

11017
Nonfunctional Behavior Checklist for Chronic Psychiatric Patients. Feitel, Barbara 1981
Descriptors: Check Lists; *Institutionalized Persons; *Patients; *Psychiatric Hospitals; *Self Care Skills
Identifiers: *Psychiatric Patients
Availability: Journal of Clinical Psychology; v37 n1 p158-60 Jan 1981
Target Audience: Adults
Notes: Items, 29

Measures the ability of regressed, chronic, psychiatric patients to perform daily living skills in the following areas: eating habits, grooming, dressing, inappropriate social behavior, and uncooperative behavior.

11019
Criminal Fantasy Technique. Schlesinger, Louis B.; Kutash, Irwin L. 1980
Descriptors: Adults; *Antisocial Behavior; *Crime; *Fantasy; *Pictorial Stimuli; *Projective Measures
Availability: Journal of Clinical Psychology; v37 n1 p210-18 Jan 1981
Target Audience: Adults
Notes: Items, 12

Projective technique which focuses on criminal fantasy to predict future antisocial behavior and to gain psychodynamic insight into offenders. Types of offenses depicted with the pictorial stimuli include drug deal, arson, bank robbery, exhibitionism, breaking and entering, assault, embezzlement, sexual assault, child molestation, organized crime, and stealing.

11022
Risk-Taking Attitudes-Values Inventory. Post High School Level. Carney, Richard E. 1976
Subtests: Background Information (5); Importance of Goals (8); Nearness to Goals (8); Utility of Behavior (25); Expectancies (Chance of Success) (25); Ways of Changing Behavior (10); Frequencies of Behavior (25)
Descriptors: Adults; Attitude Measures; *Behavior Standards; *Drug Abuse; *Social Behavior; *Values
Identifiers: *Risk Taking Behavior
Availability: Carney, Weedman and Associates; 4776 El Cajon Blvd., Ste. 203, San Diego, CA 92115
Target Audience: 17-65
Notes: Items, 106

General purpose instrument to elicit information about values and behaviors of groups or individuals; to evaluate program effectiveness; to stimulate self-analysis and group discussion; to aid in counseling; and to predict future behavior patterns of groups or individuals. Major use to date has been on mass testing associated with drug abuse prevention programs.

11032
Diagnostic Analysis of Reading Errors. Gillespie, Jacquelyn; Shohet, Jacqueline 1979
Descriptors: Adolescents; Adults; Culture Fair Tests; *Diagnostic Tests; English (Second Language); *Language Handicaps; *Learning Disabilities; *Reading Difficulties; Secondary Education; *Sensory Integration; Spelling; Two Year Colleges
Identifiers: DARE; *Transcoding; Wide Range Achievement Test; WRAT
Availability: Jastak Associates; 1526 Gilpin Ave., Wilmington, DE 19806
Target Audience: 12-65
Notes: Time, 30 approx.; Items, 46

Designed to identify adults and adolescents with language-related learning disabilities; to provide indications of the nature of each identified individual's disability as it is reflected in reading and spelling; and to elicit diagnostic information for individual assessment as part of a battery of test procedures. DARE is a one-page test form which uses the 46-item word list of the Wide Range Achievement Test (Spelling, Level II) in a 4-alternative, multiple-choice format. Four scores are provided for each individual: number of correct responses; sound substitution; omissions; and reversals.

11035
The Michigan Picture Test-Revised. Hutt, Max L. 1980
Descriptors: Adolescents; Children; *Emotional Adjustment; *Emotional Disturbances; Motifs; *Personality Traits; *Pictorial Stimuli; *Projective Measures; Psychological Needs
Identifiers: Tense (Verbs)
Availability: Grune and Stratton; 111 Fifth Ave., New York, NY 10003
Target Audience: 5-18
Notes: Items, 15

Thematic, apperceptive test to differentiate between emotionally adjusted and maladjusted individuals. Subjects' stories can be used for diagnostic and therapeutic purposes. In the Full Series, 4 cards are administered exclusively to boys and 5 others exclusively to girls. A core series, used mainly for screening, consists of 4 cards only, selected from the 7 cards used with both sexes. There are 4 indices: Tension Index; Use of Tense; Direction of Forces; and Combined Maladjustment Index.

11036
Vocational Skills Competency Checklist. Washburn, Winifred Y. 1978
Descriptors: Check Lists; Employment Experience; High Schools; *High School Students; *Learning Disabilities; Learning Modalities; *Skill Analysis; *Special Education; *Vocational Education; Vocational Interests
Availability: Special Child Publications; 4535 Union Bay Pl. N.E., Seattle, WA 98105
Grade Level: 9-12

Four-page checklist which gives special education teacher data on learning disabled students' vocational interests, job experiences, current work abilities, and learning modes. Can use this analysis of prevocational skills to determine whether students are adequately prepared to enter regular vocational training classes. Supplements vocational entry skills for secondary students.

11038
Stanford Test of Academic Skills, Braille Edition, Level II. American Printing House for the Blind, Louisville, KY 1972
Subtests: Reading; English; Mathematics
Descriptors: *Achievement Tests; *Basic Skills; *Blindness; *Braille; High Schools; *High School Students; Language Skills; *Mathematics; Multiple Choice Tests; Reading Comprehension; Spelling; Two Year Colleges; *Two Year College Students; Vocabulary
Identifiers: TASK; Test Batteries
Availability: American Printing House for the Blind; 1839 Frankfort Ave., Louisville, KY 40206
Grade Level: 11-13
Notes: Time, 120; Items, 195

Measures basic cognitive enabling skills: reading, English, and mathematics. Content assessed is usually taught before the end of grade 8. TASK may be used to assess minimal competence in the basic skills for blind students. Each subtest requires 40 minutes of working time. Two equivalent forms A and B are available. Separate manual and forms for Junior/Community College, Grade 13.

11039
Preschool Language Scale. Revised Edition. Zimmerman, Irla Lee; And Others 1979
Subtests: Auditory Comprehension Scale (40); Verbal Ability Scale (40)
Descriptors: Bilingual Students; Diagnostic Tests; Language Acquisition; *Language Tests; *Listening Comprehension; *Spanish Speaking; *Verbal Ability; Verbal Development; Young Children
Availability: The Psychological Corporation; 555 Academic Ct., San Antonio, TX 78204-0952
Target Audience: 1-7
Notes: Time, 20; Items, 80

Evaluation and screening instrument for children of all ages who function at a preschool or primary language level. Diagnoses areas of strength and deficiencies in auditory comprehension and verbal ability. Consists of a series of auditory and verbal language tasks assigned to age levels. A Spanish version is included.

11040
Developmental Profile II. 1980 Revised Edition. Alpern, Gerald D.; Shearer, Marsha S. 1980
Subtests: Physical; Self-Help; Social; Academic; Communication

Descriptors: Children; *Cognitive Ability; *Communication Skills; Developmental Stages; *Individual Development; Individualized Education Programs; *Interpersonal Relationship; Interviews; Measures (Individuals); *Physical Development; *Self Care Skills; Special Education; Student Placement
Availability: Psychological Development Publications; P.O. Box 3198, Aspen, CO 81612
Target Audience: 0-9
Notes: Time, 40 approx.; Items, 186

Can be used as a functional assessment instrument to meet requirements of the Education for All Handicapped Children Act. This is an inventory of skills designed to assess a child's development in 5 areas: physical, self-help, social, academic, and communication. Can be used for a variety of purposes, such as determining eligibility for receiving special education, planning an individualized educational program, or for pre- and posttesting.

11042
Family Relationship Inventory. Michaelson, Ruth B.; Bascom, Harry L. 1973
Descriptors: Adults; Children; *Family Relationship; *Group Dynamics; Older Adults; *Sociometric Techniques; Spanish
Availability: Family Relationship Inventory; P.O. Box 7878, Newport Beach, CA 92660
Target Audience: 4-70
Notes: Items, 50

Examines interrelational dynamics within the family. Allows each family member to examine this relationship with each member of the family. May also allow individuals to view the way family sees them. Designed to be administered to the entire family at one time. Items are also available in Spanish.

11044
Analysis of Coping Style. Boyd, Herbert F.; Johnson, G. Orville 1981
Descriptors: Behavior Problems; *Coping; *Elementary School Students; Elementary Secondary Education; Emotional Adjustment; *Interpersonal Competence; Peer Relationship; *Secondary School Students; Student Attitudes
Identifiers: ACS; Authority Figures
Availability: The Psychological Corporation; 555 Academic Ct., San Antonio, TX 78204-0952
Grade Level: K-12
Notes: Time, 10 approx.; Items, 20

For use by school psychologists, guidance counselors, and teachers in identifying children with difficulties in interpersonal relationships with peers and authority figures. May signal emotional disturbances. Subjects respond to 20 pictures of children and adults in various situations. Form C is used with elementary school students, form Y with middle and high school students. May be administered individually or to groups by using transparencies.

11046
Clinical Evaluation of Language Functions: Diagnostic Battery. American Association of Community and Junior Colleges, Washington, DC; Educational Testing Service, Princeton, NJ Semel, Eleanor Messing; Wiig, Elisabeth H. 1980
Subtests: Processing; Word and Sentence Structure; Word Classes; Linguistic Concepts; Relationships and Ambiguities; Oral Directions; Spoken Paragraphs; Producing: Word Series; Names on Confrontation; Word Associations; Model Sentences; Formulated Sentences; Speech Sounds
Descriptors: *Diagnostic Tests; *Elementary School Students; Elementary Secondary Education; Individual Testing; *Language Handicaps; *Learning Disabilities; Phonology; *Secondary School Students; Semantics; Syntax
Identifiers: CELF
Availability: The Psychological Corporation; 555 Academic Ct., San Antonio, TX 78204-0952
Grade Level: K-12
Notes: Time, 76; Items, 412

Individually administered measure designed to identify type and degree of language disabilities in school-age children. Measures phonology, syntax, semantics, memory, word finding, and retrieval. This test was reviewed by N. J. Spekman and F. P. Roth in Journal of Speech and Hearing Disorders; v49 p97-100 Feb 1984.

11049
El Circo. Educational Testing Service, Princeton, NJ 1980
Subtests: Cuanto y Cuantos (39); Para gue Sirvin las Palabras (38); What Words Are for (30); Language Check (16)
Descriptors: *Bilingual Students; Children; Early Childhood Education; English (Second Language); *Language Skills; *Mathematical Concepts; Preschool Education; Receptive Language; *Spanish Speaking; Student Placement

Availability: Publishers Test Service; 2500 Garden Rd., Monterey, CA 93940
Target Audience: 4-6
Notes: Time, 20 approx; Items, 123

Measures comprehension of simple mathematical concepts and basic linguistic structures to determine level of instruction. Receptive functional language is measured in English and Spanish. Administered individually or in small groups. A pretest is provided to check child's Knowledge of Spanish.

11050
Screening Manual: A Project APT Resource Manual. Gendreau, Joan C.; And Others 1980
Subtests: Hearing; Vision; Physical Function; Oral Motor; Maladaptive Behavior; Cognition Checklist; Home Information Questionnaire
Descriptors: Auditory Tests; Cognitive Development; *Elementary School Students; Elementary Secondary Education; Family Environment; *Multiple Disabilities; Physical Examinations; Psychomotor Skills; *Screening Tests; *Secondary School Students; *Severe Mental Retardation; Social Adjustment; Vision Tests
Identifiers: Project APT
Availability: ERIC Document Reproduction Service; 3900 Wheeler Ave., Alexandria, VA 22304 (ED192474, 74 pages)
Grade Level: K-12

Part of a series of materials developed for a program designed to foster home-school coordination in educational planning and program implementation for severely mentally retarded and/or multiply handicapped students. Provides 5 screening tools in the areas of hearing, vision, physical functioning, oral motor, and maladaptive behavior. Also available are a cognition checklist and a home information questionnaire.

11051
Developmental Achievement Wheel: A Project APT Assessment Manual. Gendreau, Joan C.; And Others 1975
Subtests: Cognition; Communication-Verbal Expressive; Communication-Nonverbal Expressive; Communication-Receptive; Gross Motor; Fine Motor; Self Help-Grooming and Toileting; Self Help-Dressing; Self Help-Feeding; Socialization
Descriptors: *Child Development; Cognitive Measurement; Daily Living Skills; Interpersonal Competence; Measures (Individuals); *Multiple Disabilities; Nonverbal Communication; Physical Disabilities; Psychomotor Skills; *Severe Mental Retardation; Verbal Ability; Young Children
Identifiers: Developmental Assessment Wheel; Project APT
Availability: ERIC Document Reproduction Service; 3900 Wheeler Ave., Alexandria, VA 22304 (ED192475, 51 pages)
Target Audience: 0-6
Notes: Items, 363

Assesses functional age level of multiply handicapped or severely mentally retarded students in 6 major areas: cognition, language, gross motor, fine motor, self-help, and socialization. The wheel consists of 5 concentric rings—0 to 6 months, 6 months-1 year, 1-2 years, 2-4 years, and 4-6 years. Permits recording student's past, present, and future levels of performance. For some skills, there are alternative sequences for physically handicapped children.

11060
Lessons for Self Instruction in Basic Skills. Revised Edition. CTB/McGraw-Hill, Monterey, CA 1979
Descriptors: *Adult Basic Education; Adults; *Basic Skills; Mastery Tests; Programed Instruction
Identifiers: LSI
Availability: CTB/McGraw Hill; Del Monte Research Park, Monterey, CA 93940
Target Audience: Adults

Series of multilevel, programed learning aids in reading, mathematics, and language for adults of limited education background. There are 53 books in the series, and various levels are included for each subject. A short mastery test for each book assesses the individual's mastery of the material covered. Diagnosis and prescription have been facilitated by keying LSI to the following tests: Test of Adult Basic Education (1976 edition); California Achievement Tests, Forms C and D; and parts of the Prescriptive Reading Inventory (PRI) and Diagnostic Mathematics Inventory (DMI).

11081
Neuropsychological Questionnaire. Children's Form. Melendez, Fernando 1978
Descriptors: *Behavior Problems; Children; *Emotional Disturbances; *Minimal Brain Dysfunction; *Neurological Impairments; Questionnaires
Identifiers: Test Batteries

Availability: Psychological Assessment Resources;
P.O. Box 998, Odessa, FL 33556
Target Audience: Children
Notes: Items, 42

Part of an overall evaluation of children who are suspected of having brain dysfunction. Designed as a set of areas of inquiry and is of little value if used alone or if answered in simple yes or no fashion. The questionnaire primarily is useful as part of an extensive battery that should include neuropsychological testing and pediatric neurological examinations. Its goal is to attempt to make a 3-way differentiation between entities that generally show very similar signs and symptoms: childhood schizophrenia, abnormal electrical functions, and posterior fossa neoplasms. The questionnaire is short and does not, in and of itself, furnish any diagnostic answers. It should stimulate the practitioner into thinking about the child in terms of possible alternative problems and to make appropriate referrals for further studies. A review of this test by Cecil R. Reynolds appears in School Psychology Review; v12 n4 p484-85 Fall 1983.

11082
Neuropsychological Questionnaire. Adult Form.
Melendez, Fernando 1978
Subtests: General Health; Substance Abuse; Psychiatric Problems; General Neurological; Right Hemisphere; Left Hemisphere; Subcortical Cerebellar Spinal; Sensory Perceptual
Descriptors: Adults; *Emotional Disturbances; *Minimal Brain Dysfunction; *Neurological Impairments; Questionnaires; *Screening Tests
Availability: Psychological Assessment Resources;
P.O. Box 998, Odessa, FL 33556
Target Audience: Adults
Notes: Time, 10 approx.; Items, 54

A screening device for neurological problems, which offers a rapid review of complaints, symptoms, and signs that may suggest underlying brain dysfunction or other organic conditions in people who have contacted a psychologist for assessment or treatment. A useful adjunct to a general intake interview and the information gained from it often leads to appropriate referrals to medical practitioners or a decision to do more comprehensive neuropsychological testing. Neuropsychological testing often will clarify or confirm the symptoms endorsed. The questionnaire is also a reliable monitor in following the course of recovery (or decline) over a period of time. The questionnaire can be self-administered, but generally it is preferable if the practitioner asks the questions and makes an inquiry as he or she goes along. A review of this test by Cecil R. Reynolds apppears in School Psychology Review; v12 n4 p484-85 Fall 1983.

11084
Special Education Teacher Profile. Westling, David L.; And Others 1978
Subtests: Personal/Professional Data; Professional Preparation; Classroom Teaching Activity; Classroom Management; Evaluation; Interaction with Other Professionals and/or Administrators; Parent Counseling and Interaction
Descriptors: Adults; Classroom Techniques; Educational Background; Interprofessional Relationship; Parent Counseling; Parent Teacher Cooperation; Profiles; Questionnaires; Special Education; *Special Education Teachers; Student Evaluation; Teacher Administrator Relationship; Teacher Background; Teaching Experience; Teaching Styles
Availability: David L. Westling; College of Education, Florida State University, Tallahassee, FL 32303
Target Audience: Adults
Notes: Items, 62

Questionnaire concerning current teaching practices and related experience of teachers designated as average or superior by their director. Used as part of a study to determine appropriate content for inservice workshops that would result in better special educators. All questions required factual answers.

11087
Test of English as a Foreign Language. Understanding TOEFL: Test Kit 1. Educational Testing Service, Princeton, NJ 1980
Subtests: Listening Comprehension; Structure and Written Expression; Reading Comprehension and Vocabulary
Descriptors: Adults; *English (Second Language); Foreign Students; *Graduate Students; Grammar; Higher Education; *High School Students; *Language Proficiency; *Language Tests; Listening Comprehension Tests; Multiple Choice Tests; Reading Comprehension; Secondary Education; Self Evaluation (Individuals); Sentence Structure; *Undergraduate Students; Vocabulary Skills; Workbooks; Writing Skills
Identifiers: Practice Tests; Self Scoring Tests; *TOEFL
Availability: TOEFL; Box 2877, Educational Testing Service, Princeton, NJ 08541

Grade Level: 11-18
Notes: Time, 120; Items, 150

Practice materials containing an actual TOEFL test. Includes a cassette tape recording of the Listening Comprehension subtest. A workbook also supplies correct answers and explanations of each answer choice. TOEFL was designed to evaluate the English proficiency of non-native speakers of English, primarily at the secondary level, who are preparing to study at North American colleges or universities.

11089
Adaptive Behavior: Street Survival Skills Questionnaire. Linkenhoker, Dan; McCarron, Lawrence 1979
Subtests: Basic Concepts; Functional Signs; Tools; Domestic Management; Health, First Aid and Safety; Public Services; Time; Money; Measurements
Descriptors: *Adjustment (to Environment); Adolescents; Adults; *Daily Living Skills; *Developmental Disabilities; Measures (Individuals); *Mental Retardation; Pictorial Stimuli; Questionnaires; *Special Education
Identifiers: SSSQ
Availability: McCarron-Dial Systems; P.O. Box 45628, Dallas, TX 75245
Target Audience: 15-55
Notes: Time, 45 approx.; Items, 216

Constructed to evaluate functional knowledge and skills necessary for independent living in the community by developmentally disabled individuals. The SSSQ consists of 9 separate 50-page volumes. Each volume has 24 pages of 4 pictures each with relevant questions on the facing page. Each volume relates to a specific area of adaptive behavior: basic concepts; functional signs; tool identification and use; domestic management; health, first aid, and safety; public services; time; money; and measurement. Normative data were obtained from developmentally disabled subjects and from a nondisabled adolescent group.

11092
Stuttering Severity Instrument for Children and Adults. Revised Edition. Riley, Glyndon D. 1980
Descriptors: Adolescents; Adults; Children; *Individual Testing; Standardized Tests; *Stuttering
Identifiers: SSI
Availability: C.C. Publications; P.O. Box 23699, Tigard, OR 97223
Target Audience: 2-65

Standardized, individually administered instrument to assess stuttering severity in adults and children. Measures frequency of repetition and prolongation of sounds and syllables; estimated duration of the longest blocks (stuttering events); and observable physical concomitants. Yields a single numerical score in a range of 0 to 45.

11094
Informal Assessment of Developmental Skills for Visually Handicapped Students. American Foundation for the Blind, New York, NY 1978
Descriptors: Adolescents; Behavior Rating Scales; Check Lists; Children; *Informal Assessment; Multiple Disabilities; *Visual Impairments; Young Children
Availability: American Foundation for the Blind; 15 W. 16th St., New York, NY 10011
Target Audience: 0-16

A compilation of informal assessment checklists or inventories developed by teachers of visually handicapped individuals. Informal assessment techniques for school-age children cover visual functioning; unique academic needs; orientation and mobility; vocational skills; and behavior in the areas of auditory comprehension and listening, spoken language, orientation; behavior, and motor skills. For younger functioning visually handicapped and multihandicapped children, informal assessment covers self-help, psychomotor, social-emotional, language, and cognition.

11102
Test of English as a Foreign Language: Sample Test. Educational Testing Service, Princeton, NJ 1981
Subtests: Listening Comprehension; Structure and Written Expression; Reading Comprehension and Vocabulary
Descriptors: Adults; *English (Second Language); Foreign Students; *Graduate Students; Grammar; Higher Education; *High School Students; *Language Proficiency; *Language Tests; Listening Comprehension Tests; Multiple Choice Tests; Reading Comprehension; Secondary Education; Sentence Structure; *Undergraduate Students; Vocabulary Skills; Writing Skills
Identifiers: Practice Tests; *TOEFL
Availability: TOEFL; Box 2877, Educational Testing Service, Princeton, NJ 08541
Grade Level: 11-18
Notes: Items, 70

Test booklet and answer key for use as practice materials for TOEFL. Half the length of an actual test. No percentile can be computed.

11103
English as a Second Language Assessment Battery. Rivera, Charlene; Lombardo, Maria 1979
Subtests: Oral Screening; Oral Competency; Aural Comprehension; Dictation Exercise; Structural Competency; Informal Reading Inventory; Writing Sample
Descriptors: *Bilingual Students; *Criterion Referenced Tests; *English (Second Language); Expressive Language; Informal Reading Inventories; Language Proficiency; Listening Comprehension; Oral Language; Reading Comprehension; Receptive Language; Secondary Education; *Secondary School Students; *Spanish Speaking; Student Placement; Writing Skills
Identifiers: ESLAB; TIM(G)
Availability: Tests in Microfiche; Test Collection, Educational Testing Service, Princeton, NJ 08541
Grade Level: 7-12
Notes: Time, 105; Items, 208

Criterion-referenced measure designed to assess the English-language proficiency of Spanish bilingual students. Covers receptive and expressive skills. For use in placing students at instructional levels in ESL classes.

11108
Figural Relations Diagnostic Test. Forms A and B. Willis, Sherry; Plemons, Judy 1977
Descriptors: *Cognitive Development; *Cognitive Measurement; Intelligence; *Older Adults; Pretests Posttests; *Spatial Ability; *Transfer of Training
Identifiers: ADEPT; *Fluid Intelligence; TIM(I)
Availability: Tests in Microfiche; Test Collection, Educational Testing Service, Princeton, NJ 08541
Target Audience: 65-99
Notes: Items, 42

Used in a study of the intellectual functioning of older adults to measure transfer of training as part of the Adult Development and Enrichment Project (ADEPT) at the Pennsylvania State University. Each form contains 4 subtests of from 7-14 nonverbal items. Item types include series classifications, matrices, and conditions. Form A is a pretest and form B a posttest.

11111
ADEPT Induction Diagnostic Test. Baltes, Paul B.; Willis, Sherry L. 1979
Subtests: Letter Sets Test; Number Series; Letter Series
Descriptors: *Cognitive Tests; *Induction; *Intelligence Differences; *Older Adults
Identifiers: ADEPT; *Fluid Intelligence; TIM(I)
Availability: Tests in Microfiche; Test Collection, Educational Testing Service, Princeton, NJ 08541
Target Audience: 65-99

Used to examine the degree to which fluid intelligence can be modified in older adults through a cognitive training program. Induction is one of the primary mental abilities to be measured in determining fluid intelligence. Two forms of the Letter Sets and Number Series are available. Used as part of the Adult Development and Enrichment Project (ADEPT).

11112
Early Identification Screening Program. Kindergarten Screening. Baltimore City Schools, MD 1982
Subtests: Xs in Circles; XO Pattern; Counting Number Sets; See-Say Letters; Matching Colors; Naming Pictures; Hear-Touch (Body Parts)
Descriptors: Auditory Stimuli; Individual Testing; *Kindergarten Children; *Learning Modalities; *Learning Problems; Primary Education; *Screening Tests; Visual Stimuli
Availability: Modern Curriculum Press; 13900 Prospect Rd., Cleveland, OH 44136
Grade Level: K
Notes: Time, 9 approx.

Meant to be used at beginning of school year to measure individual child's performance of specific tasks to predict that children may develop learning problems. It measures child's written or oral response to visual or auditory stimuli. Consists of 3 one-minute frequency measures and is given to each child over a period of 3 days. It takes approximately 20 minutes per child to complete the process and 9 minutes of screening per child. Three learning modalities that are screened are hear-write, see-write, and see-say.

11116
Language Proficiency Test. Gerard, Joan; Weinstock, Gloria 1981

Subtests: Commands; Short Answer Oral Production; Listening Comprehension; Vocabulary; Reading Comprehension; Grammar; Sentence Response; Paragraph Response; Translation
Descriptors: Adolescents; Adults; Audiolingual Skills; *Criterion Referenced Tests; Diagnostic Tests; *English (Second Language); *Language Proficiency; Learning Disabilities; Listening Comprehension; Older Adults; Oral Language; Paragraphs; Reading Skills; Sentences; Slow Learners; Translation; Vocabulary Skills; Writing Skills
Identifiers: LPT
Availability: Academic Therapy Publications; 20 Commercial Blvd., Novato, CA 94947
Target Audience: 13-65
Notes: Time, 90; Items, 99

Criterion-referenced measure designed to assess language ability for students of English as a Second Language and native speakers with learning handicaps or low level skills. Measures aural/oral, reading, and writing skills. Utilizes multiple-choice and short-answer questions. Includes an optional translation section to assess vocabulary and syntactical complexity. Two subtests measuring low level function must be individually administered.

11117
Light's Retention Scale: Revised Edition. Light, H. Wayne 1981
Descriptors: Attendance Patterns; Behavior Problems; *Elementary School Students; Elementary Secondary Education; *Grade Repetition; Intelligence; Physical Characteristics; *Rating Scales; *Secondary School Students; Sex; Student Motivation
Availability: Academic Therapy Publications; 20 Commercial Blvd., Novato, CA 94947
Grade Level: K-12
Notes: Time, 15; Items, 19

Assists the school professional in deciding whether a student would benefit from grade retention. Considers factors such as attendance, intelligence, size, age, sex, history, parent participation, student motivation, and emotional or behavior problems.

11121
Reading Comprehension Battery for Aphasia. LaPointe, Leonard L.; Horner, Jennifer 1979
Subtests: Single Word Comprehension: Visual Confusions; Single Word Comprehension: Auditory Confusions; Single Word Comprehension: Semantic Confusions; Functional Reading: Synonyms; Sentence Comprehension: Picture; Short Paragraph Comprehension: Picture; Paragraphs: Factual and Inferential Comprehension; Morpho-Syntactic Reading with Lexical Controls
Descriptors: Adults; *Aphasia; *Diagnostic Tests; *Reading Comprehension; *Reading Difficulties
Identifiers: RCBA
Availability: C.C. Publications; P.O. Box 23699, Tigard, OR 97223
Target Audience: Adults
Notes: Items, 100

Designed to provide systematic evaluation of the nature and degree of reading impairment in aphasic adults. Individually administered.

11123
Test of Auditory Comprehension. Los Angeles County Superintendent of Schools, CA 1979
Subtests: Screening Task; Linguistic and Non-Linguistic Sounds; Linguistic, Human Non-Linguistic and Environmental Sounds; Stereotypic Messages; Single Element, Core Noun Vocabulary; Recall Two Critical Elements in a Message; Recall Four Critical Elements in a Message; Sequences Three Events in a Story; Recalls Five Details of a Story; Sequences Three Events in a Story with Competing Messages; Recalls Five Details of a Story with Competing Messages
Descriptors: Audiotape Recorders; Auditory Discrimination; *Auditory Evaluation; *Auditory Tests; Children; *Diagnostic Tests; Elementary Education; *Elementary School Students; *Hearing Impairments; Individual Testing; Recall (Psychology); Student Placement
Identifiers: Figure Ground; TAC
Availability: Foreworks Publications; Box 9747, N. Hollywood, CA 91609
Target Audience: 4-12
Notes: Time, 30 approx.; Items, 154

Designed for individual administration with hearing-impaired students to assess auditory functioning. Begins with simple auditory discrimination tasks and proceeds through 10 subtests to measure child's understanding of complex stories given with a competing message background. Provides a profile of a student's auditory skills in the areas of discrimination, memory-sequencing, and figure-ground. Is

one component of the Auditory Skills Instructional Planning System. Test stimuli are recorded on an audiocassette tape.

11132
Scales of Early Communication Skills for Hearing Impaired Children. Moog, Jean S.; Geers, Ann V. 1975
Subtests: Receptive Language Skills; Expressive Language Skills; Nonverbal Receptive Skills; Nonverbal Expressive Skills
Descriptors: Communication Skills; Developmental Tasks; Expressive Language; *Hearing Impairments; *Language Skills; Nonverbal Communication; Observation; Rating Scales; Receptive Language; *Speech Communication; Teachers; Young Children
Identifiers: SECS
Availability: Central Institute for the Deaf; 818 S. Euclid Ave., St. Louis, MO 63110
Target Audience: 2-8
Notes: Items, 28

Designed to evaluate speech and language of hearing-impaired children. Developmentally ordered items describe behaviors which are rated by the teacher based on observations of the child.

11134
Knox's Cube Test (KCT). Stone, Mark H.; Wright, Benjamin D. 1980
Descriptors: Adolescents; Adults; *Attention Span; Children; Deafness; *Memory; Non English Speaking; *Nonverbal Tests; *Short Term Memory
Identifiers: KCT; Tapping Test
Availability: Stoelting Co.; 1350 S. Kostner Ave., Chicago, IL 60623
Target Audience: 2-65
Notes: Items, 51

A nonverbal test measuring attention span and shortterm memory. Incorporates all previous versions. Can be used with deaf, non-verbal, and non-English speaking persons. A Junior Form and a Senior Form are available with 16 and 22 items, respectively.

11135
Kaufman Infant and Preschool Scale. Kaufman, H. 1979
Subtests: General Reasoning; Storage; Verbal Communication
Descriptors: *Cognitive Development; *Cognitive Measurement; Intervention; Mental Age; *Mental Retardation; Screening Tests; Verbal Communication; Young Children
Identifiers: KIPS; Reasoning Ability
Availability: Stoelting Co.; 1350 S. Kostner Ave., Chicago, IL 60623
Target Audience: 0-4
Notes: Time, 30; Items, 20

Designed to measure early high-level cognition in general reasoning, storage, verbal communication. Indicates need for intervention and suggests activities. Can be used with mentally retarded subjects of all ages whose mental age using KIPS does not exceed 48 months.

11137
Millon Behavioral Health Inventory. Millon, Theodore 1974
Subtests: Introversive Style; Inhibited Style; Cooperative Style; Sociable Style; Confident Style; Forceful Style; Respectful Style; Sensitive Style; Chronic Tension; Recent Stress; Premorbid Pessimism; Future Despair; Social Alienation; Somatic Anxiety; Allergic Inclination; Gastrointestinal Susceptibility; Cardiovascular Tendency; Pain Treatment Responsibility; Life Threat Reactivity; Emotional Vulnerability
Descriptors: Adults; Attitudes; Coping; *Objective Tests; *Patients; *Physical Health; Prognostic Tests; *Psychological Patterns; Psychosomatic Disorders; Stress Variables
Identifiers: MBHI
Availability: Clinical Assessment Systems; P.O. Box 570175, Miami, FL 33157
Target Audience: Adults
Notes: Items, 150

Diagnostic tool for assessing psychological factors which affect patients with physical health or behavioral medicine problems. The 20 subscales fall into 4 major categories: coping styles, psychogenic attitudes, psychosomatic correlates, and prognostic indices.

11139
Early Identification Screening Program. First-Grade Screening. Baltimore City Schools, MD 1982
Subtests: Xs in Circles; XO Pattern; Counting Number Sets; See-Say Letters; Matching Colors; Naming Pictures; Hear-Touch (Body Parts); See-Write Letters; See-Say Numbers

Descriptors: Auditory Stimuli; *Grade 1; Individual Testing; *Learning Modalities; *Learning Problems; Primary Education; *Screening Tests; Visual Stimuli
Availability: Modern Curriculum Press; 13900 Prospect Rd., Cleveland, OH 44136
Grade Level: 1
Notes: Time, 9 approx.

Meant to be used at the beginning of the school year to measure individual child's performance of specific tasks to predict that children may develop learning problems. It measures child's written or oral response to visual or auditory stimuli. Consists of 3 one-minute frequency measures and is given to each child over a period of 3 days. It takes approximately 20 minutes per child to complete the process and 9 minutes of screening per child. Three learning modalities that are screened are hear-write, see-write, and see-say.

11140
Behavioral Deviancy Profile. Ball, Betty; Weinberg, Rita 1980
Descriptors: *Adolescents; *Behavior Rating Scales; *Children; Cognitive Development; Emotional Development; *Emotional Problems; Graphs; Interpersonal Competence; Language Acquisition; Motor Development; *Social Adjustment
Availability: Stoelting Co.; 1350 S. Kostner Ave., Chicago, IL 60623
Target Audience: 3-21
Notes: Time, 120 approx.; Items, 18

Comprehensive assessment of emotionally and socially disturbed children and adolescents in 18 areas: physical growth, gross motor development, fine motor development, motor activity, sensory perception, cognition, intelligence, speech, language, affect, aggression, relationship with mother, relationship with father, relationship with siblings, relationship with peers, relationship with adults, ego-self, supergo-conscience. The 4 major areas encompassed by these 18 factors include physical and motor development, cognitive development, speech and language, and social and emotional development.

11143
Grammatical Analysis of Elicited Language: Complex Sentence Level. GAEL-C. Moog, Jean S.; Geers, Ann E. 1980
Descriptors: Children; *Deafness; Disabilities; Grammar; *Hearing Impairments; *Language Acquisition; *Language Handicaps; *Language Tests; *Sentence Structure
Identifiers: GAEL
Availability: Central Institute for the Deaf; 818 S. Euclid Ave., St. Louis, MO 63110
Target Audience: 3-12
Notes: Time, 60 approx.; Items, 88

Designed to evaluate child's acquisition of specific grammatical structures. Consists of a set of 22 activities designed to elicit 88 target sentences exemplifying a variety of complex sentence structures. Can be used for Title I programs. Results can be used to describe child's use of grammatical structures, to delineate grammatical categories needing remediation, and to measure progress over a period of time.

11154
The Hill Performance Test of Selected Positional Concepts. Hill, Everett W. 1981
Subtests: Ability to Identify Positional Relationships of Body Parts; Ability to Move Various Body Parts to Demonstrate Positional Concepts; Ability to Move the Body in Relationship to Objects to Demonstrate Positional Concepts; Ability to Manipulate Objects to Demonstrate Positional Concepts
Descriptors: Children; Individual Testing; Perceptual Handicaps; *Performance Tests; *Spatial Ability; *Visual Impairments; *Visually Handicapped Mobility
Availability: Stoelting Co.; 1350 S. Kostner Ave., Chicago, IL 60623
Target Audience: 6-10
Notes: Items, 72

Individually administered test designed to assess spatial conceptual strengths and weaknesses of visually impaired children through their response to a series of directions. Children must have basic language abilities, be mobile and recognize body part names.

11155
The Dyslexia Screening Survey. Valett, Robert E. 1980
Subtests: Functional Reading Level; Reading Potential; Significant Reading Discrepancy; Specific Processing Skill Deficiencies; Neuropsychological Dysfunctions; Associated Factors; Developmental-Remedial Strategies

Descriptors: Auditory Perception; Check Lists; *Criterion Referenced Tests; *Dyslexia; Elementary Education; *Elementary School Students; *Learning Disabilities; Neurological Impairments; Phonetics; Psychological Characteristics; Reading Ability; *Reading Difficulties; Remedial Instruction; *Screening Tests; Visual Perception
Identifiers: Potential Ability
Availability: Fearon Education, Pitman Learning, Inc.; 6 Davis Dr., Belmont, CA 94002
Grade Level: 1-6
Notes: Items, 64

A checklist of basic neuropsychological skills involved in the reading process. For use in screening children with reading difficulties for possible inclusion in special education. Covers phonetic-auditory, visual, and multisensory processing skills in children who may be dyslexic. Recommends use of other screening techniques in addition to the checklist.

11158
Louisville Behavior Checklist. Form E3. Revised 1981. Miller, Lovick C. 1981
Subtests: Ego-Exploitive; Destructive/Assaultive; Social Delinquency; Adolescent Turmoil; Apathetic Isolation; Neuroticism; Dependent-Inhibited; Academic Disability; Neurological or Psychotic Abnormality; General Pathology; Longitudinal Scale; Severity Level; Total Pathology
Descriptors: *Adolescents; *Affective Behavior; Antisocial Behavior; Check Lists; Patients; *Personality Measures; Prosocial Behavior; *Psychopathology; *Social Behavior
Identifiers: LBC
Availability: Western Psychological Services; 12031 Wilshire Blvd., Los Angeles, CA 90025
Target Audience: 13-17
Notes: Items, 164

Inventory which covers entire range of social and emotional behaviors indicative of psychopathological disorders of childhood and adolescence from social competence to social deviance. Designed to facilitate parents' recordings of their children's behavior and to provide information to mental health workers.

11159
Louisville Behavior Checklist. Form E1. Miller, Lovick C. 1977
Subtests: Infantile Aggression; Hyperactivity; Antisocial Behavior; Aggression; Social Withdrawal; Sensitivity; Fear; Inhibition; Intellectual Deficit; Immaturity; Cognitive Disability; Normal Irritability; Prosocial Deficit; Rare Deviance; Neurotic Behavior; Psychotic Behavior; Somatic Behavior; Sexual Behavior; School Disturbance Predictor; Severity Level
Descriptors: *Affective Behavior; Antisocial Behavior; Check Lists; *Personality Measures; Prosocial Behavior; *Psychopathology; *Social Behavior; *Young Children
Identifiers: LBC
Availability: Western Psychological Services; 12031 Wilshire Blvd., Los Angeles, CA 90025
Target Audience: 4-6
Notes: Items, 164

Inventory which covers entire range of social and emotional behaviors indicative of psychopathological disorders of childhood from social competence to social deviance. Designed to facilitate parents' recordings of their children's behavior and to provide information to mental health workers.

11161
School Environment Preference Survey. Gordon, Leonard V. 1978
Subtests: Self-Subordination; Traditionalism; Rule Conformity; Uncriticalness
Descriptors: Conformity; Discipline Problems; *Educational Environment; *Elementary School Students; Elementary Secondary Education; Postsecondary Education; Rating Scales; *School Attitudes; *Secondary School Students; *Student School Relationship; Teacher Student Relationship; Work Environment
Availability: Educational and Industrial Testing Service; P.O. Box 7234, San Diego, CA 92107
Grade Level: 3-13
Notes: Time, 15; Items, 24

Designed to measure individuals' levels of commitment to the attitudes, values, and behaviors rewarded and encouraged in the school environment. High scorers seek group and institutional identification, accept authority, prefer rules, and do not question judgment. Used to gain understanding of the student in relation to disciplinary problems and in vocational education classes to determine work climate preference.

11177
Riley Motor Problems Inventory. Revised 1976. Riley, Glyndon D. 1976

Subtests: Oral Motor Tasks; Fine Motor Tasks; Gross Motor Tasks
Descriptors: Child Development; Children; *Elementary School Students; *Individual Testing; *Motor Development; *Neurological Impairments; Perceptual Motor Coordination; *Performance Tests; *Psychomotor Skills; *Screening Tests
Identifiers: Motor Problems Inventory; Oral Tests; RMPI
Availability: Western Psychological Services; 12031 Wilshire Blvd., Los Angeles, CA 90025
Target Audience: 4-9
Notes: Time, 10 approx.; Items, 10

An individually administered screening device which provides a quantified measure (of observation) of neurological signs in children. Used to estimate the severity of neurological or motor problems to determine the presence of motor problems, and to differentiate between neurogenic and psychogenic disorders. Revision of the Motor Problems Inventory (TC007407), published in 1972.

11182
Practical Articulation Kit. McDonough, Martha M. 1972
Descriptors: *Articulation (Speech); *Auditory Training; Elementary Education; *Elementary School Students; *Individual Testing; Language Acquisition; Language Skills; *Phonics; *Screening Tests; Speech Handicaps; *Speech Tests
Identifiers: Oral Tests; PAK
Availability: Interstate Printers and Publishers, 1927 N. Jackson St., Danville, IL 61834
Grade Level: K-6
Notes: Items, 81

Untimed instrument designed for use by speech and hearing therapists, particularly those traveling within an entire school system or district. Easily transportable because the instrument consists of a deck of cards. Each card contains a picture of the main word, the main word, and (below a dotted line) 2 additional words which contain the same sound. The therapists may use these cards to plan several games which involve articulation of the words on the cards, and which involve a small group of children. Alternately, the therapist may test an individual child's articulation via use of the cards. Thus, may be used as a screening or intense testing for children with many different speech and hearing problems. Also used for language building and as a tool for auditory training and sequential memory skills.

11183
Rader Visual Acuity Screening Test. Rader, K. W. 1977
Descriptors: Children; Disabilities; *Elementary School Students; *Preschool Children; *Screening Tests; *Vision Tests; *Visual Acuity
Identifiers: Visual Acuity Screening Test
Availability: Modern Education Corporation; P.O. Box 271, Tulsa, OK 74101
Target Audience: Children
Notes: Time, 10 approx.

A screening test used to measure a child's vision. Because it uses a face with either a sad mouth or a happy, smiling mouth, the test can be used with preschool children, children with learning disabilities, and children who do not know the English alphabet.

11191
Speech and Language Growth for the Mexican-American Student. Proul, Peter 1971
Subtests: Spanish Accent Sentence Completion Articulation Test; Spanish Accent Picture Stimulus Articulation Test; Spanish Accent Auditory Discrimination Test
Descriptors: *Articulation (Speech); *Auditory Discrimination; *Diagnostic Tests; Elementary Education; *Elementary School Students; *English (Second Language); Individual Testing; *Language Patterns; *Mexican Americans; *Nonstandard Dialects; Pictorial Stimuli; Remedial Instruction; *Spanish Speaking; *Speech Instruction
Identifiers: Sentence Completion Test; TIM (H)
Availability: Tests in Microfiche; Test Collection, Educational Testing Service, Princeton, NJ 08541
Grade Level: 1-6
Notes: Items, 35

Diagnostic tests of hearing and articulation and methods to aid in the diagnosis of language patterns, designed to measure deviations from standard English in those students speaking English with a Spanish accent. Hearing is tested by measuring auditory discrimination. Each subtest has between 30 and 40 items. Individually administered.

11201
The Booklet Category Test. DeFilippis, Nick A.; McCampbell, Elizabeth 1979

Descriptors: *Abstract Reasoning; Adults; Computer Assisted Testing; Computer Software; *Concept Formation; *Neurological Impairments; *Screening Tests; *Visual Measures
Identifiers: BCT; *Halstead Category Test; *Halstead Reitan Neuropsychological Tests
Availability: Psychological Assessment Resources; P.O. Box 98, Odessa, FL 33556
Target Audience: Adults
Notes: Items, 208

A booklet version of the Halstead Category Test. A visually presented test of concept formation, abstract reasoning which is a sensitive indicator of brain dysfunction in the Halstead-Reitan Neuropsychological Test Battery and is about as valid as the complete battery in detecting the presence or absence of brain damage. A review of this test by Cecil R. Reynolds appears in School Psychology Review, v12 n4 p487-88 Fall 1983. A computerized version is available for Apple IIe, II Plus, and IIc.

11202
Halstead-Reitan Neuropsychological Test Battery: Spanish Version. Manual. Melendez, Fernando; Prado, Hydee 1981
Descriptors: *Abstract Reasoning; Adults; *Concept Formation; *Neurological Impairments; Psychological Evaluation; *Screening Tests; *Spanish; Visual Stimuli
Identifiers: *Halstead Reitan Neuropsychological Tests
Availability: Psychological Assessment Resources; P.O. Box 998, Odessa, FL 33556
Target Audience: Adults

General instructions in Spanish for administering the Halstead Category Test which is a visually presented test of concept formation and abstract reasoning used to indicate brain dysfunction. Part of the Halstead-Reitan Neuropsychological Test Battery.

11203
Halstead Category Test for Young Children. Reitan, Ralph M. 1979
Subtests: Matching; Quality; Uniqueness; Lesser Quantity; Summary
Descriptors: *Abstract Reasoning; *Concept Formation; *Neurological Impairments; Psychological Evaluation; *Screening Tests; Visual Stimuli; *Young Children
Identifiers: *Halstead Reitan Neuropsychological Tests; *Reitan Indiana Neuropsychological Test Battery
Availability: Neuropsychology Laboratory; 1338 E. Edison St., Tuscon, AZ 85719
Target Audience: 5-8
Notes: Items, 80

A visually presented test of concept formation, and abstract reasoning which indicates brain dysfunction. Part of the Reitan Indiana Neuropsychological Test Battery for Children which is based on the Halstead Reitan Neuropsychological Tests. The complete battery for children includes Wechsler Intelligence Scale for Children, sensory perceptual tests, a modification of the Halstead-Wepman Aphasia Screening test, and the Reitan-Indiana Neuropsychological Test Battery for Children.

11207
The Anser System. Form 4. Self Administered Student Profile. Levine, Melvin D. 1980
Descriptors: *Data Collection; *Elementary School Students; Intermediate Grades; Interpersonal Competence; Learning Problems; *Questionnaires; Secondary Education; *Secondary School Students; Self Concept; *Self Evaluation (Individuals); Student Interests
Availability: Educators Publishing Service; 75 Moulton St., Cambridge, MA 02238
Grade Level: 4-12
Target Audience: 9-18

Integrates data in the areas of health, education, development, and behavior to assess children's school adjustment or learning problems. Compiled data can be used with direct assessments, including psychological evaluation, achievement tests, and health and developmental assessment. May also be used to help formulate individualized educational plans. Form 4 is a self-administered student profile covering student skills, interests, and perceptions of degree of ability in school, sports, cognitive ability, and social skills.

11209
Parental Diagnostic Questionnaire. Revised Edition. Tanner, Dennis C. 1978
Subtests: Speech Behavior; Parental Attitudes; Parental Responses
Descriptors: Adults; Behavior Patterns; *Behavior Rating Scales; *Diagnostic Tests; *Parent Attitudes; *Parent Child Relationship; Parent Counseling; Parents; *Questionnaires; *Speech Evaluation; *Stuttering
Identifiers: PDQ; Stuttering (Parental Diagnostic Questionnaire)

Availability: Modern Education Corporation; P.O. Box 721, Tulsa, OK 74101
Target Audience: Adults
Notes: Time, 15 approx.; Items, 81

Designed to aid a speech pathologist in the evaluation, prevention, diagnosis, and treatment of a child's stuttering problems. This untimed, Likert-styled rating scale and questionnaire is to be completed by the parents, or any adult who plays a significant role in the child's communicative environment, e.g., teacher, grandparent, guardian, etc. Based on the understanding that a relationship exists between the specific parental or adult's attitudes and behavior and the etiology and continuance of a child's stuttering. Provides a broad profile of such parental or adult attitudes, observations of the child, and reactions to the dysfluent speech that may be used in parent/teacher counseling.

11210
Developmental Articulation Profile. Tanner, Dennis C.; And Others 1977
Descriptors: *Articulation (Speech); Articulation Impairments; Child Development; *Diagnostic Tests; *Individual Testing; *Phonemes; *Profiles; *Speech Evaluation; Speech Improvement; Speech Tests; *Young Children
Identifiers: DAP; Oral Tests
Availability: Modern Education Corporation; P.O. Box 721, Tulsa, OK 74101
Target Audience: 3-7

Designed for speech and language pathologists' use in rapidly examining articulation errors of children. Includes an evaluation of the frequency of errors and an approximation of the developmental ages for each phoneme. Developed at Northern Arizona University's Speech and Hearing Center. Also used in parent/teacher counseling and as an integral part of the child's speech and language evaluation. The profile is also useful as a visual aid when retesting.

11212
The Pupil Rating Scale Revised. Screening for Learning Disabilities. Myklebust, Helmer R. 1981
Subtests: Auditory Comprehension; Spoken Language; Orientation; Motor Coordination; Personal-Social Behavior
Descriptors: *Academic Failure; Adolescents; *Behavior Rating Scales; Children; Elementary Education; *Elementary School Students; *High Risk Students; Interpersonal Competence; Language Proficiency; *Learning Disabilities; Listening Comprehension; Perceptual Development; Psychomotor Skills; *Screening Tests
Availability: Western Psychological Services; 12031 Wilshire Blvd., Los Angeles, CA 90025
Grade Level: K-6
Target Audience: 5-14
Notes: Time, 10 approx.; Items, 24

Identifies children with good mental ability, hearing and vision, adequate emotional adjustment, and without overriding physical handicaps but who have a high risk of failing in school. The auditory comprehension and spoken language scores indicate the degree of success of verbal learning. The orientation, motor coordination, and personal-social behavior scores indicate nonverbal learning. Ratings should not be made until teachers have had at least one month of experience with the children, and not more than 30 children should be rated by one teacher.

11213
School Behavior Checklist. Form A1. Miller, Lovick C. 1977
Subtests: Low Need Achievement; Aggression; Anxiety; Cognitive Deficit; Hostile Isolation; Extraversion; Normal Irritability; School Disturbance; Total Disability
Descriptors: *Affective Behavior; Antisocial Behavior; *Behavior Rating Scales; *Personality Assessment; Primary Education; *Social Adjustment; *Young Children
Availability: Western Psychological Services; 12031 Wilshire Blvd., Los Angeles, CA 90025
Target Audience: 4-6
Notes: Time, 10 approx.; Items, 104

Inventory of behaviors completed by teachers that helps them communicate their impressions of children in the classroom inventory covers a wide range of social and emotional behaviors from social competence to moderate social deviance indicative of psychopathological disorders of childhood. Inventory should be interpreted only by professional mental health workers knowledgeable in child psychopathology and who use the instrument as one component of a general clinical evaluation.

11214
School Behavior Checklist. Form A2. Miller, Lovick C. 1977
Subtests: Low Need Achievement; Aggression; Anxiety; Academic Disability; Hostile Isolation; Extraversion; Total Disability

Descriptors: *Affective Behavior; Antisocial Behavior; *Behavior Rating Scales; *Children; Elementary Education; *Personality Assessment; *Social Adjustment
Availability: Western Psychological Services; 12031 Wilshire Blvd., Los Angeles, CA 90025
Target Audience: 7-13
Notes: Time, 10 approx.; Items, 96

Inventory of behaviors completed by teachers that helps them communicate their impressions of children in the classroom. Inventory covers a wide range of social and emotional behaviors from social competence to moderate social deviance indicative of psychopathological disorders of childhood. Inventory should be interpreted only by professional mental health workers knowledgeable in child psychopathology and who use the instrument as one component of a general clinical evaluation.

11215
Quickscreen. Kindergarten. Fudala, Janet B. 1980
Subtests: Name Writing; Figure Copying; Story; Sentence Repetition
Descriptors: Auditory Perception; *Handicap Identification; *Kindergarten Children; *Learning Disabilities; *Learning Problems; Listening Comprehension; Perceptual Motor Coordination; Primary Education; *Screening Tests
Availability: Western Psychological Services; 12031 Wilshire Blvd., Los Angeles, CA 90025
Grade Level: K
Notes: Time, 25 approx.; Items, 4

Brief classroom procedure designed to screen for speech, language, and learning problems. The procedure can be administered to an average classroom at one time. The kindergarten level has 4 parallel forms. Designed as the first step to definitive diagnosis of students with learning problems.

11216
Quickscreen. First Grade. Fudala, Janet B. 1979
Subtests: Name Writing; Figures; Words; Story; Sentences
Descriptors: Auditory Perception; *Grade 1; *Handicap Identification; *Learning Disabilities; *Learning Problems; Listening Comprehension; Perceptual Motor Coordination; Primary Education; *Screening Tests
Availability: Western Psychological Services; 12031 Wilshire Blvd., Los Angeles, CA 90025
Grade Level: 1
Notes: Time, 25 approx.; Items, 8

Brief classroom procedure designed to screen for speech, language, and learning problems. The procedure can be administered to an average classroom at one time. The grade 1 level has 2 parallel forms. The subtests measure auditory comprehension, visual motor skills, and auditory vocal skills. Designed as the first step to definitive diagnosis of students with learning problems.

11217
Quickscreen. Second Grade. Fudala, Janet B. 1979
Subtests: Name Writing; Figures; Story; Cognitive; Sentences
Descriptors: Auditory Perception; Cognitive Development; *Grade 2; *Handicap Identification; *Learning Disabilities; *Learning Problems; Listening Comprehension; Perceptual Motor Coordination; Primary Education; *Screening Tests
Availability: Western Psychological Services; 12031 Wilshire Blvd., Los Angeles, CA 90025
Grade Level: 2
Notes: Time, 25 approx.; Items, 5

Brief classroom procedure designed to screen for speech, language, and learning problems. The procedure can be administered to an average classroom at one time. The grade 2 level has 2 parallel forms. The subtests measure auditory comprehension, cognitive skills, visual motor, and auditory vocal development.

11218
Vocational Adaptation Rating Scales. Malgady, Robert G.; And Others 1980
Subtests: Verbal Manners; Communication Skills; Attendance and Punctuality; Interpersonal Behavior; Respect for Property, Rules and Regulations; Grooming and Personal Hygiene
Descriptors: *Adjustment (to Environment); Adolescents; Adults; Attendance Patterns; *Behavior Problems; Communication Skills; Discipline Problems; Hygiene; Interpersonal Competence; *Mental Retardation; *Rating Scales; Verbal Communication; *Vocational Training Centers
Identifiers: VARS
Availability: Western Psychological Services; 12031 Wilshire Blvd., Los Angeles, CA 90025
Target Audience: 13-50
Notes: Time, 40 approx.; Items, 133

Measures mentally retarded individuals' maladaptive behavior likely to occur in a vocational setting, such as a sheltered workshop, job facility in the community, or vo-

cational training classroom. Rater records the behaviors of each worker who has been observed during a specified observation period (typically, about one month).

11224
Psychiatric Diagnostic Interview. Othmer, Ekkehard; And Others 1981
Subtests: Organic Brain Syndrome; Alcoholism; Drug Dependency; Mania; Depression; Schizophrenia; Antisocial Personality; Hysteria; Somatization, Briquet Syndrome; Anorexia Nervosa; Obsessive Compulsive Neurosis; Phobic Neurosis; Panic Attack Syndrome; Mental Retardation; Homosexuality; Transsexualism; Undiagnosed Psychiatric Disorders
Descriptors: Adults; Drug Abuse; *Emotional Disturbances; *Interviews; Mental Retardation; Older Adults; *Psychological Patterns; *Psychological Testing; Sexuality
Identifiers: PDI
Availability: Western Psychological Services; 12031 Wilshire Blvd., Los Angeles, CA 90025
Target Audience: 18-80
Notes: Time, 30 approx.; Items, 489

Structured diagnostic interview which can be administered by trained support personnel in 15 to 30 minutes for normals and generally about one hour for those with 2 or more syndromes. Based on a descriptive, syndromatic model of psychiatric diagnosis and is used to identify individuals currently suffering from or having previously suffered from any of the 15 most frequently encountered, established psychiatric disorders. Can be used in all phases of the diagnostic process, screening, intake, and followup. Each of the syndromes is approached separately, and each syndrome is organized into 4 sections: cardinal, social significance, auxiliary, and time profile. Individually administered and designed solely to establish presence or absence of psychiatric disorders.

11228
Self Directed Search, Form E. Spanish Edition. Holland, John L. 1979
Subtests: Realistic; Investigative; Artistic; Social; Enterprising; Conventional
Descriptors: Adolescents; Adults; *Career Guidance; Educationally Disadvantaged; High School Students; *Interest Inventories; Reading Difficulties; *Self Evaluation (Individuals); *Spanish; *Vocational Interests
Identifiers: Investigacion Auto Dirigida
Availability: Consulting Psychologists Press; 577 College Ave., Palo Alto, CA 94306
Target Audience: 15-64
Notes: Time, 60 approx.; Items, 192

Spanish version of the vocational interest measure with directions containing only 4th grade level words for those with limited reading skills.

11233
Personal Adjustment and Role Skills. Ellsworth, Robert B. 1979
Subtests: Close Relations; Alienation; Anxiety; Confusion; Alcohol-Drug; House Activity; Child Relations; Employment
Descriptors: *Adjustment (to Environment); *Adults; Drug Use; Emotional Adjustment; Homemaking Skills; Interpersonal Relationship; *Mental Health Programs; *Patients; *Rating Scales; Vocational Adjustment
Identifiers: PARS
Availability: Consulting Psychologists Press; 577 College Ave., Palo Alto, CA 94306
Target Audience: Adults
Notes: Time, 30 approx.; Items, 31

Completed by significant others for patients treated in mental hospitals and clients seen in community clinics. Used to assess clients' changes in behavioral adjustment occurring outside the treatment setting to indicate how successful a mental health program has been for the patient.

11237
Marital Satisfaction Inventory. Snyder, Douglas K. 1979
Subtests: Conventionalization; Global Distress; Affective Communication; Problem Solving Communication; Time Together; Disagreement about Finances; Sexual Dissatisfaction; Role Orientation; Family History of Distress; Dissatisfaction with Children; Conflict over Child-rearing
Descriptors: Adults; *Interpersonal Relationship; *Marital Instability; *Marriage; Marriage Counseling; *Questionnaires; *Spouses
Identifiers: MSI
Availability: Western Psychological Services; 12031 Wilshire Blvd.; Los Angeles, CA 90025
Target Audience: Adults
Notes: Items, 280

A self-report measure which identifies separately for each spouse the nature and extent of marital distress along 9 basic measured dimensions of their relationship. Also has 2 scales to measure each individual's overall dissatisfaction with the marriage. Married couples with no children answer only 239 of the 280 questions. Used as an assessment device with couples who are considering or beginning marital therapy.

11238
Single and Double Simultaneous (Face-Hand) Stimulation Test. Centofanti, Carmen C.; Smith, Aaron 1979
Descriptors: Adults; *Diagnostic Tests; *Neurological Impairments; Older Adults; *Tactual Perception
Identifiers: SDSS; *Somatosensory Functions
Availability: Western Psychological Services; 12031 Wilshire Blvd., Los Angeles, CA 90025
Target Audience: 18-75
Notes: Time, 5 approx.; Items, 20
Simple test of specific somatosensory functions to assist in diagnosing children and adults with suspected disease or injury of the central nervous system and for assessing patients with confirmed lesions. Value of the SDSS is enhanced as a diagnostic tool when used as part of an assessment battery. Use of this test with the Symbol Digit Modalities Test (SDMT) (TC007410) has been found to result in a significantly higher percentage of accurate identification of brain damaged and normal subjects than almost any single test commonly used.

11274
Comprehensive Language Program. Peoria Association for Retarded Citizens, IL 1981
Subtests: Attending; Manipulation of Objects; Mimicking; Matching; Identifying; Labeling; Following Directions; Word Combinations
Descriptors: Adults; *Check Lists; Children; Identification; Imitation; *Language Acquisition; Language Fluency; *Language Handicaps; Listening Comprehension; Motor Development; Perceptual Development; *Student Evaluation
Identifiers: CLP
Availability: Scholastic Testing Service; 480 Meyer Rd., Bensenville, IL 60106
Target Audience: 5-64
Notes: Items, 125
An inventory of speech and language behaviors that enables administrator to systematically document language-handicapped students' language abilities and progress. Profile can be used to group students for language stimulation, to develop long- and short-term goals, and to choose specific lesson plans for each student. Used with children and adults.

11299
Halstead Category Test for Older Children. Reitan, Ralph M. 1979
Subtests: Matching; Quantity; Uniqueness; Proportion; Proportion; Summary
Descriptors: *Abstract Reasoning; *Adolescents; *Children; *Concept Formation; *Neurological Impairments; Psychological Evaluation; *Screening Tests; Visual Stimuli
Identifiers: *Halstead Reitan Neuropsychological Tests
Availability: Neuropsychology Laboratory; 1338 E. Edison St., Tucson, AZ 85719
Target Audience: 9-14
Notes: Items, 168
A visually presented test of concept formation and abstract reasoning that indicates brain dysfunction. Part of the Halstead Reitan Neuropsychological Tests. Battery for children aged 9 to 14 is very similar to adult version (TC011300). The Wechsler Intelligence Scale for Children is used in place of the Wechsler Bellevue Scale, and the Minnesota Multiphasic Personality Inventory is omitted.

11300
Halstead Category Test for Adults. Reitan, Ralph M. 1979
Subtests: Matching; Quantity; Uniqueness; Identification; Proportion; Summary
Descriptors: *Abstract Reasoning; Adults; *Concept Formation; *Neurological Impairments; Psychological Evaluation; *Screening Tests; Visual Stimuli
Identifiers: *Halstead Reitan Neuropsychological Tests
Availability: Neuropsychology Laboratory; 1338 Edison St., Tucson, AZ 85719
Target Audience: Adults
Notes: Items, 208
A visually presented test of concept formation and abstract reasoning that indicates brain dysfunction. Part of the Halstead Reitan Neuropsychological Tests which also includes Wechsler Bellevue Scale (Form I), Trail Making Test, Reitan's modification of the Halstead Wepman Aphasia Screening Test, various tests of sensory-perceptual functions, and the Minnesota Multiphasic Personality Inventory.

11305
Progress Evaluation Scales. Ihilevich, David 1977
Subtests: Family Interaction; Occupation; Getting Along with Others; Feelings and Mood; Use of Free Time; Problems; Attitude toward Self
Descriptors: *Adjustment (to Environment); Adolescents; Adults; Children; Developmental Disabilities; Emotional Response; Family Relationship; Interpersonal Competence; *Mental Health Programs; *Patients; *Program Evaluation; Rating Scales
Identifiers: PES
Availability: David Ihilevich; Shiawassee County Community Mental Health Center, 826 W. King St., P.O. Box 479, Owosso, MI 48867
Target Audience: 6-65
Notes: Items, 7
Measuring device for assessing the impact of mental health programs on clients. Scales can be completed by patients, significant others, and therapists, providing different viewpoints of outcome of mental health services. Can be used to assess entry status, establish treatment goals, and measure outcomes of various aspects of personal, social, and community adjustment. There are 4 versions of the scale: for children (6-12); adolescents (13-17); adult mental health clients; developmentally disabled persons.

11306
Child Behavior Checklist. Achenbach, Thomas 1981
Subtests: Social Competence; Behavioral Problems
Descriptors: *Adolescents; Behavior Change; *Behavior Problems; *Behavior Rating Scales; Check Lists; *Children; *Interpersonal Competence
Identifiers: TIM (H)
Availability: Tests in Microfiche; Test Collection, Educational Testing Service, Princeton, NJ 08541
Target Audience: 4-16
Designed to record in standard format the behavioral problems and competencies of children aged 4 through 16, as reported by their parents or parent-surrogates. May either be self-administered or administered by an interviewer. Can also be readministered to assess reported changes in behavior over time or following treatment. Separate editions of the profile have been standardized for each sex for ages 4-5, 6-11, and, 12-16.

11310
Maine Scale of Paranoid and Nonparanoid Schizophrenia. Vojtisek, John E. 1976
Subtests: Paranoid Subscale; Nonparanoid Subscale
Descriptors: Adults; *Paranoid Behavior; *Patients; *Psychiatric Hospitals; Rating Scales; *Schizophrenia
Availability: Journal of Consulting and Clinical Psychology; v49 n3, p438-47 Jun 1981
Target Audience: 18-60
Notes: Items, 10
Used to distinguish between paranoid and nonparanoid schizophrenic patients. Paranoid items refer to delusions of grandeur, reference, persecution, grandeur, and overt expressions of hostility. Nonparanoid items refer to incongruous emotional responses, unusual postures, time disorientation, cognitive disorganization, and hallucinations.

11313
The Goodman Lock Box. Goodman, Joan F. 1979
Subtests: Competence; Organization; Aimless Actions
Descriptors: *Attention Control; Behavior Problems; Developmental Disabilities; *Goal Orientation; Individual Testing; Learning Disabilities; *Object Manipulation; Perceptual Motor Coordination; *Preschool Children; *Problem Solving
Availability: Stoelting Co.; 1350 S. Kostner Ave., Chicago, IL 60623
Target Audience: 2-5
Notes: Time, 6 approx.; Items, 10
Designed to evaluate preschool child's spontaneous approach to a novel, problematic situation. Primary clinical purpose is to identify preschool children who have difficulty controlling their attention and organizing their explorations and whose random and repetitive movements lack any apparent goal direction. Can also be used to identify children with perceptual-motor deficits. Recommended for use with children suspected of developmental delay, specific learning disability, or behavioral problem. Must always be included as part of a larger test battery because it supplements existing instruments. Except under unusual conditions, it is expected that the examiner will be a psychologist. Individually administered.

11343
Eyberg Child Behavior Inventory. Eyberg, Sheila 1980

Subtests: Frequency of Occurrence; Identification of a Problem
Descriptors: Adolescents; *Behavior Problems; *Behavior Rating Scales; *Children
Identifiers: ECBI
Availability: Sheila Eyberg; Dept. of Clinical Psychology, Box J-165 JHMHC, University of Florida, Gainesville, FL 32610
Target Audience: 2-16
Notes: Items, 36
Provides a list of most typical problem behaviors reported by parents of conduct problem children. Response format allows assessment of each item on 2 dimensions.

11349
Medida Espanola de Articulacion. San Ysidro School District, CA 1976
Descriptors: *Articulation (Speech); Bilingual Students; *Generative Phonology; Individual Testing; *Spanish; *Spanish Speaking; *Speech Tests; *Young Children
Identifiers: MEDA
Availability: San Ysidro School District; 4350 Otay Mesa Rd., San Ysidro, CA 92073
Target Audience: 4-9
Notes: Items, 54
Designed to test the phonological production of Spanish sounds. A tool to elicit the sounds to be examined. Useful for speech pathologists, linguists, and teachers of English as a Second Language. Should be administered by a native Spanish-speaker or by an English-speaker who has learned Spanish and is knowledgeable about Spanish phonological system. [Knowledge of the normal sequence of the Spanish phonological system is essential in identifying Spanish-speaking children with linguistic impairment or with linguistic abilities below expected level of development. Individually administered.]

11353
S-D Primary ESL Inventory. Sheety, John A. 1981
Subtests: Vocabulary-Nouns; Simple Comprehension and Understanding Directions; Verb Tense and Preposition Use; Spelling and Vocabulary; Sentence Structure; Reading Comprehension
Descriptors: *Achievement Tests; Elementary Education; *Elementary School Students; *English (Second Language); *Foreign Students; *Junior High School Students; *Language Skills; Language Tests; Reading Comprehension; *Second Language Learning; Student Placement
Availability: Stoelting Co.; 1350 S. Kostner Ave., Chicago, IL 60623
Grade Level: 1-8
Notes: Time, 35 approx.; Items, 60
Designed to measure foreign student's achievement in the English language. Provides a primary level of achievement based on learned material and identifies improvement within the prescribed context of the English language. Can be used as a tool for class placement. Inventory is available in 2 forms. Is primarily a power test, but working time should not exceed 35 minutes.

11358
AAMD Adaptive Behavior Scale. School Edition. Lambert, Nadine; Windmiller, Myra 1981
Subtests: Independent Functioning; Physical Development; Economic Activity; Language Development; Numbers and Time; Prevocational Activity; Self Direction; Responsibility; Socialization; Aggressiveness; Antisocial vs Social Behavior; Rebelliousness; Trustworthiness; Withdrawal vs Involvement; Mannerisms; Interpersonal Manners; Acceptability of Vocal Habits; Acceptability of Habits; Activity Level; Symptomatic Behavior; Use of Medications
Descriptors: *Adjustment (to Environment); Adolescents; *Behavior Rating Scales; Children; *Daily Living Skills; Developmental Disabilities; *Elementary School Students; Emotional Problems; Individual Testing; *Mild Mental Retardation; *Moderate Mental Retardation; *Secondary School Students; *Social Adjustment
Identifiers: ABS(SE)
Availability: Publishers Test Service; 2500 Garden Rd., Monterey, CA 93940
Target Audience: 3-16
Notes: Time, 45 approx.; Items, 95
Used to assess children whose adaptive behavior indicates possible mental retardation, emotional disturbance, or other learning handicaps. Part I is organized along developmental lines and is designed to evaluate a child's skills and habits in 9 behavior domains considered important to the development of personal independence in daily living. Part II, with 12 domains, provides measures of adaptive behavior related to personality and behavior disorders. Someone who has personal knowledge of the child, such as teachers, parents, school psychologists, speech therapists, social workers, can rate each item, or an interviewer can record the responses of someone who knows the child well.

11360
Inventory of Readiness Skills. Revised. Third Edition. Shelquist, Jack 1973
Subtests: Auditory Memory Sequential; Word Discrimination; Body Awareness; Locational and Directional Concepts; Color Discrimination; Visual-Motor Coordination; Visual Memory; Letter Perception; Letter Names
Descriptors: Concept Formation; Educationally Disadvantaged; *Grade 1; Individual Testing; *Kindergarten Children; Learning Disabilities; Mental Retardation; Perceptual Development; *Preschool Children; Preschool Education; Primary Education; Remedial Programs; *School Readiness Tests; *Student Placement
Availability: Educational Programmers; P.O. Box 332, Roseburg, OR 97470
Target Audience: 2-6
Notes: Time, 20 approx.; Items, 82
Individually administered test designed to assist the teacher in making a diagnostic assessment of a child's understanding of selected fundamental skills before a formalized instructional program is begun. Provides pretest and posttest measurement and can be used for preschool, kindergarten, first grade, Head Start, primary mentally retarded, and learning-disabled children, or for placement in remedial programs.

11366
Hannah Gardner Test of Verbal and Nonverbal Language Functioning. Hannah, Elaine P.; Gardner, Julie O. 1978
Subtests: Visual Perception; Conceptual Development; Auditory Perception; Linguistic Development; Verbal; Nonverbal
Descriptors: Auditory Perception; Bilingual Students; Concept Formation; *Language Handicaps; Nonverbal Ability; *Preschool Children; Preschool Education; *Screening Tests; Spanish; Verbal Ability; Visual Perception
Availability: Lingua Press; P.O. Box 293, Northridge, CA 91324
Target Audience: 3-5
Notes: Time, 35 approx.; Items, 42
A screening test designed for the purpose of identifying preschool children with a language deficit. Has a strong nonverbal component. To be used with children with little or no expressive language ability. Also available in Spanish and is best used with a child at least 60 percent Spanish-language functioning.

11367
Northwestern University Children's Perception of Speech. Elliott, Lois L.; Katz, Debra R. 1980
Descriptors: Adolescents; Adults; *Audiology; Children; *Hearing Impairments; *Phonemes; *Speech Evaluation; *Speech Tests
Identifiers: NUCHIPS
Availability: Auditec of St. Louis; 330 Selma Ave., St. Louis, MO 63119
Target Audience: 3-65
Developed as a speech discrimination test for use by clinical audiologists and appropriate for use with children and other patients having a language age as young as 3 years. May be administered to normal as well as hearing-impaired subjects. Individually administered.

11372
My Goal Record. Valett, Robert E. 1972
Descriptors: *Elementary School Students; Intermediate Grades; Junior High Schools; *Junior High School Students; *Objectives; *Special Education
Availability: Fearon Pitman; 6 Davis Dr., Belmont, CA 94002
Grade Level: 4-9
Notes: Items, 12
Shows special education students how to determine rewards and consequences and how to record their own progress toward attaining those goals.

11416
Project RUN: Early Education Assessment-Curriculum for the Severely-Profoundly Multiply Handicapped. North Mississippi Retardation Center, Oxford 1982
Subtests: Auditory Discrimination; Communication; Gross Motor; Visual Fine Motor
Descriptors: *Auditory Discrimination; Children; *Communication Skills; Individualized Education Programs; *Individual Testing; *Multiple Disabilities; *Psychomotor Skills; *Severe Disabilities; *Visual Learning
Availability: J.A. Preston Corporation; 60 Page Rd., Clifton, NJ 07012
Target Audience: Children
Used for planning and implementing an educational treatment program for those handicapped individuals within the 0-48 month developmental age range. Format is designed to bridge gap between assessment, IEP development, and program implementation. System lends itself to providing instructional alternatives for individual differences.

11434
Bipolar Psychological Inventory. Form A. Roe, Allan V.; And Others 1972
Subtests: Invalid-Valid; Lie-Honest; Defensive-Open; Psychic Pain-Psychic Comfort; Depression-Optimism; Self Degradation-Self Esteem; Dependence-Self Sufficiency; Unmotivated-Achieving; Social Withdrawal-Gregariousness; Family Discord-Family Harmony; Sexual Immaturity-Sexual Maturity; Social Deviancy-Social Conformity; Problem Index High-Problem Index Low; Impulsiveness-Self Control; Hostility-Kindness; Insensitivity-Empathy
Descriptors: Adults; Antisocial Behavior; Clinics; College Students; Higher Education; *Personality Assessment; *Personality Measures; Psychological Patterns
Availability: Diagnostic Specialists; 1170 N. 660 W., Orem, UT 84057
Target Audience: Adults
Notes: Time, 60 approx.; Items, 300
Designed for use with both normal and clinical populations. Primary purpose is to provide a fairly comprehensive personality assessment instrument that is useful in institutions, clinics, educational settings, industry, private work, or in any setting where personality functioning is of interest. Self-administered inventory, using true-false format. There are 2 forms, A and B. Form B does not have the sexual maturity-sexual immaturity scale but does have a Problem Index scale in its place.

11435
Bateria Woodcock de Proficiencia en el Idioma. Woodcock, Richard W. 1981
Subtests: Vocabulario sobre Dibujos; Antonimos Sinonimos; Analogias; Identificacion de Letras y Palabras; Analisis de Palabras; Comprehension de Textos; Dictado; Comprobacion; Punctuacion y Empleo de letras Mayuscalas; Ortografia; Concordancia
Descriptors: Adolescents; Adults; Children; Individual Testing; Language Dominance; *Language Proficiency; Older Adults; *Oral Language; *Reading Skills; *Spanish; *Spanish Speaking; *Writing Skills
Identifiers: WLPB; Woodcock Language Proficiency Battery
Availability: DLM Teaching Resources; P.O. Box 4000, One DLM Park, Allen, TX 75002
Target Audience: 3-80
Notes: Time, 45 approx.
Measures oral language, reading, and written language. Battery consists of 8 subtests all taken directly from the Woodcock Johnson Psycho-Educational Battery. Individually administered.

11438
EDS Diagnostic Skill Level Inventory for Advanced Reading. Henney, R. Lee 1979
Subtests: Word Meaning; Paragraph Meaning; Spelling; Language
Descriptors: *Adult Basic Education; Adults; *Diagnostic Tests; Grammar; Paragraphs; Predictive Measurement; *Pretests Posttests; *Reading Skills; Reading Tests; Semantics; Spelling
Availability: Educational Diagnostic Services; P.O. Box 347, Valparaiso, IN 46383
Target Audience: Adults
Notes: Items, 133
Developed to diagnose the strengths and weaknesses of adult students at the advanced level. Each inventory allows diagnosis of functional weaknesses within that academic discipline to concentrate on specific problems between the 5 to 8 equivalent grade levels. Can be used for predictive assessments for passing the new General Educational Development Tests (GED).

11439
EDS Diagnostic Skill Level Inventory for Advanced Mathematics. Henney, R. Lee 1979
Subtests: Mathematics Computation; Mathematical Concepts; Mathematics Application
Descriptors: *Adult Basic Education; Adults; Computation; *Diagnostic Tests; *Elementary School Mathematics; Mathematical Applications; Mathematical Concepts; Predictive Measurement; *Pretests Posttests; Problem Solving; Mathematics Tests
Availability: Educational Diagnostic Services; P.O. Box 347, Valparaiso, IN 46383
Target Audience: Adults
Notes: Items, 90
Designed to diagnose the strengths and weaknesses of adult students at the advanced level. Each inventory allows diagnosis of functional weaknesses within that aca-

demic discipline to concentrate on specific problems between the 5 to 8 equivalent grade levels. Can be used for predictive assessments for passing the new General Educational Development Tests (GED).

11440
EDS Diagnostic Skill Level Inventory for Writing Skills. Revised 1978. Henney, R. Lee 1978
Subtests: Grammatical Usage; Mechanics; Spelling; Sentence Structure; Diction and Style; Logic and Organization
Descriptors: *Adult Basic Education; Adults; Cohesion (Written Composition); *Diagnostic Tests; Grammar; Predictive Measurement; *Pretests Posttests; Punctuation; Sentence Structure; Spelling; Writing (Composition); *Writing Skills
Availability: Educational Diagnostic Services; P.O. Box 347, Valparaiso, IN 46383
Target Audience: Adults
Notes: Time, 60; Items, 65
Developed to diagnose the strengths and weaknesses of adult students at the high school level. Each inventory allows diagnosis of functional weaknesses within that academic discipline to concentrate on specific problems between the 9 to 12 equivalent grade levels. Can be used for predictive assessments for passing the new General Educational Development Tests (GED).

11441
EDS Diagnostic Skill Level Inventory for Mathematics. Henney, R. Lee 1975
Subtests: Basic Functions; Algebra; Geometry; Applications
Descriptors: *Adult Basic Education; Adults; Algebra; *Diagnostic Tests; Geometry; Mathematical Applications; Predictive Measurement; *Pretests Posttests; Problem Solving; *Secondary School Mathematics
Availability: Educational Diagnostic Services; P.O. Box 347, Valparaiso, IN 46383
Target Audience: Adults
Notes: Time, 60; Items, 40
Developed to diagnose the strengths and weaknesses of adult students at the high school level. Each inventory allows diagnosis of functional weaknesses within that academic discipline to concentrate on specific problems between the 9 to 12 equivalent grade levels. Can be used for predictive assessments for passing the new General Educational Development Tests (GED).

11442
EDS Diagnostic Skill Level Inventory for Science. Henney, R. Lee 1975
Subtests: Introduction; Physics; Chemistry; Geology; Astronomy; Biology; Physiology
Descriptors: *Adult Basic Education; Adults; Astronomy; *Biological Sciences; Biology; Chemistry; *Diagnostic Tests; Geology; *Physical Sciences; Physics; Physiology; Predictive Measurement; *Pretests Posttests; *Secondary School Science
Availability: Educational Diagnostic Services; P.O. Box 347, Valparaiso, IN 46383
Target Audience: Adults
Notes: Time, 60; Items, 40
Developed to diagnose the strengths and weaknesses of adult students at the high school level. Each inventory allows diagnosis of functional weaknesses within that academic discipline to concentrate on specific problems between the 9 to 12 equivalent grade levels. Can be used for predictive assessments for passing the new General Educational Development Tests (GED).

11443
EDS Diagnostic Skill Level Inventory for Social Studies. Henney, R. Lee 1975
Subtests: Introduction; U.S. History; Government; Economics; Geography; Behavioral Sciences
Descriptors: *Adult Basic Education; Adults; Behavioral Sciences; *Diagnostic Tests; Economics; Geography; Political Science; Predictive Measurement; *Pretests Posttests; *Social Studies; United States History
Availability: Educational Diagnostic Services; P.O. Box 347, Valparaiso, IN 46383
Target Audience: Adults
Notes: Time, 60; Items, 60
Developed to diagnose the strengths and weaknesses of adult students at the high school level. Each inventory allows diagnosis of functional weaknesses within that academic discipline to concentrate on specific problems between the 9 to 12 equivalent grade levels. Can be used for predictive assessments for passing the new General Educational Development Tests (GED).

11444
EDS Diagnostic Skill Level Inventory for Basic Mathematics. Henney, R. Lee 1979
Subtests: Mathematics Computation; Mathematics Concepts; Mathematics Application

Descriptors: *Adult Basic Education; Adults; Computation; *Diagnostic Tests; *Elementary School Mathematics; Mathematical Applications; Mathematical Concepts; Predictive Measurement; *Pretests Posttests; Problem Solving
Availability: Educational Diagnostic Services; P.O. Box 347, Valparaiso, IN 46383
Target Audience: Adults
Notes: Items, 90

Developed to diagnose the strengths and weaknesses of adult students at the basic level. Each inventory allows diagnosis of functional weaknesses within that academic discipline to concentrate on specific problems between the 0 to 4 equivalent grade levels. Can be used for predictive assessments for passing the new General Educational Development Tests (GED).

11445
EDS Diagnostic Skill Level Inventory for Basic Reading. Henney, R. Lee 1979
Subtests: Word Meaning; Paragraph Meaning; Spelling; Language
Descriptors: *Adult Basic Education; Adults; *Diagnostic Tests; Grammar; Paragraphs; Predictive Measurement; *Pretests Posttests; *Reading Skills; Reading Tests; Semantics; Spelling
Availability: Educational Diagnostic Services; P.O. Box 347, Valparaiso, IN 46383
Target Audience: Adults
Notes: Items, 88

Developed to diagnose the strengths and weaknesses of adult students at the basic level. Each inventory allows diagnosis of functional weaknesses within that academic discipline to concentrate on specific problems between the 0 to 4 equivalent grade levels. Can be used for predictive assessments for passing the new General Educational Development Tests (GED).

11446
EDS Diagnostic Skill Level Inventory for Pre-Reading. Henney, R. Lee 1980
Subtests: Pictures; Letters; Words
Descriptors: *Adult Basic Education; Adults; *Beginning Reading; *Diagnostic Tests; Letters (Alphabet); Pictorial Stimuli; Predictive Measurement; Prereading Experience; *Pretests Posttests; Word Recognition
Availability: Educational Diagnostic Services; P.O. Box 347, Valparaiso, IN 46383
Target Audience: Adults
Notes: Items, 72

Developed to diagnose the strengths and weaknesses of adult students at the prereading level. Each inventory allows diagnosis of functional weaknesses within that academic discipline to concentrate on specific problems at the equivalent grade levels. Can be used for predictive assessments for passing the new General Educational Development Tests (GED).

11447
Cuestionario Neuropsicologico para Ninos. Melendez, Fernando 1982
Descriptors: *Behavior Problems; Children; *Emotional Disturbances; *Minimal Brain Dysfunction; *Neurological Impairments; Questionnaires; *Spanish
Availability: Psychological Assessment Resources; P.O. Box 998, Odessa, FL 33556
Target Audience: Children
Notes: Items, 42

Spanish version. Part of an overall evaluation of children who are suspected of having brain dysfunction. Designed as a set of areas of inquiry and is of little value if used alone or if answered in simple yes or no fashion. The questionnaire primarily is useful as part of an extensive battery that should include neuropsychological testing and pediatric neurological examinations. Its goal is to attempt to make a 3-way differentiation between entities that generally show very similar signs and symptoms: childhood schizophrenia, abnormal electrical functions, and posterior fossa neoplasms. The questionnaire is short and does not, in and of itself, furnish any diagnostic answers. It should stimulate the pratitioner into thinking about the child in terms of possible alternative problems and to make appropriate referrals for further studies.

11448
Cuestionario Neuropsicologico de Adultos. Melendez, Fernando 1982
Subtests: General Health; Substance Abuse; Psychiatric Problems; General Neurological; Right Hemisphere; Left Hemisphere; Subcortical Cerebellar Spinal; Sensory Perceptual
Descriptors: Adults; *Emotional Disturbances; *Minimal Brain Dysfunction; *Neurological Impairments; Questionnaires; *Screening Tests; *Spanish
Availability: Psychological Assessment Resources; P.O. Box 998, Odessa, FL 33556
Target Audience: Adults
Notes: Time, 10 approx.; Items, 54

Spanish version. A screening device for neurological problems, which offers a rapid review of complaints, symptoms, and signs that may suggest underlying brain dysfunction or other organic conditions in people who have contacted a psychologist for assessment or treatment. A useful adjunct to a general intake interview, and the information gained from it often leads to appropriate referrals to medical practitioners or a decision to do more comprehensive neuropsychological testing. Neuropsychological testing often will clarify or confirm the symptoms endorsed. The questionnaire is also a reliable monitor in following the course of recovery (or decline) over a period of time. The questionnaire can be self-administered, but generally it is preferable if the practitioner asks the questions and makes an inquiry as he or she goes along.

11453
Caso Two Language Battery of Tests. Caso, Adolph 1981
Subtests: Phonetics; Comprehension Situations; Writing; Oral Proficiency
Descriptors: *Adults; *Criterion Referenced Tests; Culture Fair Tests; *Elementary School Students; Elementary Secondary Education; French; Italian; *Language Proficiency; *Language Tests; *Limited English Speaking; Portuguese; *Secondary School Students; Spanish Speaking; Student Placement; Tape Recordings; Vietnamese
Availability: Branden Press Publishers; 21 Station St., Box 843, Brookline Village, MA 02147
Grade Level: K-12
Notes: Time, 21

Used with limited English speaking or native language proficient students and adults to assess oral proficiency; written comprehension; initial letters and spelling; and reading, listening, and writing skills. Goals include determining extent of native and English language skills and proficiency, to establish current language dominance, to determine point of bilinguality, to help determine LAU categories, to help diagnose weak and strong language points, to help discover motor and/or other handicaps or disabilities, to evaluate rate of language acquisition and/or loss, to make available quick visual comparison between levels of proficiency of native language and English, to help make placement decisions, to help make program exit decisions. The Oral Proficiency section is optional. Test is available in English-Spanish, English-Italian, English-Portuguese, English-Vietnamese, and English-French.

11457
Inventario de Santa Clara de Tareas de Desenvolvimiento. Santa Clara Unified School District, CA 1978
Subtests: Coordinacion Muscular; Coordinacion Visual Muscular; Percepcion Visual; Memoria Visual; Discriminacion Auditiva; Memoria Auditiva; Desarrollo del Idioma; Desarrollo de Conceptos
Descriptors: Auditory Perception; Bilingual Education Programs; *Child Development; *Classroom Observation Techniques; Concept Formation; *Developmental Tasks; Language Acquisition; Limited English Speaking; Motor Development; Non English Speaking; Perceptual Motor Coordination; *Primary Education; Recall (Psychology); *Screening Tests; *Spanish; *Spanish Speaking; Visual Perception; *Young Children
Identifiers: Elementary Secondary Education Act Title I; Inventory of Developmental Tasks; ITD
Availability: Zweig Associates; 1711 McGaw Ave., Irvine, CA 92714
Grade Level: K-2
Target Audience: 5-7
Notes: Items, 60

Spanish version of the Santa Clara Inventory of Developmental Tasks which was developed as an ESEA Title I project. Consists of 60 tasks chosen because they represent milestones in children's development. The 60 tasks are arranged in 8 skill areas: motor coordination; visual motor performance; visual perception; visual memory; auditory perception; auditory memory; language development; conceptual development. The inventory can be used as a screening device; as a basis for parent conferences; and as a record of child's development to facilitate correct placement by student's next teacher.

11459
Early Detection Inventory. McGahan, F.E.; McGahan, Carolyn 1973
Subtests: Social Emotional Behavior; School Readiness Tasks; Motor Performance; Personal History
Descriptors: Biographical Inventories; Emotional Adjustment; Individual Testing; Interpersonal Competence; Nongraded Instructional Grouping; *Preschool Children; Primary Education; Psychomotor Skills; *School Readiness; *Screening Tests; *Underachievement
Identifiers: EDI
Availability: N.E.T. Educational Service Center; 3065 Clark Ln., Paris, TX 75460

Target Audience: 4-6

Developed to help school personnel evaluate a child's readiness for a successful school experience. Although intended primarily for preschool children, also is useful with children in transitional classes and ungraded primary classes. Is used as a screening device to facilitate detection of potential academic underachievers and for referral for diagnostic testing.

11466
The Blind Learning Aptitude Test. Newland, T. Ernest 1971
Descriptors: *Academic Aptitude; Adolescents; *Aptitude Tests; *Blindness; Children; *Individual Testing; *Manipulative Materials; Tactual Perception
Identifiers: BLAT
Availability: University of Illinois Press; 54 E. Gregory Dr., Box 5081, Station A, Champaign, IL 61820
Target Audience: 6-20
Notes: Time, 45 approx.; Items, 61

Test of learning potential designed specifically to meet the needs of blind children. Is a tactile discrimination test involving dots and lines similar to those used in Braille characters but not requiring the fine tactile discrimination needed for Braille reading.

11475
MKM Visual Letter Recognition Test. Wold, Robert M. 1970
Descriptors: Decoding (Reading); *Educational Diagnosis; Elementary Education; *Elementary School Students; Individual Testing; Learning Disabilities; Letters (Alphabet); *Phoneme Grapheme Correspondence; Phonemes; *Screening Tests; *Speech Tests
Availability: MKM, Inc.; 809 Kansas City St., Rapid City, SD 57701
Grade Level: 1-6

Designed to determine how child converts various symbols into their speech sounds. This ability is vital to the reading process. Letters of the alphabet should be presented to the child in random order. The following observations should be made during testing: posture, speed and accuracy, concentration and attention, and frustration level. The Phonic Mnemonic Method of Teaching Reading Manual of Instructions for use with this instrument is available from MKM, Inc.

11476
MKM Auditory Letter Recognition Test. Wold, Robert M. 1970
Subtests: Consonant Sounds; Consonant Blends; Consonant Digraphs; Long and Short Vowel Sounds; Vowel Combination Sounds
Descriptors: *Auditory Perception; Auditory Stimuli; *Educational Diagnosis; Elementary Education; *Elementary School Students; Individual Testing; Learning Disabilities; Phonemes; *Screening Tests; *Sensory Integration; Dictation
Availability: MKM, Inc.; 809 Kansas City St., Rapid City, SD 57701
Grade Level: 1-6

Designed to determine how children relate the things they hear to those they see and write. The lack of development of an efficient auditory-visual-motor integrative pattern is one of the most detrimental to efficient academic performance. Observations to be made during testing include: posture; speed; concentration, attention, and fatigue; vocalization or subvocalization; frustration level; and formation. The Phonic Mnemonic Method of Teaching Reading Manual of Instructions for use with this instrument is available from MKM, Inc.

11478
Language Inventory for Teachers. Cooper, Arlene; School, Beverly A. 1982
Subtests: Spoken Assessment; Written Assessment
Descriptors: Criterion Referenced Tests; *Diagnostic Tests; Elementary Education; *Elementary School Students; *Individualized Education Programs; Individual Testing; Language Patterns; *Language Tests; Remedial Instruction; Remedial Programs; *Speech Evaluation; *Writing Evaluation
Identifiers: IEP; LIT
Availability: Academic Therapy Publications; 20 Commercial Blvd., Novato, CA 94947
Grade Level: 1-6
Notes: Time, 60 approx.

Provides series of language tasks which can be used by special education teacher to assess status of students' spoken and written language, to prepare individualized educational plans (IEP), and to initiate a remedial program. Purpose of the inventory is to uncover incompetence at a specific task or a lack of basic language concept development. The checklist summarizes all information under 13 specific goals—5 for spoken language and 8 for written language. Individually administered. A review of the test by B. A. Blachman and S. I. James can be found in Reading Teacher; v37 n2 p176-79 Nov 1983. A review by Cecil R. Reynolds can be found in School Psychology Review; v12 n4 p482-83 Fall 1983.

11486
English Placement Test. Spaan, Mary; Strowe, Laura 1972
Descriptors: *College Students; *English (Second Language); Grammar; Higher Education; *Homogeneous Grouping; Listening Comprehension; Reading Comprehension; *Screening Tests; Second Language Learning; Sentences; *Student Placement; Vocabulary Skills
Availability: University of Michigan; English Language Institute, 2001 N. University Bldg., Ann Arbor, MI 48109
Grade Level: Higher Education
Notes: Time, 75 approx.; Items, 100

Nondiagnostic, objectively scored test designed to place English-as-a-Second-Language (ESL) students into homogeneous ability groups in intensive English language courses. Cutoff scores must be locally determined. Three parallel forms are available.

11487
Communicative Abilities in Daily Living: A Test of Functional Communication for Aphasic Adults. Holland, Audrey L. 1980
Descriptors: *Adults; *Aphasia; *Communication Disorders; Communication Skills; *Daily Living Skills; Individual Testing; *Speech Communication
Identifiers: CADL
Availability: University Park Press; 233 E. Redwood St., Baltimore, MD 21202
Target Audience: Adults
Notes: Time, 45 approx.; Items, 68

Used to assess functional communication skills of aphasic adults. Measures nonverbal behaviors as well as specific language forms and reveals how patient functions communicatively in everyday situations. Covers 9 general categories: reading, writing, and using numbers; speech acts; utilizing verbal and nonverbal context; role playing; sequenced and relationship-dependent communicative behavior; social conventions; divergences; nonverbal symbolic communication; deixis, humor, absurdity, metaphor. Individually administered.

11488
Functional Educability Index. McGahan, F.E.; McGahan, Carolyn 1969
Subtests: Personal Identity; Abstract Reasoning; Visual Perception; Immediate Recall; Naming of Objects; Mathematical Reasoning; Spelling; Figure Copying; Make a Picture of a Person
Descriptors: Abstract Reasoning; Adolescents; Adults; *Basic Skills; Children; *Cognitive Development; *Cognitive Measurement; *Curriculum Design; *Illiteracy; Individual Testing; Language Skills; Mathematical Concepts; *Perceptual Handicaps; Perceptual Motor Learning; Recall (Psychology); Spelling; Visual Perception
Availability: N.E.T. Educational Services; 3065 Clark Ln., Paris, TX 75460
Target Audience: 10-65
Notes: Time, 15 approx.

Individually administered instrument used to determine functional or operational academic level; to establish educational baseline of individuals; and to provide criteria for curriculum design. Originally developed to provide basic criteria for teachers to use in making judgments relative to functional educational level of illiterate adults. Later extended to use with students from upper elementary grades through high school. Instruments probe 6 basic areas necessary to the learning process. It is not intended for IQ assessment.

11489
Indice de Funcion Educativa. McGahan, F.E.; McGahan, Carolyn 1969
Subtests: Identidad Personal; Razonamiento Abstracto; Percepcion Visual; Recordatario Inmediato; Nombramiento de Objectos; Razonamiento Matematico; Deletreo; Reproducion de Figuras; Dibuje la Imagen de Una Persona
Descriptors: Abstract Reasoning; Adolescents; Adults; *Basic Skills; Children; *Cognitive Development; *Cognitive Measurement; *Curriculum Design; *Illiteracy; Individual Testing; Language Skills; Mathematical Concepts; *Perceptual Handicaps; Perceptual Motor Learning; Recall (Psychology); *Spanish; Spelling; Visual Perception
Availability: N.E.T. Educational Services; 3065 Clark Ln., Paris, TX 75460
Target Audience: 10-65
Notes: Time, 15 approx.

Individually administered instrument used to determine functional or operational academic level; to establish educational baseline of individuals; and to provide criteria for curriculum design. Originally developed to provide basic criteria for teachers to use in making judgments relative to functional educational level of illiterate adults. Later extended to use with students from upper elementary grades through high school. Instruments probe 6 basic areas necessary to the learning process. It is not intended for IQ assessment.

11491
Merrill-Demos D D Scale. Weijola, Merrill J.; Demos, George D.
Descriptors: *Attitude Measures; Community; *Delinquency; *Drug Abuse; Elementary Education; *Elementary School Students; Identification; Junior High Schools; *Junior High School Students; Police; *School Attitudes; Self Evaluation (Individuals); Teachers
Identifiers: TPSC Scale
Availability: Sheridan Psychological Services; P.O. Box 6101, Orange, CA 92667
Grade Level: 3-9
Notes: Time, 30; Items, 31

Self-administered attitude scale designed to determine whether the student understands and accepts teachers, police, school, and community. Used to identify potential or actual drug abuse and delinquent behavior.

11492
Measurement of Language Development. Melnick, Carol R. 1975
Subtests: Primary Verbs; Personal Pronouns; Negatives; Indefinite Pronouns; Interrogatives; Wh Questions; Secondary Verbs; Conjunctions
Descriptors: Achievement Gains; Emotional Disturbances; *Expressive Language; Hearing Impairments; *Language Handicaps; *Language Tests; Mental Retardation; *Receptive Language; Speech Therapy; Young Children
Identifiers: Language Delayed; MLD; Presentence Speech
Availability: Stoelting Co.; 1350 S. Kostner Ave., Chicago, IL 60623
Target Audience: 3-7
Notes: Items, 186

Developed specifically to serve as an accountability tool to enable clinicians to measure objectively receptive-expressive language gains over the course of a therapy program. It is not intended as a screening or diagnostic language test. May be used with a variety of language-impaired children, including presentence level children and those language delayed with normal intelligence, emotionally retarded, hearing impaired, and emotionally disturbed.

11521
Language Facility Test. Dailey, John T. 1977
Descriptors: *Adolescents; Bilingual Students; *Children; Deafness; Elementary Secondary Education; Individual Testing; *Language Acquisition; *Language Dominance; *Language Tests; Oral Language; *Preschool Children; Preschool Education; Speech Skills
Availability: Allington Corp.; P.O. Box 125, Remington, VA 22734
Target Audience: 3-15
Notes: Time, 10; Items, 12

Measures ability to use oral language independent of vocabulary information, pronunciation, and grammar. May be administered in Spanish, sign language, or other languages or dialects and scored by same basic scale and criteria. Particularly valuable with individuals whose family language experiences have been atypical. Test plates have copyright date of 1965.

11524
Test de g: Libre de Cultura. Escala 2, Forma A. Cattell, Raymond B.; Cattell, A. K. S. 1957
Subtests: Series; Classifications; Matrices; Conditions (Topology)
Descriptors: Adolescents; Adults; Children; *Culture Fair Tests; Individual Testing; Intelligence; *Intelligence Tests; *Nonverbal Tests; *Spanish; Spanish Speaking; Spatial Ability
Identifiers: Culture Fair Intelligence Test
Availability: Institute for Personality and Ability Testing; P.O. Box 188, Champaign, IL 61820
Target Audience: 8-64
Notes: Time, 13 approx.; Items, 46

Measures individual intelligence in a manner designed to reduce, as much as possible, the influence of verbal fluency, cultural climate, and educational level. Scale 2 may be group administered. Consists of 4 subtests involving different perceptual tasks. Spanish edition includes translations of the instructions, test booklets, and answer sheets. Scale 2 can appropriately be used with children as young as 8 years and with older children and adults. Scale 2 is appropriate for majority of subjects.

11532
Haptic Visual Discrimination Test. McCarron, Lawrence T.; Dial, Jack G. 1979
Subtests: Shape; Size; Texture; Configuration
Descriptors: Adolescents; Adults; Children; Deafness; Developmental Disabilities; *Diagnostic Tests; Neurological Impairments; Older Adults; Psychopathology; *Sensory Integration; *Tactual Perception; *Tactual Visual Tests; *Visual Discrimination
Identifiers: HVDT; McCarron Dial Work Evaluation System; MDWES
Availability: Common Market Press; 2880 LBJ Fwy., Ste. 255, Dallas, TX 75234
Target Audience: 3-90
Notes: Time, 15 approx.; Items, 48

Used to assess haptic-visual discrimination skills based on neuropsychological theory. Specifically designed to require skills in tactile sensitivity, spatial synthesis, and the ability to integrate the elements of an object into a unified whole. Useful in identifying and describing children and adults with specific developmental disabilities, severe psychopathological conditions, and cerebral dysfunctions. Is also an integral part of the McCarron-Dial Work Evaluation System (TC011533). Also found effective with deaf persons where pantomime or sign instructions can be given. The entire test for one hand can be completed in 15 minutes.

11533
McCarron-Dial Work Evaluation System. Evaluation of the Mentally Disabled—A Systematic Approach. McCarron, Lawrence T.; Dial, Jack G. 1976
Subtests: Verbal-Cognitive; Sensory; Motor; Emotional; Integration-Coping; Work Competency
Descriptors: Adjustment (to Environment); Adults; Cognitive Ability; Emotional Development; *Job Performance; *Mental Retardation; Perceptual Motor Learning; *Predictive Measurement; Psychological Patterns; *Standardized Tests
Identifiers: Haptic Visual Discrimination Test; HVDT; MDWES
Availability: Common Market Press; 2880 LBJ Fwy., Ste. 255, Dallas, TX 75234
Target Audience: Adults

Developed as a means of predicting vocational competency of mentally disabled individuals. Five basic predictor factors, which are considered essential for effective performance in a work environment, are assessed with specific tests. Factors and tests are Verbal-Cognitive (Wechster Adult Intelligence Scale or Stanford Binet Intelligence Scale and Peabody Picture Vocabulary Test); Sensory (Bender Visual Motor Gestalt Test and Haptic Visual Discrimination Test); Motor (McCarron Assessment of Neuromuscular Development: Fine and Gross Motor Abilities); Emotional (Observational Emotional Inventory); Integration-Coping (Behavior Rating Scale). System can be used to determine vocational functioning of mentally disabled individuals within the following areas: day care, work activities, extended shelter employment, transitional sheltered employment, community employment.

11534
McCarron Assessment of Neuromuscular Development. McCarron, Lawrence T. 1976
Subtests: Beads in Box; Beads on Rod; Finger Tapping; Nut and Bolt; Rod Slide; Hand Strength; Finger Nose Finger; Jumping; Heel Toe Walk; Standing on One Foot
Descriptors: Adolescents; Adults; Child Development; Children; Early Childhood Education; Mental Disorders; Neurological Impairments; *Performance Tests; *Psychomotor Skills; Screening Tests; Vocational Evaluation
Identifiers: *Fine Motor Skills; *Gross Motor Skills; MAND
Availability: McCarron Dial Systems; P.O. Box 45628, Dallas, TX 75245
Target Audience: 3-64

Designed as a standardized and quantitative procedure for assessing fine and gross motor abilities. Procedures were developed to provide developmental norms on a selected sample of gross and fine motor skills for normal individuals ranging from 3.5 years to young adult; as a component of an early childhood education screening procedure to identify children with potential developmental problems; as a clinical instrument to describe motor deficits of children with neurological dysfunctions; as a component of a work evaluation system to predict work potential of mentally disabled adults; as a research instrument to describe changes in motor behaviors associated with various physiological pathologies.

11535
Initial Communication Processes. Schery, Terris; Wilcoxen, Anne Glover 1982
Subtests: Auditory Skills; Visual Skills; Manual Fine Motor Skills; Oral Vocal Motor Skills; Object Play Skills-Manipulative; Object Play Skills-Symbolic; Problem Solving Skills; Affective Development; Communication Skills-Comprehension; Communication Skills-Expression

Descriptors: Adolescents; Affective Behavior; Auditory Evaluation; Autism; Children; *Communication Skills; *Disabilities; *Educational Objectives; Expressive Language; Individual Testing; *Item Banks; *Mental Retardation; *Observation; Problem Solving; Psychomotor Skills; Receptive Language; *Screening Tests; Speech Skills; Visual Discrimination; Young Adults
Identifiers: Education for All Handicapped Children Act; ICP
Availability: Publishers Test Service; 2500 Garden Rd., Del Monte Research Park, Monterey, CA 93940
Target Audience: 1-22

Assesses early communication processes for at-risk children and handicapped students functioning below the developmental level of 3 years. Uses observational scales for screening and then allows appropriate choice from among a bank of 250 instructional objectives to be used in improving students' skills. Appropriate for use in programs with severely-profoundly retarded, trainable mentally retarded, multiply handicapped, autistic, orthopedically handicapped, deaf or hard-of-hearing, and visually handicapped persons.

11536
Southern California Motor Accuracy Test. Revised 1980. Ayres, A. Jean 1980
Descriptors: Children; *Diagnostic Tests; *Neurological Impairments; *Perceptual Handicaps; *Perceptual Motor Coordination; Psychomotor Skills; *Sensory Integration
Identifiers: SCMAT
Availability: Western Psychological Services; 12031 Wilshire Blvd., Los Angeles, CA 90025
Target Audience: 4-8
Notes: Time, 6; Items, 1

Measures degree of, and changes in, sensorimotor integration of upper extremities of neurologically atypical children. Diagnoses perceptual motor dysfunctions. Useful with both left hands and right hands of children. Child traces a line.

11539
Receptive Expressive Language Assessment for the Visually Impaired 0-6. Anderson, Gloria M.; Smith, Annette M. 1979
Subtests: Receptive Language; Expressive Language
Descriptors: *Diagnostic Tests; *Expressive Language; *Receptive Language; *Visual Impairments; Young Children
Identifiers: Experimental Tests; Oral Tests; RELA
Availability: Ingham Intermediate School District; 2630 W. Howell Rd., Mason, MI 48854
Target Audience: 0-6

An experimental diagnostic test for use with visually handicapped preschoolers. Child uses a variety of familiar objects to respond to statements.

11554
Inventario De Associaciones. Bruce, Martin M. 1968
Subtests: Total Score; Block Score; Juvenility; Psychotic Responses; Depressed-Optimistic; Hysteric-Non-Hysteric; Withdrawal-Sociable; Paranoid-Naive; Rigid-Flexible; Schizophrenic-Objective; Impulsive-Restrained; Sociopathic-Empathetic; Psychosomapathic-Physical Contentment; Anxious-Relaxed
Descriptors: Adults; Affective Measures; *Association Measures; *Diagnostic Tests; Emotional Adjustment; *Personality Assessment; *Psychological Evaluation; *Psychological Patterns; Spanish; *Spanish Speaking
Identifiers: AAI; Kent Rosanoff Free Association Test
Availability: Martin M. Bruce, Publishers; 50 Larchmont Rd., Box 248, Larchmont, NY 10538
Target Audience: Adults
Notes: Time, 10 approx.; Items, 100

Modification of the Kent-Rosanoff Free Association Test. Designed to provide an indication of the respondent's personality and overall adjustment in terms of deviant thinking, extent of juvenile ideation, etc. The respondent circles which of 5 given words he or she associates with the item word. Untimed. Available in 2 English language forms (see TC003213) and in Spanish.

11573
The Minnesota Percepto-Diagnostic Test. 1982 Revision. Fuller, Gerald B. 1982
Descriptors: Adolescents; Adults; Behavior Problems; Children; *Diagnostic Tests; Individual Testing; Learning Disabilities; Neurological Impairments; Older Adults; *Perceptual Motor Coordination; Personality Problems; *Psychological Testing; Reading Difficulties; *Visual Measures; *Visual Perception
Identifiers: MPD

Availability: Clinical Psychology Publishing; 4 Conant Square, Brandon, VT 05733
Target Audience: 5-70
Notes: Items, 6

Used to assess and differentiate visual-motor performance in various clinical and educational groups of children and adults. Assesses brain dysfunction in children and adults and reading disabilities in children. When used with adult psychiatric populations, differentiates among normals, and those with personality disorders, psychotic or organic disorders. Also classifies learning disabilities as visual, auditory, or mixed and divides behavioral problems of children into normal, emotionally disturbed, schizophrenic, or organic. Recommended that MDP be included as part of a psychological or educational battery and that no single test is completely adequate for individual diagnosis.

11574
Ann Arbor Learning Inventory, Skill Level B. Bullock, Waneta B.; Meister, Barbara 1977
Subtests: Visual Discrimination Skills; Visual Motor Coordination Skills; Sequential Memory Skills; Aural Skills; Comprehension Skills
Descriptors: Auditory Discrimination; Criterion Referenced Tests; *Diagnostic Teaching; *Diagnostic Tests; Elementary Education; *Elementary School Students; *Learning Disabilities; *Remedial Instruction; Screening Tests; Visual Discrimination
Availability: Ann Arbor Publishers; P.O. Box 7249, Naples, FL 33940
Grade Level: 2-4

Designed to evaluate students test responses in skill areas of visual discrimination, visual motor coordination, sequential memory, auditory, and comprehension. Used to identify students with learning disabilities and provide a remediation program for them.

11576
Toronto Tests of Receptive Vocabulary. Toronto, Allen S. 1977
Descriptors: Children; *Mexican Americans; Pictorial Stimuli; *Receptive Language; *Screening Tests; *Spanish Speaking; *Vocabulary
Identifiers: English Speaking; *Oral Tests
Availability: National Educational Laboratory Publishers; 813 Airport Blvd., Austin, TX 78702
Target Audience: 4-10
Notes: Items, 40

Designed to identify English- and Spanish-speaking Mexican-American children whose performance in identifying orally presented vocabulary words is significantly below their peers. Children point to a picture in response to orally presented words.

11578
The Communication Screen. Striffler, Nancy; Willig, Sharon 1981
Descriptors: Child Language; Comprehension; Delayed Speech; *Expressive Language; *Language Handicaps; *Preschool Children; *Receptive Language; *Screening Tests
Availability: Communication Skill Builders; 3130 N. Dodge Blvd., P.O. Box 42050, Tucson, AZ 85733
Target Audience: 2-5
Notes: Items, 25

Screening tool designed to assist in early identification of speech- or language-delayed children for further evaluation. May be administered by professionals or paraprofessionals in any field associated with preschool children. Covers speech, language, language comprehension, language expression.

11579
Screening Test of Adolescent Language. Prather, Elizabeth M.; And Others 1980
Subtests: Vocabulary; Auditory Memory Span; Language Processing; Proverb Explanation
Descriptors: Auditory Stimuli; Comprehension; *Expressive Language; Individual Testing; *Language Handicaps; Language Processing; Memory; *Receptive Language; *Screening Tests; Secondary Education; *Secondary School Students; Vocabulary
Identifiers: STAL
Availability: University of Washington Press; Seattle, WA 98105
Grade Level: 7-12
Notes: Time, 7 approx.; Items, 23

Screening instrument for language disorders and linguistic development of junior and senior high school students. Test is individually administered to identify those students who may warrant further diagnostic evaluation. However, test results should not be interpreted as a comprehensive diagnostic evaluation of linguistic development. Instrument measures both receptive and expressive language through 4 subtests.

11587
Visual Functioning Assessment Tool. Costello, Kathleen Byrnes; And Others 1980
Descriptors: Adolescents; Adults; Children; Depth Perception; Eye Fixations; Eye Hand Coordination; Eye Movements; Informal Assessment; *Low Vision Aids; *Severe Disabilities; Spatial Ability; *Vision Tests; Visual Acuity; *Visual Discrimination; Visually Handicapped Mobility; *Visual Perception
Identifiers: VFAT; Visual Memory; Visual Motor Functioning
Availability: Stoelting Co.; 1350 S. Kostner Ave., Chicago, IL 60623
Target Audience: 1-65
Notes: Items, 200

Informal assessment of visual functioning for use with individuals with low vision. Administered by an eye specialist or a teacher of the visually impaired people. Assesses eye appearance, basic responses, fixation tracking, saccadic movement, visual acuity, visual field, depth perception, eye-hand and eye-foot coordination, visual imitation and memory, visual discrimination, visual perception, concept of self and others in space, pictures, visual environment, and mobility. May be used with handicapped subjects.

11596
Marysville Oral Language Assessment. Thonis, Eleanor 1981
Subtests: Receptive Language; Expressive Language
Descriptors: Bilingual Students; *Elementary School Students; Elementary Secondary Education; *English (Second Language); Expressive Language; *Language Proficiency; Morphology (Languages); Phonology; Rating Scales; Receptive Language; *Secondary School Students; Semantics; *Spanish Speaking; Vocabulary
Identifiers: MOLA
Availability: Marysville Joint Unified School District; 1919 B St., Marysville, CA 95901
Grade Level: 1-12
Notes: Items, 8

Rating scale of non-native speakers' competency in using English. Covers phonology, morphology, vocabulary, and semantics. For use in planning instruction. A Spanish-language form is available.

11597
Observational Emotional Inventory. McCarron-Dial Systems, Dallas, TX 1976
Subtests: Neuropsychological-Impulsivity; Anxiety; Depression-Withdrawal; Socialization; Self Concept
Descriptors: Adults; *Affective Behavior; *Anxiety; *Behavior Problems; *Conceptual Tempo; *Depression (Psychology); *Emotional Problems; *Interpersonal Competence; *Mental Disorders; *Observation; *Self Concept; *Sheltered Workshops; *Vocational Adjustment
Availability: McCarron-Dial Systems; P.O. Box 45628, Dallas, TX 75245
Target Audience: Adults
Notes: Time, 120; Items, 50

Record of observed dysfunctional behavior over a 5-day period. Behavior that causes social, emotional, or work dysfunction during a 2-hour observation period is scored one point for each day that the behavior is observed. For use with mentally disabled subjects in a sheltered workshop. Dial Behavior Rating Scale (TC011598) is filled out following completion of this observation inventory.

11598
Dial Behavioral Rating Scale. Dial, Jack G. 1973
Descriptors: Adults; *Behavior Problems; *Daily Living Skills; Interpersonal Competence; *Mental Disorders; Rating Scales; *Sheltered Workshops; *Vocational Adjustment
Availability: McCarron-Dial Systems; P.O. Box 45628, Dallas, TX 75245
Target Audience: Adults
Notes: Items, 13

Answers questions regarding personal, social, and work adjustment behaviors of mentally disabled adults following observations made via the Observational Emotional Inventory (TC 011 597).

11600
Test of Minimal Articulation Competence. Secord, Wayne 1981
Descriptors: Adolescents; Adults; *Articulation (Speech); *Articulation Impairments; Children; *Diagnostic Tests; Individual Testing; *Speech Tests
Identifiers: TMAC
Availability: The Psychological Corporation; 555 Academic Ct., San Antonio, TX 78204-0952
Target Audience: 5-65
Notes: Time, 10

Used to assess the severity of articulation disorders either for program placement or termination. Uses a picture identification format which allows evaluation of articulation of 24 consonant phonemes; frequently occurring s, r, and l blends; and 12 vowels, 4 diphthongs, and variations of vocalic r. Provides 2 measures: Developmental Articulation Index expressed in degree of severity and a Treatment Index which combines error type, stimulability, and frequency of occurrence values. The Treatment Index is not used to compare different children but helps the clinician target the most trainable phonemes for remediation.

11602
Fuld Object Memory Evaluation. Fuld, Paula Altman 1977
Subtests: Storage; Retrieval; Consistent Retrieval; Recall Failure-Ineffective Reminders
Descriptors: Blindness; Children; *Cognitive Measurement; Deafness; *Learning; *Memory; *Older Adults; Recall (Psychology); Schizophrenia
Availability: Stoelting Co.; 1350 S. Kostner Ave., Chicago, IL 60623
Target Audience: 70-90

Allows evaluation of memory and learning of older adults under conditions which ensure attention and minimize anxiety. Also measures ability to retrieve words rapidly from familiar semantic categories, used for dementia screening. Test has also proved easy to give to young school-age children and to blind and deaf persons.

11603
Bieger Test of Visual Discrimination. Bieger, Elaine 1982
Subtests: Letters-Larger Contrasts; Letters-Lesser Contrasts; Letters-Almost Identical; Words-Larger Contrasts; Words-Lesser Contrasts; Words-Orientation Transformation; Words-Sequencing
Descriptors: *Diagnostic Tests; Elementary Education; *Elementary School Students; *Reading Difficulties; *Visual Discrimination
Availability: Stoelting Co.; 1350 S. Kostner Ave., Chicago, IL 60623
Grade Level: 1-6
Notes: Time, 35; Items, 152

For use with nonreaders or poor readers to determine whether they have a problem with visual discrimination of letters and words. Identifies levels of mastery in discrimination between letters and words with larger and lesser contrasts and those that are almost identical.

11619
Bench Mark Measures. Cox, Aylett R. 1977
Subtests: Alphabet; Reading; Handwriting; Spelling
Descriptors: Achievement Tests; Elementary Education; *Elementary School Students; *Handwriting; Individual Testing; Language Arts; *Letters (Alphabet); *Mastery Tests; *Reading Ability; *Remedial Programs; *Spelling
Availability: Educators Publishing Service; 75 Moulton St., Cambridge, MA 02138
Grade Level: K-8
Notes: Time, 60 approx.

Three levels of mastery tests for evaluation of secondary language skills. Follows the sequence of the Alphabetic Phonics curriculum, a multiple sensory curriculum for teaching phonics and the structure of the language, based on Orton-Gillingham approach. The curriculum was developed in the Language Research and Training Laboratory of the Texas Scottish Rite Hospital for its remedial language training program. Measures are not restricted to any particular grade level but can serve as a diagnostic tool, as a measure of progress in remediation, or as a criterion for ending remediation. Each level takes between 30 and 60 minutes to administer. The alphabet and reading tests must be individually administered; handwriting and spelling tests may be administered to groups.

11623
Michigan Test of Aural Comprehension. Upshur, John; And Others 1969
Descriptors: *Achievement Tests; Auditory Stimuli; College Students; *English (Second Language); *Graduate Students; Higher Education; *Listening Comprehension; Multiple Choice Tests; Non English Speaking
Availability: English Language Institute; University of Michigan, Ann Arbor, MI 48109
Grade Level: 13-17
Notes: Time, 25; Items, 90

Designed to measure understanding of spoken English. For non-native speakers who wish to pursue academic careers in universities and colleges where English is spoken. Uses multiple-choice format. Subject selects the currect phrase in response to a spoken statement.

11624
Test of Aural Comprehension. Lado, Robert 1957
Descriptors: *Achievement Tests; Auditory Stimuli; *College Students; *English (Second Language); *Graduate Students; Higher Education; *Listening Comprehension; Multiple Choice Tests; Non English Speaking
Availability: English Language Institute; University of Michigan, Ann Arbor, MI 48109
Grade Level: 13-17
Notes: Time, 40; Items, 60

Designed to measure understanding of spoken English. For non-native speakers who wish to pursue academic careers in universities and colleges where English is spoken. Tests students' understanding of sentences and paragraphs constructed to bring out comprehension problems. Subject selects the correct picture.

11625
Michigan Test of English Language Proficiency. English Language Institute, Ann Arbor, MI 1968
Subtests: Grammar; Vocabulary; Reading Comprehension
Descriptors: *Achievement Tests; *English (Second Language); *Graduate Students; Grammar; Higher Education; *Language Proficiency; Language Tests; Reading Comprehension; *Undergraduate Students; Vocabulary
Identifiers: Test Batteries
Availability: English Language Institute; 2001 N. University Bldg., University of Michigan, Ann Arbor, MI 48109
Grade Level: 13-16
Notes: Time, 75 approx.; Items, 100

Designed as part of battery to predict academic success of non-native speakers of English in an English-language college or university. Michigan battery includes impromptu 30-minute written theme on assigned topic and a test of aural comprehension. Equivalent forms A,B,D,E,F,G, and H are available for Michigan Test of English Language Proficiency. Should not be used as a placement test.

11696
Stanford Achievement Test: 7th Edition, Primary 2. Gardner, Eric F.; And Others 1982
Subtests: Word Study Skills; Word Reading; Reading Comprehension; Vocabulary; Listening Comprehension; Spelling; Concepts of Number; Mathematics Computation; Mathematics Applications; Environment
Descriptors: *Academic Achievement; *Achievement Tests; Braille; Computation; Culture Fair Tests; Elementary School Students; *Grade 2; *Grade 3; Large Type Materials; Listening Comprehension; Mathematical Applications; Mathematics Achievement; Number Concepts; Physical Environment; Primary Education; Reading Comprehension; Social Environment; Spelling; Visual Impairments; Vocabulary Skills; Word Recognition; Word Study Skills
Identifiers: Elementary Secondary Education Act Title I; Stanford Achievement Test Series; Test Batteries
Availability: The Psychological Corporation; 555 Academic Ct., San Antonio, TX 78204-0952
Grade Level: 2-3
Notes: Time, 225 approx.; Items, 351

Designed to measure important learning outcomes of school curriculum. Provides measures of these outcomes for use in instructional improvement and evaluation of student progress. Out-of-level testing is possible where difficulty level and curriculum content make it appropriate. Meets requirements of special programs, such as Title I. Primary 2 battery includes measures of reading, listening, spelling, mathematics, and understanding of the environment. Concepts and skills assessed in each content area are those ordinarily taught during the second half of grade 2 and in grade 3. Two forms are available. Each subtest may be given at a separate sitting; no more than 2 subtests may be administered at one sitting. Available in large-type print or Braille for visually impaired students from American Printing House for the Blind, 1839 Frankfort Ave., Louisville, KY 40206.

11697
Stanford Achievement Test: 7th Edition, Primary 3. Gardner, Eric F.; And Others 1982
Subtests: Word Study Skills; Reading Comprehension; Vocabulary; Listening Comprehension; Spelling; Concepts of Number; Mathematics Computation; Mathematics Applications; Science; Social Science
Descriptors: *Academic Achievement; *Achievement Tests; Braille; Computation; Culture Fair Tests; Elementary Education; Elementary School Science; Elementary School Students; *Grade 3; *Grade 4; Language Skills; Large Type Materials; Listening Comprehension; Mathematical Applications; Mathematics Achievement; Number Concepts; Reading Comprehension; Social Sciences; Spelling; Visual Impairments; Vocabulary Skills; Word Study Skills
Identifiers: Elementary Secondary Education Act Title I; Stanford Achievement Test Series; Test Batteries
Availability: The Psychological Corporation; 555 Academic Ct., San Antonio, TX 78204-0952
Grade Level: 3-4
Notes: Time, 295 approx.; Items, 476

Designed to measure important learning outcomes of school curriculum. Provides measures of these outcomes for use in instructional improvement and evaluation of student progress. Out-of-level testing is possible where difficulty level and curriculum content make it appropriate. Meets requirements of special programs, such as Title I. Primary 3 battery includes measures of reading, listening, spelling, language, mathematics, science, and social science. Concepts and skills assessed in each content area are those ordinarily taught during the second half of grade 3 and in grade 4. Two forms are available. Each subtest may be administered at a separate sitting; no more than 2 subtests may be administered at one sitting. The total basic battery consists of 388 items and takes approximately 245 minutes to complete. Available in large-type print or Braille for visually impaired students from American Printing House for the Blind, 1839 Frankfort Ave., Louisville, KY 40206.

11698
Stanford Achievement Test: 7th Edition, Intermediate 1. Gardner, Eric F.; And Others 1982
Subtests: Word Study Skills; Reading Comprehension; Vocabulary; Listening Comprehension; Spelling; Language; Concepts of Number; Mathematics Computation; Mathematics Applications; Science; Social Science
Descriptors: *Academic Achievement; *Achievement Tests; Braille; Computation; Culture Fair Tests; Elementary School Science; *Elementary School Students; *Grade 4; *Grade 5; Intermediate Grades; Language Skills; Large Type Materials; Listening Comprehension; Mathematical Applications; Mathematics Achievement; Number Concepts; Reading Comprehension; Social Sciences; Spelling; Visual Impairments; Vocabulary Skills; Word Study Skills
Identifiers: Elementary Secondary Education Act Title I; Stanford Achievement Test Series; Test Batteries
Availability: The Psychological Corporation; 555 Academic Ct., San Antonio, TX 78204-0952
Grade Level: 4-5
Notes: Time, 315 approx.; Items, 527

Designed to measure important learning outcomes of school curriculum. Provides measures of these outcomes for use in instructional improvement and evaluation of student progress. Out-of-level testing is possible where difficulty level and curriculum content make it appropriate. Meets requirements of special programs, such as Title I. Intermediate 1 battery includes measures of reading, listening, spelling, language, mathematics, science, and social science. Concepts and skills assessed in each content area are those ordinarily taught during the second half of grade 4 and in grade 5. Two forms are available. Each subtest may be administered at a separate sitting; no more than 2 subtests should be administered at one sitting. The total basic battery contains 407 items and takes approximately 255 minutes to complete. Available in large-type print or Braille for visually impaired students from American Printing House for the Blind, 1839 Frankfort Ave., Louisville, KY 40206.

11699
Stanford Achievement Test: 7th Edition, Intermediate 2. Gardner, Eric F.; And Others 1982
Subtests: Word Study Skills; Reading Comprehension; Vocabulary; Listening Comprehension; Spelling; Concepts of Number; Mathematics Computation; Mathematics Applications; Science; Social Science
Descriptors: *Academic Achievement; *Achievement Tests; Braille; Computation; Culture Fair Tests; Elementary Education; Elementary School Science; *Elementary School Students; Language Skills; Large Type Materials; Mathematical Applications; Mathematics Achievement; Number Concepts; Reading Comprehension; Social Sciences; Spelling; Visual Impairments; Word Study Skills
Identifiers: Elementary Secondary Education Act Title I; Stanford Achievement Test Series; Test Batteries
Availability: The Psychological Corporation; 555 Academic Ct., San Antonio, TX 78204-0952
Grade Level: 5-7
Notes: Time, 315 approx.; Items, 537

Designed to measure important learning outcomes of school curriculum. Provides measures of these outcomes for use in instructional improvement and evaluation of student progress. Out-of-level testing is possible where difficulty level and curriculum content make it appropriate. Meets requirements of special programs, such as Title I. The Intermediate 2 battery includes measures of reading, listening, spelling, language, mathematics, science, and social science. Concepts and skills assessed in each content area are those ordinarily taught in the second half of grade 5 and during grades 6 and 7. Each subtest may be administered in a single setting; no more than 2 subtests should be given at one sitting. The total basic battery consists of 417 items and takes approximately 255 minutes to complete. Available in large-type print or Braille for visually impaired students from American Printing House for the Blind, 1839 Frankfort Ave., Louisville, KY 40206.

11700
Stanford Achievement Test: 7th Edition, Advanced Form. Gardner, Eric F.; And Others 1982
Subtests: Reading Comprehension; Vocabulary; Listening Comprehension; Spelling; Language; Concepts of Number; Mathematics Computation; Mathematics Applications; Science; Social Science
Descriptors: *Academic Achievement; *Achievement Tests; Braille; Computation; Culture Fair Tests; Junior High Schools; *Junior High School Students; Language Skills; Large Type Materials; Listening Comprehension; Mathematical Applications; Number Concepts; Reading Comprehension; Secondary School Science; Social Sciences; Spelling; Visual Impairments; Vocabulary Skills
Identifiers: Elementary Secondary Education Act Title I; Stanford Achievement Test Series; Test Batteries
Availability: The Psychological Corporation; 555 Academic Ct., San Antonio, TX 78204-0952
Grade Level: 7-9
Notes: Time, 280 approx.; Items, 487

Designed to measure important learning outcomes of school curriculum. Provides measures of these outcomes for use in instructional improvement and evaluation of student progress. Out-of-level testing is possible where difficulty level and curriculum content make it appropriate. Meets requirements of special programs, such as Title I. Advanced battery includes measures of reading, listening, spelling, language, mathematics, science, and social science. Concepts and skills assessed in each content area are those ordinarily taught during second half of grade 7 and in grades 8 and 9. Two forms are available. Each subtest may be administered at one sitting; no more than 2 subtests should be given at one sitting. The total basic battery consists of 367 items and takes 220 minutes approximately to complete. Available in large-type print or Braille for visually impaired students from American Printing House for the Blind, 1839 Frankfort Ave., Louisville, KY 40206.

11712
Program for the Acquisition of Language with the Severely Impaired. Owens, Robert E., Jr. 1982
Descriptors: Adolescents; Adults; Behavior Rating Scales; Children; *Communication Skills; *Diagnostic Tests; Informal Assessment; *Language Acquisition; *Language Handicaps; *Severe Disabilities; Speech Pathology
Identifiers: PALS
Availability: The Psychological Corporation; 555 Academic Ct., San Antonio, TX 78204-0952
Target Audience: 2-64

A program of assessment and training for severely language-impaired people. There are 3 assessment components in the program. The Caretaker Interview and Environmental Observation is used to record the caregiver's observations of the development level of the client's functioning and the communication strategies employed. The Diagnostic Interaction Survey (DIS) rates 10 client-caregiver behaviors and interactions which language-speech pathologists deem important. The Development Assessment Tool (DAT) includes an informally gathered speech sample and formal procedures corresponding to each training level. The purpose of the DAT is to determine the best level at which to begin training.

11714
Meadow/Kendall Social-Emotional Assessment Inventory for Deaf Students. Meadow, Kathryn P.; And Others 1980
Subtests: Social Adjustment; Self Image; Emotional Adjustment
Descriptors: Adolescents; *Behavior Rating Scales; Children; *Deafness; Elementary School Students; *Emotional Adjustment; Individualized Education Programs; Secondary School Students; *Self Concept; *Social Adjustment; Young Adults
Identifiers: Education for All Handicapped Children Act; Public Law 94 142; SEAI
Availability: OUTREACH; Pre-College Programs, Box 114, Gallaudet College, Washington, DC 20002
Target Audience: 7-21
Notes: Items, 59

Designed to be completed by teachers of deaf students or by other educational personnel closely associated with deaf students. Impetus for development of the scale was to conform to federal legislation which mandated development of individualized educational plans for handicapped

students and, therefore, required assessment of children's current status in every area of development which might be of importance to educational placement and programming.

11738
Creativity Assessment Packet. Williams, Frank 1980
Descriptors: *Creativity; Creativity Tests; *Divergent Thinking; *Elementary School Students; Elementary Secondary Education; Gifted; Rating Scales; *Screening Tests; *Secondary School Students; Self Evaluation (Individuals); Visual Measures
Identifiers: CAP; Guilfords Structure of Intellect; Structure of Intellect
Availability: D.O.K. Publishers; P.O. Box 605, E. Aurora, NY 14052
Grade Level: 3-12
Target Audience: 8-18

Initially developed to screen for gifted or talented students in schools providing federal, state, or local programs aimed at developing creative abilities. Is now available for measuring all children's creative potential. Packet consists of 2 group-administered tests plus a rating scale for parents and teachers of the same tested factors among children. The test of Divergent Thinking is a 12-item instrument which measures a combination of verbal, left brain abilities along with nonverbal, right brain visual perceptive abilities. It yields 4 scores based on Guilford's Structure of Intellect: fluency, flexibility, originality, and elaboration. The test of Divergent Feeling is a 50-item, multiple-choice instrument which evaluates how curious, imaginative, complex, and risk taking children think they are. It yields a total weighted raw score and 4 subscores. The Williams Scale is an observational checklist of 8 creativity factors measured by the tests. For each factor, the parent or teacher rates the child on 6 characteristics. There are also 4 open-ended items.

11755
Multilevel Informal Language Inventory. Goldsworthy, Candace; Secord, Wayne 1982
Descriptors: Children; *Informal Assessment; Language Acquisition; *Language Handicaps; *Oral Language; Remedial Instruction; *Semantics; Speech Pathology; *Syntax
Identifiers: *Language Sampling; MILI
Availability: The Psychological Corporation; 555 Academic Ct., San Antonio, TX 78204-0952
Target Audience: 4-12
Notes: Time, 45 approx.

Developed as an informal assessment tool to measure a child's level of oral language functioning, specifically in the production of critical semantic relations and syntactic constructions. To be used with children suspected of having oral language production problems. Intended users are practicing clinicians in speech-language pathology and specialists in learning disabilities. The assessment is designed to supplement data gathered from other assessment methods. Primary objective is to help direct the course of language intervention programs.

11756
Adaptive Behavior Inventory for Children. Mercer, Jane R.; Lewis, June F. 1977
Subtests: Family; Community; Peer Relations; Nonacademic School Roles; Earner Consumer; Self Maintenance
Descriptors: *Adjustment (to Environment); Children; Child Responsibility; Community Involvement; Culture Fair Tests; Extracurricular Activities; Family Relationship; *Interviews; Maturity (Individuals); Peer Relationship; Spanish; Spanish Speaking
Identifiers: ABIC; SOMPA; *System of Multicultural Pluralistic Assessment
Availability: The Psychological Corporation; 555 Academic Ct., San Antonio, TX 78204-0952
Target Audience: 5-11
Notes: Items, 242

Integral part of the System of Multicultural Pluralistic Assessment. May also be administered independently of other components of SOMPA. Consists of a series of questions, to be answered by child's parent or other adult who knows most about the child. Questions concern child's activities at home and in the neighborhood and yield information about child's adaptation to social systems in which he or she participates. Questions are available in both English and Spanish. Interview focuses on child's performance and behavior in nonacademic settings. The first 35 questions are asked of all respondents. The remaining questions are age-graded, and only those questions within the age range of the child are asked.

11760
Wide Range Employability Sample Test. Jastak, Joseph F.; Jastak, Sarah 1980
Subtests: Folding; Stapling; Packaging; Measuring; Stringing; Gluing; Collating; Color Matching; Pattern Matching; Assembling

Descriptors: Adolescents; *Adults; *Disabilities; *Employment Potential; *Job Skills; *Mental Retardation; Occupational Tests; Sheltered Workshops; *Work Sample Tests
Identifiers: WREST
Availability: Jastak Associates; 1526 Gilpin Ave., Wilmington, DE 19806
Target Audience: 16-54
Notes: Time, 120 approx.

Designed to measure productivity in quantity and quality. Measures "horizontal" achievement (capacity to do routine operations involved in all jobs). Measures ability to complete tasks which are carefully taught prior to testing. May also be useful in diagnosis of mental retardation.

11768
Cognitive Diagnostic Battery. Kay, Stanley R. 1982
Subtests: Color Form Preference Test; Color Form Representation Test; Egocentricity of Thought Test; Progressive Figure Drawing Test; Span of Attention Test
Descriptors: Abstract Reasoning; Adolescents; Adults; Attention Span; Children; *Cognitive Ability; *Cognitive Measurement; Concept Formation; *Diagnostic Tests; Individual Testing; *Mental Disorders; Mental Retardation; *Nonverbal Tests; Perceptual Motor Coordination; Social Development
Identifiers: *Cognitive Evaluation; *Psychiatric Patients
Availability: Psychological Assessment Resources; P.O. Box 998, Odessa, FL 33556
Target Audience: 2-64
Notes: Time, 30 approx.; Items, 46

Series of 5 tests to evaluate nature and degree of intellectual disorders and to aid in differential diagnosis. Wide range assessment of intellectual functions which helps to distinguish between mental subnormality and abnormality, assess cognitive deficits as a result of impaired development versus later regression, and differentially diagnose mental retardation versus psychosis. Designed to be suitable for a psychiatric population. Tests are brief, easily administered, self-paced, require no verbal response, demand little attention or informational knowledge, and are valid for repeated use. Suitable for psychiatric patients who are intellectually limited, nonverbal, inattentive, overtly psychotic, or otherwise untestable by conventional means. Five tests examine areas of concept formation, symbolic thinking, socialization of thought, perceptual development, and temporal attention.

11772
Trites Neuropsychological Test. Trites, D.R. 1975
Subtests: Halstead Category Test; Halstead Tactual Performance Test; Motor Steadiness Battery; Roughness Discrimination Test; Dynamometer Grip Strength Test; Finger Tapping Test; Knox Cube Test; Tactile Form Recognition Test; Grooved Pegboard Test; Foot Tapping Test
Descriptors: Academic Achievement; Adolescents; Adults; Attention Span; Children; *Diagnostic Tests; Language Skills; Memory; *Minimal Brain Dysfunction; *Neurological Impairments; *Psychomotor Skills; Visual Perception
Identifiers: Halstead Reitan Neuropsychological Tests; Reasoning Ability
Availability: Lafayette Instrument Co.; P.O. Box 5729, Sagamore Pwy., Lafayette, IN 47903
Target Audience: 6-64

Designed to detect or confirm the presence of brain dysfunction and to describe the extent of impairment and document a patient's capabilities. Consists of a variety of measures of psychomotor ability, academic achievement, reasoning ability, language functions, visual perceptual ability, attention span, and memory. Some of the tests are derived from the Halstead-Reitan Battery, the Wisconsin Motor Steadiness Battery and the Wechsler Adult Intelligence Scale.

11780
Multilevel Academic Skill Inventory: Math Component. Howell, Kenneth W.; And Others 1982
Subtests: Computation Survey; Application Survey
Descriptors: Basic Skills; Criterion Referenced Tests; *Diagnostic Teaching; *Diagnostic Tests; Elementary Education; *Elementary School Students; Mastery Learning; Mastery Tests; *Mathematics Achievement; *Mild Disabilities; *Mathematics Tests; Remedial Mathematics
Identifiers: MASI
Availability: The Psychological Corporation; 555 Academic Ct., San Antonio, TX 78204-0952
Grade Level: 1-8

Designed to aid teachers in identification of individual student needs in areas of basic math skills. The computation section assesses addition, subtraction, multiplication, division, fractions, decimals, ratios, and percent. The application section assesses areas of time and temperature, money, geometry, customary measurement, metric measurement, and problem solving. Useful with remedial and mildly handicapped students.

11783
Utah Test of Language Development and Language Sampling and Analysis. Revised Edition.
Mecham, Merlin J.; Jones, J. Jean 1978
Descriptors: Adolescents; Aphasia; Children; *Expressive Language; Individual Testing; *Language Acquisition; *Language Tests; Neurological Impairments; *Receptive Language; *Screening Tests; Young Children
Identifiers: LSA; UTLD
Availability: Pro-Ed; 5341 Industrial Oaks Blvd., Austin, TX 78735
Target Audience: 1-15
Notes: Time, 40 approx.

Objective instrument for measuring expressive and receptive language skills in both normal and handicapped children, i.e., aphasics or hyperactive brain-injured children. May be used by speech pathologists, audiologists, educators, psychologists, psychiatrists, and other specialists in clinical or educational settings.

11787
Psychological Stimulus Response Test. Mullen, Eileen M. 1977
Subtests: Auditory Language Scale; Visual Motor Scale
Descriptors: *Children; *Cognitive Development; *Cognitive Measurement; Concept Formation; Individual Testing; *Learning Modalities; *Multiple Disabilities; *Severe Disabilities; Tactual Perception; Verbal Ability; Visual Perception
Identifiers: PSR; PSR Test
Availability: Meeting St. School; 667 Waterman Ave., E. Providence, RI 02914
Target Audience: 1-10

Designed to assess the cognitive abilities of severely, multiply handicapped children. The stimulus and response item content is designed to minimize the physical aspects of the tasks while tapping behavior which demonstrates acquisition of concepts traditionally associated with levels of intellectual development. PSR Test introduces concept of functional age (F.A.) instead of mental age. Test is particularly effective with severely multiply handicapped children, ages 1 to 5, and with older, retarded, severely multiply handicapped children, ages 6 to 10. In addition to the 2 scales comprising the test, there is also a tactile differentiation section.

11788
Test of Spoken English, 1982 Edition. Educational Testing Service, Princeton, NJ 1982
Subtests: Pronunciation; Control of Grammar; Fluency
Descriptors: Colleges; Culture Fair Tests; Diagnostic Tests; *English (Second Language); Higher Education; Individual Testing; *Language Proficiency; *Language Tests; *Oral English; *Second Language Learning; Tape Recordings; *Teaching Assistants; Universities
Identifiers: TSE
Availability: Educational Testing Service; Test of Spoken English, Box 2882, Princeton, NJ 08541
Grade Level: 17-20
Notes: Time, 20 approx.

Primary purpose is to evaluate the English-speaking proficiency of persons whose native language is not English. The test is not targeted to a single academic discipline, field of employment, or other specialized language usage. Permits examinee to demonstrate general speaking proficiency. Test may also be used to diagnose strengths and weaknesses in spoken English at the end of a course of study. Was developed chiefly for use by academic institutions and has been validated in this context at present. Test is appropriate for all examinees regardless of their native language or culture. Examinee listens to tape recording of test questions and answers each question by speaking into a microphone.

11790
Let's Talk Inventory for Adolescents. Wiig, Elisabeth H. 1982
Subtests: Ritualizing; Informing; Controlling; Feeling
Descriptors: *Adolescents; *Children; Communication (Thought Transfer); *Communication Problems; *Communication Skills; *Communicative Competence (Languages); Elementary Secondary Education; Individual Testing; Pictorial Stimuli; *Speech Communication; *Speech Tests; Standard Spoken Usage; *Verbal Communication
Identifiers: *Oral Tests
Availability: The Psychological Corporation; 555 Academic Ct., San Antonio, TX 78204-0952
Grade Level: 4-12
Target Audience: 9-18
Notes: Time, 30 approx.

Designed to assist educators, clinicians, psychologists, vocational guidance counselors, and other professionals to identify preadolescents and adolescents with inadequate or delayed social-verbal communication skills. The speech acts represent the ritualizing, informing, controlling, and feeling functions of verbal communication. Used to probe speech acts germane to a standard American English language community. Inventory is purposefully biased in the direction of probing for the ability to formulate and interpret context-appropriate speech acts within the context of expectations for speakers of standard American English.

11791
Rhode Island Profile of Early Learning Behavior.
Novack, Harry S.; And Others 1982
Subtests: Observable Behavior; Written Work
Descriptors: Classroom Observation Techniques; *Cognitive Processes; Elementary School Students; *Grade 1; *Grade 2; *Kindergarten Children; *Learning Problems; Primary Education; *Screening Tests; *Student Behavior
Identifiers: Rhode Island Pupil Identification Scale; RIPELB; RIPIS
Availability: Jamestown Publishers; P.O. Box 6743, Providence, RI 02940
Grade Level: K-2
Notes: Items, 40

Scale for identifying children with learning problems in grades K-2. Can also be used to show strengths and weaknesses of children who have no serious learning problems. Test items are divided into 2 parts. Part I deals with behavior observable in the classroom and includes body perception, sensory-motor coordination, attention, memory for events, and self-concept. Part II deals with behavior which may be observed and evaluated through a review of the pupil's written work and includes memory for reproduction of symbols, directional or positional constancy, spatial and sequential arrangements of letters and symbols, and memory for symbols for cognitive operations.

11794
Adelphi Parent Administered Readiness Test.
Klein, Pnina S. 1982
Subtests: Concept Formation; Letter Discrimination; Writing Ability; Knowledge of Numbers; Visual Perception; Visual Memory; Comprehension and Memory; Auditory Sequential Memory; Creative Ability; Recognition of Facial Expression of Emotions
Descriptors: Cognitive Development; Educational Diagnosis; English (Second Language); *Kindergarten Children; Language Handicaps; Learning Disabilities; *Parent Participation; Parent School Relationship; Primary Education; Remedial Instruction; *School Readiness Tests
Identifiers: APART; Public Law 94 142
Availability: Media Materials; 2936 Remington Ave., Baltimore, MD 21211
Grade Level: K
Notes: Time, 20 approx.

Provides for building a home-school relationship by enrolling parents in testing their own children. Objectives of test are to ensure direct parental involvement in preschool evaluation activities; to provide parents with profile of child's learning abilities; to show parents relationship between specific abilities and various academic subjects; to guide parents toward activities providing necessary educational remediation; to allow for involvement of non-English speaking or bilingual parents; to provide a means of identifying specific learning disabilities and to discriminate between children with learning disabilities and children with language problems; to present teachers and school psychologists opportunity to observe parent-child interaction patterns.

11798
Kranz Talent Identification Instrument. Kranz, Bella 1982
Descriptors: Abstract Reasoning; Academically Gifted; Creativity; *Culture Fair Tests; Elementary Education; *Elementary School Students; *Gifted; Junior High Schools; *Junior High School Students; Leadership; Psychomotor Skills; *Screening Tests; Spatial Ability; *Talent Identification; Theater Arts; Underachievement; Visual Arts
Identifiers: KTII; Multidimensional Screening Device
Availability: Bella Kranz; P.O. Box 3555, Jersey City, NJ 07302
Grade Level: 3-8

A device to assist teachers, both in raising their awareness of the multiple criteria of giftedness and in screening talented children in their classes. Identifies children from all ethnic and sociological backgrounds. Involves a 3-stage procedure in which teachers are trained as raters; all children are appraised before any selections are made; a screening committee evaluates teacher ratings and pupil data to make final selections for a gifted program. Entire class is rated on each of the following areas: visual arts, performing arts, creative talent, one-sided talent, academic

talent, leadership and organizing talent, psychomotor talent, spatial and abstract thinking, underachievement talent, hidden talent.

11802
Torrance Tests of Creative Thinking, Revised Edition. Torrance, E. Paul 1974
Subtests: Fluency; Flexibility; Originality; Elaboration
Descriptors: Cognitive Processes; *Creativity; *Creativity Tests; *Elementary School Students; Elementary Secondary Education; Gifted; *Graduate Students; Higher Education; Individual Testing; *Kindergarten Children; Pictorial Stimuli; *Secondary School Students; *Undergraduate Students
Identifiers: Thinking Creatively with Pictures; Thinking Creatively with Words; TTCT
Availability: Scholastic Testing Service; 480 Meyer Rd., Bensenville, IL 60106
Grade Level: K-20

Measures creativity by assessing 4 important mental characteristics: fluency, flexibility, originality, elaboration. Comes in 2 forms, verbal and figural, which may both be administered, preferably in 2 separate sittings. The verbal forms (forms A and B) require written responses and may be administered to groups of students from grade 4 through graduate school. The verbal test may be individually administered to young children. The verbal test takes approximately 45 minutes. The figural test requires responses that are mainly drawing or pictorial in nature. Use of the figural test is recommended from kindergarten through graduate school and requires approximately 30 minutes. Streamlined scoring procedures for the figural form is a new alternative scoring procedure and yields norm-referenced measures for fluency, originality, abstractness of titles, elaboration, and resistance to premature closure.

11813
English Language Skills Assessment: Forms BC, BN, IC, AN. Ilyin, Donna; And Others 1980
Descriptors: Achievement Tests; Adult Education; Adults; Criterion Referenced Tests; *English (Second Language); *Grammar; *Immigrants; Multiple Choice Tests; *Reading Comprehension; *Reading Tests; *Screening Tests; Second Language Instruction; *Student Placement
Identifiers: ELSA
Availability: Newbury House Publishers; 54 Church St., Cambridge, MA 02138
Target Audience: Adults
Notes: Time, 30 approx.; Items, 25

Series of criterion-referenced reading tests measuring the understanding of meaning in context, as well as grammatical ability. Use multiple-choice cloze format so that students do no writing. Each passage involves common situations experienced by students and encountered in most teaching materials. Tests were developed for adult resident immigrants. Tests may also be used for students who are nonpermanent United States residents and who are in college beginning intensive English programs. May also be useful with English-as-a-Second-Language students in secondary and upper elementary grades. Tests come in 3 levels of difficulty: beginning, intermediate, and advanced. In the beginning and intermediate levels, there are a conversation format and a narrative format.

11816
Denver Developmental Screening Tests Revised.
Frankenburg, William K.; And Others 1978
Subtests: Gross Motor; Language; Fine Motor-Adaptive; Personal-Social
Descriptors: *Developmental Tasks; Individual Testing; *Infants; *Language Acquisition; Learning Disabilities; Motor Development; *Preschool Children; *Psychomotor Skills; *Screening Tests; *Social Development; Young Children
Identifiers: DDST R; Denver Developmental Screening Test; *Denver Screening Test for Preschoolers
Availability: Denver Developmental Materials; P.O. Box 6919, Denver, CO 80206-0919
Target Audience: 0-6
Notes: Time, 20 approx.; Items, 105

Designed as a screening device to identify infants and preschool children with serious developmental delays. The test is to be used only for screening purposes to alert professional child workers to the possibility of developmental delays so that appropriate diagnostic studies may be pursued. A child at any given age is administered only 20 or so simple items. DDST-R test items are arranged in a chronological step-wise order.

11817
Singer Vocational Evaluation System. The Singer Company, Rochester, NY 1977

Descriptors: Adolescents; Adults; Career Exploration; *Disadvantaged; Individual Testing; Occupational Tests; Rehabilitation Counseling; Secondary Education; *Secondary School Students; *Vocational Education; *Vocational Interests; *Work Sample Tests
Identifiers: VES
Availability: Singer Career Systems; 80 Commerce Dr., Rochester, NY 14623
Target Audience: 13-30

Designed to provide vocational assessment and occupational exploration. Identifies vocational abilities, interests, and work tolerance for vocational training. "Hands-on" procedure is individualized and self-paced using real tools and equipment. Consists of a series of work sampling stations which represent several jobs found in the Dictionary of Occupational Titles (DOT). Work stations may be purchased separately. Stations include Sample Making, Bench Assembly, Drafting, Electrical Wiring, Plumbing and Pipe Fitting, Woodworking, Air Conditioning and Refrigeration, Sales Processing, Needle Trades, Masonry, Sheet Metal Working, Cook Baker, Small Engine Service, Medical Service, Cosmetology, Data Calculation and Recording, Production Machine Operating, Household and Industrial Wiring, Filing Shipping and Receiving, Packaging and Materials Handling, Electronic Assembly, Welding and Brazing, Office Services, Typing Package, Basic Laboratory Analysis.

11818
Denver Prescreening Developmental Questionnaire (Spanish Edition). Frankenburg, William K.; And Others 1975
Descriptors: *Developmental Tasks; Individual Testing; *Infants; Language Acquisition; Learning Disabilities; Motor Development; Parents; *Preschool Children; *Screening Tests; Social Development; *Spanish; Young Children
Identifiers: PDQ; PreInvestigacion del Desarrollo Infantil en Denver
Availability: Denver Developmental Materials; P.O. Box 6919, Denver, CO 80206-0919
Target Audience: 0-6
Notes: Time, 5 approx.; Items, 97

Designed to be a "prescreening" tool used to identify those children 3 months to 6 years of age who will require further screening with the Denver Developmental Screening Test (TC003628). Used to detect developmental lags and suggest that more detailed screening is required. Parent selects the 10 age-appropriate questions for his or her child and answers these. Five color-coded forms arrange items by the chronological age at which most children can perform certain skills.

11823
Reading-Free Vocational Interest Inventory. Revised. Becker, Ralph L. 1981
Subtests: Automotive; Building Trades; Clerical; Animal Care; Food Service; Patient Care; Horticulture; Housekeeping; Personal Service; Laundry Service; Materials Handling
Descriptors: Forced Choice Technique; *Interest Inventories; *Learning Disabilities; *Mental Retardation; *Nonverbal Tests; Pictorial Stimuli; Reading Difficulties; *Vocational Interests
Identifiers: RFVII
Availability: Elbern Publications; P.O. Box 09497, Columbus, OH 43209
Target Audience: 13-64
Notes: Time, 20 approx.; Items, 55

A nonreading vocational preference test for use with mentally retarded and learning-disabled individuals from age 13 to adult. Pictorial illustrations with occupational significance are presented in forced-choice format for selections. Devised to provide systematic information on the range of interest patterns of the exceptional male or female who is diagnosed as mentally retarded or learning disabled. Provides scores in 11 interest areas of the kind and type in which this population is productive and proficient.

11826
Listening Comprehension Group Tests. Ilyin, Donna 1981
Descriptors: Adolescents; Adults; *English (Second Language); Expressive Language; Language Proficiency; *Listening Comprehension Tests; Nonverbal Tests; Older Adults; Pictorial Stimuli; Pretests Posttests; Receptive Language; Verbal Tests
Identifiers: LCPT; LCWT
Availability: Newbury House Publishers; 54 Church St., Cambridge, MA 02138
Target Audience: 14-85

The Group Test consists of 2 tests: the Listening Comprehension Picture Test (LCPT) is designed for non-native speakers of English which measures listening comprehension of basic English structures without requiring demonstration of reading or writing skills. Designed for beginning and intermediate adult education students of English as a Second Language. Has 33 multiple-choice items and may be administered in approximately 30 minutes. The Listening Comprehension Written Test (LCWT) is a test of English-language proficiency for non-native speakers of English who are intermediate or advanced students of English as a Second Language. The test consists of 30 items and assesses receptive and productive English language skills in a group testing situation. The LCWT takes approximately 45 minutes to administer.

11827
Multilevel Academic Skills Inventory; Reading and Language Arts. Howell, Kenneth W.; And Others 1982
Descriptors: Criterion Referenced Tests; *Decoding (Reading); *Diagnostic Tests; Elementary Education; *Elementary School Students; Handwriting; *Language Arts; Mastery Learning; Mastery Tests; *Mild Disabilities; *Reading Comprehension; Reading Skills; Spelling; Vocabulary
Identifiers: MASI
Availability: The Psychological Corporation; 555 Academic Ct., San Antonio, TX 78204-0952
Grade Level: 1-8

Designed to aid teachers in identification of individual needs in academic reading and language arts skills of remedial and mildly handicapped students. Designed to locate critical areas of student nonmastery, to facilitate preparing and sequencing instruction, and to monitor the effects of instruction. Covers 3 broad content areas: reading decoding including sounds, conversions, teams, clusters, modifications, complex words and passages; reading comprehension including searching for details, inference, and context-dependent vocabulary; and language arts covering content vocabulary in math/science, social studies, language/music, everyday living, and handwriting and spelling.

11862
Marshalltown Preschool Developmental Package. Donahue, Michael; And Others 1980
Descriptors: *Cognitive Development; Developmental Tasks; Diagnostic Teaching; *Disabilities; *Infants; Language Acquisition; *Preschool Children; Preschool Education; Psychomotor Skills; Screening Tests; Socialization
Identifiers: MBDP; MDSI
Availability: Marshalltown Project Area Education Agency 6; Preschool Division, 210 S. 12th St., Marshalltown, IA 50158
Target Audience: 0-6

Three-part system designed for screening assessment and curriculum retrieval. Useful for preschool handicapped population. Developmental Profile (MBDP-S) contains 216 items which evaluate development in areas of motor, cognitive, and socialization. Yields developmental quotient. Screening instrument (MDSI) has 24 items, requires about 15 minutes to administer, and was developed for quick screening. Curriculum Management system enables teacher to develop teaching prescriptions.

11865
Prueba de Lectura y Lenguaje Escrito. Hammill, Donald D.; And Others 1982
Subtests: Vocabulario; Lectura de Parrafos; Vocabulario Escrito; Composicion; Ortografia; Estilo
Descriptors: *Diagnostic Tests; Elementary Education; *Elementary School Students; Grammar; Group Testing; Individual Testing; *Reading Ability; *Reading Comprehension; Secondary Education; *Secondary School Students; *Spanish; Spanish Speaking; Spelling; Vocabulary; Writing (Composition); *Writing Evaluation; *Writing Skills
Identifiers: PLLE
Availability: Pro-Ed; 5341 Industrial Oaks Blvd., Austin, TX 78735
Grade Level: 3-10
Notes: Time, 120 approx.; Items, 75

Diagnostic test of written language proficiency. Used to identify students who have problems with written expression in comparison with their peers; to determine a student's strengths and weaknesses; to document student progress in a reading or writing program; and/or to conduct research in writing or reading. May be administered individually or to groups. Based on the Test of Reading Comprehension, 1978 (TC010394) and the Test of Written Language, 1978 (TC010392). However, Spanish version is not a translation. The subjects were specifically designed for Spanish-language version.

11866
Perfil de Evaluacion del Comportamiento. Brown, Linda; Hammill, Donald D. 1982
Descriptors: Behavior Problems; *Behavior Rating Scales; *Elementary School Students; Elementary Secondary Education; Parent Student Relationship; Peer Relationship; *Secondary School Students; Self Evaluation (Individuals); Sociometric Techniques; *Spanish; Spanish Speaking; *Student Behavior; Teacher Student Relationship
Identifiers: PEC

Availability: Pro-Ed; 5341 Industrial Oaks Blvd., Austin, TX 78735
Grade Level: 3-12

Provides an ecological evaluation of student behaviors which is standardized, reliable, experimentally validated, and normreferenced. Permits student's behaviors to be examined in a variety of settings and from several pertinent points of view. The PEC is comprised of 6 components: Student Rating Scale: Home (20 items); Student Rating Scale: School (20 items); Student Rating Scale: Peer (20 items); Teacher Rating Scale (30 items); Parent Rating Scale (30 items); Sociogram. The items from the Student Rating Scales are intermingled in a single 60-item instrument. The 6 components are independent measures and may be used alone or in combination with any other component. Spanish-language version of the Behavior Rating Profile, 1978 (TC010393).

11867
Test of Language Development—Primary. Newcomer, Phyllis L.; Hammill, Donald D. 1982
Subtests: Picture Vocabulary; Oral Vacabulary; Grammatic Understanding; Sentence Imitation; Grammatic Completion; Word Discrimination; Word Articulation
Descriptors: Articulation (Speech); Communication Problems; *Diagnostic Tests; *Elementary School Students; *Expressive Language; Grammar; Individual Testing; *Language Proficiency; Language Research; *Language Tests; *Oral Language; *Primary Education; *Receptive Language; Sentences; Vocabulary; *Young Children
Identifiers: TOLD P
Availability: Pro-Ed; 5341 Industrial Oaks Blvd., Austin, TX 78735
Target Audience: 4-8
Notes: Time, 60 approx.; Items, 170

Standardized test with reliability and validity used to measure the language skills of most children between the ages of 4 years and 8 years, 11 months. Four principal uses are to identify children significantly below their peers in language proficiency; to determine their specific strengths and weaknesses in language skills; to document progress in language as a result of special intervention programs; and to be used in research studies involving language behavior. Students who are deaf or do not speak English should not be administered the test. There are no time limits on the subtests; time to administer the entire test ranges from 30 to 60 minutes. A review of the test by Cecil R. Reynolds can be found in School Psychology Review; v12 n4 p483-84 Fall 1983.

11868
Test of Language Development—Intermediate. Hammill, Donald D.; Newcomer, Phyllis L. 1982
Subtests: Sentence Combining; Characteristics; Word Ordering; Generals; Grammatic Comprehension
Descriptors: Children; Communication Problems; *Diagnostic Tests; *Elementary School Students; *Expressive Language; Grammar; Individual Testing; *Language Proficiency; Language Research; *Language Tests; *Listening Skills; *Oral Language; *Receptive Language; Sentence Combining
Identifiers: TOLD I
Availability: Pro-Ed; 5341 Industrial Oaks Blvd., Austin, TX 78735
Target Audience: 8-12
Notes: Time, 45 approx.; Items, 160

A standardized test, with reliability and validity, to measure the language skills of most children between the ages of 8 years, 6 months and 12 years, 11 months. Test has 4 main uses: to identify children significantly below their peers in language proficiency; to determine their specific strengths and weaknesses in language skills; to document progress in language as a result of special intervention programs; and to be used in research studies involving language behavior. Students who are deaf or who do not speak English should not be administered this test. There are no time limits on the subtests; the time required to administer the entire test should take between 30 and 45 minutes.

11870
Profile of Mood States, Bi-Polar Form. McNair, Douglas M.; And Others 1982
Subtests: Composed-Anxious; Agreeable-Hostile; Elated-Depressed; Confident-Unsure; Energetic-Tired; Clearhead-Confused
Descriptors: Adults; *Affective Measures; College Students; Emotional Disturbances; Group Testing; Individual Testing; *Personality Assessment; *Personality Traits; Psychological Evaluation; *Psychological Testing
Identifiers: *Moods; POMS BI; Psychiatric Patients
Availability: Educational and Industrial Testing Service; P.O. Box 7234, San Diego, CA 92107
Target Audience: 17-64
Notes: Time, 5 approx.; Items, 72

Bipolar Form of the Profile of Mood States was constructed to measure 6 bipolar subjective mood states. Each mood state is defined by a scale comprised of 12 adjectives or phrases. Can be used with both normal subjects and persons suffering from psychiatric disorders. Some uses of POMS-BI are to identify and assess mood profile of normal subjects; to assess mood states of psychiatric outpatients; to evaluate relative effectiveness of various psychotropic drugs for reducing certain states; to assess experimentally in groups the effects of various drugs and emotional films; to assess change in mood resulting from various treatments; or to compare various personality disorders described in DSM-III, as to characteristic mood profile. May be administered to individuals or to groups.

11888
Basic School Skills Inventory—Screen. Hammill, Donald D.; Leigh, James E. 1983
Descriptors: *High Risk Students; *Kindergarten Children; *Preschool Children; Primary Education; School Readiness; *Screening Tests
Identifiers: BSSI S
Availability: Pro-Ed; 5341 Industrial Oaks Blvd., Austin, TX 78735
Target Audience: 4-6
Notes: Time, 8 approx.; Items, 20

Used to identify children who are high-risk candidates for school failure and who may need remedial work, more comprehensive evaluation, or referral for possible special services. Scores may also serve as indication of child's readiness ability. Items were selected from items on BSSI—Diagnostic (TC011864).

11890
Speaking Proficiency English Assessment Kit. Educational Testing Service, Princeton, NJ 1982
Subtests: Pronunciation; Grammar; Fluency
Descriptors: *College Students; *English (Second Language); *Graduate Students; Grammar; Higher Education; Language Fluency; *Language Proficiency; *Oral Language; Pronunciation; *Speech Tests; *Teaching Assistants
Identifiers: Oral Tests; SPEAK
Availability: Educational Testing Service; TOEFL Program Office, Princeton, NJ 08541
Grade Level: 13-18
Notes: Time, 20

A standardized test of English-speaking proficiency for internal use by colleges and universities for evaluating non-native English speaking students and applicants for positions as teaching assistants. Examinees respond orally to printed and recorded stimuli. Locally scored. May be used for pre- and posttesting in English courses and to identify those requiring additional instruction in spoken English.

11891
Stellern-Show Informal Learning Inventory. Stellern, John 1982
Descriptors: Auditory Perception; Elementary Education; *Elementary School Students; Expressive Language; Informal Assessment; *Learning Disabilities; Memory; *Screening Tests; Tactual Perception; Visual Perception
Identifiers: Graphic Ability; SILI
Availability: John Stellern; Special Education, P.O. Box 3374, University of Wyoming, Laramie, WY 82070
Grade Level: K-8
Notes: Items, 82

An informal assessment of a child's auditory; visual; haptic and multisensory input; memory and meaning processes; and verbal, graphic, and haptic output processes for use by classroom teachers, special educators, educational diagnosticians, etc. Consists of tasks to be performed by the child that can be observed and which may indicate presence of learning difficulties. Some sections require manipulative materials such as blocks.

11892
A Scale of Employability for Handicapped Persons. Jewish Vocational Service, Chicago, IL 1959
Subtests: Counseling Scale; Psychology Scale; Workshop Scale
Descriptors: Adults; *Disabilities; Emotional Problems; *Employment Potential; Mental Retardation; Physical Disabilities; Rating Scales; Social Discrimination
Availability: Materials Development Center; Stout Vocational Rehabilitation Institute, University of Wisconsin-Stout, Menomonie, WI 54751
Target Audience: Adults
Notes: Items, 124

Developed to evaluate the employability of vocationally handicapped individuals. Employability is defined as a complex set of interrelated factors which determine whether or not a client can be placed on a job and whether the client can keep the job after being placed. Vocationally handicapped people are defined as those who are disadvantaged vocationally by either mental, physical, emotional, or social disabilities. Scale consists of 3 sections: a workshop section filled out by workshop foreman, a counseling scale to be filled out by vocational counselors, and a psychology scale to be filled out by psychologists.

11917
Test of Nonverbal Intelligence: A Language Free Measure of Cognitive Ability. Brown, Linda; And Others 1982
Descriptors: Adolescents; Adults; Bilingualism; Children; *Cognitive Ability; Individual Testing; *Intelligence Tests; Language Handicaps; Learning Disabilities; Mental Retardation; Non English Speaking; *Nonverbal Tests; Older Adults; Physical Disabilities; *Problem Solving
Identifiers: TONI
Availability: Pro-Ed; 5341 Industrial Oaks Blvd., Austin, TX 78735
Target Audience: 5-85
Notes: Time, 15 approx.; Items, 50

A language-free intelligence test used to evaluate the intellectual capacity of those individuals who are difficult or impossible to test with traditional pencil-and-paper tests. These include mentally retarded, stroke patients, bilingual and non-English speaking, speech or language handicapped, or learning-disabled subjects. The basis of all the test items is problem solving and requires subjects to solve problems by identifying relationships among abstract figures. The examiner pantomimes the instructions and the subject points to the appropriate response. Test is not timed and requires approximately 15 minutes to administer. Available in 2-equivalent forms. Administered individually or to small groups.

11921
Behavioral Characteristics Progression, Spanish. Santa Cruz County Superintendent of Schools, CA 1979
Descriptors: Adolescents; *Behavior Patterns; Blindness; Children; Daily Living Skills; Deafness; *Disabilities; Job Skills; Language Skills; Mental Retardation; Perceptual Development; Physical Disabilities; Profiles; Social Behavior; *Spanish Speaking; *Special Education
Identifiers: BCP; Santa Cruz Behavioral Characteristics Progression
Availability: Vort Corporation; P.O. Box 11132, Palo Alto, CA 94306
Target Audience: 4-18
Notes: Items, 2,400

Spanish translation of the Santa Cruz Behavioral Characteristics Progression done to conform with usage and cultures in 5 Spanish speaking countries. Consists of 2,400 observable behavior characteristics grouped along 59 strands. Covers self-help, perceptual-motor language, social, academic, recreational, and vocational behaviors of special education students. For use in establishing a baseline and evaluating progress. Instrument is not standardized.

11924
Learning Accomplishment Profile: Diagnostic Screening Edition. Chapel Hill Training-Outreach Project, NC; Kentucky State Dept. of Education, Frankfort 1981
Subtests: Fine Motor; Cognitive; Language; Gross Motor
Descriptors: Cognitive Ability; *High Risk Students; *Individual Testing; *Kindergarten Children; Language Skills; Primary Education; Psychomotor Skills; *Screening Tests
Identifiers: LAP(D)
Availability: Kaplan School Supply Corporation; 1310 Lewisville-Clemmons Rd., Lewisville, NC 27023
Grade Level: K
Notes: Time, 15 approx.; Items, 17

Developed for early identification of children potentially at risk in learning and developmental areas. All items must be administered. Results obtained should be considered first or initial phase of the screening, referral, diagnostic, individualized programing, and instructional process. Items were selected from the Learning Accomplishment Profile-Diagnostic.

11930
Swassing-Barbe Modality Index. Barbe, Walter B.; Swassing, Raymond H. 1979
Subtests: Visual; Auditory; Kinesthetic
Descriptors: Adults; Auditory Stimuli; Elementary Education; *Elementary School Students; English (Second Language); *Individual Testing; Kinesthetic Perception; *Learning Modalities; Objective Tests; Preschool Children; Visual Learning
Identifiers: SBMI; Zaner Bloser Modality Kit
Availability: Zaner-Bloser; 612 N. Park St., Columbus, OH 43215
Grade Level: K-6
Notes: Time, 20 approx.

Matching-to-sample task used to assess the modality or modalities children employ in learning, specifically the visual, auditory, and kinesthetic modes. Individually administered instrument in which a stimulus item or sample is presented and the respondent is asked to duplicate the sample. Instrument can be used with preschool age children, children whose first language is not English, older children and adults, as well as with the primary group of elementary school students.

11931
Bateria Woodcock Psico-Educativa en Espanol. Woodcock, Richard W. 1982
Subtests: Vocabulario Sobre Dibujos; Relaciones Espaciales; Aprendizaje Visual-Auditivo; Conceptos Cuantitativos; Pareo Visual; Antonimos-Sinonimos; Analisis-Sintesis; Inversion de Numeros; Formacion de Conceptos; Analogias; Identificacion de Letras y Palabras; Analisis de Palabras; Comprension de Textos; Calculo; Problemas Aplicados; Dictado; Comprobacion; Puncuacion y Empleo de Letras Mayusculas
Descriptors: *Academic Achievement; *Academic Aptitude; Adolescents; Adults; Bilingualism; Children; Clinical Diagnosis; *Cognitive Ability; *Cognitive Measurement; Handicap Identification; Individualized Education Programs; Individual Testing; Older Adults; Screening Tests; *Spanish; Spanish Speaking
Identifiers: Test Batteries; Woodcock Johnson Psycho Educational Battery
Availability: DLM Teaching Resources; P.O. Box 4000, One DLM Park, Allen, TX 75002
Target Audience: 3-80

Consists of 17 subtests which measure cognitive functions, expected scholastic achievement, and actual academic achievement. To determine whether to assess a subject's psychoeducational abilities in English or Spanish, examiner may administer Oral Language Cluster (vocabulario sobre dibujos, antonimos-sinonimos, analogras) in Spanish from Bateria or in English from the Woodcock Language Proficiency Battery-English (1980). Battery may be used for clinical assessment, program evaluation, or research purposes with individuals ranging from preschool age through the geriatric level. Within the school-age range, a primary application is for students having learning and/or adjustment problems. Uses of the battery include individual evaluation, selection and placement, individual program planning, guidance, recording individual growth, program evaluation, research studies, and psychometric training.

11941
Level of Rehabilitation Scale-Revised. Carey, Raymond G.; Posavac, Emil J. 1981
Subtests: Activities of Daily Living; Mobility; Communication
Descriptors: Adults; Nonverbal Communication; *Patients; Physical Mobility; Profiles; Rating Scales; *Rehabilitation; Self Care Skills; Verbal Communication
Identifiers: LORS (II)
Availability: Raymond G. Carey; Health Care Evaluation, Parkside Medical Services Corp., 1580 N.W. Hwy., Park Ridge, IL 60068
Target Audience: Adults
Notes: Items, 17

Designed to gather and summarize functional ratings of patients from hospital-based rehabilitation programs. Completed by nurses and therapists.

11944
Prueba de Admision para Estudios Graduados. Educational Testing Service, Princeton, NJ 1980
Subtests: Verbal Ability; Quantitative Ability; English as a Second Language; Writing
Descriptors: *Academic Ability; *Aptitude Tests; *College Entrance Examinations; *College Seniors; *English (Second Language); *Graduate Students; Higher Education; *Spanish Speaking; Verbal Ability; Writing Skills
Identifiers: PAEG; Puerto Rico
Availability: Educational Testing Service; International Office, Princeton, NJ 08541
Grade Level: 16
Notes: Time, 225; Items, 205

An aptitude test designed and constructed to measure academic ability at the graduate level for use in making decisions about the admission of applicants to graduate schools in Puerto Rico. Includes a measure of English as a Second Language.

11956
Escala de Inteligencia Wechsler para Ninos—Revisada Edicion de Investigacion. Wechsler, David 1982
Subtests: Informacion; Semejanzas; Arithmetica; Vocabulario; Comprehension; Retencion de Digitos; Figuras Incompletas; Arreglo de Dibujos; Disenos con Bloques; Composicion de Objetos; Claves; Laberintos

Descriptors: Adolescents; *Bilingual Students; Children; *Elementary School Students; *Individual Testing; *Intelligence; *Intelligence Tests; *Secondary School Students; *Spanish; *Spanish Speaking
Identifiers: EIWN(R); Wechsler Intelligence Scale for Children (Revised); WISC(R)
Availability: The Psychological Corporation; 555 Academic Ct., San Antonio, TX 78204-0952
Target Audience: 6-16

Spanish adaption of the WISC-R for use with Chicano, Puerto Rican, and Cuban children. Currently a research edition published without norms. Is an individually administered measure of a child's capacity to understand and cope with the world. Intended for use by school psychologists and other trained clinical examiners. Child should not be penalized if he or she offers an acceptable response in English. Examiners should consider a bilingual administration of the test. However, the vocabulary and digit span items should be administered in Spanish only.

11977
Talent Assessment Program. Revised Edition.
Nighswonger, Wilton E. 1981
Subtests: Visualizing Structured Detail; Sorting (Size and Shape); Sorting (Color); Sorting by Touch; Handling Small Materials; Handling Large Materials; Using Small Tools; Using Large Tools; Visualizing Flow Paths; Memory for Structural Detail
Descriptors: Adolescents; Adults; *Aptitude Tests; Learning Disabilities; *Performance Tests; Secondary Education; *Secondary School Students; Skilled Occupations; Spatial Ability; Tactual Perception; Unskilled Occupations; Visual Discrimination; Visualization; *Vocational Aptitude
Identifiers: Manual Dexterity; TAP; Test Batteries
Availability: Talent Assessment, Inc.; P.O. Box 5087, Jacksonville, FL 32207
Grade Level: 7-12
Target Audience: 13-64
Notes: Time, 150 approx.

Consists of 10 tests which require hands-on work by client. Used to measure innate vocational aptitudes of all types of individuals, including handicapped, disadvantaged, and nonhandicapped vocational students. Tests measure skills applicable to work in trade, industrial, technical and professional technical lines, including skilled and unskilled occupations. Measures aptitudes in the general categories of visualization and retention, visual discrimination and manual dexterity.

11993
Special Fitness Test Manual for Mildly Mentally Retarded Persons, Revised Edition. American Alliance for Health, Physical Education, Recreation, and Dance, Reston, VA 1976
Subtests: Flexed Arm Hang; Sit-Up; Shuttle Run; Standing Long Jump; 50-yard Dash; Softball Throw for Distance; 300-yard Run
Descriptors: Adolescents; Children; *Mild Mental Retardation; *Performance Tests; *Physical Fitness; *Psychomotor Skills
Identifiers: AAHPERD
Availability: American Alliance Health, Physical Education, Recreation, and Dance; 1900 Association Dr., Reston, VA 22091
Target Audience: 8-18

Basically the same as the AAHPER Youth Fitness Test but with minor modifications. When properly administered, test yields valuable information regarding such components of physical fitness as speed, power, agility, and muscular endurance, and such basic skills as running, jumping, and throwing.

12010
Test of Individual Needs in Reading, Form B (Bidwell Form). Gilliland, Hap 1982
Subtests: Instructional Reading Level (Oral Reading); Comprehension; Word Analysis Skills
Descriptors: *Achievement Tests; Adults; American Indians; *Decoding (Reading); Elementary Education; *Elementary School Students; High School Students; *Individual Testing; Minimum Competency Testing; *Oral Reading; *Reading Achievement; *Reading Comprehension; *Reading Tests
Identifiers: Canada; United States (West)
Availability: Council for Indian Education; Box 31215, Billings, MT 59107
Grade Level: 1-7

Provides a complete analysis of a student's reading level and reading skills. Appropriate for use in grades 1 through 7 and with high school students and adult students reading below the high school level. This form was especially designed for students in the Western United States and Canada but is useful with all students.

12011
Test of Individual Needs in Reading: Red Fox Supplement. Gilliland, Hap 1982

Subtests: Auditory Sequential Memory; Visual Memory for Words; Listening Comprehension; Listening Vocabulary; Structural Analysis; Use of Context
Descriptors: *Achievement Tests; Adults; American Indians; Auditory Stimuli; Context Clues; Decoding (Reading); Elementary Education; *Elementary School Students; *Group Testing; High School Students; Listening Comprehension; *Listening Skills; Reading Comprehension; *Reading Skills; *Reading Tests; Visual Stimuli; Vocabulary Skills; Word Recognition
Availability: Council for Indian Education; Box 31215, Billings, MT 59107
Grade Level: 1-7

A group test designed to supplement the 3 parallel Forms of the Test of Individual Needs in Reading. Used to evaluate students' potential for developing both word recognition and reading comprehension.

12012
Test of Individual Needs in Reading, Form RC (Red Cloud). Gilliland, Hap 1982
Subtests: Instructional Reading Level (Oral Reading); Comprehension; Word Analysis Skills; Word Recognition; Word Meaning
Descriptors: *Achievement Tests; Adults; American Indians; *Decoding (Reading); Elementary Education; *Elementary School Students; High School Students; *Individual Testing; Minimum Competency Testing; *Oral Reading; *Reading Achievement; *Reading Tests; *Reservation American Indians; *Semantics; *Word Recognition
Identifiers: *Alaska
Availability: Council for Indian Education; Box 31215, Billings, MT 59107
Grade Level: 1-7

Provides a complete analysis of a student's reading level and reading skills. Appropriate for use in grades 1 through 7 and with high school students and adult students reading below the high school level. This form was especially designed for Native American students. Although the vocabulary was planned not to handicap reservation Indian students and the Alaskan natives, the test has been found useful with all cultures. Includes a word recognition and word meaning test, as well as subtests found in the other tests in the series.

12013
Test of Individual Needs in Reading, Form K (Kangaroo Form). Nelson, Mary Lu; Gilliland, Hap 1982
Subtests: Instructional Reading Level (Oral Reading); Comprehension; Word Analysis Skills; Word Recognition
Descriptors: *Achievement Tests; Adults; American Indians; *Decoding (Reading); Elementary Education; *Elementary School Students; High School Students; *Individual Testing; Minimum Competency Testing; *Oral Reading; *Reading Achievement; *Reading Comprehension; *Reading Tests; *Word Recognition
Identifiers: Aboriginal People; Australia (Western Australia)
Availability: Council for Indian Education; Box 31215, Billings, MT 59107
Grade Level: 1-7

Provides a complete analysis of a student's reading level and reading skills. Appropriate for use in grades 1 through 7 and with high school students and adult students reading below the high school level. This form was especially designed by teachers of Western Australia for use with Australians, including Aborigines. However, test is appropriate with nearly all students. A test of Word Recognition is also included in this test.

12014
Nonreading Aptitude Test Battery, 1982 Edition.
United States Employment Service, Division of Testing, Salem, OR 1982
Subtests: Oral Vocabulary; Number Comparison; Design Completion; Tool Matching; Three-Dimensional Space; Form Matching; GATB Mark Making; GATB Assemble; GATB Disassemble; GATB Place; GATB Turn
Descriptors: Adults; *Aptitude Tests; Career Guidance; Cognitive Ability; *Disadvantaged; *Occupational Tests; Personnel Selection; Psychomotor Skills; Spatial Ability; Verbal Ability; Visual Discrimination; Vocabulary
Identifiers: General Aptitude Test Battery; Manual Dexterity; NATB; Numerical Ability; Oral Tests; Perceptual Speed Finger Dexterity; United States Employment Service
Availability: State Employment Service Offices only
Target Audience: Adults
Notes: Time, 107; Items, 468

Developed for use with disadvantaged individuals. This revision is shorter than earlier versions and is purported to be easier to understand and administer, without loss of internal validity. Aptitudes measured are general learning ability, verbal ability, numerical ability, spatial aptitude, form perception, clerical perception, motor coordination, finger dexterity, manual dexterity. Administered by offices of the U.S. Employment Service for vocational guidance and employee selection.

12016
The Boder Test of Reading-Spelling Patterns.
Boder, Elena; Jarrico, Sylvia 1982
Subtests: Oral Reading Test; Written Spelling Test
Descriptors: Adolescents; Children; Clinical Diagnosis; *Cognitive Ability; *Diagnostic Tests; *Dyslexia; *Individual Testing; *Reading Difficulties; *Reading Processes; *Spelling
Identifiers: BTRSP
Availability: Slosson Educational Publications; P.O. Box 280, E. Aurora, NY 14052
Target Audience: 6-18
Notes: Time, 30 approx.

Test is based on premise that dyslexic reader has a characteristic pattern of cognitive strengths and weaknesses in 2 components of the reading process: the visual gestalt function and the auditory analytic function. Test is designed to clarify child's characteristic pattern of cognitive strengths and weaknesses in reading and spelling. Diagnostic purposes of test are to differentiate specific reading disability, or developmental dyslexia, from nonspecific reading disability, to classify dyslexic readers into one of 3 subtypes on basis of reading-spelling patterns and to provide guidelines for remediation of the reading disability subtypes. The test should not be used alone to make a definitive diagnosis of developmental dyslexia but should be part of a multidisciplinary neuropsychoeducational evaluation and in conjunction with other diagnostic instruments. A review of the test by M. O. Smith can be found in Journal of Reading; v27 p22-26 Oct 1983.

12017
The Western Aphasia Battery, New Version. Kertesz, Andrew 1982
Subtests: Spontaneous Speech; Auditory Verbal Comprehension; Repetition; Naming; Reading and Writing; Praxis; Constructional, Visuospatial, and Calculation Tasks
Descriptors: Adolescents; Adults; *Aphasia; Children; Clinical Diagnosis; *Language Handicaps; Language Processing; Nonverbal Ability; Nonverbal Tests; Oral Language
Identifiers: WAB
Availability: Slosson Educational Publications; P.O. Box 280, E. Aurora, NY 14052
Target Audience: 0-64

Designed to evaluate main clinical aspects of language function: content, fluency, auditory comprehension, repetition, and naming, as well as reading, writing, and calculation. Nonverbal skills are also tested, such as drawing, block design, and praxis. Raven's Colored Progressive Matrices is also administered. The oral language portion is an independent unit; the reading, writing, calculation, and praxis is another. The nonverbal tests are optional. Scoring system provides the following overall measures of severity: aphasia quotient (AQ) which uses the oral portion of language assessment and the cortical quotient (CQ) which includes the nonverbal scores.

12018
The Assessment of Phonological Processes. Hodson, Barbara Williams 1980
Descriptors: *Diagnostic Tests; *Phonemes; *Phonology; *Speech Handicaps; Speech Tests; *Young Children
Identifiers: APP
Availability: Slosson Educational Publications; P.O. Box 280, E. Aurora, NY 14052
Target Audience: 2-8
Notes: Time, 25 approx.; Items, 55

Used by clinicians to analyze and describe the most severe speech disorders to identify speech patterns which need remediation. Manual provides descriptions of over 40 phonological processes along with examples and instructions for scoring. In addition to the 55-item full-evaluation instrument, there is a quick 20-item screening test used to indicate whether any of the most common phonological processes are present. The screening test portion has also been used for limited assessment of speech performance of children under 2 years.

12019
Pretesting Orientation Techniques. United States Employment Service, Division of Testing, Salem, OR 1970
Descriptors: Adults; *Aptitude Tests; *Educationally Disadvantaged; Job Placement; *Occupational Tests; Perceptual Motor Coordination; *Personnel Selection; Spanish; Verbal Ability; Vocational Aptitude
Identifiers: Clerical Aptitude; Mathematical Aptitude; Practice Tests

Availability: U.S. Employment Service Offices only
Target Audience: 18-64
Notes: Time, 30

For use in pretesting with disadvantaged individuals who may be unfamiliar with testing procedures. Contains a brief test similar to the General Aptitude Test Battery (TC000412). A Spanish version is available. Not available to the general public. Contact a state employment service agency for further information.

12032
Pediatric Examination of Educational Readiness. Levine, Melvin D.; Schneider, Elizabeth A. 1982
Subtests: Developmental Attainment; Processing Efficiency; Selective Attention; Behavioral Adaptation; Neuromaturation
Descriptors: *Attention Span; *Behavior Development; *Cognitive Processes; *Developmental Disabilities; *Educational Diagnosis; Language Skills; Medical Evaluation; Observation; Orientation; Perceptual Motor Coordination; Psychomotor Skills; *School Readiness Tests; Sequential Learning; *Young Children
Identifiers: *Neurodevelopmental Assessment; PEER
Availability: Educators Publishing Service; 75 Moulton St., Cambridge, MA 02238-9101
Target Audience: 4-6
Notes: Time, 60; Items, 147

A combined neurodevelopmental, behavioral, and health assessment designed for use by doctors or clinicians in the identification of developmental and other disabilities after screening via another method. Six areas of development are measured: Orientation, Gross Motor, Visual-Fine Motor, Sequential, Linguistic, Preacademic Learning.

12035
Analytic Learning Disability Assessment. Gnagey, Thomas D.; Gnagey, Patricia A. 1982
Descriptors: Adolescents; Attention Span; Auditory Discrimination; *Basic Skills; Children; Concept Formation; *Diagnostic Tests; Handwriting; *Individual Testing; *Learning Disabilities; Long Term Memory; Mathematics Achievement; Psychomotor Skills; Reading Skills; Short Term Memory; Spatial Ability; Spelling; Visual Discrimination
Identifiers: ALDA
Availability: Slosson Educational Publications; P.O. Box 280, E. Aurora, NY 14052
Grade Level: K-12
Target Audience: 5-17
Notes: Time, 75 approx.; Items, 77

Used to distinguish those students with specific learning skills deficits from those not having those deficits. Tests 77 skills which underlie basic school subjects, to reveal how students go about individual processes of learning. Summary scores include conceptualization and generalization; neuropsychological efficiency and organization; subject achievement potential; grade level achievement; educational lag; age level achievement; learning lag; neuropsychological lag; neuropsychological achievement potential; mean achievement level; neuropsychological achievement proficiency; failed unit score total; pervasive school readiness dysfunction; content achievement potential.

12043
Teacher Assessment of Grammatical Structures. Moog, Jean S.; Kozak, Victoria 1983
Subtests: Pre-sentence Level; Simple Sentence Level; Complex Sentence Level
Descriptors: Achievement Rating; Children; *Delayed Speech; *Hearing Impairments; Knowledge Level; *Language Acquisition; *Syntax
Identifiers: Normal Persons; TAGS
Availability: Central Institute for the Deaf; 818 S. Euclid St., St. Louis MO 63110
Target Audience: 3-12
Notes: Items, 50

Series of rating forms developed to evaluate a child's understanding and use of the grammatical structures of English and to suggest a sequence for teaching them. Used with hearing-impaired children who use spoken and/or signed English or normal-hearing children with delayed syntax development. Used for measuring use of syntactic structures, planning instruction, recording progress, reporting to parents. The presentence level is used to rate child's understanding and use of first single words up through a variety of 2- and 3-word utterances. The simple sentence level is used to rate child's use of various grammatic structures in complete sentences of at least 4 words, and the complex sentence level rates the use of various grammatical structures in complete sentences of at least 6 words.

12044
Inventory of Language Abilities, Level II. Minskoff, Esther H.; And Others 1981

Subtests: Auditory Reception; Visual Reception; Auditory Association; Visual Association; Verbal Expression; Manual Expression; Auditory Memory; Visual Memory; Grammatic Closure; Visual Closure; Auditory Closure and Sound Blending
Descriptors: Auditory Stimuli; Disabilities; Elementary Education; *Elementary School Students; *Expressive Language; Language Proficiency; *Learning Disabilities; Psychomotor Skills; *Receptive Language; *Screening Tests; Verbal Ability; Visual Stimuli
Availability: Educational Performance Associates; 600 Broad Ave., Ridgefield, NJ 07657
Grade Level: 3-5
Notes: Items, 132

Screening device for use by classroom teacher in identifying children with possible language learning difficulties. The inventory has a separate checklist for each of the language areas of the MWM Program for Developing Language Abilities, except for auditory closure and sound blending which are combined. Each checklist has 12 behaviors or items and contains examples of everyday social and academic behaviors common in the lives of most children in grades 3, 4, and 5. Inventory may also be used by teachers of handicapped children and with other children at junior and senior high school level suspected of having severe language disabilities.

12051
Anti-Negro Scale. Steckler, George A. 1957
Descriptors: Adults; *Attitude Measures; *Black Attitudes; Interpersonal Competence; Moral Values; Opinions; *Racial Attitudes; Racial Integration; Racial Relations
Availability: Journal of Abnormal and Social Psychology; v54 no3, p396-99 May 1957
Target Audience: 18-64
Notes: Items, 16

Designed for use in a study investigating authoritarian ideologies in Black individuals. Measures their anti-Black ideologies.

12052
Anti-White Scale. Steckler, George A. 1957
Descriptors: Adults; *Attitude Measures; *Black Attitudes; Interpersonal Competence; Moral Values; Opinions; *Racial Attitudes; Racial Integration; Racial Relations
Availability: Journal of Abnormal and Social Psychology; v54 n3 p396-99 May 1957
Target Audience: 18-64
Notes: Items, 18

Designed for use in a study investigating authoritarian ideologies in Black individuals. Measures their anti-White ideologies.

12057
Social Adjustment Scale for Schizophrenics. Schooler, Nina; And Others 1978
Subtests: Work; Household; External Family; Social/Leisure
Descriptors: *Adjustment (to Environment); Adults; Affective Measures; Family (Sociological Unit); *Interpersonal Competence; Interviews; *Patients; *Schizophrenia
Identifiers: Psychiatric Patients; SAS II
Availability: Dr. Myrna A. Weissman; Depression Research Unit, Yale University, 904 Howard Ave., Ste. 2A, New Haven, CT 06519
Target Audience: Adults
Notes: Items, 69

A semistructured interview adapted from the Social Adjustment Scale (TC007619). Designed for use with schizophrenic populations. Interview formats are available for patients or significant others. Interview must be administered by a trained rater.

12085
Infant Temperament Questionnaire, Revised. Carey, William B.; McDevitt, Sean C. 1978
Descriptors: Behavior Problems; *Infants; *Personality Measures; *Problem Children; Rating Scales; Screening Tests
Identifiers: Activity (Personality); Adaptability; Approach Avoidance; Distractibility; Intensity (Personality); Moods; Persistence (Personality); Rhythmicities; Thresholds
Availability: Pediatrics; v61 n5 p 735-39 May 1978
Target Audience: 0-1
Notes: Items, 95

Developed for use as a screening device for difficult temperament in infants. Uses 6-point frequency scale and more items than the original. Describes infants' behaviors in situations, such as reactions to new foods. Uses temperament categories of activity, rhythmicity, approach, adaptability, intensity, mood, persistence, distractibility, and threshold.

12086
Peek-a-Boo Test Set. Keystone View, Davenport, IA
Descriptors: Emotional Problems; Learning Disabilities; Perceptual Handicaps; *Preschool Children; Preschool Education; Screening Tests; *Vision Tests; *Visual Acuity; Visual Impairments
Identifiers: Amblyopia; *Nonreaders; *Stereoscopes
Availability: Keystone View; Ste. 3, 736 Federal St., Davenport, IA 52803
Target Audience: 2-5
Notes: Time, 4 approx.; Items, 8

Designed for young children who are unable to read or have specific learning disabilities. Vision is tested at far point (20 feet) and reading distance (16 inches) using Keystone Telebinocular instrument. Measures visual acuity, fusion, lateral and vertical eye coordination, color discrimination, and depth perception. Valuable for testing retarded children, as well as those who have perceptual or emotional problems. Useful with semiliterates of any age.

12092
Denver Handwriting Analysis. Anderson, Peggy L. 1983
Subtests: Near Point Copying; Writing the Alphabet; Far Point Copying; Manuscript Cursive Transition; Dictation
Descriptors: *Criterion Referenced Tests; Cursive Writing; Elementary Education; *Elementary School Students; Eye Hand Coordination; *Handwriting; Letters (Alphabet); Manuscript Writing (Handlettering); Remedial Instruction; Visual Discrimination; Dictation
Identifiers: Copying Ability; DHA
Availability: Academic Therapy Publications; 20 Commercial Blvd., Novato, CA 94947-6191
Grade Level: 3-8
Notes: Time, 60 approx.

An informal, criterion-referenced test which uses a task analysis approach to identification of specific handwriting difficulties for purposes of remedial intervention. Can be administered individually or to groups by classroom teachers, remedial specialists, and educational diagnosticians. May also be extended to evaluate cursive handwriting of younger or older students. Each subtest yields a mastery level score.

12095
Bowen-Chalfant Receptive Language Inventory. Bowen, Mack L.; Chalfant, James C. 1982
Descriptors: Bilingual Students; Children; *Criterion Referenced Tests; Individual Testing; Language Acquisition; Language Handicaps; Learning Disabilities; Mental Retardation; Physical Disabilities; *Receptive Language
Identifiers: RLI
Availability: C.C. Publications; P.O. Box 23699, Tigard, OR 97223
Target Audience: 2-9

Criterion-referenced measure designed to evaluate receptive language: attending, imitating, chaining, labeling, discriminating, and concept classification. Used to measure language development in preschool and bilingual or handicapped children of any age including moderately mentally retarded, physically handicapped, learning and language disabled children. Requires individual administration.

12097
Inventory for the Assessment of Laryngectomy Rehabilitation. LaBorwit, Louis J. 1982
Subtests: Speech-Voice; Family-Social; Vocational-Occupational; Psychological-Attitudes; Physiological-Anatomy; Medical-First Aid; Laryngectomees
Descriptors: Adults; Anatomy; First Aid; Knowledge Level; Questionnaires; *Rehabilitation; Social Attitudes; *Speech Handicaps; Speech Skills; Vocational Rehabilitation
Identifiers: *Laryngectomees
Availability: C.C. Publications; P.O. Box 23699, Tigard, OR 97223
Target Audience: 18-64
Notes: Time, 45 approx.; Items, 72

Designed to obtain information on a laryngectomy patient's knowledge of his or her overall condition to determine the level of rehabilitation achieved. Covers social and psychological aspects of the condition also.

12098
Assessment of Intelligibility of Dysarthric Speech. Yorkston, Kathryn M.; Beukelman, David R. 1981
Descriptors: Adolescents; Adults; Speech; Speech and Hearing Clinics; Speech Handicaps; *Speech Tests
Identifiers: *Dysarthria
Availability: C.C. Publications; P.O. Box 23699, Tigard, OR 97223
Target Audience: 13-64

A measure of the intelligibility of speech of persons with faulty articulation as a result of lesions or defects in the central nervous system. Quantifies single word and sentence intelligibility and speaking rate. Aids in rank ordering speakers, comparing performance to normal speakers, and monitoring performance over time. Administered by clinicians.

12100
Stuttering Prediction Instrument for Young Children. Riley, Glyndon D. 1981
Descriptors: Clinical Diagnosis; Interviews; Parent Attitudes; *Prognostic Tests; Speech and Hearing Clinics; *Speech Handicaps; *Stuttering; Tape Recordings; Young Children
Identifiers: SPI
Availability: C.C. Publications; P.O. Box 23699, Tigard, OR 97223
Target Audience: 3-8

Designed to aid clinicians who work with stuttering children, to make decisions about severity and chronicity. Covers history, reactions, part-word repetitions, prolongations, and stuttering frequency. Uses parent interview, observation, and taped recording of child's speech.

12101
Screening Test for Developmental Apraxia of Speech. Blakeley, Robert W. 1981
Subtests: Expressive Language Discrepancy; Vowels and Diphthongs; Oral-Motor Movement; Verbal Sequencing; Motorically Complex Words; Articulation; Transpositions; Prosody
Descriptors: Articulation (Speech); Children; Diagnostic Tests; *Expressive Language; Individual Testing; Phonics; Psychomotor Skills; *Screening Tests; *Speech Handicaps; *Speech Skills
Identifiers: *Apraxia (Speech)
Availability: C.C. Publications; P.O. Box 23699, Tigard, OR 97223
Target Audience: 4-12
Notes: Time, 10 approx.

Individually administered measure designed to assist in the differential diagnosis of a condition which is manifested by the inability to produce words vocally in a patterned, sequential, meaningful manner. A review of the test by T. W. Guyette and W. M. Diedrich can be found in Language, Speech and Hearing Services in Schools; v14 p202-09 Oct 1983.

12102
Questionnaire for Elderly Participants in Leisure. Mellinger, Jeanne C. 1979
Descriptors: *Leisure Time; *Older Adults; Questionnaires
Availability: Jeanne C. Mellinger; Dept. of Psychology, George Mason University, Fairfax, VA 22030
Target Audience: 55-99

Questionnaire developed to compare leisure activities, attitudes toward leisure, social contacts, morale, and demographic variables of various groups of elderly people.

12103
Sexual Experiences Survey. Koss, Mary P.; Oros, Cheryl J. 1980
Descriptors: Adults; Aggression; Females; Males; Questionnaires; *Rape; *Sexuality; Victims of Crime
Availability: Journal of Consulting and Clinical Psychology; v50 n3 p455-57 Jun 1982
Target Audience: 18-45
Notes: Items, 16

Used on a college population to develop a survey capable of reflecting hidden cases of rape and of documenting a dimensional view of sexual aggression and sexual victimization. There are male and female versions, written in parallel versions and containing 12 yes or no questions which refer explicitly to sexual intercourse associated with various degrees of coercion, threat, and force. Both forms contain biographical questions. The female version has an additional question referring specifically to rape.

12104
Zukow Teacher Form. Zukow, Patricia Goldring; Zukow, Arnold H. 1968
Subtests: Attention/Excitability; Motor Coordination
Descriptors: Attention Span; *Behavior Rating Scales; Elementary Education; *Elementary School Students; Elementary School Teachers; *Hyperactivity; Perceptual Motor Coordination; *Preschool Children; Preschool Education; Preschool Teachers
Availability: Journal of Consulting and Clinical Psychology; v46 n2 p213-22 1978
Target Audience: 2-12
Notes: Items, 15

Designed for completion by teachers to aid in identification of hyperactive children.

12106
Philadelphia Geriatric Center Morale Scale, Revised. Lawton, M. Powell; And Others 1975
Subtests: Agitation; Attitude toward Own Aging; Lonely Dissatisfaction
Descriptors: *Aging (Individuals); *Anxiety; *Geriatrics; *Interpersonal Relationship; *Loneliness; *Morale; *Older Adults; *Psychological Patterns; Questionnaires
Identifiers: *Oral Tests; PGC; TIM(I)
Availability: Tests in Microfiche; Test Collection, Educational Testing Service, Princeton, NJ 08541
Target Audience: 65-99
Notes: Items, 17

A multidimensional approach to assessing the psychological state of older persons. Designed to provide a measure of morale appropriate for very old or less competent individuals. Recommended that questionnaire be administered orally. Scores on this questionnaire should not be taken as an absolute judgment but should be used in a clinical setting as one factor in helping older people and their families arrive at appropriate decisions.

12112
Hawaii Early Learning Profile. Furuno, Setsu; And Others 1979
Descriptors: *Child Development; Cognitive Development; *Developmental Disabilities; *Developmental Tasks; *Disabilities; Infants; Interpersonal Competence; Language Acquisition; Preschool Children; Profiles; Psychomotor Skills; Self Care Skills; *Young Children
Identifiers: Hawaii; HELP
Availability: Vort Corporation; P.O. Box 11757, Palo Alto, CA 94306
Target Audience: 0-3

Developed at the University of Hawaii to serve children with a wide range of handicaps and diagnoses. Designed to provide a single instrument for assessment and a comprehensive picture of a child's functional levels. A set of 3 charts display 650 skills as a horizontal continuum of sequenced skills and behaviors for children aged 0 to 3 years. Appropriate for use with handicapped infants, young children, and developmentally delayed preschool children.

12123
SRA Nonverbal Form. McMurry, Robert N.; King, Joseph E. 1973
Descriptors: Adults; *Aptitude Tests; *Clerical Occupations; *Job Placement; *Limited English Speaking; *Nonverbal Ability; Nonverbal Tests; Occupational Tests; Pictorial Stimuli; *Sales Occupations
Identifiers: *Learning Ability
Availability: Science Research Associates; 155 N. Wacker Dr., Chicago, IL 60606
Target Audience: 18-64
Notes: Time, 10; Items, 60

Designed to measure general learning ability. Uses pictorial items. Does not require reading ability. Used in industry with claims processors, office personnel, and route salespersons. Suitable for use with persons having difficulty in reading or understanding English. For placement of workers in entry level positions. Most useful for persons with less than 12 years of education.

12125
Clinical Assessment Inventory. Moss, Gene R. 1981
Subtests: Appearance; Orientation; Mood; Speech Form, Social Skills; Program Participation; Program Cooperation; Room Maintenance; Speech Content
Descriptors: Adults; Clinics; Interpersonal Competence; Measures (Individuals); *Medical Evaluation; Nurses; Older Adults; Physical Characteristics; Program Evaluation; *Psychiatric Services
Identifiers: Psychiatric Nursing; *Psychiatric Patients; TIM(I)
Availability: Tests in Microfiche; Test Collection, Educational Testing Service, Princeton, NJ 08541
Target Audience: 18-64
Notes: Items, 50

Designed to be used by nursing staff in assessing the effects of psychiatric treatment of adults in the hospital setting. Completed twice daily during staff rounds. Results are graphed.

12145
Frostig Pictures and Patterns, Revised Edition: Beginning. Frostig, Marianne 1972
Descriptors: *Elementary School Students; *Perceptual Handicaps; Perceptual Motor Coordination; Preschool Children; Preschool Education; Primary Education; Spatial Ability; Vision Tests; *Visual Perception

Identifiers: Frostig Developmental Program of Visual Perception
Availability: Modern Curriculum Press; 13900 Prospect Rd., Cleveland, OH 44136
Grade Level: K-3
Target Audience: 3-8
Notes: Items, 80

Sequentially arranged exercises designed to develop visual perception skills. Skill areas include visual-motor coordination, figure-ground perception, perceptual constancy, and perception of spatial relationships.

12146
Frostig Pictures and Patterns, Revised Edition: Intermediate. Frostig, Marianne 1972
Descriptors: *Elementary School Students; *Perceptual Handicaps; Perceptual Motor Coordination; Primary Education; Spatial Ability; Vision Tests; *Visual Perception
Identifiers: Frostig Developmental Program of Visual Perception
Availability: Modern Curriculum Press; 13900 Prospect Rd., Cleveland, OH 44136
Grade Level: K-3
Notes: Items, 112

A series of sequentially arranged exercises designed to develop visual-perception skills. Skill areas include visual-motor coordination, figure-ground perception, perceptual constancy, and perception of spatial relationships.

12147
Frostig Pictures and Patterns, Revised Edition: Advanced. Frostig, Marianne 1972
Descriptors: *Elementary School Students; *Perceptual Handicaps; Perceptual Motor Coordination; Primary Education; Spatial Ability; Vision Tests; *Visual Perception
Identifiers: Frostig Developmental Program of Visual Perception
Availability: Modern Curriculum Press; 13900 Prospect Rd., Cleveland, OH 44136
Grade Level: K-3
Notes: Items, 128

A series of sequentially arranged exercises designed to develop visual perception skills. Skill areas include visual-motor coordination, figure-ground perception, perceptual constancy, and perception of spatial relationships.

12159
Early Learning Accomplishment Profile. Glover, M. Elayne; And Others 1978
Subtests: Gross Motor; Fine Motor; Cognitive; Language; Self Help; Social Emotional
Descriptors: *Child Development; Cognitive Development; *Developmental Tasks; *Disabilities; *Infants; Interpersonal Competence; Language Acquisition; Observation; Parent Child Relationship; Pretests Posttests; Psychomotor Skills; Self Care Skills; *Spanish; Spanish Speaking; *Young Children
Identifiers: Chapel Hill Training Outreach Project; Early LAP
Availability: Kaplan School Supply Corporation; 1310 Lewisville-Clemmons Rd., Lewisville, NC 27023
Target Audience: 0-3

Used to assess developmental level of handicapped children who are functioning in the early developmental range from birth to age 3. The starting point or basal level for the Early LAP is the positive demonstration or observation of 8 consecutive skill items in each of the 6 areas of skills development. Used for pretesting and posttesting. Also available in a Spanish-language version.

12161
Brigance Diagnostic Assessment of Basic Skills—Spanish Edition. Brigance, Albert H. 1983
Subtests: Readiness; Speech; Functional Word Recognition; Oral Reading; Reading Comprehension; Word Analysis; Listening; Writing and Alphabetizing; Numbers and Computation; Measurement
Descriptors: *Bilingual Students; Criterion Referenced Tests; *Diagnostic Tests; Elementary Education; *Elementary School Mathematics; *Elementary School Students; Individual Testing; Language Dominance; *Reading Achievement; Screening Tests; *Spanish; Spanish Speaking; Student Placement
Availability: Curriculum Associates, Inc.; 5 Esquire Rd., N. Billerica, MA 01862-2589
Grade Level: K-6
Notes: Items, 102

A diagnostic assessment designed for use with Spanish-speaking, elementary-aged children. Designed to determine functioning level in Spanish; learning problems and language barriers, and basic skills. The items were translated into Spanish from the Brigance Diagnostic Inventory of Basic Skills (TC011925). Several items are provided in English and Spanish to aid in determining language dominance.

12168
Student Rights Scale. Oaster, Thomas R. 1982
Subtests: General Rights; Due Process; Academic Self Determination; Freedom of Expression; Personal Conduct
Descriptors: Age Differences; American Indians; *Attitude Measures; Comparative Analysis; *Cross Cultural Studies; Elementary School Teachers; Nonreservation American Indians; Parent Attitudes; *Parents; Reservation American Indians; Secondary Education; *Secondary School Students; *Secondary School Teachers; Student Attitudes; *Student Rights; Teacher Attitudes
Availability: Thomas R. Oaster; School of Education, Educational Research & Psychology, University of Missouri, 5100 Rockhill Rd., Kansas City, MO 64110
Grade Level: 7-12
Target Audience: 13-64
Notes: Items, 38

Designed to assess attitudes concerning student rights in junior and senior high school. Developed to gather opinions from students, teachers, and parents. Used in a study of reservation and off-reservation Native American parent, teacher, and student perceptions of student rights. Normative data are available in ERIC document ED220740.

12173
Adult Neuropsychological Evaluation. Swiercinsky, Dennis 1978
Subtests: Hand/Foot Dominance Survey; Visual Acuity; Visual Dominance; Screening Survey of Motor Functions; Finger Tapping; Hand Dynamometer; Grooved Pegboard; Trail Making Tests; Auditory Sensitivity Survey; Rhythm Test; Tactile Sensitivity Survey; Stereognosis Survey; Finger Agnosia; Graphesthesia; Visual Sensitivity and Perimetry; Spatial Relations; Tactual Performance Test; Aphasia Language Performance Scales; Speech Sounds Perception; Wechsler Adult Intelligence Scale; Shipley Institute of Living Scale; Modified Wechsler Memory Scale
Descriptors: Adults; *Aphasia; Auditory Perception; Diagnostic Tests; *Individual Testing; Intelligence Tests; Lateral Dominance; Memory; *Neurological Impairments; Psychomotor Skills; Spatial Ability; Tactual Perception; Visual Acuity
Identifiers: *Neuropsychology; Test Batteries
Availability: Charles C. Thomas Publisher; 2600 S. First St., Springfield, IL 62717
Target Audience: 18-64
Notes: Time, 480

A battery of standardized tests assembled for use in clinical neuropsychology to aid in the diagnosis of brain damage. Assesses areas of mental functioning sensitive to brain impairment. Must be administered individually by trained personnel.

12179
Grammatical Analysis of Elicited Language: Pre-Sentence Level. Moog, Jean S.; And Others 1983
Subtests: Readiness Skills; Single Words; Word Combinations
Descriptors: Expressive Language; *Hearing Impairments; *Language Acquisition; *Language Tests; Oral Language; *Preschool Children; Receptive Language; Sign Language; Total Communication
Identifiers: GAEL(P)
Availability: Central Institute for the Deaf; 818 S. Euclid, St. Louis, MO 63110
Target Audience: 3-6

Developed to evaluate spoken or signed English skills of hearing-impaired children. Can be administered in spoken and/or signed language and is appropriate for children enrolled in oral education programs and in total communication programs in English. Tests have been standardized on normal-hearing children so they can also be used to evaluate children with language disabilities who are normal hearing as well as hearing impaired. Appropriate for children at the level of not yet understanding or producing words and for children who can understand and produce short phrases. Also useful with learning-disabled, aphasic, mentally retarded, autistic, or language-impaired children.

12180
Kindergarten Language Screening Test. Gauthier, Sharon V.; Madison, Charles L. 1978
Descriptors: Expressive Language; Individual Testing; Kindergarten; *Kindergarten Children; Language Handicaps; *Language Proficiency; Language Tests; Receptive Language; *Screening Tests
Identifiers: KLST
Availability: C. C. Publications, Inc.; P.O. Box 23699, Tigard, OR 97223
Grade Level: K
Target Audience: 5-6
Notes: Items, 8

Designed to compare kindergarten children's present language abilities with a level appropriate for their age and grade. It is not meant to pinpoint the exact nature of any language problem but only to indicate the probability of a particular child having a language deficit. Items indicate abilities considered to be normal in language development of kindergarten children. Items reflect both receptive and expressive language skills.

12182
Retirement Activities Card Sort Kit. Career Research and Testing, San Jose, CA 1980
Descriptors: Aging (Individuals); Decision Making; Interests; *Older Adults; *Retirement
Identifiers: *Card Sort
Availability: Consulting Psychologists Press; 577 College Ave., Palo Alto, CA 94306
Target Audience: 65-99
Notes: Time, 120 approx.; Items, 48

Card sort which uses 48 common pastimes as an aid in planning a transition from formal employment to a fulfilling retirement lifestyle. Pastimes range from cultural events to meditation, and from entertaining to group leadership. By analyzing how they have organized and classified cards, individuals can clarify personal criteria for retirement decisions. Manual also includes 8 supplementary activities for dealing with aging and retirement.

12184
Carlson Psychological Survey. Carlson, Kenneth A. 1981
Subtests: Chemical Abuse; Thought Disturbance; Antisocial Tendencies; Self Depreciation; Validity
Descriptors: Adults; Antisocial Behavior; *Criminals; *Personality Assessment; *Prisoners; *Psychological Evaluation; Psychological Patterns; Questionnaires
Identifiers: CPS
Availability: Research Psychologists Press; P.O. Box 984, Port Huron, MI 48060
Target Audience: 18-64
Notes: Items, 50

Intended for use with those charged with or convicted of criminal offenses. Intended primarily for incarcerated adults but is satisfactory for use with criminal offenders on probation. Vocabulary is simple and written at a 4th grade reading level. Primary purpose of CPS is for initial assessment and classification of criminal offenders.

12191
Self-Rating Depression Scale. Zung, William W. K. 1974
Descriptors: Adults; *Depression (Psychology); Emotional Disturbances; Rating Scales; Self Evaluation (Individuals)
Availability: CIBA Pharmaceutical Co.; Division of CIBA-CEGY Corporation, Summit, NJ 07901
Target Audience: 18-64
Notes: Items, 20

Designed for use as a quantitative measure of depression as an emotional disorder. May be used in psychiatric research or in the doctor's office to measure "masked depression" in patients with physical symptoms having no organic basis. Items indicate pervasive affective disturbance; psychological disturbance, and physiological and psychmotor disturbances.

12199
Assessment of Basic Competencies. Somwaru, Jwalla P. 1981
Subtests: Observing Skills; Organizing Skills; Relating Skills; Understanding Words; Comprehending Expressions; Producing Expressions; Reading for Meaning; Decoding Skills; Knowing Numbers and Operations; Understanding Concepts; Solving Problems
Descriptors: *Basic Skills; *Cognitive Processes; Decoding (Reading); *Diagnostic Tests; Disadvantaged; *Elementary School Students; Elementary Secondary Education; Emotional Problems; *Individual Needs; *Junior High School Students; *Language Skills; Learning Disabilities; *Mathematics Achievement; Mild Mental Retardation; *Preschool Children; Reading Comprehension
Availability: Scholastic Testing Service; 480 Meyer Rd., Bensenville, IL 60106
Grade Level: K-9
Target Audience: 3-15
Notes: Time, 120 approx.

Part of a battery of psychoeducational tests for students with special needs. May also be used with older persons for criterion-referenced evaluation. Developed to provide assessment of students' strengths and weaknesses in basic areas of competence necessary for learning in school. The 11 subtests fall into 3 main areas: Information Processing, Language, and Mathematics. Test focuses on skills which are learned rather than on presumed abilities and processes. In addition to norm-referenced interpretation, criterion-referenced assessment can also be carried out. Can also be used for developmental assessment; items are arranged in ascending order of difficulty, and focus is on level of competence of student in developmental scale. In diagnostic assessment, items are grouped in clusters and arranged in parallel strands in ascending order of difficulty to determine which skills and clusters have been mastered.

12201
Phoneme Baseline Recording Forms. Pizzuti, Mary 1979
Descriptors: *Articulation (Speech); *Diagnostic Tests; *Elementary School Students; Elementary Secondary Education; Learning Disabilities; Mental Retardation; *Phonemes; *Secondary School Students; *Speech Therapy
Availability: Communication Skill Builders; 3130 N. Dodge Blvd., P.O. Box 42050, Tucson, AZ 85733
Grade Level: K-12

Designed to assist speech and language clinicians in public school settings. Baselines are adaptable for use with children in kindergarten through grade 6 and for use with mentally retarded and learning-disabled children. Levels are traditional: isolation, syllables, words, sentences, reading or story retelling, and spontaneous speech with topic cues given. Story retelling level of baselines was developed especially to be used with children who cannot read. Administration at all levels takes approximately 7 minutes for each phoneme.

12203
Iowa's Severity Rating Scales for Communication Disabilities: Preschool, Ages 2-5. Freilinger, J. Joseph, ed.; And Others 1978
Descriptors: *Communication Disorders; Expressive Language; *Handicap Identification; *Preschool Children; Receptive Language
Identifiers: ISRS
Availability: ERIC Document Reproduction Service; 3900 Wheeler Ave., Alexandria, VA 22304 (ED221013, 473 pages)
Target Audience: 2-5

General guidelines that may be used as part of the clinical speech and language program to obtain uniform identification of preschool children with communication disabilities. Does not include all factors which a speech and language clinician needs to consider when assigning a rating.

12204
Teste de Prontidao para a Pre-Primaria. National Portuguese Materials Development Center, Providence, RI 1980
Subtests: Linguistic; Visual; Visual Motor; Motor; Auditive
Descriptors: Behavior Patterns; Bilingual Education; Educational Diagnosis; Language Acquisition; Listening Comprehension; Portuguese; Preschool Children; Psychomotor Skills; School Readiness; School Readiness Tests; Visual Discrimination
Identifiers: Elementary Secondary Education Act Title VII; TPP
Availability: National Dissemination Center; 417 Rock St., Fall River, MA 02720
Target Audience: 4-5

Used to identify kind of behavior and level of knowledge of preschool children. Standardized test for psychoeducational assessment and the first of its kind in Portuguese. Diagnostic in nature. Is useful for providing the classroom teacher, psychologists, pupil personnel specialists, and special educators with a quick profile of a child's behavioral patterns, before entering school. Deals with 5 different behavioral areas.

12205
WISC-R Performance Scale for Deaf Children. Anderson, Richard J.; Sisco, Frankie H. 1976
Subtests: Picture Completion; Picture Arrangement; Block Design; Object Assembly; Coding; Mazes
Descriptors: Adolescents; Children; Finger Spelling; *Hearing Impairments; Individual Testing; *Intelligence Tests; Nonverbal Tests; Performance Tests; Sign Language; Total Communication
Identifiers: Oral Testing; Wechsler Intelligence Scale for Children (Revised)
Availability: Office of Demographic Studies, Gallaudet College; Washington, DC 20002
Target Audience: 6-17

A standardization of the 5 performance scales of the WISC-R for use with hearing-impaired children. Administered via total communication, oral communication, finger spelling with speech, gestures and pantomime. The test itself is available from Psychological Corporation, San Antonio, TX. Normative data are provided by the source listed here.

12206

Stanford Achievement Test for Hearing Impaired Students. Gallaudet College, Washington, DC. Office of Demographic Studies 1974
Subtests: Word Meaning; Paragraph Meaning; Spelling; Language; Arithmetic Computation; Arithmetic Concepts; Arithmetic Applications; Social Studies; Science
Descriptors: *Achievement Tests; Adolescents; *Arithmetic; Children; Finger Spelling; *Hearing Impairments; Manual Communication; *Reading Achievement; *Sciences; *Social Studies; *Spelling; Young Adults
Identifiers: Out of Level Testing; SAT HI
Availability: Center for Assessment and Demographic Studies, Gallaudet College; 800 Florida Ave., N.E., Washington, DC 20002
Target Audience: 8-19
Notes: Time, 190; Items, 400

An adjusted version of the 1973 Stanford Achievement Test. Time limits have been extended. Administration is spread over one week and is via whichever communication method is used in the classroom. Fingerspelling, as well as signing, is employed. Practice tests are used to familiarize students with tests and answer sheets. Hearing-impaired students may be tested at different levels in reading, math, and spelling because they tend to score higher in math and spelling. Normed on a nationwide sample. Subtests vary with levels.

12207

Behavior Problem Checklist-Revised. Quay, Herbert C. 1983
Subtests: Conduct Disorder; Socialized Aggression; Attention Problems-Immaturity; Anxiety-Withdrawal; Psychotic Behavior; Motor Excess
Descriptors: Adolescents; Aggression; Anxiety; Attention Span; *Behavior Problems; Children; *Diagnostic Tests; Maturity (Individuals); Physical Activity Level; Psychosis; Rating Scales; *Screening Tests
Availability: Dr. Herbert C. Quay; Applied Social Sciences, University of Miami, P.O. Box 248074, Coral Gables, FL 33124
Target Audience: 5-17
Notes: Time, 10; Items, 89

A scale for rating the severity of behavior problems. May be used by any knowledgeable observer, e.g., parent, teacher, child care worker. Used for screening in school settings, as an aid in clinical diagnosis, for measurement of behavior change, and for selection of research subjects.

12208

Stuttering Problem Profile. Silverman, Franklin H. 1973
Descriptors: Adults; Attitude Measures; Behavior Modification; Counseling Objectives; Social Behavior; *Speech Therapy; *Stuttering
Availability: Journal of Speech and Hearing Disorders; v45 n1 p119-23 Feb 1980
Target Audience: 18-64
Notes: Items, 86

Designed to identify behaviors which can be modified as goals for stuttering therapy, including aspects of the moment of stuttering, word and situation avoidances, maladaptive attitudes toward stuttering, and disturbances in the personal-social sphere. No score is computed. Qualitative data are provided only. Because instrument requires subjects to indicate behaviors they would like to occur, selected behaviors would be more likely to undergo modification through counseling.

12211

Escala de Comportamentos Para Criancas. National Portuguese Materials Development Center, Providence, RI 1980
Subtests: Linguistic; Auditory; Visual; Visual Motor; Motor; Mathematics; Emotional; Organic
Descriptors: Behavior Rating Scales; Bilingual Education; *Diagnostic Tests; Elementary Education; *Elementary School Students; Language Acquisition; Listening Comprehension; Mathematical Concepts; Personality Traits; Physical Health; *Portuguese; Psychomotor Skills; Visual Discrimination
Availability: National Dissemination Center; 417 Rock St., Fall River, MA 02720
Grade Level: K-5

A behavior scale to assess social, emotional, physical, and academic behavior of bilingual Portuguese students in kindergarten through grade 5. Diagnostic inventory intended for use by classroom teacher. Also helpful to provide a quick profile of a child's behavior patterns in school for psychologists, pupil personnel specialists, and special educators.

12212

Basic Achievement Skills Individual Screener. The Psychological Corporation, San Antonio, TX 1983
Subtests: Reading; Mathematics; Spelling; Writing

Descriptors: *Achievement Tests; *Adults; *American Indians; *Criterion Referenced Tests; Diagnostic Tests; Educational Planning; *Elementary School Students; Elementary Secondary Education; Emotional Disturbances; Gifted; Hearing Impairments; Individualized Education Programs; *Individual Testing; Learning Disabilities; *Mathematics; Mild Mental Retardation; Norm Referenced Tests; *Reading Tests; *Secondary School Students; *Spelling; Student Placement
Identifiers: BASIS; *Writing Sample
Availability: The Psychological Corporation; 555 Academic Ct., San Antonio, TX 78204-0952
Grade Level: 1-12
Notes: Time, 55

Individually administered achievement test providing norm- and criterion-referenced score interpretation in reading, mathematics, and spelling. An optional writing sample is included. For use as part of diagnostic assessment of students prior to development of IEPs or in placing students in class or text. Norms available for Native American (GR. 5-7); hearing-impaired (GR. 4-6); and emotionally handicapped (GR. 6-8); students educable mentally retarded (GR. 7-9); students gifted (GR. 2-5); and students learning-disabled (GR. 3-8). Said to be useful with a post-high school population. A review of this instrument by A. R. Fitzpatrick can be found in Journal of Educational Measurement; v21 p309-11 Fall 1984.

12218

Diagnostic Interview Schedule. National Institute of Mental Health, Washington, DC 1979
Descriptors: Adults; Counseling; *Drug Abuse; *Emotional Problems; *Interviews; *Mental Disorders; Patients; Questionnaires; Social Behavior
Identifiers: DIS; National Institute of Mental Health; NIMH
Availability: National Institute of Mental Health; Public Inquiries Section, 5600 Fishers Ln., Rockville, MD 20857
Target Audience: 18-64
Notes: Items, 254

In-depth questionnaire and screening interview designed to assess the severity of drug-related and non-drug-related emotional and mental problems prior to counseling or referral. Covers patients' background, symptoms, drug abuse, alcohol abuse, social behavior.

12232

Simmons Behavior Checklist. Reinherz, Helen Z. 1980
Descriptors: *Behavior Problems; Check Lists; Emotional Adjustment; *Parent Attitudes; Student Adjustment; Young Children
Identifiers: TIM(I)
Availability: Tests in Microfiche, Test Collection; Educational Testing Service, Princeton, NJ 08541
Target Audience: 4-5
Notes: Items, 38

Designed to assess the behavioral and emotional functioning of preschool age children. Covers a wide range of adjustment problems rather than just severe circumstances. Covers attention problems, shy or withdrawn behavior, dependency, demanding behavior, aggression, and immaturity. Unlike others, this scale is completed by parents.

12233

STILAP: State Technical Institute's Leisure Assessment Process. Navar, Nancy H.; Peterson, Carol Ann 1979
Descriptors: Adults; Behavior Problems; Check Lists; Counseling Services; Criminals; *Disabilities; Drug Abuse; Emotional Disturbances; *Interest Inventories; Learning Disabilities; *Leisure Time; Rehabilitation Counseling
Identifiers: STILAP; TIM(I)
Availability: Tests in Microfiche; Test Collection, Educational Testing Service, Princeton, NJ 08541
Target Audience: 18-64
Notes: Items, 124

An activity checklist designed to determine those leisure activities practiced by former or presently disabled counselees and their interests. Used with rehabilitation clients including disabled and behavioral, emotional and learning-disordered subjects and legal offenders. Activities are oriented toward users in the state of Michigan.

12234

Maladaptive Behavioral Record. Jenkins, W. O.; And Others 1975
Descriptors: *Adjustment (to Environment); Adolescents; Adults; Background; *Criminals; Drug Abuse; Preadolescents; Prognostic Tests; *Recidivism; Young Adults
Identifiers: *Parolees
Availability: Behavior Science Press; P.O. Drawer 28, Tuscaloosa, AL 35402

Target Audience: 10-64
Notes: Time, 40

An interview measure of degree of maladaption. Designed to predict recidivism of maladaptive persons. Items assess working conditions, amount of income, employer interactions, work attendance, alcohol use, gambling, money management, fighting, psychological adjustment, etc. For use with offenders, drug abusers and parolees to predict parole success.

12235

Environmental Deprivation Scale. Pascal, Gerald R.; Jenkins, William O. 1973
Descriptors: Adults; Background; *Criminals; *Delinquency; Individual Testing; Mental Disorders; *Patients; Preadolescents; *Recidivism
Identifiers: EDS; *Environmental Deprivation
Availability: Rehabilitation Research Foundation; P.O. Box BV, University, AL 35486
Target Audience: 10-64
Notes: Time, 40

An individually administered, hand-scored measure of the amount of environmental deprivation experienced by a person. To predict recidivism of offenders, mental hospital patients, and others who exhibit maladaption. Items cover employment, income, debts, parental relationship, education, fear, etc. Interviewer/counselor uses behavior interviewing techniques.

12237

Brief Outpatient Psychopathology Scale. Free, Spencer M.; Overall, John E. 1977
Subtests: Anxiety, Psychomotor Activation; Depression; Somatization
Descriptors: Adults; Anxiety; Depression (Psychology); Drug Therapy; *Emotional Problems; Patients; *Psychopathology; *Rating Scales
Identifiers: BOPS; *Outpatients; Psychomotor Problems; Somatization
Availability: Journal of Clinical Psychology; v33 n3 p677-88 Jul 1977
Target Audience: 18-64
Notes: Items, 15

A rating scale, designed for use with outpatients, which was developed to cover a range of clinical manifestations that are found in persons with milder forms of psychological disturbances. Said to be useful in distinguishing between the effects of drugs being used to treat the condition. A revision of the New Physician's Rating List (TC007812). Also useful for measuring degrees of change in outpatients.

12254

Sibling Inventory of Behavior. Schaefer, Earl; Edgerton, Marianna 1979
Subtests: Empathy, Concern; Avoiding; Leadership, Involvement; Hurting; Kindness; Anger; Acceptance; Embarrassment
Descriptors: *Children; *Child Role; *Congenital Impairments; *Disabilities; Rating Scales; *Siblings
Identifiers: *Child Behavior; SIB; TIM(I)
Availability: Tests in Microfiche; Test Collection, Educational Testing Service, Princeton, NJ 08541
Target Audience: 3-12
Notes: Items, 28

Developed for use in a study of families of handicapped and nonhandicapped children to determine the behavior of the nonhandicapped child toward his or her sibling. Wording of items is appropriate for older sibling behavior toward a younger child whether or not the younger child is handicapped, or for the behavior of a nonhandicapped sibling toward a handicapped child regardless of which one is the older. Inventory includes some items from Sibling Behavior Inventory (Aaronson and Schaefer, 1971) (TC008974), Relationship Inventory for Families (Schaefer and Edgerton, 1975), and Sibling Behavior to Handicapped or Younger Child Inventory (Schaefer and Edgerton, 1979).

12267

The WORD Test. Jorgensen, Carol; And Others 1981
Subtests: Associations; Synonyms; Semantic Absurdities; Antonyms; Definitions; Multiple Definitions
Descriptors: Adults; Aphasia; Auditory Stimuli; *Children; *Diagnostic Tests; *Expressive Language; *Language Handicaps; *Language Tests; Learning Disabilities; *Semantics; *Vocabulary Skills
Availability: LinguiSystems; 1630 Fifth Ave., Ste. 806, Moline, IL 61265
Target Audience: 7-12
Notes: Time, 30; Items, 83

A diagnostic test to assess expressive vocabulary and semantic abilities of school-aged children whose language problems adversely affect their academic achievement and communication skills. The 6 subtests are constructed to yield information in the following areas of expressive language: categorizing, defining, verbal reasoning, and choosing appropriate words. This test is also appropriate for older children and adults whose functional language is within the performance range of the test. Test should be administered by a trained professional, such as speech-language pathologist, psychologist, teacher of learning-disabled students, or special education consultant.

12269
Test of Articulation Performance—Screen. Bryant, Brian R.; Bryant, Deborah L. 1983
Descriptors: *Articulation (Speech); *Articulation Impairments; Expressive Language; *Individual Testing; *Phonemes; Pictorial Stimuli; *Screening Tests; Speech Therapy; *Young Children
Identifiers: TAP(S)
Availability: Pro-Ed; 5341 Industrial Oaks Blvd., Austin, TX 78735
Target Audience: 3-8
Notes: Time, 5 approx.; Items, 31

A screening test to identify children with significant articulation problems who need further diagnostic articulation assessment and therapy. Each item is a word containing key English phonemes and is elicited from the child using a stimulus picture and sentence as the prompt. The child's articulation of the word is compared to standard English production and scored as correct or incorrect. Results are compared to national norms which are provided for spontaneous and imitative formats. May be administered by anyone trained in its use.

12270
Test of Articulation Performance—Diagnostic. Bryant, Brian R.; Bryant, Deborah L. 1983
Subtests: Isolated Words; Distinctive Features; Selective Deep Test; Continuous Speech; Stimulability
Descriptors: *Articulation (Speech); Articulation Impairments; *Diagnostic Tests; Expressive Language; *Individual Testing; *Phonemes; Remedial Programs; *Young Children
Identifiers: TAP(D)
Availability: Pro-Ed; 5341 Industrial Oaks Blvd., Austin, TX 78735
Target Audience: 3-8

Used to provide information on articulation problems which will be helpful in planning and implementing remedial programs. Information is provided on phonemes a child can and cannot produce properly and is acquired by analyzing areas covered by the test: isolated words, distinctive features (place, manner, voicing), selective deep test, continuous speech, stimulability (modeling behavior). Also, attitudes of child and others about child's overall communicative competence is assessed. To gauge attitudes of child, parents, and teachers toward child's verbal communication skills, examiners may use a standarized rating scale, such as the Verbal Communication Scales (TC012271). Should be administered by those qualified to give and interpret speech and language tests. The Isolated Words Component is suggested for use with all children. The other sections are used at the examiner's discretion.

12271
Verbal Communication Scales. Bryant, Brian R.; Bryant, Deborah L. 1983
Descriptors: Adults; *Attitude Measures; Childhood Attitudes; *Children; Language Handicaps; *Oral Language; Parent Attitudes; Speech Handicaps; Teacher Attitudes
Identifiers: VCS
Availability: Pro-Ed; 5341 Industrial Oaks Blvd., Austin, TX 78735
Target Audience: 5-64
Notes: Time, 5 approx.

Provides information concerning the attitudes of parents, teachers, and students about child's speech and language skills. Used for children referred for diagnostic assessment of speech and language disorders. May be used as the attitude measure in conjunction with Test of Articulation Performance-Diagnostic (TC012270). Parent and teacher forms use a Likert-scale rating procedures and consist of 25 items about child's practical applications of spoken language. Student scale consists of 20 questions asked by examiner and requiring a yes or no answer. Norms for parent and teacher scales are for children from 3 through 8 years of age; norms for student form are for children from ages 3 through 8.

12281
Explore the World of Work. Cutler, Arthur; And Others 1980
Descriptors: *Career Exploration; Elementary Education; *Elementary School Students; Grade 4; Intermediate Grades; Mild Mental Retardation; Occupational Clusters; *Reading Difficulties; Slow Learners; *Special Education
Identifiers: EWOW
Availability: CFKR Career Materials, Inc.; P.O. Box 437, Meadow Vista, CA 95722
Grade Level: 4-6
Notes: Time, 60

A career awareness and exploration tool for use with elementary, special education students, and others who read at 4th grade level or above. Uses game-like format in which students color pictures of job activities preferred and not preferred. Intended to introduce student to concept of job clusters and to encourage job exploration.

12288
Developmental Communication Inventory. Hanna, Rosemarie P.; And Others 1982
Descriptors: Cognitive Development; *Communication Disorders; Communication Skills; Criterion Referenced Tests; Individual Testing; Informal Assessment; Language Acquisition; Language Handicaps; Speech Handicaps; *Young Children
Identifiers: DCI; Developmental Communication Curriculum
Availability: The Psychological Corporation; 555 Academic Ct., San Antonio, TX 78204-0952
Target Audience: 1-7

Part of the Developmental Communication Curriculum developed at the Rehabilitation Institute of Pittsburgh. The inventory is a 2-part informal survey of the most important aspects of a child's development of cognition, language, and communication. Results of the survey can be used in making programmatic decisions. Administration time varies. The activities manual gives curricular strategies and more than 300 activities to help the children learn.

12315
Parent as a Teacher Inventory. Strom, Robert D. 1984
Subtests: Creativity Analysis; Frustration Analysis; Control Analysis; Play Analysis; Teaching-Learning Analysis
Descriptors: Adults; Arabic; Australian Aboriginal Languages; Children; Creativity; Discipline; French; German; Greek; Hopi; Italian; Navajo; *Parent Attitudes; *Parent Child Relationship; Parent Role; Play; Serbocroatian; *Spanish Speaking; Turkish; Values
Identifiers: *Child Behavior; Frustration; PAAT; Parent Restrictiveness; Parent Teaching
Availability: Scholastic Testing Service; 480 Meyer Rd., Bensenville, IL 60106
Target Audience: 18-64
Notes: Items, 50

A measure of parental attitudes toward specific parenting and child behaviors. Designed to determine parents' feeling about the importance of various behaviors, their values, and their own responses to certain child behaviors. May be used to study cross-cultural attitudes. Available in Spanish from the publisher. Has been translated into Arabic, French, German, Greek, Italian, Serbo-Croatian, Turkish, Australian Aboriginal, and American Indian (Hopi, Navajo). For information on translations, contact: Prof. R. Strom, College of Education, Arizona State University, Tempe, AZ 85287. For use with children aged 3-9.

12329
Specific Aptitude Test Battery S-473 R82. Gambling Dealer (amuse. and rec.) 343.467-018. Employment and Training Administration (DOL), Washington, DC 1982
Subtests: General Learning Ability; Verbal Aptitude; Numerical Aptitude; Spatial Aptitude; Form Perception; Clerical Perception; Motor Coordination; Finger Dexterity; Manual Dexterity
Descriptors: Adults; *Aptitude Tests; Career Guidance; *Culture Fair Tests; *Employment Potential; Employment Qualifications; *Ethnic Groups; *Job Applicants; Job Skills; Job Training; *Minority Groups; Object Manipulation; Personnel Evaluation; *Personnel Selection; Predictive Measurement; Spatial Ability; Timed Tests; *Vocational Aptitude
Identifiers: *Gambling Dealer; GATB; General Aptitude Test Battery; Manual Dexterity; SATB; USES Specific Aptitude Test Battery
Availability: Local U.S. Employment Service Office
Target Audience: Adults

A series of aptitude tests for specific job skills. Designed to select inexperienced, or untrained, personnel for training and to predict their job proficiency. Instruments were developed to be culture fair for minorities and ethnic groups. Subtests were drawn from the General Aptitude Test Battery (TC001422). Use of these instruments is restricted to state employment agencies. Designed to assess individual's aptitude for training as a gambling dealer. Data from 4 different jobs were combined to form this test battery. The jobs were dealers for dice, roulette, baccarat, and blackjack. A report describing the development of this test can be found in the ERIC system, document ED223707.

12330
Specific Aptitude Test Battery S200 R82. Ticket Agent (any ind.) 238.367-026. Employment and Training Administration (DOL), Washington, DC 1982
Subtests: General Learning Ability; Verbal Aptitude; Numerical Aptitude; Spatial Aptitude; Clerical Perception
Descriptors: Adults; *Aptitude Tests; Career Guidance; *Culture Fair Tests; *Employment Potential; Employment Qualifications; *Ethnic Groups; Job Analysis; *Job Applicants; Job Skills; Job Training; *Minority Groups; Personnel Evaluation; *Personnel Selection; Predictive Measurement; Spatial Ability; Timed Tests; *Vocational Aptitude
Identifiers: GATB; General Aptitude Test Battery; SATB; *Ticket Agents; USES Specific Aptitude Test Battery
Availability: Local U.S. Employment Service Office
Target Audience: Adults

A series of aptitude tests for specific job skills. Designed to select inexperienced, or untrained, personnel for training and to predict their job proficiency. Instruments were developed to be culture fair for minorities and ethnic groups. Subtests were drawn from the General Aptitude Test Battery (TC001422). Use of these instruments is restricted to state employment agencies. Designed to assess individual's aptitude for training as a ticket agent. A report describing the development of this test can be found in the ERIC system, document ED223718.

12331
Specific Aptitude Test Battery S-179 R82. Waiter/Waitress, Informal (hotel and rest.) 311.477-030. Employment and Training Administration (DOL), Washington, DC 1982
Subtests: Verbal Aptitude; Numerical Aptitude; Clerical Perception; Motor Coordination; Manual Dexterity
Descriptors: Adults; *Aptitude Tests; Career Guidance; *Culture Fair Tests; *Employment Potential; Employment Qualifications; *Ethnic Groups; Job Analysis; *Job Applicants; Job Skills; Job Training; *Minority Groups; Object Manipulation; Personnel Evaluation; *Personnel Selection; Predictive Measurement; Psychomotor Skills; Timed Tests; *Vocational Aptitude
Identifiers: GATB; General Aptitude Test Battery; Manual Dexterity; SATB; USES Specific Aptitude Test Battery; *Waiters Waitresses
Availability: Local U.S. Employment Service Office
Target Audience: Adults

A series of aptitude tests for specific job skills. Designed to select inexperienced, or untrained, personnel for training and to predict their job proficiency. Instruments were developed to be culture fair for minorities and ethnic groups. Subtests were drawn from the General Aptitude Test Battery (TC001422). Use of these instruments is restricted to state employment agencies. Instrument was designed to assess aptitude for employment as a waiter or waitress. A report describing the development of this test can be found in the ERIC system, document ED223714.

12332
Specific Aptitude Test Battery S-11 R82. Carpenter (Const.) 860.381-022. Employment and Training Administration (DOL), Washington, DC 1982
Subtests: General Learning Ability; Numerical Aptitude; Spatial Manual Dexterity
Descriptors: Adults; *Aptitude Tests; Building Trades; Career Guidance; *Carpentry; *Construction (Process); *Culture Fair Tests; *Employment Potential; Employment Qualifications; *Ethnic Groups; Job Analysis; *Job Applicants; Job Skills; Job Training; *Minority Groups; Object Manipulation; Personnel Evaluation; *Personnel Selection; Predictive Measurement; Timed Tests; *Vocational Aptitude
Identifiers: GATB; General Aptitude Test Battery; Manual Dexterity; SATB; USES Specific Aptitude Test Battery
Availability: Local U.S. Employment Service Office
Target Audience: Adults

A series of aptitude tests for specific job skills. Designed to select inexperienced, or untrained, personnel for training and to predict their job proficiency. Instruments were developed to be culture fair for minorities and ethnic groups. Subtests were drawn from the General Aptitude Test Battery (TC001422). Use of these instruments is restricted to state employment agencies. Designed to assess individual's aptitude for training and employment as a carpenter. A report describing the development of this test can be found in the ERIC system, document ED223695.

12333
Specific Aptitude Test Battery S-474R82. Customer-Service Representative (Light, Heat, & Power; Telephone & Telegraph; Waterworks) 239.367-010. Employment and Training Administration (DOL), Washington, DC 1982
Subtests: General Learning Ability; Verbal Aptitude; Numerical Aptitude; Clerical Perception; Motor Coordination
Descriptors: Adults; *Aptitude Tests; Career Guidance; *Culture Fair Tests; *Employment Potential; Employment Qualifications; *Ethnic Groups; Job Analysis; *Job Applicants; Job Skills; Job Training; *Minority Groups; Personnel Evaluation; *Personnel Selection; Predictive Measurement; Timed Tests; *Utilities; *Vocational Aptitude
Identifiers: *Customer Services; GATB; General Aptitude Test Battery; SATB; USES Specific Aptitude Test Battery
Availability: Local U.S. Employment Service Office
Target Audience: Adults

A series of aptitude tests for specific job skills. Designed to select inexperienced, or untrained, personnel for training and to predict their job proficiency. Instruments were developed to be culture fair for minorities and ethnic groups. Subtests were drawn from the General Aptitude Test Battery (TC001422). Use of these instruments is restricted to state employment agencies. This instrument was designed to assess individual's aptitude for training and employment as a customer service representative. A report describing the development of this test can be found in the ERIC system, document ED223696.

12334
Specific Aptitude Test Battery S-68 R82. Refinery Operator (petrol. refin.) 549.260-010. Employment and Training Administration (DOL), Washington, DC 1982
Subtests: General Learning Ability; Numerical Aptitude; Spatial Aptitude; Form Perception; Clerical Perception; Manual Dexterity
Descriptors: Adults; *Aptitude Tests; Career Guidance; *Culture Fair Tests; *Employment Potential; Employment Qualifications; *Ethnic Groups; Job Analysis; *Job Applicants; Job Skills; Job Training; *Minority Groups; Personnel Evaluation; *Personnel Selection; Predictive Measurement; Timed Tests; *Vocational Aptitude
Identifiers: GATB; General Aptitude Test Battery; Manual Dexterity; *Refinery Operator; SATB; USES Specific Aptitude Test Battery
Availability: Local U.S. Employment Service Office
Target Audience: Adults

A series of aptitude tests for specific job skills. Designed to select inexperienced, or untrained, personnel for training and to predict their job proficiency. Instruments were developed to be culture fair for minorities and ethnic groups. Subtests were drawn from the General Aptitude Test Battery (TC001422). Use of these instruments is restricted to state employment agencies. Designed to assess aptitude for training and employment as a refinery operator. A report describing the development of this test can be found in the ERIC system, document ED223722.

12335
Specific Aptitude Test Battery S 326R82. Respiratory Therapist (Medical ser.) 079.361-010. Employment and Training Administration (DOL), Washington, DC 1982
Subtests: General Learning Ability; Spatial Aptitude; Form Perception; Motor Coordination
Descriptors: Adults; *Aptitude Tests; Career Guidance; *Culture Fair Tests; *Employment Potential; Employment Qualifications; *Ethnic Groups; *Therapists; Job Analysis; *Job Applicants; Job Skills; Job Training; *Minority Groups; Personnel Evaluation; *Personnel Selection; Predictive Measurement; Psychomotor Skills; Timed Tests; *Vocational Aptitude; Respiratory Therapy
Identifiers: GATB; General Aptitude Test Battery; SATB; USES Specific Aptitude Test Battery
Availability: Local U.S. Employment Service Office
Target Audience: Adults

A series of aptitude tests for specific job skills. Designed to select inexperienced, or untrained, personnel for training and to predict their job proficiency. Instruments were developed to be culture fair for minorities and ethnic groups. Subtests were drawn from the General Aptitude Test Battery (TC001422). Use of these instruments is restricted to state employment agencies. Designed to assess individual's aptitude for training and employment as a respiratory therapist. A report describing the development of this test can be found in the ERIC system, document ED223723.

12343
Death Anxiety Questionnaire. Conte, Hope R.; And Others 1982
Descriptors: Adults; *Anxiety; *Attitude Measures; *Death; Fear; Older Adults; Questionnaires
Identifiers: DAQ
Availability: Journal of Personality and Social Psychology; v43 n4 p775-85 1982
Target Audience: 30-82
Notes: Items, 15

Designed to measure attitudes toward death and dying. Covers fear of the unknown, fear of suffering, fear of loneliness, and fear of personal extinction.

12352
Specific Aptitude Test Battery S-471 R81 Semiconductor Occupations (Electronics). Employment and Training Administration (DOL), Washington, DC 1982
Subtests: Numerical Aptitude; Motor Coordination; Finger Dexterity; Manual Dexterity; Form Perception; Clerical Perception
Descriptors: Adults; *Aptitude Tests; Career Guidance; *Culture Fair Tests; *Electronic Technicians; *Employment Potential; Employment Qualifications; *Ethnic Groups; Job Analysis; *Job Applicants; Job Skills; Job Training; *Minority Groups; Personnel Evaluation; *Personnel Selection; Predictive Measurement; Timed Tests; *Vocational Aptitude
Identifiers: GATB; General Aptitude Test Battery; Manual Dexterity; SATB; USES Specific Aptitude Test Battery
Availability: Local U.S. Employment Service Office
Target Audience: Adults

A series of aptitude tests for specific job skills. Designed to select inexperienced, or untrained, personnel for training and to predict their job proficiency. Instruments were developed to be culture fair for minorities and ethnic groups. Subtests were drawn from the General Aptitude Test Battery (TC001422). Use of these instruments is restricted to state employment agencies. Designed to assess individual's aptitude for training or employment in electronics occupations. A report describing the development of this test can be found in the ERIC system, document ED224826.

12362
Prescriptive Analysis of Language Disorders-Expressive Syntax Assessment. Wilson, Mary Sweig 1981
Descriptors: *Expressive Language; Individualized Education Programs; *Individual Testing; *Language Handicaps; Remedial Instruction; *Screening Tests; *Syntax; *Young Children
Identifiers: PALD(ESA)
Availability: Educators Publishing Service; 75 Moulton St., Cambridge, MA 02238
Target Audience: 2-4
Notes: Time, 30 approx.

Two-part standardized procedure to identify children in need of syntax remediation therapy and to prescribe programs of treatment. Test is appropriate for use with any child whose language performance is thought to be within the range of 2 years to 4 years, 11 months. These are children whose language development stage is between beginning morphene combinations through mastery of singulary transformations. The procedure can be used to determine whether a child has a language impairment which needs syntax remediation and to help determine proper remedial techniques. Can facilitate writing of individualized education plans.

12363
The Test of Early Mathematics Ability. Ginsburg, Herbert P.; Baroody, Arthur J. 1983
Descriptors: *Achievement Tests; Arithmetic; Computation; Diagnostic Tests; *Individual Testing; Mathematical Concepts; *Mathematics Achievement; Numbers; Number Systems; Talent Identification; *Young Children
Identifiers: TEMA
Availability: Pro-Ed; 5341 Industrial Oaks Blvd., Austin, TX 78735
Target Audience: 4-8
Notes: Time, 20 approx.; Items, 50

Measures mathematics performance of children between the ages of 4 and 8 years, 11 months. May also be used as a diagnostic instrument. Items are designed to measure the following areas: informal mathematics and formal mathematics skills. Informal mathematics include concepts of relative magnitude, counting, and calculation. Skills in formal mathematics include knowledge of convention number facts, calculation, and base-10 concept. Because this test may be too difficult for most 4-year-olds, it should not be given to them for diagnostic purposes, but may be used to help identify those 4-year-olds gifted in mathematics. Results of the test may be used to identify those ahead of or behind their peers in mathematical thinking, to diagnose strengths and weaknesses, to suggest instructional practices for individual children, to document progress, or to serve as a measure in research projects. Test is individually administered.

12365
SEARCH: A Scanning Instrument for the Identification of Potential Learning Disability. Second Edition, Expanded. Silver, Archie A.; Hagin, Rosa A. 1981
Subtests: Lamb Chop Matching; Lamb Chop Recall; Designs; Rote Sequencing; Auditory Discrimination; Articulation; Initials; Directionality; Finger Schema; Grip
Descriptors: Articulation (Speech); Auditory Discrimination; Body Image; Elementary School Students; *Grade 1; Handicap Identification; Individual Testing; Kindergarten; *Kindergarten Children; *Learning Disabilities; Perceptual Handicaps; Primary Education; *Screening Tests; Visual Perception
Availability: Walker Educational Book Corp.; 720 Fifth Ave., New York, NY 10019
Grade Level: K-1
Target Audience: 5-6
Notes: Time, 20 approx.; Items, 114

A scanning measure for identifying children vulnerable to learning failure as a result of perceptual immaturity or inadequate neuropsychological maturation. Ten subtests assess development in areas of visual perception, auditory perception, intermodal dictation, and body image. Designed for children in kindergarten or early grade one. Teach, a follow-up program, is designed to prevent learning failure by teaching the skills a vulnerable child needs for progress in reading, writing, and spelling.

12366
Hoffer-Osmond Diagnostic Test. Hoffer, Abram; And Others 1981
Subtests: Perceptual; Paranoid; Depression; Ratio; Short Form
Descriptors: Adolescents; Adults; *Depression (Psychology); Diagnostic Tests; Mental Disorders; *Patients; Schizophrenia; Screening Tests
Identifiers: HOD; Psychiatric Patients
Availability: Rehabilitation Research Foundation; P.O. Box BV, University, AL 35486
Target Audience: 13-64
Notes: Time, 30 approx.; Items, 145

Designed to diagnose psychiatric illness, monitor treatment, and establish prognosis. Patient must respond to questions in booklet or sort statements into boxes marked true or false. Instrument may be used by general medical practitioners to screen for mental illness.

12376
Initial Referral Form, Revised. Southwest Georgia Psychoeducational Service, Ochlocknee, GA
Descriptors: Adolescents; Behavior Problems; Children; *Learning Disabilities; Records (Forms); *Referral; Young Adults
Availability: Southwest Georgia Psychoeducational Service; PO Box 110-A, Ochlocknee, GA 31773
Target Audience: 0-20
Notes: Items, 40

For use with learning-disabled students. Covers background information, parent approval, screening procedures used, and a behavior checklist. A special form is used with infants. Used by parents, teachers or agencies to refer students for special services. For infant form, see TC012414.

12383
Adolescent Separation Anxiety Test. Hansburg, Henry 1980
Descriptors: *Adolescents; *Adults; *Affective Measures; Anxiety; *Children; Clinical Psychology; Females; Individual Testing; Males; Personality Problems; Rejection (Psychology); *Separation Anxiety
Availability: Robert E. Kreiger Publishing Co., Inc.; P.O. Box 9542, Melbourne, FL 32902
Target Audience: 9-64
Notes: Time, 20 approx.; Items, 12

Designed to evaluate emotional and personality patterns used by children and adolescents to react to separation experiences. When adult is tested, he/she responds as he/she felt as a child in a similar situation. May be used by clinical psychologists in cases where separation disorders are suspected. Separate forms for boys and girls.

12384
Career Assessment Inventories for the Learning Disabled. Weller, Carol; Buchanan, Mary 1983
Subtests: Attributes; Ability; Interests
Descriptors: Adolescents; Adults; Elementary School Students; *Learning Disabilities; Personality Traits; Psychomotor Skills; Spatial Ability; Verbal Development; Visual Perception; *Vocational Evaluation; Vocational Interests
Identifiers: CAI
Availability: Academic Therapy Publications; 20 Commercial Blvd., Novato, CA 94947-6191

Target Audience: 12-64
Notes: Time, 30 approx.; Items, 198

Designed specifically for use by vocational counselors, psychologists, educational diagnosticians, and special education teachers who work with learning-disabled adults or children. The attributes and ability inventories are completed by the examiner after a period of observation. The interest inventory is completed by the individual being assessed. The instrument consists of 3 parts. The attributes inventory, based on John I. Holland's theories of careers, assesses individual's dominant personality characteristics. The ability inventory provides a profile of examinee's auditory, visual, and motor areas. The interest inventory can be used to determine whether the individual's interests coincide with his or her personality attributes and abilities. Suitable for use across a wide range of ages from elementary school students through adults.

12386
Rating Scale for Evaluating English as a Second Language Reading Material. Stieglitz, Ezra L. 1982
Subtests: Background Information; The Skills of Reading; Recommendations for Adoption
Descriptors: Administrators; Adults; *English (Second Language); Evaluation; Instructional Materials; *Reading Materials; *Teachers
Availability: Journal of Reading; v26 n3 p222-28 Dec 1982
Target Audience: Adults

Designed to aid in evaluation of reading materials for use with ESL (English-as-Second-Language) students. Developed to aid teachers and administrators to assess instructional reading material.

12388
Expressive One-Word Picture Vocabulary Test-Upper Extension. Gardner, Morrison F. 1983
Descriptors: *Adolescents; Bilingual Students; *Cognitive Processes; *Concept Formation; Diagnostic Tests; *Expressive Language; Group Testing; Individual Testing; Intelligence; *Language Tests; Norm Referenced Tests; Pictorial Stimuli; Spanish Speaking; *Vocabulary
Identifiers: EOWPVT; *Verbal Intelligence
Availability: Academic Therapy Publications; 20 Commercial Blvd., Novato, CA 94947-6191
Target Audience: 12-16
Notes: Time, 15 approx.; Items, 70

Purpose is to obtain a basal estimate of a student's verbal intelligence by means of his or her acquired one-word expressive picture vocabulary. Can be valuable in obtaining a valid estimate of child's verbal intelligence through child's ability to form an idea or concept from a picture. This is an upward extension of the original Expressive One-Word Picture Vocabulary Test (TC010322), published in 1979. Can also yield information on possible speech defects, possible learning disorders, bilingual child's fluency in English, auditory processing, and auditory-visual association ability. Although normed on children whose primary language is English, may also be used with bilingual students to determine extent of their English vocabulary. A Spanish version is also available. The pictures are arranged in increasing order of difficulty and range from single concrete objects to collections of objects representing abstract concepts. Students respond to each item with a single word. May be administered individually or to small groups.

12389
Scale for the Identification of School Phobia. Want, Jerome H. 1983
Subtests: School Phobia; School Truancy
Descriptors: Behavior Rating Scales; Criterion Referenced Tests; *Elementary School Students; Elementary Secondary Education; *Emotional Disturbances; *Interviews; Screening Tests; *Secondary School Students; Truancy; *School Phobia
Identifiers: *Phobic Children; SIS
Availability: United Educational Services; P.O. Box 357, E. Aurora, NY 14052
Grade Level: 1-12
Notes: Items, 24

Criterion-referenced, behavior rating scale designed to differentially identify school phobic behavior from school-truant behavior. Used as a screening instrument to aid in early identification of school phobic children as opposed to those chronically absent, to raise awareness of educators to this emotional problem, to aid phobic students through appropriate intervention strategies, and to provide school personnel with behaviors and strategies for dealing with students' school phobia. Identification of problem is done through interviews with students and significant others, such as parents and teachers. School phobia is a serious emotional problem which can lead to chronic-absenteeism. Because it is often mislabeled as truancy, educators may fail to respond appropriately to the school phobic child.

12394
Minnesota Preschool Inventory. Ireton, Harold R.; Thwing, Edward J. 1975
Subtests: Self Help; Fine Motor; Expressive Language; Comprehension; Memory; Letter Recognition; Number Comprehension; Immaturity; Hyperactivity; Behavior Problems; Emotional Problems; Motor Symptoms; Language Symptoms; Somatic Symptoms; Sensory Symptoms
Descriptors: Adjustment (to Environment); Behavior Patterns; Behavior Rating Scales; Developmental Disabilities; *Individual Development; Learning Disabilities; Mothers; *Preschool Children; Preschool Education; *School Readiness; Screening Tests
Identifiers: Minnesota Child Development Inventory; MPI
Availability: Behavior Science Systems; Box 1108, Minneapolis, MN 55440
Target Audience: 4-5
Notes: Items, 150

Designed to utilize mother's observations of her child's development, adjustment, and symptoms to determine child's readiness to enter kindergarten. Responses yield a profile of child's functioning on 7 developmental scales and 4 adjustment scales. Also detects symptoms in 4 areas.

12396
DIAL-R. Mardell-Czudnowski, Carol D.; Goldenberg, Dorothea S. 1983
Subtests: Motor; Concepts; Language
Descriptors: *Ability Identification; Concept Formation; *Gifted; Individual Testing; Language Skills; *Learning Disabilities; Performance Tests; *Preschool Children; Preschool Education; *Psychomotor Skills; *Screening Tests
Availability: Childcraft Education Corporation; 20 Kilmer Rd., Edison, NJ 08818
Target Audience: 2-6
Notes: Time, 30 approx.; Items, 24

An early childhood screening test designed to identify children who may have special educational needs. Useful in identification of gifted and learning-disabled students. Measures early motoric, conceptual, and language development. Separate norms are available for various minority groups.

12412
Child Behavior Checklist: Teacher's Report Form. Achenbach, Thomas M.; Edelbrock, Craig 1982
Descriptors: *Adolescents; *Behavior Disorders; Behavior Problems; *Behavior Rating Scales; *Children; Elementary School Students; Elementary School Teachers; Females; Males; Secondary School Students; Secondary School Teachers; *Student Evaluation
Identifiers: TRF
Availability: University Associates in Psychiatry; c/o Dr. Thomas Achenbach, One South Prospect St., Burlington, VT 05401
Target Audience: 4-16

Designed to obtain teacher's assessment of child's behavior and general adaptive characteristics. There is an area for teacher to record demographics, previous special services, and ratings of academic performance. Ratings are to be based upon previous 2 months' behavior.

12413
Classroom Behavior Description Checklist. Aaronson, May; and Others 1979
Descriptors: Academic Ability; Adjustment (to Environment); Affective Behavior; Behavior Problems; *Behavior Rating Scales; *Preschool Children; Social Behavior; *Student Behavior; Teacher Attitudes; Young Children
Identifiers: CBD; Task Orientation
Availability: ERIC Document Reproduction Service; 3900 Wheeler Ave., Alexandria, VA 22304 (ED183599, 46 pages)
Target Audience: 2-6
Notes: Items, 10

Checklist for obtaining teacher ratings of preschool children's behavior considered likely to influence school performance. Useful to identify children needing intervention. Covers child's ability; classroom adjustment; and social, emotional, and task-oriented behaviors. Suggested for use as a companion measure to the Preschool Preposition Test (TC005994), a screening measure for developmental delay.

12414
Infant Referral Form. Southwest Georgia Psychoeducational Service, Ochlocknee, GA
Descriptors: Behavior Problems; *Developmental Disabilities; *Infants; Learning Disabilities; Records (Forms); *Referral
Availability: Southwest Georgia Psychoeducational Service; P.O. Box 110-A, Ochlocknee, GA 31773
Target Audience: 0-2
Notes: Items, 40

For use with infants suspected of developmental or other problems. Used for referral to agencies for treatment. Covers identification, parent approval, previous screening, behavior.

12415
Stinchcomb Nut and Bolt Packaging Work Sample. Stinchcomb, John A. Jr. 1973
Descriptors: Adults; Job Skills; *Mental Retardation; Occupational Tests; Perceptual Motor Coordination; *Vocational Evaluation; *Work Sample Tests
Identifiers: Finger Dexterity; Manual Dexterity; *Packaging; *Packers
Availability: Materials Development Center; Work Sample Manual Clearinghouse, Stout Vocational Rehabilitation Institute, School of Education, University of Wisconsin-Stout, Menomonie, WI 54751
Target Audience: 18-64
Notes: Items, 75

Designed to assess traits and qualities necessary for successful hand packaging. Measures ability to carry out a routine, repetitive task, lift objects, count to 75, carry out simple instructions, and organize a work area. Also measures level of motor coordination, manual dexterity, and finger dexterity. Designed for use with mentally handicapped individuals. Simple materials are required.

12418
Oral Language Sentence Imitation Diagnostic Inventory. Zachman, Linda; And Others 1978
Subtests: Present Progressive; Prepositions; Plural; Past Irregular; Possessive; Uncontractible Copula; Articles; Past Regular; Third Person Regular; Third Person Irregular; Uncontractible Auxiliary; Contractible Copula; Contractible Auxiliary; Personal Pronouns; Reflexive Pronouns; Possessive Pronouns; Negatives; Wh Questions; Interrogative Reversals; Modals; DO Insertions; Embedded Sentences; Infinitives; Coordinations or Conjunctions; Future Tense
Descriptors: *Diagnostic Tests; *Expressive Language; *Grade 1; *Kindergarten Children; Primary Education; Remedial Instruction; Young Children
Identifiers: OLSIDI
Availability: Lingui Systems; Ste. 806, 1630 Fifth Ave., Moline, IL 61265
Grade Level: K-1
Target Audience: 5-7
Notes: Items, 270

Developed as effective, time-saving tool to assess expressive language abilities and plan remediation strategies. Allows speech and language clinician to deep test specific language structures previously identified as underdeveloped within child's language system. Designed as a diagnostic follow-up to the Oral Language Sentence Imitation Screening Test, Stage V, which is administered to first grade and kindergarten children (ages 5 to 7 years) (TC012419). The mean morpheme length of the sentences is the same for the OLSISI, stage V, and the OLSIDI, with the OLSIDI providing for in-depth testing of any structure produced in error on OLSIST, stage V. The OLSIDI consists of 27 subtests which evaluate 27 morphological and grammatical structures. Each subtest consists of 10 preanalyzed sentences which access a specific test structure.

12425
IEP Educational Diagnostic Inventories. Sedlak, Joseph E. 1979
Descriptors: Diagnostic Tests; Educational Diagnosis; Elementary Education; Elementary School Students; Emotional Disturbances; Exceptional Persons; Gifted; Individualized Education Programs; Individual Testing; Intelligence; Learning Disabilities; Learning Modalities; Learning Problems; Mathematics Achievement; Mild Mental Retardation; Preschool Children; Preschool Education; Reading Skills; Screening Tests; Student Behavior
Identifiers: IEP Educational Diagnostic Inventories
Availability: National Press Publishing Co.; P.O. Box 237, Belle Vernon, PA 15012
Grade Level: K-6
Target Audience: 3-12

Developed to enable classroom teachers to screen and diagnose those students with potential learning problems. The teacher may administer the entire battery or only those sections deemed suitable for the problem objectives. The instruments are individually administered and may be used for normal, gifted, educable mentally retarded, emotionally disturbed, and learning-disabled students. The battery results will yield information useful in developing an Individual Education Program for each student. The battery includes Diagnostic History Form (TC 012531), National Intelligence Test (TC012532), Behavior Reinforcement Inventory (TC012533), Near-Point Visual Screening Inventory (TC012534), Reading Inventory (TC012535-012540), Math Inventory (TC012541-012543), Spelling Inventory (TC012544-012545), Handwriting Inventory (TC012546), Psycholinguistic Inventory (TC012547), and Modality Inventory (TC012548).

12426
Social Experience Questionnaire (SOEX). Haertzen, C. A. 1978
Descriptors: Adults; Alcoholism; Antisocial Behavior; Drug Abuse; Drug Addiction; *Males; *Psychological Patterns; *Self Concept; Self Concept Measures
Identifiers: *Drug Addicts; *Psychopathy; SOEX
Availability: Dr. Charles A. Haertzen; NIDA Addiction Research Center, c/o Baltimore City Hospital, Bldg. D-5W, 4940 Eastern Ave., Baltimore, MD 21224
Target Audience: Adults
Notes: Items, 560

Designed to assess differences in psychological states between alcoholics, opiate addicts, and normal populations. Respondents must answer true or false to statements describing themselves at the time they are completing the items. Measures dimensions of psychopathy as a state, rather than a trait.

12427
Psychopathic State Inventory (PSI). Haertzen, C. A.; Martin, W. R. 1977
Subtests: High; Impulsivity; Egocentricity; Needs; Hypophoria; Sociopathy
Descriptors: Adults; *Alcoholism; Drug Abuse; *Drug Addiction; *Males; *Psychotherapy; Self Concept; Self Concept Measures
Identifiers: Drug Addicts; PSI; Psychopathy
Availability: Dr. Charles A. Haertzen; NIDA Addiction Research Center, c/o Baltimore City Hospital, Bldg. D-5W, 4940 Eastern Ave., Baltimore, MD 21224
Target Audience: Adults
Notes: Items, 90

Designed to evaluate treatment of psychopaths and distinguish opiate addicts and alcoholics from normals. Short form of Social Experience Questionnaire (TC012426) which measures dimensions of psychopathy as a state.

12428
Addiction Research Center Inventory (ARCI). Haertzen, C. A. 1974
Subtests: General Information; Interests & Drives; Sensation & Perception; Bodily Symptoms & Processes; Feelings & Attitudes
Descriptors: Adults; Affective Measures; Drug Abuse; Drug Addiction; *Illegal Drug Use; *Pharmacology; Social Attitudes
Identifiers: ARCI; Drug Addicts; Self Report Measures
Availability: Dr. Charles A. Haertzen; NIDA Addiction Research Center, c/o Baltimore City Hospital, Bldg. D-5W, 4940 Eastern Ave., Baltimore, MD 21224
Target Audience: Adults
Notes: Items, 600

Designed to assess physical, emotive, cognitive, and subjective effects of various drugs. Applicable to any literate English-speaking population, not just to opiate addicts.

12432
Child Behavior Checklist: Direct Observation Form. Achenbach, Thomas M.; Edelbrock, Craig 1981
Descriptors: *Adolescents; Behavior Change; *Behavior Disorders; Behavior Problems; Behavior Rating Scales; *Children; *Classroom Observation Techniques; *Interpersonal Competence
Identifiers: DOF
Availability: University Associates in Psychiatry; c/o Dr. Thomas Achenbach, One South Prospect St., Burlington, VT 05401
Target Audience: 4-16
Notes: Items, 96

Designed to aid in obtaining direct observational data of target child in situations such as school classrooms, lunchrooms, recess, and group activities. Experienced observer writes a narrative description of child's behavior over a 10-minute period and then rates child on the 96 behavior problem items on this instrument. Ratings from 6 10-minute observational periods spread across different days and times of day usually yield a stable behavioral score.

12437
The Five P's: Parent Professional Preschool Performance Profile. Pre-Schooler's Workshop, Syosset, NY 1982
Subtests: Self-Help; Perceptual-Motor; Language Development; Social Development; Cognitive Development

Descriptors: Adjustment (to Environment); Behavior Problems; *Behavior Rating Scales; *Child Development; Cognitive Development; *Developmental Tasks; Individualized Education Programs; Interpersonal Competence; Language Acquisition; Language Handicaps; Learning Problems; *Preschool Children; Psychomotor Skills; Self Care Skills; *Young Children
Availability: Pre-Schooler's Workshop; 47 Humphrey Dr., Syosset, NY 11791
Target Audience: 2-8
Notes: Items, 338

Assessment instrument based on developmental landmarks and observable behaviors of children. Used to record behavior of preschool child who is labeled untestable or who is delayed or deviant or older child functioning at preschool level. The checklist is completed twice yearly, each time over a 2-week period by both parents and teachers. Can be used as a basis for developing individualized education plans. Assesses children in the areas of classroom adjustment; self-help; motor skills; and language, social, and cognitive development.

12439
Miskimins Self-Goal-Other Discrepancy Scale—I. Miskimins, R. W. 1967
Descriptors: *Adults; Aspiration; Higher Education; Objectives; *Older Adults; Peer Evaluation; *Self Concept; Self Concept Measures; *Self Evaluation (Individuals)
Identifiers: *Discrepancy Measures; MSGO I; Self Administered Tests
Availability: Rocky Mountain Behavioral Science Institute, Inc.; P.O. Box 1066, Fort Collins, CO 80522
Grade Level: 13-20
Target Audience: 18-99
Notes: Items, 20

Designed to measure self-concept and related indices of psychological health through the use of discrepancy scores. The basis for calculating discrepancy scores is the respondents' ratings of self, their goals, and their belief of how others perceive them. A profile summary may be drawn from these scores. A simplified version MSGO-II (TC012440) is also available. MSGO-I is appropriate for older, well-adjusted subjects. Validity and reliability have been established for this instrument.

12440
Miskimins Self-Goal-Other Discrepancy Scale—II. Miskimins, R. W. 1972
Descriptors: *Adolescents; *Adults; Aspiration; *Children; *Educationally Disadvantaged; Individual Testing; Mental Retardation; Objectives; *Older Adults; Peer Evaluation; *Self Concept; Self Concept Measures; *Self Evaluation (Individuals)
Identifiers: *Discrepancy Measures; MSGO II; Psychiatric Patients
Availability: Rocky Mountain Behavioral Science Institute, Inc.; P.O. Box 1066, Fort Collins, CO 80522
Target Audience: 6-99
Notes: Items, 16

Designed to measure self-concept and related indices of psychological health through the use of discrepancy scores. The respondents' ratings of themselves, their goals, and how others perceive them are the basis for calculating these scores. This form is shorter and simpler in language and response format than MSGO-I (TC012439). Therefore, it is appropriate for younger subjects, psychologically impaired, or educationally disadvantaged persons. It has been designed for individual or small group administration because high rapport and personal attention from the examiner are essential. It is highly similar to MSGO-I, but reliability and validity studies have only been established for the MSGO-I.

12441
Cardboard Partition Assembly Work Sample. Hernandez, John 1974
Descriptors: Adults; Aptitude Tests; *Assembly (Manufacturing); *Disabilities; Individual Testing; *Work Sample Tests
Availability: Materials Development Center; Work Sample Manual Clearinghouse, Stout Vocational Rehabilitation Institute, School of Education, University of Wisconsin-Stout, Menomonie, WI 54751
Target Audience: 18-64
Notes: Time, 30; Items, 30

Designed for use in vocational evaluation with clients indicating interest in and potential for bench assembly work. Assesses a client's interest in fields involving manual dexterity, and gross assembly of products. Covers assembly and fitting of slotted cardboard pieces together to form partitions according to a prescribed plan. Useful with handicapped individuals.

12443
Revised Reisterer Mechanical Aptitude Work Sample. Chambers, Elzabeth Lee 1974

Descriptors: Adults; Aptitude Tests; Individual Testing; *Visual Impairments; *Vocational Evaluation; *Work Sample Tests
Identifiers: *Mechanical Aptitude
Availability: Materials Development Center; Work Sample Manual Clearinghouse, Stout Vocational Rehabilitation Institute, School of Education, University of Wisconsin-Stout, Menomonie, WI 54751
Target Audience: 18-64
Notes: Time, 10; Items, 30

Designed to measure mechanical aptitude in visually impaired and non-visually impaired persons. Evidence of ability in the area of spatial relations, form perception, and manual and finger dexterity are observed. Also useful with handicapped individuals having mental, physical, or emotional disabilities. Subject assembles blocks, bolts, and rubber tubing.

12446
Ogren Automobile Washing Work Sample. Ogren, Kenneth E. 1974
Descriptors: Adults; Aptitude Tests; Individual Testing; Mild Disabilities; *Vocational Evaluation; *Work Sample Tests
Identifiers: *Automobile Workers
Availability: Materials Development Center; Work Sample Manual Clearinghouse, Stout Vocational Rehabilitation Institute, School of Education, University of Wisconsin-Stout, Menomonie, WI 54751
Target Audience: 18-64
Notes: Time, 200

Designed to measure an individual's ability to wash the interior and exterior of an automobile. Can be used with clients having minor disabilities. Visual acuity is necessary. Washing and waxing of an entire auto are required.

12449
AGP Student Evaluation Checklist. O'Tuel, Frances S.; And Others 1983
Subtests: Critical Thinking Skills; Creative Thinking Skills; Research Skills; Social Skills; Task Commitment; Regular Classroom Participation
Descriptors: *Academically Gifted; Behavior Rating Scales; *Cognitive Processes; *Elementary School Students; Elementary Secondary Education; Grade 4; Grade 7; Grade 10; *Interpersonal Competence; *Secondary School Students; *Student Evaluation
Identifiers: Academically Gifted Program
Availability: Gifted Child Quarterly; v27 n3 p126-34 Sum 1983
Grade Level: 1-12
Notes: Items, 22

Designed to evaluate areas in which gifted students would perform in a program for the academically gifted. Teacher rates his/her students on 22 variables at the end of the academic year. The score is the total points circled by the teacher on a 4-point rating scale for each variable. The scale is constructed so that the lower the score, the more successful the student. Creative and critical thinking skills, research and social skills, task commitment, and regular classroom participation are assessed. Developed for a study of gifted students in grades 4, 7, and 10.

12450
Persistence/Dropout Rating Scale. Pascarella, Ernest T.; Terenzini, Patrick T. 1980
Subtests: Peer Group Interactions; Interactions with Faculty; Faculty Concern for Student Development and Teaching; Academic and Intellectual Development; Institutional and Goal Commitments
Descriptors: *Academic Persistence; Attitude Measures; *College Freshmen; *Dropout Attitudes; *Dropouts; Higher Education; Interpersonal Relationship; Predictive Measurement; Student Attitudes; Student Educational Objectives
Availability: Journal of Higher Education; v51 n1 p60-75 Jan-Feb 1980
Grade Level: 13
Notes: Items, 30

Designed to assess academic and social integration of college freshmen. Attempts to identify those students with a high probability of becoming dropouts.

12457
HPI Texas Preschool Screening Inventory. Haber, Julian S. 1981
Subtests: Auditory Memory for Numbers and Letters; Visual Memory for Objects; Auditory Sequencing; Articulation; Sound Discrimination; Rotations and Reversals of Numbers and Letters; Following Instructions
Descriptors: Articulation (Speech); Auditory Perception; Handicap Identification; *Kindergarten Children; Learning Problems; *Preschool Children; Primary Education; *Screening Tests; Visual Perception
Identifiers: TPSI

Availability: ERIC Document Reproduction Service; 3900 Wheeler Ave., Alexandria, VA 22304 (ED226013, 13 pages)
Grade Level: K-1
Target Audience: 4-6

Screening test to help determine children who may be at risk for learning problems as they enter kindergarten or first grade. Is not meant as a definitive test of learning problems but may be used to indicate a need for full evaluation by the local educational agency.

12461
Contributions to Neuropsychological Assessment: Temporal Orientation. Benton, Arthur L.; And Others 1983
Descriptors: Adults; Individual Testing; Mental Disorders; *Neurological Impairments; *Orientation; *Patients; Questionnaires; *Time Perspective
Identifiers: Neuropsychological Assessment; Psychiatric Patients
Availability: Oxford University Press; 1600 Pollitt Dr., Fairlawn, NJ 07410
Target Audience: Adults
Notes: Items, 5

Designed to assess temporal orientation which is an essential component of mental competence. Impaired temporal orientation implies the presence of some type of abnormal mental condition. In addition to ordering the tests separately, the 12 tests by Benton are also available in the book CONTRIBUTIONS TO NEUROPSYCHOLOGICAL ASSESSMENT: A CLINICAL MANUAL, by Arthur L. Benton and others, 1983. The book is published by Oxford University Press, 200 Madison Ave., New York, NY 10016 and serves as a manual for the 12 related tests (TC012461-TC012472).

12462
Contributions to Neuropsychological Assessment: Right-Left Orientation. Benton, Arthur L.; And Others 1983
Descriptors: Adults; Aphasia; Individual Testing; Mental Disorders; *Neurological Impairments; *Orientation; *Patients; Performance Tests
Identifiers: Neuropsychological Assessment; Oral Testing; *Right Left Discrimination
Availability: Oxford University Press; 1600 Pollitt Dr., Fairlawn, NJ 07410
Target Audience: Adults
Notes: Items, 20

Designed to assess right-left orientation of patients with brain disease. Patient is required to point to lateral body parts on verbal command. Forms A and B are available. Form B is a "mirror image" of Form A. In addition to ordering the tests separately, the 12 tests by Benton are also available in the book CONTRIBUTIONS TO NEUROPSYCHOLOGICAL ASSESSMENT: A CLINICAL MANUAL, by Arthur L. Benton and others, 1983. The book is published by Oxford University Press, 200 Madison Ave., New York, NY 10016 and serves as a manual for the 12 related tests (TC012461-TC012472).

12463
Contributions to Neuropsychological Assessment: Serial Digit Learning. Benton, Arthur L.; And Others 1983
Descriptors: Adults; Cognitive Tests; Individual Testing; Mental Disorders; *Neurological Impairments; Older Adults; *Patients; *Short Term Memory
Identifiers: Neuropsychological Assessment
Availability: Oxford University Press; 1600 Pollitt Dr., Fairlawn, NJ 07410
Target Audience: 18-75
Notes: Time, 10 approx.; Items, 3

Designed to measure short-term memory to be used in the clinical assessment of mental status. Examiner presents 8 or 9 randomly selected digits for the patient to repeat accurately for a varying number of trials up to 12. Form SD8 consists of an 8-digit sequence given to patients 65 years of age or older and those under 65 who have less than 12 years of education. Form SD9 consists of a 9-digit sequence which is given to patients under age 65 who have 12 or more years of education. In addition to ordering the tests separately, the 12 tests by Benton are also available in the book CONTRIBUTIONS TO NEUROPSYCHOLOGICAL ASSESSMENT: A CLINICAL MANUAL, by Arthur L. Benton and others, 1983 and is published by Oxford University Press, 200 Madison Ave., New York, NY 10016 and serves as a manual for the 12 related tests (TC012461-TC012472).

12464
Contributions to Neuropsychological Assessment: Facial Recognition. Benton, Arthur L.; And Others 1983
Subtests: Matching of Identical Front View Photographs. Matching of Front View with Three Quarter View Photographs. Matching of Front View Photographs Under Different Lighting Conditions
Descriptors: Adolescents; Adults; Children; Individual Testing; *Neurological Impairments; Older Adults; *Patients; Recognition (Psychology); Visual Measures; *Visual Perception
Identifiers: *Agnosia; Neuropsychological Assessment
Availability: Oxford University Press; 1600 Pollitt Dr., Fairlawn, NJ 07410
Target Audience: 6-74
Notes: Items, 54

Designed to provide a standardized objective procedure for assessing the capacity to identify and discriminate photographs of unfamiliar human faces. Facial agnosia was associated with other signs of right hemisphere dysfunction. A short form of 27 items is also available for use when examination time is limited. In addition to ordering the tests separately, the 12 tests by Benton are also available in the book CONTRIBUTIONS TO NEUROPSYCHOLOGICAL ASSESSMENT: A CLINICAL MANUAL, by Arthur L. Benton and others, 1983. The book is published by Oxford University Press, 200 Madison Ave., New York, NY 10016 and serves as a manual for the 12 related tests (TC012461-TC012472).

12465
Contributions to Neuropsychological Assessment: Judgment of Line Orientation. Benton, Arthur L.; And Others 1983
Descriptors: Adolescents; Adults; Children; Individual Testing; Mental Disorders; *Neurological Impairments; Older Adults; *Patients; Perception Tests; *Spatial Ability
Identifiers: Neuropsychological Assessment
Availability: Oxford University Press; 1600 Pollitt Dr., Fairlawn, NJ 07410
Target Audience: 7-74
Notes: Items, 30

Designed to measure visuospatial judgment. Measures a single aspect of spatial thinking. Discriminates between patients with right hemisphere lesions and those with left hemisphere lesions. In addition to ordering the tests separately, the 12 tests by Benton are also available in the book CONTRIBUTIONS TO NEUROPSYCHOLOGICAL ASSESSMENT: A CLINICAL MANUAL, by Arthur L. Benton and others, 1983. The book is published by Oxford University Press, 200 Madison Ave., New York, NY 10016 and serves as a manual for the 12 related tests (TC012461-TC012472).

12466
Contributions to Neuropsychological Assessment: Visual Form Discrimination. Benton, Arthur L.; And Others 1983
Descriptors: Adolescents; Adults; Aphasia; Individual Testing; Mental Disorders; *Neurological Impairments; Older Adults; *Patients; *Visual Discrimination; Visual Measures
Identifiers: Neuropsychological Assessment
Availability: Oxford University Press; 1600 Pollitt Dr., Fairlawn, NJ 07410
Target Audience: 16-75
Notes: Items, 16

Designed to assess capacity for complex visual form discrimination. Useful as part of a test battery to assess cognitive impairment associated with posterior right hemisphere disease. May be used with aphasic patients to determine the extent to which disabilities extend beyond the sphere of speech functions. In addition to ordering the tests separately, the 12 tests by Benton are also available in the book CONTRIBUTIONS TO NEUROPSYCHOLOGICAL ASSESSMENT: A CLINICAL MANUAL, by Arthur L. Benton and others, 1983. The book is published by Oxford University Press, 200 Madison Ave., New York, NY 10016 and serves as a manual for the 12 related tests (TC012461-TC012472).

12467
Contributions to Neuropsychological Assessment: Pantomime Recognition. Benton, Arthur L.; And Others 1983
Descriptors: Adults; *Aphasia; Individual Testing; Neurological Impairments; *Pantomime; *Patients; Perception Tests; Videotape Recordings
Identifiers: Neuropsychological Assessment
Availability: Oxford University Press; 1600 Pollitt Dr., Fairlawn, NJ 07410
Target Audience: Adults
Notes: Items, 30

Designed to provide an objective, standardized procedure for assessing a patient's ability to understand meaningful, nonlinguistic pantomimed actions. Impaired pantomine recognition was found to be closely related to defective reading comprehension in aphasic patients. In addition to ordering the tests separately, the 12 tests by Benton are also available in the book CONTRIBUTIONS TO NEUROPSYCHOLOGICAL ASSESSMENT: A CLINICAL MANUAL, by Arthur L. Benton and others, 1983. The book is published by Oxford University Press, 200 Madison Ave., New York, NY 10016 and serves as a manual for the 12 related tests (TC012461-TC012472).

12468
Contributions to Neuropsychological Assessment: Tactile Form Perception. Benton, Arthur L.; And Others 1983
Descriptors: Adolescents; Adults; Children; Individual Testing; Mental Disorders; *Neurological Impairments; Older Adults; *Patients; Perception Tests; *Spatial Ability; *Tactual Perception
Identifiers: Neuropsychological Assessment
Availability: Oxford University Press; 1600 Pollitt Dr., Fairlawn, NJ 07410
Target Audience: 8-80
Notes: Time, 15 approx.; Items, 10

Designed to assess nonverbal tactile information processing. Failing performance was associated with other indications of impaired spatial thinking in patients with brain disease. Parallel forms A and B are available. In addition to ordering the tests separately, the 12 tests by Benton are also available in the book CONTRIBUTIONS TO NEUROPSYCHOLOGICAL ASSESSMENT: A CLINICAL MANUAL, by Arthur L. Benton and others, 1983. The book is published by Oxford University Press, 200 Madison Ave., New York, NY 10016 and serves as a manual for the related tests (TC012461-TC012472).

12469
Contributions to Neuropsychological Assessment: Finger Localization. Benton, Arthur L.; And Others 1983
Descriptors: Adolescents; Adults; Children; Individual Testing; Mental Disorders; *Neurological Impairments; *Patients; Perception Tests; Tactual Perception
Identifiers: Agnosia; *Gerstmann Syndrome; Neuropsychological Assessment
Availability: Oxford University Press; 1600 Pollitt Dr., Fairlawn, NJ 07410
Target Audience: 6-64
Notes: Items, 60

Designed to assess the ability to identify tactually stimulated single fingers or pairs of fingers. Examinee may name finger or indicate finger stimulated on a chart. Finger agnosia is the loss of ability to name the fingers, show them on verbal command, or localize them after tactile stimulation. In addition to ordering the tests separately, the 12 tests by Benton are also available in the book CONTRIBUTIONS TO NEUROPSYCHOLOGICAL ASSESSMENT: A CLINICAL MANUAL, by Arthur L. Benton and others, 1983. The book is published by Oxford University Press, 200 Madison Ave., New York, NY 10016 and serves as a manual for the related tests (TC012461-TC012472).

12470
Contributions to Neuropsychological Assessment: Phoneme Discrimination. Benton, Arthur L.; And Others 1983
Descriptors: Adults; *Aphasia; Audiotape Cassettes; *Auditory Discrimination; Individual Testing; Neurological Impairments; *Patients; *Phonemes; *Screening Tests
Identifiers: Neuropsychological Assessment
Availability: Oxford University Press; 1600 Pollitt Dr., Fairlawn, NJ 07410
Target Audience: 18-64
Notes: Items, 30

Designed as a brief screening instrument for aphasic patients. In addition to ordering the tests separately, the 12 tests by Benton are also available in the book CONTRIBUTIONS TO NEUROPSYCHOLOGICAL ASSESSMENT: A CLINICAL MANUAL, by Arthur L. Benton and others, 1983. The book is published by Oxford University Press, 200 Madison Ave., New York, NY 10016 and serves as a manual for the 12 related tests (TC012461-TC012472).

12471
Contributions to Neuropsychological Assessment: Three Dimensional Block Construction. Benton, Arthur L.; And Others 1983
Descriptors: Adolescents; Adults; Aphasia; Children; Individual Testing; *Neurological Impairments; *Patients; Performance Tests; Spatial Ability
Identifiers: Neuropsychological Assessment
Availability: Oxford University Press; 1600 Pollitt Dr., Fairlawn, NJ 07410
Target Audience: 6-64
Notes: Items, 3

Designed to assess visual constructional ability. Patient must reproduce 3 block models of increasing complexity. Two alternate forms are available. An experimental version using photographs as stimuli is also available. In addition to ordering the tests separately, the 12 tests by Benton are also available in the book CONTRIBUTIONS TO NEUROPSYCHOLOGICAL ASSESSMENT: A CLINICAL MANUAL, by Arthur L. Benton and others, 1983. The book is published by Oxford University Press, 200 Madison Ave., New York, NY 10016 and serves as a manual for the related tests (TC012461-TC012472).

12472
Contributions to Neuropsychological Assessment: Motor Impersistence. Benton, Arthur L.; And Others 1983
Descriptors: Adolescents; Adults; Children; Individual Testing; Motor Development; *Neurological Impairments; *Patients; *Performance Tests
Identifiers: Neuropsychological Assessment; Psychiatric Patients
Availability: Oxford University Press; 1600 Pollitt Dr., Fairlawn, NJ 07410
Target Audience: 5-66
Notes: Items, 8

Designed to assess capacity to sustain various motor acts. Motor impersistence denotes the inability to sustain a movement which subjects were able to initiate on command. In addition to ordering the tests separately, the 12 tests by Benton are also available in the book CONTRIBUTIONS TO NEUROPSYCHOLOGICAL ASSESSMENT: A CLINICAL MANUAL, by Arthur L. Benton and others, 1983. The book is published by Oxford University Press, 200 Madison Ave., New York, NY 10016 and serves as a manual for the related tests (TC012461-TC012472).

12473
The Second Language Oral Test of English. Fathman, Ann K. 1983
Descriptors: Adolescents; Adults; Children; *English (Second Language); *Grammar; Student Placement; *Syntax
Identifiers: Oral Tests; SLOTE
Availability: The Alemany Press; 2501 Industrial Pwy., W., Hayward, CA 94545
Target Audience: 6-64

Measures the ability to produce specific syntactic structures orally. Group or individually administered for placement of beginning or intermediate students.

12476
Community Living Skills Quick Screening Test. Schalock, Robert L.; Gadwood, Linda Sweet 1980
Descriptors: Adults; Behavioral Objectives; Criterion Referenced Tests; *Daily Living Skills; *Developmental Disabilities; *Screening Tests
Availability: Mid Nebraska Mental Retardation Services; 522 E. Side Blvd., P.O. Box 1146, Hastings, NE 68901
Target Audience: Adults
Notes: Items, 174

Used to assess the integration of developmentally disabled persons into a less restrictive living environment. Screening test was developed to identify behavioral skills, which need remediation within person's current living environment before person progresses to next level of community integration, to determine when a person is ready for such movement, and to integrate assessment of specific skills with suggested prescriptive intervention strategies. This screening instrument covers the following behavior domains: personal maintenance, dressing and clothing care, eating and food management, social behavior, expressive skills, home management, time awareness and use, recreation and leisure skills, community awareness and utilization.

12477
Community Living Skills Screening Test, 2nd Edition. Schalock, Robert L.; Gadwood, Linda Sweet 1980
Descriptors: Adults; Behavioral Objectives; Criterion Referenced Tests; *Daily Living Skills; *Developmental Disabilities; *Mental Retardation; *Screening Tests
Identifiers: CLSST; Independent Living Screening Test
Availability: Mid Nebraska Mental Retardation Services; 522 E. Side Blvd., P.O. Box 1146, Hastings, NE 68901
Target Audience: Adults
Notes: Items, 174

Developed and revised to be used as part of a systematic approach to teaching community living skills within a community-based mental retardation program. Used as part of an edumetric approach to assessment and remediation which includes criterion-referenced assessment of the presence or absence of each behavioral skill, implementation of individualized programs of remediation, and a databased feedback system for assessing outcomes of intervention. The 10 behavioral domains assessed include personal maintenance, dressing and clothing care, eating and food management, social behavior, expressive skills, home living, money management, time awareness and utilization, recreation and leisure skills, community awareness and utilization.

12478
Vocational Training Screening Test, 2d edition, 1978. Addendum 1981. Mid Nebraska Mental Retardation Services, Hastings. 1981
Subtests: Self Help Skills; Personal Interpersonal Behaviors; Information Processing; Learning/Coping Strategies; Prevocational Skills; Job Related Skills; Work Performance; Work Behavior; Job Seeking Skills
Descriptors: *Adults; Behavior Rating Scales; Criterion Referenced Tests; Developmental Disabilities; Job Skills; *Mental Retardation; *Screening Tests; Sheltered Workshops; *Vocational Evaluation; Vocational Rehabilitation
Identifiers: VTST
Availability: Mid Nebraska Mental Retardation Services; 522 E. Side Blvd., P.O. Box 1146, Hastings, NE 68901
Target Audience: Adults

This instrument is a revision of the Competitive Employment Screening Test. Instrument is designed for use in assessing clients' vocational skills. Results indicate which vocational skills need to be taught in a community-based mental retardation program. Behavioral skills in prevocational areas are assessed as well as vocational skills useful in sheltered workshop situations.

12479
Vocational Training Quick Screening Test. Mid Nebraska Mental Retardation Services, Hastings. 1981
Subtests: Self Help Skills; Personal/Interpersonal Behaviors; Information Processing; Learning/Coping Strategies; Prevocational Skills; Job Related Skills; Work Performance; Work Behavior; Job Seeking Skills
Descriptors: Adults; Behavior Rating Scales; Criterion Referenced Tests; Developmental Disabilities; *Mental Retardation; *Screening Tests; Sheltered Workshops; *Vocational Evaluation; Vocational Rehabilitation
Identifiers: VTQS
Availability: Mid Nebraska Mental Retardation Services; 522 E. Side Blvd., P.O. Box 1146, Hastings, NE 68901
Target Audience: Adults
Notes: Items, 163

Designed to assess client competencies in prevocational and vocational skill areas. Used for clients with developmental disabilities to prepare them for competitive or sheltered workshop employment.

12483
Children's Adaptive Behavior Report. Kicklighter, Richard H.; Richmond, Bert O. 1982
Subtests: Language Development; Independent Functioning; Family Role Performance; Economic-Vocational Activities; Socialization
Descriptors: *Adaptive Behavior (of Disabled); *Children; *Developmental Disabilities; Family Relationship; Interpersonal Competence; Interviews; Language Acquisition; Mental Retardation; Parents; Teachers
Identifiers: CABR
Availability: Humanics Limited; P.O. Box 7447, Atlanta, GA 30309
Target Audience: 5-10
Notes: Items, 35

A structured interview guide designed to elicit an estimate of the child's adaptive behavior as rated by the parent, teacher, or other informant. May be used with the Children's Adaptive Behavior Scale (TC010637) or with other measures of adaptive behavior to obtain an estimate of child's level of functioning.

12508
Parenting Stress Index. Abidin, Richard R. 1983
Subtests: Child Characteristics; Parent Characteristics; Situational/ Demographic Characteristics
Descriptors: Adults; Behavior Problems; Family Environment; *Parent Child Relationship; Parents; Questionnaires; *Stress Variables
Identifiers: (PSI); Child Characteristics; Parent Characteristics; Parenting; Stress
Availability: Pediatric Psychology Press; 320 Terral Rd. W., Charlottesville, VA 22901
Target Audience: 18-64
Notes: Items, 120

Designed for use by clinicians and researchers who work with parents and children, to identify parent-child systems that are under stress and at risk for the development of dysfunctional parenting behaviors or behavior problems in the child. Covers child adaptability, acceptability of child to parent, child demands, child mood, distractability, reinforcement of parent, parent depression, attachment, restriction imposed by parent role, feelings of competence, social isolation, relationships with spouse, health of parent, and life stress.

12511
Perkins-Binet Tests of Intelligence for the Blind. Davis, Carl J. 1980
Descriptors: *Adolescents; *Blindness; *Children; Diagnostic Tests; Intelligence; *Intelligence Tests; Standardized Tests
Identifiers: Stanford Binet Intelligence Scale
Availability: Perkins School for the Blind; Howe Press, Watertown, MA 02172
Target Audience: 3-18

This test was adopted primarily from the Stanford Binet Intelligence Scale, third revision, forms L-M with the permission of Houghton Mifflin. Intent was to develop a scale of intelligence for the blind that would be an age level scale approximating the Stanford Binet structure and content. Two final forms of the test were developed. Form N consists of items for ages 4-18 and consists of 94 items, including alternate items. Form U is for ages 3-18 and consists of 99 items including alternate items. The Perkins-Binet is constructed so that serial tasks come first. Because of limited sampling, test-items below age 6 have limited statistical validity.

12512
Child Behavior Checklist: Youth Self Report. Achenbach, Thomas M.; Edelbrock, Craig 1981
Descriptors: Adolescents; *Behavior Disorders; Behavior Problems; Children; *Interpersonal Competence; Self Concept Measures; *Self Evaluation (Individuals)
Identifiers: Self Report Measures; YSR
Availability: University Associates in Psychiatry; c/o Dr. Thomas Achenbach, One South Prospect St., Burlington, VT 05401
Target Audience: 11-18

Designed as a self-report device for youth ages 11 to 18 years. Many social competence and problem items are the same as those used in the Child Behavior Checklist (TC011306) but are stated in the first person.

12513
Child Behavior Checklist: Revised Child Behavior Profile. Achenbach, Thomas M.; Edelbrock, Craig 1982
Subtests: Social Competence; Behavior Problems
Descriptors: *Adolescents; Behavior Change; *Behavior Disorders; Behavior Problems; *Children; Females; Interpersonal Competence; Males; Profiles
Availability: University Associates in Psychiatry; c/o Dr. Thomas Achenbach, One S. Prospect St., Burlington, VT 05401
Target Audience: 4-16

Designed for use with the Child Behavior Checklist (TC011306). Enables checklist results to be profiled with separate standardizations for each sex at ages 4-5, 6-11, and 12-16 years. Provides a comprehensive view of the behavior problems reported for a child.

12531
IEP Educational Diagnostic Inventories: Diagnostic History Form. Sedlak, Joseph E. 1979
Descriptors: Educational Diagnosis; Elementary Education; *Elementary School Students; Emotional Disturbances; *Exceptional Persons; Gifted; *Individualized Education Programs; Individual Testing; Learning Disabilities; Mild Mental Retardation; Parents; Questionnaires
Identifiers: IEP Educational Diagnostic Inventories
Availability: National Press Publishing Co.; P.O. Box 237, Belle Vernon, PA 15012
Grade Level: K-6

One instrument in a test battery developed to enable classroom teachers to screen and diagnose those students with potential learning problems. The instrument may be used to develop an Individual Education Program for gifted, educable mentally retarded, emotionally disturbed, or learning-disabled students. Brief interview form designed to gather information about the student from the parents. Questions are educationally relevant. The teacher or diagnostician should complete the form based upon information supplied by the parent.

12532
IEP Educational Diagnostic Inventories: National Intelligence Test. Sedlak, Joseph E. 1979
Descriptors: Educational Diagnosis; Elementary Education; *Elementary School Students; Emotional Disturbances; *Exceptional Persons; Gifted; *Individualized Education Programs; Individual Testing; *Intelligence; Intelligence Quotient; Intelligence Tests; Learning Disabilities; Mild Mental Retardation; *Preschool Children; Preschool Education; *Screening Tests
Identifiers: IEP Educational Diagnostic Inventories
Availability: National Press Publishing Co.; P.O. Box 237, Belle Vernon, PA 15012
Target Audience: 3-12
Notes: Time, 5 approx.; Items, 78

One instrument in a test battery developed to enable classroom teachers to screen and diagnose those students with potential learning problems. The instrument may be used to develop an Individual Education Program for gifted, educable mentally retarded, emotionally disturbed, or learning-disabled students. Designed as a screening device to estimate a student's general intellectual ability.

12533
IEP Educational Diagnostic Inventories: Behavior Reinforcement Inventory. Sedlak, Joseph E. 1979
Descriptors: Educational Diagnosis; Elementary Education; *Elementary School Students; Emotional Disturbances; *Exceptional Persons; Gifted; *Individualized Education Programs; Individual Testing; Learning Disabilities; Mild Mental Retardation; Questionnaires; *Student Attitudes
Identifiers: IEP Educational Diagnostic Inventories
Availability: National Press Publishing Co.; P.O. Box 237, Belle Vernon, PA 15012
Grade Level: K-6
Notes: Time, 5 approx.; Items, 6
One instrument in a test battery developed to enable classroom teachers to screen and diagnose those students with potential learning problems. The instrument may be used to develop an Individual Education Program for gifted, educable mentally retarded, emotionally disturbed, or learning-disabled students. Designed to assess student preferences. Useful in planning reinforcement of behaviors associated with learning. Results may aid teacher in selecting materials and rewards that stimulate effective learning.

12534
IEP Educational Diagnostic Inventories: Near-Point Visual Screening Inventory. Sedlak, Joseph E. 1979
Descriptors: *Diagnostic Tests; Educational Diagnosis; Elementary Education; *Elementary School Students; Emotional Disturbances; *Exceptional Persons; Gifted; *Individualized Education Programs; Individual Testing; Learning Disabilities; Mild Mental Retardation; Screening Tests; Secondary Education; *Secondary School Students; *Vision; *Vision Tests
Identifiers: IEP Educational Diagnostic Inventories; *Near Point Acuity
Availability: National Press Publishing Co.; P.O. Box 237, Belle Vernon, PA 15012
Grade Level: 1-12
One instrument in a test battery developed to enable classroom teachers to screen and diagnose those students with potential learning problems. The instrument may be used to develop an Individual Education Program for gifted, educable mentally retarded, emotionally disturbed, or learning-disabled students. Instrument was developed to assess near point vision of student. Measures ability to see material at a distance of 14-16 inches, such as a book or paper on a desk. Results may be used in determining whether print size in books is large enough for efficient reading instruction.

12535
IEP Educational Diagnostic Inventories: Pre-Reading Screening I and II. Sedlak, Joseph E. 1979
Descriptors: *Auditory Discrimination; *Diagnostic Tests; Educational Diagnosis; *Elementary School Students; Emotional Disturbances; *Exceptional Persons; Gifted; *Grade 1; *Individualized Education Programs; Individual Testing; *Kindergarten Children; Learning Disabilities; *Long Term Memory; Mild Mental Retardation; Primary Education; *Reading Readiness; Reading Readiness Tests; Reading Skills; Screening Tests; *Short Term Memory; *Visual Discrimination
Identifiers: IEP Educational Diagnostic Inventories
Availability: National Press Publishing Co.; P.O. Box 237, Belle Vernon, PA 15012
Grade Level: K-1
One instrument in a test battery developed to enable classroom teachers to screen and diagnose those students with potential learning problems. The instrument may be used to develop an Individual Education Program for gifted, educable mentally retarded, emotionally disturbed, or learning-disabled students. Instruments are designed to assess the skills necessary for formal reading instruction. Pre-reading I assesses visual discrimination and long-term memory. Pre-reading II assesses auditory discrimination and short-term memory.

12536
IEP Educational Diagnostic Inventories: Phonics Diagnosis. Sedlak, Joseph E. 1979
Subtests: Initial Consonant Letter Sounds; Initial Consonant Blends; Initial Consonant Diagraph; Final Letter Consonants; Final Consonant Blends; Short Vowels; Long Vowels; Diphthongs; Irregular Consonants

Descriptors: *Diagnostic Tests; Educational Diagnosis; *Elementary School Students; Emotional Disturbances; *Exceptional Persons; Gifted; *Individualized Education Programs; Individual Testing; Learning Disabilities; Mild Mental Retardation; *Phonics; Primary Education; Reading Diagnosis; Reading Skills; Reading Tests
Identifiers: IEP Educational Diagnostic Inventories
Availability: National Press Publishing Co.; P.O. Box 237, Belle Vernon, PA 15012
Grade Level: 1-3
Notes: Time, 15 approx.; Items, 175
One instrument in a test battery developed to enable classroom teachers to screen and diagnose those students with potential learning problems. The instrument may be used to develop an Individual Education Program for gifted, educable mentally retarded, emotionally disturbed, or learning-disabled students. Instrument determines whether student has learned sequential skills in phonics necessary to achieve success in formal reading instruction.

12537
IEP Educational Diagnostic Inventories: Basic Sight Vocabulary Inventory. Sedlak, Joseph E. 1979
Descriptors: *Beginning Reading; *Diagnostic Tests; Educational Diagnosis; *Elementary School Students; Emotional Disturbances; *Exceptional Persons; Gifted; *Individualized Education Programs; Individual Testing; Learning Disabilities; Mild Mental Retardation; Primary Education; Reading Diagnosis; Reading Tests; *Sight Vocabulary
Identifiers: IEP Educational Diagnostic Inventories
Availability: National Press Publishing Co.; P.O. Box 237, Belle Vernon, PA 15012
Grade Level: 1-3
Notes: Items, 250
One instrument in a test battery developed to enable classroom teachers to screen and diagnose those students with potential learning problems. The instrument may be used to develop an Individual Education Program for gifted, educable mentally retarded, emotionally disturbed, or learning-disabled students. Instrument was designed to assess student's ability to recognize and pronounce basic words found in most reading materials at the initial reading levels. There are one hundred words in the first and second grade lists and 50 words on the third grade level.

12538
IEP Educational Diagnostic Inventories: Word Recognition Screening. Sedlak, Joseph E. 1979
Descriptors: *Diagnostic Tests; Educational Diagnosis; Elementary Education; *Elementary School Students; Emotional Disturbances; *Exceptional Persons; Gifted; *Individualized Education Programs; Individual Testing; Learning Disabilities; Mild Mental Retardation; Reading Skills; Screening Tests; Student Placement; *Word Recognition
Identifiers: IEP Educational Diagnostic Inventories
Availability: National Press Publishing Co.; P.O. Box 237, Belle Vernon, PA 15012
Grade Level: K-6
Notes: Time, 5 approx.
One instrument in a test battery developed to enable classroom teachers to screen and diagnose those students with potential learning problems. The instrument may be used to develop an Individual Education Program for gifted, educable mentally retarded, emotionally disturbed, or learning-disabled students. Designed to determine proper instructional level in reading. Each word list contains 20 words. Separate lists are available for all levels from Preprimer through grade 6. Student should be tested beginning with word list approximately 2 years below his/her present grade placement. Testing should continue through levels until independent, instructional, and frustrational levels are determined.

12539
IEP Educational Diagnostic Inventories: Cloze Reading Comprehension Inventory. Sedlak, Joseph E. 1979
Descriptors: *Cloze Procedure; *Diagnostic Tests; Educational Diagnosis; Elementary Education; *Elementary School Students; Emotional Disturbances; *Exceptional Persons; Gifted; *Individualized Education Programs; Individual Testing; Learning Disabilities; Mild Mental Retardation; *Reading Comprehension; Reading Diagnosis
Identifiers: IEP Educational Diagnostic Inventories
Availability: National Press Publishing Co.; P.O. Box 237, Belle Vernon, PA 15012
Grade Level: 4-6
One instrument in a test battery developed to enable classroom teachers to screen and diagnose those students with potential learning problems. The instrument may be

used to develop an Individual Education Program for gifted, educable mentally retarded, emotionally disturbed, or learning-disabled students. Designed to measure student's reading comprehension to assist in proper placement for instructional reading. The cloze procedure is used in making the assessment. Students in grades 4 through 6 may be tested in groups.

12540
IEP Educational Diagnostic Inventories: Oral Reading Inventory. Sedlak, Joseph E. 1979
Descriptors: *Diagnostic Tests; Elementary Education; *Elementary School Students; Emotional Disturbances; *Exceptional Persons; Gifted; *Individualized Education Programs; Individual Testing; Learning Disabilities; Mild Mental Retardation; *Oral Reading; *Reading Diagnosis; Remedial Reading; Student Placement
Identifiers: IEP Educational Diagnostic Inventories
Availability: National Press Publishing Co.; P.O. Box 237, Belle Vernon, PA 15012
Grade Level: 1-6
Notes: Time, 10 approx.
One instrument in a test battery developed to enable classroom teachers to screen and diagnose those students with potential learning problems. The instrument may be used to develop an Individual Education Program for gifted, educable mentally retarded, emotionally disturbed, or learning-disabled students. Designed to determine proper instructional reading level for each student. Permits analysis of reading errors such as mispronunciation, omission, insertion, substitution, unknown, repetitions, punctuation, hesitation, and stopping.

12541
IEP Educational Diagnostic Inventories: Math Screening. Sedlak, Joseph E. 1979
Descriptors: *Diagnostic Tests; Educational Diagnosis; Elementary Education; *Elementary School Students; Emotional Disturbances; *Exceptional Persons; Gifted; *Individualized Education Programs; Individual Testing; Learning Disabilities; *Mathematics Achievement; Mild Mental Retardation; *Mathematics Tests; Screening Tests; *Student Placement
Identifiers: IEP Educational Diagnostic Inventories
Availability: National Press Publishing Co.; P.O. Box 237, Belle Vernon, PA 15012
Grade Level: 1-6
Notes: Items, 60
One instrument in a test battery developed to enable classroom teachers to screen and diagnose those students with potential learning problems. The instrument may be used to develop an Individual Education Program for gifted, educable mentally retarded, emotionally disturbed, or learning-disabled students. A screening measure used to assess a child's mathematical ability and proper instructional grade level.

12542
IEP Educational Diagnostic Inventories: Written Math Speed Diagnosis. Sedlak, Joseph E. 1979
Descriptors: *Arithmetic; *Diagnostic Tests; Educational Diagnosis; Elementary Education; *Elementary School Students; Emotional Disturbances; *Exceptional Persons; Gifted; *Individualized Education Programs; Individual Testing; Learning Disabilities; Mild Mental Retardation; Mathematics Tests; *Timed Tests
Identifiers: IEP Educational Diagnostic Inventories
Availability: National Press Publishing Co.; P.O. Box 237, Belle Vernon, PA 15012
Grade Level: 1-6
One instrument in a test battery developed to enable classroom teachers to screen and diagnose those students with potential learning problems. The instrument may be used to develop an Individual Education Program for gifted, educable mentally retarded, emotionally disturbed, or learning-disabled students. Designed to assess student's knowledge of basic facts in addition, subtraction, multiplication, and division. Each assessment sheet consists of 60 problems, 30 in vertical form and 30 in horizontal form. Sixty seconds are allotted for completion of each set of 30 problems. All students must begin with lowest level problems. Speed of response is an indication of mastery as well as necesssary for long-term retention.

12543
IEP Educational Diagnostic Inventories: Math Diagnosis. Sedlak, Joseph E. 1979
Descriptors: *Diagnostic Tests; Educational Diagnosis; Elementary Education; *Elementary School Students; Emotional Disturbances; *Exceptional Persons; Gifted; *Individualized Education Programs; Individual Testing; Learning Disabilities; *Mathematics Achievement; Mild Mental Retardation; Mathematics Tests
Identifiers: IEP Educational Diagnostic Inventories

Availability: National Press Publishing Co.; P.O. Box 237, Belle Vernon, PA 15012
Grade Level: 1-6

One instrument in a test battery developed to enable classroom teachers to screen and diagnose those students with potential learning problems. The instrument may be used to develop an Individual Education Program for gifted, educable mentally retarded, emotionally disturbed, or learning-disabled students. Designed to assess specific area of math difficulty student is experiencing. Teacher selects proper diagnostic test based on data gathered from IEP Math Screening (TC012541).

12544
IEP Educational Diagnostic Inventories: Spelling Screening. Sedlak, Joseph E. 1979
Descriptors: *Diagnostic Tests; Educational Diagnosis; Elementary Education; *Elementary School Students; Emotional Disturbances; *Exceptional Persons; Gifted; *Individualized Education Programs; Individual Testing; Learning Disabilities; Mild Mental Retardation; *Screening Tests; *Spelling
Identifiers: IEP Educational Diagnostic Inventories
Availability: National Press Publishing Co.; P.O. Box 237, Belle Vernon, PA 15012
Grade Level: 1-6
Notes: Time, 5 approx.; Items, 30

One instrument in a test battery developed to enable classroom teachers to screen and diagnose those students with potential learning problems. The instrument may be used to develop an Individual Education Program for gifted, educable mentally retarded, emotionally disturbed, or learning-disabled students. Designed to determine student's spelling grade level. The instrument consists of 30 words—5 words at each grade level from one through 6. Number of errors indicate independent, instructional, and frustrational spelling levels.

12545
IEP Educational Diagnostic Inventories: Spelling Diagnosis Inventory. Sedlak, Joseph E. 1979
Descriptors: *Diagnostic Tests; Educational Diagnosis; Elementary Education; *Elementary School Students; Emotional Disturbances; *Exceptional Persons; Gifted; *Individualized Education Programs; Individual Testing; Learning Disabilities; Mild Mental Retardation; *Spelling
Identifiers: IEP Educational Diagnostic Inventories
Availability: National Press Publishing Co.; P.O. Box 237, Belle Vernon, PA 15012
Grade Level: 1-6
Notes: Time, 10 approx.; Items, 180

One instrument in a test battery developed to enable classroom teachers to screen and diagnose those students with potential learning problems. The instrument may be used to develop an Individual Education Program for gifted, educable mentally retarded, emotionally disturbed, or learning-disabled students. Designed to diagnose specific spelling errors. Graded spelling lists of 30 words each are categorized as to type of problem area. Grade level for diagnostic test is determined by data gathered from Spelling Screening (TC012544). Students respond orally and in writing.

12546
IEP Educational Diagnostic Inventories: Handwriting Inventory. Sedlak, Joseph E. 1979
Descriptors: *Diagnostic Tests; Educational Diagnosis; Elementary Education; *Elementary School Students; Emotional Disturbances; *Exceptional Persons; Gifted; *Handwriting; *Individualized Education Programs; Individual Testing; Learning Disabilities; Mild Mental Retardation; Writing Skills
Identifiers: IEP Educational Diagnostic Inventories
Availability: National Press Publishing Co.; P.O. Box 237, Belle Vernon, PA 15012
Grade Level: 1-6
Notes: Time, 15 approx.

One instrument in a test battery developed to enable classroom teachers to screen and diagnose those students with potential learning problems. The instrument may be used to develop an Individual Education Program for gifted, educable mentally retarded, emotionally disturbed, or learning-disabled students. Designed to assess student's handwriting skills. Sample of child's handwriting is compared to writing samples of other students at the same grade level. Representative standards for each level are used for scoring. There is an "above average," "average," and "below average" standard for grades 1 through 6.

12547
IEP Educational Diagnostic Inventories: Psycholinguistic Inventory. Sedlak, Joseph E. 1979
Subtests: Reception; Memory; Expression

Descriptors: Auditory Discrimination; *Diagnostic Tests; Educational Diagnosis; Elementary Education; *Elementary School Students; Emotional Disturbances; *Exceptional Persons; Expressive Language; Gifted; *Individualized Education Programs; Individual Testing; Language Processing; Learning Disabilities; Mild Mental Retardation; *Psycholinguistics; *Receptive Language; *Short Term Memory
Identifiers: IEP Educational Diagnostic Inventories
Availability: National Press Publishing Co.; P.O. Box 237, Belle Vernon, PA 15012
Grade Level: K-6

One instrument in a test battery developed to enable classroom teachers to screen and diagnose those students with potential learning problems. The instrument may be used to develop an Individual Education Program for gifted, educable mentally retarded, emotionally disturbed, or learning-disabled students. Instrument designed to assess student's ability to communicate. The receptive process is assessed by measuring auditory and visual reception, as well as auditory discrimination. The memory process is assessed by the visual sequential memory for numbers and words and the auditory sequential memory for numbers and words. The expressive process is assessed by the expressive grammar, verbal expression, and manual expression inventories.

12548
IEP Educational Diagnostic Inventories: Modality Inventory. Sedlak, Joseph E. 1979
Subtests: Visual Learning Approach; Auditory Learning Approach; Kinesthetic Learning Approach; Eclectic Learning Approach
Descriptors: *Cognitive Style; *Diagnostic Tests; Educational Diagnosis; Elementary Education; *Elementary School Students; Emotional Disturbances; *Exceptional Persons; Gifted; *Individualized Education Programs; Individual Testing; Kinesthetic Methods; Learning Disabilities; *Learning Modalities; Mild Mental Retardation; Word Recognition
Identifiers: IEP Educational Diagnostic Inventories
Availability: National Press Publishing Co.; P.O. Box 237, Belle Vernon, PA 15012
Grade Level: K-6
Notes: Items, 40

One instrument in a test battery developed to enable classroom teachers to screen and diagnose those students with potential learning problems. The instrument may be used to develop an Individual Education Program for gifted, educable mentally retarded, emotionally disturbed, or learning-disabled students. This instrument was designed to assess student's cognitive style. Student is taught 10 unknown words through a specific approach—visual, auditory, kinesthetic, or eclectic. After all 40 words have been learned, student is tested on all 40 words. The results of this posttest, recommended for administration one or 2 weeks after learning, will be a measure of method in which student best learns new words for long-term retention.

12566
Drug Interview Schedule. Haertzen, C. A.
Descriptors: Adults; Alcoholism; Drug Abuse; Drug Addiction; *Illegal Drug Use; Interviews; Marijuana; Questionnaires; Rating Scales
Identifiers: DIS; *Drug Addicts; Heroin
Availability: Dr. Charles A. Haertzen; NIDA Addiction Research Center, c/o Baltimore City Hospital, Bldg. D-5W, 4940 Eastern Ave., Baltimore, MD 21224
Target Audience: Adults

A 3-part instrument designed for use in studies of drug and alcohol addiction. The first section asks subject to list alternate names for common drugs. The second part is an interview concerning subject's experiences with drugs. The third section consists of a rating scale to measure experiences with various drugs. The drug rating scale is composed by computer (Apple II). The program may be obtained from the author.

12567
Attitudes toward Seeking Professional Psychological Help. Fischer, Edward H.; Turner, John 1970
Subtests: Recognition of Need for Psychotherapeutic Help; Stigma Tolerance; Interpersonal Openness; Confidence in Mental Health Practitioner
Descriptors: Adults; *Attitude Measures; Emotional Problems; *Psychotherapy
Availability: Journal of Consulting and Clinical Psychology; v35 n1 p79-90 1970
Target Audience: Adults
Notes: Items, 29

A measure of attitudes toward seeking professional help for psychological disturbances was developed and standardized. Four factors were identified when the instrument was administered to college and nursing students: recognition of the need for professional psychological help;

tolerance of the stigma associated with psychiatric help; interpersonal openness regarding subject's problems; and confidence in the mental health professional.

12581
Krantz Health Opinion Survey. Krantz, David S.; And Others 1980
Subtests: Information; Behavioral Involvement
Descriptors: Adults; *Attitude Measures; Information Needs; Information Seeking; Opinions; *Patients; *Physician Patient Relationship
Identifiers: Health Care; KHOS
Availability: Journal of Personality and Social Psychology; v39 n5 p977-90 May 1980
Target Audience: Adults
Notes: Items, 16

Designed to measure a health care client's preference for an active informed role in the health care process versus an inactive, trusting role. Items cover attitudes toward self-treatment and active involvement of patients and the desire to ask questions and be informed about medical decisions.

12589
Home Environment Variable Questionnaire. Martinez, Paul E. 1981
Descriptors: *Academic Achievement; Bilingual Education; Family Characteristics; *Family Environment; Family Relationship; Grade 5; Intermediate Grades; *Language Usage; *Parent Aspiration; *Parent Attitudes; Parent School Relationship; Questionnaires; Reading Habits; Spanish Americans; *Spanish Speaking
Identifiers: New Mexico (Espanola)
Availability: ERIC Reproduction Service; 3900 Wheeler Ave., Alexandria, VA 22304 (ED 212421, 17 pages)
Target Audience: 18-64
Notes: Items, 44

The questionnaire was used to identify home environment variables which might predict academic achievement for 5th graders. The questions were given to the students' guardians and the students in bilingual-bicultural education programs in Espanola, New Mexico. The questionnaire covered parent level of education, family size, verbal interaction, learning materials in the home, encouragement of the child to read, parent aspirations toward education and future employment of the child, parental trust in school, home stability, and income levels.

12592
The Gross Geometric Forms Creativity Test for Children. Gross, Ruth Brill; And Others 1982
Descriptors: *Art Activities; *Children; *Creativity; *Creativity Tests; Performance Tests
Identifiers: GGF; *Pictorial Creativity
Availability: Stoelting Co.; 1350 S. Kostner Ave., Chicago, IL 60623
Target Audience: 3-12
Notes: Items, 10

A work sample assessment of pictorial creativity in children. Based on a theoretical rationale taken from developmental psychology and art theory. Work presumes that creativity is a manifestation of child's total personality, involving cognitive, conative, and affective dimensions. The GGF method consists of 48 felt forms (circles, rectangles, half circles, triangles, squares) in 3 colors (red, blue, yellow) from which child makes 10 spontaneous pictorial constructions according to a standardized set and inquiry. Scoring is based on productivity, communicability of ideas, and richness of thinking. Instrument is experimental and intended primarily for research purposes.

12593
Inventory of Perceptual Skills. O'Dell, Donald R. 1983
Subtests: Visual Discrimination; Visual Memory; Object Recognition; Visual Motor Coordination; Auditory Discrimination; Auditory Memory; Auditory Sequencing; Auditory Blending
Descriptors: Auditory Discrimination; *Auditory Perception; *Elementary School Students; Elementary Secondary Education; Individualized Education Programs; *Individual Testing; *Perception Tests; Perceptual Motor Coordination; Pretests Posttests; Remedial Programs; Screening Tests; *Secondary School Students; Short Term Memory; *Special Education; Visual Discrimination; *Visual Perception
Identifiers: Auditory Blending; Auditory Memory; IPS; Visual Memory
Availability: Stoelting Co.; 1350 S. Kostner Ave., Chicago, IL 60623
Grade Level: K-12
Notes: Time, 15 approx.; Items, 79

Developed to assist special education teachers in Washington County schools in Oregon. Has been used since 1979. Can be used in several ways: as pretest-posttest, as screening test to identify problem areas in resource center classrooms, or as aid in instructional planning and development of individualized education programs (IEP). Can be easily administered by teachers, aides, or specialists to individual students. No special training is required for administration. Eight perceptual skill areas are identified.

12598
Evaluation of California's Educational Services to Limited and Non English Speaking Students. Jones, Earl; And Others 1980
Descriptors: Ability Identification; Academic Achievement; Administrator Attitudes; *Bilingual Education; *Educational Assessment; Educational Finance; Elementary Secondary Education; *Limited English Speaking; Non English Speaking; Parent Attitudes; Participant Satisfaction; Program Effectiveness; *Program Evaluation; Questionnaires; State Programs; Student Attitudes; Student Placement; Teacher Attitudes
Identifiers: California
Availability: ERIC Document Reproduction Service; 3900 Wheeler Ave., Alexandria, VA 22304 (ED201652, 270 pages, microfiche only)
Target Audience: Adults

Designed to assist California policy and decision makers with planning to meet the future educational needs of limited and non-English speaking students. The services, offered to these students, were language assessment, instructional components literature, pupils, programs and instruction, satisfaction, achievement, auxiliary services, and finance. Two general information instruments were used: Program Guide (6 interview items), and Program Characteristics Guide (43 interview items). An alternate source is Development Associates, 693 Sutter St., 3rd Floor, San Francisco, CA 94102. There is a question of ownership which has not yet been settled; in the meantime, write to the address above.

12602
Vocational Assessment of the Severely Handicapped. Larson, Keith; And Others 1979
Subtests: General Appearance; Functional Academic Skills and Understanding; Physical Skills; Fine Motor/Job Skills; Self Help Skills; Social Skills; Community Mobility Skills
Descriptors: Basic Skills; Check Lists; Communication Skills; *Daily Living Skills; Hygiene; Interpersonal Competence; Mobility; Psychomotor Skills; *Self Care Skills; *Severe Disabilities; *Vocational Evaluation
Identifiers: Vocational Careers Assessment Severely Handicapped
Availability: ERIC Document Reproduction Service; 3900 Wheeler Ave., Alexandria, VA 22304 (ED198668, 92 pages)
Target Audience: 18-64
Notes: Items, 176

This document contains an instrument for the vocational assessment of severely handicapped individuals. There is a list of characteristics/procedures for each of the 8 assessment areas along with a form for recording results.

12608
Health and Daily Living—Adult Forms. Moos, Rudolf H.; And Others 1982
Subtests: Some Facts about You; Your Health in the Last 12 Months; Events in the Past Year; Your Family and Friends; Family Activities; Facts about Your Home; Facts about Your Children
Descriptors: Adjustment (to Environment); Adults; Alcoholic Beverages; Alcoholism; Biographical Inventories; *Coping; *Depression (Psychology); Drinking; Family Environment; Interpersonal Competence; Interviews; *Patients; Physical Health; Psychiatric Hospitals; Quality of Life; Questionnaires; *Self Esteem; Stress Variables
Identifiers: HDL
Availability: Stanford University School of Medicine; Dept. of Psychiatry and Behavioral Sciences TD-114, Social Ecology Laboratory, Stanford, CA 94305
Target Audience: Adults

Designed for administration as a questionnaire or interview. Instrument is a structured assessment procedure which includes sociodemographic factors as well as indices of health-related and social functioning; life stressors and strains; and coping resources and social resources. May be used with patient and community populations. Form B is recommended. Form A may be used with alcoholic patients and their families. Manual was revised in 1984.

12610
Kent Infant Development Scale. Reuter, Jeanette; Katoff, Lewis 1978
Subtests: Cognitive; Motor; Social; Language; Self Help
Descriptors: Behavior Rating Scales; Cognitive Development; *Disabilities; High Risk Persons; *Infant Behavior; *Infants; Language Acquisition; Motor Development; Parents; Self Care Skills; Social Development; Young Children
Identifiers: KID Scale
Availability: Kent Developmental Metrics; P.O. Box 3178, 126 W. College Ave., Kent, OH 44240-3178
Target Audience: 0-1
Notes: Items, 252

Designed to assess behavioral development of infants and young handicapped children chronologically or developmentally below one year of age. Behavior assessment is completed by child's parent or primary caregiver. Computerized scoring and printout furnished developmental ages; a profile of strengths and weaknesses; and a timetable indicating which developmental milestones will be acquired next. May be used in developing a prescriptive educational program.

12612
PRIDE: Preschool and Kindergarten Interest Descriptor. Rimm, Sylvia B. 1983
Descriptors: *Creativity; *Gifted; *Kindergarten Children; *Preschool Children; Preschool Education; Rating Scales; *Screening Tests; Talent Identification
Identifiers: PRIDE
Availability: Educational Assessment Service; Rt. 1, Box 139A, Watertown, WI 53094
Target Audience: 3-6
Notes: Time, 35 approx.; Items, 50

Developed to provide an easily administered, reliable, and valid instrument to screen preschool and kindergarten children for programs for the creatively gifted. Purpose of PRIDE is to identify children with attitudes and interests usually associated with preschool and kindergarten creativity, such as a variety of interests, curiosity, independence, perseverance, imagination, playfulness, humor, and originality. It is recommended that parents complete the inventory at a parent meeting or during a preschool or kindergarten screening for their child. There is no time limit to complete the inventory, but it usually takes between 20 and 35 minutes.

12683
Preschool Screening System: Non-Language Form. Hainsworth, Peter K.; Hainsworth, Marian L. 1980
Subtests: Movement Patterns; Clapping; Finger Patterns; Copy Shapes; Draw a Person
Descriptors: English (Second Language); Hearing Impairments; *Individual Testing; *Kindergarten Children; Language Handicaps; *Learning Readiness; *Nonverbal Tests; *Pantomime; *Preschool Children; Preschool Education; *Screening Tests
Identifiers: PSS
Availability: ERISys; Box 1635, Pawtucket, RI 02862
Target Audience: 2-6

A nonlanguage version of the Preschool Screening System (TC012681) for use with children with a hearing language problem or with children whose first language is not English. Score is used as a rough indicator of whether child should be tested further. Subtests used are movement patterns, clapping, finger patterns, copy shapes, and draw a person. Should be followed by complete evaluation if score is low.

12693
Geriatric Sentence Completion Form. LeBray, Peter R. 1982
Subtests: Physical; Psychological; Socioenvironmental; Temporal Orientation
Descriptors: *Gerontology; *Individual Characteristics; *Older Adults; *Projective Measures
Identifiers: GSCF; *Sentence Completion Method
Availability: Psychological Assessment Resources; P.O. Box 998, Odessa, FL 33556
Target Audience: 60-99

Developed as a projective measure of selected personal characteristics of geriatric patients or older adults (age 60 and over). Is a sentence completion form which requires an older client to complete fragmentary sentence stems either in writing or orally. Elicits personal responses in 4 content domains: physical, psychological, social, and temporal orientation. Can be used in hospitals, long-term care facilities, group settings, outpatient, community care programs, and private office settings.

12694
Neuropsychological Status Examination. Psychological Assessment Resources, Odessa FL 1983
Descriptors: Adults; *Clinical Psychology; Court Litigation; *Medical Care Evaluation; Neurological Impairments; *Patients; *Psychological Evaluation; *Psychologists; Questionnaires
Identifiers: Neuropsychology; NSC; NSE; *Psychiatric Patients
Availability: Psychological Assessment Resources; P.O. Box 998, Odessa, FL 33556
Target Audience: 25-64

Comprehensive status exam forms to organize and collate all data required in completion of a neuropsychological evaluation. Designed to accomplish 3 goals: provide a complete and exhaustive database for neuropsychological assessment, provide a logical format to help in completing assessment report and provide a thorough record of clinician's contact with patient for purposes of court proceedings. The NSE has 13 sections including patient and referral data; neuropsychological symptom checklist; premorbid status; physical, emotional, and cognitive status; results of neuropsychological testing; diagnostic comments; follow-up and treatment recommendations. The Neuropsychological Symptom Checklist (NCS) can be completed by clinician, patient, or significant other and is intended as a screening instrument to assess the status of all potential neurological and neuropsychological signs and symptoms.

12696
Janus Job Planner. Jew, Wing; Tong, Robert 1976
Descriptors: Career Choice; *Interest Inventories; *Learning Problems; Secondary Education; *Secondary School Students; Self Concept; *Self Evaluation (Individuals); Values; *Vocational Interests; Work Environment; Work Experience
Availability: Janus Book Publishers; 2501 Industrial Pwy., W., Hayward, CA 94545
Grade Level: 7-12

For use with secondary school students who have had little experience with the process of self-assessment necessary to make effective career decisions, especially students with limited learning ability or other academic handicaps. This job planner is a combination of activities, exercises, and inventories for each of the following: work interests, work experience, working conditions, personal values, earnings and expenses, choosing a vocation, individual attitudes which may influence job performance, students' goals, and plans.

12697
The Ullman ESL Achievement Test for Beginning ESL Students. Ullman, Ann 1984
Descriptors: *Achievement Tests; Adolescents; *Adults; *Adult Students; *English (Second Language); *Grammar; Program Evaluation; Secondary Education; *Secondary School Students; *Student Placement
Identifiers: ESL
Availability: The Alemany Press; 2501 Industrial Pwy., W., Hayward, CA 94545
Grade Level: 7-12
Target Audience: 12-64
Notes: Time, 30 approx.; Items, 50

Used to measure achievement and to assist in placement; of beginning ESL (English-as-a-Second-Language) students in secondary and adult programs. Purpose of test is to estimate English ability at beginning levels. Test has also been used as a tool in developing and assessing program effectiveness. Test with two alternate forms is group administered. Either form may be used for initial placement, or Form A may be used as a pretest and form B as a posttest.

12698
The Henderson-Moriarty ESL/Literacy Placement Test. Henderson, Cindy; Moriarty, Pia 1982
Subtests: Oral; Written
Descriptors: *Adults; *Adult Students; *English (Second Language); *Individual Testing; Limited English Speaking; Non English Speaking; Oral English; Reading Skills; *Screening Tests; *Student Placement; Writing Skills
Identifiers: HELP Test
Availability: The Alemany Press; 2501 Industrial Pwy., W., Hayward, CA 94545
Target Audience: 18-64

Individually administered test for adult learners of English as a Second Language (ESL) who have minimal or no oral English skills and who fall into one of the following categories: no reading or writing skills in any language; minimal reading or writing skills in their native language; or reading and writing skills in a language which does not use the Roman alphabet. The HELP test has 3 components: intake information (first language assessment), oral English assessment (including reading and manipulative skills), and written English assessment (including reading skills). Test helps with appropriate class placement and identifies literacy levels of students. Test is untimed.

12710
Language Background Questionnaire for the Bilingual Child. Redlinger, Wendy E. 1977
Descriptors: *Bilingualism; *Bilingual Students; Child Language; Children; Cultural Influences; Demography; Elementary School Students; *Family Environment; Hispanic Americans; Language Acquisition; *Language Role; Language Tests; *Language Usage; Minority Group Children; *Preschool Children; Questionnaires; Social Influences; Sociocultural Patterns; Socioeconomic Influences; Sociolinguistics; Spanish Americans
Availability: ERIC Document Reproduction Service; 3900 Wheeler Ave., Alexandria, VA 22304 (ED148184, 21 pages)
Target Audience: 2-12

This questionnaire is designed for use in gathering information on the home linguistic background on both pre- and school-aged bilingual children. The questionnaire probes a series of demographic and environmental variables which define a bilingual child's sociolinguistic milieu and is directed to the mother or the caretaker of the child. The questionnaire is appropriate for use by both researchers and educators in studying and evaluating language development in bilingual children.

12712
Nonreturning or Former Student Questionnaire.
Bower, Cathleen P.; Renkiewicz, Nancy K. 1977
Descriptors: Academic Persistence; College Attendance; *College Students; Community Colleges; Demography; Dropouts; Higher Education; Participant Satisfaction; Questionnaires; *School Attitudes; *Student Characteristics; *Two Year College Students; Withdrawal (Education)
Identifiers: Student Outcomes Questionnaires
Availability: ERIC Document Reproduction Service; 3900 Wheeler Ave., Alexandria, VA 22304 (ED147330, 80 pages)
Grade Level: 13-16

The Nonreturning Student Questionnaire is for 4-year college and university students, and the Former Student Questionnaire is designed for community college students. These questionnaires can be administered to any student who leaves the institution without receiving a degree or certificate. In addition to demographic and background data concerning students' experiences and progress at the institution, a survey of nonreturning students using these questionnaires would provide detailed information about why students did not return to this school (both positive and negative reasons), and their satisfaction with various institutional services. This is one of 4 student outcomes questionnaires developed by the National Center for Higher Education Management Systems. Student outcomes are defined as the results or consequences of a student's enrollment in a postsecondary educational program. The student outcomes measured by these questionnaires include information on student's background, goals, aspirations, plans, attitudes, activities, educational plans, occupational choices, and reasons for making certain decisions. The questionnaires were intended to be used in sequence so that longitudinal data can be collected on students. By the periodic administration of these questionnaires to the appropriate students, colleges and universities will be able to measure the progress of their students and the impacts of college on their students. Each questionnaire was designed to collect from students the most important information colleges and universities want at the most appropriate point in time. An alternate source is National Center for Higher Education Management Systems Publications, P.O. Drawer P, Boulder, Colorado 80302.

12715
Wisconsin Administrative Practice Scale: Special Education. Lietz, Jeremy Jon 1975
Subtests: Informal Communication; Responsibility Delegation; Parent Involvement; Systems Development; Organizational Change; Child Centeredness; Administrative Control
Descriptors: *Administrative Policy; Adults; Clinical Diagnosis; Communication (Thought Transfer); Cooperative Programs; *Disabilities; Elementary Secondary Education; Organizational Change; Parent Participation; *Policy Formation; *Special Education; Student Participation; Surveys
Identifiers: Self Administered Tests; WAPS
Availability: ERIC Document Reproduction Service; 3900 Wheeler Ave., Alexandria, VA 22304 (ED144945, 22 pages)
Target Audience: 18-64
Notes: Time, 45 approx.; Items, 162

The Wisconsin Administrative Practice Scale: Special Education (WAPS) is a self-administering survey instrument designed to measure implementation of 162 selected administrative practices and policies used to coordinate diagnostic units for handicapped children. Originally developed to measure the implementation of Wisconsin Ch. 115 relating to the education of children with exceptional educational needs, WAPS was subsequently refined to measure 162 general items associated with the development of a quality school-level multidisciplinary diagnostic unit. One hundred thirty-five items are grouped into 7 subscales each consisting of 20 items. The WAPS takes approximately 45 minutes to complete.

12724
The ACT Evaluation/Survey Service for Educational Institutions and Agencies: Adult Learner Needs Assessment Survey. American College Testing Program, Iowa City, IA 1981
Descriptors: *Adult Learning; Adults; *Adult Students; *Higher Education; *Institutional Research; *Needs Assessment; *Organizational Objectives; *Postsecondary Education; Questionnaires
Identifiers: ACT Evaluation Survey Service; ESS
Availability: ACT; Evaluation/Survey Service, P.O. Box 168, Iowa City, IA 52243

Grade Level: 13-16
Target Audience: 18-64
Notes: Time, 25 approx.; Items, 89

Primary purpose of the ACT Evaluation/Survey Service (ESS) is to assist postsecondary educational institutions and agencies in the collection, interpretation, and use of student survey data for such purposes as institutional planning, research, evaluation, and self-study. There are 9 survey instruments currently available, and each is designed to address a single educational topic and audience. Items are broad enough in scope to be applicable to most postsecondary institutions but specific enough to provide data which may be readily translatable into institutional action. Purpose of the Adult Learner Needs Assessment Survey is to explore the perceived educational and personal needs of adult students enrolled at the institution and of prospective students in the community. The 89 questions cover background information, educational plans and preferences, personal and educational needs. There is room for up to 30 additional questions from the individual institution as well as a comments and suggestions section. Untimed questionnaire which takes approximately 25 minutes to complete.

12731
The ACT Evaluation/Survey Service for Educational Institutions and Agencies: Withdrawing/Nonreturning Student Survey. American College Testing Program, Iowa City, IA 1979
Descriptors: *College Students; *Dropouts; Higher Education; *Institutional Research; *Organizational Objectives; Questionnaires; School Holding Power; *Withdrawal (Education)
Identifiers: ACT Evaluation Survey Service; ESS
Availability: ACT; Evaluation/Survey Service, P.O. Box 168, Iowa City, IA 52243
Grade Level: 13-16
Notes: Time, 20 approx.; Items, 110

Primary purpose of the ACT Evaluation/Survey Service (ESS) is to assist postsecondary educational institutions and agencies in the collection, interpretation, and use of student survey data for such purposes as institutional planning, research, evaluation, and self-study. There are 9 survey instruments currently available, and each is designed to address a single educational topic and audience. Items are broad enough in scope to be applicable to most postsecondary institutions but specific enough to provide data which may be readily translatable into institutional action. The Withdrawing/Nonreturning Student Survey is used to determine the reasons students leave an institution before completing a degree or certification program. Untimed instrument which takes approximately 20 minutes to complete and covers background information, reasons for leaving college, college services and characteristics. There is room for institution to add up to 30 additional questions and for respondents to write in comments and suggestions.

12732
The ACT Evaluation/Survey Service for Educational Institutions and Agencies: Withdrawing/Nonreturning Student Survey (Short Form). American College Testing Program, Iowa City, IA 1981
Descriptors: *College Students; *Dropouts; Higher Education; *Institutional Research; *Organizational Objectives; Questionnaires; School Holding Power; *Withdrawal (Education)
Identifiers: ACT Evaluation Survey Service; ESS
Availability: ACT; Evaluation/Survey Service, P.O. Box 168, Iowa City, IA 52243
Grade Level: 13-16
Notes: Time, 10 approx.; Items, 62

Primary purpose of the ACT Evaluation/Survey Service (ESS) is to assist postsecondary educational institutions and agencies in the collection, interpretation, and use of student survey data for such purposes as institutional planning, research, evaluation, and self-study. There are 9 survey instruments currently available, and each is designed to address a single educational topic and audience. Items are broad enough in scope to be applicable to most postsecondary institutions but specific enough to provide data which may be readily translatable into institutional action. Short form of the Withdrawing/Nonreturning Student Survey may be more suitable for certain audiences than the longer form (TC012731). Is used to determine the reasons students leave an institution before completing a degree or certification program. Untimed instrument which takes approximately 10 minutes to complete and covers background information and reasons for leaving college. There is room for an institution to add up to 20 additional questions.

12735
The Mini-Check System. Ilyin, Donna 1981
Descriptors: *Achievement Tests; Adults; Advanced Students; Children; Communication Skills; *English (Second Language); Grammar; Language Proficiency; Listening Skills; Testing
Identifiers: Oral Tests
Availability: The Alemany Press; 2501 Industrial Pwy., W., Hayward, CA 94545
Target Audience: 12-64

A method of testing and scoring tests in classes of English as a Second Language. Booklets of questions are provided in the areas of listening for structural cues, grammatical form and communicative function, and other miscellaneous areas. Questions are read to the students. Answers are marked on answer sheets and scored immediately via sets of precut answer keys. For use with intermediate through advanced students including adults.

12736
Alemany English Second Language Placement Test, Revised. Ilyin, Donna; And Others 1977
Descriptors: *Achievement Tests; Adults; *Adult Students; *English (Second Language); *Student Placement
Availability: Alemany Press; 2501 Industrial Pwy., W., Hayward, CA 94545
Target Audience: Adults

An English language placement test for adults who are learning English as a second language.

12737
MAC Checklist for Evaluating, Preparing and/or Improving Standardized Tests for Limited English Speaking Students. Maculaitis, Jean D'Arcy 1981
Subtests: Evidence of Validity; Evidence of Examinee Appropriateness; Evidence of Proper Item Construction; Evidence of Technical Merit; Evidence of Administrative Excellence
Descriptors: Adults; Bilingual Students; Check Lists; *Evaluation Criteria; *Limited English Speaking; *Second Language Learning; *Standardized Tests; Test Construction; Test Selection; Test Validity
Availability: The Alemany Press; 2501 Industrial Pwy., W., Hayward, CA 94545
Target Audience: Adults
Notes: Items, 103

A checklist designed to assist in evaluation of standardized second-language tests. The appendices include a list of helpful hints for, and basic rights of, test takers, selected sources of bilingual tests and testing information, and a list of commercially available tests.

12738
The Maculaitis Assessment Program: Basic Concept Test. Maculaitis, Jean D'Arcy 1982
Subtests: Identification of Color; Identification of Shapes; Counting; Number Identification; Alphabet; Letter Identification; Identification of Relationships
Descriptors: *Achievement Tests; *Admission Criteria; Criterion Referenced Tests; *Diagnostic Tests; Elementary School Students; *English (Second Language); *Grade 1; Group Testing; Individual Testing; *Kindergarten Children; *Language Proficiency; Listening Comprehension; Norm Referenced Tests; *North American English; Oral Language; Primary Education; Reading Comprehension; *Screening Tests; *Standard Spoken Usage; *Student Placement; Vocabulary; Writing Skills
Identifiers: MAC; Test Batteries
Availability: The Alemany Press; 2501 Industrial Pwy., W., Hayward, CA 94545
Grade Level: K-1
Notes: Time, 15; Items, 46

A multipurpose test for non-native speakers of English in kindergarten through grade 12. The MAC battery can be used to provide an indication of a student's global as well as specific language proficiency; provide an indication of student's academic achievement in English (i.e., student's second language); provide specific diagnostic information; determine whether non-native student will be chosen for selection into the ESL/BE program provided by a school district; and assist in establishing exit criteria from the program. MAC focuses on the functional meaning of language and emphasizes the vocabulary and structures needed by the learner to respond appropriately in specific situations. Skills tested by the battery include oral expression, listening comprehension, vocabulary knowledge, reading comprehension, writing ability. In the battery, item difficulty increases gradually. All components are color coded so that students can be given subtests from different levels. Many of the subtests must be individually administered; others may be group administered. The battery has both norm-referenced and criterion-referenced applications. Target language of MAC is standard American English.

12739
The Maculaitis Assessment Program: K-1. Maculaitis, Jean D'Arcy 1982
Subtests: Asking Questions; Connected Discourse; Comprehension of Commands; Situational Comprehension; Minimal Pairs; Identification of Consonants and Vowels

Descriptors: *Achievement Tests; *Admission Criteria; Criterion Referenced Tests; *Diagnostic Tests; Elementary School Students; *English (Second Language); *Grade 1; Group Testing; Individual Testing; *Kindergarten Children; *Language Proficiency; Listening Comprehension; Norm Referenced Tests; *North American English; Oral Language; Primary Education; Reading Comprehension; *Screening Tests; *Standard Spoken Usage; *Student Placement; Vocabulary; Writing Skills
Identifiers: MAC; Test Batteries
Availability: The Alemany Press; 2501 Industrial Pwy., W., Hayward, CA 94545
Grade Level: K-1
Notes: Time, 25; Items, 43

A multipurpose test for non-native speakers of English in kindergarten through grade 12. The MAC battery can be used to provide an indication of a student's global as well as specific language proficiency; provide an indication of student's academic achievement in English (i.e., student's second language); provide specific diagnostic information; determine whether non-native student will be chosen for selection into the ESL/BE program provided by a school district; and assist in establishing exit criteria from the program. MAC focuses on the functional meaning of language and emphasizes the vocabulary and structures needed by the learner to respond appropriately in specific situations. Skills tested by the battery include oral expression, listening comprehension, vocabulary knowledge, reading comprehension, writing ability. In the battery, item difficulty increases gradually. All components are color coded so that students can be given subtests from different levels. Many of the subtests must be individually administered; others may be group administered. The battery has both norm-referenced and criterion-referenced applications. Target language of MAC is standard American English.

12740
The Maculaitis Assessment Program: 2-3.
Maculaitis, Jean D'Arcy 1982
Subtests: Answering Questions; Connected Discourse; Identification of Consonants and Vowels; Definition of Nouns; Identifying Words; Counting Words; Answering Questions; Comprehending Statements; Alphabetizing; Recognizing Vowels and Consonants; Recognizing Long and Short Vowels; Using Word Families; Singular and Plural Forms; Recognizing Silent Letters; Reading Outcomes
Descriptors: *Achievement Tests; *Admission Criteria; Criterion Referenced Tests; *Diagnostic Tests; *Elementary School Students; *English (Second Language); *Grade 2; *Grade 3; Group Testing; Individual Testing; *Language Proficiency; Listening Comprehension; Norm Referenced Tests; *North American English; Oral Language; Primary Education; Reading Comprehension; *Screening Tests; *Standard Spoken Usage; *Student Placement; Vocabulary; Writing Skills
Identifiers: MAC; Test Batteries
Availability: The Alemany Press; 2501 Industrial Pwy., W., Hayward, CA 94545
Grade Level: 2-3
Notes: Time, 79; Items, 111

A multipurpose test for non-native speakers of English in kindergarten through grade 12. The MAC battery can be used to provide an indication of a student's global as well as specific language proficiency; provide an indication of student's academic achievement in English (i.e., student's second language); provide specific diagnostic information; determine whether non-native student will be chosen for selection into the ESL/BE program provided by a school district; and assist in establishing exit criteria from the program. MAC focuses on the functional meaning of language and emphasizes the vocabulary and structures needed by the learner to respond appropriately in specific situations. Skills tested by the battery include oral expression, listening comprehension, vocabulary knowledge, reading comprehension, writing ability. In the battery, item difficulty increases gradually. All components are color coded so that students can be given subtests from different levels. Many of the subtests must be individually administered; others may be group administered. The battery has both norm-referenced and criterion-referenced applications. Target language of MAC is standard American English.

12741
The Maculaitis Assessment Program: 4-5.
Maculaitis, Jean D'Arcy 1982
Subtests: Asking Questions; Connected Discourse; Vocabulary Knowledge; Positional Auditory Discrimination; Answering Questions; Comprehending Statements; Comprehending Dialogues; Recognizing Homonyms; Recognizing Antonyms; Recognizing Abbreviations; Reading Outcomes; Grammatical Structure; Paragraph Construction

Descriptors: *Achievement Tests; *Admission Criteria; Criterion Referenced Tests; *Diagnostic Tests; *Elementary School Students; *English (Second Language); *Grade 4; *Grade 5; Group Testing; Individual Testing; Intermediate Grades; *Language Proficiency; Listening Comprehension; Norm Referenced Tests; *North American English; Oral Language; Reading Comprehension; *Screening Tests; *Standard Spoken Usage; *Student Placement; Vocabulary; Writing Skills
Identifiers: MAC; Test Batteries
Availability: The Alemany Press; 2501 Industrial Pwy., W., Hayward, CA 94545
Grade Level: 4-5
Notes: Time, 119; Items, 126

A multipurpose test for non-native speakers of English in kindergarten through grade 12. The MAC battery can be used to provide an indication of a student's global as well as specific language proficiency; provide an indication of student's academic achievement in English (i.e., student's second language); provide specific diagnostic information; determine whether non-native student will be chosen for selection into the ESL/BE program provided by a school district; and assist in establishing exit criteria from the program. MAC focuses on the functional meaning of language and emphasizes the vocabulary and structures needed by the learner to respond appropriately in specific situations. Skills tested by the battery include oral expression, listening comprehension, vocabulary knowledge, reading comprehension, writing ability. In the battery, item difficulty increases gradually. All components are color coded so that students can be given subtests from different levels. Many of the subtests must be individually administered; others may be group administered. The battery has both norm-referenced and criterion-referenced applications. Target language of MAC is standard American English.

12742
The Maculaitis Assessment Program: 6-8.
Maculaitis, Jean D'Arcy 1982
Subtests: Answering Questions (Oral Expression); Asking Questions (Oral Expression); Connected Discourse; Answering Questions (Listening Comprehension); Comprehending Statements; Comprehending Dialogues; Vocabulary; Reading Outcomes; Grammatical Structure; Paragraph Construction
Descriptors: *Achievement Tests; *Admission Criteria; Criterion Referenced Tests; *Diagnostic Tests; *English (Second Language); *Grade 6; Group Testing; Individual Testing; Junior High Schools; *Junior High School Students; *Language Proficiency; Listening Comprehension; Norm Referenced Tests; *North American English; Oral Language; Reading Comprehension; Screening Tests; *Standard Spoken Usage; *Student Placement; Vocabulary; Writing Skills
Identifiers: MAC; Test Batteries
Availability: The Alemany Press; 2501 Industrial Pwy., W., Hayward, CA 94545
Grade Level: 6-8
Notes: Time, 108; Items, 112

A multipurpose test for non-native speakers of English in kindergarten through grade 12. The MAC battery can be used to provide an indication of a student's global as well as specific language proficiency; provide an indication of student's academic achievement in English (i.e., student's second language); provide specific diagnostic information; determine whether non-native student will be chosen for selection into the ESL/BE program provided by a school district; and assist in establishing exit criteria from the program. MAC focuses on the functional meaning of language and emphasizes the vocabulary and structures needed by the learner to respond appropriately in specific situations. Skills tested by the battery include oral expression, listening comprehension, vocabulary knowledge, reading comprehension, writing ability. In the battery, item difficulty increases gradually. All components are color coded so that students can be given subtests from different levels. Many of the subtests must be individually administered; others may be group administered. The battery has both norm-referenced and criterion-referenced applications. Target language of MAC is standard American English.

12743
The Maculaitis Assessment Program: 9-12.
Maculaitis, Jean D'Arcy 1982
Subtests: Answering Questions (Oral Expression); Asking Questions (Oral Expression); Connected Discourse; Answering Questions (Listening Comprehension); Comprehending Statements; Comprehending Dialogues; Vocabulary; Reading Outcomes; Grammatical Structure; Paragraph Construction

Descriptors: *Achievement Tests; *Admission Criteria; Criterion Referenced Tests; *Diagnostic Tests; *English (Second Language); Group Testing; High Schools; *High School Students; Individual Testing; *Language Proficiency; Listening Comprehension; Norm Referenced Tests; *North American English; Oral Language; Reading Comprehension; *Screening Tests; *Standard Spoken Usage; *Student Placement; Vocabulary; Writing Skills
Identifiers: MAC; Test Batteries
Availability: The Alemany Press; 2501 Industrial Pwy., W., Hayward, CA 94545
Grade Level: 9-12
Notes: Time, 108; Items, 112

A multipurpose test for non-native speakers of English in kindergarten through grade 12. The MAC battery can be used to provide an indication of a student's global as well as specific language proficiency; provide an indication of student's academic achievement in English (i.e., student's second language); provide specific diagnostic information; determine whether non-native student will be chosen for selection into the ESL/BE program provided by a school district; and assist in establishing exit criteria from the program. MAC focuses on the functional meaning of language and emphasizes the vocabulary and structures needed by the learner to respond appropriately in specific situations. Skills tested by the battery include oral expression, listening comprehension, vocabulary knowledge, reading comprehension, writing ability. In the battery, item difficulty increases gradually. All components are color coded so that students can be given subtests from different levels. Many of the subtests must be individually administered; others may be group administered. The battery has both norm-referenced and criterion-referenced applications. Target language of MAC is standard American English.

12759
Should You Return to School?
Descriptors: Adults; *Adult Students; Higher Education; Nontraditional Students; Questionnaires
Identifiers: Self Administered Tests; Self Scoring Tests
Availability: Norback, Craig T.; Check Yourself Out. New York: Times Books, 1980
Target Audience: Adults
Notes: Items, 20

Designed to enable adults to determine the practicality of returning to college. Aids in clarifying motivation for returning to school.

12770
How Do You Rate as a Single Parent? Parents without Partners, Inc.
Subtests: Single Parents and Their Children; Separated/Divorced Single Parents; Widowed Single Parents; Never-Married Single Parents
Descriptors: Adults; *Attitude Measures; *Divorce; *One Parent Family; *Parent Attitudes; *Parent Child Relationship; Parents; Self Evaluation (Individuals); Social Attitudes; *Widowed
Identifiers: Self Administered Tests; Self Scoring Tests
Availability: Norback, Craig T.; Check Yourself Out. New York: Times Books, 1980
Target Audience: Adults
Notes: Items, 37

Designed to assess understanding of single parent roles, attitudes, and expectations which influence a single parent's effectiveness. Items are concerned with problems faced by single, divorced or separated, and widowed parents.

12776
Do You Need Psychotherapy? O'Brien, John S.; Brennan, John H. 1980
Descriptors: *Adults; *Emotional Adjustment; Emotional Problems; Psychological Patterns; Psychotherapy; Self Concept Measures; *Self Evaluation (Individuals)
Identifiers: Self Administered Tests; Self Report Measures; Self Scoring Tests
Availability: Norback, Craig T.; Check Yourself Out. New York: Times Books, 1980
Target Audience: Adults
Notes: Items, 20

Designed to enable subjects to determine their need for psychotherapy. Items enable respondent to assess their emotional adjustment and behavior. Instrument is also available in Family Circle Magazine, May 19, 1978.

12781
What Are the Signs of Alcoholism? National Council on Alcoholism, Inc. 1980
Descriptors: Adults; *Alcoholism; Questionnaires
Identifiers: Self Administered Tests; Self Report Measures; Self Scoring Tests
Availability: Norback, Craig T.; Check Yourself Out. New York: Times Books, 1980
Target Audience: Adults
Notes: Items, 26

Designed to determine presence of alcoholism symptoms which may require assistance. May be used by suspected alcoholic or a friend or family member of patient.

12786
Are You Financially Prepared for Retirement?
1980
Descriptors: *Adults; Financial Needs; Knowledge Level; Older Adults; Questionnaires; *Retirement; *Retirement Benefits
Identifiers: Medicare; Self Administered Tests; Self Scoring Tests; *Social Security
Availability: Norback, Craig T.; Check Yourself Out. New York: Times Books, 1980
Target Audience: Adults
Notes: Items, 30
Designed to assess respondent's knowledge of Social Security and pension regulations. Developed to enable one to plan for financial security after retirement.

12803
Spanish Culture Fair Intelligence Test: Scale 2.
Cattell, Raymond B.; Cattell, A.K.S. 1957
Descriptors: Adolescents; *Adults; Children; Culture Fair Tests; *Elementary School Students; Elementary Secondary Education; Individual Testing; Intelligence; *Intelligence Tests; Nonverbal Tests; *Secondary School Students; *Spanish; *Spanish Speaking; Spatial Ability
Identifiers: Cattell Culture Fair Intelligence Test
Availability: Institute for Personality and Ability Testing; P.O. Box 188, Champaign, IL 61820
Target Audience: 8-64
Notes: Items, 46
A Spanish-language translation of the Culture Fair Intelligence Test, Scale 2 (TC001660) which is designed to assess individual intelligence in a manner that reduces the influence of verbal fluency, cultural climate, and educational level. Forms A and B are available for use with children ages 8-14 and adults of average intelligence. Scale 2 is appropriate for majority of subjects.

12804
Spanish Culture Fair Intelligence Test: Scale 3.
Cattell, Raymond B.; Cattell, A.K.S. 1963
Subtests: Series; Classifications; Matrices; Conditions (Topology)
Descriptors: Adults; College Students; *Culture Fair Tests; Higher Education; High Schools; High School Students; Individual Testing; Intelligence; *Intelligence Tests; Nonverbal Tests; *Spanish; *Spanish Speaking; *Spatial Ability; Timed Tests
Identifiers: Cattell Culture Fair Intelligence Test
Availability: Institute for Personality and Ability Testing; P.O. Box 188, Champaign, IL 61820
Target Audience: 15-64
Notes: Time, 13 approx.; Items, 50
A Spanish translation of the Culture Fair Intelligence Test, Scale 3 (TC001661). Test booklets, administration instructions, and answer sheets are in Spanish. Instrument is designed to measure individual intelligence in a manner intended to reduce the influence of verbal fluency, cultural climate, and educational level. Forms A and B are available for Scale 3.

12819
Survey of Metropolitan Public Schools Administrators. Nashville-Davidson County Metropolitan Public Schools, TN 1976
Descriptors: *Administrators; Adult Education; *Community Education; *Community Schools; Elementary Secondary Education; Lifelong Learning; *Program Evaluation; Questionnaires; *School Community Programs; School Community Relationship; Surveys
Identifiers: Nashville Davidson County Tennessee Schools
Availability: ERIC Document Reproduction Service; 3900 Wheeler Ave., Alexandria, VA 22304 (ED132689, 92 pages)
Target Audience: 18-64
Notes: Items, 12
This is one of 3 questionnaires used in the evaluation of the Community Education Program of the Nashville-Davidson County, Tennessee, Metropolitan Public Schools. The questions are multiple choice and open ended and ask information about their perceptions of the program for the community, the greatest strength and weakness, how to improve the program, inform the community, and to fund the program.

12820
Survey of Community Agencies Using Community Education Facilities. Nashville-Davidson County Metropolitan Public Schools, TN 1976

Descriptors: Adult Education; *Community Education; *Community Involvement; Community Organizations; *Community Schools; Elementary Secondary Education; Lifelong Learning; *Program Evaluation; Questionnaires; *School Community Programs; School Community Relationship
Identifiers: Nashville Davidson County Tennessee Schools
Availability: ERIC Document Reproduction Service; 3900 Wheeler Ave., Alexandria, VA 22304 (ED132689, 92 pages)
Target Audience: 18-64
Notes: Items, 7
This is one of 3 questionnaires used in the evaluation of the Community Education Program of the Nashville-Davidson County, Tennessee, Metropolitan Public Schools. The questions are multiple choice and open ended and ask for the agency's perceptions of the program, how to improve it, the greatest strength and weakness, what services the agency can offer the community through the program, and whether the program meets a community need.

12821
Survey of Community Education Participants.
Nashville-Davidson County Metropolitan Public Schools, TN 1976
Descriptors: Adult Education; Adult Students; *Community Education; *Community Schools; Elementary Secondary Education; Evening Programs; Lifelong Learning; *Participant Satisfaction; *Program Evaluation; Questionnaires; School Community Programs; School Community Relationship; Surveys
Identifiers: Nashville Davidson County Tennessee Schools
Availability: ERIC Document Reproduction Service; 3900 Wheeler Ave., Alexandria, VA 22304 (ED132689, 92 pages)
Target Audience: 18-64
Notes: Items, 11
This is one of 3 questionnaires used in the evaluation of the Community Education Program of the Nashville-Davidson County, Tennessee, Metropolitan Public Schools. The questions are multiple choice and open ended and ask about how the respondent felt the program reflected its need. This questionnaire was sent to all the participants in the 7 community schools who had taken part in the education program.

12844
Mexican American Youth and Vocational Education in Texas Questionnaire. Houston Univ. Texas Center for Human Resources 1976
Descriptors: *Academic Aspiration; Attitude Measures; Career Choice; High Schools; *High School Students; *Mexican Americans; *Occupational Aspiration; *Student Attitudes; Student Educational Objectives; *Vocational Education; Youth
Identifiers: Texas
Availability: ERIC Document Reproduction Service; 3900 Wheeler Ave., Alexandria, VA 22304 (ED124368, 39 pages)
Grade Level: 9-12
Notes: Items, 287
This questionnaire was used to survey the attitudes, program at school; and plans for the future of Mexican-American high school students in Texas. Almost all of the questions consist of circling a number or checking one or more answers. A few require written answers. Topics covered by the questions are the student's family background; school activities; attitudes about school, work, and life in general; what their parents do, feel, and think about their school; kinds of problems encountered while "job hunting"; careers, jobs; the labor market; how to go about getting a job; employers' attitudes about high school students; students' attitudes about employers; education or training necessary for certain jobs; and future educational and employment plans. There is one section for vocational students only.

12863
Brief Behavior Rating Scale. Kahn, Paul; Ribner, Sol 1977
Subtests: Abrasiveness; Inattentiveness; Dependency; Restlessness; Self Involvement; Bizarreness; Frustration Tolerance
Descriptors: *Behavior Rating Scales; Elementary Education; Elementary School Students; Emotional Disturbances; Neurological Impairments; Social Adjustment; *Special Education; *Student Behavior
Identifiers: BBRS; TIM(K)
Availability: Tests in Microfiche; Test Collection, Educational Testing Service, Princeton, NJ 08541
Grade Level: K-6
Notes: Items, 28
Developed to be part of an assessment battery administered to children referred to the Committee on the Handicapped for placement in special education classes.

Constructed to aid teacher evaluators of diagnostic classrooms in organizing and clarifying behavior patterns of children, as a guide to formulate prescriptive teaching recommendations, as an adjunct in making special education recommendations, and as an instrument to measure behavioral change over time. Measures 7 personality traits.

12866
Bessemer Screening Test. Jones, Evelyn V.; Sapp, Gary L. 1981
Subtests: Name Writing; Human Figure Drawing; Work Knowledge; Design Copying; Math
Descriptors: Adolescents; Arithmetic; *Behavior Problems; *Educational Diagnosis; Elementary Education; *Elementary School Students; *Handicap Identification; Handwriting; *Learning Disabilities; Preadolescents; *Screening Tests
Identifiers: BST; Public Law 94 142
Availability: Stoelting Co.; 1350 S. Kostner Ave., Chicago, IL 60623
Target Audience: 8-14
Notes: Time, 15 approx.; Items, 97
This test is to identify children with handicapping conditions who may require special services. It identifies potential school-related deviance which is behavioral, sociocultural, and normative in nature. The features incorporated into the Bessemer Screening Test (BST) are group administration, coverage of a broad age range, short administration time, objective scoring, little training required for administration and scoring, little preparation required by examiner prior to administration, and classroom-related task similarity. There are 5 individual subtests.

12867
Fisher Language Survey (and Process). Fisher, Alyce F. 1978
Descriptors: Achievement Tests; Auditory Tests; *Criterion Referenced Tests; Educational Diagnosis; Elementary Education; Elementary School Students; Grammar; Handwriting; *Learning Disabilities; Learning Modalities; Minimum Competency Testing; Spelling
Identifiers: *Auditory Reception; FLS
Availability: Stoelting Co.; 1350 S. Kostner Ave., Chicago, IL 60623
Grade Level: 1-4
The FLS is a criterion-referenced test and is administered by dictation of sentences that students must write in their entirety. It is a test of auditory reception with written expression on the part of the pupil. An evaluation is made of spelling, handwriting, 2 specific English rules, plus many types of errors typically made by students who have difficulty learning.

12891
EDS Diagnostic Skill Level Inventory for Reading Skills, Revised. Henney, R. Lee 1978
Subtests: General Reading; Practical Reading; Prose Interpretation; Poetry Interpretation; Drama Interpretation
Descriptors: *Adult Education; Adults; *Diagnostic Tests; Drama; Multiple Choice Tests; Poetry; *Pretests Posttests; Prose; Reading Comprehension; *Reading Difficulties; Reading Skills
Availability: Educational Diagnostic Services; P.O. Box 347, Valparaiso, IN 46383
Target Audience: 18-64
Notes: Time, 60; Items, 65
This instrument was developed so that teachers could quickly diagnose the strengths and weaknesses of students. The Pre-Instructional Test is to be used to diagnose the student's initial skills in the subject matter. The Post-Instructional Test is to be used following the instructional process to test the student's progress. The student must demonstrate his/her ability to read and correctly interpret each of 5 types of literary material. These categories provide the instructor with the opportunity to determine exactly which type of material causes difficulty in interpretation for the adult so that a productive instructional program can be developed. This test is one part of the 5 which are part of the Diagnostic Program. The test is used in the GED (General Education Development) preparation programs conducted by public schools, manpower training organizations, industrial training departments and private schools, in Freshman Literature courses, for remediation in high school and college, in industrial instruction programs, and in self-study programs.

12893
Childhood Psychosis Scale. Haworth, Mary R. 1981
Descriptors: Child Development; *Children; Clinical Diagnosis; *Developmental Disabilities; *Psychomotor Skills; *Psychosis; *Screening Tests
Identifiers: Primary Visual Motor Test; PVM; TIM(K)
Availability: Tests in Microfiche; Test Collection, Educational Testing Service, Princeton, NJ 08541

Target Audience: 6-12

Developed to explore visual motor deviations of psychotic children who have completed the Primary Visual Motor Test. Developed on the basis of features reported in Bender Gestalt literature and from observations of psychotic children working on the Primary Visual Motor Test while it was being normed. Ten categories comprise the Childhood Psychosis Scale: elaboration, line emphasis, shading, border deviation, use of 3 spaces, overlap or fuse, perseveration, delayed response, personalization, titles. Scale may be useful as an initial screening device.

12906
Cuban Behavioral Identity Questionnaire. Garcia, Margarita; Lega, Leonor I. 1979
Descriptors: Acculturation; Adults; *Cubans; *Cultural Awareness; *Ethnicity; Hispanic Americans; Questionnaires; Rating Scales
Identifiers: CBIQ; El Cuestionario de Identidad Conductual Cubano; Likert Scales
Availability: Hispanic Journal of Behavioral Sciences; v1 n3 p247-61 Sep 1979
Target Audience: 18-64
Notes: Items, 8

The Cuban Behavioral Identity Questionnaire (CBIQ) was constructed to assess the degree of Cuban ethnic identity. The instrument is a short, 8-item questionnaire answerable in a 7-point Likert scale format. It inquires about the frequency with which respondents engage in several ethnic behaviors and the degree to which they are familiar with Cuban idiomatic expressions and Cuban artists/musicians.

12952
Trainee Performance Sample. Irvin, Larry K.; And Others 1982
Descriptors: Adolescents; Adults; Individual Testing; Job Skills; *Performance Tests; *Severe Mental Retardation; *Student Placement; *Trade and Industrial Education; Vocational Education
Identifiers: TPS
Availability: Ideal Developmental Labs; P.O. Box 27142, W. Allis, WI 53227
Target Audience: 13-64
Notes: Items, 26

The Trainee Performance Sample (TPS) was designed as an individually administered test to measure the type and amount of resources required for vocational skill training of severely retarded adolescents and adults. The utility of TPS scores is in providing information on the amount and type of training resources that a severely retarded person may be expected to require relative to other similar clients in specific types of tasks.

12953
Parent Questionnaire: Preschool Handicapped Program. Center for Resource Management, Yorktown Heights, NY
Descriptors: *Attitude Measures; *Disabilities; *Parent Attitudes; Parents; *Parent School Relationship; *Preschool Children; *Preschool Education; *Program Evaluation; Questionnaires
Availability: Director of Preschool Program; Board of Cooperative Educational Services, Yorktown Heights, NY 10598
Target Audience: 18-64
Notes: Items, 35

This instrument allows parents to evaluate the regional program for preschool handicapped children with anonymity in 5 major domains. The questionnaire consists of checklists, rating scales, and detailed instructions. Open-ended questions are asked regarding major program strengths, weaknesses, and recommendations for changes.

12954
Reading Assessment for Language Learning Youngsters. Mineola Union Free School District, NY 1975
Descriptors: *Bilingual Students; *Criterion Referenced Tests; Elementary Education; *Elementary School Students; *English (Second Language); Portuguese; Reading Achievement; *Reading Tests
Identifiers: RALLY; TIM(K)
Availability: Tests in Microfiche; Test Collection, Educational Testing Service, Princeton, NJ 08541
Grade Level: K-6

Reading assessment consisting of 9 parts to evaluate reading attainment of bilingual students. Parts I and II are appropriate for students in kindergarten through grade 3. The 9 parts cover word association, picture word association, life situation questions, classification-categorization, basic numerical computation, analogies, sentence completion-basic conceptual knowledge, sentence completion-own words, and story comprehension.

12967
Parent Observation Index. Anderson, Esther; Jobson, Sharon G. 1981

Subtests: Organization of the Child's Home Environment; Behavior Management Style; Interactions with Child; Attitudes and Perceptions; Coping Abilities and Emotional Well-Being; Teaching Style; Parent Relationship to Staff and Program
Descriptors: Adults; Behavior Rating Scales; Child Caregivers; *Developmental Disabilities; *Disabilities; Family Environment; Intervention; Observation; *Parent Attitudes; *Parent Child Relationship; *Parents; Special Education; Young Children
Identifiers: Me Too Program; Parent Behavior Profile
Availability: The Me Too Program; Solano County Superintendent of Schools, 655 Washington St., Fairfield, CA 94533
Target Audience: Adults

Designed for use by staff of early intervention programs to assess and observe parents' behaviors, skills, and needs in regard to their handicapped or delayed child. Scale was developed for use with families of children ages birth to 5 years.

12969
Writing Attitude Survey. Coleman, Dona R. 1980
Descriptors: *Attitude Measures; *Gifted; Primary Education; Student Evaluation; Surveys; *Writing (Composition)
Identifiers: Faces Scale
Availability: Dona R. Coleman; Friends University, 2100 University, Wichita, KS 67213
Grade Level: 1-3
Notes: Items, 12

Measures student attitudes toward writing, prewriting, teacher evaluation of writing, and student's evaluation of their own writing. A face scale is used with 5 points ranging from happy face to sad face. The test was designed to measure change after student participation in a writing project for gifted students. A discussion of the project evaluation can be found in Gifted Child Quarterly; v27 n3 p114-21 Sum 1983.

13015
Monthly Parent Advisor Evaluation Form. SKI HI Outreach, Logan, UT 1978
Descriptors: Adults; Auditory Perception; Expressive Language; *Hearing Aids; *Hearing Impairments; Interviews; *Language Acquisition; *Parents; *Young Children
Availability: Home Oriented Program Essentials (HOPE); 1780 N. Research Pwy., Ste. 110, Logan, UT 84321
Target Audience: Adults

Designed to assess young child's progress at home in hearing-aid use and auditory and language development. Parental behaviors which may affect the child's progress are also assessed, as well as parental competency in managing child's hearing aid and encouraging language and auditory development. Instrument is also available from ERIC Document Reproduction Service; PO Box 190, Arlington, VA 22210 (ED162451, 386 pages).

13027
Thought Stopping Survey Schedule. Cautela, Joseph R. 1977
Descriptors: Adults; *Behavior Modification; Counseling Techniques; *Patients; Rating Scales; Self Concept
Identifiers: *Thought Stopping; TSSS
Availability: Prof. Joseph R. Cautela; Dept. of Psychology, Boston College, Chestnut Hill, MA 02167
Target Audience: Adults
Notes: Items, 51

Designed to identify negative thoughts behavior therapy clients have about themselves. Instrument is used to train clients in thought stopping, a thought control procedure.

13028
Evaluating Ourselves in Head Start. Nomland, Ella Kube; And Others 1973
Subtests: Education; Health Services; Social Services; Mental Health; Parent Involvement; Training and Career Development; Nutrition; Volunteer Program; Administration
Descriptors: Administration; Biculturalism; Bilingual Education; Career Development; Child Development; Disabilities; *Disadvantaged Youth; *Federal Programs; Health; Mental Health; Nutrition; Parent Participation; *Preschool Children; Preschool Education; Preschool Teachers; *Program Evaluation; Rating Scales; Social Services; Volunteers
Identifiers: California; *Project Head Start
Availability: ERIC Document Reproduction Service; 3900 Wheeler Ave., Alexandria, VA 22304 (ED109141, microfiche only)
Target Audience: 2-5
Notes: Items, 360

This Head Start Evaluation System was developed at the request of the California Head Start Directors Association. The system includes evaluation schedules for components in Education (Bilingual, Bicultural, Handicapped Children, Facilities), Health Services, Social Services, Mental Health Services, Parent Involvement, Training and Career Development, Nutrition, Volunteers (Other than Parents), and Administration. The format is a 4-point rating scale on which the evaluator reacts to a performance standard indicating performance exceeds the standard, performance meets the standard, performance is somewhat below the standard and needs improvement, and performance is substantially below the standard and needs immediate improvement. Space is provided for comments and recommendations.

13069
Fine Finger Dexterity Work Task Unit: Electromechanical Vocational Assessment. Mississippi State Univ., Rehabilitation Research and Training Center 1983
Descriptors: Adults; *Blindness; Individual Testing; *Kinesthetic Perception; *Performance Tests; Psychomotor Skills; *Visual Impairments; *Vocational Evaluation
Identifiers: *Bilateral Dexterity; Electromechanical Vocational Assessment; Finger Dexterity; Frustration; Mississippi State University
Availability: Rehabilitation Research and Training Center; P.O. Box 5365, Mississippi State, MS 39762
Target Audience: Adults
Notes: Time, 50

Designed to provide a flexible system of evaluating a variety of work abilities including kinesthetic memory, bimanual coordination, finger dexterity, and frustrating tolerance. Purpose is to assist National Industries for the Blind and vocational evaluators to improve assessment of the vocational potential of blind and severely visually impaired persons, particularly multiply handicapped blind persons. Subject is taught the task, then works for a 50-minute period and receives feedback on the rate and accuracy of work. Used to compare visually impaired person's performance with the sighted standard. The Methods-Time Measurement Procedure was used to develop the average sighted standard for this work task.

13070
Foot Operated Hinged Box Work Task Unit: Electromechanical Vocational Assessment. Mississippi State Univ., Rehabilitation Research and Training Center 1983
Descriptors: Adults; *Blindness; *Individual Testing; *Performance Tests; Psychomotor Skills; *Visual Impairments; *Vocational Evaluation
Identifiers: Bilateral Dexterity; Electromechanical Vocational Assessment; Finger Dexterity; *Hand Foot Coordination; Mississippi State University
Availability: Rehabilitation Research and Training Center; P.O. Box 5365, Mississippi State, MS 39762
Target Audience: Adults
Notes: Time, 50

Designed to provide a flexible system of evaluating a variety of work abilities including hand foot coordination, bimanual coordination, and finger dexterity. Purpose is to assist National Industries for the Blind and vocational evaluators to improve assessment of the vocational potential of blind and severely visually impaired persons, particularly multiply handicapped blind persons. Subject is taught the task, then works for a 50-minute period and receives feedback on the rate and accuracy of work. Provides an objective method of comparing a blind, or visually impaired person's performance in these work abilities against the performance expected from an average sighted worker. The Methods-Time Measurement Procedure was used to develop the average sighted standard for this work task.

13071
Hinged Box Work Task Unit: Electromechanical Vocational Assessment. Mississippi State Univ., Rehabilitation Research and Training Center 1983
Descriptors: Adults; *Blindness; Individual Testing; *Performance Tests; Psychomotor Skills; *Tactual Perception; *Visual Impairments; *Vocational Evaluation
Identifiers: Bilateral Dexterity; Electromechanical Vocational Assessment; Frustration; Mississippi State University
Availability: Rehabilitation Research and Training Center; P.O. Box 5365, Mississippi State, MS 39762
Target Audience: Adults
Notes: Time, 50

Designed to provide a flexible system of evaluating a variety of work abilities including tactual perception, material control, bimanual coordination, and frustration tolerance. Purpose is to assist National Industries for the Blind and vocational evaluators to improve assessment of the vocational potential of blind and severely visually impaired persons, particularly multiply handicapped blind persons. Subject is taught the task, then works for a 50-minute period and receives feedback on the rate and accuracy of work. Used to compare visually impaired person's performance with the sighted standard. The Methods-Time Measurement Procedure was used to develop the average sighted standard for this task.

13072
Index Card Work Task Unit: Electromechanical Vocational Assessment. Mississippi State Univ., Rehabilitation Research and Training Center 1983
Descriptors: Adults; *Blindness; Individual Testing; *Memory; *Performance Tests; Psychomotor Skills; *Visual Impairments; *Vocational Evaluation
Identifiers: *Bilateral Dexterity; Electromechanical Vocational Assessment; Finger Dexterity; Frustration; Mississippi State University
Availability: Rehabilitation Research and Training Center; P.O. Box 5365, Mississippi State, MS 39762
Target Audience: Adults
Notes: Time, 50

Designed to provide a flexible system of evaluating a variety of work abilities including bimanual coordination, finger dexterity, frustration tolerance, and memory for sequence of operations. Purpose is to assist National Industries for the Blind and vocational evaluators to improve assessment of the vocational potential of blind and severely visually impaired persons, particularly multiply handicapped blind persons. Subject is taught the task, then works for a 50-minute period and receives feedback on the rate and accuracy of work. An objective method of comparing visually impaired person's performance with the sighted standard. The Methods-Time Measurement Procedure was used to develop the average sighted standard for this task.

13073
Multifunctional Work Task Unit: Electromechanical Vocational Assessment. Mississippi State Univ., Rehabilitation Research and Training Center 1983
Descriptors: Adults; Assembly (Manufacturing); *Blindness; Individual Testing; *Kinesthetic Perception; *Performance Tests; Psychomotor Skills; *Visual Impairments; *Vocational Evaluation
Identifiers: *Bilateral Dexterity; Electromechanical Vocational Assessment; Mississippi State University
Availability: Rehabilitation Research and Training Center; P.O. Box 5365, Mississippi State, MS 39762
Target Audience: Adults
Notes: Time, 50

Designed to provide a flexible system of evaluating a variety of work abilities including bimanual coordination, material control, and kinesthetic memory. Purpose is to assist National Industries for the Blind and vocational evaluators to improve assessment of the vocational potential of blind and severely visually impaired persons, particularly multiply handicapped blind persons. Subject is taught the task, then works for a 50-minute period and receives feedback on the rate and accuracy of work. Used to compare visually impaired person's performance with the sighted standard. The Methods-Time Measurement Procedure was used to develop the average sighted standard for this task.

13074
Revolving Assembly Table Work Task Unit: Electromechanical Vocational Assessment. Mississippi State Univ., Rehabilitation Research and Training Center 1983
Descriptors: Adults; *Blindness; *Individual Testing; Interpersonal Competence; *Kinesthetic Perception; *Performance Tests; Psychomotor Skills; *Visual Impairments; *Vocational Evaluation
Identifiers: Bilateral Dexterity; Electromechanical Vocational Assessment; Finger Dexterity; Mississippi State University
Availability: Rehabilitation Research and Training Center; P.O. Box 5365, Mississippi State, MS 39762
Target Audience: Adults
Notes: Time, 50

Designed to provide a flexible system of evaluating a variety of work abilities including bimanual coordination, finger dexterity, kinesthetic memory, and ability to work with others. Purpose is to assist National Industries for the Blind and vocational evaluators to improve assessment of the vocational potential of blind and severely visually impaired persons, particularly multiply handicapped blind persons. Subject is taught the task, then works for a 50-minute period and receives feedback on the rate and accuracy of work. Used to compare performance of visually impaired persons with the sighted standard.

13075
PEECH Parent Questionnaire. Peech Project, Champaign, IL
Descriptors: Adults; *Attitude Measures; *Disabilities; Elementary Education; *Handicap Identification; *Parent Attitudes; Parent Participation; *Parents; Parent School Relationship; *Preschool Children; *Program Evaluation
Identifiers: PEECH Outreach Project
Availability: PEECH Project; Colonel Wolfe School, 403 E. Healey St., Champaign, IL 61820
Target Audience: Adults
Notes: Items, 15

Designed for completion by parents of children in the PEECH project. Assesses parents' satisfaction with program for their child; their perceptions of the child's progress and the usefulness of parent involvement activities; and the level of parent involvement. Program PEECH (Program for Early Identification of Children with Handicaps) is a home-based program for handicapped preschool children.

13082
Compton Phonological Assessment of Foreign Accent. Compton, Arthur J. 1983
Subtests: Background Information; Stimulus Word Response; Spontaneous Speech; Oral Reading Passage Script; Phonetic Transcription of Oral Reading Passage; Pattern Analysis
Descriptors: Adults; Audiotape Recordings; *English (Second Language); Limited English Speaking; *Pronunciation; *Speech Evaluation; Speech Tests
Identifiers: Accents
Availability: Carousel House, P.O. Box 4480, San Francisco, CA 94101
Target Audience: Adults
Notes: Time, 100 approx.

A phonological assessment procedure designed to analyze the accented sounds of American English for the foreign born. May be used to determine specific areas of pronunciation difficulty for each individual.

13090
IEA Six-Subject Survey Instruments: English Student Questionnaires. International Association for the Evaluation of Educational Achievement, Stockholm (Sweden) 1975
Subtests: Questions about Learning English; English Student Questionnaire
Descriptors: *Academic Achievement; College Bound Students; *Comparative Education; *Cross Cultural Studies; *English (Second Language); Foreign Countries; Grade 12; Questionnaires; Secondary Education; *Secondary School Students; *Second Language Learning; *Student Attitudes; Student Interests
Identifiers: International Evaluation Educational Achievement; Sweden
Availability: ERIC Document Reproduction Service; 3900 Wheeler Ave., Alexandria, VA 22304 (ED102182, 24 pages)
Target Audience: 14-15; 17-18
Notes: Items, 63

In 1965 the International Association for the Evaluation of Educational Achievement (IEA) inaugurated a cross-national survey of achievement in 6 subjects: science, reading comprehension, literature, English as a Foreign Language, French as a Foreign Language, and civic education. The overall aim of the project was to use international tests to relate student achievement and attitudes to instructional, social, and economic factors, and from the results, to establish generalizations of value to policymakers worldwide. These questionnaires survey information regarding the student and his or her study of English and the students' outside interests and activities for students in Populations II, IV. Population II consists of students aged 14 to 15 years; Population IV, those students enrolled in the final year of preuniversity training.

13091
IEA Six-Subject Survey Instruments: English as a Foreign Language, Listening, Population II. International Association for the Evaluation of Educational Achievement, Stockholm (Sweden) 1975
Descriptors: *Academic Achievement; *Comparative Education; *Cross Cultural Studies; *English (Second Language); Foreign Countries; *Listening Comprehension Tests; Secondary Education; *Secondary School Students; Second Language Learning; Tape Recorders
Identifiers: International Evaluation Educational Achievement; Sweden
Availability: ERIC Document Reproduction Service; 3900 Wheeler Ave., Alexandria, VA 22304 (ED102181, 123 pages)
Target Audience: 14-15
Notes: Items, 24

In 1965 the International Association for the Evaluation of Educational Achievement (IEA) inaugurated a cross-national survey of achievement in 6 subjects: science, reading comprehension, literature, English as a Foreign Language, French as a Foreign Language, and civic education. The overall aim of the project was to use international tests to relate student achievement and attitudes to instructional, social, and economic factors, and from the results, to establish generalizations of value to policymakers worldwide. This test is in 3 sections: discrimination of sounds, listening comprehension, and dictation. In the first section, students are given pictures and are asked to listen to 3 words and pick the one corresponding to the pictures. The second section is meant to discover whether the students understand what they hear. They listen to a tape asking questions, and the students are to choose the corresponding sentence in their native language. In the dictation section, a short piece of prose is read, and the students are to write it as they have heard it. This test is for Population II which consists of students aged 14 to 15 years.

13092
IEA Six-Subject Survey Instruments: English as a Foreign Language, Listening, Population IV. International Association for the Evaluation of Educational Achievement, Stockholm (Sweden) 1975
Descriptors: *Academic Achievement; *College Bound Students; *Comparative Education; *Cross Cultural Studies; *English (Second Language); Foreign Countries; *Grade 12; High Schools; *Listening Comprehension Tests; *Second Language Learning; Tape Recorders
Identifiers: International Evaluation Educational Achievement; Sweden
Availability: ERIC Document Reproduction Service; 3900 Wheeler Ave., Alexandria, VA 22304 (ED102181, 123 pages)
Target Audience: 12
Notes: Items, 36

In 1965 the International Association for the Evaluation of Educational Achievement (IEA) inaugurated a cross-national survey of achievement in 6 subjects: science, reading comprehension, literature, English as a Foreign Language, French as a Foreign Language, and civic education. The overall aim of the project was to use international tests to relate student achievement and attitudes to instructional, social, and economic factors, and from the results to establish generalizations of value to policymakers worldwide. Population IV consists of students enrolled in the final year of preuniversity training. The test is in 4 parts, and the students listen to the questions on a tape recorder and mark their answer on an answer sheet. The first section is discrimination of sounds, and the students listen to 3 words on the tape and mark the picture which corresponds to the words. Section II is recognition of meaning though intonation. In this section, a question is asked in the students' native language, and they determine the answer to the question by listening to the way the voice rises and falls in the 3 sentences. In section III, listening comprehension, the students listen to a sentence or short paragraph and select from their book the one they heard. The last section is listening comprehension (conversation) in which the students listen to a conversation and then answer a question

13093
IEA Six-Subject Survey Instruments: English as a Foreign Language, Reading, Population II. International Association for the Evaluation of Educational Achievement, Stockholm (Sweden) 1975
Descriptors: *Academic Achievement; *Achievement Tests; *Comparative Education; *Cross Cultural Studies; *English (Second Language); Foreign Countries; Multiple Choice Tests; *Reading Comprehension; Reading Tests; Secondary Education; *Secondary School Students; *Second Language Learning
Identifiers: International Evaluation Educational Achievement; Sweden
Availability: ERIC Document Reproduction Service; 3900 Wheeler Ave., Alexandria, VA 22304 (ED102181, 123 pages)
Target Audience: 14-15
Notes: Items, 60

In 1965 the International Association for the Evaluation of Educational Achievement (IEA) inaugurated a cross-national survey of achievement in 6 subjects: science, reading comprehension, literature, English as a Foreign Language, French as a Foreign Language, and civic education. The overall aim of the project was to use international tests to relate student achievement and attitudes to instructional, social, and economic factors, and from the results, to establish generalizations of value to policymakers worldwide. This test is for Population II which consists of students aged 14- to 15-years-old. The test consists of 6 sections: recognition of antonyms, sound correspondences, recognition of structural features, vocabulary-recognition, reading comprehension (short sentences), and reading comprehension (continuous passages).

13094
IEA Six-Subject Survey Instruments: English as a Foreign Language, Reading, Population IV. International Association for the Evaluation of Educational Achievement, Stockholm (Sweden) 1975
Descriptors: *Academic Achievement; *Achievement Tests; *College Bound Students; *Comparative Education; *Cross Cultural Studies; *English (Second Language); *Grade 12; Multiple Choice Tests; *Reading Comprehension; Reading Tests; *Second Language Learning
Identifiers: International Evaluation Educational Achievement; Sweden
Availability: ERIC Document Reproduction Service; 3900 Wheeler Ave., Alexandria, VA 22304 (ED102181, 123 pages)
Grade Level: 12
Notes: Items, 60

In 1965 the International Association for the Evaluation of Educational Achievement (IEA) inaugurated a cross-national survey of achievement in 6 subjects: science, reading comprehension, literature, English as a Foreign Language, French as a Foreign Language, and civic education. The overall aim of the project was to use international tests to relate student achievement and attitudes to instructional, social, and economic factors, and from the results, to establish generalizations of value to policymakers worldwide. This test is for Population IV, students enrolled in the final year of preuniversity training. The test is divided into sections which are recognition of word stress, collocations, recognition of grammatical structures, reading comprehension (short sentences), reading comprehension (continuous passages).

13095
IEA Six-Subject Survey Instruments: English as a Foreign Language, Writing Populations II, IV. International Association for the Evaluation of Educational Achievement, Stockholm (Sweden) 1975
Descriptors: *Academic Achievement; *Achievement Tests; College Bound Students; *Comparative Education; *Cross Cultural Studies; *English (Second Language); Foreign Countries; Grade 12; Secondary Education; *Secondary School Students; *Second Language Learning; *Writing (Composition)
Identifiers: International Evaluation Educational Achievement; Sweden
Availability: ERIC Document Reproduction Service; 3900 Wheeler Ave., Alexandria, VA 22304 (ED102181, 123 pages)
Target Audience: 14-15; 17-18
Notes: Items, 31

In 1965 the International Association for the Evaluation of Educational Achievement (IEA) inaugurated a cross-national survey of achievement in 6 subjects: science, reading comprehension, literature, English as a Foreign Language, French as a Foreign Language, and civic education. The overall aim of the project was to use international tests to relate student achievement and attitudes to instructional, social, and economic factors, and from the results, to establish generalizations of value to policymakers worldwide. Population II consists of students aged 14 to 15 years and Population IV, students enrolled in the final year of preuniversity training. This test is divided into 4 sections. The first 2 sections are sentence completion requiring one word; the third section requires the students to rearrange 3 words or phrases to complete the sentence; and the last section is composition. The student must use 12 words that are given and write no more than 200 words.

13096
IEA Six-Subject Survey Instruments: English as a Foreign Language, Speaking Populations II, IV. International Association for the Evaluation of Educational Achievement, Stockholm (Sweden) 1975
Descriptors: *Academic Achievement; *Achievement Tests; College Bound Students; *Comparative Education; *Cross Cultural Studies; *English (Second Language); Foreign Countries; Grade 12; *Language Fluency; Secondary Education; *Secondary School Students; *Second Language Learning; Tape Recordings
Identifiers: International Evaluation Educational Achievement; Sweden
Availability: ERIC Document Reproduction Service; 3900 Wheeler Ave., Alexandria, VA 22304 (ED102181, 123 pages)
Target Audience: 14-15; 17-18

In 1965 the International Association for the Evaluation of Educational Achievement (IEA) inaugurated a cross-national survey of achievement in 6 subjects: science, reading comprehension, literature, English as a Foreign Language, French as a Foreign Language, and civic education. The overall aim of the project was to use international tests to relate student achievement and attitudes to instructional, social, and economic factors, and from the results, to establish generalizations of value to policymakers worldwide. Population II consists of students aged 14 to 15 years and Population IV, students enrolled in the final year of preuniversity training. This test is divided into sections on speaking, oral reading, and fluency. The students are asked to answer questions on tape recorders.

13126
Rating Scale for Visually Handicapped Children's Exploratory Behavior. Olson, Myrna R. 1983
Descriptors: Children; *Classroom Observation Techniques; *Exploratory Behavior; Rating Scales; Videotape Recordings; *Visual Impairments
Availability: Exceptional Children; v50 n2 p130-38 1983
Target Audience: 4-9
Notes: Items, 14

Child was observed and videotaped while examining a novel and an ordinary toy. Behavior was rated in 10 areas chosen on the basis of literature review related to exploratory behavior and visual impairment. Covers interest, method of examination, senses used, assistance, verbalization.

13146
Adaptive Performance Instrument. Consortium on Adaptive Performance Evaluation, Moscow, ID 1980
Subtests: Physical Intactness; Reflexes and Reactions; Gross Motor; Fine Motor; Self-Care; Sensori-Motor; Social; Communication
Descriptors: *Adaptive Behavior (of Disabled); Communication Skills; Deaf Blind; *Developmental Stages; Hearing Impairments; Infant Behavior; Infants; *Multiple Disabilities; Observation; Perceptual Development; Physical Activity Level; Self Care Skills; *Severe Disabilities; Social Behavior; Visual Impairments; *Young Children
Identifiers: API
Availability: Project CAPE; Special Education Dept., University of Idaho, Moscow, ID 83843
Target Audience: 0-8

The API measures functional skills (those enabling a child to perform in his or her environment). Small steps versus general developmental milestones are measured to discriminate progress of the exceptionally slow learner. Behaviors are assessed through observation while the child is in "routine environment." Adaptations are utilized, when appropriate (for children with sensory and motoric impairments), which change either the directions given or the required behavioral response. The adaptations allow for handicapping conditions for deaf/blind, visually impaired, hearing-impaired, and motorically impaired students. The API is divided into 8 domains: physical intactness, reflexes and reactions, gross motor, fine motor, self-care, sensorimotor, social, and communication. This instrument is to assess any child functioning developmentally under 2 years (and most appropriate for individuals under the chronological age of 9). May be used by direct service personnel, such as teachers, therapists, psychologists. This is an experimental edition and is being field tested.

13151
Compton Speech and Language Screening Evaluation: Spanish Adaptation. Compton, Arthur J.; Kline, Marlaine 1983
Descriptors: Articulation (Speech); *Bilingual Students; Check Lists; *Language Acquisition; Language Fluency; *Preschool Children; *Primary Education; Spanish; *Spanish Speaking; *Speech Evaluation; Student Evaluation
Availability: Carousel House, P.O. Box 4480, San Francisco, CA 94101
Grade Level: K-1
Target Audience: 4-6
Notes: Time, 10 approx.; Items, 40

This instrument is a tool for a rapid and descriptive estimate of both the articulation and language development of preschool, kindergarten, and first grade children. This device assesses both comprehension and production. The areas surveyed include articulation, vocabulary, colors, shapes, memory span, language, spontaneous language, fluency, voice, and oral mechanism.

13152
Neuropsychological Screening Exam, Second Edition. Preston, John 1983
Descriptors: Adolescents; Adults; *Learning Disabilities; *Neurological Impairments; *Patients; Psychological Evaluation; Questionnaires; *Screening Tests
Identifiers: NPSE
Availability: The Wilmington Collection; 13315 Wilmington Dr., Dallas, TX 75234
Target Audience: 13-64
Notes: Time, 50 approx.

Screening procedure for learning disabilities or suspected neurological impairment. Includes areas of consciousness, handedness, brain and behavioral abnormalities, emotional and verbal functions, memory, cognitive functions, and motor development. For use with adolescent and adult patients. Is not considered a psychometric instrument, per se. Purpose of NPSE is to provide additional, important neuropsychological data lacking in a traditional psychometric test battery. Although the WAIS-R and the Halstead-Reitan Neuropsychological Battery are not technically a part of NPSE, the user is encouraged to administer the WAIS-R and the Seashore Rhythm Test, Trail Making Test and Fingertip Number Writing Test from the Halstead Reitan to supplement the NPSE.

13154
Clinical Interview Technique: Adults-Children, Third Edition. Gordon, Robert 1983
Descriptors: *Adolescents; Adults; *Children; *Clinical Diagnosis; *Patients; *Psychological Evaluation; Questionnaires
Availability: The Wilmington Collection; 13315 Wilmington Dr., Dallas, TX 75234
Target Audience: 2-64
Notes: Time, 50 approx.

Systematic approach to initial clinical interviewing of a patient or of a parent about a child. Form is completed by a clinician or an assistant under supervision. Can be used as a well-documented record covering referral information procedures, social history, cognitive functioning, family dynamics, physical and emotional status, life history, diagnosis, treatment goals, prognosis. Contains patient rights checklist and clinical notes insert.

13155
The Mental Health Check-Up. Gordon, Robert; Harris, Alan 1982
Descriptors: Adults; Emotional Adjustment; Emotional Problems; *Mental Health; Physical Health; Questionnaires; *Screening Tests
Identifiers: MHCU; Self Administered Tests
Availability: The Wilmington Collection; 13315 Wilmington Dr., Dallas, TX 75234
Target Audience: 18-64
Notes: Time, 30 approx.

Surveys patient's emotional health, including physical symptoms. Based on DSM III descriptions and are referenced to DSM III categories to aid the clinician in diagnosis. This questionnaire is given in association with a diagnostic interview procedure, such as the Clinical Interview Technique (TC013154). May be given annually to serve as an early warning system of emotional difficulty and as a preventative clinical strategy. Patient responds to questions and clinician scans patient's responses and then explores with patient those responses which patient has identified as areas of emotional difficulty. Form covers 5 areas: clinical syndromes, personality and specific developmental disorders, physical disorders and conditions, severity of psychosocial stressors, highest level of adaptive functioning the past year.

13156
Children's Mental Health Check-Up. Gordon, Robert; Harris, Alan 1983
Descriptors: Adolescents; Children; Emotional Adjustment; Emotional Problems; *Mental Health; Physical Health; Questionnaires; *Screening Tests
Identifiers: MHCU; Self Administered Tests
Availability: The Wilmington Collection; 13315 Wilmington Dr., Dallas, TX 75234
Target Audience: 2-17
Notes: Time, 30 approx.

To be completed by parent or guardian of child or adolescent. Surveys patient's emotional health, including physical symptoms. Based on DSM III descriptions and are referenced to DSM III categories to aid the clinician in diagnosis. This questionnaire is given in association with a diagnostic interview procedure, such as the Clinical Interview Technique (TC013154). May be given annually to serve as an early warning system of emotional difficulty and as a preventative clinical strategy. Patient responds to questions and clinician scans patient's responses and then explores with patient those responses which patient has identified as areas of emotional difficulty. Form covers 5 areas: clinical syndromes, personality and specific developmental disorders, physical disorders and conditions, severity of psychosocial stressors, highest level of adaptive functioning the past year.

13157
Relationship Satisfaction Survey. Lucas, Rose 1982
Descriptors: Adults; Check Lists; Clinical Diagnosis; *Interpersonal Relationship; Marital Instability; Psychological Evaluation
Identifiers: RSS
Availability: The Wilmington Collection; 13315 Wilmington Dr., Dallas, TX 75234
Target Audience: Adults
Notes: Time, 25 approx.

Aid to use in assessing marital conflict or for identifying relationship issues in couples. May be used to alert clinician to significant issues in human relationships that a patient is experiencing. Relationship may be marital, premarital, or otherwise intimate. May be administered when relationship is focus of therapeutic concern or as part of a healthy relationship maintenance strategy. Self-report survey. Part 1 is a checklist covering communication patterns, psychological/emotional, child rearing practices, health and personal habits, affection, careers, financial well-being, social activities and recreation, household, values. Part 2 consists of a relationship-oriented sentence completion form which provides clinical information for projective interpretation. Recommended that this form be used with other assessment tools available from publisher.

13158
Professional Service Survey. Gordon, Robert; And Others 1983
Descriptors: Adults; *Counselor Evaluation; *Feedback; Patients; *Professional Services; *Psychologists; *Psychotherapy; Questionnaires
Availability: The Wilmington Press; 13315 Wilmington Dr., Dallas, TX 75234
Target Audience: Adults

Brief questionnaire to send to patients following psychotherapy. Asks for feedback about the quality of care, effectiveness of delivery system, reaction to fees, and office policies. Useful for designing more effective office or agency procedures. To accompany therapist's personal letter.

13159
Wisconsin Behavior Rating Scale, Revised. Central Wisconsin Ctr. for Developmentally Disabled, Madison 1979
Subtests: Gross Motor; Fine Motor; Expressive Language; Expressive Language for Deaf/Blind; Receptive Language; Receptive Language for Deaf/Blind; Play Skills; Socialization; Socialization for Deaf/Blind; Domestic Activities; Eating; Toileting; Dressing; Grooming
Descriptors: *Adaptive Behavior (of Disabled); Adolescents; Adults; *Behavior Rating Scales; Check Lists; Children; *Deaf Blind; *Developmental Tasks; Expressive Language; *Institutionalized Persons; Intervention; Interviews; Language Acquisition; Measures (Individuals); Motor Development; Multiple Disabilities; Older Adults; Play; Receptive Language; Self Care Skills; Severe Disabilities; *Severe Mental Retardation; Socialization
Identifiers: Public Law 94 142; WBRS
Availability: Central Wisconsin Center for the Developmentally Disabled; 317 Knutson Dr., Madison, WI 53704
Target Audience: 1-72
Notes: Time, 15 approx.; Items, 176

The WBRS was developed for the developmentally disabled persons and is applicable to individuals of all ages functioning at a developmental level under approximately 3 years. The entire scale can be completed through an interview technique by a professional staff person in about 10-15 minutes and provides a least-biased adaptive behavior scale to provide adequate assessment, intervention, and evaluation of the severely and profoundly retarded institutionalized individuals. The items have a 3-point rating and are developmentally arranged and sequenced under 11 subcategories of adaptive behavior. These 11 subscales contain alternative items for deaf/blind persons. The instrument can be used for (1) assessing an overall level of functioning, (2) ascertaining a quick profile of development in basic behavioral areas to identify areas of strengths and weaknesses for evaluation and programing, (3) following up individual development or monitoring progress following training and/or improved opportunity, and (4) programing and remediation. Standardization data were obtained from residents of the Central Wisconsin Center for the Developmentally Disabled ranging in age from one year to 72 years.

13161
Primary Test of Higher Processes of Thinking. Williams, Winnie 1978
Subtests: Convergent Production; Convergent Analogies; Sequential Relationships; Logic; Deductive Reasoning; Divergent Thinking
Descriptors: *Academically Gifted; *Cognitive Processes; *Cognitive Tests; Convergent Thinking; Deduction; Divergent Thinking; *Elementary School Students; Intermediate Grades; Logic; Primary Education
Identifiers: Analogies; Sequential Relationship; TIM(J)
Availability: Tests in Microfiche; Test Collection, Educational Testing Service, Princeton, NJ 08541
Grade Level: 2-4
Notes: Time, 45; Items, 55

Designed to determine the gifted student's level of cognitive ability in higher-level thinking processes. The first 50 items are multiple choice. Items 51-55 require a written response in the form of a list of solutions to a problem.

13162
Reflex Testing Methods for Evaluating CNS Development, Second Edition. Fiorentino, Mary R. 1979

Descriptors: *Developmental Stages; Motor Development; *Neurological Impairments; Neurological Organization; Physical Mobility; Screening Tests; Special Health Problems; *Young Children
Availability: Charles C. Thomas, Publisher; 2600 S. First St., Springfield, IL 62717
Target Audience: 0-6
Notes: Time, 30 approx.; Items, 37

These testing methods are used to evaluate neurophysiological reflexive maturation of the central nervous system (CNS) at the spinal, brain stem, midbrain, and cortical levels. The manual presents a normal sequential development of reflexive maturation and possible abnormal responses found in individuals with CNS disorders, such as cerebral palsy. Photographs and explanations of reflex responses and test positions with normal and abnormal responses are illustrated. Each reflex tested can be rated on a Reflex Testing Chart and resulting functional responses on a Motor Development Chart.

13163
Developmental Learning Profile. Cuyahoga Special Education Service Center, OH 1975
Descriptors: Career Development; *Developmental Continuity; *Developmental Disabilities; *Elementary School Students; Elementary Secondary Education; *Individual Development; Language Arts; Mathematics; Perceptual Development; Physical Development; Profiles; Sciences; *Secondary School Students; Skill Development; Social Development; Social Sciences; Special Education
Availability: Creative Learning Systems; 936 C St., San Diego, CA 92101
Grade Level: K-12

This instrument was designed by classroom teachers and instructional supervisors for use by teachers of children with special developmental needs. The profile is used to record a child's accomplishments of the basic "survival skills" throughout his/her school years. Its developmental nature is designed to facilitate the teacher's planning of an individualized curriculum for the student. The profile has a format and a marking system that enable quick assessment of appropriate next learning goals in any one of 7 major curriculum areas. The Performance Objectives within each Terminal Objective are sequentially ordered to help prevent skill development gaps. The profile provides a convenient, comprehensive, ongoing record of the student's accomplishments which can be used by classroom teachers, tutors, psychologists, principals, counselors, and parents on a daily, weekly, monthly, and yearly basis to determine short- and long-range learning goals specific to a student's profile of accomplishments. The 7 curriculum areas are language arts, science, social studies, physical and perceptual development, career development, mathematics, personal-social development.

13164
Assessment of Fluency in School-Age Children. Thompson, Julia 1983
Descriptors: Articulation Impairments; *Criterion Referenced Tests; Elementary School Students; Elementary Secondary Education; Interviews; *Screening Tests; Secondary School Students; *Speech Evaluation; Speech Therapy; *Stuttering; Tape Recordings; Therapists
Identifiers: AFSC
Availability: The Interstate Printers and Publishers; 19-27 N. Jackson St., Danville, IL 61832-0594
Grade Level: K-12
Target Audience: 5-18
Notes: Time, 45

The Assessment of Fluency in School-Age Children (AFSC) is a criterion-referenced instrument to be used with children between the ages of 5 and 18. The assessment tool incorporates a multisourced, multifactored format. Parent/teacher/child interview forms are included with the differential evaluation, as well as sequenced tasks to determine speech, language, and physiological functioning. This tool assists in determining which young children would benefit from early intervention. There are complete directions for administration plus reference information describing management procedures in public school settings. The purpose is to direct speech therapists to appropriate procedures for children who stutter.

13166
Early Intervention Developmental Profile, Revised Edition. Rogers, Sally J.; And Others 1981
Subtests: Perceptual/Fine Motor; Cognition; Language; Social Emotional; Self-Care; Gross Motor
Descriptors: Cognitive Development; *Developmental Stages; *Disabilities; Emotional Development; Evaluation Methods; Infant Behavior; Language Processing; Motor Development; Perceptual Development; Profiles; Self Care Skills; Social Development; *Young Children
Identifiers: Developmental Programming Infants; Young Children

Availability: University of Michigan Press; 615 E. University, Ann Arbor, MI 48106
Target Audience: 0-3
Notes: Time, 60 approx.; Items, 299

This infant/preschool assessment instrument is made up of 6 scales which provide developmental milestones in the following areas: perceptual/fine motor, cognition, language, social/emotional, self-care, and gross motor development. The profile contains 274 items and yields information for planning comprehensive developmental programs for children with various handicaps who function below the 36-month developmental level. It is intended to supplement, not replace, standard psychological, motor, and language evaluation data. The profile is not to be used to predict future capabilities or handicaps and should not be used to diagnose handicapping conditions such as mental retardation, emotional disturbance, cerebral palsy, etc. The profile indicates which skills are expected to emerge next in the child's development. Identification of emerging skills enables the teacher/therapist to plan appropriate activities to facilitate the emergence of these skills. There are 5 volumes in the series: Assessment and Application, Early Intervention Development Profile, Stimulation Activities, Preschool Assessment and Application, and Preschool Development Profile.

13170
Escala de Desarrollo Infantil de Kent, Version Experimental. Reuter, Jeanette; Katoff, Lew 1978
Subtests: Cognitive; Motor; Social; Language; Self Help
Descriptors: Behavior Rating Scales; Child Development; Cognitive Development; Disabilities; High Risk Persons; *Infant Behavior; *Infants; Language Acquisition; Motor Development; Self Care Skills; Social Development; *Spanish; Young Children
Identifiers: EDIK; Kent Infant Development Scale; KID Scale
Availability: Kent Developmental Metrics; P.O. Box 3178, 126 W. College Ave., Kent, OH 44240-3178
Target Audience: 0-1
Notes: Items, 252

Spanish version of the Kent Infant Development Scale (TC012610) designed to assess behavioral development of infants and young handicapped children chronologically or developmentally below one year of age. Behavior assessment is completed by child's parent or primary caregiver. Computerized scoring and printout furnishes developmental ages; a profile of strengths and weaknesses; and a timetable indicating which developmental milestones will be acquired next. May be used in developing a prescriptive educational program.

13185
Clinical Record Keeping System. Wilmington Press, Dallas, TX 1983
Descriptors: Adults; Children; *Clinical Diagnosis; *Patients; *Psychological Evaluation; Recordkeeping; Records (Forms)
Availability: The Wilmington Collection; 13315 Wilmington Dr., Dallas, TX 75234
Target Audience: Adults
Notes: Time, 50 approx.

A systematic approach to initial clinical interviewing of a patient or of a parent about a child. Completed by the clinician or assistant under supervision. Includes referral information, procedures, social history, cognitive functioning, family dynamics, personal and emotional status, life history, diagnosis, treatment goals, and prognosis. Consists of following forms: clinical interview technique, progress note method, treatment plan and review, mental health checkup, health history, and professional service survey, career-path strategy, and others.

13189
Barclay Classroom Assessment System. Barclay, James R. 1983
Subtests: Self Competency; Group Nomination; Vocational; Teacher Rating; Reinforcer; Attitude; Factor
Descriptors: *Affective Measures; Check Lists; Elementary Education; *Elementary School Students; *High Risk Students; *Peer Evaluation; Questionnaires; *Screening Tests; *Self Concept; *Self Evaluation (Individuals); Sociometric Techniques; Student Characteristics; *Student Evaluation; *Vocational Interests
Identifiers: BCAS
Availability: Western Psychological Services; 12031 Wilshire Blvd., Los Angeles, CA 90025
Grade Level: 3-6
Notes: Time, 40 approx.; Items, 192

Developed to assist educators in early identification of potential problems that may interfere with learning progress of children. Provides information from 3 viewpoints: child, child's classmates, and teachers. Measures are obtained from self, peer, and teacher ratings on a broad range of skills, feelings, and attitudes which child displays in classroom setting. Provides means of assessing individual social and affective interactions of children in the classroom. Highest purpose is early identification of at-risk children for learning-related problem. BCAS is scored by computer only, using the Western Psychological Services Test Report Service. In addition to the items completed by the students, there is a 63-item checklist to be completed by the teacher for each student. Sections that the student completes cover vocational interests, assessment of skills and ability to complete various activities, attitudes toward school, preferred activities, description of peers' characteristics. Formerly known as the Barclay Classroom Climate Inventory.

13190
Early Language Milestone Scale. Coplan, James 1983
Subtests: Auditory Expressive; Auditory Receptive; Visual
Descriptors: Expressive Language; Handicap Identification; *Infants; *Language Acquisition; Language Handicaps; Preschool Children; Receptive Language; *Screening Tests; Visual Stimuli
Identifiers: ELM Scale
Availability: Modern Education Corporation; P.O. Box 721, Tulsa, OK 74101
Target Audience: 0-3
Notes: Time, 3 approx.; Items, 41

Norm-referenced, validated language screening instrument covering the entire age range from birth to 36 months. Performance on most items may be ascertained by parental report. The scale is sensitive to various causes of speech or language delay, including mental retardation, hearing loss, dysarthria, and communicative disorders. It does not yield a specific developmental diagnosis. It is designed as a rapid, reliable screening test capable of detecting language-impaired children at the earliest possible age. Potential users of the scale include pediatricians, family practitioners, public health nurses, preschool teachers, speech pathologists, psychologists, and specialists in infant development.

13231
The Developmental Sequence Performance Inventory. Univ. of Washington, Seattle 1980
Subtests: Gross Motor; Fine Motor; Cognitive; Communication; Social Self-Help
Descriptors: Check Lists; Children; *Cognitive Development; Daily Living Skills; Developmental Disabilities; *Developmental Tasks; *Downs Syndrome; *Exceptional Persons; Infants; Language Skills; Mental Retardation; *Motor Development; Performance Tests; *Preschool Education; *Social Development; Student Evaluation
Identifiers: Downs Syndrome Performance Inventory; DSPI
Availability: Experimental Education Unit; Child Development Center, University of Washington, Seattle, WA 98165
Target Audience: 0-7

This inventory is based on normal sequential developmental patterns. Skills are arranged linearly from simple to complex assuring the mastery of requisite skills at each level of attainment within the following levels: birth to 18 months, 18 months-3 years, 3-4 years, 4-5 years, 5-6 years, 6-9 years. Focus is on sequence of skill development, not age level scores. This instrument is intended primarily as an assessment tool and as a guide for planning specific curriculum objectives for Down's Syndrome children. It is, however, applicable for any developmentally delayed child. The inventory uses a checklist format with a wide sampling of tasks within each skill area to develop a fairly complete profile of skill mastery.

13233
Diamond Technique for the Assessment of Child Custody. Diamond, Leonard 1983
Descriptors: Adolescents; Attitudes; Biographical Inventories; *Child Custody; Children; *Divorce; *Interviews; Marital Instability; Marriage Counseling; *Parents
Identifiers: DTACC
Availability: Judicare Press; 350 N. Lantana, Ste. 774, Box 3000, Camarillo, CA 93011
Target Audience: 9-64

There are 2 forms for this instrument; one is for the parents and the other for the child. This has been designed to be used as an interview and should never be used as a paper-and-pencil questionnaire. The instrument covers 9 major areas: general information, perceptions of the current issues, information regarding previous and current court actions, marriage data, occupational information, education, relationship with the child, additional information, and general descriptions. All of the areas covered will assist in making the custody decision, and none should be eliminated. This interview form was designed to be used in making custody evaluations. The author recommends that, to make as much information as possible available to the courts during a custody inquiry, other specific psychological instruments should be used in addition to this interview to uncover the most important information; the testing should be tailored for each custody matter. The areas that the child's interview covers are general information, current issue, school, friends and siblings, parents, current situation, stepparents, fantasy productions, and general descriptions.

13239
Comprehensive Developmental Evaluation Chart. El Paso Rehabilitation Center, TX 1975
Subtests: Reflexes; Gross Motor; Manipulation; Feeding; Receptive Language; Expressive Language; Cognitive-Social; Vision, Hearing
Descriptors: Cerebral Palsy; Cognitive Development; *Developmental Stages; Expressive Language; Hearing (Physiology); High Risk Persons; *Infant Behavior; Language Acquisition; Motor Development; *Physical Development; Receptive Language; Vision; *Young Children
Identifiers: CDE
Availability: El Paso Rehabilitation Center; 2630 Richmond, El Paso, TX 79930
Target Audience: 0-3

This evaluation chart is specific for young children who are developmentally between the ages of birth to 3 years. The test items of each area are detailed so that the quality of the child's functioning can be adequately assessed. The chart is divided into small time intervals to allow for observations of minute changes in developmental stages. This instrument was designed to fill a gap in the total approach toward the treatment of young children with developmental delays. It was designed to be comprehensive, specific, and consistent.

13241
Skills Inventory, Revised Edition. The Oregon Project for Visually Impaired and Blind Preschool Children. Brown, Donnise; And Others 1979
Descriptors: *Blindness; *Child Development; Cognitive Development; Curriculum Design; Developmental Stages; Individual Development; Individual Needs; *Infants; Language Acquisition; Measures (Individuals); Motor Development; Performance; Self Care Skills; Skill Development; Socialization; *Visual Impairments; *Young Children
Identifiers: Oregon (Jackson County)
Availability: OREGON Project; Jackson County Education Service District, 101 N. Grape St., Medford, OR 97501
Target Audience: 0-6
Notes: Items, 700

The Skills Inventory assesses the blind or visually handicapped child's development in the areas of cognition, language, self-help, socialization, fine motor, and gross motor. The skills are organized by one-year intervals. A total of 700 skills are assessed. The items that may not be appropriate for a totally blind child and those that may be acquired by a totally blind child are marked. The items that are appropriate either for the child who will need orientation and mobility training or will be a braille reader are also marked. The items are presented in behavioral terms and are generally clearly stated. Scoring criteria are not provided, but examples are offered for some of the items. The purpose is not to obtain a precise score but rather the child's performance level. The Skills Inventory is not a normed-assessment instrument but is a curriculum guide and enables educators to find a visually impaired or blind child's performance level, select long- and short-range objectives and record the child's progress. It contains items that are unique to the development of the visually handicapped child.

13250
Biographical Inventory, Form U. Institute for Behavioral Research in Creativity, Salt Lake City, UT 1976
Subtests: Academic Performance; Creativity; Artistic Potential; Leadership; Career Maturity; Educational Orientation
Descriptors: Academic Achievement; Academic Aspiration; *Biographical Inventories; Creativity; Leadership Qualities; Secondary Education; *Secondary School Students; Talent; Vocational Maturity
Identifiers: BI
Availability: Institute for Behavioral Research in Creativity; 1570 S. 1100, E., Salt Lake City, UT 84105
Grade Level: 7-12
Notes: Time, 60 approx.; Items, 150

Instrument used to obtain and analyze information about a person's characteristics and background. Form U was developed primarily to help identify talents that are typically difficult to measure. May also be used in counseling, guidance, and talent teaching. Results of inventory are most effectively used when combined with other information to recognize and develop student potential. Use of inventory with students below grade 7 should be based on evidence of satisfactory reading ability (at least 5th grade reading level). No time limit, but most should complete inventory in about one hour. Form U has been designed so that responses can be optically scanned and computer scored at the availablity source. Is a research instrument.

13252
A Motor Development Checklist. Doudlah, Anna M. 1976
Descriptors: Check Lists; Developmental Disabilities; Developmental Tasks; *Infants; *Motor Development; Observation; Rating Scales; Spontaneous Behavior
Identifiers: *Gross Motor Skills
Availability: Human Services Information Center; 317 Knutson Dr., Madison, WI 53704
Target Audience: 0-1

To be used with infants from birth to walking (approximately 15 months) to record the developmental progress in the gross motor area of nondisabled and developmentally disabled infants. Used most accurately by those who have viewed and studied the sequence of motor development described in the videotape "Motor Development: Birth to Walking." Can be used as a basis for planning and evaluating effectiveness of motor development programs for children with developmental disabilities. Checklist may be used in one of 2 ways: as a checklist by placing a mark in the appropriate area noting which motor behaviors were seen during observation; or as a 4-point rating scale from "does not perform task" to "performs task skillfully." Videotape is available from address listed in availability paragraph. Checklist was derived from movie records of spontaneous motor behavior of 20 normal infants filmed monthly at home over a 15-month period.

13254
Giannetti On-Line Psychosocial History. Giannetti, Ronald A. 1984
Subtests: Current Living Situation; Family of Origin; Client Development; Educational History; Marital History-Present Family; Occupational History-Current Finances; Legal History; Symptom Screening-Physical; Symptom Screening-Psychological; Military History
Descriptors: Adults; *Biographical Inventories; *Computer Assisted Testing; Criminals; Job Applicants; *Microcomputers; Multiple Choice Tests; Online Systems; Personnel Selection; Psychological Evaluation; *Psychological Testing
Identifiers: GOLPH; *Psychosocial Development; Sentence Completion Method
Availability: National Computer Systems; Professional Assessment Services, P.O. Box 1416, Minneapolis, MN 55440
Target Audience: Adults

Multiple-choice and completion-type items that can be computer administered and scored using the Psychometer microcomputer-based service. The instrument can be used to gather information about 10 aspects of a client's background and current life circumstances. Items are written at an 8th grade reading level. Inventory will take between 30 and 120 minutes depending on areas chosen for exploration and extent of client's problem. May be used for comprehensive psychosocial history for general medical or psychiatric patients; evaluation of a job applicant's work history; a criminal offender's history of legal difficulties; or a training applicant's educational history. Psychometer is a computer-based interactive testing system which administers and scores tests and provides printed evaluations. For information on hardware and software requirements, contact National Computer Systems.

13255
Gifted and Talented Scale. Dallas Educational Services, Richardson, TX 1983
Subtests: Numerical Reasoning; Vocabulary; Synonyms-Antonyms; Similarities; Analogies
Descriptors: Abstract Reasoning; *Academically Gifted; *Elementary School Students; Intermediate Grades; Logical Thinking; *Screening Tests; *Talent; Talent Identification; Verbal Ability; Vocabulary
Identifiers: Antonyms; Synonyms
Availability: Dallas Educational Services; P.O. Box 1254, Richardson, TX 75080
Grade Level: 4-6
Notes: Items, 50

Designed to identify children with special skills in grades 4, 5, and 6. Limited to identifying those children with talent only in those areas necessary for success in gifted and talented school programs in the classroom environment. A group test and essentially a power test rather than a timed test. The items in all 5 subtests are designed to measure abstract concepts.

13327
Bader Reading and Language Inventory. Bader, Lois A. 1983
Subtests: Word Recognition Lists; Supplemental Word Lists; Graded Reading Passages; Phonics and Word Analysis Tests; Spelling Tests; Cloze Tests; Visual Discrimination Tests; Auditory Discrimination Test; Unfinished Sentences; Arithmetic Test, Oral Language; Written Language

Descriptors: Achievement Tests; *Adult Reading Programs; Arithmetic; Auditory Discrimination; Cloze Procedure; *Diagnostic Tests; *Elementary School Students; Elementary Secondary Education; Language Skills; Oral Language; Phonics; Reading Achievement; Reading Comprehension; *Reading Diagnosis; Reading Difficulties; *Secondary School Students; Spelling; Student Placement; Visual Discrimination; Word Recognition
Availability: Macmillan Publishing Co.; 866 Third Ave., New York, NY 10022
Grade Level: K-12

This inventory was constructed for use by reading specialists, resource teachers, and classroom teachers. The graded passages, the major section of the battery, were designed to determine appropriate placement of students in instructional materials. Because students experiencing difficulty in learning to read may have problems in other areas, several informal tests are provided to assess the reader's needs and level. Three sets of reading passages have been constructed for each level. The content of the first set has been adapted from the kinds of materials used in basals on the primary levels and content-area materials on the upper levels for children. Another set has been designed for use with children, adolescents, or adults, and the third set, written on a primary level, is intended for use with adults who are just beginning to read.

13341
Criterion Referenced Curriculum: Reading Assessment. Stephens, Thomas M. 1982
Descriptors: *Achievement Tests; Auditory Discrimination; *Criterion Referenced Tests; Diagnostic Tests; *Elementary School Students; *Learning Disabilities; Oral Reading; Reading Comprehension; *Reading Diagnosis; Reading Improvement; *Remedial Programs; *Special Education; Structural Analysis (Linguistics)
Identifiers: CRC
Availability: The Psychological Corporation; 555 Academic Ct., San Antonio, TX 78204-0952
Grade Level: K-6
Notes: Items, 267

The Criterion-Referenced Curriculum is a comprehensive system of criterion-referenced tests and teaching strategies organized by objective sequences in reading. It is designed specifically for remedial and special education classes K-6 and includes virtually all of the basic reading objectives which normally achieving students are expected to master during the first 3 to 4 years of elementary school. Major categories in reading include auditory discrimination, sight words, phonic analysis, structural analysis, oral reading, and comprehension.

13342
Criterion Referenced Curriculum: Mathematics Assessment. Stephens, Thomas M. 1982
Descriptors: *Achievement Tests; Arithmetic; *Criterion Referenced Tests; *Diagnostic Tests; Educational Strategies; *Elementary School Mathematics; *Elementary School Students; *Learning Disabilities; *Mastery Learning; Metric System; Numbers; *Remedial Programs; Sequential Approach; *Special Education
Identifiers: CRC
Availability: The Psychological Corporation; 555 Academic Ct., San Antonio, TX 78204-0952
Grade Level: K-6
Notes: Items, 378

The Criterion-Referenced Curriculum is a comprehensive system of criterion-referenced tests and teaching strategies organized by objective sequences in mathematics. It is designed specifically for remedial and special education classes K-6 and includes virtually all of the basic mathematics objectives which normally achieving students are expected to master during the first 3 to 4 years of elementary school. Major categories in mathematics include numbers, numerals and numeration systems, operations and their properties, sets, measurements, and metric skills and concepts.

13356
Scales of Independent Behavior: Woodcock Johnson Psycho-Educational Battery, Part 4. Bruininks, Robert H.; And Others 1984
Subtests: Gross-Motor Skills; Fine-Motor Skills; Social Interaction; Language Comprehension; Language Expression; Eating and Meal Preparation; Toileting; Dressing; Personal Self-Care; Domestic Skills; Time and Punctuality; Money and Value; Work Skills; Home/Community Orientation; Problem Behaviors
Descriptors: *Adjustment (to Environment); Adolescents; Adults; Behavior Problems; Behavior Rating Scales; Child Development; Children; *Daily Living Skills; Homemaking Skills; Hygiene; Individual Development; *Individual Testing; Interpersonal Relationship; *Interviews; *Language Skills; *Motor Development; Preadolescents; *Self Care Skills; *Social Behavior; Young Adults; Young Children
Identifiers: SIB
Availability: DLM Teaching Resources; One DLM Park, Allen, TX 75002
Target Audience: 0-65
Notes: Time, 60 approx.; Items, 226

The Scales of Independent Behavior (SIB) is a wide-age-range, comprehensive set of tests for measuring functional independence in motor development, social development, language, self-help, and community adaptation. The tests are individually administered through a structured interview, and norms are provided from the infant level to the mature adult level. SIB includes 14 subscales of developmental and social independence, a short-form scale, an early development scale, and a measure of problem behaviors. There are a total of 226 items although the short form contains 32 tasks selected from all of the 14 subscales. This form is designed for use when a brief, overall screening or evaluation is appropriate. The administration time is approximately 10-15 minutes. The scale used gives 4 ratings: 0 for never or rarely performs the task to 3, does the task very well always or almost always. An Early Development (ED) Scale is provided. This scale is designed for use with subjects whose development level is below approximately 2 1/2 years of age. There are 32 tasks in this scale sample from 12 of the 14 developmental areas. This scale may be particularly suitable for assessing the development of young children and of severely and profoundly handicapped children and adults. The administration time is approximately 10 to 15 minutes. In addition to evaluating functional independence and adaptive behavior, the SIB includes a scale for identifying problem behaviors that often limit personal adaptation and community adjustment. The SIB is statistically linked to the Woodcock-Johnson Psycho-educational Battery. The SIB may be administered and interpreted independently of the Woodcock-Johnson.

13360
Screening Kit of Language Development. Bliss, Lynn S.; Allen, Doris V. 1983
Subtests: Vocabulary Comprehension; Story Completion; Sentence Comprehension; Paired Sentence Repetition with Pictures; Individual Sentence Repetition with Pictures; Individual Sentence Repetition without Pictures; Comprehension of Commands
Descriptors: *Black Dialects; Individual Testing; *Language Acquisition; *Language Handicaps; *Preschool Children; *Screening Tests; *Standard Spoken Usage
Identifiers: SKOLD
Availability: Slosson Educational Publications; P.O. Box 280, E. Aurora, NY 14052
Target Audience: 2-4
Notes: Time, 15

Developed as a standardized test to meet the needs of speech-language pathologists and paraprofessionals as a screening test to identify children with language impairments. The manual contains normative data for preschool children who speak Black English or Standard English so that test administrators can avoid misidentifying a nonstandard speaker as one with language impairments. The battery consists of 6 subtests to screen Standard English speaking children at 30 to 36 months, 37 to 42 months, and 43-48 months and equivalent subtests for the same age children whose responses are in Black English. There are approximately 35 items in each subtest.

13363
Teacher Rating Scale. Conners, C. Keith 1969
Subtests: Defiance or Aggressive Conduct Disorder; Daydreaming Inattentive; Anxious Fearful; Hyperactivity; Health
Descriptors: *Attention Deficit Disorders; *Behavior Disorders; Behavior Rating Scales; *Drug Therapy; Elementary Education; *Elementary School Students; Elementary School Teachers; *Hyperactivity; *Student Behavior
Availability: American Journal of Psychiatry; v126 n6 p152-56 Dec 1969
Grade Level: 1-8
Notes: Items, 39

Designed for use by teachers of children with behavior disorders, hyperactivity, or poor attention span associated with learning disorders. Teachers assess their student's behavior on a rating scale prior to medication and during the last week of treatment. Subjects in this drug study received either dextroamphetamine sulfate or a matched placebo.

13364
Performance Assessment of Syntax-Elicited and Spontaneous. Coughran, Lila 1980
Subtests: Articles; Personal Pronouns; Possessive Pronouns; Adjectives; Verbs-is/are (Present Progressive); Verbs-has/have; Verbs (Past Tense); Plurality; Negation; Interrogation-(who, what, where, why); Interrogation-(is/are); Conjunctions
Descriptors: Adjectives; *Criterion Referenced Tests; Diagnostic Tests; Elementary Education; Elementary School Students; *Expressive Language; *Form Classes (Languages); *Individualized Education Programs; *Individual Testing; *Language Handicaps; Preschool Education; Pronouns; Speech Tests; *Syntax; Tenses (Grammar); Verbal Development; Verbs; *Visual Measures; *Young Children
Identifiers: IEP; PASES
Availability: PRO-ED; 5341 Industrial Oaks Blvd., Austin, TX 78735
Target Audience: 3-8
Notes: Items, 113

Performance Assessment of Syntax: Spontaneous and Elicited (PASES) was developed to simplify and expedite the development of an appropriate individual educational program (IEP) by speech-language pathologists and other personnel committed to educating speech/language/learning disabled children. PASES can be used as a preremedial evaluative/postremedial evaluative process. It taps only the most frequently exhibited errors in children so other evaluative measures might be administered to analyze errors for those not included in PASES (adverbs and contractions). This is a criterion-referenced assessment instrument that may be used to prescribe developmental language training programs for individual children. It measures expressive syntax in children, and the items are developmentally sequenced in order of appearance in normal children's repertoires. This instrument is designed to be a teaching test, and a unique feature is the controlled procedure to elicit samples of spontaneous speech where possible and to obtain speech samples imitatively, if necessary. It is individually administered and specific subtests rather than the entire battery may be administered.

13365
Test of Early Socioemotional Development. Hresko, Wayne P.; Brown, Linda 1984
Descriptors: *Behavior Problems; *Behavior Rating Scales; *Emotional Development; *Identification; *Interpersonal Competence; Parent Attitudes; Peer Evaluation; Primary Education; *Problem Children; Self Evaluation (Individuals); Sociometric Techniques; *Student Evaluation; Teacher Attitudes; *Young Children
Identifiers: TOESD
Availability: PRO-ED; 5341 Industrial Oaks Blvd., Austin, TX 78735
Target Audience: 3-7

Norm-referenced instrument which may be used to help identify students who are believed to be emotionally disturbed, behaviorally disordered, or learning disabled; to identify settings or environments in which child is perceived to be deviant; to document degree of behavioral difficulty; to help plan intervention programs with children, parents, and teachers; to identify goals for behavioral change. Is a downward extension of the Behavior Rating Profile (TC010393) and consists of 4 components: a 30-item student rating scale; a 34-item parent rating scale in which parents rate child's behavior; a 36-item teacher rating scale in which teacher rates child's behavior, and a sociogram which provides peer perceptions of child being evaluated. By using 4 sets of respondents, TOESD examines behavioral perceptions at home, in school, and in interpersonal relationships.

13366
Developmental Activities Screening Inventory II. Fewell, Rebecca R.; Langley, Mary Beth 1984
Descriptors: *Child Development; *Developmental Disabilities; Developmental Tasks; Individual Testing; *Infants; *Nonverbal Tests; Performance Tests; *Screening Tests; Visual Impairments; *Young Children
Identifiers: DASI(II)
Availability: PRO-ED; 5341 Industrial Oaks Blvd., Austin, TX 78735
Target Audience: 0-5
Notes: Items, 67

Revision of the original Developmental Activities Screening Inventory (DASI). Designed as an informal screening measure to provide early detection of developmental disabilities in children functioning between the ages of birth and 5 years. Individually administered. Developmental skills assessed cover 15 skill categories: imitation, sensory intactness, means-ends relationships, causality, memory, seriation, reasoning, sensorimotor organization, visual pursuit, object permanence, behaviors relating to objects, discrimination, association, quantitative reasoning, spatial relationships. The 67 items can be administered in different sequences and in one or 2 sittings. Instructions are given either verbally or visually. Each test item includes adaptations for use with visually impaired persons.

13367
Computer Aptitude, Literacy, and Interest Profile. Poplin, Mary S.; And Others 1984
Subtests: Estimation (Aptitude); Graphic Patterns (Aptitude); Logical Structures (Aptitude); Series (Aptitude); Interest; Literacy

Descriptors: *Achievement Tests; *Adolescents; *Adults; *Aptitude Tests; Career Counseling; *College Students; *Computer Literacy; *Computers; Higher Education; *Interest Inventories; Knowledge Level; *Programing; Secondary Education; *Secondary School Students
Identifiers: CALIP
Availability: PRO-ED; 5341 Industrial Oaks Blvd., Austin, TX 78735
Grade Level: 7-16
Target Audience: 12-60
Notes: Time, 45 approx.; Items, 138
Comprehensive, standardized test battery designed to assess computer-related abilities. Can be administered individually, in groups. Measures aptitudes relevant to computer programing and aptitudes relevant to a wide variety of computer-related uses, e.g., graphics, systems analysis, and repair. Also assesses computer literacy, interest, and experience. In addition to use in educational settings, may also be used in business and industry for personnel decisions. Designed to accomplish 4 main purposes: identify talented minorities, women, individuals with reading disabilities and disadvantaged persons; broaden range of realistic career options; provide an empirical basis for administrators, business, managers, and teachers to allocate organizational resources; and document person's progress as a result of training.

13368
The Behavior Evaluation Scale. McCarney, Stephen B.; And Others 1983
Descriptors: *Behavior Disorders; *Behavior Rating Scales; Disabilities; *Elementary School Students; Elementary Secondary Education; Individualized Education Programs; Intervention; Learning Disabilities; Mental Retardation; Physical Disabilities; *Secondary School Students; *Special Education; Student Evaluation
Identifiers: BES
Availability: PRO-ED; 5341 Industrial Oaks Blvd., Austin, TX 78735
Grade Level: K-12
Notes: Time, 20 approx.; Items, 52
Provides results to assist school personnel in making decisions about eligibility, placement, and programing for any student with behavior problems who has been referred for evaluation. May be used with students who have learning disabilities, mental retardation, physical handicaps, or other handicapping conditions. May be used for 6 primary purposes: to screen for behavior problems; to assess behavior for any referred student; to assist in the diagnosis of behavior disorders or emotional disturbances; to develop individual education programs; to document progress resulting from intervention; to collect data for research. Standardized as a general behavior rating scale with regular class or special education students who exhibit behavior problems which call for assessment and intervention. A review by K. A. Kavale can be found in Education and Training of the Mentally Retarded; v18 p326-28 Dec 1983.

13369
The Pyramid Scales: Criterion Referenced Measures of Adaptive Behavior in Severely Handicapped Persons. Cone, John D. 1984
Subtests: Tactile Responsiveness; Auditory Responsiveness; Visual Responsiveness; Gross Motor; Eating; Fine Motor; Toileting; Dressing; Social Interaction; Washing and Grooming; Receptive Language; Expressive Language; Recreation and Leisure; Writing; Domestic Behavior; Reading; Vocational; Time; Money; Numbers
Descriptors: *Adaptive Behavior (of Disabled); Adolescents; Adults; Children; *Criterion Referenced Tests; Daily Living Skills; Language Processing; Mild Disabilities; Older Adults; Perception; Self Care Skills; *Severe Disabilities
Identifiers: West Virginia Assessment and Tracking System
Availability: PRO-ED; 5341 Industrial Oaks Blvd., Austin, TX 78735
Target Audience: 0-78
Notes: Time, 45 approx.; Items, 160
A revision of the former West Virginia Assessment and Tracking System used to assess adaptive behavior in moderately to severely handicapped persons of all ages. Designed for following uses: to provide picture of person's functioning in 20 skill areas; to provide comprehensive descriptions of clients; to permit monitoring of changes in functioning; to assist in establishing relevant training priorities; to monitor overall programs involving numbers of individuals. The 20 skills are arranged in 3 categories: sensory, primary (9 basic skills), and secondary (8 skills appropriate for older, higher-functioning persons). Scales may be administered in one of 3 ways: by interview, by informant, by direct observation. Scales are both criterion referenced and curriculum referenced to many programs. The author says that, although the scales have undergone field testing and databased revision, data are best viewed as preliminary and potential users should consider whether additional information is needed.

13385
Preschool Screening System: Vietnamese Adaptation. Hainsworth, Peter K.; Hainsworth, Marian L. 1981
Subtests: Movement Patterns; Clapping; Body Directions; Finger Patterns; Copy Shapes; Visual Integration; Spatial Directions; Draw a Person; Serial Counting; Phrases; Sentences; Verbal Reasoning; General Information; Quantity Recognition; Read Shapes
Descriptors: Bilingual Education; Bilingual Teachers; Human Body; *Individual Testing; *Kindergarten Children; Language Proficiency; *Learning Readiness; *Preschool Children; Preschool Education; Psychomotor Skills; *Screening Tests; *Vietnamese
Identifiers: PSS
Availability: Early Recognition Intervention Network; 376 Bridge St., Dedham, MA 02026
Target Audience: 2-6
Notes: Time, 20 approx.
This foreign-language adaptation of the Preschool Screening System is an individually administered screening test of learning efficiency. It is used as an initial screening device for identifying the special learning needs of preschool or kindergarten children. Primary use is to quickly survey learning skills of children entering nursery school or kindergarten so that curriculum can be adapted to their needs. Can also serve as part of a more detailed assessment of individual children. May be group administered by having a team of several adults meet with 8 children at a time. Test assesses body awareness, visual-perceptual-motor skills, and language skills. Subtests may be combined to yield a short form or nonlanguage form. Several subtests may also be compiled to yield imitation and learned skills scores. English-language manual is necessary for administration. This instrument is a Vietnamese adaptation of the Preschool Screening System (TC012681).

13386
Preschool Screening System: Spanish Adaptation. Hainsworth, Peter K.; Hainsworth, Marian L. 1981
Subtests: Movement Patterns; Clapping; Body Directions; Finger Patterns; Copy Shapes; Visual Integration; Spatial Directions; Draw a Person; Serial Counting; Phrases; Sentences; Verbal Reasoning; General Information; Quantity Recognition; Read Shapes
Descriptors: Bilingual Education; Bilingual Teachers; Human Body; *Individual Testing; *Kindergarten Children; Language Proficiency; *Learning Readiness; *Preschool Children; Preschool Education; Psychomotor Skills; *Screening Tests; *Spanish
Identifiers: PSS
Availability: Early Recognition Intervention Network; 376 Bridge St., Dedham, MA 02026
Target Audience: 2-6
Notes: Time, 20 approx.
This foreign-language adaptation of the Preschool Screening System is an individually administered screening test of learning efficiency. It is used as an initial screening device for identifying the special learning needs of preschool or kindergarten children. Primary use is to quickly survey learning skills of children entering nursery school or kindergarten so that curriculum can be adapted to their needs. Can also serve as part of a more detailed assessment of individual children. May be group administered by having a team of several adults meet with 8 children at a time. Test assesses body awareness, visual-perceptual-motor skills, and language skills. Subtests may be combined to yield a short form or nonlanguage form. Several subtests may also be compiled to yield imitation and learned skills scores. English-language manual is necessary for administration. This instrument is a Spanish adaptation of the Preschool Screening System (TC012681).

13387
Preschool Screening System: Portuguese Adaptation. Hainsworth, Peter K.; Hainsworth, Marian L. 1981
Subtests: Movement Patterns; Clapping; Body Directions; Finger Patterns; Copy Shapes; Visual Integration; Spatial Directions; Draw a Person; Serial Counting; Phrases; Sentences; Verbal Reasoning; General Information; Quantity Recognition; Read Shapes
Descriptors: Bilingual Education; Bilingual Teachers; Human Body; *Individual Testing; *Kindergarten Children; Language Proficiency; *Learning Readiness; *Portuguese; *Preschool Children; Preschool Education; Psychomotor Skills; *Screening Tests
Identifiers: PSS
Availability: Early Recognition Intervention Network; 376 Bridge St., Dedham, MA 02026
Target Audience: 2-6
Notes: Time, 20 approx.
This foreign-language adaptation of the Preschool Screening System is an individually administered screening test of learning efficiency. It is used as an initial screening device for identifying the special learning needs of preschool or kindergarten children. Primary use is to quickly survey learning skills of children entering nursery school or kindergarten so that curriculum can be adapted to their needs. Can also serve as part of a more detailed assessment of individual children. May be group administered by having a team of several adults meet with 8 children at a time. Test assesses body awareness, visual-perceptual-motor skills, and language skills. Subtests may be combined to yield a short form or nonlanguage form. Several subtests may also be compiled to yield imitation and learned skills scores. English-language manual is necessary for administration. This instrument is a Portuguese adaptation of the Preschool Screening System (TC012681).

13388
Preschool Screening System: Italian Adaptation. Hainsworth, Peter K.; Hainsworth, Marian L. 1981
Subtests: Movement Patterns; Clapping; Body Directions; Finger Patterns; Copy Shapes; Visual Integration; Spatial Directions; Draw a Person; Serial Counting; Phrases; Sentences; Verbal Reasoning; General Information; Quantity Recognition; Read Shapes
Descriptors: Bilingual Education; Bilingual Teachers; Human Body; *Individual Testing; *Italian; *Kindergarten Children; Language Proficiency; *Learning Readiness; *Preschool Children; Preschool Education; Psychomotor Skills; *Screening Tests
Identifiers: PSS
Availability: Early Recognition Intervention Network; 376 Bridge St., Dedham, MA 02026
Target Audience: 2-6
Notes: Time, 20 approx.
This foreign-language adaptation of the Preschool Screening System is an individually administered screening test of learning efficiency. It is used as an initial screening device for identifying the special learning needs of preschool or kindergarten children. Primary use is to quickly survey learning skills of children entering nursery school or kindergarten so that curriculum can be adapted to their needs. Can also serve as part of a more detailed assessment of individual children. May be group administered by having a team of several adults meet with 8 children at a time. Test assesses body awareness, visual-perceptual-motor skills, and language skills. Subtests may be combined to yield a short form or nonlanguage form. Several subtests may also be compiled to yield imitation and learned skills scores. English-language manual is necessary for administration. This instrument is an Italian adaptation of the Preschool Screening System (TC012681).

13389
Preschool Screening System: Greek Adaptation. Hainsworth, Peter K.; Hainsworth, Marian L. 1981
Subtests: Movement Patterns; Clapping; Body Directions; Finger Patterns; Copy Shapes; Visual Integration; Spatial Directions; Draw a Person; Serial Counting; Phrases; Sentences; Verbal Reasoning; General Information; Quantity Recognition; Read Shapes
Descriptors: Bilingual Education; Bilingual Teachers; *Greek; Human Body; *Individual Testing; *Kindergarten Children; Language Proficiency; *Learning Readiness; *Preschool Children; Preschool Education; Psychomotor Skills; *Screening Tests
Identifiers: PSS
Availability: Early Recognition Intervention Network; 376 Bridge St., Dedham, MA 02026
Target Audience: 2-6
Notes: Time, 20 approx.
This foreign-language adaptation of the Preschool Screening System is an individually administered screening test of learning efficiency. It is used as an initial screening device for identifying the special learning needs of preschool or kindergarten children. Primary use is to quickly survey learning skills of children entering nursery school or kindergarten so that curriculum can be adapted to their needs. Can also serve as part of a more detailed assessment of individual children. May be group administered by having a team of several adults meet with 8 children at a time. Test assesses body awareness, visual-perceptual-motor skills, and language skills. Subtests may be combined to yield a short form or nonlanguage form. Several subtests may also be compiled to yield imitation and learned skills scores. English-language manual is necessary for administration. This instrument is a Greek adaptation of the Preschool Screening System (TC012681).

13390
Preschool Screening System: French Adaptation. Hainsworth, Peter K.; Hainsworth, Marian L. 1981
Subtests: Movement Patterns; Clapping; Body Directions; Finger Patterns; Copy Shapes; Visual Integration; Spatial Directions; Draw a Person; Serial Counting; Phrases; Sentences; Verbal Reasoning; General Information; Quantity Recognition; Read Shapes

Descriptors: Bilingual Education; Bilingual Teachers; *French; Human Body; *Individual Testing; *Kindergarten Children; Language Proficiency; *Learning Readiness; *Preschool Children; Preschool Education; Psychomotor Skills; *Screening Tests
Identifiers: PSS
Availability: Early Recognition Intervention Network; 376 Bridge St., Dedham, MA 02026
Target Audience: 2-6
Notes: Time, 20 approx.

This foreign-language adaptation of the Preschool Screening System is an individually administered screening test of learning efficiency. It is used as an initial screening device for identifying the special learning needs of preschool or kindergarten children. Primary use is to quickly survey learning skills of children entering nursery school or kindergarten so that curriculum can be adapted to their needs. Can also serve as part of a more detailed assessment of individual children. May be group administered by having a team of several adults meet with 8 children at a time. Test assesses body awareness, visual-perceptual-motor skills, and language skills. Subtests may be combined to yield a short form or nonlanguage form. Several subtests may also be compiled to yield imitation and learned skills scores. English-language manual is necessary for administration. This instrument is a French adaptation of the Preschool Screening System (TC012681).

13391
Preschool Screening System: Chinese Adaptation. Hainsworth, Peter K.; Hainsworth, Marian L. 1981
Subtests: Movement Patterns; Clapping; Body Directions; Finger Patterns; Copy Shapes; Visual Integration; Spatial Directions; Draw a Person; Serial Counting; Phrases; Sentences; Verbal Reasoning; General Information; Quantity Recognition; Read Shapes
Descriptors: Bilingual Education; Bilingual Teachers; *Chinese; Human Body; *Individual Testing; *Kindergarten Children; Language Proficiency; *Learning Readiness; *Preschool Children; Preschool Education; Psychomotor Skills; *Screening Tests
Identifiers: PSS
Availability: Early Recognition Intervention Network; 376 Bridge St., Dedham, MA 02026
Target Audience: 2-6
Notes: Time, 20 approx.

This foreign-language adaptation of the Preschool Screening System is an individually administered screening test of learning efficiency. It is used as an initial screening device for identifying the special learning needs of preschool or kindergarten children. Primary use is to quickly survey learning skills of children entering nursery school or kindergarten so that curriculum can be adapted to their needs. Can also serve as part of a more detailed assessment of individual children. May be group administered by having a team of several adults meet with 8 children at a time. Test assesses body awareness, visual-perceptual-motor skills, and language skills. Subtests may be combined to yield a short form or non-language form. Several subtests may also be compiled to yield imitation and learned skills scores. English-language manual is necessary for administration. This instrument is a Chinese adaptation of the Preschool Screening System (TC012681).

13392
Preschool Screening System: Cape Verdean Adaptation. Hainsworth, Peter K.; Hainsworth, Marian L. 1981
Subtests: Movement Patterns; Clapping; Body Directions; Finger Patterns; Copy Shapes; Visual Integration; Spatial Directions; Draw a Person; Serial Counting; Phrases; Sentences; Verbal Reasoning; General Information; Quantity Recognition; Read Shapes
Descriptors: Bilingual Education; Bilingual Teachers; Human Body; *Individual Testing; *Kindergarten Children; Language Proficiency; *Learning Readiness; *Preschool Children; Preschool Education; Psychomotor Skills; *Screening Tests
Identifiers: *Cape Verdeans; PSS
Availability: Early Recognition Intervention Network; 376 Bridge St., Dedham, MA 02026
Target Audience: 2-6
Notes: Time, 20 approx.

This foreign-language adaptation of the Preschool Screening System is an individually administered screening test of learning efficiency. It is used as an initial screening device for identifying the special learning needs of preschool or kindergarten children. Primary use is to quickly survey learning skills of children entering nursery school or kindergarten so that curriculum can be adapted to their needs. Can also serve as part of a more detailed assessment of individual children. May be group administered by having a team of several adults meet with 8 children at a time. Test assesses body awareness, visual-perceptual-motor skills, and language skills. Subtests may be combined to yield a short form or nonlanguage form. Several subtests may also be compiled to yield imitation and learned skills scores. English-language manual is necessary for administration. This instrument is a Cape Verdean adaptation of the Preschool Screening System (TC012681).

13393
Preschool Screening System: Armenian Adaptation. Hainsworth, Peter K.; Hainsworth, Marian L. 1981
Subtests: Movement Patterns; Clapping; Body Directions; Finger Patterns; Copy Shapes; Visual Integration; Spatial Directions; Draw a Person; Serial Counting; Phrases; Sentences; Verbal Reasoning; General Information; Quantity Recognition; Read Shapes
Descriptors: *Armenian; Bilingual Education; Bilingual Teachers; Human Body; *Individual Testing; *Kindergarten Children; Language Proficiency; *Learning Readiness; *Preschool Children; Preschool Education; Psychomotor Skills; *Screening Tests
Identifiers: PSS
Availability: Early Recognition Intervention Network; 376 Bridge St., Dedham, MA 02026
Target Audience: 2-6
Notes: Time, 20 approx.

This foreign-language adaptation of the Preschool Screening System is an individually administered screening test of learning efficiency. It is used as an initial screening device for identifying the special learning needs of preschool or kindergarten children. Primary use is to quickly survey learning skills of children entering nursery school or kindergarten so that curriculum can be adapted to their needs. Can also serve as part of a more detailed assessment of individual children. May be group administered by having a team of several adults meet with 8 children at a time. Test assesses body awareness, visual-perceptual-motor skills, and language skills. Subtests may be combined to yield a short form or nonlanguage form. Several subtests may also be compiled to yield imitation and learned skills scores. English-language manual is necessary for administration. This instrument is an Armenian adaptation of the Preschool Screening System (TC012681).

13394
Preschool Screening System: Cambodian Adaptation. Hainsworth, Peter K.; Hainsworth, Marian L. 1981
Subtests: Movement Patterns; Clapping; Body Directions; Finger Patterns; Copy Shapes; Visual Integration; Spatial Directions; Draw a Person; Serial Counting; Phrases; Sentences; Verbal Reasoning; General Information; Quantity Recognition; Read Shapes
Descriptors: Bilingual Education; Bilingual Teachers; *Cambodian; Human Body; *Individual Testing; *Kindergarten Children; Language Proficiency; *Learning Readiness; *Preschool Children; Preschool Education; Psychomotor Skills; *Screening Tests
Identifiers: PSS
Availability: Early Recognition Intervention Network; 376 Bridge St., Dedham, MA 02026
Target Audience: 2-6
Notes: Time, 20 approx.

This foreign-language adaptation of the Preschool Screening System is an individually administered screening test of learning efficiency. It is used as an initial screening device for identifying the special learning needs of preschool or kindergarten children. Primary use is to quickly survey learning skills of children entering nursery school or kindergarten so that curriculum can be adapted to their needs. Can also serve as part of a more detailed assessment of individual children. May be group administered by having a team of several adults meet with 8 children at a time. Test assesses body awareness, visual-perceptual-motor skills, and language skills. Subtests may be combined to yield a short form or nonlanguage form. Several subtests may also be compiled to yield imitation and learned skills scores. English-language manual is necessary for administration. This instrument is a Cambodian adaptation of the Preschool Screening System (TC012681).

13395
Preschool Screening System: Farsi Adaptation. Hainsworth, Peter K.; Hainsworth, Marian L. 1981
Subtests: Movement Patterns; Clapping; Body Directions; Finger Patterns; Copy Shapes; Visual Integration; Spatial Directions; Draw a Person; Serial Counting; Phrases; Sentences; Verbal Reasoning; General Information; Quantity Recognition; Read Shapes
Descriptors: Bilingual Education; Bilingual Teachers; Human Body; *Individual Testing; *Kindergarten Children; Language Proficiency; *Learning Readiness; *Persian; *Preschool Children; Preschool Education; Psychomotor Skills; *Screening Tests
Identifiers: PSS
Availability: Early Recognition Intervention Network; 376 Bridge St., Dedham, MA 02026
Target Audience: 2-6
Notes: Time, 20 approx.

This foreign-language adaptation of the Preschool Screening System is an individually administered screening test of learning efficiency. It is used as an initial screening device for identifying the special learning needs of preschool or kindergarten children. Primary use is to quickly survey learning skills of children entering nursery school or kindergarten so that curriculum can be adapted to their needs. Can also serve as part of a more detailed assessment of individual children. May be group administered by having a team of several adults meet with 8 children at a time. Test assesses body awareness, visual-perceptual-motor skills, and language skills. Subtests may be combined to yield a short form or nonlanguage form. Several subtests may also be compiled to yield imitation and learned skills scores. English-language manual is necessary for administration. This instrument is a Farsi or Persian adaptation of the Preschool Screening System (TC012681).

13396
Preschool Screening System: Japanese Adaptation. Hainsworth, Peter K.; Hainsworth, Marian L. 1981
Subtests: Movement Patterns; Clapping; Body Directions; Finger Patterns; Copy Shapes; Visual Integration; Spatial Directions; Draw a Person; Serial Counting; Phrases; Sentences; Verbal Reasoning; General Information; Quantity Recognition; Read Shapes
Descriptors: Bilingual Education; Bilingual Teachers; Human Body; *Individual Testing; *Japanese; *Kindergarten Children; Language Proficiency; *Learning Readiness; *Preschool Children; Preschool Education; Psychomotor Skills; *Screening Tests
Identifiers: PSS
Availability: Early Recognition Intervention Network; 376 Bridge St., Dedham, MA 02026
Target Audience: 2-6
Notes: Time, 20 approx.

This foreign-language adaptation of the Preschool Screening System is an individually administered screening test of learning efficiency. It is used as an initial screening device for identifying the special learning needs of preschool or kindergarten children. Primary use is to quickly survey learning skills of children entering nursery school or kindergarten so that curriculum can be adapted to their needs. Can also serve as part of a more detailed assessment of individual children. May be group administered by having a team of several adults meet with 8 children at a time. Test assesses body awareness, visual-perceptual-motor skills, and language skills. Subtests may be combined to yield a short form or nonlanguage form. Several subtests may also be compiled to yield imitation and learned skills scores. English-language manual is necessary for administration. This instrument is a Japanese adaptation of the Preschool Screening System (TC012681).

13397
Preschool Screening System: Laotian Adaptation. Hainsworth, Peter K.; Hainsworth, Marian L. 1981
Subtests: Movement Patterns; Clapping; Body Directions; Finger Patterns; Copy Shapes; Visual Integration; Spatial Directions; Draw a Person; Serial Counting; Phrases; Sentences; Verbal Reasoning; General Information; Quantity Recognition; Read Shapes
Descriptors: Bilingual Education; Bilingual Teachers; Human Body; *Individual Testing; *Kindergarten Children; Language Proficiency; *Lao; Laotians; *Learning Readiness; *Preschool Children; Preschool Education; Psychomotor Skills; *Screening Tests
Identifiers: PSS
Availability: Early Recognition Intervention Network; 376 Bridge St., Dedham, MA 02026
Target Audience: 2-6
Notes: Time, 20 approx.

This foreign-language adaptation of the Preschool Screening System is an individually administered screening test of learning efficiency. It is used as an initial screening device for identifying the special learning needs of preschool or kindergarten children. Primary use is to quickly survey learning skills of children entering nursery school or kindergarten so that curriculum can be adapted to their needs. Can also serve as part of a more detailed assessment of individual children. May be group administered by having a team of several adults meet with 8 children at a time. Test assesses body awareness, visual-perceptual-motor skills, and language skills. Subtests may be combined to yield a short form or nonlanguage form. Several subtests may also be compiled to yield imitation and learned skills scores. English-language manual is necessary for administration. This instrument is a Laotian adaptation of the Preschool Screening System (TC012681).

13398
Preschool Screening System: Samoan Adaptation. Hainsworth, Peter K.; Hainsworth, Marian L. 1981

Subtests: Movement Patterns; Clapping; Body Directions; Finger Patterns; Copy Shapes; Visual Integration; Spatial Directions; Draw a Person; Serial Counting; Phrases; Sentences; Verbal Reasoning; General Information; Quantity Recognition; Read Shapes
Descriptors: Bilingual Education; Bilingual Teachers; Human Body; *Individual Testing; *Kindergarten Children; Language Proficiency; *Learning Readiness; *Preschool Children; Preschool Education; Psychomotor Skills; *Samoan; *Screening Tests
Identifiers: PSS
Availability: Early Recognition Intervention Network; 376 Bridge St., Dedham, MA 02026
Target Audience: 2-6
Notes: Time, 20 approx.

This foreign-language adaptation of the Preschool Screening System is an individually administered screening test of learning efficiency. It is used as an initial screening device for identifying the special learning needs of preschool or kindergarten children. Primary use is to quickly survey learning skills of children entering nursery school or kindergarten so that curriculum can be adapted to their needs. Can also serve as part of a more detailed assessment of individual children. May be group administered by having a team of several adults meet with 8 children at a time. Test assesses body awareness, visual-perceptual-motor skills, and language skills. Subtests may be combined to yield a short form or nonlanguage form. Several subtests may also be compiled to yield imitation and learned skills scores. English-language manual is necessary for administration. This instrument is a Samoan adaptation of the Preschool Screening System (TC012681).

13399
Preschool Screening System: Tagalog Adaptation. Hainsworth, Peter K.; Hainsworth, Marian L. 1981
Subtests: Movement Patterns; Clapping; Body Directions; Finger Patterns; Copy Shapes; Visual Integration; Spatial Directions; Draw a Person; Serial Counting; Phrases; Sentences; Verbal Reasoning; General Information; Quantity Recognition; Read Shapes
Descriptors: Bilingual Education; Bilingual Teachers; Human Body; *Individual Testing; *Kindergarten Children; Language Proficiency; *Learning Readiness; *Preschool Children; Preschool Education; Psychomotor Skills; *Screening Tests; *Tagalog
Identifiers: PSS
Availability: Early Recognition Intervention Network; 376 Bridge St., Dedham, MA 02026
Target Audience: 2-6
Notes: Time, 20 approx.

This foreign-language adaptation of the Preschool Screening System is an individually administered screening test of learning efficiency. It is used as an initial screening device for identifying the special learning needs of preschool or kindergarten children. Primary use is to quickly survey learning skills of children entering nursery school or kindergarten so that curriculum can be adapted to their needs. Can also serve as part of a more detailed assessment of individual children. May be group administered by having a team of several adults meet with 8 children at a time. Test assesses body awareness, visual-perceptual-motor skills, and language skills. Subtests may be combined to yield a short form or nonlanguage form. Several subtests may also be compiled to yield imitation and learned skills scores. English-language manual is necessary for administration. This instrument is a Tagalog adaptation of of the Preschool Screening System (TC012681).

13408
The Drug-Abuse Questionnaire. Ferneau, E.; Mueller, S. 1971
Descriptors: *Attitude Measures; *College Students; *Drug Abuse; Drug Addiction; Drug Education; Higher Education; Rating Scales; *Student Attitudes
Identifiers: Alcoholism Questionnaire; Marcus (A)
Availability: ERIC Document Reproduction Service; 3900 Wheeler Ave., Alexandria, VA 22304 (ED071091, 18 pages)
Grade Level: 13-16
Notes: Time, 20 approx.; Items, 40

This questionnaire was used to survey college student attitudes on drug abuse. It is identical to the alcoholism questionnaire except for word changes appropriate to the subject matter. The subject responds to the 40 statements by checking a position on the 1-7 rating scale. It takes about 20 minutes to complete this instrument.

13409
CID Preschool Performance Scale. Geers, Ann E.; Lane, Helen S. 1984
Subtests: Manual Planning; Manual Dexterity; Form Perception; Perceptual Motor Skills; Preschool Skills; Part Whole Relationships
Descriptors: Early Childhood Education; *Hearing Impairments; *Intelligence Tests; Kindergarten Children; *Language Handicaps; *Nonverbal Tests; Predictive Measurement; *Preschool Children; Preschool Tests
Identifiers: Randalls Island Performance Series
Availability: Stoelting Co.; 1350 S. Kostner Ave., Chicago, IL 60623
Target Audience: 2-5

An adaptation of the Randall's Island Performance Series (1931) which was used to measure the intelligence of mentally retarded children at Randall's Island, a New York City institution. Test is nonverbal, both in instructions and in response. The CID was revised and standardized. It retains most of the items from the earlier test, but the items have been regrouped into 6 subtests with point scores that can be converted into scaled scores and a deviation IQ. The test can now be administered to hearing- and language-impaired children. The subtests are administered individually and take varying amounts of time to complete. Validity and reliability data are reported.

13410
Assessment of a Deaf-Blind Multiply Handicapped Child, Third Edition. Rudolph, James M.; And Others
Subtests: Gross Motor Development; Fine Motor Development; Personal—Self-Help Skills; Communication; Auditory Development; Visual Development; Cognition; Social Development; Mobility
Descriptors: Adolescents; Auditory Stimuli; Children; Cognitive Development; Communication Skills; Daily Living Skills; *Deaf Blind; *Educational Assessment; Elementary School Students; Elementary Secondary Education; Employment Potential; Interpersonal Competence; Motor Development; Multiple Disabilities; Performance Tests; Physical Mobility; Rating Scales; Secondary School Students; Self Care Skills; *Severe Disabilities; Sheltered Workshops; Visual Stimuli
Availability: Midwest Regional Center for Services to Deaf-Blind Children; P.O. Box 30008, Lansing, MI 48909
Target Audience: 5-18

This manual is designed to measure a student's progress in individual skill areas that often overlap. It is not intended to be a curriculum guide but is an instrument for measuring the performance of students. It should be used to supplement the total assessment endeavor. The manual is to be used to assess the deaf-blind child and provides an opportunity to alert parents and staff to general developmental directions, to the student's present level of development, and to the focus of training needs. This guide identifies the minimum skills in 5 skill areas required for entrance into most protected work environments. It is an assessment tool, an aid for planning long-range goals and short-term objectives, and a guide to developing activities for the classroom. The guide will indicate the student's present skill level in relationship to the minimum skills necessary for entrance into the sheltered work environment.

13428
Preliminary Test of English as a Foreign Language. Educational Testing Service, Princeton, NJ 1984
Subtests: Listening Comprehension; Structure and Written Expression; Reading Comprehension and Vocabulary
Descriptors: College Students; *English (Second Language); Foreign Students; Higher Education; High School Students; *Language Proficiency; *Language Tests; Listening Comprehension; Reading Comprehension; Secondary Education; Sentence Structure; Student Placement; Vocabulary Skills; Writing Skills
Identifiers: Nonnative Speakers; TOEFL
Availability: Educational Testing Service (TOEFL); Box 899, Princeton, NJ 08541
Grade Level: 13-16
Notes: Time, 70

Designed to measure the English proficiency of non-native speakers of the language at the beginning and intermediate levels. For use by schools, colleges and universities to place students in ESL programs, to measure progress after instruction, or to determine if student can function in an English-language instructional setting. Scored by publisher. Part and total scores are reported.

13462
Parent Appraisal of Needs. Numata, Wendy
Descriptors: Adults; Child Rearing; *Disabilities; *Needs Assessment; *Parents; Preschool Education; Questionnaires; *Young Children
Identifiers: *Public Law 94 142
Availability: Preschool Training Coordination; Educational Service District 101, W. 1025 Indiana Ave., Spokane, WA 99205
Target Audience: Adults

Designed to assess parent's needs and preferred method of training. Allows parents of young handicapped children to identify areas about which they would like more training, or information, and ways they prefer to receive it.

13463
Photo Articulation Test, Second Edition. Pendergast, Kathleen; And Others 1984
Descriptors: *Articulation (Speech); *Articulation Impairments; Check Lists; Consonants; Diagnostic Tests; Diction; *Individual Testing; Pronunciation; Speech Improvement; *Speech Tests; Visual Measures; Vowels; *Young Children
Identifiers: Articulation Tests; PAT
Availability: Slosson Educational Publications; P.O. Box 280, E. Aurora, NY 14052
Target Audience: 3-8
Notes: Time, 5 approximately; Items, 72

The Photo Articulation Test (PAT) is designed to elicit spontaneous speech from children with articulation problems. It consists of 72 color photographs with 9 pictures on each of 8 sheets. The first 69 pictures test consonants and all but one vowel and one diphthong. The concluding 3 pictures test connected speech and the remaining vowel and diphthong. In addition, a deck of the same 72 color photographs, each on a separate card, is provided for further diagnosis and for use in speech therapy and speech improvement. The test cards are also used to test subjects with visual problems and others who would have difficulty with more than one picture being presented at a time. The test is administered individually and is recommended for ages from 3.5 to 8 years. Responses are recorded on the PAT recording sheet which has a provision for both consonants and vowels. Articulation Age Overlays (AA) are given for each age group and provide an instant picture of the subject's articulation development. It is recommended that PAT be administered in its entirety, but it can be adapted for screening when a rapid evaluation of articulation is desired.

13467
Eby Elementary Identification Instrument. Eby, Judy W. 1984
Descriptors: *Ability Identification; *Academically Gifted; Elementary Education; *Elementary School Students; Junior High Schools; *Junior High School Students; *Screening Tests; *Student Placement
Identifiers: EEII
Availability: Slosson Educational Publications; P.O. Box 280, E. Aurora, NY 14052
Grade Level: K-8

Developed to provide administrators of gifted programs an easily administered, objective, and comprehensive process to select students for gifted programing on the basis of performance and behavior. Emphasis is on academic talent or gifted behavior. Assessment areas are based on Joseph Renzulli's work. The instrument consists of 3 components: general selection matrix, teacher recommendation form, and unit selection matrix.

13468
Arlin Test of Formal Reasoning. Arlin, Patricia Kennedy 1984
Subtests: Volume; Probability; Correlations; Combinations; Proportions; Momentum; Mechanical Equilibrium; Frames of Reference
Descriptors: *Abstract Reasoning; Adults; Cognitive Development; *Cognitive Tests; Gifted; Individual Testing; Learning Disabilities; *Logical Thinking; *Middle Schools; Multiple Choice Tests; Screening Tests; Secondary Education; *Secondary School Students
Identifiers: ATFR; Inhelder Piaget System; *Reasoning Ability
Availability: Slosson Educational Publications; P.O. Box 280, E. Aurora, NY 14052
Grade Level: 6-12
Notes: Time, 60 approx.; Items, 32

Designed for large-group administration to assess students' levels of cognitive development. Also yields specific subtest scores which refer to each of Inhelder and Piaget's 8 formal schemata. May be used diagnostically by teachers in instructional planning. May also be used in conjunction with other instruments to screen students for programs for the gifted and for early admission to special science and mathematics classes. Can also be individually administered to students with reading and other learning disabilities, to probe their logical reasoning skills separately from general achievement and intelligence tests. In addition to testing the instrument on students in grades 6-12, some selected adult samples were also used. The majority of those in the norm sample represents White middle-class students for whom English is a first language. The publisher is planning to provide a wider range of forms for other representative populations in North America.

13471
Automobile Mechanic Assistant Work Sample. Shawsheen Valley Regional Vocational-Technical High School, Billerica, MA 1979

Descriptors: *Aptitude Tests; *Auto Mechanics; *Disabilities; High Schools; High School Students; Job Performance; Job Skills; Occupational Tests; Prevocational Education; Trade and Industrial Education; *Vocational Aptitude; *Vocational Evaluation; Vocational Interests; *Work Sample Tests
Availability: ERIC Document Reproduction Service; 3900 Wheeler Ave., Alexandria, VA 22304 (ED236421, 40 pages)
Grade Level: 9-12

The Automobile Mechanic Assistant Work Sample is intended to assess a handicapped student's interest in and potential to successfully pass a Training Program in Automotive Mechanics or in a similar automotive job. On this Work Sample, the student is to look over and inspect the thermostat housing to intake manifold setup. The student is to remove the thermostat housing, gasket, and thermostat in order to replace a new thermostat in the intake manifold. The sample involves physical demands and must be done by a 2-armed person standing in front of the work sample. The work sample is timed from the moment the student signifies he/she is ready to begin until the last tool needed is put down and he/she indicates completion.

13472
Automotive Work Sample. Shawsheen Valley Regional Vocational-Technical High School, Billerica, MA 1979
Descriptors: *Aptitude Tests; *Auto Mechanics; *Disabilities; High Schools; *High School Students; Job Performance; Job Skills; Occupational Tests; Prevocational Education; Trade and Industrial Education; *Vocational Aptitude; *Vocational Evaluation; Vocational Interests; *Work Sample Tests
Availability: ERIC Document Reproduction Service; 3900 Wheeler Ave., Alexandria, VA 22304 (ED236422, 34 pages)
Grade Level: 9-12

The Automotive Mechanic Assistant Work Sample II is intended to assess a handicapped student's interest in and potential to successfully pass a Training Program in Automotive Mechanics or in a similar automotive job. The work sample is timed from the moment the student signifies that he/she understands the instructions and picks up the first tool or piece of equipment and indicates that he/she is ready to begin the removal phase, until the last tool or piece of equipment needed for the replacement phase is finished and the student indicates completion. This work sample deals with oil filters, and the student is to replace the old filter with a new one. The sample involves physical demands and must be done by a 2-armed person standing in front of the work sample.

13473
Bagger Work Sample. Shawsheen Valley Regional Vocational-Technical High School, Billerica, MA 1979
Descriptors: *Aptitude Tests; *Disabilities; *Distributive Education; High School Students; Job Performance; Job Skills; Occupational Tests; Prevocational Education; Service Occupations; *Vocational Aptitude; *Vocational Evaluation; Vocational Interests; *Work Sample Tests
Identifiers: *Baggers
Availability: ERIC Document Reproduction Service; 3900 Wheeler Ave., Alexandria, VA 22304 (ED236423, 25 pages)
Grade Level: 9-12

The Bagger Work Sample is intended to assess a handicapped student's interest in and to screen interested students into a training program in Distributive Education I in the Shawsheen Valley Regional Vocational-Technical High School. The course is based upon the entry level of a bagger job. The sample involves medium work, and must be performed by a person with both hands or one who has equivalent manual and finger dexterity from a chair or wheelchair. The work sample is timed from the moment the student signifies he/she understands the instructions and is ready to begin until the student has placed the last grocery bag in the basket and indicates that he/she is finished.

13474
Clerical Machine Operator Work Sample. Shawsheen Valley Regional Vocational-Technical High School, Billerica, MA 1979
Descriptors: *Aptitude Tests; *Clerical Occupations; Clerical Workers; *Disabilities; High Schools; *High School Students; Job Performance; Job Skills; Occupational Tests; *Office Machines; Office Occupations Education; Prevocational Education; *Typewriting; *Vocational Aptitude; *Vocational Evaluation; Vocational Interests; *Work Sample Tests
Availability: ERIC Document Reproduction Service; 3900 Wheeler Ave., Alexandria, VA 22304 (ED236424, 42 pages)
Grade Level: 9-12

The Clerical Machine Operator-Typist Work Sample is intended to assess a handicapped student's interest in and potential to successfully pass a clerical business machine course (typing) in a comprehensive or vocational high school. This test can be done by a 2-armed person sitting in a wheel chair. The sample is designed to simulate the functions and methods of a typist in the clerical area as it may exist in a training program or a comprehensive or technical school. The work sample is timed from the moment the student signifies he/she understands the instruction and is ready to begin until the student indicates completion.

13475
Color Discrimination Work Sample. Shawsheen Valley Regional Vocational-Technical High School, Billerica, MA 1979
Descriptors: *Aptitude Tests; *Color; *Disabilities; High Schools; *High School Students; Industrial Arts; Job Performance; Job Skills; Occupational Tests; Painting (Industrial Arts); Prevocational Education; *Visual Perception; *Vocational Aptitude; *Vocational Evaluation; Vocational Interests; *Work Sample Tests
Identifiers: *Color Discrimination
Availability: ERIC Document Reproduction Service; 3900 Wheeler Ave., Alexandria, VA 22304 (ED236425, 21 pages)
Grade Level: 9-12

The Color Discrimination Work Sample is intended to assess a handicapped student's ability to see likenesses or differences in colors or shades, by identifying or matching certain colors and selecting colors which go together. The sample can be done by a one- or 2-armed person from a chair or wheelchair. The sample is timed from the moment the student signifies that the instructions are understood and begins until the student signifies that the sample is completed.

13476
Drafting Work Sample. Shawsheen Valley Regional Vocational-Technical High School, Billerica, MA 1979
Descriptors: *Aptitude Tests; *Disabilities; *Drafting; Engineering Drawing; High Schools; *High School Students; Industrial Arts; Job Performance; Job Skills; Occupational Tests; Prevocational Education; *Vocational Aptitude; *Vocational Evaluation; Vocational Interests; *Work Sample Tests
Availability: ERIC Document Reproduction Service; 3900 Wheeler Ave., Alexandria, VA 22304 (ED236426, 31 pages)
Grade Level: 9-12

The Drafting Work Sample is intended to assess a handicapped student's interest in and to screen interested students into a training program in basic mechanical drawing. The sample involves sedentary work and must be performed by a person with both hands or one who has equivalent manual and finger dexterity from a chair or wheelchair. This sample is limited to a right-handed student; a left-handed drafting machine must be substituted if the student is left-handed. The work sample is timed from the moment the student signifies he/she understands the instructions until the student indicates that he/she is finished.

13477
Drill Press Work Sample. Shawsheen Valley Regional Vocational-Technical High School, Billerica, MA 1979
Descriptors: *Aptitude Tests; *Disabilities; High Schools; *High School Students; Job Performance; Job Skills; *Machine Tool Operators; *Machine Tools; Machinists; Occupational Tests; Prevocational Education; Trade and Industrial Education; *Vocational Aptitude; *Vocational Evaluation; Vocational Interests; *Work Sample Tests
Availability: ERIC Document Reproduction Service; 3900 Wheeler Ave., Alexandria, VA 22304 (ED236427, 27 pages)
Grade Level: 9-12

The Drill Press Work Sample is intended to assess a student's interest in and screen interested students into a training program in Basic Machine Shop I. The sample involves light work and must be performed by a person with both hands or one who has equivalent manual and finger dexterity from a chair or wheelchair. The sample is timed from the moment the student signifies he/she is ready to begin until he/she idicates that he/she is finished.

13478
Electrical Wiring Work Sample. Shawsheen Valley Regional Vocational-Technical High School, Billerica, MA 1979
Descriptors: *Aptitude Tests; *Disabilities; *Electricians; *Electricity; High Schools; *High School Students; Industrial Arts; Job Performance; Job Skills; Occupational Tests; Prevocational Education; Trade and Industrial Education; *Vocational Aptitude; *Vocational Evaluation; Vocational Interests; *Work Sample Tests
Identifiers: *Electrical Wiring
Availability: ERIC Document Reproduction Service; 3900 Wheeler Ave., Alexandria, VA 22304 (ED236428, 27 pages)
Grade Level: 9-12

The Electrical Work Sample is intended to assess a handicapped student's interest in and to screen interested students into a training program in basic electricity. The work sample involves light work and must be performed by a person with both hands or one who has equivalent manual and finger dexterity from a chair or wheelchair. The work sample is timed from the moment the student is ready to begin until he/she indicates that the sample is completed. The test is to wire an electrical duplex outlet.

13479
Electronics Assembly Work Sample. Shawsheen Valley Regional Vocational-Technical High School, Billerica, MA 1979
Descriptors: *Aptitude Tests; *Assembly (Manufacturing); *Disabilities; *Electronics; High Schools; *High School Students; Industrial Arts; Job Performance; Job Skills; Occupational Tests; Prevocational Education; *Vocational Aptitude; *Vocational Evaluation; Vocational Interests; *Work Sample Tests
Identifiers: *Electronics Assemblers
Availability: ERIC Document Reproduction Service; 3900 Wheeler Ave., Alexandria, VA 22304 (ED236429, 26 pages)
Grade Level: 9-12

The Electronics Assembler Work Sample is intended to assess a handicapped student's interest in and potential to enter a training program in electronics assembly or a similar program. The sample involves sedentary work and can be done by a 2-armed person from a chair or wheelchair. Time is not a factor in this work sample.

13480
Finger Dexterity Work Sample. Shawsheen Valley Regional Vocational-Technical High School, Billerica, MA 1979
Descriptors: *Aptitude Tests; *Disabilities; High Schools; *High School Students; Job Performance; Job Skills; *Motor Development; *Object Manipulation; Occupational Tests; Prevocational Education; *Vocational Aptitude; *Vocational Evaluation; Vocational Interests; *Work Sample Tests
Availability: ERIC Document Reproduction Service; 3900 Wheeler Ave., Alexandria, VA 22304 (ED236430, 22 pages)
Grade Level: 9-12

The Finger Dexterity Work Sample is intended to assess a handicapped student's ability to move the fingers and manipulate small objects with fingers, rapidly and accurately. The sample can be done by a one- or 2-armed person from a chair or wheelchair. The sample is timed from the moment the student signifies readiness to completion of the task.

13481
Manual Dexterity Work Sample. Shawsheen Valley Regional Vocational-Technical High School, Billerica, MA 1979
Descriptors: *Aptitude Tests; *Disabilities; High Schools; *High School Students; Job Performance; Job Skills; *Motor Development; *Object Manipulation; Occupational Tests; Prevocational Education; *Vocational Aptitude; *Vocational Evaluation; Vocational Interests; *Work Sample Tests
Identifiers: *Manual Dexterity
Availability: ERIC Document Reproduction Service; 3900 Wheeler Ave., Alexandria, VA 22304 (ED236431, 21 pages)
Grade Level: 9-12

The Manual Dexterity Work Sample is intended to assess a handicapped student's ability to move the hands easily and skillfully and the ability to move the hands in placing and turning motions. The sample can be done by a 2-armed person from a chair or wheelchair. Time is not a factor in this work sample.

13482
Small Parts Assembler Work Sample. Shawsheen Valley Regional Vocational-Technical High School, Billerica, MA 1979

Descriptors: *Aptitude Tests; *Assembly (Manufacturing); *Disabilities; High Schools; *High School Students; Job Performance; Job Skills; Occupational Tests; Prevocational Education; Secondary Education; Secondary School Students; Trade and Industrial Education; *Vocational Aptitude; *Vocational Evaluation; Vocational Interests; *Work Sample Tests
Identifiers: *Assemblers
Availability: ERIC Document Reproduction Service; 3900 Wheeler Ave., Alexandria, VA 22304 (ED236432, 29 pages)
Grade Level: 9-12

The Small Parts Assembler Work Sample is intended to assess a handicapped student's interest in and potential to enter a training program in small parts assembly or in a similar job. The sample involves light to medium work and can be done by a 2-armed person with good eyesight from a chair or wheelchair. Time is not a factor in scoring this work sample but is kept for informational purposes only.

13495
The Clinical Articulation Profile. Rilla, Donna; Hurvitz, Judith 1983
Descriptors: *Articulation (Speech); *Articulation Impairments; *Speech Tests; *Young Children
Identifiers: CAP
Availability: Modern Education Corporation; P.O. Box 721, Tulsa, OK 74101
Target Audience: 3-8

Designed to assess young children with moderate to severe articulation disorders. Child's ability to say sounds can be tested at isolation level or syllable level as well as at word level. Provides information which is useful in development of individualized education plans and as a visual aid in conferences with parents and teachers.

13498
Washer Visual Acuity Screening Technique. Washer, Rhonda Wiezer 1984
Descriptors: Adolescents; Adults; Children; Mental Retardation; Older Adults; *Screening Tests; *Severe Disabilities; *Vision Tests; *Visual Acuity
Availability: Scholastic Testing Service; 480 Meyer Rd., Bensenville, IL 60106
Target Audience: 2-80

Developed as an acuity screening test for near and far vision for severely handicapped and low functioning populations. Skills required for individuals to be screened are gross visual discrimination skills, visual matching skills, and ability to indicate selections via touch, eye movements, or verbally. Can also be used for very young children. Using conditioning and reinforcement, test has been used to screen children as young as 18-months-old.

13502
Adaptive Behavior Scale for Infants and Early Childhood. Leland, Henry; And Others 1981
Subtests: Eating and Drinking; Toileting; Dressing; Travel Skills; Sensory Development; Body Control; Locomotion; Receptive Language; Speech Content; Personal Identification Skills; Conceptual Skills; Play; Self; Personal Responsibility and Socialization
Descriptors: *Adjustment (to Environment); Behavior Disorders; *Behavior Rating Scales; Criterion Referenced Tests; Daily Living Skills; Developmental Disabilities; *Emotional Adjustment; *Handicap Identification; *Infants; *Mental Retardation; Personality Traits; *Preschool Children; *Young Children
Identifiers: ABSI
Availability: Ohio State University; Nisonger Center Publication, 1580 Cannon Dr., Columbus, OH 43210
Target Audience: 0-6

Behavior rating scale for mentally retarded, emotionally maladjusted, and/or developmentally disabled infants and young children. Can also be used with other handicapped individuals. Designed to provide objective descriptions and evaluations of adaptive behavior in infants and young children from 2 weeks to 6 years of age. Consists of 2 parts. Part 1 is organized along developmental lines to evaluate skills and habits in 7 domains: independent functioning, physical development, communication skills, conceptual skills, play, self-direction, and personal responsibility and socialization. Part 2 provides measures of maladaptive behavior related to personality and behavior disorders.

13514
S-ESL Spoken English Test (The Standard English as a Second Language Spoken Test), Tests A, B, C. Pedersen, Elray L. 1978
Descriptors: Adult Education; *Communication Skills; Elementary School Students; Elementary Secondary Education; *English (Second Language); *Language Tests; *Oral Language; Secondary School Students; Tape Recorders; Vocabulary Skills
Identifiers: The Research Instruments Project
Availability: ERIC Document Reproduction Service; 3900 Wheeler Ave., Alexandria, VA 22304 (ED236648, 67 pages)
Grade Level: K-12
Target Audience: 18-64
Notes: Time, 20; Items, 90

This is one of 3 tests which is designed to assess the oral communication, grammatical fluency, and vocabulary development of students for whom English is a second language. The spoken English test comes in 2 versions: one with 90 items on a cassette tape, the other with 90 items to be read aloud by the examiner. Each version is available in 3 forms that employ a multiple-choice format requiring the selection of the semantically and grammatically correct response. The test does not assume knowledge of grammatical terminology. Each test is of 20 minutes duration and may be machine or hand scored.

13515
S-ESL Spoken English Test (The Standard English as a Second Language Grammar Test), Forms O, A, B, C. Pedersen, Elray L. 1978
Descriptors: Adult Education; College Students; *Communication Skills; Elementary School Students; Elementary Secondary Education; *English (Second Language); *Grammar; Higher Education; *Language Tests; Secondary School Students
Identifiers: The Research Instruments Project
Availability: ERIC Document Reproduction Service; 3900 Wheeler Ave., Alexandria, VA 22304 (ED236648, 67 pages)
Grade Level: K-16
Notes: Time, 15; Items, 35

This is one of 3 tests which is designed to assess the oral communication, grammatical fluency, and vocabulary development of students for whom English is a second language. Two levels of the Grammar Test have been developed: Form O tests the grammatical fluency of primary graders; Forms A, B, and C are similar tests for secondary or college and university students. The 35 questions on each form require no formal knowledge of grammatical terminology, require 15 minutes to complete, and can be machine or hand scored.

13516
S-ESL Spoken English Test (The Standard English as a Second Language Vocabulary Tests), Forms O, A, B, C. Pedersen, Elray L. 1978
Descriptors: Adult Education; College Students; *Communication Skills; Elementary School Students; Elementary Secondary Education; *English (Second Language); Higher Education; Language Tests; Multiple Choice Tests; Secondary School Students; *Vocabulary Development; Vocabulary Skills
Identifiers: The Research Instruments Project
Availability: ERIC Document Reproduction Service; 3900 Wheeler Ave., Alexandria, VA 22304 (ED236648, 67 pages)
Grade Level: K-16
Notes: Time, 15; Items, 37

This is one of 3 tests which is designed to assess the oral communication, grammatical fluency, and vocabulary development of students for whom English is a second language. Two levels of the vocabulary test have been developed: Form O tests the vocabulary development of primary grades; Forms A, B, and C are similar tests for secondary or college and university students. Each form of the test has 37 multiple-choice questions of 3 types: the student fills in a blank with a syntactically and semantically appropriate choice; the students respond to a question about the meaning, value, or usage of underlined words; the student matches a brief description with one of the choices provided. Administration of each form requires 15 minutes, and the tests can be machine or hand scored. Items come from survival and daily life contexts.

13529
Salamon-Conte Life Satisfaction in the Elderly Scale. Salamon, Michael J.; Conte, Vincent A. 1984
Subtests: Daily Activities; Meaning; Goals; Mood; Self Concept; Health; Finances; Social Contacts
Descriptors: Adults; *Attitude Measures; *Life Satisfaction; *Older Adults; Rating Scales; *Self Evaluation (Individuals)
Identifiers: LSES; Self Report Measures
Availability: Psychological Assessment Resources; P.O. Box 998, Odessa, FL 33556
Target Audience: 55-90
Notes: Time, 25 approx.; Items, 40

Designed to measure reliably life satisfaction among aged persons in a variety of settings. Assesses older adult reactions to their ecological, emotional, and social environments. Key areas found to be significant to this age group and which are evaluated by the LSES include taking pleasure in daily activities; regarding life as meaningful; goodness of fit between desired and achieved goals; positive mood; positive self-concept; and perceived health, financial security, and satisfaction with number and quality of social contacts.

13530
Rogers Criminal Responsibility Assessment Scales. Rogers, Richard 1984
Descriptors: Adults; *Court Litigation; *Crime; *Criminals; *Decision Making; *Legal Problems; Models; Questionnaires; *Responsibility
Identifiers: Insanity Plea (M Naghten); RCRAS
Availability: Psychological Assessment Resources; P.O. Box 998, Odessa, FL 33556
Target Audience: Adults
Notes: Items, 30

Purpose of scale is to provide a systematic and empirically based approach to evaluations of criminal responsibility. Designed to quantify essential psychological and situational variables at the time of the crime and to implement criterion-based decision models for criminal responsibility. Allows clinician to quantify impairment at the time of the crime, to conceptualize the impairment with respect to appropriate legal standards, and to render an expert opinion with respect to that legal standard. Instrument is designed to be used by qualified professionals who have had experience in forensic evaluations or who will obtain supervision from a qualified professional. Part I is used to establish the degree of impairment on psychological variables significant to the determination of insanity. Part II aids in the decision process toward rendering an accurate opinion on criminal responsibility with the American Law Institute Standard. Also contains experimental decision models for guilty-but-mentally-ill (GBMI) under the M'Naghten standards.

13532
C.U.B.E. Learning Disabilities Empirical Mapping Instrument. Vincennes University, IN 1979
Descriptors: *Adult Basic Education; Adults; Cognitive Mapping; *Cognitive Style; *Diagnostic Tests; Educational Environment; *Individual Testing; Interviews; *Learning Disabilities; Learning Modalities
Identifiers: Continuity and Unity in Basic Education Program; CUBE
Availability: ERIC Document Reproduction Service; 3900 Wheeler Ave., Alexandria, VA 22304 (ED211833, 437 pages)
Target Audience: 18-64
Notes: Items, 38

A simplified cognitive style mapping technique. Consists of an interview type survey, given individually, which results in a pictorial "map" of the adult basic education student's preferred learning style. Covers preferred modality, physical environment, organization of learning materials, and instruction.

13533
C.U.B.E. Learning Disabilities Diagnostic Test. Vincennes University, IN 1979
Subtests: Early's Informal Test of Cognitive Overloads; Copying (Far Point); Copying (Near Point); Writing from Dictation; Spelling (Oral); Spelling (Written); Sentence Formation (Oral); Sentence Formation (Written)
Descriptors: *Adult Basic Education; Adults; Cognitive Processes; *Diagnostic Tests; Instructional Development; *Learning Disabilities; *Learning Processes
Identifiers: Continuity and Unity in Basic Education Program; CUBE
Availability: ERIC Document Reproduction Service; 3900 Wheeler Ave., Alexandria, VA 22304 (ED211833, 437 pages)
Target Audience: 18-64

Series of instruments designed to indicate the presence of learning disabilities in general. Does not identify specific disabilities. Used to gather information that will help the teacher of adult basic education students to understand their learning processes and develop an instructional plan. See also ERIC Documents ED211831 and ED211832 for further information on reading and vocabulary tests.

13534
C.U.B.E. Program Administration Forms. Monroe County Community Schools Corp., Bloomington, IN 1979
Descriptors: Academic Achievement; *Adult Basic Education; Adults; Attendance Records; Enrollment; *Records (Forms)
Identifiers: Continuity and Unity in Basic Education Program; CUBE
Availability: ERIC Document Reproduction Service; 3900 Wheeler Ave., Alexandria, VA 22304 (ED211834, 66 pages)
Target Audience: 18-64

A series of forms for use in administering an adult basic education teaching/learning management system, C.U.B.E. (Continuity and Unity in Basic Education). Includes daily attendance records, enrollment forms, student performance forms. An additional fiche discusses program goals (ED211829, 29 pages).

13535
C.U.B.E. Math Mastery Tests. Monroe County Community Schools Corp., Bloomington, IN 1979
Descriptors: *Achievement Tests; *Adult Basic Education; Adults; Arithmetic; Fractions; Geometry; Mastery Tests; *Mathematics; Percentage
Identifiers: Continuity and Unity in Basic Education Program; CUBE
Availability: ERIC Document Reproduction Service; 3900 Wheeler Ave., Alexandria, VA 22304 (ED211830, 467 pages)
Target Audience: Adults
Notes: Items, 400

For use in measuring achievement in an adult basic education teaching/learning management system. Tests cover operations, graphs, algebra, fractions, decimals, percent measurements, formulas, geometry.

13536
C.U.B.E. Math Placement Inventory. Monroe County Community Schools Corp., Bloomington, IN 1979
Descriptors: Achievement Tests; *Adult Basic Education; Adults; Arithmetic; Fractions; Geometry; Mathematics; Percentage; Mathematics Tests; *Student Placement
Identifiers: Continuity and Unity in Basic Education Program; CUBE
Availability: ERIC Document Reproduction Service; 3900 Wheeler Ave., Alexandria, VA 22304 (ED211830, 467 pages)
Target Audience: Adults
Notes: Items, 80

For use as part of an adult basic education teaching/learning management system. Covers operations, fractions, percents, geometry, and money. Places adult students into a workbook series.

13553
Aston Index, Revised: A Classroom Test for Screening and Diagnosis of Language Difficulties. Newton, Margaret; Thompson, Michael 1982
Subtests: Picture Recognition; Vocabulary Scale; Goodenough Draw-A-Man Test; Copying Geometric Designs; Grapheme/Phoneme Correspondence; Schonell Reading Test; Spelling Test; Visual Discrimination; Child's Laterality; Copying Name; Free Writing; Visual Sequential Memory Picture; Auditory Sequential Memory; Sound Blending; Visual Sequential Memory Symbolic; Sound Discrimination; Graphomotor Test
Descriptors: Academic Aptitude; *Diagnostic Tests; Elementary Education; *Elementary School Students; Individual Testing; Junior High Schools; *Junior High School Students; *Language Handicaps; *Learning Disabilities; *Screening Tests; *Written Language
Availability: United Educational Services; P.O. Box 357, E. Aurora, NY 14052
Grade Level: K-8
Target Audience: 5-14

Consists of 17 subtests used to indicate the nature of a child's learning potential for literacy. Used as a screening and diagnostic tool for early recognition of educationally at-risk children. Can be used to indicate the particular learning pattern of a child and to identify specific types of learning patterns. May be used to identify specific written language difficulties, slow learners, culturally different children, neurologically damaged children, language-disordered children, specific auditory difficulties, specific visual difficulties, or specific graphic difficulties. The 17 subtests are organized on 2 levels. Level 1 is used as a screening test for children who have been in school approximately 6 months. Level 2 is for use with children over age of 7 years. Some of the tests can be group administered; others must be given individually. Total administration time for Level 1 is 45 minutes and for level 2, approximately 60 minutes. It is best to give the test over a period of several days.

13561
Profile of Occupational Interests. Dunne, Faith 1978
Descriptors: Academic Aspiration; *Attitude Measures; *Career Development; *Females; High Schools; *High School Students; Marriage; *Needs Assessment; Occupational Aspiration; Profiles; Questionnaires; *Rural Youth; School Attitudes; Sex Role; Surveys; *Vocational Interests; Womens Education; Work Attitudes
Identifiers: Options Project; POI; TIM(J)
Availability: Tests in Microfiche; Test Collection, Educational Testing Service, Princeton, NJ 08541
Grade Level: 9-12
Notes: Items, 61

A needs assessment questionnaire designed for use in a career development project for rural high school students, especially women. It covers career and educational aspirations, perceptions of school and work, attitudes about marriage and the division of labor, responsibility within the home, and suitability of various jobs for men and women. Has separate forms for males and females.

13567
Offer Self-Image Questionnaire for Adolescents, Revised. Offer, Daniel, M. D. 1977
Subtests: Impulse Control; Emotional Tone; Body Image and Self-Image; Social Relationships; Morals; Sexual Attitudes; Family Attitudes; Mastery of the External World; Vocational Goals and Educational Goals; Psychopathology; Superior Adjustment
Descriptors: *Adjustment (to Environment); *Adolescents; Anorexia Nervosa; Attitude Measures; Body Image; Cancer; Child Abuse; Coping; Delinquency; Emotional Adjustment; Empathy; Family Relationship; Gifted; Group Testing; *Interpersonal Relationship; Moral Values; Occupational Aspiration; Patients; Personality Measures; *Personality Traits; Psychopathology; Questionnaires; Rating Scales; *Self Concept; Self Concept Measures; Self Control; Sex Role; Student Educational Objectives; Teacher Attitudes; *Young Adults
Identifiers: Conscience; Ego Strength; OSIQ; Psychiatric Patients; Superego
Availability: Daniel Offer, M.D.; Director, Center for the Study of Adolescence, Michael Reese Hospital and Medical Center, 2959 S. Cottage Grove Ave., Chicago, IL 60616
Target Audience: 13-19
Notes: Time, 40 approx.; Items, 130

A personality test that can be used to measure the adjustment of teenage boys and girls. Contains 11 scored subscales. Has been used with delinquents (hospitalized and nonhospitalized), abused children, cancer patients, anorexics, normals, psychiatric patients, gifted. Profiles are included for these groups. Scale is group administered. Has separate male and female versions. Further information is in Archives of General Psychiatry; v27 p529-37 1972. Statements are rated on a 6-point scale from describing the respondent very well to not descriptive at all.

13568
Offer Teacher-Student Questionnaire. Offer, Daniel, M. D. 1977
Descriptors: *Adjustment (to Environment); *Adolescents; Anorexia Nervosa; Attitude Measures; Body Image; Cancer; Child Abuse; Coping; Delinquency; Emotional Adjustment; Empathy; Family Relationship; Gifted; Group Testing; *Interpersonal Relationship; Moral Values; Occupational Aspiration; Patients; Personality Measures; *Personality Traits; Psychopathology; Rating Scales; *Self Concept; Self Control; Sex Role; Student Educational Objectives; Teacher Attitudes; *Young Adults
Identifiers: Conscience; Ego Strength; OTSQ; Psychiatric Patients; Superego
Availability: Daniel Offer, M.D.; Director, Center for the Study of Adolescence, Michael Reese Hospital and Medical Center, 2959 S. Cottage Grove Ave., Chicago, IL 60616
Target Audience: 13-19
Notes: Items, 50

A rating scale, completed by a teacher, that describes the adjustment of teenage boys and girls. Covers impulse control, emotional tone, body and self-image, social relationships, morals, sexual attitudes, mastery of the external world, vocational and educational goals, psychopathology, and superior adjustment. Parallels the Offer Self-Image Questionnaire for Adolescents (TC013567). Other forms for completion by parent (TC013570) and therapist (TC013569) are available. The questionnaire for adolescents has been used with delinquents (hospitalized and nonhospitalized), abused children, cancer patients, anorexics, normals, gifted, and psychiatric patients.

13569
Offer Therapist Adolescent Questionnaire. Offer, Daniel, M. D. 1977
Descriptors: *Adjustment (to Environment); *Adolescents; Anorexia Nervosa; Attitude Measures; Body Image; Cancer; Child Abuse; Coping; Delinquency; Emotional Adjustment; Empathy; Family Relationship; Gifted; Group Testing; *Interpersonal Relationship; Moral Values; Occupational Aspiration; Patients; Personality Measures; *Personality Traits; Psychopathology; Rating Scales; *Self Concept; Self Control; Sex Role; Student Educational Objectives; Therapists; *Young Adults
Identifiers: Conscience; Ego Strength; OTAQ; Psychiatric Patients; Superego
Availability: Daniel Offer, M.D.; Director, Center for the Study of Adolescence, Michael Reese Hospital and Medical Center, 2959 S. Cottage Grove Ave., Chicago, IL 60616
Target Audience: 13-19
Notes: Items, 50

A rating scale, completed by a therapist, that describes the adjustment of teenage boys and girls. Separate forms are available for each sex. Covers impulse control, emotional tone, body and self-image, social relationships, morals, sexual attitudes, mastery of the external world, vocational and educational goals, psychopathology, and superior adjustment. This scale parallels the Offer Self-Image Questionnaire for Adolescents (TC013567). Other forms for completion by teacher (TC013568) and parent (TC013570) are available. The questionnaire for adolescents has been used with delinquents (hospitalized and nonhospitalized), abused children, cancer patients, anorexics, normals, gifted, and psychiatric patients.

13570
Offer Parent-Adolescent Questionnaires. Offer, Daniel, M. D. 1977
Descriptors: *Adjustment (to Environment); *Adolescents; Anorexia Nervosa; Attitude Measures; Body Image; Cancer; Child Abuse; Coping; Delinquency; Emotional Adjustment; Empathy; Family Relationship; Females; Gifted; Group Testing; *Interpersonal Relationship; Males; Moral Values; Occupational Aspiration; Parent Attitudes; Parents; Patients; Personality Measures; *Personality Traits; Psychopathology; Rating Scales; *Self Concept; Self Control; Sex Role; Student Educational Objectives; *Young Adults
Identifiers: Conscience; Ego Strength; OPAQ; Psychiatric Patients; Superego
Availability: Daniel Offer, M.D.; Director, Center for the Study of Adolescence, Michael Reese Hospital and Medical Center, 2959 S. Cottage Grove Ave., Chicago, IL 60616
Target Audience: 13-19
Notes: Items, 50

A rating scale, completed by parents, that describes the adjustment of teenage boys and girls. Separate forms are available for each sex. Covers impulse control, emotional tone, body and self-image, social relationships, morals, sexual attitudes, mastery of the external world, vocational and educational goals, psychopathology, and superior adjustment. This scale parallels the Offer Self-Image Questionnaire for Adolescents (TC013567). Other forms for completion by teacher (TC013568) and therapist (TC013569) are available. The questionnaire for adolescents has been used with delinquents (hospitalized and nonhospitalized), abused children, cancer patients, anorexics, normals, gifted, and psychiatric patients.

13572
C.U.B.E. English/Vocabulary. Monroe County Community Schools Corp., Bloomington, IN 1979
Descriptors: Achievement Tests; *Adult Basic Education; Adults; English; *Grammar; Language Skills; *Vocabulary
Identifiers: Cambridge English (Examinations); Continuity and Unity in Basic Education Program; CUBE; Mott Basic Language Skills Program
Availability: ERIC Document Reproduction Service; 3900 Wheeler Ave., Alexandria, VA 22304 (ED211832, 235 pages)
Target Audience: Adults

A part of an adult basic education teaching/learning management system. Consists of a series of tests for use in teaching English and vocabulary skills to adult basic education students. Includes several tests from other sources the "Mott Tests" and Cambridge language tests. Others cover recognition of parts of speech, tense, subject verb agreement, punctuation, capitalization, parts of a sentence, style and clarity, sentence structure, prefixes, and suffixes.

13575
C.U.B.E. Reading. Vincennes University, IN 1979
Descriptors: Achievement Tests; *Adult Basic Education; Adult Reading Programs; Adults; Reading Difficulties; *Reading Tests
Identifiers: Continuity and Unity in Basic Education Program; CUBE
Availability: ERIC Document Reproduction Service; 3900 Wheeler Ave., Alexandria, VA 22304 (ED211831, 767 pages)
Target Audience: Adults

Part of the Continuity and Unity in Basic Education Program, an adult basic education teaching/learning management system. Contains one group of inventories, answer sheets, and checklists geared to reading levels from primer to grade 6.9, and another covering grades 8-10. These measure skills commonly taught at those grade levels.

13576
Migrant Handicapped Teaching Competencies Questionnaire. Salend, Spencer J.; And Others 1984

Descriptors: Adults; Bilingual Education; *Disabilities; Elementary School Students; Elementary Secondary Education; Migrant Children; *Migrant Education; Multicultural Education; Questionnaires; Rating Scales; Secondary School Students; *Teachers; *Teaching Skills
Availability: Exceptional Children; v51 n1 p50-55 Sep 1984
Target Audience: Adults
Notes: Items, 45

A questionnaire rating the importance of specific competencies reported as necessary for success in teaching migrant handicapped students at elementary and secondary levels. It is based on a review of bilingual/multicultural education teacher training literature. Competencies relate to special education (managing behavior, producing IEPs) and to the unique needs of migrant families. Though child-change data is lacking, the competencies may be useful in designing programs for educators of this population.

13579
SEVTC Assessment Scales for Community Integration of the Severely/Profoundly Handicapped, Post-Entry Monitoring Instrument, Adolescent-Adult Form. Southeastern Virginia Training Center for the Mentally Retarded, Chesapeake, VA 1977
Subtests: Motor Development; Self-Help; Academic/Cognitive; Language; Socialization
Descriptors: Adolescents; Adults; Behavioral Objectives; Check Lists; Children; Cognitive Development; Daily Living Skills; *Deinstitutionalization (of Disabled); Language Acquisition; Motor Development; Observation; *Severe Disabilities; Social Development
Availability: ERIC Document Reproduction Service; 3900 Wheeler Ave., Alexandria, VA 22304 (ED167565, 52 pages)
Target Audience: 8-64

For use in a program to deinstitutionalize mentally retarded individuals and return them to a less restrictive environment. This instrument measures observed behavioral change and progress through a short rehabilitation period. Each subscale has 5 levels from minimally to independently functioning. Each item appears as a behavioral objective. Scoring depends on whether the behavior was self-initiated, cued, or not performed.

13580
SEVTC Assessment Scales for Community Integration of the Severely/Profoundly Handicapped, Part I, Maladaptive Behavior Inventory. Southeastern Virginia Training Center for the Mentally Retarded, Chesapeake, VA 1977
Descriptors: Adolescents; Adults; *Antisocial Behavior; *Behavior Problems; Check Lists; Children; *Deinstitutionalization (of Disabled); Observation; *Severe Disabilities; *Social Development
Availability: ERIC Document Reproduction Service; 3900 Wheeler Ave., Alexandria, VA 22304 (ED167564, 31 pages)
Target Audience: 0-64
Notes: Items, 25

For use with institutionalized mentally retarded individuals to determine suitability for participation in a program to return them to a less restrictive living environment. Observer checks off behaviors exhibited by the individual.

13581
Flowers-Costello Tests of Central Auditory Abilities. Flowers, Arthur; And Others 1970
Subtests: Low Pass Filtered Speech; Competing Messages
Descriptors: *Audiotape Cassettes; *Audiotape Recordings; Auditory Discrimination; *Auditory Perception; Auditory Stimuli; *Auditory Tests; *Distinctive Features (Language); Elementary Education; *Elementary School Students; Hearing Impairments; Screening Tests
Identifiers: CAA
Availability: Perceptual Learning Systems; P.O. Box 864, Dearborn, MI 48121
Grade Level: K-6
Notes: Items, 48

The Central Auditory Abilities (CAA) tests are to assist the educator, the psychologist, and the physician in identifying the young child whose auditory perceptual deficit will interfere or is interfering with his/her ability to acquire normal language facility and with his/her ability to learn in school. The tests are designed to aid the professional worker in early identification of potentially learning disabled young children and older children whose learning deficit is in some way associated with auditory perceptual malfunction. The CAA tests are only one approach by which the total perceptual system is evaluated. This instrument may be utilized in 2 ways: at the kindergarten level—to identify children with general CAA dysfunction and to establish probabilities for future success in reading, and 2 at grades 1 through 6 to identify children with general CAA dysfunction and to identify, among low achieving children, those whose low CAA scores suggest a specific learning disability which may be presumed to be interfering with the child's progress in learning. The CAA test battery represents evaluation of the central hearing function and the subject must have a routine audio-metric screening examination prior to the CAA. The battery consists of 2 parts—low pass filtered speech and competing messages. The low pass filtered speech measures the child's ability to resist distortion with the auditory perceptual system and the competing messages test measures the ability to select and differentiate a significant foreground stimulus from a non-relevant background stimulus. The test is recorded on a tape. After the child listens to the sentence, he/she completes it by pointing to a picture representing the word that would correctly complete the sentence. Each section has 24 items which are preceded by 9 practice items.

13582
Lawrence Psychological-Forensic Examination, 1983 Revision. Lawrence, Stephen B. 1983
Subtests: Life Clinical History; Psychological Test Results; Diagnosis; DSM III; Interview Behavior and Mental Status; Lawrence Present Mental Competency Test; Report Evaluation Form; Workman's Compensation Rating Schedule
Descriptors: Adults; Behavior; Biographies; *Clinical Diagnosis; *Criminals; Evaluation Methods; Interviews; Mental Disorders; *Predictive Measurement; *Psychological Evaluation; Records (Forms); Reports; Test Results; Workers Compensation
Identifiers: LAW(PSI); *Mental Status Examination
Availability: Associates in Forensic Psychology; Lawrence Psychological Center, 407 E. Gilbert St., Ste. 6, San Bernardino, CA 92404
Target Audience: Adults
Notes: Items, 550

Guidelines developed to assist clinicians in making psychological assessments of clients in the criminal justice system, and in determining a client's present legal, mental capacity to stand trial. Also useful in the prediction of future behavior. Administered via interview.

13584
Wide Range Achievement Test, Revised. Jastak, Sarah; Wilkinson, Gary S. 1984
Subtests: Reading; Spelling; Arithmetic
Descriptors: *Achievement Tests; Adolescents; Adults; *Arithmetic; Braille; Children; Diagnostic Tests; Large Type Materials; Older Adults; *Reading Skills; *Spelling; Visual Impairments
Identifiers: Test Batteries; WRAT(R)
Availability: Jastak Assessment Systems; 1526 Gilpin Ave., Wilmington, DE 19806
Target Audience: 5-74
Notes: Time, 30 approx.

A restandardization of the Wide Range Achievement Test available in 2 levels. Level 1 is designed for use with children from age 5 through age 11. Level 2 is designed for use for people from age 12 through age 74. The purpose of the WRAT is to measure the codes needed to learn the basic skills of reading, spelling, and arithmetic. It was intentionally designed to eliminate as much as possible the effects of comprehension. Can be used to determine if and where individual is having difficulty and to prescribe remedial/educational programs to treat the deficit. Available in large-type print or Braille for the visually impaired from American Printing House for the Blind, 1839 Frankfort Ave., Louisville, KY 40206.

13591
Prueba Illinois de Habilidades Psicolinguisticas. Isser, Aldine von; Kirk, Winifred 1980
Subtests: Auditory Reception; Visual Reception; Visual Sequential Memory; Auditory Association; Auditory Sequential Memory; Visual Association; Visual Closure; Verbal Expression; Grammatic Closure; Manual Expression; Auditory Closure; Sound Blending
Descriptors: Auditory Perception; *Children; Diagnostic Tests; Expressive Language; Individual Testing; *Preschool Children; *Psycholinguistics; Receptive Language; *Spanish; *Spanish Speaking; Visual Perception
Identifiers: Illinois Test of Psycholinguistic Abilities; ITPA; Sequential Memory
Availability: Aldine von Isser; SITPA Enterprises, 5300 Camino Escuela, Tucson, AZ 85718
Target Audience: 2-10

A Spanish adaptation of the Illinois Test of Psycholinguistic Abilities, an individually administered test of abilities and disabilities in psycholinguistic functions of children, including channels of communication, psycholinguistic processes, and levels of organization. It is not a translation of the North American English version. Norms are based on testing of 436 children ages 3, 5, 7,and 9 in Mexico, Columbia, Peru, Chile, and Puerto Rico who were monolingual only. It is suggested that the test should be used only for research when used with bilingual children.

13592
Minnesota Multiphasic Personality Inventory: Group Form, Minnesota Report. Hathaway, Starke R.; McKinley, J. C. 1982
Subtests: Cannot Say Score; Lie; Infrequency; Defensiveness; Dissimulation Index; Hypochondriasis; Depression; Hysteria; Psychopathic Deviate; Masculinity-Feminity; Paranoia; Psychasthenia; Schizophrenia; Mania; Social Introversion-Extraversion
Descriptors: Adolescents; Adults; *Correctional Institutions; *Medical Services; *Mental Health Programs; *Personality Assessment; *Personality Measures; Personality Traits
Identifiers: MMPI
Availability: NCS Interpretive Scoring Systems; P.O. Box 1416, Minneapolis, MN 55440
Target Audience: 17-64
Notes: Items, 566

A report derived from use of the MMPI intended to assess medical, mental health, and correctional populations.

13602
Psychological Screening Inventory, Spanish Form. Lanyon, Richard I. 1968
Descriptors: *Adolescents; Adults; *Mental Health; Psychological Evaluation; Questionnaires; *Screening Tests; Self Evaluation (Individuals); Spanish; *Spanish Speaking
Identifiers: PSI
Availability: Research Psychologists Press; P.O. Box 984, 1110 Military St., Port Huron, MI 48061-0984
Target Audience: 13-64
Notes: Time, 15 approx.; Items, 130

The Psychological Screening Inventory (PSI) is a mental health screening device used to identify people who might benefit from more extensive examination and professional attention. It can be given individually or in a group setting. It is a true or false test, and there is both an English and Spanish test. It is appropriate for use with adults and adolescents in community clinics, hospitals, high school and college counseling offices, referral agencies, medical facilities, courts, reformatories, and similar settings. It can be used to decide whether to refer people to a formal mental health agency, retain them for counseling, or to select another alternative.

13607
The Waksman Social Skills Rating Scale. 1983
Subtests: Aggressive; Passive
Descriptors: *Aggression; *Antisocial Behavior; Classroom Observation Techniques; *Elementary School Students; Elementary Secondary Education; Interpersonal Competence; *Secondary School Students
Identifiers: *Passivity; WSSRS
Availability: Asiep Education Co.; 3216 N.E. 26th St., Portland, OR 97212
Grade Level: K-12
Notes: Items, 21

Developed to assist psychologists, educators, and other clinicians to identify specific and clinically important social skills deficits in children and adolescents. WSSRS should be completed by classroom teachers, counselors, or childcare workers who have daily contact with the subject. Ratings should be based on observation or first-hand knowledge.

13609
Developmental Inventory of Learned Skills: Detailed Version. Early Recognition Intervention Newtork, Dedham, MA 1981
Descriptors: Check Lists; *Child Development; *Criterion Referenced Tests; Expressive Language; Individual Needs; *Language Skills; *Perceptual Motor Coordination; Receptive Language; Special Education; *Young Children
Identifiers: DILS; ERIN
Availability: Early Recognition Intervention Network; 376 Bridge St., Dedham, MA 02026
Target Audience: 0-8

Criterion-referenced checklists of skills of children from birth to 8 years old. Created as part of the assessment component of the ERIN method of assessing young children with special needs in regular and special education settings. Assessment of visual-perceptual-motor skills includes visual attention, form discrimination, form sequences, understanding sequence/position, visual memory and association, planning with a tool, motor control of arms/hands/fingers, and formulating visual-motor ideas. Assessment of the language component includes auditory attention, sound discrimination, word sentence sequences, language memory and association, planning sentence construction, motor control of speech, and formulating language ideas. Should be used by highly trained special education teachers or teacher-therapist team.

13621
Michigan Alcoholism Screening Test, Revised. Selzer, Melvin L. 1980

Descriptors: Adults; *Alcoholism; Questionnaires; *Screening Tests
Identifiers: MAST
Availability: American Journal of Psychiatry, v129 n3 p342-45 Sept 1972
Target Audience: Adults
Notes: Items, 24

A screening test used to detect alcoholism in individuals. An earlier version of MAST can be found in The American Journal of Psychiatry; v129 n3 p342-45 Sep 1972.

13624
Letter Comparison Test. Cunningham, Walter R. 1975
Descriptors: *Cognitive Measurement; *Older Adults; *Perception Tests
Identifiers: *Perceptual Speed
Availability: Walter C. Cunningham; Psychology Dept., University of Florida, Gainesville, FL 32611
Target Audience: 60-99
Notes: Time, 3

Used in a study to assess correlations between age and factor scores of abilities drawn from the domains of intellectual functioning and information processing tasks. The letter comparison test assessed perceptual speed.

13629
Global Assessment Scale. Spitzer, Robert L.; And Others 1978
Descriptors: Adults; *Emotional Disturbances; *Mental Health; *Patients; Rating Scales
Identifiers: GAS
Availability: New York State Psychiatric Institute; Research Assessment and Training Unit, 722 W. 168 St., Rm. 341, New York, NY 10032
Target Audience: Adults
Notes: Items, 10

Used to evaluate the overall functioning of a patient or subject during a specified time period in terms of psychological well-being or sickness. Time period assessed is generally one week prior to evaluation. For special studies, a longer period of assessment may be preferable. Scale covers entire range of severity and can be used in any situation or study where an overall evaluation of the severity of the illness or degree of health is needed.

13630
Family History—Research Diagnostic Criteria, Third Edition. Endicott, Jean; And Others 1978
Descriptors: Adolescents; Adults; Clinical Diagnosis; *Emotional Disturbances; Etiology; *Evaluation Criteria; *Medical Case Histories; *Medical Evaluation; Older Adults; Psychiatric Services
Identifiers: FHRDC
Availability: New York State Psychiatric Institute; Research Assessment and Training Unit, 722 W. 168 St., Rm. 341, New York, NY 10032
Target Audience: 13-75

Developed to enable research investigators to use a consistent set of criteria to diagnose psychiatric illness in relatives of subjects when it is not possible to examine relatives directly. The instrument describes specific operational criteria for determining a diagnosis on the basis of information obtained by the family history method.

13632
Wichita Auditory Fusion Test. McCroskey, Robert L. 1984
Descriptors: Adolescents; Adults; *Auditory Tests; Children; Individualized Education Programs; Language Handicaps; Magnetic Tape Cassettes; Older Adults
Identifiers: *Auditory Timing; WAFT
Availability: Modern Education Corporation; P.O. Box 721, Tulsa, OK 74101
Target Audience: 3-80

Used to assess auditory timing through determining an Auditory Fusion Threshold to aid in the diagnosis and treatment of verbally disabled persons. Stimuli on cassette tapes consist of tone pairs separated by brief silent intervals ranging from 0 to 300 milliseconds between each tone. Subjects must be able to distinguish between the concepts one and 2 so that they can indicate whether they have heard one or 2 sounds. Test provides academic specialists, speech and language pathologists, and audiologists with a means of determining subjects' auditory age and underlying neural transmission differences which may impede educational progress. Test has implications for use in the areas of remedial articulation, learning disabilities, remedial reading, dialect remediation, mental retardation, assessment of elderly persons, and academic achievement.

13644
Eating Disorder Inventory. Garner, David M.; And Others 1983
Subtests: Drive for Thinness; Bulimia; Body Dissatisfaction; Ineffectiveness; Perfectionism; Interpersonal Distrust; Interoceptive Awareness; Maturity Fears
Descriptors: *Adolescents; *Anorexia Nervosa; Body Weight; Computer Assisted Testing; *Eating Habits; Emotional Disturbances; Forced Choice Technique; Microcomputers; Rating Scales; *Young Adults; *Bulimia
Identifiers: EDI; Self Report Measures
Availability: Psychological Assessment Resources; P.O. Box 998, Odessa, FL 33556
Target Audience: 14-25
Notes: Items, 64

Designed to assess a broad range of psychological and behavorial traits common in anorexia nervosa and bulimia. Consists of 8 subscales which can be used to measure specific cognitive and behavioral dimensions which may differentiate among subgroups of individuals with eating disorders. Is useful as a screening tool, outcome measure, as an aid in typological research or as an aid in clinical judgments with eating disorder patients. It is a self-report instrument. May also be computer-administered, using Apple II or IIe or IBM/PC.

13645
Comprehensive Drinker Profile. Marlatt, G. Alan; Miller, William R. 1984
Descriptors: Adults; *Alcoholism; Clinical Diagnosis; Interviews
Identifiers: CDP
Availability: Psychological Assessment Resources; P.O. Box 998, Odessa, FL 33556
Target Audience: 18-64
Notes: Time, 120 approx.

Intended to be administered as a structured clinical interview with both male and female clients entering various treatment programs for alcoholism in either inpatient or outpatient settings. Provides comprehensive history and status of client concerning his or her use or abuse of alcohol. Can also be used as an intake instrument for clinics and research programs doing pretreatment and follow-up evaluations.

13647
Vineland Adaptive Behavior Scales: Interview Edition, Survey Form. Sparrow, Sara S.; And Others 1984
Subtests: Communication; Daily Living Skills; Socialization; Motor Skills
Descriptors: *Adjustment (to Environment); Adolescents; Adults; Children; *Communication Skills; *Daily Living Skills; Expressive Language; *Interviews; Mental Retardation; *Psychomotor Skills; Receptive Language; *Socialization; Verbal Ability
Identifiers: Vineland Social Maturity Scale
Availability: American Guidance Service; Publishers' Bldg., Circle Pines, MN 55014
Target Audience: 0-64
Notes: Time, 60 approx.; Items, 297

Provides a general assessment of adaptive behavior and is useful for determining areas of strength or weakness in individuals from birth through 18 years of age and in low-functioning adults. The scales are administered by a trained interviewer to the parent or caregiver of the subject being assessed. A maladaptive behavior domain is also included as an optional section. This is a revision of the Vineland Social Maturity Scale and is applicable to both handicapped and nonhandicapped individuals.

13648
Vineland Adaptive Behavior Scales: Interview Edition, Survey Form, Spanish. Sparrow, Sara S.; And Others 1984
Subtests: Communication; Daily Living Skills; Socialization; Motor Skills
Descriptors: *Adjustment (to Environment); Adolescents; Adults; Children; *Communication Skills; *Daily Living Skills; Expressive Language; *Interviews; Mental Retardation; *Psychomotor Skills; Receptive Language; *Socialization; *Spanish; *Spanish Speaking; Verbal Ability
Identifiers: Vineland Social Maturity Scale
Availability: American Guidance Service; Publishers' Bldg., Circle Pines, MN 55014
Target Audience: 0-64
Notes: Time, 60 approx.; Items, 297

Provides a general assessment of adaptive behavior and is useful for determining areas of strength or weakness in individuals from birth through 18 years of age and in low-functioning adults. The scales are administered by a trained interviewer to the parent or caregiver of the subject being assessed. A maladaptive behavior domain is also included as an optional section. This is a revision of the Vineland Social Maturity Scale and is applicable to both handicapped and nonhandicapped individuals.

13649
Vineland Adaptive Behavior Scales: Interview Edition, Expanded Form. Sparrow, Sara S.; And Others 1984
Subtests: Communication; Daily Living Skills; Socialization; Motor Skills
Descriptors: *Adjustment (to Environment); Adolescents; Adults; Children; *Communication Skills; *Daily Living Skills; Expressive Language; *Interviews; Mental Retardation; *Psychomotor Skills; Receptive Language; *Socialization; Verbal Ability
Identifiers: Vineland Social Maturity Scale
Availability: American Guidance Service; Publishers' Bldg., Circle Pines, MN 55014
Target Audience: 0-64
Notes: Time, 90 approx.; Items, 577

This is a revision of the Vineland Social Maturity Scale and is used to assess personal and social sufficiency of people from birth to adulthood. The scales are applicable to both handicapped and nonhandicapped individuals. This form offers a more comprehensive assessment of adaptive behavior than the interview edition, survey form and includes 297 items from the survey form. It is administered in a semistructured interview with a parent or caregiver of an individual from birth through 18 years of age or of a low functioning adult. A maladaptive behavior domain is included in this form as an optional section.

13650
Parent/Family Involvement Index. Cone, John D.; And Others 1984
Descriptors: Adults; *Disabilities; *Family Involvement; *Family School Relationship; Parent Participation; *Parent School Relationship; *Parent Teacher Cooperation; Questionnaires
Identifiers: PFII
Availability: University Affiliated Center; W. Virginia University, 311 Oglebay Hall, Morgantown, WV 26506
Target Audience: 18-64
Notes: Items, 63

The purpose of this index is to assess the degree to which parents participate in the education of their handicapped child. By using it, educators can discover the type of involvement parents have in their specific program and whether parents are involved as much as they would like for them to be. It is designed to be completed by a teacher and/or aide after sufficient contact with the parent(s) to be able to judge such involvement, at least 6 months. There are 4 answers to the questions: yes, no, not applicable, and don't know. The areas covered are (1) contact with teacher, (2) participation in special education process, (3) transportation, (4) observations at school, (5) educational activities at home, (6) attending parent education/consultation meetings, (7) classroom volunteering, (8) parent-parent contact and support, (9) involvement with administration, (10) involvement in fund-raising activities, (11) involvement in advocacy groups, (12) disseminating information, and (13) overall.

13657
Computerized Assessment of Intelligibility of Dysarthric Speech. Yorkston, Kathryn M.; And Others
Descriptors: Adolescents; Adults; Articulation (Speech); *Computer Assisted Testing; Microcomputers; *Speech; Speech and Hearing Clinics; *Speech Handicaps; *Speech Tests
Identifiers: Apple II; Apple IIe; *Dysarthria
Availability: Pro-Ed. Inc.; 5341 Industrial Oaks Blvd., Austin, TX 78735
Target Audience: 13-65

A measure of the intelligibility of speech of those with faulty articulation resulting from lesions or defects in the central nervous system. Software disks are available for use with Apple II and Apple IIe computers. The software selects 50 words and 20 sentences from the stimuli contained in the program. Clients respond to tasks presented at timed intervals. Responses are recorded on a cassette tape and judged by a third person. The computer stores the data and provides a score sheet listing percentage of correct responses, rate of intelligible words per minute, and an efficiency ratio that can be used to rank dysarthric speakers, monitor changing performance, and contrast a dysarthric speaker to a normal speaker.

13660
Community Talent Miner. Jenkins, Reva C.W.; Stewart, Emily D. 1977
Descriptors: *Academically Gifted; *Adults; *Community Resources; Questionnaires; *Surveys
Availability: Creative Learning Press; P.O. Box 320, Mansfield Center, CT 06250
Target Audience: 18-64
Notes: Items, 30

This survey was designed to identify community resources for an intellectually gifted or artistically talented program. The purpose was to find people in the community who could provide these students with challenging experiences and stimulating personal interactions, to provide them with more opportunities for community involvement, a wide exposure to people and ideas, and a chance for some in-depth explorations. The questions dealt with hobbies, professional activities, experiences, and college major.

13661
Strength-a-Lyzer. Renzulli, Joseph S.; Smith, Linda H. 1978
Descriptors: Academically Gifted; *Elementary School Students; Elementary Secondary Education; Guides; *Individualized Education Programs; *Secondary School Students; Talent
Identifiers: IEP
Availability: Creative Learning Press; P.O. Box 320, Mansfield Center, CT 06250
Grade Level: 3-12
Notes: Items, 42

The Strength-a-Lyzer is one of 3 items in the Individualized Educational Programing (IEP) Guide which is designed to assist teachers in personalizing educational experiences for gifted and talented students. The Strength-a-Lyzer gives a comprehensive picture of both the cognitive and affective dimensions of each child. Information relating to general intelligence, aptitude, and creativity is combined with interest and learning style. The instrument is to help the teacher with individual and group activities that capitalize on the strengths of each child.

13668
Temple University Short Syntax Inventory. Gerber, Adele; Goehl, Henry 1984
Descriptors: Adolescents; Children; *Delayed Speech; Emotional Disturbances; Error Analysis (Language); *Expressive Language; *Form Classes (Languages); Individualized Education Programs; Individual Testing; *Language Acquisition; *Language Handicaps; Mental Retardation; *Morphemes; Sentence Structure; *Syntax; *Visual Measures; *Young Children
Identifiers: IEP; IPP; TUSSI
Availability: Edmark Corporation; P.O. Box 3903, Bellevue, WA 98009-9990
Target Audience: 3-18
Notes: Time, 15 approx.; Items, 32

The Temple University Short Syntax Inventory (TUSSI) is designed as a clinical tool for obtaining descriptive information about selected aspects of delayed language that will contribute to the establishment of goals for remedial training. Although the TUSSI is primarily designed to serve as a descriptive instrument, its use will provide certain data relevant to decisions about normative performance that can be applied to the writing of individual educational programs (IEP) and individual preschool programs (IPP). The instrument consists of 4 multipicture boards, each with 8 pictures, 32 picture cards that match the pictures on the large multipicture boards, test form, and scoring sheet. A tape recorder is recommended. It is a picture lotto game. It is essential that administration procedures foster and maintain a game-playing atmosphere to ensure willing participation and spontaneity of response. The use of the tape recorder reduces the need for extensive written recording of responses which tend to disrupt the play of the game. The game is designed to assess and describe children's acquisition of early patterns of syntax and morphology in a way that is fun. Its target populations are normal preschool children, mentally retarded children and adolescents, and learning disabled and emotionally disturbed children.

13669
Normative Adaptive Behavior Checklist. Adams, Gary L. 1984
Descriptors: Adaptive Behavior (of Disabled); *Adjustment (to Environment); Adolescents; Check Lists; Children; *Daily Living Skills; Developmental Tasks; Mental Retardation; Young Adults
Identifiers: NABC
Availability: The Psychological Corporation; 555 Academic Ct., San Antonio, TX 78204-0952
Target Audience: 0-21
Notes: Time, 20 approx.; Items, 120

The Normative Adaptive Behavior Checklist (NABC) was designed to fill the need for a valid, descriptive test of adaptive behavior that could be administered in a relatively short amount of time. The intent was to design an instrument from which a test administrator could examine how well a child compares to peers of his/her age (birth to 21 years) in performing skills needed for independent living.

13670
Comprehensive Test of Adaptive Behavior. Adams, Gary L. 1984
Subtests: Self-Help Skills; Home Living Skills; Independent Living Skills; Social Skills; Sensory and Motor Skills; Language and Academic Skills
Descriptors: Academic Achievement; *Adaptive Behavior (of Disabled); Adolescents; Adults; Check Lists; Children; *Daily Living Skills; *Individualized Education Programs; Interpersonal Competence; *Mental Retardation; Performance Tests; Psychomotor Skills; *Self Care Skills; *Speech Communication
Identifiers: CTAB; IEP
Availability: The Psychological Corporation; 555 Academic Ct., San Antonio, TX 78204-0952

Target Audience: 0-64

The Comprehensive Test of Adaptive Behavior was designed to be both a descriptive and prescriptive test. It assesses 6 skill categories and samples 497 male behaviors and 527 female behaviors. It is used for prescribing instructional objectives and sequences by teachers of retarded students. The purpose of the CTAB is to evaluate how well a retarded student is functioning independently in the environment. It provides information about the student's adaptive behavior level in comparison to handicapped and nonhandicapped peers. The CTAB was designed for accountability and fits well into the Individualized Education Plan (IEP) process.

13671
VITAS: Vocational Interest, Temperament and Aptitude System. Vocational Research Institute, Philadelphia, PA
Descriptors: Adolescents; *Aptitude Tests; *Disadvantaged Youth; *Mild Mental Retardation; Performance Tests; Personality Traits; *Vocational Aptitude; *Vocational Evaluation; Vocational Interests; *Work Sample Tests; Young Adults
Identifiers: VITAS
Availability: Vocational Research Institute; Jewish Employment and Vocational Service, 2100 Arch St., 6th Floor, Philadelphia, PA 19103
Target Audience: 18-30

The Vocational Interest, Temperament and Aptitude System (VITAS) includes 22 different work samples and was developed for use with disadvantaged and educable mentally retarded persons. It requires less than 6th grade level reading ability. In each of the work samples, the individual performs a task which is identical or similar to a job experience. Performance and reaction to work samples form the basis of vocational recommendations. VITAS assesses aptitudes, vocational interests, and work-related temperaments. The work samples are nuts, bolts, and washers assembly; packing matchbooks; tile sorting and weighing; collating material samples; verifying numbers; pressing linens; budget book assembly; nail and screw sorting (2 parts); pipe assembly; filing by letters; lock assembly; circuit board inspection; calculating; message taking; bank teller; proofreading; payroll computation; census interviewing; spot welding; laboratory assistant; and drafting. It takes about 2 1/2 days to administer VITAS.

13672
VIEWS: Vocational Information and Evaluation Work Samples. Vocational Research Institute, Philadelphia, PA
Descriptors: Adolescents; Adults; *Aptitude Tests; Individualized Education Programs; *Mild Mental Retardation; *Moderate Mental Retardation; Performance Tests; Personality Traits; *Prevocational Education; *Severe Mental Retardation; *Vocational Aptitude; Vocational Evaluation; Vocational Interests; *Work Sample Tests
Identifiers: IEP; Public Law 94 142; VIEWS
Availability: Vocational Research Institute; Jewish Employment and Vocational Service, 2100 Arch St., 6th Floor, Philadelphia, PA 19103
Target Audience: 12-64

The Vocationally Information and Evaluation Work Samples (VIEWS) instrument is a vocational assessment for mentally retarded individuals. It is a hands-on assessment system which includes 16 work samples to be used in a simulated work environment. VIEWS requires no reading ability and, because it was developed specifically for the mentally retarded, allows for repeated instruction. Each work sample incorporates a period of training prior to the measurement of time and quality of performance. This instrument meets prevocational and vocational requirements for Individualized Education Programs (IEPs); is suitable for mildly, moderately, and severely retarded individuals; measures rate of learning, quality of work, and productivity; and provides industrial time standards (MODAPTS) for each work sample. VIEWS assesses aptitudes, vocational interests, and work-related behaviors. During the 4 to 5 day period of evaluation, the subjects perform a variety of tasks including sorting, cutting, collating, assembling, weighing, typing, measuring, using hand tools, tending a drill press, and electric machine feeding.

13674
J.E.V.S. Work Samples. Vocational Research Institute, Philadelphia, PA
Descriptors: Adults; *Aptitude Tests; *Career Guidance; Interest Inventories; *Interpersonal Competence; Job Skills; Occupational Tests; Physical Disabilities; Vocational Aptitude; *Vocational Evaluation; *Vocational Interests; Vocational Rehabilitation; *Work Sample Tests
Availability: Vocational Research Institute; Jewish Employment and Vocational Service, 2100 Arch St., 6th Floor, Philadelphia, PA 19103
Target Audience: 18-64

J.E.V.S. Work Samples are hands-on activities to assess aptitudes, vocational interests, and work-related behaviors. It is a complete vocational evaluation program which

includes hardware for 28 work samples, recording, report, and evaluation forms, consultation, and training for users. The work samples involve tasks, materials and tools which are identical or similar to those in actual jobs and are administered in a work-like environment over 5-7 days. Reading is necessary only in work samples related to occupational areas where reading is required. This instrument can be used with disadvantaged or unsuccessful students who have no idea what they like or want to do, students with emotional problems who are failing to adjust in school, a physically injured person whose current physical capabilities must be assessed, an emotionally disabled person whose behavior on the job needs analysis, a psychiatric patient reentering the community after hospitalization, and persons with little or no work history. The evaluation report includes information on discriminatory abilities, manipulative skills, communication, behavior in interpersonal situations, worker characteristics, learning and comprehension, physical appearance, and interests. Recommendations are made for apppropriate areas of employment and/or training and supportive services that may be needed. The work samples are nut, bolt, and washer assembly; rubber stamping; washer threading; budget book assembly; sign making; tile sorting; nut packing; collating leather samples; grommet assembly; union assembly; belt assembly; ladder assembly; metal square fabrication; hardware assembly; telephone assembly; lock assembly; filing by numbers; proofreading; filing by letters; nail and screw sorting; adding machine; payroll computation; computing postage; resistor reading; pipe assembly; blouse making; vest making; and condensing principle.

13675
Bloomer Learning Test. Bloomer, Richard H. 1978
Subtests: Activity; Visual Short Term Memory; Auditory Short Term Memory; Visual Apprehension Span; Serial Learning; Recall and Relearning; Free Association; Paired Associate Learning; Concept Recognition and Concept Production; Problem Solving
Descriptors: *Elementary School Students; Elementary Secondary Education; *Learning Modalities; Learning Problems; *Screening Tests; *Secondary School Students; Teaching Methods
Identifiers: BLT
Availability: Dr. Richard Bloomer; Decker Hill Rd., Willimantic, CT 06226
Grade Level: 1-12

Developed to provide an instrument which would give a profile indicating strengths and weaknesses in a child's learning process. Profile could be used as a guide to appropriate teaching strategies. BLT should be used as a starting point in planning instructional strategies. Standardization population included reading or learning disabled, emotionally disturbed, and gifted, as well as nonhandicapped subjects.

13676
The London Procedure, Revised Edition. Weissel, Laura Peltz 1977
Descriptors: *Adult Basic Education; Adults; Auditory Discrimination; Auditory Perception; Decoding (Reading); *Diagnostic Tests; *Reading Processes; *Screening Tests; Visual Acuity; *Visual Perception
Availability: Ohio State University; Instructional Materials Center, 154 W. 12th Ave., Columbus, OH 43210
Target Audience: Adults
Notes: Time, 45 approx.

Designed to provide a screening of visual and auditory functions and a diagnosis of visual perception, auditory perception, and reading as an encoding and decoding process for adult basic education students functioning below the 8th-grade level. The procedure is divided into 15 short tests organized into 5 major areas: visual functions, auditory functions, visual perception, auditory perception, and reading encoding and decoding.

13684
Hester Evaluation System. Human Services Data Center, Chicago, IL
Descriptors: Adults; *Aptitude Tests; Culture Fair Tests; Deafness; Disabilities; Gifted; Illiteracy; Mental Retardation; Non English Speaking; Nonverbal Tests; *Occupational Tests; Perceptual Motor Coordination; *Physical Disabilities; Psychomotor Skills; *Vocational Aptitude
Identifiers: Finger Dexterity; HES; Manual Dexterity; Mechanical Aptitude; Perceptual Motor Skills; Verbal Aptitude
Availability: Lafayette Instrument Co., Inc.; P.O. Box 5729, Sagamore Pwy., Lafayette, IN 47903
Target Audience: Adults

A series of 26 tests measuring factor-pure abilities actually used in a wide range of occupations. Relates to the Dictionary of Occupational Titles. Raw scores can be compared to profiles for 1500 jobs. This test is useful for aptitude testing for gifted, nonhandicapped, physically handicapped, mentally handicapped, deaf, illiterate, and non-English-speaking people.

13688
Goldberg Anorectic Attitude Scale. Goldberg, Solomon C. 1980
Descriptors: Adolescents; Adults; *Anorexia Nervosa; *Attitude Measures; Body Weight; Eating Habits; *Emotional Disturbances; *Preadolescents; *Rating Scales; *Self Evaluation (Individuals)
Identifiers: GAAS
Availability: Journal of Psychiatric Research; v15 p239-51, 1980
Target Audience: 10-30
Notes: Items, 63

This scale is part of a study designed to evaluate the effectiveness of drug treatment and of behavior modification on anorexia nervosa patients. The items were constructed from a number of attitude dimensions hypothesized on the basis of clinical experience. The scale was given to female anorexia nervosa patients in 3 hospitals: University of Iowa, University of Minnesota, and the Illinois State Psychiatric Institute. The factors covered are staff, fear of fat, parents, denial, hunger, hypothermia, bloated, self-care, effort for achievement, food sickens me, my problems—mental or physical, helpful authority, physical problems, hobby cooking, and heterosexual disinterest. The responses were on a 4-point scale in which the patient indicated the extent to which the statement reflected her feelings. The patients had to be between 10 and 40 years of age and had to have had the onset of their illness between 10 and 30 years.

13696
The Therapeutic Evaluation and Treatment Center Intake and Evaluation Forms. Southeast Mental Health and Retardation Center, Fargo, ND
Descriptors: *Clinics; *Disabilities; Family Characteristics; Imitation; Measures (Individuals); Psychomotor Skills; *Records (Forms); Verbal Stimuli; Young Children
Identifiers: Outpatient Care
Availability: Red River Human Services Foundation; Publications Division, 15 Broadway, Ste. 510, Fargo, ND 58126
Target Audience: 0-6

A series of forms and scales used for gathering information on handicapped children prior to out-patient treatment. Included are mentally retarded, emotionally or behaviorally disordered, and developmentally delayed persons. Forms cover staff training records, request for services, family information form, child information form, treatment plans. Scales cover motor skills and verbal imitation.

13697
Rosewell-Chall Diagnostic Reading Test of Word Analysis Skills (Revised and Extended). Rosewell, Florence G.; Chall, Jeanne S. 1978
Subtests: Words; Decoding Test; Letter Names; Encoding
Descriptors: Adults; Consonants; *Decoding (Reading); *Diagnostic Tests; Elementary School Students; Elementary Secondary Education; Encoding (Psychology); *Reading Diagnosis; *Reading Difficulties; Reading Skills; Secondary School Students; Word Recognition
Availability: Essay Press; P.O. Box 2323, La Jolla, CA 92038
Grade Level: 1-12
Notes: Time, 10 min.

The Rosewell-Chall Diagnostic Reading Test (Revised and Extended) is designed to evaluate the basic word analysis (decoding) and word recognition skills of children and adults reading at approximately first to 4th grade levels. It may also be used for those reading at higher levels where difficulty in decoding and basic word recognition are suspected. The areas covered by the test are high frequency words, consonant sounds, consonant blends, short vowel sounds (in CVC words), short and long vowel sounds (in isolation), rule of silent e, vowel digraphs, diphthongs and vowels controlled by r, syllabication (and compound words), naming capital letters, naming lower case letters, encoding single consonants, and encoding regular (CVC) words.

13702
La Prueba Riverside de Realizacion en Espanol. Cote, Nancy S. and Others 1984
Subtests: Reading Comprehension; Vocabulary; Study Skills; Grammar; Punctuation; Capitalization; Spelling; Math Computation; Math Problem Solving; Social Studies; Science
Descriptors: *Achievement Tests; Bilingual Students; Capitalization (Alphabetic); Elementary Secondary Education; Grammar; Language Skills; Literacy; Mathematics; Punctuation; Mathematics Tests; Reading; Reading Comprehension; Sciences; Social Studies; *Spanish; Spanish Speaking; Spelling; Study Skills; Vocabulary
Identifiers: 3 Rs Test; Test Batteries
Availability: Riverside Publishing Co.; 8420 Bryn Mawr Ave., Chicago, IL 60631
Grade Level: K-9
Notes: Time, 100 approx.

This Spanish-language edition of the 3 R's Test (TC011502-TC011505) is designed to assess the achievement of students whose primary language is Spanish and to determine the degree to which students are literate in Spanish. It is recommended that the school district select the level of the test that will be administered in each grade, according to the students' level of Spanish literacy. Results are reported in terms of local norms based on the use of a specific test level in a particular grade. Test times vary from 80 to 165 minutes by grade level.

13703
Denman Neuropsychology Memory Scale. Denman, Sidney B. 1984
Subtests: Presentation and Immediate Recall of a Story; Paired Associate Learning and Immediate Recall; Copying a Complex Figure; Immediate Recall of the Complex Figure; Memory for Digits; Memory for Musical Tones and Memories; Remotely Stored Verbal Information; Memory for Human Faces; Remotely Stored Non-Verbal Information; Delayed Recall of Complex Figures; Delayed Recall of Paired Associates; Delayed Recall of the Story
Descriptors: Adolescents; Adults; Children; *Individual Testing; *Long Term Memory; Older Adults; Psychological Evaluation; Psychological Testing; *Recall (Psychology); *Short Term Memory
Availability: Sidney B. Denman; Clinical Neuropsychology, 1040 Fort Sumter Dr., Charleston, SC 29412
Target Audience: 10-69
Notes: Time, 60 approx.

Designed for use in clinical situations where there is a need of quantitative assessment of immediate recall, short-term memory, and long-term memory in verbal and non-verbal areas. Scale has the capacity to assess a variey of memory functions, and to help in differentiating normal subjects from those with memory dysfunction. It should also be able to help in differentiating memory dysfunction from psychiatric depression. Examiners should be trained in the use of individually administered psychological tests and should follow the specific directions in the manual.

13704
The Portland Problem Behavior Checklist, Revised. Waksman, Steven A. 1984
Descriptors: *Adjustment (to Environment); *Behavior Problems; Check Lists; Elementary Education; Elementary School Students; Individualized Education Programs; Junior High Schools; Junior High School Students; Learning Disabilities; Learning Problems; *Problem Children
Identifiers: IEP; PPBC
Availability: ASIEP Education Co.; 3216 N.E. 27th, Portland, OR 97212
Grade Level: K-8
Notes: Items, 29

The purpose of the Portland Problem Behavior Checklist (PPBC) is to provide specific information to specialists and support personnel who may need to further evaluate or prescribe services to children. It is designed to identify and rate the specific problems which classroom teachers perceive to warrant professional intervention, services. The PPBC may also be used to assist in diagnostic or classification decisions. It is intended to be used as a screening instrument or as a supplement in a more comprehensive evaluation process. The identified problem behaviors may be used to design specific intervention programs for certified special education students or noncertified students with less severe problems. The targeted problem behaviors could be included into Individual Education Programs (IEP). The PPBC is a quick, useful aid for clinical referrals, personality assessment, behavioral intervention and special education evaluation. The PPBC can be used for children from K-6, and there are 2 forms—one for males and another for females.

13705
Martinez Assessment of the Basic Skills: Criterion-Referenced Diagnostic Testing of Basic Skills. Martinez, David 1983
Subtests: Reading; Primary Language Concepts; Arithmetic; Spelling; Counting and Numerals; Time Telling
Descriptors: Arithmetic; *Basic Skills; Computation; *Criterion Referenced Tests; *Diagnostic Tests; Education; *Educationally Disadvantaged; *Elementary School Students; Elementary Secondary Education; Fractions; *Handicap Identification; Individualized Education Programs; *Junior High School Students; Language; *Mild Disabilities; Reading; *Spanish Speaking; Spelling; Time
Identifiers: IEP; PL 94 142
Availability: ASIEP Education Co.; 3216 N.E. 27th, Portland, OR 97212
Grade Level: K-9
Notes: Time, 180 approx.

The 6 diagnostic criterion areas in this assessment instrument are appropriate for mildly handicapped students in the regular classroom as well as those served in resource and self-contained settings. Mildly handicapped generally refers to students identified under PL 94-142 and other noncategorical underachievers who may profit from a criterion-referenced skill assessment. No attempt should be made to assign grade level achievement to the 6 areas. There is a list of behavioral objectives with each area which may be used in the development of individual education programs (IEPs). A Spanish version is available for 4 of the tests: Arithmetic; Counting and Numerals; Time Telling and Primary Language Concepts.

13706
Adolescents into the Mainstream: Community and Student Assessment Manual. Arick, Joel; And Others 1983
Subtests: Phase I—Finding Community Placements; Phase II—Community and Peer Model Assessment
Descriptors: *Adolescents; *Autism; Behavior Rating Scales; Community Involvement; Community Role; *Community Surveys; Individualized Education Programs; Job Placement; Mainstreaming; *Normalization (Handicapped); *Severe Disabilities; Student Evaluation; Surveys; Task Analysis
Identifiers: AIM; CCABOI; IEP
Availability: ASIEP Education Co.; 3216 N.E. 27th, Portland, OR 97212
Target Audience: 18-64

Adolescents Into the Mainstream (AIM) is a curriculum that presents procedures for determining what to teach the autistic and severely handicapped adolescent, how to teach skills that generalize across community settings, how to change the tolerances of community members. AIM also provides procedures for working with community members beginning the first day of the school year. The structured community procedures ensure positive community interactions. There are 2 sections to the instrument. The first phase provides procedures to gather information about community sites, conduct community and student assessments, and to program the information. Phase 2 activities include prioritizing of students for community placement; selecting the most appropriate potential residence and job placement for each student; determining placement site criterion levels for success; developing daily activity sequences; prioritizing survival skills for programming; task analysis of survival skills; probing the student's skills and competencies in the community; and establishing IPE recommendations. The surveys were developed to determine the attitude and tolerances of the staff of school facilities for specific maladaptive behaviors and the management procedures in facilities for mentally handicapped persons, and to get a better understanding from companies of what is expected for autistic and severely handicapped individuals if they were to work in the community after their schooling ends. Another instrument which can be used with the AIM is the Classroom/Community Adaptive Behavior Observation Instrument (C/CABOI). An observer uses a data sheet and observes the individual for 15 continuous seconds. It helps to evaluate a student's adaptive and maladaptive behavior in contrast to the same behaviors exhibited by a peer model.

13707
La Marcacion del Comportamiento Autismo. Krug, David A.; And Others 1978
Descriptors: Adolescents; Adults; *Autism; *Behavior Rating Scales; *Check Lists; Children; Individualized Education Programs; *Spanish
Identifiers: ABC; Autism Behavior Checklist
Availability: ASIEP Education Co.; 3216 N.E. 27th, Portland, OR 97212
Target Audience: 1-64
Notes: Time, 20 approx.; Items, 57

One of 5 subtests that comprise the Autism Screening Instrument for Educational Planning. Consists of 57 observable behaviors which can be used to discriminate autism from other severely handicapped conditions. This subtest is available in Spanish. The subtest and overall battery are appropriate for use by psychologists, psychiatrists, special educators, speech therapists, social workers, and psychometrists, who are assessing, developing educational plans, and evaluating progress of autistic, severely handicapped, or developmentally delayed students.

13708
Jansky Diagnostic Battery. Jansky, Jeannette
Descriptors: *Diagnostic Tests; Expressive Language; High Risk Persons; *Individual Testing; *Kindergarten Children; Primary Education; *Reading Diagnosis; *Reading Readiness; *Reading Readiness Tests; Receptive Language
Availability: Jeannette Jansky; 120 E. 89th St., New York, NY 10028
Grade Level: K
Notes: Time, 30 approx.

Assesses reading readiness ability of kindergarten children who have been identified as at risk by the Jansky Screening Index (TC008031). Assesses oral language;, pattern matching; pattern memory; visuomotor organization; receptive language; and ability to work alone, persist, and think independently. Instructions for administration and scoring can be found in PREVENTING READING FAILURE by Jansky and Hirsch and published by Harper and Row.

13709
Academic and Social Behavior Assessment Kit. University of Washington, Seattle. Child Development and Mental Retardation Center
Subtests: Screening Probes for Academic Battery; Academic Assessment Probes; Social Behavior Assessment
Descriptors: Antisocial Behavior; Arithmetic; Check Lists; *Diagnostic Tests; Elementary Education; *Elementary School Students; Evaluation Utilization; Handwriting; Interpersonal Competence; Learning Disabilities; *Learning Problems; *Measures (Individuals); *Observation; Reading; *Screening Tests
Identifiers: AAB; SPAAB; University of Washington
Availability: Child Development and Mental Retardation Center, WJ-10; Experimental Education Unit, University of Washington, Seattle, WA 98105
Grade Level: K-8

The Academic and Social Behavior Assessment Kit was developed at the Experimental Education Unit, University of Washington, to provide an assessment tool which could (1) assess performance levels in specific skill areas systematically, (2) be administered by untrained personnel, (3) provide relevant information for lesson planning, (4) be used for continuous measurement of performance, (5) be administered in short periods of time, and (6) use individual probes in selected skill areas separately. It was designed to pinpoint academic and social deficits in relation to peer skill levels and to be used on a regular basis to describe the progress made by the pupil. There are 2 parts to the assessment, Academic Deficiencies and Social Behavior Observation Procedures. The Screening Probe for the Academic Assessment Battery (SPAAB) identifies possible academic deficits in specific areas. The appropriate Academic Assessment Battery probes are then selected to be administered to the student. The AAB probes are administered over 5 consecutive days. Each probe is timed for one minute, and the total daily time depends on the number of probes given. Probes requiring a written response may be given to a group of students; those requiring an oral or pointing response must be administered individually. In assessing the social behaviors, the establishment of the behaviors may be based on the social observation data collected for 5 consecutive days in conjunction with the AAB data. After the behaviors are pinpointed, the frequency of occurrence is recorded for 5 consecutive days.

13710
Weiss Intelligibility Test. Weiss, Curtis E. 1982
Subtests: Intelligibility of Isolated Words; Intelligibility of Contextual Speech
Descriptors: *Adolescents; Adults; Audiotape Recordings; *Children; *Communication Disorders; *Oral Language; *Speech Tests
Identifiers: *Intelligibility (Speech)
Availability: C.C. Publications; P.O. Box 23699, Tigard, OR 97223
Target Audience: 3-64
Notes: Time, 15 approx.; Items, 31

Designed to quantify intelligibility of isolated words, contextual speech, and overall intelligibility of children and adolescents. Standardization sample included subjects ranging in age from 3 years to 64 years. A sample of subject's speech is tape recorded and judged from the audio playback. There is no visual feedback. Test may be administered and judged by speech-language clinicians or by untrained judges. Test is appropriate for use with subjects with a wide range of communicative disorders. There is an option form, Scale for Rating Factors that Influence Intelligibilitiy. The following factors may be rated: adventitious sounds, articulation, communicative dysfluency, inflection, juncture, mean length of utterance, morphology, morphophonemics, pauses, physical posture, pitch, pronunciation, rate, redundancy, resonation, rhythm, semantics stress, syntax, voice quality, intensity, pragmatics, and other.

13711
Basic Language Concepts Test. Engelmann, Siegfried,; And Others 1982
Descriptors: *Elementary School Students; *Expressive Language; Individualized Education Programs; Language Handicaps; *Language Skills; *Preschool Children; Primary Education; *Receptive Language; *Screening Tests
Identifiers: Basic Concept Inventory
Availability: C.C. Publications; P.O. Box 23699, Tigard, OR 97223
Grade Level: K-1
Target Audience: 4-6
Notes: Time, 15 approx.; Items, 81

A screening test of language skills of children from ages 4 to 6.5 years. Assesses receptive language, expressive language, and analogy skills in which responses require an awareness of patterns. Test may also be used with older language-deficient children in elementary schools or in a clinical setting. Other purposes for using the test include diagnosing specific skill deficiencies for instructional remediation, serving as a basis for individualized education programs, obtaining baseline measures against which to evaluate progress, providing norms against which children may be compared in language concept development. Test is especially useful with children in special programs, such as Head Start.

13712
New England Pantomime Tests. Duffy, Robert J.; Duffy, Joseph R. 1984
Descriptors: *Adults; *Aphasia; *Communication Disorders; *Nonverbal Communication; *Nonverbal Tests
Availability: C.C. Publications; P.O. Box 23699, Tigard, OR 97223
Target Audience: Adults
Notes: Items, 46

Consists of the Pantomime Recognition Test, Forms A and B, Pantomime Expression Test, and the Pantomime Referential Abilities Test. Tests are used to assess the nonverbal sending and receiving abilities of aphasic or communication disordered adults. Pantomime Recognitive Test assesses subject's ability to recognize mimed acts associated with common objects. Pantomime Expression Test evaluates pantomimic performance of aphasic subjects. Pantomime Referential Abilities Test measures communicative effectiveness of subject on a simple pantomimic referential task.

13713
Hoja de Cotejo o Perfil de Desarrollo de Carolina del Norte. Lillie, David L.; Harbin, Gloria L. 1977
Subtests: Cross Motor; Fine Motor; Reasoning; Visual Perception; Receptive Language; Expressive Language; Social-Emotional
Descriptors: *Child Development; Criterion Referenced Tests; Expressive Language; Interpersonal Competence; Language Acquisition; Measures (Individuals); *Preschool Children; Profiles; Psychomotor Skills; Receptive Language; Spanish; Spanish Speaking; Visual Perception
Identifiers: Carolina Developmental Profile; Reasoning Ability
Availability: Kaplan School Supply Corporation; 1310 Lewisville-Clemmons Rd., Lewisville, NC 27023
Target Audience: 2-5
Notes: Items, 100

A criterion-referenced behavioral checklist designed for use with the Developmental Task Instructional System contained in Early Childhood Education—An Individual Approach to Developmental Instruction. Palo Alto: Science Research Associates, 1975. The goal of the system is to increase developmental abilities in the 6 subtest areas to prepare the child for academic tasks in elementary school. The checklist is used to determine a baseline of the child's highest level of functioning. It is not standardized. After testing, the teacher translates findings into behavioral objectives.

13716
Sheltered Employment Work Experience Program, Second Revised Edition. Gertrude A. Barber Center, Erie, PA. 1982
Descriptors: *Adolescents; *Adults; *Mental Retardation; Rating Scales; *Sheltered Workshops; *Vocational Evaluation
Identifiers: SEWEP
Availability: The Barber Center Press; 136 E. Ave., Erie, PA 16507
Target Audience: 12-64

Designed to assess and program the development of vocational capabilities of mentally retarded adolescents and adults. Focuses on subject who has achieved a minimal development in vocational independence and adequate independence in personal and social skills. Vocational skills assessed are those designed to facilitate success in traditional programs, such as sheltered workshops. SEWEP identifies 10 major vocational competency areas: factory work, carpentry, print shop, laundry, building maintenance, general and outdoor maintenance, transportation aide, library aide, food service, and housekeeping. The vocational competency areas are divided into 50 specific skill areas which are subdivided into 504 specific skills. Two other competency areas are also assessed: personal-social development and general vocational development.

13717
Continuing Education Assessment Inventory for Mentally Retarded Adults, Second Revised Edition. Dr. Gertrude A. Barber Center, Erie, PA 1982
Descriptors: *Adolescents; *Adult Day Care; *Adults; Communication Skills; *Daily Living Skills; Interpersonal Competence; *Mental Retardation; Rating Scales; Self Care Skills
Identifiers: CEAI
Availability: The Barber Center Press; 136 E. Ave., Erie, PA 16507
Target Audience: 12-64

Designed to measure development of somatic, personal, social, and vocational capabilities of mentally retarded teenagers and adults. Geared toward a population which has not yet reached minimal development in vocational independence and/or personal and social skills and who are found in work activity centers and adult day care centers. CEAI identifies 7 major competencies: independence, leisure time, pre-vocational, self-care, mobility, communication, and personal and social development. These 7 competencies are divided into 34 specific skill areas which are subdivided into 434 specific skills.

13718
EMI Assessment Scale. University of Virginia School of Medicine, Dept. of Pediatrics, Charlottesville
Subtests: Gross Motor Skills; Fine Motor Skills; Socialization; Cognition; Language
Descriptors: Behavioral Objectives; *Child Development; Cognitive Development; Developmental Stages; *Infants; Intervention; Language Acquisition; Measures (Individuals); *Multiple Disabilities; *Psychomotor Skills; Socialization
Identifiers: Developmental Age
Availability: University of Virginia School of Medicine; Dept. of Pediatrics, Education for Multihandicapped Infants, Box 232, Medical Center, Charlottesville, VA 22901
Target Audience: 0-2
Notes: Time, 45 approx.; Items, 360

Designed to provide information about levels of functioning in multihandicapped infants to assist in planning intervention activities. Can be used as a checklist of instructional objectives or to obtain a score to compare individuals or assess growth over time. This scale was developed by sequencing items from other, standardized, scales. The EMI is not standardized. It is untimed. Each skill is evaluated with 15 items. A method of ordinal scoring is used to arrive at a developmental age. A series of common items, such as ball and crayons, are required for administration.

13719
The Spanish Oral Reading Test. Romero, Cesar; Miller, Robert 1982
Descriptors: *Achievement Tests; *Bilingual Students; Diagnostic Tests; Elementary Education; Individual Testing; Native Speakers; *Oral Reading; Phonics; Reading Comprehension; Reading Difficulties; *Reading Tests; *Spanish; Spanish Speaking; Student Placement; Word Lists
Identifiers: Oral Tests; SORT
Availability: Paradox Press; P.O. Box 1438, Los Gatos, CA 95031
Grade Level: 1-6

Designed to detect reading problems of bilingual Spanish speakers in reading material in the Spanish language. Identifies reading level and detects various phoneme grapheme problems. Consists of 2 word lists, 12 graded paragraphs, and 6 phonics tests. The tests are individually administered, orally. The test takers read each section aloud until they achieve a specified failure rate.

13720
The Ber-Sil Spanish Test, Revised Edition. Beringer, Marjorie L. 1976
Descriptors: *Bilingual Students; Elementary Education; *Elementary School Students; English (Second Language); *Individual Testing; Language Dominance; *Language Proficiency; Magnetic Tape Cassettes; *Screening Tests; *Spanish Speaking
Availability: The Ber-Sil Co.; 3412 Seaglen Dr., Rancho Palos Verdes, CA 90274
Grade Level: K-6
Target Audience: 5-11
Notes: Time, 30 approx.; Items, 118

Developed as an individual screening instrument to evaluate Spanish-speaking children in southern California. Non-Spanish-speaking examiner can observe the way the child responds to his or her native language. Test is divided into 3 sections: vocabulary, action responses to directions, and visual-motor activity involving writing and drawing. Directions and vocabulary are on tape. Test assists examiner in determining direction for further study of child. Test was developed in response to California legislation mandating that child be screened for language dominance before an approved intelligence test could be administered and before child can be placed in a special education program.

13721
The Ber-Sil Spanish Test, Secondary Level, Revised. Beringer, Marjorie L. 1984
Descriptors: *Bilingual Students; English (Second Language); *Individual Testing; Language Dominance; *Language Proficiency; Magnetic Tape Cassettes; *Screening Tests; Secondary Education; *Secondary School Students; *Spanish Speaking
Availability: The Ber-Sil Co.; 3412 Seaglen Dr., Rancho Palos Verdes, CA 90274
Grade Level: 7-12
Target Audience: 13-17
Notes: Time, 45 approx.; Items, 175

Developed as a quick individual screening test to evaluate Spanish-speaking secondary students in southern California. Test was developed in response to state legislation mandating that child be screened for language dominance before an approved intelligence test can be administered and before child can be placed in a special education program. Test assesses knowledge and ability in 4 areas of Spanish: vocabulary, grammar, punctuation, and spelling. Also assesses knowledge of basic processes in mathematics. Can be administered by non-Spanish evaluators, using a cassette tape. Also translated into Phillipine languages of Tagalog and Ilokano.

13724
The Hand Test, Revised 1983. Wagner, Edwin E. 1983
Descriptors: Adolescents; Adults; Children; *Clinical Psychology; *Diagnostic Tests; Emotional Disturbances; Individual Testing; *Mental Disorders; Neurosis; *Personality Assessment; *Pictorial Stimuli; *Projective Measures; Psychological Patterns; Tape Recorders
Availability: Western Psychological Services; 12031 Wilshire Blvd., Los Angeles, CA 90025
Target Audience: 6-64
Notes: Items, 10

The Hand Test is a diagnostic technique that uses pictures of hands as the projective medium. The stimulus materials are a set of 10 cards, 9 of which have simple line drawings of hands in various positions on them; the 10th card is blank. Cards are presented one at a time and the examinee tells what the hand is doing. For the blank card, the examinee must imagine a hand and explain what it is doing. Responses are recorded verbatim, scored, and interpreted according to prescribed procedures. Initial response,, time and other relevant behaviors are also noted. This test can be done with any individual old enough to verbalize a response, but it is not recommended for those under 6 years of age. The test should be integrated into a battery of tests because it is intended as an ancillary clinical technique. There are 4 combined quantitative categories—interpersonal, environmental, maladjustive, withdrawal—and 17 qualitative categories identified for formal scoring. This is a psychologically sophisticated test and should be administered, scored, and interpreted by individuals at or beyond the graduate level who are familiar with personality dynamics and projective theory.

13725
An Adaptation of the Wechsler Preschool and Primary Scale of Intelligence for Deaf Children. Ray, Steven; Ulissi, Stephen Mark 1982
Subtests: Animal House; Picture Completion; Mazes; Geometric Design; Block Design
Descriptors: *Deafness; *Hearing Impairments; *Intelligence Tests; *Preschool Children; *Young Children
Identifiers: WPPSI
Availability: Steven Ray Publishing; P.O. Box 751, Sulphur, OK 73086
Target Audience: 4-7

This test was adapted from the Wechsler Preschool and Primary Scale of Intelligence (WPPSI) for use with hearing-impaired children in the lower age ranges. It is designed to supplement the regular WPPSI manual and to facilitate the testing of hearing-impaired children. No attempt has been made to change the test items or their scoring procedure. The instructions have been adapted to meet the necessity posed by communication methods other than spoken English.

13726
An Adaptation of the Wechsler Intelligence Scales for Children-Revised for the Deaf. Ray, Steven 1979
Subtests: Picture Completion; Picture Arrangement; Block Design; Object Assembly; Coding
Descriptors: *Adolescents; *Children; *Deafness; Elementary School Students; *Hearing Impairments; *Intelligence Tests
Identifiers: WISC
Availability: Steven Ray Publishing; P.O. Box 751, Sulphur, OK 73086
Target Audience: 6-17

This test is an adaptation of the "Wechsler Intelligence Scales for Children—Revised" for deaf persons. The psychologist administering this test does not have to be a skilled signer, but the test can be administered by one having limited ability to communicate with deaf children. It was developed so that children possessing only minimal standard language could receive an appropriate assessment. The instrument contains alternate and supplemental materials designed to minimize the adverse effects of handicapping conditions within the testing situation.

13730
Inventario Multifasico de la Personalidad-Minnesota Version Hispana. Hathaway, Starke R.; McKinley, J. C. 1984
Subtests: Hypochondraisis; Depression; Hysteria; Psychopathic Deviate; Masculinity-Feminity; Paranoia; Psychasthenia; Schizophrenia; Hypomania; Social Introversion; Anxiety; Repression; Ego Strength
Descriptors: Adolescents; Adults; Anxiety; Depression (Psychology); Older Adults; Paranoid Behavior; *Personality Measures; Personality Problems; Psychopathology; Schizophrenia; Self Concept; Spanish; *Spanish Speaking
Identifiers: Femininity; Hypochondria; Hypomania; Hysteria; Introversion; Masculinity; MMPI; Psychastenia; Repression
Availability: National Computer Systems; P.O. Box 1416, Minneapolis, MN 55440
Target Audience: 16-65
Notes: Time, 45; Items, 566

A Spanish translation of the Minnesota Multiphasic Personality Inventory (TC001190), made in 1984 by Rose E. Garcia and Alex A. Azan. The MMPI is designed for clinical use in identifying psychological and psychiatric problems of adolescents and adults.

13731
Rhode Island Test of Language Structure. Engen, Elizabeth; Engen, Trygg 1983
Descriptors: Adolescents; Bilingual Education Programs; Children; Criterion Referenced Tests; Educational Planning; *Hearing Impairments; *Language Acquisition; Language Handicaps; *Language Tests; Learning Disabilities; Mental Retardation; Norm Referenced Tests; *Receptive Language; Young Adults
Identifiers: RITLS
Availability: Edmark Corporation; P.O. Box 3903, Bellevue, WA 98009-9990
Target Audience: 3-20
Notes: Time, 30 approx.; Items, 100

Developed to provide a measure of language development and to provide assessment data to allow for educational planning. Goal is to achieve a profile of a child's receptive language through use of a representative sample of sentence structures. Designed primarily for use with hearing-impaired children but is also useful in other areas where language development is of concern, such as mental retardation, learning disability, and bilingual programs. Test focuses on syntax. Test can be interpreted as either a norm-referenced or criterion-referenced test.

13737
Detroit Tests of Learning Aptitude, DTLA-2. Hammill, Donald D. 1985
Subtests: Word Opposites; Sentence Imitation; Oral Directions; Word Sequences; Story Construction; Design Reproduction; Object Sequences; Symbolic Relations; Conceptual Matching; Word Fragments; Letter Sequences
Descriptors: *Academic Aptitude; *Adolescents; *Aptitude Tests; *Children; *Cognitive Ability; Diagnostic Tests; Individual Testing; Intelligence; Learning Disabilities; Long Term Memory; Nonverbal Ability; Psychomotor Skills; Short Term Memory; Verbal Ability
Identifiers: DTLA2; Test Batteries
Availability: Pro-Ed; 5341 Industrial Oaks Blvd., Austin, TX 78735
Target Audience: 6-17

A revision and restandardization of a test battery to assess specific abilities. Used to isolate individual strengths and weaknesses and to identify students deficient in general or specific aptitudes. Useful for diagnosing learning disabilities. Subtests should be administered in same order they were used when tests were standardized. Time required to administer entire battery varies from 50 minutes to 2 hours. Subtests are also used to formulate 9 composite scores in 4 domains: linguistic, attention, cognitive, and motor. DTLA-2 has 3 main uses: to determine strengths and weaknesses among intellectual abilities; to identify children and adolescents significantly below their peers in aptitude; and to use in research studies investigating aptitude, intelligence, and cognitive behavior. There are also 3 special use composites for testing blind, deaf, or physically impaired persons.

13739
The Preverbal Assessment-Intervention Profile. Connard, Patricia 1984
Descriptors: Adolescents; Adults; Children; *Communication Skills; Developmental Stages; *Diagnostic Tests; *Individual Testing; *Multiple Disabilities; *Nonverbal Ability; Observation; Perceptual Handicaps; *Perceptual Motor Learning; Physical Disabilities; *Severe Disabilities; Severe Mental Retardation
Identifiers: PAIP; Piagetian Tasks; *Preverbal Communication; Public Law 94 142
Availability: ASIEP Education Co.; 3216 N.E. 27th, Portland, OR 97212
Target Audience: 2-65

Developed as an individualized assessment for severely and multihandicapped preintentional learners. The sensorimotor domains of auditory, visual, vocal/oral, and motor are evaluated and yield an individualized preverbal/motor assessment profile. Test incorporates Piagetian sensorimotor framework, stages I-III. Test is used to evaluate prelinguistic behavior of subjects on whom the profile was standardized: severely mentally, physically, and sensory handicapped persons.

13742
The Behavior Rating Index for Children. Stiffman, Arlene R.; And Others 1984
Descriptors: Adolescents; *Behavior Problems; Behavior Rating Scales; Children
Identifiers: BRIC
Availability: Measurement and Evaluation in Counseling and Development; v17 n2 p83-90 Jul 1984
Target Audience: 7-15
Notes: Time, 3 approx.; Items, 13

Can be used as a screening device. Measures the degree of a behavior problem rather than the direction or type of behavior problem. In addition to this form, there is a form used to evaluate a single individual. This instrument was developed for a program of preventive mental health research. Form can be completed by both children being evaluated and by parents and/or teachers. Can be easily administered at intervals over a course of treatment.

13743
Geriatric Hopelessness Scale. Fry, P.S. 1984
Descriptors: *Affective Measures; *Aging (Individuals); *Depression (Psychology); Geriatrics; *Older Adults
Identifiers: GHS; *Hopelessness
Availability: Journal of Counseling Psychology; v31 n3 p322-31 Jul 1984
Target Audience: 65-80
Notes: Items, 30

Designed to assess specific and generalized cognitions of pessimism and futility among the elderly towards themselves and their future. Designed for use with nonpsychiatric, nonpatient populations. Factor analysis yielded 4 major factors of hopelessness: about recovering lost physical and cognitive abilities, about recovering lost personal and interpersonal worth and attractiveness, about recovering spiritual faith and receiving spiritual grace, and about receiving nuturance and recovering respect and remembrance both in the present and after death.

13748
Frenchay Dysarthria Assessment. Enderby, Pamela M. 1983
Subtests: Reflex; Respiration; Lips; Jaw; Palate; Laryngeal; Tongue; Intelligibility
Descriptors: Adolescents; Adults; *Diagnostic Tests; Foreign Countries; Older Adults; Rating Scales; Speech Communication; *Speech Evaluation; *Speech Handicaps; Speech Pathology; *Speech Tests
Identifiers: *Dysarthria
Availability: College Hill Press; 4284 41st St., San Diego, CA 92105
Target Audience: 15-99

This assessment instrument was developed at the Frenchay Hospital in Bristol, England, to be used by speech pathologists to categorically diagnose dysarthria. There are 8 major sections with subtests within them. It is used in hospital and clinical settings as the primary assessment procedure for dysarthric patients. A 9-point rating scale is used to score the response for each subtest. The instrument has been used with people as young as 15 and as old as 99.

13749
Autistic Behavior Composite Checklist and Profile. Riley, Anita Marcott 1984
Descriptors: Adolescents; *Autism; *Behavior Disorders; Check Lists; Children; *Developmental Disabilities; Individual Development; *Profiles; Young Adults
Availability: Communication Skill Builders; 3130 N. Dodge Blvd., P.O. Box 42050, Tucson, AZ 85733
Target Audience: 4-22
Notes: Items, 225

The Autistic Behavior Composite checklist and profile are inventories of interfering behaviors associated with the syndrome of autism but are also applicable to other populations having severe learning and behavioral problems such as mentally impaired and severely emotionally impaired persons. The instruments may be used to establish and support a diagnosis of autism, to follow a student's behavioral patterns over a period of time, and to aid in prioritizing problem areas as a basic for establishing a Behavioral Intervention Plan. There are 8 categories included in the checklist: prerequisite learning behaviors; sensory perceptual skills; motor development; prelanguage skills; speech, language, and communication skills; developmental rates and sequences; learning behaviors; and relating skills. The profile includes a graph for each of the 8 categories contained in the checklist which enables the clinician or teacher to gain an overview of the student's interfering behaviors through a visual display. A scale is used to score the existence of an interfering behavior from frequent (70 to 100 percent of the time) to not applicable; it is a 4-step scale.

13751
Evaluating Acquired Skills in Communication. Riley, Anita Marcott 1984
Descriptors: Adolescents; *Autism; Children; *Communication Skills; Expressive Language; Informal Assessment; Language Handicaps; Mental Retardation; Preschool Children; Receptive Language; Young Adults; Young Children
Identifiers: EASIC; Prelanguage
Availability: Communication Skill Builders; 3130 N. Dodge Blvd., P.O. Box 42050, Tucson, AZ 85733
Target Audience: 2-26

A 5-level informal communication skills inventory for the preschool, language impaired, mentally impaired, and autistic student. The informal communication skills inventories include the areas of semantics, syntax, morphology, and pragmatics. Each assessment level is organized into skill clusters ordered from easy to difficult.

13756
Schedule for Affective Disorders and Schizophrenia, Third Edition. Spitzer, Robert L.; Endicott, Jean 1979
Descriptors: Adults; *Affective Behavior; Anxiety; *Behavior Development; Behavior Patterns; *Clinical Psychology; Depression (Psychology); *Emotional Problems; Interviews; *Mental Disorders; Paranoid Behavior; Personality Problems; Psychopathology; *Psychosis; *Schizophrenia
Identifiers: Psychiatric Patients; SADS
Availability: New York Psychiatric Institute; Research Assessment and Training Unit, 722 W. 168th St., New York, NY 10032
Target Audience: 18-64

This instrument is designed for use as a form to record information regarding a subject's functioning and symptoms. This contains an interview guide and assumes that the subject will be interviewed, but the judgments should be based on all available sources of information, such as interviews with family members, case records and referral notes. In most instances, the SADS evaluation should follow the initial clinical workup and should be done when the subject is drug free. There are 2 parts to the SADS. Part I focuses on details of the current episode, and Part II focuses primarily on historical information. Both parts may be given in one sitting with a short break in between. SADS is used with schizophrenic or emotionally disturbed persons.

13757
Quality of Life Dimensions. Flanagan, John C.
Descriptors: Adults; Attitude Measures; Interpersonal Relationship; *Life Satisfaction; Living Standards; Older Adults; Physical Fitness; *Quality of Life; Questionnaires; Rating Scales; Self Evaluation (Individuals); Socioeconomic Status; *Values
Availability: Education; v100 n3 p194-202 Spr 1980
Target Audience: 30; 50; 70
Notes: Items, 15

This instrument was used to define the main determinants of quality of life. It is an empirical approach and 3 groups of Americans were surveyed: 30-year-olds, 50-year-olds and 70-year-olds. Both male and female were in the 3 age groups. The items covered physical and material well-being; relations with other people; social, community, and civic activities; personal development and fulfillment; and recreation. The adults were asked to respond to 2 questions: At this time in your life, how important is (the list of items)? and How well are your needs and wants being met in this regard? (for those aged 30, the question read How satisfied are you with your status in this respect?)

13758
Haptic Memory Matching Test. McCarron, Lawrence; Dial, Jack G. 1976
Descriptors: Adults; Blindness; Kinesthetic Perception; Mental Retardation; Nonverbal Tests; Perception Tests; Recognition (Psychology); *Sensory Integration; *Short Term Memory; *Tactile Adaptation; *Visual Impairments; *Visualization
Identifiers: HMMT
Availability: McCarron-Dial Systems; Common Market Press, P.O. Box 45628, Dallas, TX 75245
Target Audience: 18-64
Notes: Items, 48

The Haptic Memory Matching Test (HMMT) was designed to assess a person's capacity to function and accommodate to the loss of vision; to assess the tactile-matching skills, short-term haptic memory and spatial localization skills. The subjects are asked to manipulate objects which vary in shape, size, texture, and spatial configuration and, after they have had an opportunity to feel all of the objects in a set, will be presented another object which matches one of those they have felt; and their task is to return to the previous set and find an identical object. The subjects are instructed to give their best performance because the information is important for determining the rehabilitation program and training strategies. This test has been used with nonhandicapped subjects as well as mentally retarded adults with visual impairments.

13767
Student Evaluation of Teacher Instrument II. University of Texas, Austin, Research and Development Ctr. for Teacher Education 1972
Descriptors: Elementary School Students; Objective Tests; *Primary Education; Self Esteem; *Student Evaluation of Teacher Performance; Teacher Response; Teacher Student Relationship
Identifiers: SET
Availability: University of Texas; Dissemination Dept., Research and Development Center for Teacher Education, Education Annex 3.203, Austin, TX 78712
Grade Level: 1-3
Notes: Time, 20 approx.; Items, 20

Designed to secure evaluations of teachers by students below grade 4. May also be appropriate for use with disadvantaged students through grade 6. Use of this instrument with kindergarten children should be limited to those children who are average or above average in classroom ability and performance. Analysis indicates that there are 3 factors upon which primary grade children make their evaluations of teachers. One is stimulating interactive style which involves child-teacher rapport and teacher competence. The second factor is unreasonable negativity which deals with the teacher's emotionality. Factor 3 is fosterance of self-esteem among the students.

13775
Informal Reading Comprehension Placement Test. Insel, Eunice; Edson, Ann
Subtests: Word Comprehension; Passage Comprehension
Descriptors: Achievement Tests; Computer Assisted Testing; *Elementary School Students; Elementary Secondary Education; *Junior High School Students; *Microcomputers; *Reading Comprehension; *Reading Tests; Remedial Reading; *Student Placement
Identifiers: Apple (Computer); TRS80
Availability: Educational Activities, Inc.; P.O. Box 392, Freeport, NY 11520
Grade Level: 1-8

Sequentially designed reading comprehension placement test for students in grades 1 through 8 and in remedial secondary programs. Administered, scored, and managed on either an Apple microcomputer (48K) or a TRS 80III or IV (32K). Word comprehension section has 60 items to measure students' knowledge of word meanings and uses an analogy format. Passage comprehension section consists of 8 graded selections and questions at varying degrees of difficulty.

13795
Life Satisfaction Index. Neugarten, Bernice; And Others 1961
Descriptors: *Attitude Measures; Check Lists; *Life Satisfaction; Middle Aged Adults; *Older Adults; Questionnaires; *Self Evaluation (Individuals); *Well Being
Identifiers: LSI
Availability: Journal of Gerontology; v16 n2 p134-43 Apr 1961
Target Audience: 50-90
Notes: Items, 18

The Life Satisfaction Index is an attitude inventory which is used to measure psychological well-being of older people. The subjects respond to statements about life, in general, by checking whether they agree, disagree, or are not sure. The LSI was used for men and women aged 50 to 90.

13796
Autism Screening Instrument for Educational Planning, First Edition. Krug, David A.; And Others 1980
Descriptors: *Adaptive Behavior (of Disabled); Adolescents; Adults; Articulation (Speech); *Autism; Check Lists; Children; Expressive Language; Interpersonal Competence; Learning Problems; Observation; Preschool Children; Psychomotor Skills; Receptive Language; *Screening Tests; Toddlers; Young Adults
Identifiers: ASIEP; Learning Rate
Availability: ASIEP Educational Co.; 3216 N.E. 27th, Portland, OR 97212
Target Audience: 3-35
Notes: Time, 90

Includes a checklist of nonadaptive behaviors that provides a profile for comparison of the test taker to other populations with handicapping conditions. Four other observation measures are included: a vocal sample, social interaction observation, functional education assessment, and a learning rate assessment. The client performs simple tasks in a standardized setting.

13812
Sequenced Inventory of Communication Development, Revised Edition. Hedrick, Dona Lea; And Others 1984
Subtests: Receptive Scale; Expressive Scale
Descriptors: Autism; *Communication Skills; Diagnostic Tests; Eskimos; *Expressive Language; *Language Acquisition; *Language Handicaps; Language Patterns; Language Processing; Measures (Individuals); Nonverbal Communication; Profiles; *Receptive Language; Remedial Programs; Spanish Speaking; Speech Habits; Syntax; *Young Children
Identifiers: SICD(R)
Availability: Slosson Educational Publications; P.O. Box 280, E. Aurora, NY 14052

The Sequenced Inventory of Communication Development-Revised (SICD-R) is to assist clinicians in remedial programing for the deviant child. It can be used to assign communication ages and in screening broad spectrums of behavior for more intensive study or for initial management goals. The test items are the original ones in the SICD but have been classified according to semantic-cognitive, syntactic, and pragmatic aspects of communication. The test may be given by one person, but it is easier if there is another to act as a recorder. The Receptive Scale is usually administered first, followed by the Expressive Scale. The complete test is never given to a child, but testing begins where consistent success is anticipated. The testing continues until a ceiling is reached; this is when 3 consecutive items are failed. Behaviors included in the Receptive Scale are awareness, discrimination, nd understanding. The behaviors included in the Expressive Scale are motor response, vocal response, verbal response, imitating behaviors, initiating behaviors, and responding behaviors. The SICD has been modified and standardized for special populations: Yup'ik Eskimo, autistic and other difficult-to-test children, and hearing-impaired children. There is a Spanish translation of the instrument also.

13818
Geriatric Depression Scale. Brink, Terry L.; Yesavage, Jerome A. 1983
Descriptors: *Attitude Measures; *Depression (Psychology); Geriatrics; *Older Adults; *Screening Tests; Self Evaluation (Individuals)
Identifiers: GDS
Availability: Journal of Psychiatric Research; v17 n1 p37-49 1983
Target Audience: 55-90

Scale designed specifically to rate depression in the elderly. Has a yes-no format that can be used as a self-rating scale.

13820
Children's Dysfunctional Cognition Scale. Wasserman, Theodore H. 1984
Descriptors: *Affective Measures; Children; Elementary Education; *Elementary School Students; *Emotional Disturbances; *Student Behavior
Identifiers: CDCS; *Cognitive Dysfunction
Availability: Theodore Wasserman; Astor Child Guidance Center, 750 Tilden St., Bronx, NY 10467
Grade Level: K-6
Target Audience: 6-12
Notes: Items, 45

Scale is used to differentiate between normal and disturbed children and is used to assess the effects of inappropriate cognitions as they relate to emotional disturbance and classroom behavior of elementary school students. Studies indicate a relationship between specific cognitions hypothesized to cause emotional dysfunction and teacher reports of behavior.

13824
Sklar Aphasia Scale, Revised 1983. Sklar, Maurice 1983
Subtests: Auditory Decoding; Visual Decoding; Oral Encoding; Graphic Encoding
Descriptors: Adults; *Aphasia; *Language Handicaps; *Neurological Impairments; *Speech Handicaps
Identifiers: SAS
Availability: Western Psychological Services; 12031 Wilshire Blvd., Los Angeles, CA 90025
Target Audience: Adults
Notes: Items, 100

Provides objective measurements and evaluations of speech and language disturbances resulting from brain damage. Designed for use with adults suspected of having some speech or language impairment as a result of damage to the cerebral cortex. Aphasia is generally diagnosed by a physician. SAS is used to determine type and extent of speech and language disturbances and patient's potential for benefiting from aphasia therapy. Is easily administered, scored, and interpreted by clinician or speech pathologist with knowledge of the aphasic syndrome.

13829
Computer Managed Screening Test. Fitch, James L. 1984
Descriptors: *Articulation (Speech); *Computer Assisted Testing; *Expressive Language; *Language Fluency; Microcomputers; *Receptive Language; *Screening Tests; *Voice Disorders; *Young Children
Availability: Communication Skill Builders; 3130 N. Dodge Blvd., Tucson, AZ 85733
Target Audience: 3-8
Notes: Time, 4 approx.; Items, 32

A screening test to evaluate child's articulation, expressive and receptive language, voice, and fluency. Administrator reads instrutions from the screen, child responds, and administrator keys in whether the response was correct or incorrect. The test can be administered using the program that runs on the Apple II, IIe, or IIc.

13830
Receptive One-Word Picture Vocabulary Test. Gardner, Morrison F. 1985
Descriptors: *Basic Vocabulary; Bilingual Students; Children; *Cognitive Development; Elementary School Students; Emotional Disturbances; Physical Disabilities; Pictorial Stimuli; Preschool Children; *Receptive Language; *Screening Tests; Spanish; Spanish Speaking; Speech Handicaps; Visual Measures
Identifiers: Oral Tests; ROWPVT
Availability: Academic Therapy Publications; 20 Commercial Blvd., Novato, CA 94947-6191
Target Audience: 2-11
Notes: Time, 20 approx.

Individually administered, norm-referenced, untimed test developed to obtain an estimate of a child's one-word hearing vocabulary based on what child has learned from home and formal education. When used alone, provides a means for evaluating receptive vocabulary of those with expressive difficulties, such as bilingual, speech-impaired, immature and withdrawn, and emotionally or physically impaired children. Norms for the Receptive One-Word Picture Vocabulary Test and the Expressive One-Word Picture Vocabulary Test are equivalent. When both tests are used, comparison of results provides information about differences in these language skills that could be a result of specific language impairment, language delay, bilingualism, nonstimulating home environment, cultural differences, learning difficulties, or other factors to be investigated. Spanish forms are also available to obtain an estimate of a child's Spanish vocabulary.

13832
The Gordon Diagnostic System. Clinical Diagnostics, Golden, CO 1983
Descriptors: Adolescents; *Attention Deficit Disorders; Children; *Clinical Diagnosis; *Diagnostic Tests; Electronic Equipment; Hyperactivity; Learning Disabilities; *Self Control
Identifiers: ADD; GDS
Availability: Psychological Assessment Resources; P.O. Box 998, Odessa, FL 33556
Target Audience: 3-16
Notes: Time, 20 approx.

A portable electronic device designed to assess deficits in attention and impulse control in children. Developed for use by clinicians to aid in the diagnosis of attention deficit disorders with or without hyperactivity, and some forms of learning disabilities. Presents 2 tasks: the delay task that measures a child's ability to refrain from pressing a button to win points and the vigilance task that assesses how well a child sustains attention over a long period of time.

13833
Miller-Yoder Language Comprehension Test, Clinical Edition. Miller, Jon F.; Yoder, David E. 1984
Descriptors: Cognitive Processes; *Developmental Disabilities; *Educational Diagnosis; *Language Handicaps; *Language Processing; Language Tests; *Mental Retardation; Standard Spoken Usage; *Visual Measures; *Young Children
Identifiers: *Language Comprehension; MY
Availability: Slosson Educational Publications; P.O. Box 280, E. Aurora, NY 14052
Target Audience: 4-8
Notes: Time, 30 approx.; Items, 42

The Miller-Yoder Language Comprehension Test (MY) (Clinical Edition) is a measure of mainstream American-English language comprehension and was designed as a clinical research tool for exploring the grammatical comprehension abilities of mentally retarded persons. The test can also be used with children who are not diagnosed as mentally retarded but who are suspected to be delayed in their understanding of language. The 84 sentences,, forming 42 sentence pairs, represent 10 basic grammatical forms: active, preposition, possessive, negative/affirmative, pronoun, singular/plural, verb inflection, modification, passive, reflexivization. Each sentence is represented by a line drawing, and there are 42 different test plates with 4 pictures on each plate. Two of the pictures represent stimulus sentences, and 2 are distractors. The distractor pictures represent sentences of the same grammatical form as the experimental sentences but vary in either subject, verb, or object vocabulary from the stimulus sentences. The stimulus sentence is read to the child, and the child points to one of the 4 pictures as the answer. The time for administration varies, dependent on how much of the test the examiner chooses to present.

13834
Visual Skills Appraisal. Richards, Regina G. 1984
Subtests: Pursuits; Scanning; Aligning; Locating; Eye-hand Coordination; Fixation Unity
Descriptors: Diagnostic Tests; Elementary Education; *Elementary School Students; *Eye Fixations; *Eye Hand Coordination; *Eye Movements; *Screening Tests; *Visual Impairments
Identifiers: Scanning; VSA
Availability: Academic Therapy Publications; 20 Commercial Blvd., Novato, CA 94947-6191
Grade Level: K-4
Notes: Time, 15 approx.

The Visual Skills Appraisal (VSA) was developed to assist educators and other professionals in the identification of children with vision inefficiencies and related problems. It assesses visual skills related to classroom tasks and is divided into 2 main categories: (1) eye movement skills and (2) eye teaming skills. The eye movement skills assess 4 patterns: pursuit movements, scanning movements, aligning, and locating movements. The eye teaming skills assessed are: eye-hand coordination and fixation unity. To administer the test a basic understanding of visual skills is helpful but not essential. Although the VSA subtests have been established for use with children in kindergarten through 4th grade, the tests may be used with older students with the assumption that, if they score below the 4th grade level, they definitely have some visual skills difficulties or inefficiencies.

13838
McDermott Multidimensional Assessment of Children. McDermott, Paul A.; Watkins, Marley W. 1985
Descriptors: *Academic Achievement; *Adjustment (to Environment); Children; *Cognitive Ability; *Computer Software; *Diagnostic Tests; *Emotional Adjustment; *Exceptional Persons; *Individualized Education Programs; Microcomputers; *Student Evaluation
Identifiers: MMAC
Availability: The Psychological Corporation; 555 Academic Ct., San Antonio, TX 78204-0952
Target Audience: 3-12

Comprehensive system of over 100 computer programs that integrates data from psychological evaluations, classifies childhood exceptionality, and designs individualized education programs. The system has 2 major levels. The Classification Level provides a diagnosis of exceptionality along 4 dimensions: general intellectual functioning, academic achievement, adaptive behavior, and social-emotional adjustment. The Program Design Level generates behavioral objectives for individualized educational planning based on skills identified by criterion-referenced evaluation in reading, mathematics, general learning style, or adaptive skills. The following classifications are generated: exceptional talent, normal intellectual functioning, borderline intellectual functioning, mental retardation, intellectual retardation, educational retardation, and commensurate achievement.

13842
Walker Problem Behavior Identification Checklist, Revised 1983. Walker, Hill M. 1983
Subtests: Acting Out; Withdrawal; Distractibility; Disturbed Peer Relations; Immaturity
Descriptors: Adjustment (to Environment); *Behavior Disorders; *Behavior Problems; Check Lists; Elementary Education; *Elementary School Students; *Kindergarten Children; *Preschool Children; *Screening Tests
Identifiers: WPBIC
Availability: Western Psychological Services; 12031 Wilshire Blvd., Los Angeles, CA 90025
Grade Level: K-6
Target Audience: 2-12
Notes: Items, 50

Used by elementary school teachers to identify children with behavior problems and disorders who should be referred for further psychological evaluation, referral, and treatment. Checklist is to be used as a supplement in the total identification process rather than as an instrument to simply classify children as emotionally disturbed or maladjusted. There are separate checklists for female and male students.

13844
Texas Preschool Screening Inventory, Revised. Haber, Julian S.; Norris, Marylee 1984
Subtests: Auditory Memory for Numbers and Letters; Visual Memory for Objects; Auditory Sequencing; Articulation; Sound Discrimination; Rotations and Reversals of Letters and Numbers; Following Instructions and Understanding Prepositions
Descriptors: Articulation (Speech); Auditory Perception; *Handicap Identification; *High Risk Students; Learning Problems; *Preschool Children; Preschool Education; Primary Education; *Screening Tests; Visual Perception
Identifiers: Coping Skills; Following Directions
Availability: ERIC Document Reproduction Service; 3900 Wheeler Ave., Alexandria, VA 22304 (ED246057, 15 pages)
Target Audience: 4-6

This instrument is a revision of the Texas Preschool Screening Inventory (TPSI). It is a screening test designed to identify children who may be at risk for learning problems as they enter kindergarten or first grade. The components include Auditory Memory for Numbers and Letters; Visual Memory for Objects; Auditory Sequencing; Articulation; Sound Discrimination; Rotations and Reversals of Letters and Numbers; and Following Instructions and Understanding Prepositions.

13845
The Behavior Evaluation Scale. McCarney, Stephen B. 1983
Descriptors: Behavior Problems; *Behavior Rating Scales; Diagnostic Tests; Elementary School Students; *Elementary Secondary Education; *Emotional Disturbances; *Handicap Identification; Individualized Education Programs; Observation; Rating Scales; Screening Tests; Secondary School Students; Special Education
Identifiers: BES; IEP
Availability: ERIC Document Reproduction Service; 3900 Wheeler Ave., Alexandria, VA 22304 (ED244460, 39 pages).
Grade Level: K-12
Notes: Time, 20 approx.

The Behavior Evaluation Scale (BES) was designed to help school personnel reach and document decisions regarding diagnosis, placement, and programing for children and adolescents with behavior disorders/emotional disturbance. It can be used as a general behavior rating scale with regular class or special education student who exhibits behavior problems which warrant assessment and intervention. The BES may be used to screen for behavior problems, assess behavior for any referred student, assist in the diagnosis of behavior disorders/emotional disturbance, develop individual education programs, and document intervention progress. The 7-point rating scale ranges from 1 (Never or Not Observed) to 7 (Continuously Throughout the Day).

13870
California Adaptive Behavior Scale. Gardner, James M.; Breuer, Anne Marie 1984
Subtests: Toileting; Dressing; Fastening; Eating; Bathing; Grooming; Toothbrushing; Personal Interaction; Group Participation; Leisure; Receptive Language; Expressive Language; Gross Motor; Perceptual Motor; Prevocational; Work; Academic; Translocation; Money Handling; Personal Management; Home Management; Health Care; Community Awareness; Responsibility
Descriptors: *Adaptive Behavior (of Disabled); *Adjustment (to Environment); Adolescents; Adults; Children; *Computer Assisted Testing; *Daily Living Skills; Gifted; *Microcomputers; Older Adults; Severe Mental Retardation
Identifiers: CABS
Availability: Planet Press Enterprises; P.O. Box 3477, Newport Beach, CA 92663-3418
Target Audience: 0-81
Notes: Time, 15 approx.; Items, 329

Computerized assessment instrument to measure significant developmental milestones across 24 areas. Is applicable to gifted children as well as with severely and profoundly retarded persons. Behavioral items have age equivalencies ranging from less than one year to 19 years of age. Also provides estimates of school readiness and vocational readiness. Various versions are available including practitioner version, school version, workshop version, and residential version.

13875
Perceptual Motor Development Series. Capon, Jack J. 1975
Descriptors: Disabilities; *Performance Tests; *Preschool Education; *Primary Education; *Psychomotor Skills
Availability: Pitman Learning, Inc.; 6 Davis Dr., Belmont, CA 94002
Grade Level: K-1
Target Audience: 2-6
Notes: Items, 6

Used to evaluate student's level of motor proficiency in several areas. Administered before beginning a program in motor development. Information on child's skills can aid in planning program activities or in evaluating student progress and the effectiveness of an existing program in motor development. Tasks include identifying body parts, walking a board, hopping, jumping and landing, completing an obstacle course, and catching a ball.

13888
Brief Symptom Inventory. Derogatis, Leonard R.; Spencer, Phillip M. 1975
Subtests: Somatization; Obsessive-Compulsive; Interpersonal Sensitivity; Depression; Anxiety; Hostility; Phobic Anxiety; Paranoid Ideation; Psychoticism
Descriptors: *Patients; *Psychological Patterns; Psychological Testing; Rating Scales; Self Evaluation (Individuals)
Identifiers: BSI
Availability: Clinical Psychometric Research; P.O. Box 425, Riderwood, MD 21139
Notes: Items, 53

A self-report symptom inventory designed to reflect the psychological symptom patterns of psychiatric and medical patients as well as nonpatients. It is essentially the brief form of the SCL-90-R and is one of a matched series of tests and rating scales called the Psychopathology Rating Scale Series.

13891
Geriatric Depression Scale. Brink, T. L.; And Others 1982
Descriptors: Aging (Individuals); *Attitude Measures; *Depression (Psychology); *Older Adults; Psychological Evaluation
Identifiers: GDS
Availability: Clinical Gerontologist; v1 n1 p37-43 Fall 1982
Target Audience: 65-90
Notes: Items, 30

A self-rating scale used to identify depression in the elderly. Items represent core of geriatric depression and include items on lowered affect, inactivity, irritability, withdrawal, distressing thoughts, and negative outlook on past, present, and future. A copy of the scale can also be found in Journal of Psychiatric Research; v17 n1 p37-49 1983.

13937
Counseling Needs of Ethnic-Minority Students. King, Bradford D. 1983
Descriptors: *College Students; *Counseling Services; Higher Education; *Minority Groups; *Needs Assessment
Identifiers: Boston University; TIM(K)
Availability: Tests in Microfiche; Test Collection, Educational Testing Service, Princeton, NJ 08541
Grade Level: 13-16

Questionnaire developed to conduct a minority counseling needs assessment and intervention at Boston University. Uses a format which adapts both a problem checklist and environmental assessment methodologies. Designed to provide students with opportunity to identify individual concerns, concerns related to the university environment, and to suggest areas of improvement in underutilized services.

13940
Rehabilitation Client Rating Scale. United Cerebral Palsy of Queens, Inc., Jamaica, NY Hicks, John S. 1974
Descriptors: Adults; Antisocial Behavior; Cerebral Palsy; Counseling; Neurological Impairments; *Personality Measures; *Rating Scales; Social Adjustment; *Vocational Adjustment; Vocational Rehabilitation; Work Attitudes
Identifiers: Adjective Rating Scale

Availability: John S. Hicks; Fordham University, School of Education at Lincoln Center, New York, NY 10023
Target Audience: Adults
Notes: Items, 90

A counselor rates each client's performance in the areas of work attributes, impulsivity, emotional maladjustment, social adjustment, and devious behavior. The scale was developed at the vocational training center of United Cerebral Palsy of Queens, Inc., Jamaica, NY. The scale uses 5 points from very low to very high to rate the client according to each adjective. The adjectives and a description of the scale are also contained in Training School Bulletin; v71 n2 p71-79 Aug 1984.

13941
Oral Language Dominance Measure. El Paso Public Schools, TX 1979
Descriptors: Achievement Tests; Bilingualism; Bilingual Students; Diagnostic Tests; *English; English (Second Language); Grouping (Instructional Purposes); Individual Testing; Language Arts; *Language Dominance; *Language Tests; *Native Speakers; Primary Education; Reading Skills; Spanish; *Spanish Speaking; *Student Placement; Transfer of Training
Identifiers: Oral Tests; Spanish (Second Language)
Availability: El Paso Independent School District; Business Office, 6531 Boeing Dr., El Paso, TX 79925
Grade Level: K-3
Notes: Time, 7; Items, 28

An informal, individually administered measure of oral language dominance that uses 3 colorful cartoon-like pictures and a series of questions to compare a student's proficiency in English and Spanish. It is used as a placement test for grouping children for instruction in language arts, English or Spanish as a second language, Spanish for Spanish speakers, and transfer of reading skills. Can be used as a diagnostic test because it elicits specific language structures. Should be administered by a trained bilingual only.

13942
Oral Language Proficiency Measure. El Paso Public Schools, TX 1979
Descriptors: Achievement Tests; Bilingualism; Bilingual Students; Diagnostic Tests; *English; English (Second Language); Grouping (Instructional Purposes); Individual Testing; Intermediate Grades; Language Arts; *Language Dominance; *Language Proficiency; *Language Tests; *Native Speakers; Reading Skills; Spanish; *Spanish Speaking; *Student Placement; Transfer of Training
Identifiers: Oral Tests; Spanish (Second Language)
Availability: El Paso Independent School District; Business Office, 6531 Boeing Dr., El Paso, TX 79925
Grade Level: 4-6
Notes: Time, 7; Items, 32

A measure of students' proficiency in Spanish and English that elicits speech in each language and compares it to the performance of bilingual and monolingual students. Can be used to determine language dominance, as a placement test for grouping in English- or Spanish-as-a-Second-Language classes, Spanish for Spanish Speakers, transfer of reading skills, and language arts. May be used as a rough diagnostic measure because it elicits specific structures. Should be administered and scored by those with native proficiency in the languages tested.

13950
Vineland Adaptive Behavior Scales, Classroom Edition. Sparrow, Sara S.; And Others 1985
Subtests: Communication; Daily Living Skills; Socialization; Motor Skills
Descriptors: *Adjustment (to Environment); Children; *Communication Skills; *Daily Living Skills; Elementary Education; *Elementary School Students; Expressive Language; Mental Retardation; *Psychomotor Skills; Receptive Language; *Socialization; *Student Adjustment; Verbal Ability
Identifiers: Vineland Social Maturity Scale
Availability: American Guidance Service; Publishers' Bldg., Circle Pines, MN 55014-1796
Grade Level: K-6
Target Audience: 3-12
Notes: Time, 20 approx.; Items, 244

A revision of the Vineland Social Maturity Scale used to assess personal and social sufficiency of subjects. Scales are applicable to handicapped and nonhandicapped individuals. The classroom edition provides an assessment of adaptive behavior in the classroom. It includes items from both the Survey Form and Expanded Form plus additional items related to academic functioning. The classroom edition is a questionnaire independently completed by a teacher of students from 3 years of age to 12 years, 11 months.

13954
Pre-Mod. Kaplan, Joseph; Kent, Sandy 1983
Descriptors: *Behavior Problems; *Computer Assisted Testing; *Computer Software; *Diagnostic Tests; Elementary School Students; Elementary Secondary Education; Individualized Education Programs; Intervention; Microcomputers; *Secondary School Students; *Special Education
Availability: Asiep Education Co.; 3216 N.E. 27th Ave., Portland OR 97212
Grade Level: K-12

A software package used by a teacher or specialist to diagnose behavior problems and prescribe appropriate interventions. Used to diagnose 14 of the most common behavior problems found in the classroom, including physical aggression, abusive or provocative language, noncompliance, hyperactive or impulsive behavior, and withdrawn behavior. May also be used to generate objectives for individualized education programs in the affective domain and in social skills areas. Teacher enters a behavior problem into computer. Program then provides a socially appropriate behavior plus prerequisite skills, knowledge, and attitudes necessary for student to engage in appropriate behavior. Based on prerequisites student lacks, computer provides corresponding performance objectives and suggested interventions. Program diskette is suitable for use with Apple II and Apple IIe.

13964
Severely Handicapped Progress Inventory. Dunlap, William C.; And Others 1983
Subtests: Motor Development; Perceptual; Self Care; Cognition and Language; Social; Individual Living
Descriptors: *Achievement Gains; Adolescents; Adults; Children; Communicative Competence (Languages); Daily Living Skills; *Deaf Blind; Individualized Programs; Interpersonal Competence; Motor Development; Perceptual Development; Questionnaires; Self Care Skills; Severe Disabilities
Identifiers: TIM(K)
Availability: Tests in Microfiche; Test Collection, Educational Testing Service, Princeton, NJ 08541
Target Audience: 0-64
Notes: Time, 30 approx.; Items, 199

Specifically developed for use with deaf-blind persons to provide assessment necessary for individual program planning and for measuring progress. Organized into 6 major categories with 19 subsections. Major categories are motor development, perceptual skills, self-care skills, cognition and language, social skills, independent living.

13970
A Family Violence Scale. Bardis, Panos D. 1973
Descriptors: Adolescents; Adults; Family Environment; Family Problems; *Family Violence; Rating Scales
Availability: Panos D. Bardis; Sociology Dept., University of Toledo, Toledo, OH 43606
Target Audience: Adults
Notes: Items, 25

A 5-point measure of the frequency of family violence. Items concern actual physical violence, anger, violent language, threats.

13988
Staggered Spondaic Word Test. Katz, Jack 1960
Descriptors: Adults; Auditory Evaluation; *Auditory Perception; *Auditory Tests; Children; Individual Testing; *Neurological Impairments; Older Adults
Identifiers: SSW
Availability: Arnst, Dennis and Katz, Jack, eds.; Central Auditory Assessment: The SSW Test, Development and Clinical Use, San Diego, CA: College Hill Press
Target Audience: 7-65
Notes: Time, 10; Items, 40

A dichotic speech procedure designed for use as a technique to identify dysfunction in auditory centers in the brain. Each item is made up of 2 spondaic words, e.g., upstairs and downtown, presented at the same time, one to each ear. Said to be free from the influence of peripheral hearing loss and discrimination difficulty.

13993
Systematic Approach to Vocational Evaluation. S.A.V.E. Enterprises, Rome, GA
Descriptors: Adults; Educationally Disadvantaged; High Schools; High School Students; Mental Retardation; Predictive Measurement; *Vocational Aptitude; *Vocational Evaluation; Work Sample Tests
Identifiers: SAVE
Availability: S.A.V.E. Enterprises; P.O. Box 5871, Rome, GA 30161
Grade Level: 9-12
Target Audience: Adults

Employs a concept of evaluating vocational potential by worker trait groups as found in volume II of the Dictionary of Occupational Titles (D.O.T.), 1965 edition. There are 2 separate packages. Package A includes 16 worker trait groups and is specifically targeted toward the academically deprived, culturally and socially deprived, educable mentally handicapped, learning disabled, and trainable mentally handicapped persons. Package B encompasses 46 worker trait groups and is geared to the general population. No tools or equipment are furnished with either package.

14000
The SOI Behavioral Checklist to Identify Dysintegral Learning Systems. Meeker, Mary 1982
Descriptors: Check Lists; *Elementary School Students; Elementary Secondary Education; *Learning Disabilities; Neurological Impairments; *Secondary School Students; Speech; Student Behavior; Vision
Identifiers: Symptoms
Availability: SOI Institute; 343 Richmond St., El Segundo, CA 90245
Grade Level: 1-11
Notes: Items, 100
Includes lists of proprioceptor symptoms, and behavioral symptoms, vision symptoms, speech symptoms, and tactile and academic symptoms. For determination of learning-related deficiencies. Used in association with the SOI Learning Abilities Test (TC009264).

14001
Sequential Assessment of Mathematics Inventories. Reisman, Fredricka K. 1985
Subtests: Mathematical Language; Ordinality; Number and Notation; Computation; Measurement; Geometric Concepts; Mathematical Applications; Word Problems
Descriptors: *Achievement Tests; Diagnostic Tests; Elementary Education; *Elementary School Mathematics; *Elementary School Students; Individual Testing; Junior High Schools; *Junior High School Students; *Mathematics Tests; *Secondary School Mathematics; Special Education; Standardized Tests
Identifiers: SAMI
Availability: The Psychological Corporation; 555 Academic Ct., San Antonio, TX 78204-0952
Grade Level: K-8
Notes: Time, 60 approx.
Primarily intended for those educators who assess or instruct students who have difficulty in learning mathematics. May also be administered by teachers in regular classrooms to normally achieving students but is mainly intended for use by school personnel who normally assess student performance in mathematics, including school psychologists, educational diagnosticians, and special education teachers. Consists of 2 instruments to assess mathematics performance: the SAMI Standardized Inventory and a parallel program for classroom use, the SAMI Informal Inventory, may be used independently or in combination to develop a comprehensive profile of a student's overall standing in the mathematics curriculum. Test is individually administered because takes from 20 to 60 minutes, depending on student's level.

14002
Motor Skills Inventory. Aulenta, John 1984
Descriptors: Disabilities; *Preschool Children; *Psychomotor Skills; *Screening Tests; *Young Children
Identifiers: *Fine Motor Skills; *Gross Motor Skills; MSI
Availability: Stoelting Co.; 1350 S. Kostner Ave., Chicago, IL 60623
Target Audience: 0-6
Notes: Time, 15 approx.
Developed to assess skill development in the gross motor and fine motor areas. Designed as a brief screening instrument to evaluate motor functioning of normal and handicapped preschool and primary-aged children. Use of the instrument can contribute to differential diagnosis and gives the clinician a quick and practical measure of motor skill development. Helps to establish child's motor functioning levels and the possible need for more in-depth evaluation or remedial services.

14025
Needs Assessment Inventory. Albright College, PA. Family Centered Resource Project
Descriptors: Adults; Disabilities; Emotional Adjustment; *Family Environment; *Needs Assessment; Parent Child Relationship; Parents; Rating Scales; Social Work
Availability: Gilbert M. Foley; Albright College, 13th and Exeter St.s, Reading, PA 19603
Target Audience: Adults
Notes: Items, 75
Designed for use by social workers to identify areas of need after observation of the family in the home environment or at the agency. Each item in the scale is rated quantitatively and qualitatively. For use with families of handicapped children. Items cover nutrition, parent con-

cept of the child, marriage and the family, parent as teacher, parent's emotional well-being, home environment, medical needs.

14042
The Self-Directed Search, Revised, Form E. Holland, John L. 1985
Descriptors: *Adolescents; *Adults; Career Counseling; *Interest Inventories; *Reading Difficulties; Self Evaluation (Individuals); *Vocational Interests
Identifiers: SDS
Availability: Psychological Assessment Resources; P.O. Box 998, Odessa, FL 33556
Target Audience: 15-70
Self-administered, self-scored, and self-interpreted vocational counseling tool. Form E is for the benefit of those with limited reading ability, and the vocabulary employed is at the 4th grade reading level. This is a vocational interest inventory based on Holland's theory of careers. Individual completes the assessment booklet and obtains a 2-letter occupational code. Code is then used to locate suitable occupations in the booklet, the Jobs Finder.

14044
BCD Test: The Maryland/Baltimore County Design for Adult Basic Education. 1982
Subtests: Personal Data on Form; Calendar; Time; Money; Recognition of Printed Letters; Recognition of Cursive Letters; Reproduction of Printed Letters; Reproduction of Cursive Letters; Sequence of the Alphabet; Discrimination of Words; Recognition of Symbols for Beginning Sounds; Discrimination of Syllables; Directional/Spatial Information; Visual Perception of Symbols; Visual Discrimination among Symbols; Visual Perception of Words; Visual Discrimination among Words; Traffic Signs; Words in Isolation; Words in a Functional Setting; Sight Word Recognition in Context
Descriptors: *Adult Basic Education; *Adult Literacy; Adults; Criterion Referenced Tests; *Diagnostic Tests; Visual Discrimination; Word Recognition
Identifiers: Maryland
Availability: Cambridge, the Adult Education Co.; 888 Seventh Ave., New York, NY 10106
Target Audience: Adults
A series of 5 diagnostic/prescriptive tests designed to identify prereading instructional needs of the adult basic education student. It is made up of 21 different criterion-referenced subtests in skill areas necessary for literacy. Used with adult nonreaders at the Federal Level I grouping (levels 0-4 on standardized reading tests). No special training is necessary to administer or score the test. A chart of suggested remedial activities is included.

14045
The Body Image of Blind Children. Cratty, Bryant J.; Sams, Theressa A. 1968
Descriptors: Adolescents; *Blindness; *Body Image; Children; Concept Formation; Individual Testing
Identifiers: Lateral Awareness
Availability: The American Foundation for the Blind; 15 W. 16th St., New York, NY 10011
Target Audience: 5-16
Notes: Items, 80
Designed to measure the concept of body image in blind children. The child responds to simple commands concerned with the identification of body planes, body parts, body movements, laterality, and directionality. Data are available from a norming administration to a group of 90 blind children in a school for the blind.

14047
Eating Attitudes Test. Garner, David M.; Garfinkel, Paul E. 1982
Descriptors: Adolescents; *Anorexia Nervosa; *Attitude Measures; *Eating Habits; *Females; Rating Scales; Young Adults
Identifiers: EAT
Availability: Dr. David M. Garner; Toronto General Hospital, 101 College St., Toronto, Ontario M5G 9Z9, Canada
Target Audience: 13-25
Notes: Items, 26
Data suggest EAT is an objective and valid index of symptoms frequently seen in cases of anorexia nervosa. Has been used to detect abnormal eating habits in female adolescents and young adults. An earlier 40-item version can be found in Psychological Medicine; v9 p278 1979.

14049
Pediatric Examination of Educational Readiness at Middle Childhood. Levine, Melvin D. 1985
Descriptors: Adolescents; Behavior Problems; *Child Development; *Developmental Stages; Language Acquisition; Learning Problems; Motor Development; Neurological Organization; Preadolescents; Time Perspective; Visual Stimuli

Identifiers: Fine Motor Skills; Gross Motor Skills; PEERAMID
Availability: Educators Publishing Service; 75 Moulton St., Cambridge, MA 02238-9101
Target Audience: 9-15
A neurodevelopmental assessment procedure for use by health care and other professionals. Purpose is to generate part of a functional profile or empirical description of child's development and current neurological status. Can help in assessing children between ages of 9 and 15 who may be experiencing difficulties that affect learning, overall academic achievement, or behavioral adjustment. This inventory should always be used as part of a complete evaluation of a subject's problems and never be used in isolation. Inventory is divided into 6 major sections: minor neurological indicators, fine motor functions, language, gross motor functions, temporal-sequential organization, and visual processing.

14053
Hopkins Psychiatric Rating Scale. Derogatis, Leonard R. 1978
Descriptors: Adults; Anxiety; Clinical Diagnosis; Depression (Psychology); Hostility; Interpersonal Competence; Paranoid Behavior; Patients; Personality Measures; Psychomotor Skills; *Psychopathology; Psychosis; Psychosomatic Disorders; Rating Scales; Sleep
Identifiers: Abjection; Hysterical Personalities; Obsessive Compulsive Behavior; *Psychiatric Patients
Availability: Clinical Psychometric Research; P.O. Box 425, Riderwood, MD 21139
Target Audience: Adults
Notes: Items, 18
A rating scale of 17 psychiatric symptoms and a global level of pathology for use with psychiatric patients. Symptoms are somatization, obsessive-compulsive, interpersonal sensitivity, depression, anxiety, hostility, phobic anxiety, paranoid ideation, psychoticism, sleep disturbance, psychomotor retardation, hysterical behavior, abjection-disinterest, conceptual dysfunction, disorientation, excitement, and euphoria. Training in psychopathology is essential for use.

14067
Psychosocial Adjustment to Illness Scale—Self Report. Derogatis, Leonard R. 1983
Subtests: Health Care Orientation; Vocational Environment; Domestic Environment; Sexual Relationships; Extended Family Relationships; Social Environment; Psychological Distress
Descriptors: Adults; *Diseases; *Emotional Adjustment; *Patients; Questionnaires; Self Evaluation (Individuals); *Social Adjustment
Identifiers: PAIS
Availability: Clinical Psychometric Research; P.O. Box 425, Riderwood, MD 21139
Target Audience: Adults
Notes: Time, 30 approx.; Items, 46
Self-report, multidimensional questionnaire to quantify and assess the psychological and social adjustment of medical patients to their own illness or to the illness of a family member, such as a spouse or child. Subjects are asked to refer to the past 30 days when answering the questions. Profile forms are available for mixed cancer patients and cardiac patients.

14068
Psychosocial Adjustment to Illness Scale. Derogatis, Leonard R. 1983
Subtests: Health Care Orientation; Vocational Environment; Domestic Environment; Sexual Relationships; Extended Family Relationships; Social Environment; Psychological Distress
Descriptors: Adults; *Diseases; *Emotional Adjustment; Interviews; *Patients; Questionnaires; *Social Adjustment
Identifiers: PAIS
Availability: Clinical Psychometric Research; P.O. Box 425, Riderwood, MD 21139
Target Audience: Adults
Notes: Time, 30 approx.; Items, 46
A multidimensional, semistructured interview to quantify and assess the psychological and social adjustment of medical patients to their own illness or to the illness of a family member, such as a spouse or child. Subjects are asked to refer to the past 30 days when answering the questions. Interviews should be conducted by a trained health professional or interviewer. Adjustment profiles are available for lung cancer and renal dialysis patients.

14069
SCL-90-R. Derogatis, Leonard R. 1975
Subtests: Somatization; Obsessive-Compulsive; Interpersonal Sensitivity; Depression; Anxiety; Hostility; Phobic Anxiety; Paranoid Ideation; Psychoticism

Descriptors: Adults; *Anxiety; Computer Software; *Depression (Psychology); *Hostility; *Interpersonal Competence; *Paranoid Behavior; Patients; *Personality Measures; *Psychosis; *Psychosomatic Disorders; Scoring; Screening Tests; Self Evaluation (Individuals); Summative Evaluation
Identifiers: Obsessive Compulsive Behavior
Availability: Clinical Psychometric Research; P.O. Box 425, Riderwood, MD 21139
Target Audience: Adults
Notes: Items, 90

A self-report measure of the symptoms of psychological distress. Used for screening and measuring outcome of treatment or status of a patient. Norms are available for males and females who are inpatients, outpatients, or nonpatients. A scoring program is available for microcomputers (Apple and IBM-PC). This instrument has been translated into 20 languages. Contact the publisher for further information.

14075
The Nisonger Questionnaire for Parents. Loadman, William E.; And Others 1983
Descriptors: Adults; *Biographical Inventories; *Multiple Disabilities; *Parents; Questionnaires; *Young Children
Identifiers: NQP
Availability: Nisonger Center; Ohio State University, 1580 Cannon Dr., Columbus, OH 43210
Target Audience: Adults
Notes: Items, 57

Nontechnical questionnaire used to collect preliminary information on a multiply-handicapped child from the parents' perspective. Emphasizes current information on child's problems. Best used with children between 2 and 8 years old but can be used with younger or older children. Not a diagnostic instrument, NQP provides review of child's status and can be used prior to direct client contact to identify problem areas needing investigation. Areas covered by questionnaire include identifying information, services provided to the child, parent concerns, health care history, motor skills, diet and eating habits, communication, social-emotional issues, play and leisure time, and family life. Questionnaire results may be used by individual professionals, interdisciplinary clinical teams, day care and preschool staff, and university clinical training programs.

14076
PRG Interest Inventory. Nevil Institute for Rehabilitation and Service, Philadelphia, PA
Subtests: Mechanical; Computational; Scientific; Persuasive; Artistic; Literary; Musical; Social Service; Clerical; Outdoor
Descriptors: Adults; *Blindness; *Interest Inventories; Science Interests; Visual Impairments; *Vocational Interests
Availability: Associated Services for the Blind; 919 Walnut St., Philadelphia, PA 19107
Target Audience: Adults
Notes: Items, 150

A large-print list of job activities in 10 areas, e.g., mechanical, computational, scientific. Partially sighted persons can read the list themselves and make selections on an enlarged answer sheet. It is suggested that a tape may be prerecorded for totally blind testees. Separate norms are included for males and females. Used as a vocational interest measure.

14077
Non-Language Learning Test. Bauman, Mary K. 1947
Descriptors: Adults; Aptitude Tests; *Blindness; Clinical Diagnosis; *Learning; Nonverbal Tests; Performance Tests; *Predictive Measurement; Tactual Perception
Availability: Associated Services for the Blind; 919 Walnut St., Philadelphia, PA 19107
Target Audience: Adults
Notes: Time, 5

A formboard said to be useful for observing learning in blind adults in a standard way, rather than a test in the usual sense. It is for clinical use by experienced administrators to supplement a verbal I.Q. Said to be useful in predicting success on jobs involving concrete materials, though no statistical data are given. Abilities observed are learning with insight, superficial memorization, dealing with complexity, discrimination by touch. Plans for construction of the board by the user are included.

14080
Multilingual Aphasia Examination. Benton, A.L.; Hamsher, K de S. 1983
Subtests: Visual Naming; Sentence Repetition; Controlled Oral Word Association; Oral Spelling; Written Spelling; Block Spelling; MAE Token Test; Aural Comprehension; Reading Comprehension; Rating of Articulation; Rating of Praxic Features of Writing

Descriptors: Adults; *Aphasia; Articulation (Speech); Clinical Diagnosis; *Diagnostic Tests; Individual Testing; Rating Scales; Speech Skills; Spelling; Writing Difficulties
Availability: Psychological Assessment Resources; P.O. Box 998, Odessa, FL 33556
Target Audience: 16-69
Notes: Items, 119

Consists of 11 tests and rating scales to assess visual naming, repetition, fluency, articulation, spelling, aural comprehension, reading and writing (from a test of written spelling). This test is designed to evaluate the presence, severity, and type of aphasic disorder. The name derives from the translation of this instrument into various languages. None of these versions is standardized for clinical use. Further information on them can be obtained by writing AJA Associates, 504 Manor Dr., Iowa City, IA 52240.

14082
Color Span Test. Richman, Lynn C. 1978
Subtests: Visual Presentation-Visual Response; Visual Presentation-Verbal Response; Verbal Presentation-Visual Response; Verbal Presentation-Verbal Response
Descriptors: Children; Color; *Hearing Impairments; *Language Handicaps; *Learning Disabilities; *Memory; Verbal Tests
Identifiers: *Sequential Memory; Verbal Memory
Availability: Lynn C. Richman; Dept. of Pediatrics, 2523 JCP, University of Iowa Hospitals, Iowa City, IA
Target Audience: 8-12

Measures a child's verbal memory by requiring the child to remember color names in sequences of increasing length, to minimize the effects of other factors aiding memory. Designed for use with clinical populations such as learning-disabled, language-disordered, and hearing-impaired children.

14100
Carolina Picture Vocabulary Test (for Deaf and Hearing Impaired). Layton, Thomas L.; Holmes, David W. 1985
Descriptors: Adolescents; Children; *Deafness; *Hearing Impairments; Individual Testing; Pictorial Stimuli; Receptive Language; *Sign Language; *Vocabulary
Availability: Modern Education Corporation; P.O. Box 721, Tulsa, OK 74101
Target Audience: 2-16
Notes: Time, 15; Items, 130

Designed to measure the receptive sign language vocabulary in individuals where manual signing is the primary mode of communication. It was normed on a sample of deaf and hearing-impaired children who use manual signs as their primary means of communication. Items contain nouns, verbs, and adjectives which could be illustrated by sign. Uses photos of someone signing. Requires a pointing response to select a line drawing.

14105
Evaluating Educational Programs for Intellectually Gifted Students. Whitmore, Joanne Rand 1984
Descriptors: *Academically Gifted; Adults; *Decision Making; *Elementary Secondary Education; *Program Evaluation
Identifiers: EEPIGS
Availability: United Educational Services; P.O. Box 357, E. Aurora, NY 14052
Grade Level: K-12
Target Audience: Adults

Developed to assist educators with decision making based on professional judgments concerning the extent to which the special needs of the academically talented students from kindergarten through grade 12 are being met. It is a process tool used to guide the evaluation of educational programing for the intellectually gifted. Used to assist educational administrators, school psychologists, and teachers in seeking answers to evaluative questions. Questionnaires cover socioemotional needs and cognitive development and intellectual needs.

14106
Reversals Frequency Test. Gardner, Richard A. 1978
Subtests: Execution; Recognition; Discrimination
Descriptors: Adolescents; Children; *Dyslexia; Learning Disabilities; *Minimal Brain Dysfunction; Neurological Impairments; *Screening Tests; Visual Discrimination
Availability: Creative Therapeutics; P.O. Box R, Cresskill, NJ 07626
Target Audience: 5-15
Notes: Items, 52

Designed for the purpose of gathering normative data on the number of reversals of single letters and numbers a normal (not dyslexic) child will perform when writing, recognizing, or matching them. Assesses long-term visual storage and retrieval of linguistic symbols and visual dis-

criminatory capacity. Used as a screening test for dyslexia in combination with other instruments that detect minimal brain dysfunction.

14109
Functional Skills Screening Inventory. Becker, Heather; And Others 1984
Subtests: Basic Skills and Concepts; Communication; Personal Care; Homemaking; Work Skills and Concepts; Community Living; Social Awareness; Problem Behaviors
Descriptors: Adolescents; Adults; *Behavior Rating Scales; Children; *Computer Assisted Testing; *Criterion Referenced Tests; *Daily Living Skills; *Mild Disabilities; *Severe Disabilities
Identifiers: FSSI
Availability: Functional Resources Enterprises; 2734 Trail of the Madrones, Austin, TX 78746
Target Audience: 10-64
Notes: Items, 343

Used to assess critical living and working skills of moderately to severely handicapped persons. It is a criterion-referenced, behavioral checklist that covers a wide range of functional levels. Inventory is divided into 8 scales. Within each scale, items have been grouped into subscales and into 3 priority levels. Priority 1 are the basic elements of life and work skills training. Priority II items are required for successful group home living and/or sheltered employment. Priority III items facilitate independent living and working in the community. The inventory is available in print and in software for the IBM and Apple IIe personal computers. It can be used to assess current functioning, identify placement needs and options, identify and prioritize training needs and goals, document progress in training, and facilitate transition to adult living.

14112
Language Assessment Battery, 1982. New York City Board of Education, NY 1982
Subtests: Reading; Writing; Listening; Speaking
Descriptors: *Achievement Tests; Cloze Procedure; *Elementary School Students; Elementary Secondary Education; *English (Second Language); Language Dominance; Language Proficiency; *Limited English Speaking; Listening; Reading; *Secondary School Students; *Spanish Speaking; Speech Skills; *Student Placement; Writing (Composition)
Identifiers: LAB
Availability: Dr. Muriel M. Abbott; Board of Education of the City of New York, 131 Livingston St., Rm. 621, Brooklyn, NY 11201
Grade Level: K-12
Notes: Time, 60; Items, 130

A revised version of the Language Assessment Battery (1977, Riverside Publishing Company, Chicago) for use in the New York City Schools. It was designed to be of average difficulty for limited English speakers, and separate norms are available for them and the English proficient student so that comparisons can be made for placement purposes. The test is group administered and multiple choice, except for the speaking subtest which is individually administered and requires free-response from the student to each of a series of line drawings. The Reading, Writing, and Listening subtests use modified cloze procedure. The Writing subtest measures knowledge of language usage elements necessary for good writing. The Spanish version is not a translation but parallel in content and is used to measure language dominance. Parallel forms are available to measure gain in proficiency.

14118
Michigan English Language Assessment Battery. English Language Institute, Ann Arbor, MI
Subtests: Composition; Listening or Oral Rating; Objective Test
Descriptors: *Achievement Tests; Adults; Cloze Procedure; *English (Second Language); Grammar; Higher Education; Language Fluency; *Language Proficiency; Listening Skills; Rating Scales; Reading; Reading Comprehension; Vocabulary; Writing Skills
Identifiers: Oral Tests; Writing Samples
Availability: English Language Institute; Testing and Certification, University of Michigan, 3023 N. University Bldg., Ann Arbor, MI 48109-1057
Target Audience: Adults
Notes: Time, 150 approx.

Designed to measure the English-language proficiency, of adult non-native speakers who will use the language for academic purposes at the university level. The essay is judged on the clarity, fluency, and accuracy of the English. The Listening Test is tape recorded. An oral rating is optional. The Objective Test is of 100-items in multiple-choice format covering grammar, cloze reading, vocabulary, and reading passages. Administered at testing centers arranged by the publisher after registration by the test taker.

14126
Teacher Treatment Inventory. Weinstein, Rhona S. 1978

Subtests: Supportive Help; Negative Feedback and Teacher Direction; Work and Rule Orientation; High Expectations; Opportunity and Choice
Descriptors: Adults; Elementary Education; Elementary School Students; *Elementary School Teachers; Feedback; Helping Relationship; High Achievement; Low Achievement; Rating Scales; *Teacher Behavior; *Teacher Student Relationship
Availability: Rhona S. Weinstein; Psychology Dept., University of California, Berkeley, CA 94720
Grade Level: 4-6
Target Audience: Adults
Notes: Items, 44

Students rate the frequency with which 44 teacher behaviors might be used in situations with hypothetical target students. Four forms were administered according to whether the hypothetical student was male or female and a high or low achiever. Student perceptions of teacher treatment of male and female high and low achievers were measured.

14128
Smoker Complaint Scale, Revised. Schneider, Nina 1984
Descriptors: Adults; *Drug Abuse; Drug Rehabilitation; Rating Scales; *Smoking
Identifiers: Symptoms
Availability: Dr. Nina Schneider; VA Medical Center, Brentwood T350, Mail Code 691-5151D, Los Angeles, CA 90073
Target Audience: Adults
Notes: Time, 2; Items, 20

A self-report of physiological, emotional, craving states associated with smoking cessation. Items reflect the current state of the respondent. Has been used to measure withdrawal symptoms with or without nicotine replacement.

14133
Mobile Vocational Evaluation. Hester, Edward J.
Subtests: Finger Dexterity; Wrist-Finger Speed; Arm-Hand Steadiness; Manual Dexterity; Two-Arm Coordination; Two-Hand Coordination; Perceptual Accuracy; Spatial Perception; Aiming; Reaction Time; Abstract Reasoning; Verbal Reasoning; Numerical Reasoning; Reading; Arithmetic; Leadership Consideration; Leadership Structure; Sales; Following Directions
Descriptors: *Abstract Reasoning; *Adults; *Aptitude Tests; Arithmetic; Clinics; *College Students; *Disabilities; Eye Hand Coordination; Group Testing; Higher Education; High Schools; *High School Students; Individual Testing; Leadership; Reaction Time; Reading; Rehabilitation Centers; Salesmanship; *Spatial Ability; *Vocational Evaluation
Identifiers: Finger Dexterity; Following Directions; *Manual Dexterity
Availability: Hester Evaluation Systems; 2709 W. 29th St., Topeka, KS 66614
Grade Level: 9-16
Target Audience: Adults
Notes: Time, 240

A measure of vocationally related abilities. Given in a series of group and brief individual tests. The test is portable, weighing less than 30 pounds. All electronic parts are battery powered, and it may be administered by nonprofessional staff. The ability factor scores are combined with 17 personal characteristics to identify specific jobs out of a database of 700. For use by colleges, high schools, technical schools, rehabilitation agencies, hospitals and clinics.

14146
Grammatical Analysis of Elicited Language-Simple Sentence Level, Revised. Moog, Jean S.; Geers, Ann E. 1985
Descriptors: *Children; *Deafness; Expressive Language; *Hearing Impairments; Individual Testing; *Language Acquisition; *Language Tests; Oral Language; Sign Language; Total Communication
Identifiers: GAEL(S)
Availability: Central Institute for the Deaf; 818 S. Euclid, St. Louis, MO 63110
Target Audience: 4-9
Notes: Items, 94

Designed to evaluate hearing-impaired child's acquisition of specific grammatical structures. Consists of 21 activities used to elicit 94 target sentences exemplifying simple sentence structures. The grammatical categories include articles, noun modifiers, pronouns, subject nouns, object nouns, WH-questions, verbs, verb inflections, copulas, prepositions, and conjunctions and negatives. Revisions include expansion of the normative sample to 3 groups of hearing-impaired persons, changes in age range of hearing-impaired groups, and revision of the scoring system.

14147
Playfulness Instrument. Barnett, Lynn A.; Fiscella, Joan 1985
Subtests: Physical Spontaneity; Manifest Joy; Sense of Humor; Social Spontaneity; Cognitive Spontaneity
Descriptors: *Behavior Rating Scales; Gifted; *Play; *Preschool Children
Availability: Gifted Child Quarterly; v29 n2 p61-66 Spr 1985
Target Audience: 2-5
Notes: Items, 33

Developed to assess the degree of composite playfulness and 5 dimensions of playfulness of gifted and nongifted children. Results of one study indicated higher degrees of physical, social, and cognitive play styles among the gifted. Both groups were comparable in sense of humor and manifest joy.

14148
Inventory of Career Attitudes. Pinkney, James W.; Ramirez, Marty 1985
Descriptors: *Attitude Measures; *Career Planning; *Cultural Traits; High Schools; *High School Students; *Mexican Americans; Rating Scales; *Student Attitudes
Identifiers: *Chicanos; ICA
Availability: Journal of College Student Personnel; v26 n4 p300-05 Jul 1985
Grade Level: 11-12
Notes: Items, 28

Developed to study the career planning assumptions and beliefs of Chicano high school students and the cultural influences that affect their career planning process. Findings from using the inventory in a research study indicated Chicano students were less realistic in their career-planning attitudes than were White students.

14149
Attitudes toward College Inventory. Johanson, Roger P.; Vopava, Judy R. 1985
Descriptors: *Attitude Measures; *College Attendance; *Disadvantaged Youth; *Economically Disadvantaged; High Schools; *High School Students; Rating Scales; *Student Attitudes
Identifiers: ATCI
Availability: Journal of College Student Personnel; v26 n4 p339-42 Jul 1985
Grade Level: 9-12
Notes: Items, 30

Developed to assess high school students' attitudes toward college. Used in a study that investigated college attendance of economically disadvantaged students.

14150
Written Language Syntax Test. Berry, Sharon A. 1981
Descriptors: *Elementary School Students; Elementary Secondary Education; *Hearing Impairments; *Screening Tests; *Secondary School Students; *Syntax; *Written Language
Availability: Gallaudet College Press; Distribution Office, 800 Florida Ave., N.E., Washington, DC 20002
Grade Level: K-12

Screening instrument used to provide information on the performance of hearing-impaired students in written language syntax. Appropriate for use with students who have basic language skills. Tests are based on 69 instructional objectives. Information from the test can be used to design instructional language programs. Test contains a screening level to determine appropriate level for administration and 3 levels of assessment referenced to the objectives.

14154
SOI Learning Abilities Test: A Screening Form for Atypical Gifted. Meeker, Mary; Meeker, Robert 1975
Subtests: Convergent Production; Evaluation of Figural Classes; Evaluation of Symbolic Classes; Cognition of Symbolic Relations; Memory of Symbolic Units-Auditory; Memory of Symbolic Systems-Auditory; Cognition of Figural Systems; Cognition of Figural Transformations; Convergent Production of Symbolic Transformation; Convergent Production of Symbolic Implications
Descriptors: Abstract Reasoning; *Academic Ability; Adults; *Aptitude Tests; Attention; Convergent Thinking; Decision Making; Elementary Secondary Education; *Gifted Disadvantaged; Language Handicaps; Listening; Memory; Psychomotor Skills; Spatial Ability; Word Recognition
Identifiers: Convergent Production; Guilfords Structure of Intellect; Sequencing Skills; Symbols
Availability: SOI Institute; 343 Richmond St., El Segundo, CA 90245
Grade Level: K-12

Target Audience: Adults
Notes: Time, 60

A version of the SOI Learning Abilities Test (TC009264) for use in identifying gifted low-socioeconomic students and those who may be nonlanguage proficient but gifted. The SOI series is based on Guilford's multifactor model of intelligence. Instead of giving a single I.Q., the SOI series of tests provides a profile of learning abilities. Form AG covers psychomotor readiness, judging similarities, understanding abstract relations, auditory attending and sequencing, spatial perceptions, word recognition, reasoning with forms.

14157
SOI Learning Abilities Test: Developmental Vision Form. Meeker, Mary; Meeker, Robert 1975
Subtests: Cognition of Figural Units; Cognition of Semantic Units; Memory of Symbolic Systems-Visual; Memory of Symbolic Units-Visual; Convergent Production of Figural Units; Divergent Production of Semantic Units; Evaluation of Figural Units; Convergent Production of Symbolic Transformations; Cognition of Figural Transformations
Descriptors: *Academic Ability; Aptitude Tests; Cognitive Ability; Convergent Thinking; Creative Writing; Creativity; Decision Making; Diagnostic Tests; Divergent Thinking; *Elementary School Students; Elementary Secondary Education; *Learning Disabilities; Memory; Psychomotor Skills; School Readiness; *Screening Tests; *Secondary School Students; Spatial Ability; *Vision; Visual Discrimination; Vocabulary; Word Recognition
Identifiers: Closure; Guilfords Structure of Intellect
Availability: SOI Institute; 343 Richmond St., El Segundo, CA 90245
Grade Level: K-12

A use of the SOI Learning Abilities Test (TC009264) subtests that will screen for vision problems which affect learning. This test is for use by teachers, nurses and health personnel. It covers visual closure, vocabulary, visual attending, visual concentraion for sequencing, psychomotor readiness, creativity with words and ideas, visual discrimination, speed of word recognition, and spatial conservation. A checklist of behaviors that accompany severe subtle vision problems is included.

14163
Windward Rating Scale. Hamada, Roger S.; Tomikawa, Sandra 1984
Descriptors: *Behavior Rating Scales; Elementary Education; *Elementary School Students; *Handicap Identification; Learning Disabilities; *Screening Tests; Student Behavior
Identifiers: Hawaii; WRS
Availability: ERIC Document Reproduction Service; 3900 Wheeler Ave., Alexandria, VA 22304 (ED248263, 36 pages)
Grade Level: K-6
Notes: Items, 54

A locally developed teacher rating scale of student behavior to be used as a screening test in deciding whether or not to refer students for diagnostic evaluations for specific learning disabilities.

14165
The BULIT. Smith, Marcia C.; Thelen, Mark H. 1984
Descriptors: *Eating Habits; *Emotional Disturbances; *Females; *Self Evaluation (Individuals); *Bulimia
Availability: Journal of Consulting and Clinical Psychology; v52 n5 p863-72 Oct 1984
Target Audience: 18-22
Notes: Items, 32

A 32-item, self-report test developed to assess the symptoms of bulimia, which is classified as a distinct psychiatric disorder and is characterized by binge eating. The binge eating may be accompanied by self-induced vomiting, strict dieting, or laxative abuse.

14168
Decoding Skills Test. Richardson, Ellis; And Others 1979
Subtests: Basal Word Recognition; Phonic Decoding; Oral Passage Reading
Descriptors: *Criterion Referenced Tests; *Decoding (Reading); *Diagnostic Tests; *Dyslexia; Elementary Education; *Elementary School Students; Oral Reading; Phoneme Grapheme Correspondence; Remedial Reading; Word Recognition
Availability: ERIC Document Reproduction Service; 3900 Wheeler Ave., Alexandria, VA 22304 (ED193304, microfiche only)
Grade Level: 1-5
Notes: Items, 180

Designed as a measure of decoding skills for use in research on developmental dyslexia. May be used as a diagnostic-prescriptive measure to evaluate children needing remedial reading. A brief reading comprehension test is included. This test is criterion referenced. Words used in subtest one are embedded in the oral passages.

14178
Research Diagnostic Criteria, Third Edition Updated. Endicott, Jean; And Others 1981
Subtests: Formal Thought Disorder; Schizophrenia; Manic Syndrome; Depressive Syndrome; Schizoaffective Disorders; Schizophrenia; Briquet's Disorder; Cyclothymic; Hypomania; Intermittent Depressive Disorder; Minor Depressive Disorder; Labile Personality; Generalized Anxiety Disorder; Panic Disorder; Phobic Disorder; Obsessive Compulsive Disorder; Antisocial Personality; Alcoholism; Drug Use Disorder; Unspecified Functional Psychosis; Schizotypal Features
Descriptors: Adults; Alcoholism; Anxiety; *Clinical Diagnosis; Depression (Psychology); Drug Use; Interviews; Personality Problems; *Psychopathology; Psychosis; Research Tools; Schizophrenia
Identifiers: RDC
Availability: New York State Psychiatric Institute; Research Assessment and Training Center, 722 W. 168th St., Rm. 341, New York, NY 10032
Target Audience: 18-65

Criteria for the description of research subjects with functional psychiatric illnesses. Used to obtain homogeneous groups of subjects. Completed based on an interview, or with detailed case record material. The specific criteria refer to either symptoms, duration or course of illness, or level of severity or impairment. They also allow for assignment of subjects on the basis of episode diagnosis as well as longitudinal diagnosis. This instrument should only be used after study of the Schedule for Affective Disorders and Schizophrenia (TC013756).

14230
Manual for the Assessment of a Deaf-Blind Multiply Handicapped, Child, Third Edition. Rudolph, James M.; And Others 1978
Subtests: Gross Motor Development; Fine Motor Development; Personal-Self Help Skills; Communication; Auditory Development; Cognition; Social Development; Mobility
Descriptors: Adolescents; Auditory Perception; *Child Development; Children; Cognitive Ability; *Deaf Blind; Elementary Secondary Education; Interpersonal Communication; Job Skills; *Multiple Disabilities; Physical Fitness; Psychomotor Skills; Self Care Skills; *Sheltered Workshops; Social Development
Identifiers: Fine Motor Skills; Gross Motor Skills
Availability: Midwest Regional Center for Services to Deaf-Blind Children; P.O. Box 30008, Lansing, MI 48909
Target Audience: 6-18
Notes: Items, 1000

A collection of scales for use in measuring a deaf-blind student's development and progress. They are said to possess more accuracy for this population than do scales designed for students without sensory impairments. May be used by parents, houseparents, teacher aides, and other staff. A training guide is included. Used to measure skills necessary for entrance into the protected work environment.

14237
Classroom Teachers' Self Reported Attitudes toward Mainstreaming Emotionally Disturbed Children. Vacc, Nicholas A.; Kirst, Nancy 1977
Descriptors: Adults; *Attitude Measures; Depression (Psychology); Elementary Education; Elementary School Teachers; *Emotional Disturbances; Hyperactivity; *Mainstreaming; Rating Scales; *Teacher Attitudes; Withdrawal (Psychology)
Availability: Elementary School Journal; v77 n4 p309-17 Mar 1977
Target Audience: Adults
Notes: Items, 20

A measure of elementary school teachers' attitudes toward the mainstreaming of emotionally disturbed children, those who exhibit deviant behavior such as hyperactivity, impulsive or depressive behavior, or withdrawal. Ratings were made on a 5-point Likert scale. Items covered special class versus mainstreaming; effects of mainstreaming on the nonhandicapped children; and effects of mainstreaming on the regular classroom teacher.

14275
Test of Computational Processes. Kingston, Neldon D. 1985

Descriptors: *Achievement Tests; Addition; *Computation; Criterion Referenced Tests; Decimal Fractions; Division; Elementary Education; *Elementary School Students; Fractions; Multiplication; Norm Referenced Tests; Remedial Instruction; *Screening Tests; Subtraction; Whole Numbers
Identifiers: TCP
Availability: DLM Teaching Resources; One DLM Park, Allen, TX 75002
Grade Level: 1-8
Notes: Items, 122

Developed to measure students' ability to add, subtract, multiply, and divide with whole numbers, fractions, and decimals. Some measurement facts and calculations are also included. Contains computational processes most commonly found in grades 1 through 8. Untimed test independent of vocabulary and reading level. Appropriate for use with students in grades 1 through 8. Administration time can range from 20 to 80 minutes. Developed using criterion-referenced principles, also using a norm-referenced test standardized on more than 6,000 subjects. Can be useful in identifying remedial and mathematically handicapped students.

14283
Preschool Development Inventory. Ireton, Harold 1984
Descriptors: *Behavior Problems; *Child Development; *Disabilities; *Preschool Children; *Screening Tests; Young Children
Identifiers: PDI
Availability: Behavior Science Systems; Box 1108, Minneapolis, MN 55440
Target Audience: 3-5
Notes: Items, 84

Brief screening inventory for use with preschool children from age 3. Parent completes questionnaire which is designed to help identify children with developmental and other problems that may interfere with child's ability to learn. Inventory consists of a 60-item measure of child's general developmental status and a 24-item symptoms and behavior problems list. The parent also describes the child in his/her own words, reports special problems or handicaps of the child, and expresses any concerns about child.

14285
Pain and Distress Scale. Zung, William W. K. 1983
Descriptors: Adolescents; Adults; Health; Older Adults; *Patients; Rating Scales; Self Evaluation (Individuals)
Identifiers: PAD; *Pain; Self Report Measures
Availability: Psychosomatics; v24 n10 p887-90, 892-94 Oct 1983
Target Audience: 16-90
Notes: Items, 20

Scale to assess pain and distress. Scale is intended to assess various aspects of dysfunction which pain patients experience, be short and simple, be quantitative so that results can be analyzed statistically, and be self-administering. Scale was constructed on basis of clinical diagnostic criteria based on most commonly found characteristics involved in pain and associated distress. The clinical criteria include presence of somatosensory pain, mood changes, and behavioral changes. Scale can be used in research and clinical settings to provide an overall index of pain and distress present, to determine a pain profile of the subject, and to evaluate the effectiveness of various forms of pain treatment.

14290
Test of Language Competence. Wiig, Elisabeth H.; Secord, Wayne 1985
Subtests: Understanding Ambiguous Sentences; Making Influences; Recreating Sentences; Understanding Metaphoric Expressions
Descriptors: Adolescents; Adults; Children; Individual Testing; *Language Handicaps; *Language Tests; *Screening Tests
Identifiers: TLC
Availability: The Psychological Corporation; 555 Academic Ct., San Antonio, TX 78204-0952
Target Audience: 9-64
Notes: Time, 60 approx.

Design to aid speech-language pathologists, psychologists, and special educators to identify children ages 9 and above and adults with language disabilities. Expected to identify those who have not attained the expected levels of competence in semantics, syntax, and/or pragmatics. The test is not designed to provide in-depth assessment at the level of phonology. Test is individually administered.

14291
Test of Gross Motor Development. Ulrich, Dale A. 1985
Subtests: Locomotion; Object Control
Descriptors: *Elementary Education; *Individual Testing; *Performance Tests; *Preschool Education; Primary Education; *Psychomotor Skills; *Special Education
Identifiers: *Gross Motor Skills; TGMD

Availability: Pro-Ed; 5341 Industrial Oaks Blvd., Austin, TX 78735
Target Audience: 3-10
Notes: Items, 12

Individually administered test that evaluates gross motor functioning of children ages 3 to 10 years. Measures 12 gross motor skills frequently taught to preschoolers and children in the primary grades and in special education classes. Skills are grouped into 2 subtests: locomotion and object control. Locomotion subtest assesses the run, gallop, hop, leap, horizontal jump, skip, and slide. Object control subtest measures the 2-hand strike, stationary bounce, catch, kick, and overhand throw. Purposes of developing the test include designing a measure that represents content frequently taught to children ages 3 to 10, developing a test that can be used by a wide variety of professionals with minimum training, that provides norm- and criterion-referenced interpretations, and that places a priority on the gross motor skill sequence rather than the product of performance.

14296
Adolescent and Adult Psychoeducational Profile. Mesibov, Gary B.; And Others 1982
Subtests: Direct Observation Scale; School/Work Scale
Descriptors: Adolescents; Adults; *Autism; *Clinical Diagnosis; Cognitive Ability; Communication Skills; *Daily Living Skills; *Educational Diagnosis; Interpersonal Competence; *Job Skills; Mental Retardation; Observation; Perceptual Motor Coordination; Psychoeducational Clinics; *Psychomotor Skills; Verbal Ability
Identifiers: AAPEP
Availability: Orange Industries; 229 W. Tyron St., Hillsborough, NC 27278
Target Audience: 13-65

An adolescent and adult version of the Psychoeducational Profile (TC010778) designed to measure an autistic person's functioning: imitation, perception, fine and gross motor skills, eye-hand integration, cognitive performance, verbal performance, pathology. Also includes observations of skills at home and in the school or work environment. Each scale covers 6 areas: vocational skills, independent functioning, leisure, vocational behavior, functional communication, and interpersonal behavior. Used with autistic persons functioning intellectually within the moderately to severely retarded range, higher functioning autistic persons, and retarded persons.

14313
Adult Growth Examination. Morgan, Robert 1986
Descriptors: *Adults; *Aging (Individuals); *Human Body; *Older Adults; *Physical Development; *Standardized Tests
Identifiers: AGE; *Body Age; *Physiological Age
Availability: Dr. Robert Morgan; 1350 M St., Fresno, CA 93721
Target Audience: 19-71
Notes: Time, 15 approx.

A standardized test for body age in humans based on research data acquired over a 20-year period. Quick procedure for quantifying adults' physiological age. Built mainly on 3 subtests: auditory, visual, and cardiovascular. Provides supplementary indices also. Uses include research, program evaluation, individual counseling, industrial assessment, and personal health awareness. May be used by individuals to monitor their own body age and professionally by psychologists, physicians, mental health workers, nurses, researchers, and other professionals in the health or life sciences.

14315
Boston Naming Test. Kaplan, Edith; And Others 1983
Descriptors: Adults; Aphasia; Elementary Education; *Elementary School Students; *Individual Testing; Language Processing; *Pictorial Stimuli; *Visual Measures; *Vocabulary
Identifiers: Boston Diagnostic Aphasia Examination
Availability: Lea & Febiger; 600 S. Washington Square, Philadelphia, PA 19106
Grade Level: K-5
Target Audience: Adults
Notes: Items, 60

Visual test which may be purchased separately or as part of the materials for the Boston Diagnostic Aphasia Examination. Subject is asked to name stimulus pictures within 20 seconds. Authors believe test is useful in detecting mild word-retrieval problems and may be useful with subjects who demonstrate dementia or with children demonstrating developmental reading and speech problems.

14339
Test of Written Spelling-2. Larsen, Stephen C.; Hammill, Donald D. 1986
Subtests: Predictable Words; Unpredictable Words
Descriptors: *Achievement Tests; *Elementary School Students; Elementary Secondary Education; Remedial Programs; *Secondary School Students; *Spelling

Identifiers: TWS2
Availability: Pro-Ed; 5341 Industrial Oaks Blvd., Austin, TX 78735
Grade Level: 1-12
Notes: Items, 100

Revision of an earlier test. Is used to assess students' ability to spell words. Consists of 2 subtests, both employing a dictated word format. One subtest measures predictable words that conform to rules and generalizations. The second subtest measures unpredictable words. Normed on a large national sample of students in grades 1 through 12. Appropriate for use with remedial students as well as for regular students.

14340
Detroit Tests of Learning Aptitude—Primary. Hammill, Donald D.; Bryant, Brian R. 1986
Subtests: Verbal Aptitude; Nonverbal Aptitude; Conceptual Aptitude; Structural Aptitude; Attention-Enhanced Aptitude; Attention-Reduced Aptitude; Motor Enhanced Aptitude; Motor-Reduced Aptitude
Descriptors: *Academic Aptitude; *Aptitude Tests; *Cognitive Ability; Individual Testing; Intelligence; Learning Problems; Long Term Memory; Nonverbal Ability; Psychomotor Skills; Screening Tests; Short Term Memory; Verbal Ability; *Young Children
Identifiers: DTLA(P)
Availability: Pro-Ed; 5341 Industrial Oaks Blvd., Austin, TX 78735
Target Audience: 3-9
Notes: Time, 45 approx.; Items, 130

Designed to measure intellectual abilities of children ages 3-9. Measures the same basic theoretical domains as the Detroit Tests of Learning Aptitude, Revised (TC013737): linguistics, cognition, attention, and motor. Items are arranged in developmental order from easiest to most difficult. Particularly useful with low-functioning school-aged children. Can be used to isolate special individual strengths and weaknesses and to identify children deficient in general and specific aptitudes. May also be used in research studies investigating aptitude, intelligence, and cognitive behavior.

14342
Twenty-Two Item Screening Score. Langner, Thomas S. 1962
Descriptors: Adults; Group Testing; *Patients; *Psychiatry; Psychosomatic Disorders; *Screening Tests; Surveys
Identifiers: Midtown Community Mental Health Study; Somatization
Availability: Journal of Health and Human Behavior; v3 p269-76 1962
Target Audience: Adults
Notes: Items, 22

Designed to provide a rough indication of where psychiatric patients lie on a continuum of impairment in life functioning resulting from common types of psychiatric symptoms. May be used in mass surveys to select candidates for further examination or to measure gross symptomatology of groups. Many items were included because they are typical of complaints that psychiatrists hear in their practices. Items are primarily psychophysiological.

14364
Preschool Preposition Test. Aaronson, May R. 1980
Descriptors: *Cognitive Development; Developmental Disabilities; Mental Retardation; *Preschool Children; *Receptive Language; *Screening Tests
Availability: May R. Aaronson; National Institute of Mental Health, 5600 Fishers Ln., Rockville, MD 20857
Target Audience: 3-5
Notes: Time, 5; Items, 23

A quick screening method for determining delay in cognitive development. Uses receptive language. Can be used with mentally retarded, autistic, emotionally disturbed, and physically handicapped children. A test board and a magnetized ball are required for administration. These are loaned by the author upon request. The test taker places a ball into position on a board in compliance with a direction containing a preposition.

14365
Pre-Vocational Readiness Battery. Valpar International, Tucson, AZ
Subtests: Developmental Assessment; Workshop Evaluation; Vocational Interest Screening; Interpersonal Social Skills; Independent Living Skills
Descriptors: Adolescents; Adults; Aptitude Tests; Daily Living Skills; Interpersonal Competence; Job Skills; *Mental Retardation; Occupational Tests; Personnel Evaluation; Vocational Interests; *Vocational Rehabilitation; *Work Sample Tests
Availability: Valpar International Corporation; 3801 E. 34th St., Tucson, AZ 85713
Target Audience: 13-65

Designed to assess the trainable retarded person's ability to function in a vocational or independent living setting. Uses hands-on work samples that require little or no language or reading skills. Identifies the subject's barriers to competitive employment. Performance is compared to 9 norm groups: independent living, competitive employment, special learning disabilities, high school special needs, rehabilitation workshop, sheltered workshop, activity center, homebound employment, institutionalized work, and institutionalized nonworking. Uses kit materials, photos, and manipulative devices.

14366
Missouri Children's Behavior Checklist. Sines, Jacob O.; Pauker, Jerome D. 1969
Subtests: Aggression; Inhibition; Activity Level; Sleep Disturbance; Somatization; Sociability
Descriptors: Adolescents; Aggression; *Behavior Patterns; *Behavior Problems; Check Lists; Children; Hyperactivity; Inhibition; Interpersonal Competence; *Personality Measures; Psychosomatic Disorders; Sleep
Availability: Journal of Consulting and Clinical Psychology; v33 n6 p728-34 1969
Target Audience: 5-16
Notes: Items, 70

A set of descriptions of children's behaviors to be rated by a child's parent. Items measure 6 dimensions or scales. Used to identify groups of children at the extreme of the several clinically significant dimensions of children's behavior. Developed as part of a research study to develop a personality test.

14371
Steps Up Developmental Screening Program for Children Birth to Three. Carr, Diane; And Others 1977
Descriptors: *Child Development; Cognitive Ability; Developmental Disabilities; Hearing (Physiology); *Infants; Interpersonal Competence; Language Skills; Physical Development; Physical Disabilities; Psychomotor Skills; *Screening Tests; *Toddlers; Vision; Young Children
Identifiers: SUDS
Availability: El Paso Rehabilitation Center; 2630 Richmond, El Paso, TX 79930
Target Audience: 0-3
Notes: Time, 5

Designed for use as a brief screening tool to identify children who need further evaluation, for wholesale screening in the community, in clinics, doctors' offices, by social workers, day care staff, and others not experienced with developmental problems. There are 33 test cards with different cards for each 2-week age category for children under 1 year and for 3-month categories for children between ages 1 and 3. Each card contains items covering gross and fine motor skills, language skill, cognitive-social skills, vision, hearing, head circumference, dislocated hip, and convulsions.

14375
JOBTAP: Job Training Assessment Program. Educational Testing Service, Princeton, NJ 1984
Descriptors: Adults; Blue Collar Occupations; *Dislocated Workers; Job Search Methods; Job Skills; *Job Training; Knowledge Level; *Measures (Individuals); *Unemployment; Unskilled Workers; Vocational Interests; Work Experience
Identifiers: *Test Batteries
Availability: CTB/McGraw Hill; Del Monte Research Park, 2500 Garden Rd., Monterey, CA 93940
Target Audience: Adults

Integrated system of materials and services that provides information leading to placement of individuals in job training programs. Target populations for whom JOBTAP is designed include unemployed workers, displaced or dislocated blue-collar workers, new unskilled labor force entrants, and disadvantaged, chronically unemployed workers. The system includes 3 phases: assessment, planning, and implementation. During assessment, subject completes a battery of tests and inventories that include assessment of job searching skills; job knowledge; an interest and work experience inventory; and an inventory of employment skills. The assessment results can be used in the planning phase by the counselor and client to determine training and employment opportunities. Implementation phase includes a description of recommended steps and activities for client to follow with the help of the counselor.

14379
Parent and Teacher Rating Forms for the Assessment of Hyperkinesis in Children. Conners, C. Keith
Descriptors: Adolescents; Children; *Hyperactivity; *Minimal Brain Dysfunction; Parent Attitudes; Rating Scales; Teacher Attitudes
Availability: Keller, Peter A.; Ritt, Lawrence G., eds. Innovations in Clinical Practice: A Source Book. Volume 1. Sarasota, FL: Professional Resource Exchange, 1982
Target Audience: 3-17

Useful in assessment of children diagnosed as hyperkinetic as a result of minimal brain dysfunction. May also be useful to clinician in identifying other symptoms which appear as factors on the scale. The parent's questionnaire consists of 48 items and assesses 5 primary factors: conduct problems, learning problems, psychosomatic, impulsive hyperactive, and anxiety. The teacher's questionnaire has 28 items and assesses 3 primary factors: conduct problems, hyperactivity, and inattentive-passive.

14380
Suicidal Death Prediction Scales. Lettieri, Dan J.
Descriptors: Adolescents; Adults; *Crisis Intervention; *Hotlines (Public); Older Adults; Questionnaires; *Suicide
Availability: Keller, Peter A.; Ritt, Lawrence G., eds. Innovations in Clinical Practice: A Source Book. Volume 1. Sarasota, FL: Professional Resource Exchange, 1982
Target Audience: 13-75

Four suicide risk scales to measure and predict the risk of a person engaging in future suicidal ideations, threats, attempts, or suicidal completion. These are to be used in phone work at crisis prevention centers. The 4 scales are for older males (40 years and older), younger males (under 40 years), older females (40 years and older), and younger females (under 40 years). When using the scales, if it is impossible to ask subject all the questions on the scale, volunteer may use a shortened form of the scale. This instrument was included in this volume by permission of the original publisher and can be found on pages 163-92, chapter 11 of The Prediction of Suicide edited by Aaron T. Beck and others, and published by The Charles Press Publishers, Bowie, MD, 1975. The scales were developed by the author in collaboration with the staff of the Los Angeles Suicide Prevention Center.

14381
A Substance Abuse Screening Check List. Foreman, Bruce D.
Descriptors: Adolescents; Adults; *Alcoholism; Check Lists; Court Litigation; *Drinking; *Drug Abuse; *Intervention; Older Adults; *Screening Tests; Self Evaluation (Individuals)
Availability: Keller, Peter A.; Ritt, Lawrence G., eds. Innovations in Clinical Practice: A Source Book. Volume 1. Sarasota, FL: Professional Resource Exchange, 1982
Target Audience: 16-75
Notes: Time, 3 approx.; Items, 15

A screening instrument developed for use by counselors in a pretrial intervention program in Columbia, SC. Self-administered and self-scored inventory in which items were worded for applicability to either alcohol or drug use. Can be used as an aid to clinical interviewing. Items can be reworded into questions for use in a diagnostic interview to determine how much a client's life revolves around substance use.

14383
Current Symptom Checklist for Children. Walker, C. Eugene
Descriptors: *Affective Behavior; *Behavior Problems; *Children; Parent Attitudes; *Psychological Evaluation; Psychotherapy; Questionnaires
Availability: Keller, Peter A.; Ritt, Lawrence G., eds. Innovations in Clinical Practice: A Source Book. Volume 2. Sarasota, FL: Professional Resource Exchange, 1983
Target Audience: 6-12
Notes: Time, 10 approx.; Items, 71

Developed for use in an outpatient clinic for children to serve as an interview guide during the initial diagnostic assessment of child therapy cases. Questionnaire is completed by child's parents. Questionnaire is to serve only as a guide to interviewing child and makes no claims for reliability, validity or other psychometric properties.

14384
Hendler Screening Test for Chronic Back Pain Patients. Hendler, Nelson 1979
Descriptors: Adults; Diseases; *Medical Evaluation; *Patients; Questionnaires; *Screening Tests
Identifiers: *Back Pain; *Pain
Availability: Keller, Peter A.; Ritt, Lawrence G., eds. Innovations in Clinical Practice: A Source Book. Volume 2. Sarasota, FL: Professional Resource Exchange, 1983
Target Audience: Adults

Brief screening test useful in assisting with clinical evaluation of patients with chronic back pain. Information obtained can be helpful in discriminating between patients who may or may not benefit from surgery, as a therapy for back pain. Author emphasizes that this is not a refined test and that important decisions regarding treatment should not be made on basis of this instrument alone nor should it be substituted for other more formal tests. It should be used as only one aid in the diagnostic process.

14391
Valpar Component Work Sample 1 (Small Tools-Mechanical). Valpar International, Tucson, AZ
Descriptors: Adults; Aptitude Tests; Blindness; Deafness; Disabilities; *Hand Tools; Job Skills; *Mechanical Skills; Occupational Tests; Personnel Evaluation; Sign Language; *Work Sample Tests
Identifiers: Finger Dexterity; Manual Dexterity
Availability: Valpar International Corporation; 3801 E. 34th St., Tucson, AZ 85713
Target Audience: Adults
Notes: Time, 60
A measure of the ability to work with small tools such as screwdrivers and pliers, motor coordination, manual dexterity, finger dexterity, ability to perform long repetitious tasks, physical perseverance, and frustration tolerance. Can also be used with disabled persons. A special kit is available for use with blind persons. Videotaped, signed instructions are available for the deaf testees.

14392
Valpar Component Work Sample 2 (Size Discrimination). Valpar International, Tucson, AZ
Descriptors: Adults; Blindness; Deafness; Disabilities; Occupational Tests; Personnel Evaluation; Sign Language; *Visual Discrimination; *Work Sample Tests
Identifiers: Size Discrimination
Availability: Valpar International Corporation; 3801 E. 34th St., Tucson, AZ 85713
Target Audience: Adults
Measures a person's ability to perform work tasks requiring visual size discrimination, motor coordination, and manual dexterity. Also provides the opportunity to observe worker characteristics such as decision-making, acceptance of supervision, tolerance of time pressure, and concentration on tasks. Can be used with disabled persons. A special kit is available for use with blind persons. Videotaped, signed instructions are available for deaf persons.

14393
Valpar Component Work Sample 3 (Numerical Sorting). Valpar International, Tucson, AZ
Descriptors: Adults; *Clerical Occupations; Deafness; Disabilities; Filing; *Numbers; Occupational Tests; Perceptual Motor Coordination; Personnel Evaluation; Sign Language; *Work Sample Tests
Identifiers: Finger Dexterity; Manual Dexterity
Availability: Valpar International Corporation; 3801 E. 34th St., Tucson, AZ 85713
Target Audience: Adults
Measures a person's ability to perform work tasks requiring the use of numbers and numerical series, sorting, filing, categorizing by numerical arrangement, form perception, clerical aptitude, motor coordination, and finger and manual dexterity. Used with occupations involving examining, grading and sorting, keeping records and receipts, and recording information. Can be used with disabled persons. Videotaped, signed instructions are available for deaf persons.

14394
Valpar Component Work Sample 4 (Upper Extremity Range of Motion). Valpar International, Tucson, AZ
Descriptors: Adults; Blindness; Deafness; Disabilities; Fatigue (Biology); *Motion; Occupational Tests; Perceptual Motor Coordination; Personnel Evaluation; Sign Language; Visual Impairments; *Work Sample Tests
Identifiers: Finger Dexterity; Manual Dexterity
Availability: Valpar International Corporation; 3801 E. 34th St., Tucson, AZ 85713
Target Audience: Adults
A measure of a person's range of motion and work tolerance of the upper torso, including the use of shoulders, upper arms, forearms, elbows, wrists, hands, and fingers. Useful also for measuring fatigue and discomfort, finger dexterity, and sense of touch. A special kit is available for use with visually impaired or blind persons. Signed, videotaped instructions are available for deaf persons. This kit is also useful with nondisabled persons. Consists of a box to which bolts must be attached from various directions.

14395
Valpar Component Work Sample 5 (Clerical Comprehension and Aptitude). Valpar International, Tucson, AZ
Descriptors: Adults; Aptitude Tests; Bookkeeping; *Clerical Occupations; Deafness; Disabilities; Occupational Tests; Personnel Evaluation; Sign Language; Spatial Ability; Typewriting; *Work Sample Tests
Identifiers: Finger Dexterity; Manual Dexterity

Availability: Valpar International Corporation; 3801 E. 34th St., Tucson, AZ 85713
Target Audience: Adults
Measures a person's ability to learn and perform a variety of clerical tasks. Measures verbal and numerical ability, spatial and form perception, finger and manual dexterity. Three sections measure general clerical, bookkeeping, and typing skills. The kit includes a modified typewriter and requires the use of an adding machine. Can also be used with disabled persons. Signed, videotaped instructions are available for use with deaf persons.

14396
Valpar Component Work Sample 6 (Independent Problem Solving). Valpar International Corporation, Tucson, AZ
Descriptors: Adults; Color; Deafness; Disabilities; Occupational Tests; Perceptual Motor Coordination; Personnel Evaluation; *Problem Solving; Sign Language; Spatial Ability; Visual Discrimination; *Work Sample Tests
Identifiers: Finger Dexterity; Manual Dexterity
Availability: Valpar International Corporation; 3801 E. 34th St., Tucson, AZ 85713
Target Audience: Adults
Measures a person's ability to perform work tasks requiring the visual comparison and proper selection of a series of abstract designs. The purpose of the work sample is to determine a person's basic independent problem-solving ability. Also measures verbal and numerical skills, spatial and form perception, motor coordination, finger and manual dexterity, and color discrimination. May be used with disabled persons. Evaluee must be sighted.

14397
Valpar Component Work Sample 7 (Multi-Level Sorting). Valpar International Corporation, Tucson, AZ
Descriptors: Adults; Color; Deafness; *Decision Making Skills; Disabilities; Occupational Tests; Personnel Evaluation; Sign Language; Visual Discrimination; *Work Sample Tests
Identifiers: Finger Dexterity; Manual Dexterity
Availability: Valpar International Corporation; 3801 E. 34th St., Tucson, AZ 85713
Target Audience: Adults
Measures a person's ability to make decisions while performing work tasks requiring physical manipulation and visual discrimination of colors, numbers, letters, and combinations of these. Useful in observing decision-making skills that would determine entry level into a position requiring them, such as laboratory tester, sales agent, equipment assembler. Can be used with the disabled. Signed, videotaped instructions are available for deaf persons. Evaluee must be sighted.

14398
Valpar Component Work Sample 8 (Simulated Assembly). Valpar International Corporation, Tucson, AZ
Descriptors: Adults; Aptitude Tests; *Assembly (Manufacturing); Blindness; Deafness; Disabilities; Job Skills; Occupational Tests; Perceptual Motor Coordination; Personnel Evaluation; Sign Language; Visual Impairments; *Work Sample Tests
Identifiers: Finger Dexterity; Manual Dexterity
Availability: Valpar International Corporation; 3801 E. 34th St., Tucson, AZ 85713
Target Audience: Adults
Notes: Time, 20
Measures a person's ability to work at an assembly task requiring repetitive physical manipulation, bilateral use of the upper extremities, finger and manual dexterity, and motor coordination. Useful with conveyor-assembly positions in which materials move toward and then away from workers. Can be used with disabled or nondisabled workers. A special kit has been developed for use with blind or visually impaired persons. Signed, videotaped instructions for deaf persons are also available.

14399
Valpar Component Work Sample 9 (Whole Body Range of Motion). Valpar International Corporation, Tucson, AZ
Descriptors: Adults; Blindness; Deafness; Disabilities; *Motion; Occupational Tests; Perceptual Motor Coordination; Personnel Evaluation; *Physical Mobility; Sign Language; Visual Impairments; *Work Sample Tests
Identifiers: Manual Dexterity
Availability: Valpar International Corporation; 3801 E. 34th St., Tucson, AZ 85713
Target Audience: Adults
Measures the agility of a person's gross body movements of the trunk, arms, hands, legs, and fingers as they relate to the ability to perform job tasks. Also concerns manual dexterity and spatial and form perception, and fatigue. The evaluator observes physical reactions to the muscular stress necessary to the performance of the tasks. Can be

administered to disabled and nondisabled. A special kit is available for the blind. Signed, videotaped instructions are available for deaf persons.

14400
Valpar Component Work Sample 10 (Tri-Level Measurement). Valpar International Corporation, Tucson, AZ
Descriptors: Adults; Aptitude Tests; Blindness; Deafness; Decision Making; Disabilities; *Inspection; Job Skills; *Measurement; Occupational Tests; Perceptual Motor Coordination; Personnel Evaluation; Sign Language; Visual Impairments; *Work Sample Tests
Identifiers: Finger Dexterity; Manual Dexterity
Availability: Valpar International Corporation; 3801 E. 34th St., Tucson, AZ 85713
Target Audience: Adults
Measures a person's ability to perform very simple to very precise inspection and measurement tasks. The evaluee makes increasingly difficult decisions about whether machined parts fall within specific tolerances. Skills needed are reasoning, clerical aptitude, finger and manual dexterity, and motor coordination. Can be administered to disabled or nondisabled persons. A special kit is available for the blind. Signed, videotaped instructions are available for deaf persons.

14401
Valpar Component Work Sample 11 (Eye-Hand-Foot Coordination). Valpar International Corporation, Tucson, AZ
Descriptors: Adults; Deafness; Disabilities; Occupational Tests; *Perceptual Motor Coordination; Personnel Evaluation; Physical Mobility; Sign Language; *Spatial Ability; *Work Sample Tests
Identifiers: Manual Dexterity
Availability: Valpar International Corporation; 3801 E. 34th St., Tucson, AZ 85713
Target Audience: Adults
Measures the ability of a person to use eyes, hands, and feet simultaneously and with coordination. Abilities measured are spatial perception, and finger and manual dexterity. May be used with disabled and nondisabled persons, but they must be sighted. Signed, videotaped instructions for deaf persons are also available.

14402
Valpar Component Work Sample 12 (Soldering and Inspection Electronic). Valpar International Corporation, Tucson, AZ
Descriptors: Adults; Deafness; Disabilities; *Electronics; Evaluative Thinking; Inspection; Occupational Tests; Personnel Evaluation; Sign Language; Spatial Ability; Visual Perception; *Work Sample Tests
Identifiers: *Soldering
Availability: Valpar International Corporation; 3801 E. 34th St., Tucson, AZ 85713
Target Audience: Adults
Measures a person's ability to acquire and apply the basic skills necessary to perform soldering tasks that vary in difficulty. Also concerns evaluee's ability to follow instructions, visual acuity, frustration tolerance, attentiveness, judgment, reasoning ability, and spatial and form perception. Can be used with disabled and nondisabled persons, but they must have a reasonable level of sight and coordination. Signed, videotaped instructions for deaf persons are available.

14403
Valpar Component Work Sample 13 (Money Handling). Valpar International Corporation, Tucson, AZ
Subtests: Money Recognition; Change Making; Economics
Descriptors: Adults; Clerical Occupations; Deafness; Disabilities; *Economics; *Money Management; Numbers; Occupational Tests; Personnel Evaluation; Sign Language; Spatial Ability; Verbal Ability; *Work Sample Tests
Availability: Valpar International Corporation; 3801 E. 34th St., Tucson, AZ 85713
Target Audience: Adults
Designed to measure an individual's skills in dealing with monetary concepts ranging from basic money recognition to consumer economics. Cash register use is simulated. Useful with occupations such as cashier, teller, clerk, or loan counselor. Can be used with disabled or nondisabled persons. Signed, videotaped instructions for the deaf are available. Abilities required are verbal and numerical skills, reasoning, spatial perception, and clerical aptitude.

14404
Valpar Component Work Sample 14 (Integrated Peer Performance). Valpar International Corporation, Tucson, AZ

Descriptors: Adults; Assembly (Manufacturing); Color; Disabilities; *Interpersonal Competence; Occupational Tests; *Peer Relationship; Perceptual Motor Coordination; Personnel Evaluation; Spatial Ability; *Visual Impairments; *Work Sample Tests
Identifiers: Finger Dexterity; Manual Dexterity
Availability: Valpar International Corporation; 3801 E. 34th St., Tucson, AZ 85713
Target Audience: Adults

Designed to encourage observable interaction of 3 to 5 evaluees working together, during completion of actual assembly tasks. Also measures reasoning skills, spatial and form perception, finger and manual dexterity, motor coordination, and color discrimination. Can be used with sighted disabled and nondisabled persons.

14405
Valpar Component Work Sample 15 (Electrical Circuitry and Print Reading). Valpar International Corporation, Tucson, AZ
Descriptors: Adults; Blueprints; Deafness; Disabilities; *Electrical Systems; Engineering Drawing; Occupational Tests; Perceptual Motor Coordination; Personnel Evaluation; Sign Language; Spatial Ability; *Work Sample Tests
Identifiers: Finger Dexterity; Manual Dexterity
Availability: Valpar International Corporation; 3801 E. 34th St., Tucson, AZ 85713
Target Audience: Adults

Measures a person's ability to understand and apply principles of electrical circuits and to use pictorial materials such as blueprints, drawings, and schematics. Also concerns reasoning, spatial and form perception, finger and manual dexterity, and motor coordination. Not recommended for those with severe visual or coordination problems. Signed, videotaped instructions are available for deaf persons.

14406
Valpar Component Work Sample 16 (Drafting). Valpar International Corporation, Tucson, AZ
Descriptors: Adults; *Blueprints; Deafness; Disabilities; *Drafting; Occupational Tests; Perceptual Motor Coordination; Personnel Evaluation; Sign Language; Spatial Ability; *Work Sample Tests
Identifiers: Finger Dexterity; Manual Dexterity
Availability: Valpar International Corporation; 3801 E. 34th St., Tucson, AZ 85713
Target Audience: Adults

Measures a person's potential for jobs involving drafting and blueprint reading, from minimal needs to high-level performance. Also covers reasoning, spatial and form perception, finger and manual dexterity, and motor coordination. May be used with disabled or nondisabled persons. Signed, videotaped instructions are available for deaf persons. Disabled persons must be sighted.

14413
Test of Oral Structures and Functions. Vitali, Gary J. 1986
Subtests: Speech Survey; Verbal Oral Functioning; Nonverbal Oral Functioning; Orofacial Structures; History/Behavioral Survey
Descriptors: Adolescents; Adults; Children; *Clinical Diagnosis; Screening Tests; Speech Handicaps; *Speech Pathology; *Speech Skills
Identifiers: TOSF
Availability: Slosson Educational Publications; P.O. Box 280, E. Aurora, NY 14052
Target Audience: 7-64
Notes: Time, 20

Assesses oral structures, nonverbal oral functioning, and verbal oral functioning in a standardized manner. Used to help establish nature of disorders, including structural, neurological, or functional. Descriptive information and expected subtest performance given for dysarthria, apraxia, Broca's aphasia, velopharyngeal incompetence-insufficiency, and functional disorders. Effective for many uses, including screening, differential diagnosis, caseload management decisions, pre- and posttreatment assessment. Designed for speech pathologists in clinical and educational settings.

14414
Alcohol Dependence Scale. Skinner, Harvey A.; Horn, John L. 1984
Descriptors: Adolescents; Adults; *Alcoholism; Drug Addiction; Foreign Countries; Interviews; Questionnaires
Identifiers: ADS; Alcohol Use Questionnaire; Canada
Availability: Addiction Research Foundation; Marketing Services, Dept. 898, 33 Russell St., Toronto, Ontario, Canada M5S 2S1
Target Audience: 15-65
Notes: Time, 10 approx.; Items, 25

Provides a brief measure of the extent to which the use of alcohol has progressed from psychological involvement to impaired control. Designed to provide a brief but psychometrically sound measure of the alcohol dependence syndrome, to be used as both a research and clinical diagnostic tool. May be administered in either a questionnaire or interview format.

14416
Children of Alcoholics Screening Test. Jones, John W. 1983
Descriptors: Adolescents; Adults; *Affective Measures; *Alcoholism; *Attitude Measures; Children; Parent Child Relationship; Screening Tests
Identifiers: CAST
Availability: Camelot Unlimited; 17 N. State St., Ste. 1222, Dept. 18, Chicago, IL 60602
Target Audience: 6-35
Notes: Time, 10 approx.; Items, 30

Measures children's attitudes, feelings, perceptions, and experiences related to their parent's drinking behavior. Assesses children's psychological distress, perceptions of drinking-related marital discord between the parents, attempts to control a parent's drinking, efforts to escape from the alcoholism, exposure to drinking-related family violence, tendencies to perceive parents as alcoholic, and desire for professional counseling. Inventory can be used to identify children of alcoholics and to assist in the diagnosis of a parent's alcoholism, as a clinical counseling tool and as a valid and reliable research instrument.

14419
Survival Skills Profile, 2nd Edition. Cuyahoga Special Education Service Center, Ohio 1981
Descriptors: Behavior Patterns; Behavior Rating Scales; Check Lists; *Daily Living Skills; *Elementary School Students; Elementary Secondary Education; *Emotional Disturbances; *Secondary School Students; *Social Development
Availability: Creative Learning Systems, Inc.; 936 C St., San Diego, CA 92101
Grade Level: K-12

Designed by classroom teachers for use with children who are emotionally disturbed. Focuses on 2 major areas: skills directly related to daily living and personal development, such as managing criticism or controlling aggression. May also be used as an adjunct to Developmental Learning Profile (TC013163) or Student Learning Profile (TC014420).

14420
Student Learning Profile, 2nd Edition. Cuyahoga Special Education Service Center, OH 1980
Descriptors: *Achievement Gains; Adjustment (to Environment); Basic Skills; Career Development; Check Lists; *Elementary School Students; Elementary Secondary Education; Individualized Instruction; *Learning Disabilities; Learning Modalities; Perceptual Development; *Secondary School Students
Availability: Creative Learning Systems, Inc.; 936 C St., San Diego, CA 92101
Grade Level: K-12

Designed by classroom teachers and instructional supervisors for use by teachers who work with learning-disabled children. Profile is used to record a child's accomplishments of the basic skills throughout his or her school years. Profile covers the following areas: modality preference, study skills, language arts, perceptual development, career development, mathematics, and social or coping skills.

14428
The Senior Apperception Technique, Revised. Bellak, Leopold; Bellak, Sonya Sorel 1985
Descriptors: Aging (Individuals); *Older Adults; *Projective Measures; *Psychological Evaluation
Identifiers: SAT
Availability: C.P.S., Inc.; P.O. Box 83, Larchmont, NY 10538
Target Audience: 65-90

Consists of 16 pictures designed to reflect thoughts and feelings of the elderly. Pictures are meant to be ambiguous enough to give individual leeway and which also reflect the problems and situations faced by the elderly, such as loneliness, illness, uselessness as well as pictures which reflect happy sentiments. Pictures are designed to elicit possible psychological problems. For use by psychologists, physicians, psychiatrists, rehabilitation workers, nurses, therapists, and other professionals concerned with caring for the aged.

14431
Khan-Lewis Phonological Analysis. Khan, Linda M.L.; Lewis, Nancy P. 1986
Descriptors: Articulation Impairments; Children; *Diagnostic Tests; *Phonetic Analysis; Remedial Instruction; *Young Children
Identifiers: Goldman Fristoe Test of Articulation; KLPA
Availability: American Guidance Service; Publishers' Bldg., Circle Pines, MN 55014-1796
Target Audience: 2-5

Provides a means of assessing the use of 15 phonological processes in the speech of young children 2 through 5 years of age. Analysis may also be used with children 6 years and older who have articulation/phonological disorders. To perform the analysis, one must use the Sounds-in-Words subtest of the Goldman-Fristoe Test of Articulation. The Khan-Lewis Phonological Analysis is recommended for use in the diagnosis and description of articulation or phonological disorders in preschool children. Norms are provided for children between the ages of 2.0 through 5.11. Of the 15 phonological processes assessed, 12 are characteristic of normal speech development, and 3 are not.

14437
Paced Auditory Serial Addition Task (PASAT). NeuroTech, Galveston, TX
Descriptors: Adults; *Cognitive Processes; Injuries; Minimal Brain Dysfunction; *Neurological Impairments; Timed Tests
Identifiers: PASAT
Availability: NeuroTech; 10 Quintana Dr., Galveston, TX 77551
Target Audience: Adults
Notes: Items, 124

A method of assessing the recovery of information processing speed after a head injury. Subject listens to a tape recording of numbers and pauses and adds spoken number to the previously spoken number. Norms are available for persons age 21-56 with 12-20 years of education (mean 15.7). Four series of numbers are presented.

14453
Behavioral Dimensions Rating Scale. Bullock, Lyndal M.; And Others 1970
Descriptors: Adolescents; *Behavior Disorders; *Behavior Rating Scales; Children; Correctional Institutions; Psychiatric Hospitals; Residential Institutions; Resource Room Programs; Self Contained Classrooms
Identifiers: BDRS
Availability: Exceptional Children; v52 n2 p123-30 Oct 1985
Target Audience: 5-18
Notes: Items, 30

Designed to obtain an overview of behavioral patterns demonstrated by students. Instrument consists of 30 pairs of adjectives and rater indicates on a 7-point scale which of the 2 adjectives in each pair best describes the behavior typically demonstrated by the student. Rating scale was used in a research study to analyze behaviors demonstrated by behaviorally disordered children and youth and adjudicated children and youth and differences in behavioral characteristics of students assigned to public school resource rooms, self-contained classrooms in public schools, psychiatric hospitals, state residential treatment centers, and state training schools for adjudicated children and youth.

14459
Schaie-Thurstone Adult Mental Abilities Test, Forms A and OA. Schaie, K. Warner 1985
Subtests: Recognition Vocabulary; Figure Rotation; Letter Series; Number Addition; Word Fluency; Object Rotation (Form OA); Word Series (Form OA)
Descriptors: Abstract Reasoning; Addition; Adults; *Cognitive Ability; Cognitive Processes; *Cognitive Tests; Older Adults; Spatial Ability; Vocabulary
Identifiers: *Primary Mental Abilities Test; STAMAT; Thurstone Scales
Availability: Consulting Psychologists Press; 577 College Ave., Palo Alto, CA 94306
Target Audience: 22-84
Notes: Time, 30 approx.

Research and assessment tool for measuring mental abilities of adults. Represents an extension of the seminal work of L.L. and T.G. Thurstone on measurement of primary mental abilities. There are 2 forms: form A for adults and form OA for older adults. Form A is essentially the Thurstone Primary Mental Abilities Test Form 11-17 with new adult norms. Form OA has 2 additional scales designed specifically for use with persons over age 55 and has new norms for older adults. STAMAT has so far been used primarily for research purposes to investigate patterns of stability and decline in intellectual processes. May have use in counseling returning adult students, assessing skills necessary for independent living, counseling adults for second careers, making diagnostic judgments about individual competence in disability examinations.

14469
Structured Photographic Expressive Language Test—Preschool. Werner, Ellen O'Hara; Kresheck, Janet Dawson 1983
Descriptors: Articulation (Speech); Black Dialects; *Expressive Language; Grammar; Individual Testing; Morphology (Languages); Photographs; Preschool Education; *Screening Tests; Syntax; *Young Children
Identifiers: SPELT

Availability: Janelle Publications; P.O. Box 12, Sandwich, IL 60548

Target Audience: 3-5

Notes: Time, 10; Items, 50

Designed as a screening tool to identify children who may have difficulty in their expression of early morphological and syntactic features. Not for diagnosis, but indicates the need for further evaluation. Uses photographs of children in various activities. Contains a section on Black English usage. The structures covered are plural and possessive nouns, present and past tense, auxiliary verbs, copulas, prepositions and personal pronouns. Normed on Caucasion, monolingual children, from middle-class rural and urban families. An optional test of articulation is included.

14472

CST: Comprehensive Screening Tool for Determining Optimal Communication Mode. House, Linda Infante; Rogerson, Brenda S. 1984

Subtests: Oral Skills; Manual Skills; Pictographic Skills

Descriptors: Adolescents; Adults; Children; *Communication Disorders; *Communication Skills; *Criterion Referenced Tests; *Individual Testing; Nonverbal Communication; Older Adults; Psychomotor Skills; *Screening Tests; *Speech Pathology; Speech Skills

Availability: United Educational Services; P.O. Box 357, E. Aurora, NY 14052

Target Audience: 1-75

Notes: Time, 45 approx.

Designed to assess the communicative behaviors of verbally limited or nonspeaking persons. Usually client's functional communication deficit is secondary to other impairments, such as mental retardation, cerebral palsy, or other neurological problems. Serves as a tool for the speech language pathologist to use to evaluate nonspeaking clients. Includes tasks which evaluate client's neurological, motoric, cognitive, and social-communicative behaviors in relation to his or her potential for developing a functional communication system. Three major areas are assessed. The Oral Skills Battery consists of 3 subtests: prespeech and oral awareness, prearticulatory and articulatory skills, and auditory awareness. The Manual Skills Battery includes subtests for manual training prerequisites, movement patterning, and cognitive correlates for manual communication. The Pictographic Skills Battery also has 3 subtests: visual training prerequisites, attending behavior and accuracy of movement, and cognitive correlates for pictographic skills.

14473

ASSETS: A Survey of Students' Educational Talents and Skills-Later Elementary. Grand Rapids Public Schools, MI 1978

Descriptors: *Elementary School Students; *Enrichment Activities; Gifted; Intermediate Grades; Needs Assessment; Parent Attitudes; Rating Scales; Student Attitudes; *Student Interests; *Talent Identification; Teacher Attitudes

Availability: Learning Publications; P.O. Box 1326, Holmes Beach, FL 33509

Grade Level: 4-6

Helps in identification of children's gifts and talents and in planning enrichment activities and experiences for these students. Provides a means of surveying individual student interests and creative abilities as well as academic strengths and talents. Can serve a variety of purposes such as selecting students for special programs, individualizing curricula in the classroom, enhancing curriculum planning, discovering knowledge and skills students bring to the classroom, and helping parents and teachers to discuss student's needs. There are separate forms for parents, students, and teachers to fill out. Information from all 3 sources is combined in a single profile and can be viewed together to obtain a thorough and balanced assessment of each student's educational talents and skills, including academic aptitude, motivational characteristics, creative thinking ability, and visual and performing arts aptitude/talent.

14474

ASSETS: A Survey of Students' Educational Talents and Skills-Early Elementary. Grand Rapids Public Schools, MI 1979

Descriptors: Elementary School Students; *Enrichment Activities; Gifted; Needs Assessment; Parent Attitudes; *Primary Education; Rating Scales; Student Attitudes; *Student Interests; *Talent Identification; Teacher Attitudes

Availability: Learning Publications; P.O. Box 1326, Holmes Beach, FL 33509

Grade Level: K-3

Helps in identification of children's gifts and talents and in planning enrichment activities and experiences for these students. Provides a means of surveying individual student interests and creative abilities as well as academic strengths and talents. Can serve a variety of purposes such as selecting students for special programs, individualizing curricula in the classroom, enhancing curriculum planning, discovering knowledge and skills students bring to the classroom, and helping parents and teachers to discuss student's needs. There are separate forms for parents,

students, and teachers. Information from all 3 sources is combined in a single profile and can be viewed together to obtain a thorough and balanced assessment of each student's educational talents and skills, including academic aptitude, motivational characteristics, creative thinking ability, and visual and performing arts aptitude/talent.

14483

Conceptual Understanding through Blind Evaluation. Valpar International Corporation, Tucson, AZ

Descriptors: Adults; Blindness; Disabilities; Occupational Tests; *Perceptual Motor Coordination; Physical Mobility; Spatial Ability; *Visual Impairments; *Work Sample Tests

Identifiers: CUBE

Availability: Valpar International Corporation; 3801 E. 34th St., Tucson, AZ 85713

Target Audience: Adults

Designed to measure the perceptive abilities that help compensate for visual handicaps. It is a performance test that assesses the perceptual skills necessary to meet basic needs, including judgment, mobility, orientation, discrimination, and balance.

14493

Treatment Evaluation Inventory. Kazdin, A.E. 1980

Descriptors: Adolescents; Adults; Antisocial Behavior; *Behavior Modification; Children; Institutionalized Persons; Intervention; *Medical Care Evaluation; Parent Attitudes; Patients; Positive Reinforcement; Professional Personnel; Psychiatry; Rating Scales

Identifiers: Mediation

Availability: Journal of School Psychology; v24 n1 p23-35 Spr 1986

Target Audience: 6-18

Notes: Items, 15

A rating scale through which child psychiatric inpatients with severe behavior problems, their parents and institutional staff rated the acceptability of 4 treatments: positive reinforcement of incompatible behavior, positive practice, medication, and time out from reinforcement.

14494

Children's Intervention Rating Profile. Witt, J.C.; Elliott, S.N. 1985

Descriptors: Adolescents; *Antisocial Behavior; Behavior Modification; Children; *Intervention; Rating Scales; Student Attitudes; *Student Behavior; *Student Evaluation of Teacher Performance; Teachers

Identifiers: CIRP

Availability: Journal of School Psychology; v24 n1 p23-35 Spr 1986

Target Audience: 6-18

Notes: Items, 7

A scale to measure children's reactions to 12 interventions by a teacher for classroom misbehavior involving a male student who either destroyed property or frequently talked out of turn. Written at a 5th grade reading level.

14510

Achievement Identification Measure. Rimm, Sylvia B. 1985

Subtests: Competition; Responsibility; Control; Achievement; Communication; Respect

Descriptors: *Elementary School Students; Elementary Secondary Education; Gifted; Identification; *Parent Attitudes; Rating Scales; *Secondary School Students; *Underachievement

Identifiers: AIM

Availability: Educational Assessment Service; Rt. 1, Box 139-A, Watertown, WI 53094

Grade Level: K-12

Notes: Time, 20 approx.; Items, 77

Developed to identify students who have characteristics of underachievers. Purpose of inventory is to determine the degree to which children exhibit the characteristics of underachievers, so that preventive or remedial efforts can be administered. Parents complete the inventory by marking the responses that best describe their child's present behavior and environment. There is no time limit for completing the questionnaire. It usually takes about 20 minutes for each child.

14523

Matrix Analogies Test, Expanded Form. Naglieri, Jack A. 1985

Descriptors: *Abstract Reasoning; *Adolescents; *Children; *Cognitive Tests; Disabilities; *Individual Testing; Limited English Speaking; *Nonverbal Ability; *Spatial Ability

Identifiers: MAT

Availability: The Psychological Corporation; 555 Academic Ct., San Antonio, TX 78204-0952

Target Audience: 5-17

Notes: Time, 30 approx.; Items, 64

Designed as an individually administered measure of nonverbal ability. Allows individuals to either point or say aloud the number of their answers. Uses 64 abstract designs of the standard progressive matrix type. Test format reduces the effects of such variables as motor coordination, verbal skills, time pressure, and primary language. Can be used with individuals with limited English-language skills, or those with a handicap, such as deafness, cerebral palsy, or communication disorders. May also be useful with exceptional populations, such as hearing-impaired or mentally retarded persons. Items are organized in 4 item groups: pattern completion, reasoning by analogy, serial reasoning, and spatial visualization. Designed to be used as part of a comprehensive testing battery.

14524

Evaluating Communicative Competence, Revised Edition. Simon, Charlann S. 1986

Descriptors: Adolescents; Children; *Communication Skills; Criterion Referenced Tests; *Elementary School Students; Elementary Secondary Education; *Expressive Language; Individual Testing; *Informal Assessment; Language Handicaps; Learning Disabilities; *Listening Skills; *Secondary School Students

Identifiers: ECC

Availability: Communication Skill Builders; 3130 N. Dodge Blvd., P.O. Box 42050, Tucson, AZ 85733

Grade Level: 4-12

Target Audience: 9-18

Notes: Items, 21

A series of 21 informal evaluation probes in 2 categories: auditory tasks and expressive tasks. It is useful for clinicians to use to aid in obtaining descriptive data, on metalinguistic and communication skills. Information from the probes allows clinician to decide whether a student should be included in the case load, to determine the frequency of remediation contacts, and to determine a realistic baseline upon which specific pragmatic individualized education program (IEP) objectives can be written. Cognitive level of the 21 tasks is appropriate for those who have reached or are entering Piaget's concrete operational stage and who have a mean length of utterance of at least 4.5 words.

14528

Aberrant Behavior Checklist. Aman, Michael G.; Singh, Nirbhay N. 1986

Subtests: Irritability; Lethargy; Stereotypy; Hyperactivity; Inappropriate Speech

Descriptors: *Adaptive Behavior (of Disabled); Adolescents; Adults; Behavior Disorders; Children; *Mental Retardation; Rating Scales; *Residential Institutions

Identifiers: ABC

Availability: Slosson Educational Publications; P.O. Box 280, E. Aurora, NY 10452

Target Audience: 5-64

Notes: Time, 5 approx.; Items, 58

Rating scale to assess inappropriate and maladaptive behavior of mentally retarded individuals in residential settings. Scale may be completed by personnel who have regular contact with the patients and know them well.

14532

The Conley-Vernon Idiom Test. Conley, Janet; Vernon, McCay 1975

Descriptors: *Achievement Tests; *Context Clues; *Deafness; Elementary Education; *Elementary School Students; *Idioms; *Vocabulary Skills

Availability: Janet Conley; 1105 River Rd., Sykesville, MD 21784

Grade Level: 1-6

Notes: Items, 50

May be used with either deaf or hearing students to assess their skills in use of idiomatic English.

14548

Facts on Aging Quiz. Palmore, Erdman B. 1977

Descriptors: Adults; *Aging (Individuals); Aging Education; *Knowledge Level; Older Adults; Social Bias

Identifiers: FAQ

Availability: The Gerontologist; v20 n6 p669-72 1980

Target Audience: Adults

Notes: Time, 5; Items, 25

A self-scoring measure covering basic factual information on aging including basic physical, mental, and social facts and common misconceptions about aging. For use as a stimulus to group discussion and clarification of misconceptions and for detection of bias toward older adults.

14550

The Facts on Aging Quiz, Alternate Form. Palmore, Erdman B.

Descriptors: Adults; *Aging (Individuals); Aging Education; Attitude Measures; *Knowledge Level; Older Adults; Social Bias

Identifiers: FAQ

Availability: The Gerontologist; v21 n4 p431-37 1981
Target Audience: Adults
Notes: Items, 25

Designed for use in assessing knowledge level about the aging process for use in stimulating discussion, for identifying misconceptions, and for measuring the effects of education in gerontology. Also measures bias toward the aged.

14562
Language Processing Test. Richard, Gail; Hanner, Mary Anne 1985
Subtests: Associations; Categorization; Similarities; Differences; Multiple Meanings; Attributes
Descriptors: Children; *Diagnostic Tests; *Individual Testing; Language Handicaps; *Language Processing; Remedial Instruction
Identifiers: LPT
Availability: Linguisystems; 716 17th St., Moline, IL 61265
Target Audience: 5-12
Notes: Time, 30 approx.

Used to identify childrens' language processing strengths and weaknesses in a hierarchical framework so that professionals can determine special program placement, remedial placement, the point at which children's language processing breaks down, and which behaviors contribute to the processing disorders. These disorders may be caused by word retrieval difficulties, inappropriate word substitutions, nonspecific word usage, inability to correct recognized errors, avoidance of responding, rehearsal of responses, or unusual responses. Hierarchy of tasks used in test was based on A.R. Luria's model of brain organization.

14571
Slosson Oral Reading Test, Form A for Adults and Visually/Verbally Handicapped. Slosson, Richard L. 1986
Descriptors: Achievement Tests; *Adult Literacy; Adults; Individual Testing; *Oral Reading; *Reading Tests; *Speech Handicaps; *Visual Impairments
Identifiers: SORT
Availability: Slosson Educational Publications; P.O. Box 280, E. Aurora, NY 10452
Target Audience: Adults
Notes: Items, 200

Word lists are identical to those in the Slosson Oral Reading Test (TC011187). Scoring instructions have been revised to accommodate adult literacy programs and visually and verbally or speech handicapped persons. For visually handicapped individuals, the reading lists have been enlarged and placed on separate cards for ease of presentation.

14586
Social-Emotional Dimension Scale. Hutton, Jerry B.; Roberts, Timothy G. 1986
Subtests: Avoidance of Peer Interaction; Aggressive Interaction; Avoidance of Teacher Interaction; Inappropriate Behavior; Depressive Reaction; Physical/Fear Reaction
Descriptors: *Behavior Problems; Behavior Rating Scales; *Elementary School Students; Elementary Secondary Education; *High Risk Persons; Norm Referenced Tests; *Secondary School Students
Identifiers: SEDS
Availability: Pro-Ed; 5341 Industrial Oaks Blvd., Austin, TX 78735
Grade Level: K-12
Notes: Items, 32

Highly structured, norm-referenced rating scale to be used by school personnel to identify students who are at risk for problematic behaviors. Designed to provide school personnel, such as teachers, counselors, administrators, diagnosticians, and psychologists, with a means for rating student behaviors. Measures nonacademic behaviors judged to cause problems in the classroom and which may interfere with the student's and/or other students' learning.

14595
Multilevel Academic Survey Test. Howell, Kenneth W.; And Others 1985
Descriptors: Achievement Tests; Criterion Referenced Tests; *Elementary School Students; Elementary Secondary Education; *Low Achievement; *Mathematics Achievement; Norm Referenced Tests; *Reading Achievement; *Secondary School Students
Identifiers: MAST
Availability: The Psychological Corporation; 555 Academic Ct., San Antonio, TX 78204-0952
Grade Level: K-12

Intended for use by school personnel who make decisions about student performance in reading or mathematics. Test is intended primarily for those students who have academic difficulties. There are 2 basic instruments: a grade level test and a curriculum level test. If the primary need is to rank a student's performance versus that of his

or her peers, the grade level test provides a short, wide-range measure of academic achievement. It is a norm-referenced measure. If the primary goal is to collect criterion-referenced information on specific areas of curriculum performance, the curriculum level test surveys critical clusters of reading and math skills. The 2 basic instruments may be used independently or in combination.

14599
Diagnostic Reading Inventory, Second Edition. Jacobs, H. Donald; Searfoss, Lyndon W. 1979
Descriptors: Decoding (Reading); *Diagnostic Tests; Elementary Education; *Elementary School Students; Individual Testing; Listening Comprehension Tests; Oral Reading; *Reading Diagnosis; *Reading Difficulties; *Reading Tests; Silent Reading
Identifiers: Frustration Reading Level; Independent Reading Level; Instructional Reading Level
Availability: Kendall Hunt Publishing Co.; 2460 Kerper Blvd., Dubuque, IA 52001
Grade Level: 4-8

This test is designed for use with students who have already been identified as having reading problems. It is individually administered. It consists of 8 each of graded oral reading passages, word lists, phrase lists, silent reading passages, listening passages, and a decoding inventory. A profile is drawn for each child. Identifies independent, instructional, and frustration reading levels. Parts of the test are timed.

14602
Child Behavior Checklist for Ages 2-3. Achenbach, Thomas M.; Edelbrock, C. 1986
Subtests: Social Withdrawal; Depressed; Sleep Problems; Aggressive; Destructive; Other Problems
Descriptors: *Behavior Problems; *Behavior Rating Scales; *Young Children
Identifiers: CBCL
Availability: University Associates in Psychiatry; One S. Prospect St., Burlington, VT 05401
Target Audience: 2-3
Notes: Items, 99

Consists of 99 problem items, 57 of which have counterparts on the Child Behavior Checklist for Ages 4-16 (TC011306). Form is completed by parent or parent-surrogate. Subscores include social withdrawal, depressed, sleep problems, somatic problems, aggressive, and destructive.

14604
Southern California Ordinal Scales of Development: Scale of Fine Motor Abilities. California State Department of Education 1977
Descriptors: Behavior Rating Scales; Children; *Criterion Referenced Tests; Culture Fair Tests; *Developmental Disabilities; *Developmental Tasks; *Learning Disabilities; *Multiple Disabilities; *Psychomotor Skills
Identifiers: *Fine Motor Skills; Piaget (Jean); *Piagetian Tests; SCOSD
Availability: Foreworks; Box 9747, N. Hollywood, CA 91609
Target Audience: 2-12

Developed by the Diagnostic School for Neurologically Handicapped Children, Southern California, State Department of Education as a complete Piagetian system that combines classroom and clinical assessment. The series consists of 6 cross-referenced Piagetian developmental scales. Each scale assesses all levels of development from sensorimotor through formal operations. Useful for comparative assessments, ability grouping, research, and individualized education program (IEP) development. Designed especially for use with multiply handicapped, developmentally delayed, and learning-disordered persons but may be used with all other children. Scales are considered to be culture-free and nonsexist. Administration of the scale consists of informal observation of the child within the environment. This scale assesses fine motor abilities within a Piagetian framework. Areas assessed include dexterity, perceptual motor, and graphomotor development.

14605
Southern California Ordinal Scales of Development: Scale of Gross Motor Abilities. California State Department of Education 1977
Descriptors: Behavior Rating Scales; Children; *Criterion Referenced Tests; Culture Fair Tests; *Developmental Disabilities; *Developmental Tasks; *Learning Disabilities; *Multiple Disabilities; *Psychomotor Skills
Identifiers: *Gross Motor Skills; Piaget (Jean); *Piagetian Tests; SCOSD
Availability: Foreworks; Box 9747, N. Hollywood, CA 91609
Target Audience: 2-12

Developed by the Diagnostic School for Neurologically Handicapped Children, Southern California, State Department of Education as a complete Piagetian system that combines classroom and clinical assessment. The series consists of 6 cross-referenced Piagetian developmental

scales. Each scale assesses all levels of development from sensorimotor through formal operations. Useful for comparative assessments, ability grouping, research, and individualized education program (IEP) development. Designed especially for use with multiply handicapped, developmentally delayed, and learning-disordered persons but may be used with all other children. Scales are considered to be culture-free and nonsexist. Administration of the scale consists of informal observation of the child within the environment. This scale assesses a continuum of abilities ranging from simple reflexes to complex motor actions. Developmental areas assessed include strength, balance, mobility, and coordination.

14606
Southern California Ordinal Scales of Development: Scale of Practical Abilities. California State Department of Education 1977
Descriptors: Behavior Rating Scales; Children; *Criterion Referenced Tests; Culture Fair Tests; *Daily Living Skills; *Developmental Disabilities; *Developmental Tasks; *Learning Disabilities; *Multiple Disabilities; *Self Care Skills
Identifiers: Piaget (Jean); *Piagetian Tests; SCCSD
Availability: Foreworks; Box 9747, N. Hollywood, CA 91609
Target Audience: 2-12

Developed by the Diagnostic School for Neurologically Handicapped Children, Southern California, State Department of Education as a complete Piagetian system that combines classroom and clinical assessment. The series consists of 6 cross-referenced Piagetian developmental scales. Each scale assesses all levels of development from sensorimotor through formal operations. Useful for comparative assessments, ability grouping, research, and individualized education program (IEP) development. Designed especially for use with multiply handicapped, developmentally delayed, and learning-disordered persons but may be used with all other children. Scales are considered to be culture-free and nonsexist. Administration of the scale consists of informal observation of the child within the environment. This scale is designed to assess personal independence and the ability to care for basic needs. Developmental areas assessed include eating, dressing, personal-hygiene, safety, and social awareness.

14607
Southern California Ordinal Scales of Development: Scale of Social-Affective Behavior. California State Department of Education 1977
Descriptors: *Affective Behavior; Behavior Rating Scales; Children; *Criterion Referenced Tests; Culture Fair Tests; *Developmental Disabilities; *Developmental Tasks; *Interpersonal Relationship; *Learning Disabilities; *Multiple Disabilities
Identifiers: Piaget (Jean); *Piagetian Tests; SCOSD
Availability: Foreworks; Box 9747, N. Hollywood, CA 91609
Target Audience: 2-12

Developed by the Diagnostic School for Neurologically Handicapped Children, Southern California, State Department of Education as a complete Piagetian system that combines classroom and clinical assessment. The series consists of 6 cross-referenced Piagetian developmental scales. Each scale assesses all levels of development from sensorimotor through formal operations. Useful for comparative assessments, ability grouping, research, and individualized education program (IEP) development. Designed especially for use with multiply handicapped, developmentally delayed, and learning-disordered persons but may be used with all other children. Scales are considered to be culture-free and nonsexist. Administration of the scale consists of informal observation of the child within the environment. This scale assesses 2 areas: self-awareness and relationships with others. Assessment procedures include observation, interviews, and simulations.

14608
Southern California Ordinal Scales of Development: Scale of Communication. California State Department of Education 1977
Descriptors: Behavior Rating Scales; Children; *Communication Skills; *Criterion Referenced Tests; Culture Fair Tests; *Developmental Disabilities; *Developmental Tasks; *Expressive Language; *Learning Disabilities; *Multiple Disabilities; *Receptive Language
Identifiers: Piaget (Jean); *Piagetian Tests; SCOSD
Availability: Foreworks; Box 9747, N. Hollywood, CA 91609
Target Audience: 2-12

Developed by the Diagnostic School for Neurologically Handicapped Children, Southern California, State Department of Education as a complete Piagetian system that combines classroom and clinical assessment. The series consists of 6 cross-referenced Piagetian developmental scales. Each scale assesses all levels of development from sensorimotor through formal operations. Useful for comparative assessments, ability grouping, research, and individualized education program (IEP) development. Designed especially for use with multiply handicapped, developmentally delayed, and learning-disordered persons but may be used with all other children. Scales are considered to be culture-free and nonsexist. Administration of the scale consists of informal observation of the child within the environment. This scale is designed to assess the full range of oral and gestural expression and comprehension within a framework of Piaget's model of development. Scale is divided into receptive and expressive behavior, and within each area, the development strands assessed include awareness of self and environment, imitation, communicative mediation, and symoblization.

14609
Southern California Ordinal Scales of Development: Scale of Cognition. California State Department of Education 1977
Descriptors: Behavior Rating Scales; Children; *Cognitive Ability; *Criterion Referenced Tests; Culture Fair Tests; *Developmental Disabilities; *Developmental Tasks; *Learning Disabilities; *Multiple Disabilities
Identifiers: Piaget (Jean); *Piagetian Tests; SCOSD
Availability: Foreworks; Box 9747, N. Hollywood, CA 91609
Target Audience: 2-12

Developed by the Diagnostic School for Neurologically Handicapped Children, Southern California, State Department of Education as a complete Piagetian system that combines classroom and clinical assessment. The series consists of 6 cross-referenced Piagetian developmental scales. Each scale assesses all levels of development from sensorimotor through formal operations. Useful for comparative assessments, ability grouping, research, and individualized education program (IEP) development. Designed especially for use with multiply handicapped, developmentally delayed, and learning-disordered persons but may be used with all other children. Scales are considered to be culture-free and nonsexist. Administration of the scale consists of informal observation of the child within the environment. This scale relies on Piaget's model of intellectual development to determine child's level of cognitive functioning and to assess quality of sensory and information processing at that level. Areas assessed are development of means, object, concept, and imitation.

14610
Iowa Screening Battery for Mental Decline. Eslinger, Paul J.; And Others 1985
Descriptors: Aging (Individuals); *Older Adults; *Screening Tests
Identifiers: *Dementia; ISBMD; *Mental Decline; Neuropsychological Assessment
Availability: University of Iowa; Alzheimer's Disease Research Center, Dept. of Neurology, Iowa City, IA 52242
Target Audience: 60-90

Used as a brief neuropsychological test for examining older adults suspected of experiencing abnormal mental decline. Screening battery is composed of 3 tests available from other sources: Temporal Orientation (TC012461), Visual Retention of Designs (TC002068), and Controlled Oral Word Association from the Multilingual Aphasia Examination (TC014080).

14619
Valpar Physical Functioning Questionnaire. Valpar Corp., Tucson, AZ 1977
Descriptors: Adults; Mexican Americans; *Patients; *Physical Disabilities; Physical Mobility; Puerto Ricans; Questionnaires; Self Evaluation (Individuals); *Spanish; *Vocational Rehabilitation
Availability: Valpar Corporation; 3801 E. 34th St., Ste. 105, Tucson, AZ 85713
Target Audience: Adults
Notes: Items, 18

This questionnaire was designed for use by rehabilitation personnel in determining clients' perceptions of their own physical condition. It is available in Formal Spanish, as well as English, and in Regional Spanish (Puerto Rican or Mexican American). The English version is at the grade 7 or grade 8 reading level.

14633
Steck-Vaughn Placement Survey for Adult Basic Education. Phillips, Beth Ann 1981
Subtests: Reading; Mathematics; Language
Descriptors: *Adult Basic Education; Adults; Arithmetic; *Diagnostic Tests; Language Skills; Language Usage; Mathematics; Mathematics Tests; Punctuation; Reading; Reading Diagnosis; *Student Placement
Availability: Steck-Vaughn Co.; P.O. Box 2028, Austin, TX 78768
Target Audience: Adults
Notes: Time, 45; Items, 141

Designed to obtain diagnostic and prescriptive information on the academic skills of adult learners. Measures skills from nonreading levels through grade 8. The reading subtest covers comprehension, vocabulary, and phonics. The language subtest covers capital letters, punctuation, spelling, and English usage. The mathematics subtest cov-

ers money, word problems, and operations with whole numbers. Two levels are available: and Level I covers reading levels for grades 1-3.9; and Level II covers reading levels for grades 6 through 8.9. Two parallel forms are available at each level.

14634
Study Behavior Inventory, Form D. Mueller, Richard J. 1984
Descriptors: Adults; Adult Students; *Attitude Measures; Higher Education; *Metacognition; Rating Scales; Self Evaluation (Individuals); Student Behavior; *Study Habits
Identifiers: Study Habits Inventory (Wrenn)
Availability: ERIC Document Reproduction Service; 3900 Wheeler Ave., Alexandria, VA 22304 (ED254535, 28 pages)
Target Audience: Adults
Notes: Items, 46

An inventory developed to measure the study habits and behaviors of adult students in a variety of college settings. It covers general study habits and behaviors, reading and note-taking techniques, and coping with examinations. Data were collected on over 1,000 students. Statements about general study attitudes and behavior are rated on a 4-point frequency scale. It is the third revision on an instrument first developed by C. Gilbert Wrenn.

14643
Risk Assessment Tool. Hwalek, Melanie; And others 1984
Descriptors: Background; Client Characteristics (Human Services); *Elder Abuse; Family Characteristics; Family Violence; Geriatrics; Interviews; Older Adults; Prevention; Questionnaires
Availability: ERIC Document Reproduction Service; 3900 Wheeler Ave., Alexandria, VA 22304 (ED257016, 41 pages)
Target Audience: Adults
Notes: Items, 93

Designed to identify elderly victims of abuse, and neglect for use in planning services and targeting resources for prevention. Data were collected by social service agencies on 50 cases of abuse and 50 controls. There are 4 sections: questions asked directly of elderly, demographic and background questions, evaluation by the service provider, and risk indicators. The questions cover physical and pychological abuse and neglect, material abuse, and violation of personal rights.

14648
Keystone Adaptive Behavior Profile. Keystone Area Education, Elkader, IA 1983
Subtests: School Coping Behaviors; Social Skills; Emotional Development; Language Skills; Self Care Skills; Applied Cognitive Skills; Academic Development
Descriptors: Academic Aptitude; *Adaptive Behavior (of Disabled); Cognitive Processes; Coping; *Elementary School Students; Elementary Secondary Education; Emotional Development; Family Environment; Interpersonal Competence; Language Skills; Rating Scales; *Secondary School Students; Self Care Skills; *Special Education
Availability: ERIC Document Reproduction Service; 3900 Wheeler Ave., Alexandria, VA 22304 (ED250867, 59 pages)
Grade Level: K-12

Designed to measure adaptive behavior of special education students in Northeastern Iowa. A school-related scale and a home-related scale are included. The school scale emphasizes the child's behavior in the school setting. The home scale was devised to describe the child's adaptation to home and community. Both scales assess the same domains for comparison. The home scale has 2 additional subtests, the community and the family. The family scale covers relationships, participation, responsibility, and self-concept. The home scale has not been normed. It is completed by either parent.

14652
Pictorial Inventory of Careers. Talent Assessment, Jacksonville, FL
Descriptors: Adults; Affective Measures; Career Awareness; Disabilities; Disadvantaged; Filmstrips; *Interest Inventories; Job Training; Nonverbal Tests; Pictorial Stimuli; Sex Bias; Technical Occupations; *Vocational Interests
Identifiers: PIC
Availability: Talent Assessment; P.O. Box 5087, Jacksonville, FL 32247-5087
Target Audience: Adults
Notes: Time, 20; Items, 119

This instrument is an interest inventory on a 35-mm filmstrip and is designed to help an individual identify areas of occupational preference and training on the basis of his or her affective response to actual work scenes. This test is nonverbal and said to be sex fair. It may be used with disadvantaged and handicapped individuals. No reading is necessary. It emphasizes vocational and technical careers.

14655
Aphasia Screening Test for Adults and Older Children. Reitan, Ralph M. 1984
Descriptors: Adolescents; Adults; *Aphasia; Children; Expressive Language; *Individual Testing; Language Handicaps; *Neurological Impairments; Receptive Language; *Screening Tests; Spatial Ability; Speech Communication
Availability: Neuropsychology Press; 1338 E. Edison St., Tucson, AZ 85719
Target Audience: 9-64

An adaptation of the Halstead-Wepman Aphasia Screening Test used to evaluate deficits in the ability to use aspects of language for communication purposes in brain-injured persons. It covers areas of language and verbal expression including: oral speech; letter recognition; number recognition; simple arithmetic, reading, spelling, and writing; receptive and expressive language; right-left orientation; and spatial abilities. The test is individually administered via flashcards. A version for young children is available (see TC014656).

14656
Aphasia Screening Test for Young Children. Reitan, Ralph M. 1984
Descriptors: *Aphasia; Expressive Language; *Individual Testing; Language Handicaps; *Neurological Impairments; Receptive Language; *Screening Tests; Spatial Ability; Speech Communication; *Young Children
Availability: Neuropsychology Press; 1338 E. Edison St., Tucson, AZ 85719
Target Audience: 5-8

An adaptation of the Halstead Wepman Aphasia Screening Test used to evaluate deficits in the ability to use language for communication purposes in brain-damaged or learning-disabled children whose dysphasia does not have a demonstrated neurological basis. Covers oral speech, letter or number recognition, simple arithmetic, reading, perception of communication (both expressive and receptive), right-left orientation, and spatial abilities. The test is individually administered.

14661
Learning Accomplishment Profile, Revised Edition. Sanford, Anne R.; Zelman, Janet G. 1981
Descriptors: *Child Development; Cognitive Ability; *Criterion Referenced Tests; Disabilities; Early Childhood Education; Interpersonal Competence; Language Skills; Preschool Education; Primary Education; Profiles; Psychomotor Skills; *Spanish; Student Behavior; Writing Skills; *Young Children
Identifiers: Fine Motor Skills; Gross Motor Skills
Availability: Kaplan School Supply Corporation; 1310 Lewisville-Clemmons Rd., Lewisville, NC 27023
Target Audience: 3-6

A criterion-referenced assessment of a young nonhandicapped or handicapped child's skills. Designed for use in identifying developmentally appropriate learning objectives for each child. Measures child's progress in 7 developmental areas: gross motor skills, fine motor skills, personal skills, social skills, self-help, prewriting, cognitive and language skills. The difference between this revised edition and the earlier one is the translation of general descriptors of developmental milestones into behavioral objectives. Another edition is available for ages 0-36 months. See the Early Learning Accomplishments Profile (TC012159). A Spanish edition is available.

14716
Adaptive Behavior Inventory. Brown, Linda; Leigh, James E. 1986
Subtests: Self Care Skills; Communication Skills; Social Skills; Academic Skills; Occupational Skills
Descriptors: Academic Achievement; *Adjustment (to Environment); *Adolescents; *Children; Communication Skills; Daily Living Skills; Developmental Disabilities; Interpersonal Competence; Job Skills; *Mental Retardation; Norm Referenced Tests
Identifiers: ABI
Availability: Pro-Ed; 5341 Industrial Oaks Blvd., Austin, TX 78735
Target Audience: 5-18
Notes: Items, 150

Norm-referenced test consisting of 5 subtests designed to aid in the assessment of students suspected of being mentally retarded or otherwise developmentally disabled. Appropriate for use with mentally retarded students from ages 6 through 18 and with students of normal intelligence or giftedness from ages 5 through 18. Is used to evaluate student's day-to-day ability to take care of himself/herself, communicate with others, interact socially, perform academic tasks, and perform work-related prevocational tasks. The evaluator or respondent is the classroom teacher or other professional who has regular, relevant contact with the student being assessed. The ABI is meant to supplement or complement other data, including intelligence quotients, that are gathered in the course of clinical assessment. There is also a 50-item short form which can be used by professionals to conduct a primary screening to reevaluate students already in special education programs, or to investigate overall adaptive behavior in research studies.

14718
Employment Screening Test. Schalock, Robert L.; And Others 1985
Descriptors: Adults; *Developmental Disabilities; Job Analysis; Personality Traits; Physical Development; *Screening Tests; *Vocational Evaluation
Identifiers: EST
Availability: Mid-Nebraska Mental Retardation Services; Box 1146, 522 E. Side Blvd., Hastings, NE 68901
Target Audience: Adults
Notes: Items, 37

Used to evaluate a developmentally disabled person's behavioral capabilities in reference to 26 physical demands and 11 temperament requirements to determine which jobs are suitable for this handicapped population. The EST is used to assess the performance requirements for a particular job and the client's behavioral capabilities in relation to those requirements. This instrument reflects the ecobehavioral perspective which analyzes a person's behavioral capabilities as they relate to the performance requirements identified through a job analysis. The instrument also attempts to meet 2 current needs of vocational rehabilitation/employment service programs: a brief, standardized person-job assessment tool to use for client evaluation and a means of identifying the specific matches and mismatches between job requirements and a person's behavioral capabilities.

14728
SAGE Vocational Assessment System. Train-Ease Corp., Pleasantville, NY 1985
Subtests: Vocational Interest Inventory; Cognitive and Conceptual Abilities; Vocational Aptitude Battery; Assessment of Attitudes; Temperament Factor Assessment
Descriptors: Adults; Aptitude Tests; Attitude Measures; *Cognitive Ability; *Employee Attitudes; Hearing Impairments; Interest Inventories; Interpersonal Relationship; Personality Measures; *Personality Traits; Reading Difficulties; Visual Impairments; *Vocational Aptitude; *Vocational Evaluation; *Vocational Interests
Availability: KeySystems; 2055 Long Ridge Rd., Stamford, CT 06903
Target Audience: Adults

A system that matches the aptitudes, interests, educational levels, attitudes, and temperaments of people to jobs and training. May be used with handicapped populations and may be group or individually administered. The system consists of 5 units. The Vocational Interest Inventory assesses areas of interest related to the 12 interest areas of the Guide for Occupational Exploration. May be used with hearing impaired, visually impaired, or nonreaders. The Cognitive and Conceptual Abilities unit measures the 3 General Educational Development (GED) factors of reasoning, mathematics, and language. The Vocational Aptitude Battery has been validated against the General Aptitudes Test Battery (GATB) and assesses 11 aptitudes by means of the following individual job-related tests: general, verbal, numerical, spatial, form perception, clerical perception, motor coordination, finger dexterity, manual dexterity, eye-hand-foot coordination, and color discrimination. The Assessment of Attitudes presents real-life situations in which the individual must evaluate on-the-job social situations, such as dealing with coworkers, supervisors, or employers. The Temperament Factor Assessment provides an objective measure of an individual's temperament.

14764
FAST Test: Flowers Auditory Screening Test. Flowers, Arthur 1986
Descriptors: *Auditory Evaluation; *Auditory Tests; Children; Disabilities; Individual Testing; Listening; *Screening Tests
Identifiers: Central Auditory Deficiencies; FAST
Availability: Perceptual Learning Systems; P.O. Box 864, Dearborn, MI 48121
Target Audience: 6-10
Notes: Time, 5

Designed for use as a screening device to identify children with potential central auditory deficiencies, not as a final assessment in the identification of central auditory problems. This test is experimental. It is individually administered "freefield" without use of earphones. It uses a form of selective listening (auditory-figure-ground) function using 2 almost simultaneous words and pictures requiring a pointing response.

14769
Matrix Analogies Test, Short Form. Naglieri, Jack A. 1985
Subtests: Pattern Completion; Reasoning by Analogy; Serial Reasoning; Spatial Visualization
Descriptors: Abstract Reasoning; Adolescents; Children; *Cognitive Ability; Culture Fair Tests; Deafness; Disabilities; Elementary Secondary Education; Group Testing; Learning Disabilities; Limited English Speaking; Mental Retardation; *Nonverbal Tests; Norm Referenced Tests; Pattern Recognition; *Screening Tests; Spatial Ability; Underachievement
Availability: The Psychological Corporation; 555 Academic Ct., Austin, TX 78204-0952
Grade Level: K-12
Notes: Items, 34

Designed to provide a measure of nonverbal reasoning that could be administered as a screening test in a group setting. Uses abstract designs of the standard progressive matrix type and brief directions. It was based on factors identified for the Raven's Progressive Matrices (TC810027). Said to be especially useful for those with limited English skills, a handicap, or other cause for lack of verbal ability. It is norm referenced and standardized on a national sample of children living in the United States. May be used in screening for learning problems in the case of an ability/achievement discrepancy. Some training in group testing is required for administration. Because of its nonverbal nature, the test is said to be culture reduced. It may be used with deaf and mentally retarded individuals as well. Percentile ranks, stanines and age equivalent scores can be computed.

14779
Educational Goals Inventory. National Council on the Aging, Washington, DC 1984
Descriptors: *Adult Education; *Adult Programs; Career Development; Community Relations; Counseling Objectives; Creative Expression; Educational Administration; Educational Change; Educational Environment; Educational Improvement; *Educational Objectives; Educational Planning; Health Education; Individual Development; Knowledge Level; Leadership Training; *Older Adults; Outreach Programs; *Program Evaluation; Social Problems
Identifiers: Community College Goals Inventory
Availability: The National Council on the Aging; Attn: Dr. Bella Jacobs, W. Wing 100, 600 Maryland Ave. S.W., Washington, DC 20024
Target Audience: 65-75
Notes: Items, 60

This adaptation of the Community College Goals Inventory (see TC010454) was designed for use by community-based groups concerned with educational programs related to preparing older adults to participate in the social, economic, and political aspects of our society. It can be used to assess the status of existing programs and determine changes necessary. There are 15 goal areas. For each goal a response is sought that indicates what the present importance of each goal is and what it should be. Goals cover general knowledge, leadership development, personal growth, basic education, community education, cultural/creative expression, social concerns/advocacy, vocational development, health education, counseling and advising, outreach, educational climate, community relations, education administration, planning, and evaluation.

14787
IDEA Oral Language Proficiency Test I, Form A. Ballard, Wanda S.; And Others 1982
Descriptors: *Diagnostic Tests; Elementary Education; *English (Second Language); *Language Proficiency; *Language Tests; Listening Comprehension; Morphology (Languages); *Oral English; Phonology; Pictorial Stimuli; Syntax; Vocabulary
Identifiers: IPT; Oral Testing
Availability: Ballard and Tighe; 480 Atlas St., Brea, CA 92621
Grade Level: K-6
Notes: Items, 83

This test was developed for use in determining students' levels of oral language proficiency and also for use as a diagnostic tool. It covers syntax, morphology, lexicon, and phonology. It is organized by developmental or sequential levels of difficulty. For use with students whose primary language is other than English to determine adequacy of English Skills (comprehending and responding) prior to the introduction of reading skills. Verbal and visual stimuli were used. Normed in California.

14791
PACE. Barclay, Lisa K.; Barclay, James R. 1986
Subtests: Motor Coordination; Visual Perception; Recognizing Rhythm Patterns; Listening; Visual Matching; Tactile Skills; Motor Behavior Memory; Verbal Memory; Attending; Social Development
Descriptors: Attention Span; *Behavior Rating Scales; *Computer Assisted Testing; *Learning Disabilities; Listening Skills; Memory; Parents; Perceptual Motor Coordination; *Preschool Education; Psychomotor Skills; *Screening Tests; Social Development; *Student Placement; Tactual Perception; Verbal Ability; Visual Perception
Identifiers: Rhythm
Availability: Institute for Personality and Ability Testing; P.O. Box 188, Champaign, IL 61822
Target Audience: 3-5

A behavior rating designed to identify deficits in learning skills of preschool children for screening, educational placement, and remediation. Uses parent observation and classroom findings to generate a developmental report. Currently runs on Apple IIe and 2 drives and on 64kb RAM or IBM-PC and compatibles.

14794
Pre Las English. Duncan, Sharon E.; Avila, Edward A. 1985
Subtests: Simon Says; Choose a Picture; What's in the House; Say What You Hear; Finishing Stories; Let's Tell Stories
Descriptors: *English (Second Language); *Expressive Language; Individual Testing; Language Proficiency; Morphology (Languages); *Oral English; Pictorial Stimuli; *Receptive Language; *Semantics; Syntax; *Young Children
Identifiers: Oral Testing
Availability: Linguametrics Group; P.O. Box 3495, San Rafael, CA 94912-3495
Target Audience: 4-6
Notes: Time, 10; Items, 53

Designed to measure young children's expressive and receptive abilities in 3 linguistic components of oral language morphology, syntax, and semantics. Uses a cassette tape and pictorial stimuli. May be administered by qualified teachers or school personnel who speak proficient standard English. It is individually administered outside the classroom. Covers receptive language, expressive language, morphology, and syntax via repetition of oral stimulus sentences, sentence completion/expressive language, expressive language via story retelling. Two forms are available. Classifies children by age, level of proficiency (1-5) and NES/FES/LES.

14798
Meadow-Kendall Social-Emotional Assessment Inventory for Deaf and Hearing Impaired Students. Meadow, Kathryn P. 1983
Subtests: Sociable, Communicative Behaviors; Impulsive Dominating Behaviors; Developmental Lags; Anxious, Compulsive Behaviors; Special Items Related to Deafness
Descriptors: Affective Behavior; *Deafness; Emotional Adjustment; *Hearing Impairments; Measures (Individuals); Preschool Children; Preschool Education; Social Behavior; Young Children
Identifiers: SEAI
Availability: OUTREACH Pre College Programs; Box 114, Gallaudet College, Washington, DC 20002
Target Audience: 7-21
Notes: Items, 49

This inventory is completed by teachers or other educational personnel who have close contact with their deaf students. There are 4 subscales. Norms are provided for girls and boys based on responses from 2,400 students in 10 schools and programs for deaf persons.

14799
Bilingual Vocational Oral Proficiency Test. Melton Peninsula, Dallas, TX 1981
Descriptors: Adults; *Bilingualism; Bilingual Students; *Criterion Referenced Tests; *English (Second Language); Expressive Language; Language Proficiency; Oral Language; Pictorial Stimuli; Pretests Posttests; Receptive Language; *Vocational Education
Identifiers: BVOPT; Oral Testing
Availability: Melton Peninsula; 111 Leslie St., Dallas, TX 75207
Target Audience: Adults
Notes: Time, 30

This test is designed to determine the language needs of limited English speaking applicants to vocational training programs and to determine how much English a trainee has learned during the training program. The test is criterion-referenced and based on a study of actual langage in the vocational setting. There are 2 parallel forms for pre- and posttesting. The test measures oral proficiency and consists of questions and answers; an open-ended interview; elicited imitation (repetition); and imperatives (receptive language).

14800
Comprehensive English Language Test. Harris, David P.; Palmer, Leslie A. 1986
Subtests: Listening; Structure; Vocabulary

Descriptors: *Achievement Tests; Adolescents; Adults; *College Students; *English (Second Language); Expressive Language; Grammar; Higher Education; *High School Students; *Language Proficiency; Listening; Oral Language; Receptive Language; Secondary Education; Student Placement; Vocabulary
Identifiers: CELT; Oral Testing
Availability: Delta Systems; 570 Rock Rd. Dr., Unit H, Dundee, IL 60118
Grade Level: 9-16
Notes: Time, 135

This test is designed to measure the English-language proficiency of non-native speakers. It is used with students in high school, college, or adult programs of English as a Second or Foreign Language, at the intermediate and advanced levels. May be used for placement or measuring achievement. Covers the ability to comprehend short statements, questions, and dialogues spoken by native speakers; manipulate grammatical structures in spoken English; understand lexical items in advanced English reading.

14900
Test of Auditory-Perceptual Skills. Gardner, Morrison F. 1985
Subtests: Auditory Number Memory; Auditory Sentence Memory; Auditory Word Memory; Auditory Interpretation of Directions; Auditory Word Discrimination; Auditory Processing; Hyperactivity Index Scale
Descriptors: *Auditory Perception; *Auditory Tests; *Children; *Diagnostic Tests; Hyperactivity; Language Handicaps
Identifiers: TAPS
Availability: Slosson Educational Publications; P.O. Box 280, E. Aurora, NY 14052
Target Audience: 4-12
Notes: Time, 25 approx.

Developed to measure how a child performs auditorily, based on performance on various auditory subtests. Test was normed on children whose primary language is English and children having normal hearing who were believed to be neither mentally retarded nor to have a language disorder. Is used to aid examiners to diagnose children with language disorders and measures 6 areas of auditory skills. May be administered by psychologists, speech and language pathologists, learning specialists, diagnosticians, and other professionals. The Hyperactivity Index Scale, developed by Dr. C. Keith Connors, to assess a child's hyperactivity as observed by the parent, also provides information about the child's behavioral characteristics. It was included mainly to assist the examiner in determining how a child's behavior may affect test results.

14902
Scales of Creativity and Learning Environment. Slosson, Steven W. 1986
Subtests: Scale of Divergent/Convergent Thinking; Scale of Gifted Students
Descriptors: Classroom Environment; *Classroom Observation Techniques; Cognitive Style; Creativity; *Divergent Thinking; *Elementary School Students; Elementary Secondary Education; *Gifted; *Secondary School Students; Self Concept
Identifiers: SCALES
Availability: Slosson Educational Publications; P.O. Box 280, E. Aurora, NY 14052
Grade Level: K-12

Two descriptive, 5-point Likert-type rating scales designed to assist school personnel to recognize students' gifted characteristics and the traits of creative, divergent thinkers. Both scales are based on Bloom's theory of taxonomy. Ratings are based on teacher's observations of student behavior over the previous month. The Scale of Gifted Students is designed to aid in the recognition of gifted characteristics in exceptionally talented students. The form is divided into the following areas: cognitive, comprehension, language, affective, problem solving, hobbies, and play. The Scale of Divergent/Convergent Thinking is used to assist in recognizing attributes of the divergent versus convergent thinker. It covers knowledge, ability, creativity, task commitment, synthesis, and evaluation. The manual also includes self-evaluation questionnaires for teachers to assess their teaching environment, and students to assess their learning style and their self-image.

14911
Assessment of Phonological Processes, Revised. Williams, Barbara Hodson 1986
Descriptors: Diagnostic Tests; Elementary Education; *Elementary School Students; *Language Handicaps; Outcomes of Treatment; *Phonology; *Preschool Children; *Preschool Education; Screening Tests
Identifiers: APP R; Phonological Deviancy
Availability: Interstate Printers and Publishers; 19-27 N. Jackson St., Danville, IL 61832
Grade Level: K-8
Notes: Time, 20; Items, 50

This instrument is designed for use with children who are highly unintelligible. Administration time is short. Analysis requires approximately one hour. Results show presence and severity of the disorder, for the design of more efficient individualized remediation programs, as a reliable posttreatment measure. Each child's responses are recorded on a transcription form. Two screening protocols are available, one for preschoolers, one for elementary school children.

14927
Hughes Basic Gross Motor Assessment. Hughes, Jeanne E. 1979
Subtests: Static Balance; Stride Jump; Tandem Walk; Hopping; Skipping; Target; Yo-Yo; Ball Handling Skills
Descriptors: *Children; *Diagnostic Teaching; Elementary Education; *Elementary School Students; Individual Testing; Motor Development; Performance Tests; Physical Education; *Psychomotor Skills; *Screening Tests; Special Education
Identifiers: BGMA; Gross Motor Skills
Availability: G.E. Miller, Inc.; 484 S. Broadway, Yonkers, NY 10705
Target Audience: 6-12

Designed to screen basic gross motor skills of children believed to have minor motor dysfunction and lead to the development of remedial programs. May indicate that the child needs physical therapy evaluation, occupational therapy evaluation, or medical attention. It is not to be used to assess developmental delay. Includes 8 subtests and notes 36 additional observations. Contains information on reliability and validity and sex differences in selected subtests. Several pieces of physical education equipment are needed to complete assessment.

14939
Oral Speech Mechanism Screening Examination, Revised. St. Louis, Kenneth O.; Ruscello, Dennis M. 1987
Descriptors: Adolescents; Adults; Anatomy; Children; Health Personnel; *Language Handicaps; Physiology; *Screening Tests; *Speech Evaluation; *Speech Handicaps; *Speech Tests; Standardized Tests
Identifiers: OSMSE R
Availability: Pro-Ed; 5341 Industrial Oaks Blvd., Austin, TX 78735
Target Audience: 5-65
Notes: Time, 10 approx.

Designed as a screening test for those who have structural or functional deviations of the oral speech mechanism. Intended to assess those anatomical structures and physiological functions that are most often considered to be potentially related to speech and language disorders. To be administered primarily by speech/language pathologists or other health professionals. This test was revised to make it more clinically useful. Exam is reliable, relatively easy and quick to administer, and appropriate for children and adults in a diagnostic or therapy setting.

14946
Chronic Pain Battery—Oncology. Pain Resource Center, Durham, NC
Descriptors: Adults; *Cancer; Check Lists; Health Personnel; *Medical Evaluation; *Oncology; *Psychological Testing; Questionnaires; Rating Scales
Identifiers: CPB; *Pain; Pain Assessment Questionnaire; Symptom Checklist
Availability: Pain Resource Center; P.O. Box 2836, Durham, NC 27705
Target Audience: Adults
Notes: Time, 60 approx.; Items, 204

Chronic Pain Battery—Oncology is identical to Chronic Pain Battery (CPB) except that it assumes the CPB was completed by a person undergoing evaluation or treatment for pain of malignancy. CPB is a comprehensive pain questionnaire. Comprised of Pain Assessment Questionnaire-Revised (PAQ-R) by Stephen R. Levitt and the Symptom Checklist 90-Revised (SCL-90-R) by Leonard R. Derogatis. The PAQ-R collects medical, psychological, and social information. The SCL-90 allows psychological screening. The information is formulated into the Chronic Pain Battery (CPB) Report. This Report is an assessment of the patient's pain problem based on the patient's self-report and inferences drawn from the 2 questionnaires. The Report cannot rule out physical disorders and does not make diagnoses nor definitive judgments. Designed for use by health professionals as an adjunct to clinical evaluation. A self-administered test developed for patients over 18 years old with an 8th grade reading level. Appropriate for patients undergoing evaluation or treatment for all varieties of pain. Organizes and simplifies chronic pain assessment.

14947
Adolescent Emotional Factors Inventory. Bauman, Mary K.

Subtests: Sensitivity; Somatic Symptoms; Social Competency; Attitudes of Distrust; Family Adjustment; Boy-Girl Adjustment; School Adjustment; Morale; Attitudes about Blindness; Validation
Descriptors: *Adolescents; *Blindness; *Personality Assessment; *Personality Measures; Projective Measures; Questionnaires; Tape Recorders
Identifiers: AEFI
Availability: Associated Services for the Blind; 919 Walnut St., Philadelphia, PA 19107
Target Audience: Adolescents
Notes: Items, 150

A personality assessment for blind adolescents. This is a questionnaire type instrument with a validation scale which is made up of 10 subscales, each consisting of approximately 15 items. This test is useful to point up problems, show the need for counseling, and help administrators work with children. This can be read to blind clients, but many examinees prefer to use a tape recorder. When using a tape recorder, the client can indicate his or her responses by using numbered cards or tickets.

14967
Identi-Form System for Gifted Programs. Weber, Patricia; Battaglia, Catherine 1982
Descriptors: *Academically Gifted; Elementary Education; *Elementary School Students; *Identification; Parent Attitudes; Peer Evaluation; Personality Traits; Records (Forms); *Screening Tests; Student Placement; Surveys
Identifiers: Task Orientation
Availability: D.O.K. Publishers; P.O. Box 605, E. Aurora, NY 14052
Grade Level: 2-5

This series of instruments and procedures designed for the identification of gifted students includes a matrix record form for data management and display which is said to simplify the procedure for including and excluding students from a program. It includes test performance and anecdotal measurement tools, including a Personal Characteristics Appraisal, Peer Survey, Parent Survey, Self Survey, Work Style Survey.

14968
Evaluating Gifted Programs. Nasca, Don 1983
Descriptors: *Academically Gifted; Educational Objectives; Elementary Education; *Elementary School Students; Formative Evaluation; Needs Assessment; Profiles; *Program Evaluation; Staff Role; Student Evaluation; Summative Evaluation
Availability: D.O.K. Publishers; P.O. Box 605, E. Aurora, NY 14052
Grade Level: 2-5

This guide to the evaluation of programs for gifted students includes measures for both formative and summative evaluation; needs assessment; goals and objectives report; screening profile form; a rating scale covering the relationship between the instructional program and program goals; staffing profile; a student evaluation; and a profile form for summarizing data.

14998
Screening for Problem Parenting. Avison, William R.; And Others 1986
Descriptors: Adults; *Child Abuse; Child Rearing; High Risk Persons; *Mothers; *Screening Tests
Identifiers: Likert Scales
Availability: Child Abuse and Neglect; v10 n2 p157-70 1986
Target Audience: Adults
Notes: Items, 20

Screening instrument used to identify mothers who may be at risk for problems in parenting which may result in child abuse. Those identified may be recommended for intervention programs. Examines social support the mother receives as well as her parenting attitudes, behaviors, and perceptions. Not to be used as a clinical or diagnostic instrument.

15005
COACH-Cayuga-Onondago Assessment for Children with Handicaps, Second Edition. Giangreco, Michael F. 1986
Descriptors: *Cognitive Processes; Criterion Referenced Tests; *Curriculum; *Disabilities; Educational Needs; *Elementary School Students; Elementary Secondary Education; *Environmental Influences; Integrated Curriculum; Secondary School Students; Special Education; Student Evaluation
Identifiers: COACH; *Function Based Curriculum
Availability: National Clearinghouse of Rehabilitation Training Materials; 115 Old USDA Bldg., Oklahoma State University, Stillwater, OK 74078
Grade Level: 1-12
Notes: Time, 60 approx.

Designed for use with school-aged learners having moderate, severe, or profound handicapping conditions. Designed to assist in educational planning and evaluation process. A curriculum-based criterion-referenced assessment tool generated from a functional curriculum model which combines environmental and cognitive curriculum components. Functional curriculum refers to teaching activities which have practical applications in daily life within the context of domestic school, community, and vocational settings for use in the learner's current and future environment. Cognitive curriculum is geared toward teaching concepts in communication and math via functional activities. Blends the environmental and cognitive curricula to maximize general learning and simultaneously teach relevant skills to the learner. To be administered by special education professionals in conjunction with the families of the learner.

15016

Adult Basic Learning Examination, Level 1, Second Edition. Karlsen, Bjorn; Gardner, Eric F. 1986
Subtests: Vocabulary; Reading Comprehension; Spelling; Number Operations; Problem Solving
Descriptors: *Achievement Tests; *Adult Basic Education; *Adult Education; *Adult Students; *Basic Skills; Language Arts; Mathematics Achievement; Reading Achievement
Identifiers: ABLE
Availability: Psychological Corporation; 555 Academic Ct., San Antonio, TX 78024-0952
Target Audience: Adults
Notes: Time, 130; Items, 142

Battery of tests measuring the level of educational achievement among adults. Determines general educational level of adults who have not completed 12 years of schooling and evaluates efforts to raise the educational level of these adults. Has adult oriented content and a nonthreatening format. Covers basic skills in reading, mathematics, and the language arts. Easy to administer. No single subtest requires more than 35 minutes. Content of ABLE, second edition, is totally new. The 3 levels were developed to accommodate meaningful segments of 12 years of schooling. The grade designation of each level refers to the achievement level that can be assessed most readily. At each level, 2 forms are available, Form E and Form F, which are parallel in content and difficulty. Two forms are to be used when reevaluation or periodic testing is desired. SelectABLE is a screening device to determine which level is most suitable for a particular individual if prior educational information is not available. Level 1 is for adults who have had one to 4 years of formal education (the primary grades). Many subtests are dictated to allow assessment of adults who do not have the necessary reading skills.

15017

Adult Basic Learning Examination, Level 2, Second Edition. Karlsen, Bjorn; Gardner, Eric F. 1986
Subtests: Vocabulary; Reading Comprehension; Spelling; Number Operations; Problem Solving; Applied Grammar; Capitalization and Punctuation
Descriptors: *Achievement Tests; *Adult Basic Education; *Adult Education; *Adult Students; *Basic Skills; Language Arts; Mathematics Achievement; Reading Achievement
Identifiers: ABLE
Availability: Psychological Corporation; 555 Academic Ct., San Antonio, TX 78024-0952
Target Audience: Adults
Notes: Time, 175; Items, 206

Battery of tests measuring the level of educational achievement among adults. Determines general educational level of adults who have not completed 12 years of schooling and evaluates efforts to raise the educational level of these adults. Has adult oriented content and a nonthreatening format. Covers basic skills in reading, mathematics, and the language arts. Easy to administer. No single subtest requires more than 35 minutes. Content of ABLE, second edition, is totally new. The 3 levels were developed to accommodate meaningful segments of 12 years of schooling. The grade designation of each level refers to the achievement level that can be assessed most readily. At each level, 2 forms are available, Form E and Form F, which are parallel in content and difficulty. Two forms are to be used when reevaluation or periodic testing is desired. SelectABLE is a screening device to determine which level is most suitable for a particular individual if prior educational information is not available. Level 2 is for adults who have had 5 to 8 years of schooling (the intermediate grades).

15018

Adult Basic Learning Examination, Level 3, Second Edition. Karlsen, Bjorn; Gardner, Eric F. 1986
Subtests: Vocabulary; Reading Comprehension; Spelling; Number Operations; Problem Solving; Applied Grammar; Capitalization and Punctuation
Descriptors: *Achievement Tests; *Adult Education; *Adult Students; *Basic Skills; Language Arts; Mathematics Achievement; Reading Achievement
Identifiers: ABLE

Availability: Psychological Corporation; 555 Academic Ct., San Antonio, TX 78024-0952
Target Audience: Adults
Notes: Time, 175; Items, 210

Battery of tests measuring the level of educational achievement among adults. Determines general educational level of adults who have not completed 12 years of schooling and evaluates efforts to raise the educational level of these adults. Has adult oriented content and a nonthreatening format. Covers basic skills in reading, mathematics, and the language arts. Easy to administer. No single subtest requires more than 35 minutes. Content of ABLE, second edition, is totally new. The 3 levels were developed to accommodate meaningful segments of 12 years of schooling. The grade designation of each level refers to the achievement level that can be assessed most readily. At each level, 2 forms are available, Form E and Form F, which are parallel in content and difficulty. Two forms are to be used when reevaluation or periodic testing is desired. SelectABLE is a screening device to determine which level is most suitable for a particular individual if prior educational information is not available. Level 3 is for adults who have had at least 8 years of schooling, but who have not graduated from high school (the high school grades).

15037

Brand Emotions Scale for Writers. Brand, Alice G.
Descriptors: Adults; *Affective Measures; *Authors; Creative Writing; Personality Measures; Self Evaluation (Individuals); *Writing Research
Identifiers: BESW
Availability: ERIC Document Reproduction Service; 3900 Wheeler Ave., Alexandria, VA 22304 (ED268152, 38 pages)
Target Audience: Adults

A 20-item scale designed to measure the emotions of writers immediately before writing, immediately after writing, and when writing in general. In general, the Brand Emotions Scale for Writers appears to be an internally consistent instrument capable of measuring positive and negative emotions in the above-mentioned situations.

15041

Tests of Adult Basic Education, Forms 5 and 6, Level E (Easy), Complete Battery. CTB/McGraw-Hill, Monterey, CA 1987
Subtests: Vocabulary; Comprehension; Mathematics Computation; Mathematics Concepts and Applications; Language Mechanics; Language Expression; Spelling
Descriptors: *Achievement Tests; *Adult Basic Education; Adults; *Adult Students; *Basic Skills; Language Skills; Mathematics Achievement; Norm Referenced Tests; Reading Achievement; Spelling
Identifiers: TABE
Availability: CTB/McGraw-Hill; 2500 Garden Rd., Monterey, CA 93940
Target Audience: Adults
Notes: Time, 293

Norm-referenced tests designed to measure achievement in reading, mathematics, language, and spelling, the subjects most commonly found in adult basic education curricula. Test focuses on the basic skills required for an individual to function in society. Tests combine the characteristics of norm-referenced and criterion-referenced tests and provide information about the relative ranking of examinees against a norm group and specific information about the instructional needs of the examinees. Results allow teachers and administrators to diagnose, evaluate, and place examinees in adult education programs. There is a correlation between scores on this test and the scores on the General Educational Development (GED) tests. Items on this test reflect language and content appropriate for adults and measure the understanding and application of conventions and principles. Test items are not intended to measure specific knowledge or recall of facts. There are 4 overlapping levels and 2 parallel forms for each level. The 4 levels and their estimated grade ranges are E (easy) with a grade range of 2.6-4.9; M (medium) with a grade range of 4.6-6.9; D (difficult) with a grade range of 6.6-8.9; and A (advanced) with a grade range of 8.6-12.9. There is also a survey form which is a subset of the complete battery and can be used to quickly screen examinees for appropriate placement in programs of instruction.

15042

Tests of Adult Basic Education, Forms 5 and 6, Level M (Medium), Complete Battery. CTB/McGraw-Hill, Monterey, CA 1987
Subtests: Vocabulary; Comprehension; Mathematics Computation; Mathematics Concepts and Applications; Language Mechanics; Language Expression; Spelling
Descriptors: *Achievement Tests; *Adult Basic Education; Adults; *Adult Students; *Basic Skills; Language Skills; Mathematics Achievement; Norm Referenced Tests; Reading Achievement; Spelling
Identifiers: TABE

Availability: CTB/McGraw-Hill; 2500 Garden Rd., Monterey, CA 93940
Target Audience: Adults
Notes: Time, 293; Items, 263

Norm-referenced tests designed to measure achievement in reading, mathematics, language, and spelling, the subjects most commonly found in adult basic education curricula. Test focuses on the basic skills required for an individual to function in society. Tests combine the characteristics of norm-referenced and criterion-referenced tests and provide information about the relative ranking of examinees against a norm group and specific information about the instructional needs of the examinees. Results allow teachers and administrators to diagnose, evaluate, and place examinees in adult education programs. There is a correlation between scores on this test and the scores on the General Educational Development (GED) tests. Items on this test reflect language and content appropriate for adults and measure the understanding and application of conventions and principles. Test items are not intended to measure specific knowledge or recall of facts. There are 4 overlapping levels and 2 parallel forms for each level. The 4 levels and their estimated grade ranges are E (easy) with a grade range of 2.6-4.9; M (medium) with a grade range of 4.6-6.9; D (difficult) with a grade range of 6.6-8.9; and A (advanced) with a grade range of 8.6-12.9. There is also a survey form which is a subset of the complete battery and can be used to quickly screen examinees for appropriate placement in programs of instruction.

15043

Tests of Adult Basic Education, Form 5, Level D (Difficult), Complete Battery. CTB/McGraw-Hill, Monterey, CA 1987
Subtests: Vocabulary; Comprehension; Mathematics Computation; Mathematics Concepts and Applications; Language Mechanics; Language Expression; Spelling
Descriptors: *Achievement Tests; *Adult Basic Education; Adults; *Adult Students; *Basic Skills; Language Skills; Mathematics Achievement; Norm Referenced Tests; Reading Achievement; Spelling
Identifiers: TABE
Availability: CTB/McGraw-Hill; 2500 Garden Rd., Monterey, CA 93940
Target Audience: Adults
Notes: Time, 293; Items, 263

Norm-referenced tests designed to measure achievement in reading, mathematics, language, and spelling, the subjects most commonly found in adult basic education curricula. Test focuses on the basic skills required for an individual to function in society. Tests combine the characteristics of norm-referenced and criterion-referenced tests and provide information about the relative ranking of examinees against a norm group and specific information about the instructional needs of the examinees. Results allow teachers and administrators to diagnose, evaluate, and place examinees in adult education programs. There is a correlation between scores on this test and the scores on the General Educational Development (GED) tests. Items on this test reflect language and content appropriate for adults and measure the understanding and application of conventions and principles. Test items are not intended to measure specific knowledge or recall of facts. There are 4 overlapping levels and 2 parallel forms for each level. The 4 levels and their estimated grade ranges are E (easy) with a grade range of 2.6-4.9; M (medium) with a grade range of 4.6-6.9; D (difficult) with a grade range of 6.6-8.9; and A (advanced) with a grade range of 8.6-12.9. There is also a survey form which is a subset of the complete battery and can be used to quickly screen examinees for appropriate placement in programs of instruction.

15044

Tests of Adult Basic Education, Form 5, Level a (Advanced), Complete Battery. CTB/McGraw-Hill, Monterey, CA 1987
Subtests: Vocabulary; Comprehension; Mathematics Computation; Mathematics Concepts and Applications; Language Mechanics; Language Expression; Spelling
Descriptors: *Achievement Tests; *Adult Basic Education; Adults; *Adult Students; *Basic Skills; Language Skills; Mathematics Achievement; Norm Referenced Tests; Reading Achievement; Spelling
Identifiers: TABE
Availability: CTB/McGraw-Hill; 2500 Garden Rd., Monterey, CA 93940
Target Audience: Adults
Notes: Time, 293; Items, 263

Norm-referenced tests designed to measure achievement in reading, mathematics, language, and spelling, the subjects most commonly found in adult basic education curricula. Test focuses on the basic skills required for an individual to function in society. Tests combine the characteristics of norm-referenced and criterion-referenced tests and provide information about the relative ranking of examinees against a norm group and specific information about the instructional needs of the examinees. Results allow teachers and administrators to diagnose, evaluate, and place examinees in adult education programs. There is a correlation between scores on this test and the scores on the

General Educational Development (GED) tests. Items on this test reflect language and content appropriate for adults and measure the understanding and application of conventions and principles. Test items are not intended to measure specific knowledge or recall of facts. There are 4 overlapping levels and 2 parallel forms for each level. The 4 levels and their estimated grade ranges are E (easy) with a grade range of 2.6-4.9; M (medium) with a grade range of 4.6-6.9; D (difficult) with a grade range of 6.6-8.9; and A (advanced) with a grade range of 8.6-12.9. There is also a survey form which is a subset of the complete battery and can be used to quickly screen examinees for appropriate placement in programs of instruction.

15055
Arizona Basic Assessment and Curriculum Utilization System. McCarthy, Jeanne M.; And Others 1986
Subtests: Body Management; Self-Care; Communication; Preacademic; Socialization
Descriptors: *Communication Skills; *Criterion Referenced Tests; *Developmental Disabilities; *Handicap Identification; *Hygiene; Individualized Education Programs; *Preschool Education; *Self Care Skills; *Social Development; Young Children
Identifiers: ABACUS; IEP
Availability: Love Publishing; 1777 S. Bellaire St., Denver, CO 80222
Target Audience: 2-5
Notes: Items, 214

An early education program for young handicapped children functioning in the developmental age range from 2 to 5.5 years. Contains several individual instruments used for different purposes. The ABACUS assessment is a criterion-referenced instrument which contains 214 items referenced to the 5 broad areas of the program's curriculum: Body Management, Self-Care, Communication, Pre-Academics, and Socialization. Meant to be used after the child has been screened, using the program-supplied PASS I (Pre ABACUS Screening Scale) and PASS II instruments. Based on the results of The Assessment data, placement decisions are made and an individualized education program is developed for the child. Also included in the program is a Teaching Behavior Inventory to monitor the quality of classroom teaching. A Modified Teaching Behavior Inventory can be used for observation of aides, home teachers, and volunteers.

15058
Dysarthria Profile. Robertson, J. J. 1987
Subtests: Respiration; Phonation; Examination of Facial Musculature; Diadochokinesis; Reflexes; Articulation; Intelligibility; Prosody and Rate
Descriptors: Adolescents; Adults; Individual Testing; Profiles; *Speech Evaluation; *Speech Handicaps; *Speech Tests; Speech Therapy
Identifiers: *Dysarthria
Availability: Communication Skill Builders; P.O. Box 42050, Tuscon, AZ 85733
Target Audience: 13-65

A brief, objective assessment procedure for dysarthria which provides the practicing speech therapist with a profile of the client's abilities and disabilities; descriptive information to help in classification of the dysarthric problem; and a sound basis on which to build a therapy and management program. Does not classify types of dysarthria. Designed to describe dysarthric clients' problems, whatever the underlying neurological etiology. Profile has been compiled with treatment planning as a priority. Dysarthric Profile is divided into 8 sections: respiration, phonation, examination of facial musculature, diadochokineses, reflexes, articulation, intelligibility, and prosody and rate. Individually administered. Designed for adolescents and adults.

15092
Gifted and Talented Screening Scale. Cicione, Frank J.; Latham, Jefferson M. 1977
Descriptors: *Elementary School Students; Elementary Secondary Education; *Gifted; *Program Development; Rating Scales; *Screening Tests; *Secondary School Students; *Talent
Identifiers: GTSS
Availability: ERIC Document Reproduction Service; 3900 Wheeler Ave., Alexandria, VA 22304-5110 (ED180153, 18 pages)
Grade Level: K-12
Target Audience: 5-18
Notes: Time, 5 approx.; Items, 25

Screening scale used to determine the students in a class or group who are gifted and talented. Teachers of the students rate them according to a 4-point scale. Scale focuses on day-to-day experiences teachers have with students. Should be used with entire school or grade so results are norm based upon school or grade. Scale may be used to help define, implement, and administer a Gifted and Talented program in the grade or school.

15137
STIM/CON. Sommers, Ronald K. 1987
Descriptors: *Articulation Impairments; *Grade 1; *Kindergarten; Kindergarten Children; *Primary Education; *Prognostic Tests; Speech Evaluation; *Speech Tests
Availability: United Educational Services; P.O. Box 357, E. Aurora, NY 14052
Grade Level: K-1
Notes: Time, 20 approx.

A prognostic inventory for misarticulating kindergarten and first grade children which incorporates 2 valid prognostic measures: stimulability for defective sounds and consistency of error of defective sounds. Stimulability scores are derived by comparing the spontaneous responses to pictures with the child's imitation of nonsense syllables that test the same positional context. Inconsistency scores are determined by recording the percentages of correct productions across various phonetic contexts by having the child repeat sentences spoken by the clinician. Results are useful in determining whether intervention to correct misarticulation is necessary.

15139
Spellmaster Revised. Greenbaum, Claire R. 1987
Subtests: Regular Word Test; Irregular Word Test; Homophone Test; Entry Level Test
Descriptors: *Adult Basic Education; Adults; *Criterion Referenced Tests; *Diagnostic Tests; *Elementary School Students; Elementary Secondary Education; Remedial Instruction; *Secondary School Students; *Spelling; Spelling Instruction
Availability: Pro-Ed; 5341 Industrial Oaks Blvd., Austin, TX 78735
Grade Level: K-10
Target Audience: 6-65
Notes: Time, 20 approx.

A criterion-referenced, self-contained assessment and teaching system used in both remedial and regular classroom spelling instruction. Allows for the identification of specific problem areas as tests are scored, and later yields a rapid analysis of an individual's progress or a whole class's ability. The manual contains teaching methods and strategies, learning activities, and supplemental word lists. Suitable for use with students of varying ability levels; and can be integrated with other spelling programs already in use. A revision of The Spellmaster system originally published in 1974.

800086
Kindergarten Behavioral Index: A Screening Technique for Reading Readiness. Banks, Enid M. 1972
Descriptors: Behavior Patterns; Foreign Countries; *Grade 1; Handicap Identification; *Kindergarten Children; Learning Disabilities; Perceptual Development; Primary Education; *Reading Readiness; School Readiness; *School Readiness Tests; Screening Tests
Identifiers: Australia
Availability: Australian Council for Educational Research; P.O. Box 210, Hawthorn 3122, Australia
Grade Level: K-1
Notes: Items, 37

Designed for use at the end of a child's first year in school when he or she is at least 5.5 years of age. Developed for use in assessing academic readiness and identification of children with potential learning disabilities.

800147
Language Imitation Test. Berry, Paul; Mittler, Peter
Subtests: Sound Imitation; Word Imitation; Syntactic Control; Word Organisation Control; Sentence Completion
Descriptors: Children; Foreign Countries; *Imitation; *Language Skills; Language Tests; Psycholinguistics; Severe Disabilities; *Severe Mental Retardation
Identifiers: England; Great Britain; LIT
Availability: NFER-Nelson Publishing Co.; Darville House, 2 Oxford Rd. E., Windsor, Berks SL4 1DF, England
Target Audience: 2-12

Designed for use as a language assessment technique for the severely educational subnormal (ESN) population. Assesses linguistic competence.

800167
Test of English for Migrant Students. Australian Council for Educational Research, Hawthorn 1977
Descriptors: Achievement Tests; Children; *Diagnostic Tests; Disadvantaged Environment; *Elementary School Students; *English (Second Language); Foreign Countries; Individual Testing; *Kindergarten; *Language Proficiency; Language Skills; Language Tests; Pictorial Stimuli; *Primary Education; Second Language Learning; *Speech Skills; Verbal Tests; Visual Measures
Identifiers: Australia; TEMS
Availability: Australian Council For Educational Research, Ltd.; P. O. Box 210, Hawthorn, Victoria, Australia 3122
Target Audience: 5-9

A collection of 84 tests and checklists designed to measure the competence of Australian migrant students in various aspects of the English language such as sounds and symbols, grammar, vocabulary and idioms, integrated comprehension and production, communicative competence, and nonverbal communication. Migrant students are defined as students who experience difficulties with English because they were born in a non-English speaking country and/or because they have at least one parent whose native language is not English. The speaking tests are individually administered; all others are to be administered to individuals or to a small group. Many tests are visual measures, with little written text. Some tests require the use of prerecorded tape and related equipment for playing it.

800169
Edinburgh Articulation Test. Anthony, A.; And Others 1971
Descriptors: Articulation (Speech); *Articulation Impairments; Foreign Countries; *Individual Testing; Pictorial Stimuli; *Preschool Children; Preschool Education; Speech Handicaps; Speech Tests; *Speech Therapy; *Therapists
Identifiers: Australia; EAT
Availability: Australian Council for Educational Research, Ltd.; Radford House, Frederick St., Hawthorn, Victoria 3122, Australia
Target Audience: 3-5
Notes: Time, 20 approx.; Items, 35

Designed to assess phonological maturation of preschool children whose speech development is abnormal or slow. Booklet of pictures is designed to elicit spontaneous responses. Instrument should be individually administered by a speech therapist or someone with training in phonetic procedures.

800193
ACER Early School Series. Rowe, Helga A.H. 1981
Subtests: Auditory Discrimination; Recognition of Initial Consonant Sounds; Number; Figure Formation; Prepositions; Verb Tense; Pronouns; Negation; Comprehension; Word Knowledge
Descriptors: Adults; Auditory Discrimination; Basic Vocabulary; *Cognitive Development; *Cognitive Measurement; Concept Formation; Consonants; Diagnostic Tests; Disabilities; *Elementary School Students; Foreign Countries; Individual Testing; Numbers; Primary Education; Remedial Instruction; *Screening Tests; Syntax
Identifiers: Australia; Power Tests
Availability: Australian Council for Educational Research; Frederick St., Hawthorn 3122, Victoria, Australia
Grade Level: K-3
Notes: Time, 200 approx.; Items, 150

Designed to provide a series of estimates of a child's cognitive development and maturity. In addition to identifying particular strengths and weaknesses of individual school beginners, tests may also be useful as counseling and guidance tools in lower grades of primary schools and with certain groups of handicapped adults. Also useful with children who cannot read and for remedial students because reading is not required with this series. All tests are power tests. Suitable for administration with small groups, but more valid results obtained when individually administered.

800201
Australian Second Language Proficiency Ratings—English. Ingram, D. E.; Wylie, Elaine 1982
Subtests: Speaking; Listening; Writing; Reading
Descriptors: Achievement Tests; Adults; *English (Second Language); Foreign Countries; *Individual Testing; Interviews; *Language Proficiency; Linguistic Performance; Listening Comprehension Tests; Oral Language; Rating Scales; Reading Comprehension; Writing Skills
Identifiers: ASLPR; Australia; Oral Tests
Availability: David E. Ingram; Dept. of Languages and Literature, Mt. Gravatt College of Advanced Education, Messines Ridge Rd., Brisbane CAE, Mt. Gravatt, Queensland, Australia 4122
Target Audience: Adults
Notes: Items, 31

An individual interview rating of language proficiency and a written test. Originally designed for use with immigrants. Uses natural real-life language activities requiring speaking, listening, reading and writing. Each subscale describes 9 levels of proficiency from zero to native-like, plus 3 additional plus/minus gradings. Versions are available for use with French (TC800202), Italian (TC800200), and Japanese (TC 800199).

810028
Progressive Matrices, Coloured. Raven, J.C. 1965

Descriptors: Adults; Children; *Cognitive Ability; *Culture Fair Tests; Foreign Countries; *Moderate Mental Retardation; Multiple Choice Tests; *Nonverbal Tests
Identifiers: CPM; England; Great Britain
Availability: The Psychological Corporation; 555 Academic Ct., San Antonio, TX 78204-0952
Target Audience: 5-11
Notes: Items, 36

A nonverbal test designed to assess mental ability via problems concerning colored abstract figures and designs. Also useful with mentally handicapped adults. Individual or small group administration is necessary. Norms are available for several English groups. Purported to be culture fair.

810100
Progressive Matrices, Advanced Sets I and II. Raven, John C. 1965
Descriptors: *Academically Gifted; Adolescents; Adults; *Cognitive Measurement; *Cognitive Processes; Foreign Countries; *Intellectual Development; Nonverbal Tests
Identifiers: APM I; APM II; England; Great Britain
Availability: The Psychological Corporation; 555 Academic Ct., San Antonio, TX 78204-0952
Target Audience: 12-64
Notes: Time, 40 approx.; Items, 48

A nonverbal test designed for use as an aid in assessing mental ability. Requires the examinee to solve problems presented in abstract figures and designs. Scores are said to correlate well with comprehensive intelligence tests. This form is designed for use with persons having above average intellectual ability. Norms are estimated for a British population at ages 11.5, 14, 20, 30, and 40. Said to be culture fair. Set I covers all intellectual processes covered by the Standard Progressive Matrices Sets. Set II provides a means of assessing all the analytical and integral operations involved in the higher thought processes and differentiates between people of superior intellectual ability.

810122
Group Test of General Intelligence AH4. Heim, A.W. 1973
Subtests: Verbal and Numerical; Diagrammatic
Descriptors: *Adolescents; *Adults; *Children; *Deduction; Foreign Countries; *Intelligence; *Intelligence Tests; *Mental Retardation; Multiple Choice Tests; Timed Tests; Visual Measures
Identifiers: England; Great Britain
Availability: NFER-Nelson Publishing Co. Ltd.; Darville House, 2 Oxford Rd. E., Windsor, Berks, SL4 1DF, England
Target Audience: 10-64
Notes: Time, 20; Items, 130

Developed in England to measure general intelligence of the adult population, some groups with below average intelligence, and for all children over 10 years of age. The qualities tested are ability to reason, to obey simple instructions, to understand the meaning of everyday words, and to observe details accurately. The emphasis is mainly on deductive reasoning. The author recommends one administrator for groups of up to 25 and an assistant for each additional 5 to 20 people. The distribution is restricted, available only to recognized professional institutions and qualified psychologists.

810313
The Stycar Hearing Tests (Revised Edition, 1968). Sheridan, Mary D. 1968
Descriptors: *Auditory Tests; Foreign Countries; Infants; *Listening Comprehension; *Mental Retardation; *Screening Tests; *Young Children
Identifiers: England; Great Britain
Availability: NFER-Nelson Publishing Co.; Darville House, 2 Oxford Rd. E., Windsor, Berks SL4 1DF, England
Target Audience: 0-7

Designed to assess the ability of infants and young children to hear with comprehension. The battery consists of a series of simple clinical auditory screening tests, using durable toys to involve children.

810339
The Stycar Vision Tests (Revised Edition, 1969). Sheridan, Mary D.
Descriptors: Foreign Countries; *Infants; Mental Retardation; Preschool Children; Preschool Education; *Vision; *Vision Tests; *Visual Impairments; *Young Children
Identifiers: England; Great Britain
Availability: NFER-Nelson Publishing Co.; Darville House, 2 Oxford Rd. E., Windsor, Berks SL4 1DF, England
Target Audience: 0-7

Designed to assess distant and near vision of young non-handicapped and handicapped children. Procedures are organized into 4 groups—3 by age and the 4th with reference to very low vision. The procedures are infants (6

months to 2.5 years), pre-school children (2.5 to 4 years), and school entrants (5-7 years). The Panda Test is for children with severe visual handicaps.

810368
Stycar Language Test. Sheridan, Mary D. 1976
Subtests: Common Objects Test; Miniature Toys Test; Picture Book Test
Descriptors: Developmental Disabilities; *Diagnostic Tests; Foreign Countries; Individual Testing; *Infants; Language Acquisition; *Language Handicaps; Medical Evaluation; Mental Retardation; *Speech Handicaps; *Young Children
Identifiers: England; Great Britain
Availability: NFER-Nelson Publishing Co.; Darville House, 2 Oxford Rd. E., Windsor, Berks SL4 1DF, England
Target Audience: 1-7
Notes: Time, 30 approx.

A series of clinical test procedures for the differential diagnosis and management of developmental disorders of speech and language in young children, including those who are mentally handicapped. Instruments should be administered by speech therapists, medical doctors, specialist language teachers, or clinically experienced psychologists.

810369
Symbolic Play Test: Experimental Edition. Lowe, Marianne; Costello, Anthony J. 1976
Descriptors: *Concept Formation; *Diagnostic Tests; Foreign Countries; Nonverbal Tests; *Speech Handicaps; *Young Children
Identifiers: England; Great Britain; *Symbolic Play; Symbolic Thinking
Availability: NFER-Nelson Publishing Co.; Darville House, 2 Oxford Rd. E., Windsor, SL41DF, Berkshire, England
Target Audience: 1-3
Notes: Time, 15; Items, 24

Diagnostic measure using children's spontaneous nonverbal play activities in a structured situation to identify the level of a child's symbolic thinking and early concept formation. To be used with children who have failed to develop receptive or expressive language. Unlike performance tests in that it measures semantic rather than spatial relationships and ability to deal with symbols in their simplest form, main function is to identify children whose failure to communicate is because of an environmental cause, not a lack in the area of symbolization, or a developmental delay.

810374
SPAR Spelling and Reading Tests. Young, D. 1976
Subtests: Spelling; Reading: Pictures; Reading: Sentences
Descriptors: Academic Ability; Adolescents; Basic Skills; Children; *Elementary School Students; Foreign Countries; Language Skills; Learning Problems; *Literacy; *Low Achievement; Multiple Choice Tests; Pictorial Stimuli; Reading Difficulties; *Reading Tests; *Screening Tests; *Secondary School Students; *Spelling; Student Evaluation; Verbal Ability; Verbal Development; Visual Measures
Identifiers: England; Great Britain; Group Reading Test; SPAR Reading Test; SPAR Spelling Test
Availability: Hodder And Stoughton Educational; P.O. Box 702, Mill Rd., Dunton Green, Sevenoaks, Kent TN 13 2YD, England
Target Audience: 7-16
Notes: Time, 30 approx.; Items, 75

Designed to provide a complementary approach to the testing of literacy at a simple level; to alert the teacher to the need for remedial measures; and to be used as a means of following the literacy progress of primary school students and/or older, less able students in the secondary schools. This instrument is designed to discriminate particularly among the lower ability levels. The author emphasizes that (1) this instrument is not a diagnostic test, but a screening test; and (2) the reading and spelling tests may be used independently of each other even though this separation would prevent the comparison and contrasting of the results. The spelling items are divided into 2 banks, Bank A and Bank B, so that the administrator may select 10 matched tests without any overlap or a much larger number of words with only a partial overlap. Thus, the author feels that these spelling banks give a distinct advantage, especially in charting the student's progress over a number of years. Forms A and B of the reading test follow the same formula as that of the author's Group Reading Test (GRT), and the marking templates for the GRT can be used for this reading test. Spelling test is not timed but usually takes about 10 minutes; the 2 sections of the reading test are timed separately.

810385
Reynell Developmental Language Scales (Revised). Reynell, Joan K. 1977
Subtests: Expressive Language; Verbal Comprehension

Descriptors: *Disabilities; *Expressive Language; Foreign Countries; *Hearing Impairments; Individual Testing; *Language Handicaps; *Language Tests; *Neurological Impairments; Physical Disabilities; *Receptive Language; Vocabulary; *Young Children
Identifiers: England; Great Britain; RDLS
Availability: The NFER-Nelson Publishing Co., Ltd.; Darville House, 2 Oxford Rd. E., Windsor, Berkshire, SL4 1DF, England
Target Audience: 1-6

Designed to assess expressive language and verbal comprehension of children suspected of having some language deficit. Suitable for handicapped or hearing-impaired children ages 1.5 through 6 years of age. Verbal comprehension scale needs no spoken response, and verbal comprehension needed for the expressive language scale is minimal.

810388
Neale Analysis of Reading Ability, Braille Adaptation. Neale, Marie D.; Lorimer, J. 1977
Descriptors: *Blindness; *Braille; Children; *Diagnostic Tests; Elementary Education; *Elementary School Students; Foreign Countries; Individual Testing; Oral Reading; *Reading Achievement; Reading Diagnosis; *Reading Difficulties; Reading Tests
Identifiers: England; Great Britain; Oral Tests
Availability: NFER-Nelson Publishing Co.; Darville House 2 Oxford Rd. E., Windsor, Berkshire SL4 1DF, England
Target Audience: 6-12
Notes: Time, 45 approx.

Adaptation by J. Lorimer of Neale Analysis of Reading Ability (TC830315) for use with blind children. Individually administered test designed to provide diagnostic information which can be used to help remedy reading difficulties. Comes in Forms A, B, and C. Pictures used in print edition are replaced by introductory sentences, also used to arouse interest in the story. M. Lorimer strongly recommends that the test be administered only by experienced teachers of blind children who have a sound knowledge of grade II Braille, who have taught Braille, and, thus, understand the problems of reading by touch.

810416
Group Tests of High-Level Intelligence AH 6. Heim, A.W.; And Others 1970
Subtests: Verbal; Numerical; Diagrammatic
Descriptors: *Adolescents; *Adults; College Students; Foreign Countries; *Gifted; High School Students; *Intelligence; *Intelligence Differences; *Intelligence Tests; Multiple Choice Tests; Professional Personnel; Timed Tests; Visual Measures; Vocational Schools
Identifiers: England; Great Britain
Availability: NFER-Nelson Publishing Co., Ltd.; Darville House, 2 Oxford Rd. E., Windsor, Berkshire, SL4 1DF, England
Target Audience: 14-64
Notes: Time, 40; Items, 72

Developed in England to effect discrimination among the highly intelligent students and potential students at universities and colleges, potential entrants to professions and senior students at grammar, public, and technical schools. Two forms exist: AG and SEM. SEM is for potential or qualified scientists, engineers, and mathematicians; has 72 questions; and is timed for 40 minutes. AG (Arts and General) is for everyone else; has 60 questions; and is timed for 35 minutes. Subjects may answer the questions in any order that they choose because the aim is to allow the subject to work at his/her own natural tempo on those questions which appeal most to him/her and to determine which chosen questions he/she can correctly answer. The author recommends one administrator for groups up to 25 and an assistant for each additional 5 to 20 people.

810442
The Anxiety Symptom Rating Scale. Hamilton, Max 1959
Descriptors: Adults; *Anxiety; Emotional Problems; Foreign Countries; Patients; Rating Scales
Identifiers: England; Great Britain
Availability: The British Journal of Medical Psychology; v32 pt1 p50-55 1959
Target Audience: Adults

Scale intended for use with patients already diagnosed as suffering from neurotic anxiety states; not for assessing anxiety in patients suffering from other disorders. A 5-point scale is used. Is to be used for the qualification of symptoms.

810464
PIP Developmental Charts. Jeffree, Dorothy M.; McConkey, Roy 1976
Descriptors: Behavior Rating Scales; *Child Development; Daily Living Skills; *Disabilities; Eye Hand Coordination; Foreign Countries; *Infants; Language Acquisition; Parents; Physical Development; *Young Children
Identifiers: England; Great Britain

Availability: Hodder & Stoughton Educational; P.O. Box 6, Mill Rd., Dunton Green Sevenoaks, Kent TN13 2XX, England
Target Audience: 0-5

Developed to provide a profile of child's development in 5 major areas. Used to determine disabled child's level of ability. Completed by parent. Areas assessed include physical development, social development, eye-hand development, development of play, and language development.

810476
National Adult Reading Test. Nelson, Hazel E. 1982
Descriptors: Adults; Alcoholism; Drug Use; Foreign Countries; Individual Testing; *Intelligence; *Mental Disorders; Older Adults; *Pronunciation; *Reading Tests; *Word Recognition
Identifiers: *Dementia; England; Great Britain; NART; *Premorbid Intelligence
Availability: NFER-Nelson Publishing Co.; Darville House, 2 Oxford Rd. E., Windsor, Berkshire SL4 1DF, England
Target Audience: 20-70
Notes: Items, 50

Represents a new technique for estimating premorbid intelligence in the assessment of elements. Consists of 50 words in which the correct pronunciation is based on word recognition. This measure is stable despite deterioration of other intellectual functions. From subject's score, IQ can be predicted which closely approximates premorbid IQ level. Will also be useful in measuring effects of alcohol, drugs, or illness on intellectual functioning of 20-70 year olds.

810477
The Claybury Selection Battery. Caine, T.M.; And Others 1982
Descriptors: Adults; *Attitude Measures; *Counselor Attitudes; Expectation; Foreign Countries; *Interests; Patients; *Psychotherapy; Questionnaires; Rating Scales
Identifiers: ATQ; DIQ; England; Great Britain; Psychiatric Patients; TEQ; *Treatment Expectancies
Availability: NFER-Nelson Publishing Co.; Darville House, 2 Oxford Rd. E., Windsor, Berkshire SL4 1DF, England
Target Audience: Adults

Battery consists of 3 measures which assess elements of personal style which research has demonstrated to have clinical implications, particularly in the area of treatment selection. Based on evidence that patient expectancies and staff attitudes are a major influence on the outcome of treatment for psychological therapies, the Direction of Interest Questionnaire (DIQ) is a 14-item forced-choice questionnaire which distinguishes between an interest in ideas, theories, emotions, and an interest in facts, practical problems, common sense, power, and action. The Treatment Expectancies Questionnaire (TEQ) is a 15-item factor-analytically derived questionnaire which measures patients' expectancies regarding psychological and psychiatric treatment. The Attitudes to Treatment Questionnaire (ATQ) is a 19-item factor-analytically derived scale incorporated in a 24-item questionnaire which measures staff attitides toward approaches to psychological and psychiatric treatment. Intended for psychologists, psychiatrists, occupational therapists, nurses, educational counselors, and personnel and training officers.

810483
NIIP Verbal Test 91. National Institute of Industrial Psychology, London, England 1968
Descriptors: *Abstract Reasoning; Adolescents; Adults; *Aptitude Tests; *Cognitive Ability; Cognitive Tests; Dropouts; *Employees; Foreign Countries; *Job Applicants; *Occupational Tests; Problem Solving; Timed Tests; Verbal Ability; *Verbal Tests; Vocational Aptitude
Identifiers: England; Great Britain; Group Test 91; *Reasoning Ability
Availability: NFER-Nelson Publishing Co.; Darville House, 2 Oxford Rd. E., Windsor, Berkshire SL4 1DF, England
Target Audience: 15-64
Notes: Time, 15; Items, 110

Measures verbal general intelligence. Used with employees and job applicants for positions requiring verbal reasoning and usually with subjects who are high school dropouts or have a lower level of educational attainment. Distribution limited to persons who are registered with NIIP as qualified to use it.

810488
NIIP Engineering Arithmetic Test, EA 2A and EA4. National Institute of Industrial Psychology, London, England
Descriptors: Ability Identification; Achievement Tests; Adolescents; Adults; Career Choice; Career Counseling; Computation; Dropouts; *Employees; *Employment Potential; Foreign Countries; High School Graduates; Job Placement; Mathematics; *Mathematics Achievement; *Metric System; Occupational Tests; *Mathematics Tests; Timed Tests; Vocational Education
Identifiers: EA2A; EA4; Engineering Selection Test Battery; England; Great Britain; *Imperial (Measurement); NIIP Engineering Selection; Test Battery
Availability: NFER-Nelson Publishing Co.; Darville House, 2 Oxford Rd. E., Windsor, Berkshire SL4 1DF, England
Target Audience: 15-64
Notes: Time, 20; Items, 49

Timed, group-administered instrument designed to test the attainment in mathematics for those entering the work field, high school dropouts and graduates, or those considering a career change. Used in the selection of suitable courses, apprenticeships, and occupations. Test EA2A (49 items) uses imperial measures while Test EA4 measures knowledge in metric system. One of the tests included in the Engineering Apprentice Selection Battery (TC810481). Includes items using square roots and percentages. Restricted distribution.

810493
NIIP Clerical Test 61A (Speed and Accuracy). National Institute of Industrial Psychology, London, England 1978
Subtests: Filing; Classification; Checking
Descriptors: Adolescents; Adults; *Clerical Workers; *Dropouts; Foreign Countries; *Occupational Tests
Identifiers: *Clerical Aptitude; *Clerical Skills; England; Great Britain
Availability: NFER-Nelson Publishing Co.; Darville House, 2 Oxford Rd. E., Windsor, Berks SL4 1DF, England
Target Audience: 15-64
Notes: Time, 20; Items, 456

A test of speed and accuracy in filing, classifying, and checking. Useful for selecting candidates for clerical positions, and especially suitable for use with school dropouts. Test usage is limited.

810494
NIIP Group Test 64. National Institute of Industrial Psychology, London, England 1978
Descriptors: *Achievement Tests; Adolescents; Adults; *Clerical Workers; *Dropouts; Foreign Countries; *Spelling
Identifiers: *Clerical Skills; England; Great Britain
Availability: NFER-Nelson Publishing Co., Darville House, 2 Oxford Rd. E., Windsor, Berkshire SL4 1DF, England
Target Audience: 15-64
Notes: Time, 15 approx.; Items, 118

An untimed test of spelling useful in selecting candidates for clerical positions. Suitable for use with school dropouts.

810507
The Bereweeks Skill Teaching System: Assessment Checklist. Jenkins, Judith; And Others 1983
Subtests: Cognitive Skills; Receptive Language; Expressive Language; Self Care; Gross Motor Skills; Social Practical
Descriptors: Adolescents; Adults; *Check Lists; Children; Cognitive Ability; Daily Living Skills; Expressive Language; Foreign Countries; Individual Testing; Interpersonal Competence; Moderate Mental Retardation; Older Adults; Psychomotor Skills; Receptive Language; *Residential Institutions; Self Care Skills; *Severe Mental Retardation
Identifiers: Bereweeke Assessment Checklist; England; Great Britain; Gross Motor Skills
Availability: NFER-Nelson Publishing Co.; Darville House, 2 Oxford Rd. E., Windsor, Berks SL4 1DF, England
Target Audience: 6-80
Notes: Time, 360 approx.; Items, 285

Part of a teaching-assessment system developed to provide individual training programs for profoundly or severely mentally retarded or most moderately mentally retarded adults in residential institutions. The Skill-Teaching System is also appropriate for children, adolescents and older adults. The checklist covers the major areas of daily behavior and items are phrased in behavioral terms. The checklist is not designed to be an exhaustive list of behaviors. There may be cases where items will have to be broken down into smaller steps to obtain a practical long-term goal. The assessment should be conducted over a period of a few days.

810510
Social Behaviour Assessment Schedule. Third Edition. Platt, Stephen; And Others 1983
Descriptors: *Emotional Disturbances; Foreign Countries; *Interpersonal Competence; Interviews; *Physical Health
Identifiers: England; Great Britain; *Psychiatric Patients; SBAS
Availability: NFER-Nelson Publishing Co.; Darville House, 2 Oxford Rd. E., Windsor, Berks SL4 1DF, England
Target Audience: Adults
Notes: Time, 90 approx.

Used as a semistructured interview with a relative or close friend of acutely ill psychiatric patients. Can also be adapted for use with those close to the physically or chronically ill. Designed to assess patient's social behavior and its effect on others. May be used to assess effects of different treatments on patient or in comparing different patients. Original edition of the SBAS was the Patient Behaviour Assessment Schedule.

810513
Wessex Revised Portage Language Checklist. White, Mollie; East, Cathy 1983
Descriptors: Check Lists; *Developmental Disabilities; Foreign Countries; *Language Acquisition; *Mental Retardation; *Young Children
Identifiers: England; Portage Guide to Early Education
Availability: NFER-Nelson Publishing Co.; Darville House, 2 Oxford Rd. E., Windsor, Berks SL4 1D7, England
Target Audience: 0-4

A revision and extension of the original Checklist of Behaviors, a component of the Portage Guide to Early Education. Designed for use with children between the mental ages of birth and 4, especially the developmentally delayed or mentally handicapped children. Used as a guide to the design of teaching activities for the individual child and provides a framework for the teaching of language skills. This version has been updated, expanded, and anglicized. Behaviors listed under other headings in the original checklist have been added to the Wessex Checklist, especially those particularly relevant to child's growth in language skills.

810514
Bexley-Maudsley Automated Psychological Screening and Bexley-Maudsley Category Sorting Test. Acker, William; Acker, Clare 1982
Subtests: Visual Spatial Ability-Little Men; Symbol Digit Coding-Perceptual Motor Speed; Visual Perceptual Analysis; Verbal Recognition Memory; Visual Spatial Recognition Memory; Abstract Problem Solving-Bexley Maudsley Category Sorting Test
Descriptors: Adults; *Alcoholism; Cognitive Processes; *Computer Assisted Testing; Foreign Countries; Memory; *Microcomputers; *Neurological Impairments; Problem Solving; *Psychological Evaluation; *Psychomotor Skills; *Screening Tests; Spatial Ability
Identifiers: BMAPS; BMCST; England; Great Britain
Availability: NFER-Nelson Publishing Co.; Darville House, 2 Oxford Rd. E., Windsor, Berks SL4 1DF, England
Target Audience: 18-64

Designed to screen patients for psychological defects resulting from organic brain damage. Emphasizes testing for deficits in nonverbal skills often found when verbal intelligence is intact. Administered via microcomputer. Originally designed for use with alcoholics.

810525
Behavior Assessment Battery. Second Edition. Kiernan, Chris; Jones, Malcolm C. 1982
Subtests: Reinforcement and Experience; Inspection; Tracking; Visuo-Motor; Auditory; Postural Control; Exploratory Control; Constructive Play; Search Strategies; Perceptual Problem Solving; Social, Communication; Self Help Skills
Descriptors: Adolescents; Adults; Behavior Rating Scales; Children; *Cognitive Ability; *Communication Skills; Foreign Countries; Individual Testing; Interviews; *Self Care Skills; *Severe Mental Retardation; *Training Methods
Identifiers: BAB; England; Great Britain; Test Batteries
Availability: NFER-Nelson Publishing Co.; Darville House, 2 Oxford Rd. E., Windsor SL4 1DF, Berkshire, England
Target Audience: 2-64
Notes: Time, 260 approx.

Developed for use by psychologists, teachers, doctors and others who have experience with severely mentally handicapped individuals. Battery is based on premise that children should achieve certain target or criterion behaviors to function adequately in their environment. Battery is not meant to replace other methods of assessing profoundly retarded but to complement other techniques by providing additional or unique details. Each section consists of items and a lattice, which is a visual representation of the sequencing of items. Designed to provide a basis for macroassessment of profoundly handicapped. Battery is teaching- or training-oriented so that purpose is to aid in setting up training programs. Battery consists of 2 types of items: interview items for use with teacher and parent or guardian of child and behavioral items to assess child's general behavior. Sections of the battery may be administered in the order indicated or in another order. Evaluates cognitive, communicative, and self-help skills. During development of the BAB, 174 children ranging in age from 2 years to 17 years were tested.

810528
General Occupational Interest Inventory. Holdsworth, Ruth; Cramp, Lisa 1982
Subtests: Medical; Welfare; Personal Services; Selling Goods; Selling Services; Supervision; Clerical; Office Equipment; Control; Leisure; Art and Design; Crafts; Plants; Animals; Transport; Construction; Electrical; Mechanical
Descriptors: Adolescents; Adults; Career Counseling; Dropouts; Foreign Countries; *Interest Inventories; Personnel Selection; *Semiskilled Occupations; *Supervisors; *Vocational Interests
Identifiers: England; Great Britain
Availability: Saville and Holdsworth, Ltd.; N. Lodge, 4 Esher Park Ave., Esher, Surrey KT10 9NP, England
Target Audience: 16-64
Notes: Time, 40 approx; Items, 216

Designed as an interest inventory for school dropouts and those with average educational attainment. Includes activities suitable for semiskilled to supervisory level occupations. Untimed inventory which should take between 20 to 40 minutes to complete. Suitable for use in business, industry, and education and also for such purposes as vocational guidance, career counseling and planning, job relocation, retirement counseling, and for organizational decision making in employee selection and placement.

810529
Advanced Occupational Interest Inventory. Holdsworth, Ruth; Cramp, Lisa 1982
Subtests: Medical; Welfare; Education; Control; Commercial; Managerial; Administration; Legal; Financial; Data Processing; Information; Media; Art and Design; Biological; Physical; Process; Mechanical; Electrical; Construction
Descriptors: Adolescents; Adults; Career Counseling; Dropouts; Foreign Countries; *Interest Inventories; *Managerial Occupations; Personnel Selection; *Professional Occupations; *Skilled Occupations; Supervisors; *Vocational Interests
Identifiers: England; Great Britain
Availability: Saville and Holdsworth, Ltd.; The Old Post House, 81 High St., Esher, Surrey, KT10 9QA, England
Target Audience: 16-64
Notes: Time, 40 approx.; Items, 228

Designed as a vocational interest inventory for adults and school leavers with higher educational attainments. Includes activities in 19 job categories ranging from skilled and supervisory jobs up to professional and managerial levels. Inventory is untimed but should take between 20 to 40 minutes to complete. Suitable for use in business, industry, and education and for such purposes as vocational guidance, career planning, job relocation, retirement counseling, and for organizational decision making in employee selection and placement.

810531
Graded Naming Test. McKenna, Pat; Warrington, Elizabeth K. 1983
Descriptors: Adolescents; Adults; Clinical Diagnosis; Foreign Countries; *Handicap Identification; *Language Handicaps; *Language Tests; *Neurological Impairments; Older Adults
Identifiers: England; Great Britain
Availability: NFER-Nelson Publishing Co.; Darville House, 2 Oxford Rd. E., Windsor, Berks SL4 1DF, England
Target Audience: 12-70
Notes: Items, 30

Used to identify naming deficits in brain-damaged patients and to assess presence and degree of language disorders. Particularly useful for clinical psychologists working in neurology, neurologists, and speech therapists. Names in test avoid both words in common usage and specialist terms, and presents objects to the patient in order of difficulty. Test is effective across a wide range of intellectual ability and can accurately assess even patients with above average premorbid intelligence.

810532
Mossford Assessment Chart for the Physically Handicapped. Whitehouse, Janet 1983

Subtests: Sitting and Walking; Mobility; Bathing and Dressing; Personal Hygiene; Health; Leisure and Social Activities; Reading and Writing; Mathematics; Financial Skills; Domestic Skills; Manipulative and Perceptual Skills; Communication and Aids
Descriptors: *Adolescents; Check Lists; *Children; *Daily Living Skills; Foreign Countries; *Physical Disabilities
Identifiers: England; Great Britain; MACPH
Availability: NFER-Nelson Publishing Co.; Darville House, 2 Oxford Rd. E., Windsor, Berks SL4 1DF, England
Target Audience: 5-18

A checklist for daily living activities relevant to physically handicapped children, including those with severe physical handicaps. Provides a visual record of a child's abilities and, if the assessment is conducted at regular intervals, a convenient way to compare a child's progress over time. May be useful in many situations such as transition to a new school or residential center, for employment considerations, when a child is being considered for adoption or a foster home, or in the work of occupational therapists, psychologists, teachers, physiotherapists, social workers, and others. Parents may also complete the checklist.

810542
Snijders-Oomen Non-Verbal Intelligence Scale. Snijders, J. Th.; Snijders-Oomen, N. 1976
Subtests: Sorting; Mosaic; Combination; Memory; Copying
Descriptors: *Deafness; Foreign Countries; Hearing Impairments; *Intelligence Tests; *Nonverbal Tests; Preschool Children; *Young Children
Identifiers: Netherlands; SON
Availability: NFER-Nelson Publishing Co.; Darville House, 2 Oxford Rd. E., Windsor, Berks, SL4 1DF, England
Target Audience: 2-7
Notes: Items, 50

An intelligence test intended chiefly for use by practicing psychologists. This is a revised and newly standardized version of the original test. Test was standardized on both a hearing sample and a deaf sample.

810544
Group Literacy Assessment. Spooncer, Frank A. 1982
Descriptors: Achievement Tests; Cloze Procedure; Context Clues; Foreign Countries; Grammar; *Group Testing; Literacy; Logical Thinking; Perceptual Development; *Reading Achievement; *Reading Tests; Screening Tests; Secondary Education; *Secondary School Students; Short Term Memory; *Slow Learners; *Spelling
Identifiers: England; GLA; Great Britain
Availability: Hodder and Stoughton; P.O. Box 702, Mill Rd., Dunton Green, Sevenoaks, Kent TN13 2YD, England
Grade Level: 7-12
Notes: Time, 30 approx.

Used to indicate what students in intermediate grades have achieved not only in reading but in overall efficiency with written materials. Also used as students enter secondary level as a screening test. Test has 2 sections. The first contains a story with misspellings which students must correct. The second part is a modified cloze procedure with words or parts of words missing which students must fill in. A major aim of test is to provide information on slow learners. Test requires students to use and combine perceptual, contextual, and grammatical clues. It tests their ability to note particular details, to carry information in short-term memory and to make judgments about plausible inferences. Also provides useful information about their spelling.

810548
Behaviour Problems: A System of Management. Galvin, Peter; Singleton, Richard 1984
Descriptors: *Behavior Problems; Check Lists; *Elementary School Students; Elementary Secondary Education; Foreign Countries; *Problem Children; Records (Forms); *Secondary School Students
Identifiers: England; Great Britain
Availability: NFER Nelson Publishing Co.; Darville House, 2 Oxford Rd. E., Windsor, Berks SL4 1DF, England
Grade Level: K-12
Target Audience: 5-16

Provides a systematic means of recording and analyzing information on children's disruptive behavior. Can be used by specialist and nonspecialist teachers and by educational psychologists. System consists of a manual and 3 forms. The first 2 forms, the Behavior Checklist and the Daily Record, record the child's behaviors; moving from an overall profile to a deeper analysis of areas of special concerns. The third form, the Monthly Progress Chart, records the progress of trying to modify these behaviors. The Behaviour Checklist contains over 111 behaviors classified into 7 main sections: classroom conformity, task

orientation, emotional control, acceptance of authority, self-worth, peer relationships, self-responsibility-problem solving.

810551
Specific Test in English for Everyday International Use. Pergamon Press, Oxford, England 1983
Subtests: Reading; Writing; Listening; Oral Interview
Descriptors: *Achievement Tests; Adults; *English (Second Language); Foreign Countries; Interviews; Listening Skills; Oral English; Reading Comprehension; Speech Skills; *Student Placement; Writing Skills
Identifiers: England; Great Britain; Oral Tests; Writing Sample
Availability: Pergamon Press Inc.; Maxwell House, Fairview Park, Elmsford, NY 10523
Target Audience: Adults
Notes: Time, 117; Items, 73

Designed to measure proficiency in English of learners of English as a Second Language for decisions on placement and as an achievement test. Includes a reading comprehension measure, writing sample, a recorded listening test, and a person-to-person interview. Scoring is on a 9-point scale.

810568
Group Tests of High Level Intelligence, AH6:AG. Heim, A.W.; and Others 1983
Subtests: Verbal; Numerical and Diagrammatic
Descriptors: *Abstract Reasoning; *Academically Gifted; Adolescents; *Cognitive Ability; College Students; Foreign Countries; High School Students; *Intelligence Differences; *Intelligence Tests; Liberal Arts; Professional Personnel; Young Adults
Identifiers: England; Great Britain
Availability: NFER-Nelson Publishing Co.; Darville House, 2 Oxford Rd. E., Windsor, Berks SL4 1DF, England
Target Audience: 16-25
Notes: Time, 35 approx.; Items, 60

Test of general reasoning designed for use with selected, highly intelligent subjects such as candidates for or students at university and colleges of education, potential entrants to the professions, and senior students at schools and colleges. Form AG is intended for those in liberal arts and social sciences, such as historians, linguists, economists, philosophers, and teachers. Test is meant to discriminate among the intelligent population. Half of the questions in form AG (arts and general subjects) are verbal, one-quarter are numerical, and one-quarter are diagrammatic. Tests may be group administered.

810574
Family Relations Test: Children's Version, Revised 1978 Edition. Bene, Eva; Anthony, James 1978
Descriptors: *Adolescents; Attitude Measures; *Children; *Emotional Disturbances; *Family Counseling; Family Influence; *Family Relationship; Foreign Countries; *Parent Child Relationship; *Parent Role
Identifiers: England; Great Britain
Availability: NFER-Nelson Publishing Co.; Darville House, 2 Oxford Rd. E., Windsor, Berks SL4 1DF, England
Target Audience: 3-15
Notes: Time, 25 approx.

The test material of the Family Relations Test was designed to give a concrete representation of the child's family. It consists of 20 figures representing people of various ages, shapes, and sizes, sufficiently stereotyped to stand for members of any child's family, yet ambiguous enough to become, under suggestion, a specific family. They range from grandparents to a baby in a carriage, and from these the child is able to create his or her own significant circle. There is also a figure "Nobody" which serves to accommodate those items that are not felt to apply to any in the family. Each figure is attached to a box-like base which has a slit in the top. The items are printed on small individual cards. The child is told that the cards contain messages, and that his or her task is to put each card "into the person" for whom the message fits best. This is an objective technique for exploring emotional attitudes in children. There are 2 scoring sheets, one for younger children, ages 3-7, and another for older children, ages 7-15. There are 3 tests in the series: The Children's Version, The Adult Version and The Married Couples' Version of the Family Relations Test. There are 99 items on the older children's test and 47 on the younger children's.

810575
Recognition Memory Test. Warrington, Elizabeth 1984
Descriptors: Adults; Foreign Countries; *Neurological Impairments; Older Adults; Screening Tests; *Short Term Memory; Verbal Stimuli; Visual Stimuli
Identifiers: England; Great Britain; RMT

Availability: NFER-Nelson Publishing Co.; Darville House, 2 Oxford Rd. E., Windsor, Berks SL4 1DF, England
Target Audience: 18-70
Notes: Time, 15 approx.; Items, 100

Developed to detect minor visual and verbal memory deficits which may indicate organic neurological disease. Two subtests assess verbal and visual recognition and enable clinicians to distinguish between right and left hemisphere damage.

810578
Group Tests of High Level Intelligence, AH6: SEM. Heim, A.W.; and Others 1983
Subtests: Verbal; Numerical; Diagrammatic
Descriptors: *Abstract Reasoning; *Academically Gifted; Adolescents; *Cognitive Ability; College Students; Foreign Countries; High School Students; *Intelligence Differences; *Intelligence Tests; Professional Personnel; *Scientific Personnel; Young Adults
Identifiers: England; Great Britain
Availability: NFER-Nelson Publishing Co.; Darville House, 2 Oxford Rd. E., Windsor, Berks SL4 1DF, England
Target Audience: 16-25
Notes: Time, 40; Items, 72

Test of general reasoning ability designed to discriminate among selected, highly intelligent subjects such as candidates for and students at universities and colleges of education, potential entrants to the professions, and senior students at schools and colleges. SEM is intended for use with scientists, engineers, and mathematicians. On form SEM, questions are divided among verbal, numerical, and diagrammatic. Tests may be group administered.

810587
Kendrick Cognitive Tests for the Elderly. Kendrick, Donald 1985
Subtests: Object Learning; Digit Copying
Descriptors: *Depression (Psychology); Diagnostic Tests; Foreign Countries; *Older Adults; *Patients; Reaction Time; *Schizophrenia; *Screening Tests; Short Term Memory
Identifiers: England; Great Britain; KDCT; Test Batteries
Availability: NFER-Nelson Publishing Co.; Darville House, 2 Oxford Rd. E., Windsor, Berks SL4 1DF, England
Target Audience: 56-99
Notes: Time, 15 approx.

Battery of 2 tests to detect early dementia and depressive psychosis among patients over 55 years old. Two subtests detect early dementia and depressive psychosis by assessing those cognitive abilities which seem most sensitive to age changes: short-term memory and speed of processing and recording information. Administered to patients upon admission and 6 weeks later. Is a revision of the Kendrick Battery for the Detection of Dementia in the Elderly (TC810441).

810608
Phonological Assessment of Child Speech. Grunwell, Pamela 1985
Descriptors: *Articulation (Speech); Child Development; *Children; Clinical Diagnosis; English; Foreign Countries; Native Speakers; *Oral English; *Phonemes; *Speech Evaluation; *Speech Handicaps; Speech Tests; Stress (Phonology); Syllables
Identifiers: *England; PACS
Availability: NFER-Nelson Publishing Co.; Darville House, 2 Oxford Rd. E., Windsor, Berks SL4 1DF, England
Target Audience: 6-10

This series of procedures for clinical assessment of children's speech disorders was designed for use in England. It consists of a developmental assessment of speech and analyses of the child's pronunciation of common words with emphasis on the production of beginning, middle, and ending consonants. It covers use of phonemes, homophones, and syllables. Included are forms for summarizing results.

830235
A Scale of Real Life Ability. Stott, D. H.; Duncan, L. H.
Subtests: Emotional Barrier; Managing Own Clothes; Doing Classroom Jobs; Understanding of Pictures; Drawing; Powers of Observation; General Alertness; Counting Money; Telling Time, Day & Age; General Competence; Hobbies or Specialized Accomplishments; Speech Disability; Communication
Descriptors: Behavior Rating Scales; Daily Living Skills; Elementary Education; *Elementary School Students; Foreign Countries; *Interpersonal Competence; Mental Retardation; *Preschool Children; Preschool Education; *Student Adjustment
Identifiers: Canada

Availability: Dr. D. H. Stott; 30 Colborn St., Guelph, Ontario, Canada
Target Audience: 2-12

Designed for teacher use in assessing social competence of young children. Teaching may indicate existence of physical handicap or emotional barrier which would preclude certain behaviors.

830244
Test of Motor Impairment. Stott, D. H.; And Others 1972
Descriptors: *Adolescents; Behavior Disorders; *Children; *Diagnostic Tests; Foreign Countries; Handicap Identification; Individual Testing; Learning Disabilities; *Neurological Impairments; Nonverbal Tests; Performance Tests; Psychomotor Skills
Identifiers: Canada
Availability: NFER-Nelson Publishing Co.; Darville House, 2 Oxford Rd., E., Windsor, Berks, SL4 1DF, England
Target Audience: 5-14
Notes: Time, 15 approx.; Items, 8

Designed to assist in diagnosis of neural dysfunction by assessing degree of motor impairment. Behavior and learning problems may result from neurological impairments.

830313
Vulpe Assessment Battery. Vulpe, Shirley German 1977
Subtests: Basic Senses and Functions; Gross Motor Behaviors; Fine Motor Behaviors; Language Behaviors; Cognitive Processes and Specific Concepts; Organizational Behaviors; Activities of Daily Living; Assessment of Environment
Descriptors: *Behavior Patterns; *Child Development; *Cognitive Processes; Cognitive Style; Daily Living Skills; *Developmental Disabilities; *Diagnostic Tests; Foreign Countries; *Individual Development; Individual Testing; Learning Readiness; Observation; Perceptual Handicaps; Preschool Evaluation; School Readiness; Sensory Experience; *Young Children
Identifiers: Canada; VAB
Availability: Vulpe Assessment Battery; National Institute on Mental Retardation, Kinsmen, NIMR Bldg., York University Campus, 4700 Keele St., Toronto, Ontario, Canada M3J 1P3
Target Audience: 0-5

A developmental assessment procedure for atypically developing children. Used for individualized programing and therapy, child development tracking, and counseling with parents and teachers. Individually administered; based on observations and interactions with the child.

830315
Neale Analysis of Reading Ability, Second Edition. Neale, Marie D. 1966
Descriptors: Blindness; *Braille; Children; *Diagnostic Tests; Elementary Education; *Elementary School Students; Foreign Countries; Individual Testing; *Oral Reading; *Reading Achievement; *Reading Diagnosis; *Reading Difficulties; Reading Tests
Identifiers: Oral Tests; United Kingdom
Availability: NFER-Nelson Publishing Co.; Darville House, 2 Oxford Rd. E., Windsor, Berkshire SL4 1DF, England
Target Audience: 6-12
Notes: Time, 15 approx.

Individually administered test designed to provide diagnostic information which can be used to help remedy reading difficulties. Comes in Forms A, B, and C. Booklet includes all 3 forms for all graded passages and a supplementary diagnostic test for each form. Also available in braille (TC810388).

830358
Aptitude Assessment Battery: Programming. Wolfe, Jack M. 1967
Descriptors: Adults; *Aptitude Tests; Blindness; Braille; *Data Processing Occupations; Employers; Foreign Countries; French; Left Handed Writer; Occupational Tests; *Personnel Evaluation; *Personnel Selection; *Programers; *Programing; *Simulation; Spanish
Identifiers: AABP; Canada
Availability: Wolfe Computer Aptitude Testing; Box 319, Oradell, NJ 07649
Target Audience: Adults
Notes: Time, 180 approx.; Items, 5

Designed to measure 2 major requirements which programmers should have: the ability to analyze a problem in a reasonable and logical manner and the ability to perform highly detailed work with a high degree of accuracy. Although not timed, most persons who have taken the test in the past have finished in 3 hours or less. If necessary, the test taker may return to finish the test either later that day or the following day. The test consists of 5 problems which require multiple answers and which simulate on-the-job tasks. All figuring, etc. is to be done on the test

booklet, not on a separate sheet of scrap paper. The test is mailed to the company for evaluation; is available in English, French, and Spanish and in an English version for left-handed persons; and is available only to employers of programmers. Also available in Braille.

830362
Wolfe Spence Programming Aptitude Test. Wolfe, Jack M. 1977
Descriptors: Adults; *Aptitude Tests; Blindness; Braille; *Data Processing Occupations; Job Training; Occupational Tests; Partial Vision; Personnel Selection; Problem Solving; *Programing; Screening Tests
Identifiers: *Self Scoring
Availability: Wolfe Computer Aptitude Testing, Ltd.; Box 1104, St. Laurent Station, Montreal, Quebec, Canada H4L 4W6
Target Audience: Adults
Notes: Items, 10

A self-administered, self-scoring screening-out test for use in selecting job candidates for further testing. This is a take home test which includes answers. If applicants still want to be considered for the position, they are then tested further with the Aptitude Assessment Battery: Programming. Also available in Braille and large print for partially sighted persons.

840062
Test de Retention Visuelle. Benton, Arthur L. 1965
Descriptors: Adolescents; Adults; Children; *Diagnostic Tests; *Foreign Countries; *French; *Memory; *Neurological Impairments; *Visual Perception
Identifiers: *France
Availability: Editions du Centre de Psychologie Appliquee, 48, avenue Victor-Hugo 75783 Paris Cedex 16, France
Target Audience: 8-65
Notes: Time, 5 approx.; Items, 10

Clinical and research instrument designed to assess visual perception and visual memory. Useful in experimental research and as a supplement to mental examinations of persons suspected of abnormality or impairment.

885031
BETA (Revised Beta Examination). Kellogg, C. E.; Morton, N. W. 1969
Subtests: Labyrinths; Key of Symbols; Recognition of Errors; Formboard; Incomplete Figures; Differences
Descriptors: Adolescents; Adults; Aptitude Tests; *Cognitive Ability; Cognitive Tests; *Educationally Disadvantaged; Employees; Employment Potential; Foreign Countries; *Illiteracy; Job Applicants; Job Skills; *Nonverbal Ability; Nonverbal Tests; Spanish; *Spanish Speaking; Timed Tests; Visual Measures; *Visual Stimuli; *Vocational Aptitude
Identifiers: BETA II; Revised Beta Examination; Spain
Availability: TEA Ediciones, S.A.; Fray Bernardino de Sahagun 24, Madrid, 16, Spain
Target Audience: 14-64
Notes: Items, 200

Spanish version of Revised Beta Examination, Second Edition (TC008875). Nonverbal measure of mental abilities; thus, useful with illiterate persons, non-English speaking, or handicapped persons employed in unskilled jobs in industrial organizations. English version does include instructions in Spanish.

990002
Tests of English Consonants. University of Jyvaskyla, Finland Moisio, Risto; Valento, Eero 1976
Descriptors: Auditory Discrimination; Consonants; *English (Second Language); Finnish; Foreign Countries; *Language Proficiency; Listening Skills; Pronunciation; Secondary Education; *Secondary School Students; Speech Skills
Identifiers: *Finland
Availability: ERIC Document Reproduction Service; 3900 Wheeler Ave., Alexandria, VA 22304 (ED135214, 109 pages)
Grade Level: 7-12
Notes: Items, 200

A measure of English as a Second Language for Finnish students. Consists of a substitution test to determine which sounds Finns substitute for English sounds, a discrimination test, a sound analogy test, a written analogy test, and a production test.

SUBJECT INDEX

Ability
Self-Concept Test — 9554

Ability Identification
DIAL — 1793
DIAL-R — 12396
Eby Elementary Identification Instrument — 13467
Oregon Academic Ranking Test — 715
Scales for Rating the Behavioral Characteristics of Superior Students — 7933
SOI Screening Form for Gifted — 9267

Abstract Reasoning
An Abstraction Test for Use with Cerebral Palsied Children — 2632
Arlin Test of Formal Reasoning — 13468
The Booklet Category Test — 11201
Employee Aptitude Survey: Prueba 10—Razonamiento Simbolico (Forma A) — 7983
Goldstein-Scheerer Tests of Abstract and Concrete Thinking — 3257
Group Tests of High Level Intelligence, AH6:AG — 810568
Group Tests of High Level Intelligence, AH6:SEM — 810578
Halstead Category Test for Adults — 11300
Halstead Category Test for Older Children — 11299
Halstead Category Test for Young Children — 11203
Halstead-Reitan Neuropsychological Test Battery: Spanish Version. Manual — 11202
Kasanin-Hanfmann Concept Formation Test — 2451
Matrix Analogies Test, Expanded Form — 14523
Mobile Vocational Evaluation — 14133
NIIP Verbal Test 91 — 810483
Otis-Lennon Mental Ability Test, Advanced Level — 2590
Otis-Lennon Mental Ability Test, Intermediate Level — 2589
Otis-Lennon Mental Ability Test, Level II, Elementary — 2588
Proverbs Test: Best Answer Form — 2048
Proverbs Test: Forms I, II and III — 2047
SRA Pictorial Reasoning Test — 1557
Test of Non-Verbal Reasoning, Long Form — 3839
Test of Non-Verbal Reasoning, Short Form — 3854
Wisconsin Card Sorting Test — 4891

Academic Ability
Metropolitan Readiness Tests: 1976 Edition, Level I — 7971
Metropolitan Readiness Tests: 1976 Edition, Level II — 7972
Peabody Picture Vocabulary Test—Revised, Form L — 10877
Peabody Picture Vocabulary Test—Revised, Form M — 10878
Prueba de Admision para Estudios Graduados — 11944
SOI Learning Abilities Test: A Screening Form for Atypical Gifted — 14154
SOI Learning Abilities Test: Developmental Vision Form — 14157

Academic Achievement
Bateria Woodcock Psico-Educativa en Espanol — 11931
Criterion Referenced Test: MGS/CRTest Eastern Navajo Agency, Level B — 9903
Criterion-Referenced Test: MGS/CRTest Eastern Navajo Agency, Level C — 9904
Criterion-Referenced Test: MGS/CRTest Eastern Navajo Agency, Level D — 9905
Criterion-Referenced Test: MGS/CRTest Eastern Navajo Agency, Level E — 9906
Criterion-Referenced Test: MGS/CRTest Eastern Navajo Agency, Level F — 9907
Criterion-Referenced Test: MGS/CRTest Eastern Navajo Agency, Level G — 9908
Criterion-Referenced Test: MGS/CRTest Eastern Navajo Agency, Level H — 9909
Criterion-Referenced Test: MGS/CRTest Eastern Navajo Agency, Level I — 9910
Criterion-Referenced Test: MGS/CRTest Eastern Navajo Agency, Level J. — 9911
Home Environment Variable Questionnaire — 12589
IEA Six-Subject Survey Instruments: English as a Foreign Language, Listening, Population II — 13091
IEA Six-Subject Survey Instruments: English as a Foreign Language, Listening, Population IV — 13092
IEA Six-Subject Survey Instruments: English as a Foreign Language, Reading, Population II — 13093
IEA Six-Subject Survey Instruments: English as a Foreign Language, Reading, Population IV — 13094
IEA Six-Subject Survey Instruments: English as a Foreign Language, Speaking Populations II, IV — 13096
IEA Six-Subject Survey Instruments: English as a Foreign Language, Writing Populations II, IV — 13095
IEA Six-Subject Survey Instruments: English Student Questionnaire — 13090
McDermott Multidimensional Assessment of Children — 13838

Stanford Achievement Test: 7th Edition, Advanced Form — 11700
Stanford Achievement Test: 7th Edition, Intermediate 1 — 11698
Stanford Achievement Test: 7th Edition, Intermediate 2 — 11699
Stanford Achievement Test: 7th Edition, Primary 2 — 11696
Stanford Achievement Test: 7th Edition, Primary 3 — 11697
Tests of General Educational Development: High School Level — 610

Academic Aptitude
Bateria Woodcock Psico-Educativa en Espanol — 11931
The Blind Learning Aptitude Test — 11466
Detroit Tests of Learning Aptitude, DTLA-2 — 13737
Detroit Tests of Learning Aptitude—Primary — 14340
Gilliland Learning Potential Examination: 1970 Revision — 5378
Motor Academic Perceptual Skill Development Checklist — 8297
Otis-Lennon Mental Ability Test, Advanced Level — 2590
Otis-Lennon Mental Ability Test, Intermediate Level — 2589
Otis-Lennon Mental Ability Test, Level I, Elementary — 2587
Otis-Lennon Mental Ability Test, Level I, Primary — 2585
Otis-Lennon Mental Ability Test, Level II, Elementary — 2588
Otis-Lennon Mental Ability Test, Level II, Primary — 2586
Relevant Aspects of Potential — 10917

Academic Aspiration
Mexican American Youth and Vocational Education in Texas Questionnaire — 12844

Academic Failure
The Pupil Rating Scale Revised. Screening for Learning Disabilities — 11212

Academic Persistence
Persistence/Dropout Rating Scale — 12450

Academically Gifted
AGP Student Evaluation Checklist — 12449
Community Talent Miner — 13660
Eby Elementary Identification Instrument — 13467
Evaluating Educational Programs for Intellectually Gifted Students — 14105
Evaluating Gifted Programs — 14968
Gifted and Talented Scale — 13255
Gifted and Talented Screening Form — 8980
Group Tests of High Level Intelligence, AH6:AG — 810568
Group Tests of High Level Intelligence, AH6:SEM — 810578
Identi-Form System for Gifted Programs — 14967
Oregon Academic Ranking Test — 715
Primary Test of Higher Processes of Thinking — 13161
Progressive Matrices, Advanced Sets I and II — 810100
Revised Pre-Reading Screening Procedures to Identify First Grade Academic Needs — 10529

Acculturation
Acculturation Rating Scale for Mexican Americans — 10984

Achievement Gains
Severely Handicapped Progress Inventory — 13964
Student Learning Profile, 2nd Edition — 14420

Achievement Tests
Adult Basic Learning Examination, Level 1, Second Edition — 15016
Adult Basic Learning Examination, Level 2, Second Edition — 15017
Adult Basic Learning Examination, Level 3, Second Edition — 15018
Adult Basic Learning Examination: Level I Forms A and B — 1822
Adult Basic Learning Examination—Level II — 1823
Adult Basic Learning Examination—Level III — 6001
Alemany English Second Language Placement Test, Revised — 12736
Basic Achievement Skills Individual Screener — 12212
Bilingual Test Battery — 10196
Bryant-Schwan Design Test — 7464
Comprehensive English Language Test — 14800
Computer Aptitude, Literacy, and Interest Profile — 13367
The Conley-Vernon Idiom Test — 14532
Criterion Referenced Curriculum: Mathematics Assessment — 13342
Criterion Referenced Curriculum: Reading Assessment — 13341
CTBS Espanol, Level 1 — 9788
CTBS Espanol, Level 2 — 9789
CTBS Espanol, Level 3 — 9790
CTBS Espanol, Level B — 9786
CTBS Espanol, Level C — 9787

C.U.B.E. Math Mastery Tests — 13535
Educational Goal Attainment Tests — 8081
Educational Goal Attainment Tests: Spanish Version — 8083
Examen en Francais — 9996
Examination in Structure (English as a Foreign Language) — 2698
French Achievement Test: Language Arts, Grade 1 — 7848
French Achievement Test: Language Arts, Grade 2 — 7849
French Achievement Test: Language Arts, Grade 3 — 7850
French Achievement Test: Language Arts, Grade 4 — 7851
French Achievement Test: Language Arts, Grade 5 — 7852
French Achievement Test: Language Arts, Kindergarten — 7847
French Achievement Test: Mathematics, Grade 1 — 7854
French Achievement Test: Mathematics, Grade 2 — 7855
French Achievement Test: Mathematics, Grade 3 — 7856
French Achievement Test: Mathematics, Grade 4 — 7857
French Achievement Test: Mathematics, Grade 5 — 7858
French Achievement Test: Mathematics, Kindergarten — 7853
Gilmore Oral Reading Test — 3822
IEA Six-Subject Survey Instruments: English as a Foreign Language, Reading, Population II — 13093
IEA Six-Subject Survey Instruments: English as a Foreign Language, Reading, Population IV — 13094
IEA Six-Subject Survey Instruments: English as a Foreign Language, Speaking Populations II, IV — 13096
IEA Six-Subject Survey Instruments: English as a Foreign Language, Writing Populations II, IV — 13095
The Instant Word Recognition Test — 6870
Inter-American Series: Test of Reading, Level 1, Primary — 863
Inter-American Series: Test of Reading, Level 2, Primary — 864
Inter-American Series: Test of Reading, Level 3, Elementary — 865
Inter-American Series: Test of Reading, Level 4, Intermediate — 866
Inter-American Series: Test of Reading, Level 5, Advanced — 867
La Prueba Riverside de Realizacion en Espanol — 13702
Language Assessment Battery, 1982 — 14112
The Maculaitis Assessment Program: 2-3 — 12740
The Maculaitis Assessment Program: 4-5 — 12741
The Maculaitis Assessment Program: 6-8 — 12742
The Maculaitis Assessment Program: 9-12 — 12743
The Maculaitis Assessment Program: Basic Concept Test — 12738
The Maculaitis Assessment Program: K-1 — 12739
Michigan English Language Assessment Battery — 14118
Michigan Test of Aural Comprehension — 11623
Michigan Test of English Language Proficiency — 11625
The Mini-Check System — 12735
Multilevel Academic Survey Test — 14595
NIIP Group Test 64 — 810494
Oral Placement Test — 10632
Oral Production Tests: Levels One-Three — 10633
Peabody Picture Vocabulary Test—Revised, Form L — 10877
Peabody Picture Vocabulary Test—Revised, Form M — 10878
S-D Primary ESL Inventory — 11353
Secondary Level English Proficiency Test — 10649
Sequential Assessment of Mathematics Inventories — 14001
Socio-Sexual Knowledge and Attitudes Test — 10140
Spanish Oral Proficiency Test — 8717
The Spanish Oral Reading Test — 13719
Speaking Test in Spanish/English — 9933
Specific Test in English for Everyday International Use — 810551
Stanford Achievement Test: 7th Edition, Advanced Form — 11700
Stanford Achievement Test: 7th Edition, Intermediate 1 — 11698
Stanford Achievement Test: 7th Edition, Intermediate 2 — 11699
Stanford Achievement Test: 7th Edition, Primary 2 — 11696
Stanford Achievement Test: 7th Edition, Primary 3 — 11697
Stanford Achievement Test; Braille Edition, Advanced Level — 10903
Stanford Achievement Test: Braille Edition, Intermediate, Level I — 10901
Stanford Achievement Test: Braille Edition, Intermediate, Level II — 10902
Stanford Achievement Test: Braille Edition, Primary, Level II — 10899
Stanford Achievement Test: Braille Edition, Primary, Level III — 10900
Stanford Achievement Test for Hearing Impaired Students — 12206
Stanford Early School Achievement Test; Level 1. Navajo Edition — 9816
Stanford Test of Academic Skills, Braille Edition, Level I — 10904

Dialect Studies

Directionality

Disabilities

Disadvantaged

SUBJECT INDEX

AUTHOR INDEX

TITLE INDEX